D1319816

ITALO SVEVO

ITALO SVEVO

A Double Life

... it is wrong to sign a masterpiece, a discovery
with a single name; a date would be better; its
true authors are the author's predecessors and
contemporaries.

Italo Svevo (signing E. Samigli)
'Un individualista' (III.605)
(Following Hippolyte Taine)

JOHN GATT-RUTTER

CLARENDON PRESS · OXFORD

1988

Oxford University Press, Walton Street, Oxford OX2 6DP

Oxford New York Toronto
Delhi Bombay Calcutta Madras Karachi
Petaling Jaya Singapore Hong Kong Tokyo
Nairobi Dar es Salaam Cape Town
Melbourne Auckland

and associated companies in
Beirut Berlin Ibadan Nicosia

Oxford is a trade mark of Oxford University Press

Published in the United States
by Oxford University Press, New York

British Library Cataloguing in Publication Data

Gatt-Rutter, John
Italo Svevo: a double life.
1. Svevo, Italo—Biography   2. Authors—
Italian—19th century—Biography
3. Authors, Italian—20th century—
Biography
I. Title
853'.8   PQ4841.C482Z/
ISBN 0-19-815848-3

Library of Congress Cataloging in Publication Data

Gatt-Rutter, John.
Italo Svevo: a double life.
Bibliography: p
Includes index.
1. Svevo, Italo, 1861–1928—Biography.   2. Authors,
Italian—19th century—Biography.   3. Authors, Italian—
20th century—Biography.   I. Title.
PQ4841.C482Z664 1988   853'.8   87–11240
ISBN 0-19-815848-3

Printed in Great Britain by
Butler & Tanner Ltd, Frome and London

ACKNOWLEDGEMENTS

The making of a book involves the skill and labour of numerous people who will never see the book and whom the author will never know. To all of these I am grateful. My special thanks are due to those who have contributed more personally and directly to the making of this biography of Svevo, first and foremost the writer's daughter, Letizia Fonda Savio, for her unfailing kindness and inestimable help, particularly in granting me access to manuscript and other personal material and for her generous permission to quote freely from her mother's, her husband's and her own writings on Svevo and to use family photographs as illustrations. Anna and Fulvio Anzellotti and their families have likewise been unstinting in their friendship, hospitality, help and encouragement and have done much to convey to me Trieste's special atmosphere. I was greatly advantaged in writing this book by being allowed to look in on the making of Fulvio's *Il segreto di Svevo*. I owe much to other Triestine friends, the late Signora Jole Ferro, Ida Ferro and Sabina Chiggiato de Minerbi. Dr Sauro Pesante of the Biblioteca Civica and Dottoressa Jona of the Archivio di Stato in Trieste, and their staffs, were invariably obliging. Professor Claudio Magris and Professor Bruno Maier gave encouragement and useful advice. In Vienna I received help from the Staatsarchiv, the Finanzarchiv, the Verwaltungsarchiv and the Kriegsarchiv. The British Library and the Greenwich Libraries Local History Collection and the Biblioteca Civica and the Biblioteca Nazionale in Turin provided invaluable service. Herr Otto Selzer in Marktbreit kindly gave me useful information. I am particularly grateful to the staff of the University of Hull, and especially of its library, for all they have done to help me over the years. I am grateful to Professor P. N. Furbank for permission to quote from his book *Italo Svevo—The Man and the Writer*.

I also wish to thank good friends and colleagues who have patiently read and commented on my text at various stages and helped to improve it: Professor Brian Moloney, Dr Edward Timms, Elizabeth Mahler-Schächter and Dr Stephen Kolsky. Julia Cook and Margaret Mackay put in a large amount of work on the typescript.

Finally, my gratitude is due to the British Academy for a European Exchange Grant awarded to me in 1976, which enabled me to follow Svevo's tracks in Italy, Austria and Germany; and to the University of Hull for financially supporting my studies in various places.

All errors are my own.

JOHN GATT-RUTTER

CONTENTS

Contents

LIST OF ILLUSTRATIONS

AUTHOR'S NOTE

All translations from Italian or other languages are my own unless otherwise indicated. Except for works which are familiar under an English title (e.g. *A Doll's House*, *The Psychopathology of Everyday Life*), I have usually given the original title, followed, where necessary, and usually at first mention, by its English translation—either in my own version or in that most widely accepted, as seemed more appropriate in each particular case.

Part I

THE ELUSIVE SELF

THE FACE IN THE MIRROR

Fame, smiling briefly on Italo Svevo just as his life was ending, subjected him to the embarrassing prospect of talking about himself in public. He agonized over this for months, then opted to talk about his friend James Joyce instead.

The text of the funked autobiographical talk survives,[1] but it gives little away about the man Ettore Schmitz who bore the pseudonym Italo Svevo. 'There is one thing in the world which I think I know something about,' he started, '— myself.' Conceding that 'the ancients made quite a to-do about the fact that even one's self is a mystery', he tried looking into the mirror, to find that 'while you are looking at yourself, it is hard to think.' And Svevo, or Schmitz, at the sight of 'those great whiskers' of his, an evolutionary relic that adorns but does not serve him in the least, cannot help laughing. 'At once my reflection laughs too. We laugh together. And laughter is an expression which conceals thought instead of revealing it.'

This is Svevo's cue for introducing Freud as the scientist of the self, but Svevo is as teasingly elusive about Freud as about himself. Yet Svevo's writing always presented itself as a science of the self: an arduous endeavour to capture subjectivity within objectivity without traducing either term; to dissect the butterfly under the microscope without damaging it or killing it. To this end, in all his narrative writings, a version of himself is subjected to critical scrutiny, explored, excavated to levels which may be felt to be common to all.

This is what makes Svevo an uncannily representative writer. He writes about contemporary man at his most ordinary, the man in the street. In the person of Schmitz he experienced the petty bourgeois and the bourgeois condition thoroughly, lucidly and painfully. The ordinariness of his life is the subject of his books, and has the suspect yet compulsive 'originality' discovered in it by the protagonist of *La coscienza di Zeno* (The Confessions of Zeno*). His characters embody the equivocations, delusions, frustrations and flabby adaptations of everyday living, the reality which never gets to grips with itself, which does not determine but is determined, and which is the reality of many or most of us. His books are remarkable for the sensitive registering of the almost imperceptible seismic tremors that run to and fro beneath the apparently even, uneventful flux of this drab existence. His subject is Everyman in modern dress.

In *La coscienza di Zeno*, the chronicle of unlived life turns almost miraculously and quizzically into burlesque, only to be overshadowed by the

---

* *Coscienza* in Italian embraces more than 'conscience' or 'conscientiousness', taking in 'consciousness', 'awareness', and therefore also 'the conscious' as opposed to 'the unconscious'.

convulsion of the Great War. History throws off its drab disguise and turns Zeno's farce into epic, improbable but true. Private history reveals itself as public history, however lopsidedly. This is where Svevo most overtly—though still obliquely, quizzically—approaches the history of his town and of our time, which his first two novels, *Una vita* (A Life) and *Senilità* (Senility*), written long before the revelation of Sarajevo and after, had expressed through the broader themes of competition and delusion among individuals.

Trieste's peculiar situation goes a long way towards explaining—though by no means straightforwardly—this most unemphatic and insinuating of writers. The town's complex character, at once Austrian and Italian, and more than a little Slav, compounds a cultural predicament for the young Ettore Schmitz trying to define his own identity and for a writer of Svevo's sceptical awareness. The reality underlying the 'Habsburg myth'—of an anachronistic dynasty artificially preserving but shackling an economic and bureaucratic bourgeoisie threatened by its own warring nationalities—converged with the Italian sense of the failure, or at least of the disappointments, of the Risorgimento, which the rhetoric of nationalistic writers such as D'Annunzio could not conceal. This sense of historic failure or frustration, of the death or decay of once bright ideals or of their unreality, runs deep in Svevo. All the combatants saw the Great War as the answer to their historic problems. It can be no accident that Svevo leaves the protagonist of his greatest novel suspended at the height and mid-point of that war, when every historic issue seemed furthest from solution.

In Italy, from the Enlightenment to the Risorgimento, writing was a public and political act whose efficacy was never doubted and which could be worth a battle won. So too no one doubted the writer's share of responsibility for his world and its history. But as the nineteenth century drew towards its close, this confidence ebbed away, in Italy as elsewhere. Writers now began to realize how puny is the individual in the face of history, of man's world, and how problematical the authority and the influence of literature. In Svevo, a critical point is reached. Society, and the individual, and the act of writing itself—despite its 'scientific' aspirations—are seen as being in crisis. Irony quickly asserts itself as the characteristic and controlling mode of Svevo's literary fictions.

Discovering Schopenhauer, therefore, brought theoretical confirmation of an outlook which Svevo had already established before he was twenty. The 'philosopher of pessimism' presented the world as an illusory projection of an underlying blind Universal Will: the individual and his mental products are themselves mere delusions, fragmented phenomena doomed to endless conflict and misrepresentation. What we think of as life is merely a great charade painfully obscuring the undifferentiated oneness of being—in other words, an all-embracing irony.

*The book is known in English by the title suggested by James Joyce, *As a Man Grows Older*. This is to take 'senility' in a misleadingly literal sense. The characters in the novel are old in heart, not body.

Svevo proclaimed this metaphysical irony in 1896 in his attempt to establish a complete union of mind and soul with his fiancée:

everything's still a make-believe [*commedia*], for in the end the curtain will fall. Besides, indifference towards life is the essence of my intellectual life. In so far as what I say is witty and forceful, it is nothing but irony, and I fear that on the day when you succeed in making me believe in life (which is impossible) I would find myself greatly diminished.[2]

The unreality of individual existence can, for Svevo as for Schopenhauer, be tentatively transcended by a realized ethical impulse or by artistic vision. (Svevo does not follow Schopenhauer in seeing mystical experience as also a valid way of going beyond self.)

Writing, like other forms of art, is, at its best, a precarious attempt at such a transcendence. Most of Svevo's narrative fictions incorporate the theme of the failed writer, or of writing which serves the individual and his illusory ends of self-gratification. Such a writer and such writing are themselves subjects to the Schopenhauerian irony of Svevo's own writing, which encompasses them. The ultimate case is that of *La coscienza di Zeno* and its fragmentary sequel. In the latter, the book consists *only* of Zeno writing his confessions; in the former, there is also the psychoanalyst writing his brief but tell-tale preface. Svevo has performed an elementary disappearing trick. But his controlling irony remains, of course, in the novel's structure: in its internal structure, juxtaposing the rival perspectives of analyst and patient; and in the external structure of its historical setting.

The writer who called himself Italo Svevo led a double life. Indeed, he badly needed Schopenhauer's help in explaining the 'mystery' of Ettore Schmitz: that is, his own scrambled everyday self, his divided will, the contradictions in his existence: between his literary vocation and his lifetime spent as a bank-clerk and a factory manager; between his Jewish origins, his atheistic convictions and his nominal Catholicism; between his German name and background and his chosen Italian nationality; between his nationalist aspirations for Trieste's union with Italy, his internationalist Socialist sympathies, and his Austrian business interests. The demands and allegiances multiply, and the conflicts between them intensify, as the course of Ettore Schmitz's life carries him towards, through and beyond the cataclysm of the Great War.

Such a personality could not possibly be the construct of a rational will, or the product of a rational society or universe. (Perhaps none is.) In everyday life, Italo Svevo the writer remained submerged beneath the semblance of Ettore Schmitz: with an invisibility so complete that there was never a public mention of him (beyond a few reviews) right up to 1925. In fact, the close but subtle connexion between Svevo and his milieu, between text and context, is most signally proved precisely by the politically motivated conspiracy of silence that enfolded the writer almost to the end of his life.

To the biographer, the sparseness in the documentation of Svevo's life is dispiriting. On the one hand there is an untidy riot of biographical and autobiographical material, much of it not greatly enlightening and some of it downright misleading; on the other, large areas of silence. Hardly ever did Svevo bare his soul. His attempt to do so to his wife was severely curtailed by the limits of her interests and receptiveness. His only bosom friend appears to have been the painter Umberto Veruda, who was not given to committing himself to paper.

The relation between Svevo's literary works and their audience therefore has to be worked out mostly by implication: that is, by juxtaposing the two as faithfully as possible. Which is one of the major endeavours of this book. Another is to define the role of writing in Svevo's life. The Schopenhauerian perspective already outlined suggests that for Svevo writing was a metaphysical act: only through writing could he hope to know the world and to know himself and be himself.

If writing, implying the will to be among such 'geniuses' or 'gods' as Schiller, Heine or Zola, is an impulse towards self-aggrandizement and therefore subject to Schopenhauerian irony, this irony itself can control and redeem the writing if it is integral to it. And since consciousness, when it takes analytic and ironic forms, is always one step ahead of itself, the cognitive function prevails over both self-aggrandizement and ironic self-deprecation, and invests the whole of what is written. At its acme—in *La coscienza di Zeno* and some later works, the process becomes yet more complex: Svevo's protagonist undertakes writing with impure motives, the analytic intent being undermined at key points by mystification or special pleading or discarded altogether, as when Zeno abandons his confessions to plunge into another form of self-aggrandizement in the practical world of business, the world of the fathers to which he has so long aspired. The context for this is war, the most naked form of that *lotta* (strife or struggle) which, for Svevo as for his intellectual masters, is the first and last reality in life: the metaphysical conflict of individuation for Schopenhauer; the biological struggle to survive for Darwin; the socio-economic struggle between the classes for Marx; conflict within and between psyches for Freud.

Yet Ettore Schmitz lives in that same world which the irony of Italo Svevo dismantles. He lives in it, but does not belong to it. On his twenty-eighth birthday, at the moment of his greatest apparent involvement in politics, he confesses that his life is a systematic social fiction. He adapts to life by living it as a fiction or *commedia* and can be himself, outside social fictions, only through literary fiction, where he is protected by complex ironies. It is at this point, just as he is trying to get his first novel published, that he assumes the pseudonym Svevo.

The journalist Roberto Graff, at the moment when Svevo at last achieved celebrity, was to see this split between Schmitz and Svevo, the outside and the inside, more sharply than any other observer. The author was for Graff 'the man with the split personality':

Even in Trieste, where he lived, he felt a stranger and out of place. Irony welded and cemented together his two personalities into a unity ... he believed art to be the supreme going beyond self ... he embraced what was in the first half of the twentieth century called the religion of art ... Literary expression was the supreme endeavour of the man with the split personality to be human ... and he turned the rationale for his own personal salvation into a universal role for modern man. Like André Gide, Svevo overcame his sense of guilt and his neurasthenia through the discipline of his art.[3]

Guilt and neurasthenia indeed figure largely both in the life of Ettore Schmitz and in the works of Italo Svevo.

Another journalist who knew Svevo in the same period as Graff, Dora Salvi, recollects a remark of Svevo's: 'How can you help being yourself on the first day as on the last and how can you desire not to be?' And his avowal: 'I wasn't meaning to produce literature.'[4]

Literature here, as always for Svevo, is quite a different thing from 'writing'. Svevo lives through writing, as he frequently admits: in his reflections of December 1902 on 'my habit and that of all impotent people of being unable to think except pen in hand';[5] in his disclosure in the preface to the 1927 edition of *Senilità*: 'That title was my guide and I lived by it.'[6] And the voice of the ageing Zeno might well be that of Svevo cocooned in his social fictions:

I have to think and write in order to feel alive, because this life I lead, what with all my virtues, and those I'm credited with, and all the affections and obligations that bind and paralyse me, deprives me of all freedom.[7]

And again: 'I feel as if I'd lived only that part of my life which I described.'[8]

But the writer, no less than the paterfamilias and businessman, has to play an exacting social role. He has to reconstruct his own past so as to make it acceptable to the public at large, to publishers and critics, to relatives and business associates, to official Trieste and Italy, and he does this in the letters he sends in answer to enquiries and in his *Profilo autobiografico*.[9] He manufactures another social image of himself as the writer who sacrificed literature to the well-being of his family by devoting himself to business and vowing himself to silence for twenty years. To throw light on the real Ettore Schmitz who was so well protected by the fictions and ironies of Italo Svevo and so well camouflaged by the obscurity of his life, and on the real Italo Svevo who was in turn put on show by Ettore Schmitz—this is no easy task.

One of the most difficult skeins to disentangle is the exact weight and character of Schmitz's, or Svevo's, political interests. From the execution of the Italian nationalist Oberdan for high treason in 1882, Ettore Schmitz became a regular contributor to *L'Indipendente*, the newspaper that mostly closely identified itself with Oberdan's cause. All his political acts and affiliations were associated with that cause. Yet, apart from some veiled hints in his newspaper articles, it figures in none of his writings. Even more strikingly, as we have seen, it was just when he was doing most for the nationalist cause that he privately avowed that it was all systematic simulation on his part. Moreover,

La coscienza di Zeno shows up in sardonic light a Triestine's attitude to what
the nationalists saw as the sublimely heroic war to 'redeem' Trieste for Italy.

The writer's 'Socialism' is equally problematic. It appears to be a matter
of attitude and intellectual development, whose lack of personal practical
commitment finds an ironic echo in the treatment of Emilio Brentani's socialism
in *Senilità*. It compounds the social and political awareness of Svevo's writing—
always acute—which becomes a subtly insistent element in the ethical perspectives of most of his work from the Great War onwards. Certainly, Trieste's
special relevance to the Great War, and to the rise of Fascism, and the complexities and double-dealing of Triestine politics, provide an essential context
against which we may hope to define Svevo's response to the world he lived
in.

Ettore Schmitz seems generally to have compromised with circumstances;
sometimes, like some of his protagonists, accommodating himself to them in
the most blatant bad faith. He delegates his real responses and responsibilities
to the writer Italo Svevo. So arises one of his central dilemmas: whether writing
is an alternative to living, or the only possible mode of living. In the last year
of his life he declared himself on the matter. He divided mankind into doers
and thinkers, leaning on Schopenhauer, who 'considered the observer to be as
much a finished product of nature as the fighter'.[10] Svevo presented this as an
accident of personality, but it could be viewed, in part, in the context of a
historical development: the collapse of individualism. Corporate capital and
the corporate State now render the individual consciousness and conscience
increasingly peripheral and ineffectual. The consciousness survives in the solitude of the act of writing—in which alone, for Svevo, one can be oneself—and
of reading. We can carry over into the context of his reflections of December
1902 a phrase which Svevo penned on 2 October 1899: 'In a word, there is no
salvation outside the pen.'[11] This book attempts to follow the trail of Svevo's
obscure quest to be himself and to establish a link between living and writing.

Part II

SPLITS
to 1878

2

THE TRIESTINE MELTING-POT

Ettore Schmitz's pseudonym, Italo Svevo, indicates Italy and Germany (Swabia) as his double homeland. Svevo's home town, Trieste, while linguistically and culturally Italian, was politically subject to the (Germanic) Austrian House of Habsburg. But the pseudonym excludes as much as it includes of Trieste, for a third party, the Slavs, dominated the surrounding countryside and became an increasingly important element in the town's population. And, at the writer's birth in 1861, the town was an intricate mosaic of different tongues, cultures and creeds, remarkable even for the multilingual Babel of the Habsburg Empire.

Trieste, then known as Tergeste, had been Romanized in the time of Augustus and had preserved Roman traditions of law and internal government ever since. During the national struggles that accompanied and outlasted Svevo's lifetime, the Italians of Trieste made the most of their town's Roman past and of its subsequent development as a typical Italian city-state. Trieste's Latin character survived its subjection to the Habsburgs in 1382, since for centuries the dynasty hardly interfered with the city's internal affairs. It was only towards the end of the nineteenth century, when Trieste not only still had German-speaking rulers but saw Slav workers pouring in from the countryside to man the town's expanding industry, that the leaders of the Italian National Liberal party revived the frontier mentality of Imperial Roman Tergeste.

In this cosmopolis, the Jewish community, to which Svevo's family belonged, amounted to 6.5 per cent of the town population. This was much less than in most towns in Austria-Hungary, but nevertheless, the Jews controlled much of Trieste's trade and finance. The Greeks also had a large share.

Census figures were politically contentious, as nationality was defined by 'language of use'. This consistently overstated the politically dominant national-ities—Italian and German—and understated the number of the subordinate Slavs, who were generally employed by Italian- or German-speakers. The 1880 returns show a population of 72,344 living in the town and about the same number in the surrounding district. Over two-thirds (104,951) declared them-selves Italian 'users'. Sixteen thousand of these were in fact citizens of Italy. There were 26,000 Slavs, nearly 5,000 Germans and almost 6,000 assorted foreigners.[1] Trieste's powers of assimilation were such that many thousands of Germans and Slavs and others quickly came to feel themselves to be, and were accepted as, Triestines. James Joyce was to be among them, and Triestine (a variant of Venetian dialect) became the home language in his family.

The considerable number of foreign residents reflected Trieste's status as a free port, which brought it a flourishing entrepôt trade and a good deal of shipping, insurance and finance business. The Free Port was a shop-window for the world commodity market and Trieste was the most important financial centre in the Austrian half of the Empire, but, by the time Ettore Schmitz was growing up, was losing out commercially through having lagged behind in the Industrial Revolution and the age of steam.

Most of the German speakers belonged to upper ranks of the Imperial administration, the armed forces or the police. The Slavs were mainly Catholic Slovenes and Croats from around Trieste, usually unskilled labourers and domestic servants. Towards the end of the century many Slavs entered the lower ranks of the civic administration and the police, as they readily learnt Italian and German, whilst Italians and Germans disdained to learn Slovene. The monarchy encouraged the Slavs in Trieste as a counterweight to the dominant Italians, and the latter were indeed far more hostile to the 'Slav peril' than to Vienna and the German-speaking Austrians. Svevo, though he evinced no national prejudice, never gave the slightest sign of interest in the Slovenes, their language or any aspect of their culture. He ironically reflects the national relationships of Trieste in *La coscienza di Zeno*: when the war breaks out, Zeno is confronted by malodorous Slav border-guards with whom he has only one word in common, *Zurück!* ('Back!'), but is then able to have a conversation of sorts with a German officer.[2] And in 'Una burla riuscita' (A Hoax) the failed writer Mario Samigli is embarrassed that it is an illiterate Slav who admires him so much that he keeps him supplied with valuable food in wartime.[3] James Joyce dismissed the Slavs of Istria as ignorant peasants.

These staunchly Catholic peasants or recent urban immigrants certainly did not care for the Italian nationalists, who were mostly anticlerical free-thinkers and whose leaders were Freemasons or Jews or both at once (though anti-Semitism never took root in Trieste). Most Italian-speaking Triestines in fact had no contact with the Slav world except through their Slovene maids.[4] Isabel Burton, whose husband, the explorer, was British consul-general in Trieste from 1872 to 1890, described how the supercilious townspeople on holiday on the Carso plateau above Trieste treated the religious festivities of the Slav villagers as a curious spectacle and did not deign to bend their knees.[5]

Trieste is more happily situated geographically than politically. The city faces west over a broad bay in the north-east Adriatic. To the south lie the small hilly peninsula of Muggia and the larger, mountainous peninsula of Istria. To the north-west, the low Venetian and Friulan coastline of Italy is out of sight. Behind Trieste rises the limestone Carso, which forms steep cliffs all along the sea-coast for a dozen miles to the north, as far as the Isonzo, beyond Duino with its Roman and medieval castles. It is riddled with potholes, crevasses and labyrinthine underground caverns and has an interesting but sparse vegetation, except for scattered rich pockets where grow the vines that produce the sharp *terrano* wines. Here on the Carso, Triestines have always loved to escape the summer heat of the town below, exploring the rugged terrain or simply enjoying the cool, clean air. A cable tramway linked the town to Opicina, or Obcina, on the Carso's edge.

The historic centre of Trieste is the hill surmounted by the Castle and the Basilica of San Giusto, the city's patron and symbol of its municipal identity. Around this are the working-class districts of San Giacomo and Città Vecchia. North of San Giusto lay the salt-pans on which the Triestine economy had depended from pre-Roman times. This space between the sea and the Carso was drained during the reigns of Maria Teresa and Joseph II to make way for the Città Nuova, built in a rectangular layout of imposing buildings three or four storeys high. A new harbour (the present Porto Vecchio), adjoining Città Nuova, was completed in 1884. Here much of the characteristic bustle of pre-1914 Trieste was concentrated and the short canal that cuts right through Città Nuova to stop beneath the steps of the stately neoclassical church of Sant'Antonio Taumaturgo was thronged with the masts of sailing-ships. (See Plate 3.)

Lady Burton described Trieste as 'a city dear and unhealthy to live in, over-ventilated and ill-drained'.[6] The violent north wind that blows from the Alps in winter, the *bora*, is legendary. Handrails had to be put up and Triestines are full of stories of horses, wagons and even trams being blown into the sea. In summer comes the humid, enervating, southerly sirocco, from which Ettore particularly suffered, and which blew the drainage back into the town.[7]

Several stone piers reach out into the bay of Trieste. The longest, the Molo San Carlo (now Molo Audace), is where Triestines take their quiet evening stroll. The mid-nineteenth-century German Triestine poet Robert Hammerling indulged in a Schopenhauerian reflection on this habit: he saw the money-minded Triestines as finding at the end of the pier, in the darkness of night, the mystical spell of nature, 'recalling the secret rites of some mysterious deity', as they gazed 'into emptiness, into nothingness', a nothingness which 'bears an alluring likeness to Infinity', as conceived by 'the contemplative religions of India'.[8] Svevo, a lifelong devotee of Schopenhauer, must have been particularly sensitive to the mystique of the pier.

3

THE RISE OF THE NATIONALITIES

The contemplative calm of the Triestines was threatened not only by money-making, but also by politics. Trieste was particularly affected by the rise of nationalism which was ultimately to destroy the empire of the Habsburgs and shatter the Italian community on the eastern shore of the Adriatic. The Italian nation-state and Ettore Schmitz were born in the same year, 1861. The prospect of joining a united Italy now became both more realistic and more appealing for many Triestines, and the Austrians accordingly abandoned the cruel repression and penal horrors of Metternich's time, and adopted the more discreet methods of strict censorship and legal prosecution for 'treasonable' offences. Diplomacy was preferred to force, and it produced results. As early as 1864 Italy renounced any claim to Trieste, and consequently the nationalists in the town suffered an eclipse for some years. However, the Società di Ginnastica had been founded in 1863 to foster Italian patriotism in Trieste, and as national rivalries intensified, the Germans and Slavs formed their own gymnastic societies.

When Austria lost Venice in 1866, the frontier was brought much closer to Trieste, but the town acquired a new importance in being now Austria's only major seaport—a position whose advantages the business-minded Triestines were in no hurry to throw away, preferring to encourage Vienna to extend the port's facilities.

In the aftermath of their defeat in 1866, the Habsburgs set about re-ordering, modernizing, and strengthening their Empire. The act of *Ausgleich*, or 'Parity', divided the Empire between Germans and Hungarians by a line which left Trieste just on the Austrian side. The 'Dual System' or 'Dualism' of 1867 guaranteed equal political and civil rights to all the nationalities of Austria-Hungary, but this hardly squared with the fact that millions of Slavs were ruled from German Vienna and Magyar Budapest under a German dynasty, and national tensions within Austria-Hungary were as fierce as anywhere in Europe. Competition raged, especially over language—the language of instruction in schools and universities, the language used in public administration and in the law-courts and even in the census. The politically dominant nationalities vigorously strove to 'Germanize', 'Magyarize', or, in Trieste's case, 'Italianize', the population of 'their' territory.

The Italians of Trieste were apt to regard their own very considerable success in assimilating Slovenes, Croats and even Germans and others as a token both of their cultural superiority and of their benevolence and openness to foreigners. 'The idea never crossed the mind of any Triestine that anyone might be the less Triestine in spirit or Italian in sentiment merely on account of having been born in Malta, Zagreb or Dublin,' argued Alberto Spaini.[9] It was difficult for Italians to understand that their offer of the gift of Italian culture must have looked to many Slavs like the kiss of death.

Conflict between nationalities was easily aroused but much less easily to be quelled in a mainly Italian town surrounded by a mainly Slav countryside. Industry was developing in Trieste. The first railway link with Vienna came at last in 1857 and new port facilities were built in 1869–83. These works brought in large numbers of Slav labourers. As early as 1868 feelings between Italians and Slavs had run so high that a large crowd of Slovenes assaulted Italians at the Volti di Chiozza near the town centre, only a few streets away from the Schmitzes' house. The police appear to have supported the Slovenes with swords and firearms and two people were killed and twenty-three, mostly Italians, injured. A few days earlier, the Austrian police had intervened against an angry Italian crowd after a stormy scene in the Triestine Diet. Five people had received bayonet wounds.[10]

The nationalists rarely lost even the most trivial opportunity to provoke the Austrian authorities. An Italian royal birthday or anniversary, an Italian military success or the anniversary of a political event, would bring cheering crowds out on the squares, many people waving the prohibited red-white-and-green tricolour. Police intervention was often brutal. The worst incident of this kind occurred on 21 September 1870, when the news reached Trieste that Italian troops had at last entered Rome. Austrian soldiers trying to control the demonstration wounded several people. The police were aware of the existence of conspiratorial societies working to unite Trieste to Italy and, like police in even the most liberal countries, they kept a watch on every organization, from the Triestine Hairdressers' Friendly Society to the Trieste Girls' Hospice.[11]

The Italian National Liberal Party in Trieste was quick to come to terms with the new Austria-Hungary of the *Ausgleich*. In 1868 it founded the Società del Progresso to advance the Italian national character of Trieste and to organize culturally, socially and politically. In 1869 this in turn produced the Società Operaia Triestina, whose avowed intention was to keep Italian workers in Trieste within the national movement and (especially after the shock of the 1871 Paris Commune) to prevent the rise of Socialist or revolutionary organizations.[12] Indeed, the National Liberals, according to their own historian Tamaro, displayed a 'phoney left-wing extremism' which they could control or disclaim as circumstances advised.[13] They sought in this way to exploit the new 'Irredentist' movement of old and young Garibaldians and radicals in Italy and in Trieste, who aspired to bring into the Kingdom of Italy the as yet 'unredeemed' Italian territories ('terre irredente', 'Italia irredenta'), including, of course, Trieste and its neighbouring provinces.

Opponents of the National Liberal leadership always accused it of caring less for union with Italy than for keeping control of Trieste for the ruling financial and business interests which it represented. And recent historians have shown how, at least until the introduction of an element of manhood suffrage in 1896, the Liberals did not work towards 'redeeming' Trieste for Italy: rather, they used Irredentist sentiment to preserve Trieste's municipal privileges, particularly its political autonomy as *città immediata*, directly subject to the monarchy, but not to the Vienna Parliament, outside the political structure of the Imperial domains. The Party's own control of the self-governing city was therefore its first concern.

This attitude became even clearer in 1873: direct elections to the Austrian Parliament replaced the previous system whereby each Provincial Diet selected its own representatives to go to Vienna; the Italian party now boycotted the parliamentary elections, as to participate would have implied recognition of Trieste's dependence on Vienna. Since the right to vote depended on a property qualification, the Italians (who formed the bulk of the upper and middle classes) virtually monopolized political power, more as a class than as a nationality (the bulk of the working class was also Italian).[14]

Irredentism in Trieste therefore presented a double face: its patriotic idealism could be used as a political myth and an instrument of control. In such matters as the Empire's transport and communications policy (especially with regard to railways) or its military budget, the National Liberals regularly pursued policies which bound Trieste more closely to Austria. Their equivocations were to be the essential political education of Ettore Schmitz, alias Italo Svevo.

4

THE SCHMITZ FAMILY

Hardly anything about Svevo is straightforward: not his name or date of birth, nor his family origins. The register of births of the Jewish community in Trieste records the birth of 'Schmitz, Aron called Ettore' on 20 December 1861 to Raffaele (Francesco) Schmitz and Allegra Moravia, but, at least as far back as 1889, Ettore always celebrated his birthday on 19 December. Besides having the names Aron and Ettore, he was called Tajè *en famille*.

Just as the ethnic composition of his home town was more complex than the pseudonym Italo Svevo indicates, so too were Ettore's family origins: the roots of the Schmitz family tree straddle Europe. While Ettore's mother came from an Italian Jewish family, his paternal grandfather was a German-speaking Jew, originally from the Rhineland, who moved to Köpchen, or Klein Kopitz in Siebenbürgen (Transylvania). In 1867 this went to the Hungarian half of Austria-Hungary and has belonged since 1919 to Romania.

Svevo's *Profilo autobiografico* is evasive about the German and Austrian side of his family background. The *Profilo* was drafted by Giulio Césari, Svevo's old friend and a lifelong nationalist, in 1928, at the height of the nationalistic Fascist regime, and revised by Svevo. Germany and Austria were then still remembered as Italy's adversaries in the Great War. The *Profilo*, therefore, explains away, with evident embarrassment, the author's Germanic pseudonym 'which seems to imply a brotherhood between the Italian and Germanic races'; and likewise minimizes the importance of Ettore's 'distant German forebear', his paternal grandfather, Adolfo Schmitz, an Austrian government employee at Treviso. It disparages Ettore's German schooling and makes the most of his credentials as an Italian patriot.[15]

Svevo's widow, Livia Veneziani, similarly disclaimed any German or Austrian allegiance for Ettore's father, Francesco Schmitz, but disclosed that his grandfather Adolfo's family came from the Rhineland. This seems likely enough. Ettore was once working in Mülheim, near the Rhine: out of his seven workhands, three were called Schmitz.[16] In Austria, Schmitzes are far less numerous: not one appears in the nineteenth-century tax register of the Vienna Finanzarchiv.

Ettore's younger brother, Elio, kept a diary which is the only source of information on the Schmitz family and on Ettore's early years, except for Svevo's own *Profilo autobiografico*, to which it is an indispensable corrective. It is Elio who states that in 1855 his father Francesco had a paternal uncle living in Köpchen in Hungary, 'which is where our family probably comes from'; and, more positively: 'My grandfather was Hungarian, and came from Köpchen.'[17] A German-speaking Jew from the Rhineland may indeed easily have made the move to one of the large German-speaking colonies in the eastern Habsburg domains, especially after the Emperor Joseph II, by his Edict of Tolerance of 1783, had abolished many of the legal restrictions imposed on the residence and movements of his Jewish subjects. Köpchen now appears on the map under its Romanian name of Copşa Mică. It is a small township in the Carpathian foothills of Transylvania north of the Danube, on the road between Alba Iulia and Sighişoara.

Transylvania underwent a vigorous Magyarization campaign to assimilate its very mixed population which included, besides Magyars, or Hungarians, and Germans, a very large number of Romanians and a fairly strong Jewish contingent. The Jews controlled most of the commerce of the area, as they did over much of eastern Europe. As they also enthusiastically accepted Magyarization, they roused jealousies among other groups, particularly among the Romanians, and the neighbouring kingdom of Romania was always hostile to Jews. In 1928, Svevo was to talk of 'that blessed Romania with all those anti-Semites'.[18] The Germans in the area around Köpchen spoke a Swabian dialect, which earned the district the nickname of Schwabenland, or Swabia—a first link with the pseudonym Svevo.

Elio reports that his paternal grandparents, Abramo Adolfo Schmitz and Paolina Macerata, were married in Trieste.[19] The Jewish marriage register in Trieste indeed records the marriage of 'Abramo di Raffael Smitz', aged twenty-five, to Allegra Macerata, aged twenty-four, on 30 July 1828. I have found no explanation for the different versions of the bride's first name. She may have used several. Less than two months after the marriage, on 17 September 1828, she had a son, Raffael (that is, Svevo's father, Francesco), and her name is entered on the register of births as Rosa Macerata. The fact that Francesco Schmitz's first child was to be named Paolina supports the supposition that that was the name used by his mother, who, according to Elio, was a Triestine.

The uncertain spelling of Abramo's surname could be put down to illiteracy.

According to Elio, Abramo and Paolina were extremely poor, and also ill-matched. Elio was never able to find out his grandfather's occupation. He makes no mention of Abramo's ever having been a state official (*funzionario*) at Treviso, or anywhere.

In 1910, Svevo's aunt Marietta, a compulsive and over-imaginative story-teller then over seventy, told him two tales going back to a time before she was born. One of them is about grandmother Schmitz appearing before the Emperor in her best clothes to petition him to allow her family to settle in Leopoldstadt, the mainly Jewish quarter of Vienna. This would have taken place around 1830. Marietta's other story describes grandfather Schmitz hiding in a cellar full of garbage in Udine to avoid military service. When he was eventually drafted, 'like the wily Jew that he was, he turned victualler and sent home bags of Napoleons'.[20] This must have been in the war against Piedmont in 1821.

In Vienna, to resume Elio's narrative, Raffael Francesco received his schooling, but his family was still so poor that on 20 March 1842, when he was thirteen, his father, having no more food, sent him out to earn his living as a pedlar with two florins in his pocket and a little bundle of knick-knacks. Francesco Schmitz sometimes told his family of the hardships he had endured as he wandered from town to town selling his wares in the cafés. One winter in Padua he was saved from freezing and starving to death by a dealer in fancy goods whom Francesco in his turn saved from bankruptcy many years later.[21]

Francesco found his way back to Hungary, where he became an overseer in railway construction and, 'when the insurrection broke out in '48, he fought for liberty and constitution. When the insurrection had been quelled, he was sent to Venice', where the Austrians were dealing with yet another rebellion. At the citadel in Palmanuova he was arrested as a deserter and imprisoned for a few months. However, as Triestines were, until 1867, exempt from military service, he was eventually freed.[22]

Elio is unclear about the subsequent history of the family of Adolfo Schmitz and Rosa (or Paolina, or Allegra) Macerata. At some time in the 1840s they moved back with their young daughter Marietta from Vienna to Udine. Francesco's brother Vito was born there around 1848, followed some two years later by his second sister, Peppina, who, Elio remarks, 'as she emerged into the light of day, killed her mother'.[23] Francesco was then away in Dalmatia but returned home at the news of his mother's death only to find his father also on his death-bed. Abramo Adolfo must have died of cholera, which Elio elsewhere says took off three of his grandparents.

Francesco, now about twenty-two, moved to Trieste in 1850 or 1851 with his orphaned brother and sisters. Marietta was about twelve years old, Vito two, and Giuseppina (or Peppina) an infant. Francesco found work with a glassware merchant called Straulino for miserable wages. He made ends meet by giving lessons to children in the evenings and improved his education by exchanging German lessons for instruction in book-keeping. He had moved on to a job with Trieste's leading glassware firm, Leiss, when he fell in love with Allegra Moravia. She was born in 1833, the eldest of a large family, and was said to be one of the prettiest girls in Trieste. Of her three suitors, Francesco was the poorest and the least attractive to her, owing to his habit of following everything he said with a laugh.

Just then Allegra's father was carried off by what was thought to be a mild attack of cholera. The night after he died he appeared to her in a dream and 'directed her to accept the hand of Francesco Schmitz, and no one else's, and the next morning she gave the said Schmitz a good round yes for an answer, sent the others packing, and never had cause to regret her decision.'[24]

When Francesco married, on 2 December 1855, he was still supporting Vito and Peppina. Marietta, then about seventeen, had, it seems, already married Ferdinando Ziffer. Allegra's first child, Paola, was born on 8 May 1856, and when Noemi was born, on 15 June of the following year, Francesco could not afford a midwife, but was often to remark, with the good humour that characterized the first twenty or so years of his married life: 'Providence came to my aid as always, as Noemi was born in a few minutes without any need of a midwife.' 'Any other father but mine', writes Elio, 'would have been in despair at not having had a son in place of Noemi, but not he. Noemi's arrival was welcomed and celebrated, from what I am told, as much as Paola's, and as if she were a boy.'[25] There was yet a third daughter, Natalia, before the boys started arriving: Adolfo in 1860, Ettore in 1861, Elio in 1863. 'My father, ever modest in his ideas, used to tell us, and still does, that that brought his happiness to its peak.'[26] At every birth Francesco would exclaim: 'Today my capital has increased by a million!' Elio's birth was hailed as his sixth million.[27]

Two more Schmitz children were to survive infancy: Ortensia, born in 1870, and Ottavio, the eighth of the family, who came in 1872. Thus there were four sisters and four brothers in all. Allegra had no less than sixteen deliveries,[28] so that she must have been continually either pregnant or nursing or both. She was, Elio tells us, of poor but honest family, with five brothers and two sisters, and 'was educated after the manner of the times, not so as to pass as clever, but to be a good housekeeper'. She breast-fed all her children except Elio, for whom a wet-nurse had to be found.[29] She was a warmly affectionate and indulgent mother. Her father, Abramo, had come to Trieste from San Daniele del Friuli, not far from Udine, and set up as a butcher. A family legend, suppressed in the published version of Elio's diary, had it that the family was of partly aristocratic descent in an illegitimate line and had been done out of a promised inheritance.

Francesco Schmitz set up his own glassware business, Schmitz & Co., in 1861, in partnership first with one Finzi, who provided the capital, then with a man called Cuzzi. Finally, having built up his own capital, he went into partnership around 1870 with his own brother Vito, twenty years his junior. Elio, writing in 1879 or 1880, describes his father as 'in every sense of the word a good businessman', of absolute integrity and with a strong sense of order, quite creditably self-educated, but exceptionally strict with his children.[30] A generous man, he not only looked after his own brothers and sisters but also helped numerous needy relatives.

5

A SHELTERED CHILDHOOD

By the time Ettore was born, the Schmitz family were occupying a fine third-floor apartment in Via dell'Acquedotto (now Viale XX Settembre), where the foothills of the Carso reach furthest into Trieste. In this house Ettore grew up, his father's strict but benevolent authority balanced by the gentler manner of his mother. His uncle Vito and aunt Peppina, his seniors by only about thirteen and eleven years respectively, lived at home, as well as his three elder sisters and an affectionate resident family servant, Cati Moro (who appears as Catina in *La coscienza di Zeno*). All the children slept in one large room and aunt Peppina washed them and combed their hair in the mornings and taught them to read and to say their prayers. They would play hide-and-seek and ball-games, at which Noemi excelled. Until Ortensia and Ottavio were born in 1870 and 1872, Elio, as the youngest, was the pet of the family.[31]

At the age of six the boys were sent to a school run by Trieste's senior Rabbi, Melli. Svevo's fragment 'Le confessioni del vegliardo' (An Old Man's Confessions) seems to be straightforwardly autobiographical. The protagonist, Giovanni Respiro, is born on the same day as Ettore. His earliest memory goes back to somewhere around 1866:

I had so wanted to go to school and eventually did so. Having got to school, however, I must have been hurt, badgered or threatened by some schoolmate or by my teacher, because I remember clinging to the door that led to the staircase exit, that is, the place nearest to my home and my mother. I stayed there for hours because they would not let me leave school, nor could they tear me from the spot ... Left alone, my whimpering gradually grew softer ...[32]

But subsequently Respiro reflects that the tears may have been caused simply by leaving his mother.

In 1872 the Schmitz boys transferred to a private school run by another Jew, Emanuele Edeles, which was supposed to give its pupils a commercial education. The teaching was poor and the headmaster, though an able man, was, according to Elio, extremely stingy and unfair. Elio humorously relates a brief dialogue between the headmaster, Edeles, and one of the teachers, Ciatto. Ciatto wants to give the first two prizes to Adolfo and Ettore, but Edeles won't have two prizes awarded to the same family, so Ettore has to go without. The three brothers learned very little and Adolfo and Ettore, the latter particularly, devoured French novels without their father's knowledge. 'That is partly the cause', remarks Elio, 'of Ettore's state of excitement [*esaltazione*].'[33]

The Schmitzes, then, were a typical close-knit, middle-class Jewish-Italian family. Pretty well all their matrimonial and business connections were with other members of Trieste's Jewish community. They were clearly practising Jews, but easy-going and open-minded. Elio mentions without any disapproval his uncle Giuseppe Moravia's marriage to a Catholic. Noemi Schmitz fell in love with an Orthodox Slav called Dedovich, but Elio does not explain why nothing came of the affair.[34] Abramin Ancona, who had married Allegra's sister Giuditta, took his religion very seriously and looked down on the Schmitzes on both religious and social grounds.[35]

Some time before 1870 came the first of a series of family disasters. Francesco's sister Peppina, not yet twenty, fell in love with the twenty-year-old Ignazio Tedeschi, whom Elio describes as small and unattractive, an idler given over to novel-reading and other vices. Francesco was against the match, but as Vito stood surety for Tedeschi the elder Schmitz gave way and made over to the bridegroom a dowry of 10,000 florins, with which to open an oil-shop. There was a great wedding-feast, and the newly married couple set off on their honeymoon. Next morning Peppina awoke to find that her husband had made off with all their money, having pawned everything he could. Three months later, Tedeschi was arrested upon landing at Alexandria, having squandered the lot. Nine months after her wedding day Peppina gave birth to her child. Ignazio Tedeschi rejoined her after serving six months in prison, but the child, Mario, died at the age of two, as a result, Elio says, of a venereal disease which his father had contracted.[36]

Politics also severely impinged on the family's serenity. When the Franco-Prussian war broke out in 1870, Francesco, feeling himself an Austrian, backed the Prussians as brother Germans, while Vito, brought up in Trieste, and Allegra's brother Giacomo, were ardent supporters of Italy and therefore of France, for whom Garibaldi was fighting.[37] However, it was the collapse of France which made possible the Italian entry into Rome on 20 September 1870. This led to enthusiastic demonstrations in Trieste. The arguments between Francesco and Vito greatly upset the family, but Elio gives a brief account of the three main political parties in Trieste (the Irredentist *italianissimi*, the Austrian and the Slav) without any partisan comment other than that by 1880 the Irredentists had gained a great deal of ground. He adds only that 'nowadays we are in a continual state of apprehension as to what one or other of the parties will do next.' One of the most impressive demonstrations of Italian national feeling in Trieste took place near the Schmitz home on Sunday 23 March 1874. Twenty or twenty-five thousand people gathered in Via dell'Acquedotto for the unveiling of the bust of Domenico Rossetti, who had been one of Trieste's foremost Italian patriots and scholars.

In the early 1870s, the Schmitz household followed a peaceful routine. The three older boys used to rise at eight, go to school, come home to play ball with Noemi at midday, lunch and go back to school until five. Then the girls would play some music, there would be dinner and bed. However, one morning in 1873, Francesco came home and ordered the trunks to be packed. There was cholera in Trieste. Three of the children's grandparents had died of it, and a hundred deaths had been reported in the town the previous day. The whole family took the train to Celje in Slovenia, between Ljubljana and Maribor, then a pleasant country town of a few thousand inhabitants on the Savinja.[38] The Schmitzes escaped the cholera and liked Celje enough to return there for several summer holidays.

There is no hint that Francesco's business suffered from the great Austrian 'Black Friday' crash of 1873. It was in fact his prosperity which brought the first of the few great upheavals in Ettore's life. Francesco foresaw careers in commerce for his sons and felt that their education could not be completed at home.

6

A SCHOOL IN GERMANY

Francesco Schmitz, prosperous, kindly, but strong-minded, bred independence. He bent his children—Paolina, Noemi (perhaps), Ettore and Elio—to his will. 'My father', relates Elio, 'ever ready to make any sacrifice for us, whether of the heart or of the pocket, held the maxim: boys do not grow up into able men under their parents' eyes.' He therefore scanned the newspaper advertisements for a boarding-school which was strong in teaching but did not accustom its pupils to the soft ways of the wealthy.[39] Elio accepted his father's idea that his son's education should consist of a good commercial training with a knowledge of at least four languages, including a perfect knowledge of German and Italian, essential in Triestine commerce. Ettore's mangling of a German name was one incident that led his father to send the boys to school in Germany.[40] Good business Italian (though not the literary language), a Triestine could pick up at home.

Profilo autobiografico offers another reason why the Schmitz boys were sent off to boarding-school: 'his mother being of gentle character and not in the least authoritarian, his father thought it necessary to relieve her of the burden of dealing with so many children.'[41] Allegra's elder daughters, then aged respectively eighteen, seventeen and fifteen, could help her deal with the younger children, and the servant Cati Moro was still with the family as late as 1880. Was Svevo being sardonic in suggesting that Francesco was seeking to please his wife by sending away the children of whom she was so fond?

On 16 May 1874 (not 1873, as is usually stated*), Adolfo and Ettore left home for their school in Segnitz. This is a tiny village on the right (northern) bank of the Main, where the river makes its southernmost bend. On the opposite bank stands the small, ancient and picturesque walled town of Marktbreit, which is on the railway line about a dozen miles south-east of Würzburg. Ettore's stay there is one of the several reasons given in the *Profilo* for his choice of pseudonym,[43] but Segnitz is not in Swabia. That region lies over a hundred miles further south, along the course of the upper Danube (which threads its way through the Swabian Alps) as far as Lake Constance and the Swiss border. However, much nearer to Segnitz than that, one finds such place-names as Schwabisch Hall and Schwabische Gmünd, towards Stuttgart, and Schwabach, towards Nuremburg. 'Swabian' can be taken as synonymous with 'German', but distinct from 'Prussian' or 'Austrian'.

Why did Francesco send his sons to a school in Germany rather than somewhere in the Habsburg domains, where they might have learnt, in addition to German, Hungarian or Polish or Czech? A wave of anti-Semitism swept Austria-Hungary after the 1873 financial crash, for which many clerical and reactionary politicians blamed the Jews who dominated the Dual Monarchy's finance, industry and commerce. This may have discouraged Svevo's father from looking in that direction. The German, French and English taught at the Segnitz School, and its commercial emphasis, probably appeared better nourishment for the business career which Francesco had in mind for his sons. Perhaps the headmaster, Spier, who came to Trieste to recruit pupils, personally impressed their father, for Elio describes him as 'a teacher with a profound knowledge of his subjects and a practical man to the very marrow of his bones'.

---

* The *Profilo*, as well as several of Svevo's letters, mentions that Ettore went off to school in Segnitz at the age of twelve. This would set his departure in 1874. Elio's memories of the Vienna Exhibition and the Trieste cholera epidemic of 1873, with the family's evacuation to Celje, make it clear that his brothers could not have left for Segnitz that year. Elio remembers very clearly that Adolfo and Ettore set off on 16 May, but his account is confused as to the year. In one place he gives 1875 as the year of his brothers' first journey to Segnitz and says that he went with them when they returned there after a holiday at Celje and Trieste, on 24 October 1877. He talks of 'that year' he spent in Segnitz, and, as all three brothers returned to Trieste permanently on 1 September 1878, this account of the chronology hangs together. However, in another diary entry, Elio states that he first went to Segnitz three days after his thirteenth birthday—a date which a Jewish boy might be expected to remember, as it is when he goes through his *bar mitzvah* (though Elio makes no mention of this). If this latter statement is correct, he must have left for Segnitz on 24 October 1876, and therefore his brothers, who had already been there for two years, must have started in 1874. This chronology fits in better with Svevo's frequent statements that he was at Segnitz from the age of twelve till seventeen, and means that he would have spent four full years there. In another entry, Elio mentions that a family catastrophe brought him home after one year at Segnitz, and that he then returned to Segnitz for a second year. This supports 1874 as the year of Ettore and Adolfo's first departure, and 1876 for Elio's first departure.[42]

The elder Schmitz may also have found out that Spier, like himself, had played an active part in the revolutionary activity of 1848. Spier was a member of the Frankfurt Pan-German Constituent Assembly and on account of this had been confined to living in Segnitz.[44]

Elio—not yet eleven in May 1874—was utterly distressed at the prospect of leaving home and Trieste, having been, he says, thoroughly spoilt in all things. He fell ill, so Adolfo and Ettore set off with their parents, leaving him behind, and Elio woke the following morning dismayed to find his brothers no longer there, and particularly missing Ettore. His brothers seem to have been more cheerful about going away, at least after their first stay in Segnitz, but Ettore confided to Elio that he too, when he first left, thought that he would never again see those familiar places and their family which they loved so much. Years later, Ettore wrote to his wife: 'I remember that even as a boy I used to loathe chasing from pillar to post and seeing all those strange faces [musi nuovi].'[45]

The only information about Ettore's first journey to Segnitz is the fictionalized account which he wrote after revisiting the place in middle age, 'L'avvenire dei ricordi' (Memories and their Future).[46] The reminiscing character is called Roberto. His memories centre on the 'crisis' of the 'enormous journey'. He remembers arriving at a hotel in Verona in the hotel omnibus after a day's train travel, and leaving in the same vehicle, which had large windows and two decorated mirrors, that 'sang' as it jogged over the cobbles. Then the train over the Brenner Pass 'and an Englishman who explained to the child in terrible Italian that one could reach the mountain-top quicker on foot than by the railway's enormous climbing loops'. Of Innsbruck he could remember only the snow everywhere, no houses, and nothing of the nights he had spent either there or at Verona.

Some hours after leaving Innsbruck, eleven-and-a-half-year-old Roberto has a fearful tantrum at 'the discovery of his own inferiority': his parents entrust him to the charge of his thirteen-year-old brother, Armando. (These ages, if taken as straightforwardly and reliably autobiographical, would point to 1873.) Up to now, Roberto, the 'violent' one, had taken the lead. 'They were being sent to boarding-school precisely in order to tame Roberto who had hardly stuck his nose outside his nest before he turned out to be too much [troppo forte] for his weak mother and for his father who was busy in his office all day long.' He had got into bad company, disappeared mysteriously for hours at a time, was ashamed of his new clothes, which he quickly reduced to tatters, smoked and knew a great many obscene words—which were all he had learned of the Divine Comedy.

Roberto remembers a long wait on the platform beside their baggage at Kufstein (on Austria's border with Bavaria) on that cold June day. Perhaps, the writer surmises, Roberto felt divided by the Alps from his home and realized that he would now be journeying into that endless plain with its hills which his memory made naïvely regular.

He then leaps the huge distance to Würzburg, a clean, elegant and uncrowded city full of blue-capped schoolboys. The family visits an enormous palace where they see Italian paintings (the Prince-Bishop's palace with its great ceiling frescoes by Tiepolo) and a hall whose echo impresses Roberto, making the noise of ripping paper sound like a trumpet-blast.

At the hotel, however, as Svevo's story has it, the hotel owner refused to accept Triestine banknotes and 'descended from a sort of throne behind a wooden bar, alarmed that anyone should try to palm off such a currency on to him by way of payment, and came to keep an eye on his guest. He yelled, he actually yelled.' Roberto's father had to go off to draw some local currency from the bank, leaving his family and his luggage 'in pawn'. Roberto, who had never had to worry about money, was not in the least frightened, but his mother burst out crying and had to mop the tears off her cheeks under her veil, being already distraught at shortly having to part from her sons and at having left a third son sick at home.

His father returned in bitter humour, his pockets bulging with silver coins, and complained to his wife in Italian at the exchange rate and at this nation of robbers and ignoramuses who had never heard of the notes issued by the Bank of Trieste. 'There were the first words against Germany that Roberto had ever heard him utter.'

The travellers then took the train to Marktbreit, where they were met. Roberto remembers the schoolmaster Beer's face as 'wooden' (Elio calls Spier 'bony'). The school porter, a lad with a slight limp, panted as he trundled all the luggage down the slope.

The party crossed the river on a punt with tall sides and moored at the other side on a huge sandbank, making their way along wooden planks up the foreshore to a stone landing-stage, and from there to the village. At this point a later memory interferes with Roberto's earlier impressions. Like Svevo himself, he had returned there 'ten or twelve years earlier' (before the Great War) with his wife and daughter and had found the place greatly changed. The school had gone, and now there were dung-heaps around the village. (Elio had remembered the dung-heaps and open sewers.) The hill-tops were no longer wooded, the river-bed had been deepened, and its flood-pools filled in and put under cultivation. The punt had been replaced by a 'majestic' stone toll-bridge that vaulted over the river and the beet-fields on the Segnitz side. Swift steamboats had replaced the narrow sand-lighters and the log-rafts a kilometre long which would be steered downriver all the way to Belgium by two or three lumberjacks.

Roberto remembers the grassy unpaved lanes of Segnitz with their poor houses, some of them with a small flight of steps leading up to a terrace or parapet of wood that had been weathered shiny. There was the paved main street with its better-looking houses, its little Gothic church and tidy lawn, and a few oak trees and horse-chestnuts then in flower. A lady, matching Elio's description of Frau Spier, beautiful, elegant, tall and dark, with large expressive eyes and a pure profile with an aquiline nose, came to meet them. The reminiscing Roberto lingers on her gay smile and graceful movements which, as a boy, he had never noticed.

His recollections end with a significant little incident. Both the mother and the boys were grief-stricken at having to part, so the headmaster took the father aside and suggested a ruse. He then told the boys to follow him quickly to a spot where they could catch a last glimpse of their parents as they left. The two boys, hand in hand, followed the headmaster along a path screened from the river by tall reeds and other plants. Beer soon fell into a reverie (as Spier was wont to do), and, to hurry him up, the elder brother, Armando, started trotting along with short quick steps, imitated by Roberto. Beer, unconsciously, also quickened his pace, to Armando's amusement. Roberto, however, 'was anxious to see his parents again. In his young heart he hoped to be able to hold on to his mother again, once and for all. Why did the threatened parting have to take place?' Eventually the boys found that they had been led around the outskirts of the village and back to the place they had started from. 'Roberto's heart was beating. Tears of distress sprang at once to Armando's eyes, but already he seemed on the way to resigning himself to the situation.' Roberto, less easily resigned, rushed up the stairs to where he had last seen his parents.

This is the Freud-conscious Svevo's most pointed expression of his own 'family romance'. Beer (or Spier) visibly takes over the paternal role of driving the boys out of the family into the world, despite the strong emotional bond between them and their mother. Roberto is quickly established as a threat, from the moment he sticks his 'nose' out of his nest. He takes over his mother' in the father's absence and undermines his father's respectability by ruining his clothes, and his sexual domination by learning the obscene words in the *Divine Comedy*.

The incomplete 'L'avvenire dei ricordi' thus draws a pattern of rebellion ending in dependence and impotence. We may at least see a link between the fiction and the life. The young Ettore is the prisoner of the material comfort and security provided by his father. His father proves too strong for him. The school at Segnitz is too far away for him to run home, and by the time Ettore has learned the language of the country (his father's first language), he will have settled down there. The rebellion is displaced to the realm of fiction. Ettore had already developed a clandestine taste for reading fiction, in the face of his father's disapproval. His psychological independence was gradually to be transferred from reading to writing, and the middle-aged author of 'L'avvenire dei ricordi' was still using his pen to protect and restore his threatened personality. Life outside the page consisted mostly of imposed social behaviour. The 'true' self expressed itself in writing.

Eleven Jewish families, amounting to thirty-six souls, were living in Segnitz by 1866. The school had three Jewish teachers and eighty-two Jewish pupils. The resident population of the village was then 677. A sizeable paint factory was owned by the Jews, but all they had for a synagogue was a shabby little house.

The Brussel'sche Handels- und Erziehungsinstitut in Segnitz had been founded in 1838 and was quite famous. The school buildings were 'fine stone buildings, still the most handsome in Segnitz'.[47] Spier himself was Jewish. The pupils included local Catholics, but not Protestants. Nothing is known of the religious attitudes or practices of the school. It was closed down when all the Jewish families were expelled from Segnitz in 1882.

The pupils' accommodation was Spartan. Elio shared a room two metres square with two other pupils. 'Everything in that room was in miniature', for into it were crammed three beds, a table, a stove, three chairs, three stools, and a wash-stand so small that the basin 'wouldn't hold a litre'. Elio's descriptions of life there are invariably coloured by his home-sickness:

School meals are the most boring thing there could possibly be. You're not allowed to open your mouth much. Amongst ourselves we were not supposed to speak Triestine but German ... Everything proceeds the same slow way. And there were only the occasional jokes of Ettore Luzzatto, one of our fellow pupils from Trieste, to interrupt the monotony for a few moments.[48]

Lessons were held in the *Curs*, or school-house, on the bank of the Main. Svevo always said that he learned even less than he was taught, and did not speak highly of the quality of the instruction.[49] Nevertheless, at Segnitz he rapidly picked up the German language and a lifelong affection and admiration for things German. The great writers of German Romanticism and Weimar Classicism were his first introduction to serious literature, and fired him with a literary passion that never left him.

Bismarck's *Realpolitik* of 'blood and iron' had achieved the unification which the liberal democrats of 1848 had failed to bring about, and created the Reich under a Prussian Kaiser. The new Germany was authoritarian (and increasingly anti-Semitic), but in the 1870s the Germans' patriotic pride probably made itself felt also among the teachers and pupils at Segnitz. To the Italians, Prussia was a friend who had helped them to win Venetia in 1866 and Rome in 1870.

In the summer of 1876 Adolfo and Ettore returned for their first holiday, staying with their family in Celje. Upon the return of the Schmitzes to Trieste, Adolfo and Ettore prepared to go back to Segnitz. Elio was still most reluctant to leave home and to forgo the privilege, even at the age of thirteen, of falling asleep in his mother's arms, but he had been quite impressed by the results—including fluent German—which their education at Segnitz had had on his brothers.[50] On the evening of 24 October, the three Schmitz brothers, including a tearful Elio, were at the station to catch the train to Vienna. Spier was there, collecting other pupils from Trieste and points south. The other pupils were joking cheerfully as if they were coming home instead of leaving, remarked Elio, who had to be thrust into his compartment and shrank into a corner as the cliffs of the Carso cut out his last view of the city and its beautiful bay. He felt Spier's authority, though Spier as ever was buried in a book. However, even when he was not reading, he was so absorbed in his own thoughts as to be oblivious to all around him. The schoolboys had nicknamed him *Halomespeter*, from the Hebrew word for 'dream'.

The train reached Vienna at 10.30 the following night. The Segnitz party spent four days there, staying at the Hotel Metropole, which in view of Spier's reputation for stinginess, Elio found surprisingly luxurious—until he was told that Spier had shares in the hotel. Elio spent his five florins of pocket money on the entertainments of the Prater before they set off again, reaching Budweiss (České Budějovice) on the Bohemian border at midnight. All the pupils slipped out furtively to the station bar to have their last drink of coffee while Spier was asleep, Ettore explaining to Elio that at Segnitz they would have to drink chicory. By morning the train was at Fürth near Nuremburg, and there were now twenty of the blue caps of Segnitz (another detail corresponding to 'L'avvenire dei ricordi'). Ettore told Elio of the system of bullying and fagging that prevailed at Segnitz: 'the strongest had the right of command and they had to be obeyed.' Elio was dismayed, as, though excessively tall for his age, he was of feeble build. Ettore had to assure him that he and Adolfo were quite capable of protecting him.

The party reached Marktbreit in the evening, and was met at the station by a dozen 'blue-caps' and four masters. They set off down the hill, then along the smelly Marktbreit canal, Elio stumbling on the cobblestones. He wondered how the higgledy-piggledy houses, so different from the rectilinear streets of Trieste's modern quarters, managed not to tumble down. The oil lanterns hung at intervals on the house fronts were unlit.

At last there was the moonlit vista of the Main and the sound of a weir and on the other side, on the narrow plain below the Waldspitz hill, was Segnitz. To the right could be seen the ruins of a feudal castle. The party crossed the river in a large boat, used for ferrying ox-carts.

As they turned into the main street of Segnitz they were met by Frau Spier, who gave Elio a kiss and a lecture in German of which he understood not a word. Ettore led him into the school dining-room, a fine columned hall with four parallel tables in it. The deafening din suddenly ceased as the school sat down to dinner, during which Elio made the acquaintance of Caroline, Spier's daughter, and Anna Herz, his wife's niece, who greeted him in broken Italian. Fräulein Herz was 'very attractive, on the short side, but slim'. Like her aunt, she had her hair cut short and falling loosely behind her neck, instead of combed up after the fashion. Elio liked her very much indeed, with her 'easy, good-humoured laugh and large, knowing eyes'. Frau Spier and Caroline, on the other hand, put him off from their very first meeting by their affected manners. He was always on very cool terms with Spier himself.[51]

7

POETIC YOUTH

Through Elio's eyes we now get a closer look at Ettore's life at Segnitz. It was Ettore who had infected Elio with a passion for Dumas *père*, having given him a copy of *The Three Musketeers*. Now Elio was amazed to find that Ettore devoted all his free time to the modern classics, frequently dragging Elio into his room and reading him some passage of German literature. In a pen-portrait, probably written in 1881, Elio recapitulates the course of Ettore's literary obsession:

He appears apathetic, because he finds the greater part of his life within his own mind, and in himself. Little by little he conceived the idea of becoming a writer. Oh! to become famous was his highest hope. Little by little he became so accustomed to this idea that even today it dominates him totally.

Ettore studied all the German classics as thoroughly as he could. In his Segnitz days, Schiller and Goethe were his best friends. He collected a library out of his savings—the only thing that was neat and tidy in their room at home. Elio reads off the names of some of the authors on Ettore's bookshelves: Schiller, Hauff, Körner, Heine. Ettore had bought Goethe's works, read them, written his own commentary on them and then made them the prize in a raffle at Segnitz, with the proceeds of which he bought the works of Shakespeare in German translation. He read right through several nights learning *Hamlet* by heart, and then wanted to go on to *King Lear*. But his sleepless nights had made him pale, Spier found out the cause, and confiscated the book. Still Ettore lay awake for several more nights brooding over 'To be or not to be'. When Elio suggested that he should read the Italian classics, Dante and Petrarch, rather than Schiller and Goethe, Ettore laughed in his face: 'Schiller is the world's greatest genius,' he replied.[52]

Of his readings at Segnitz, Svevo's *Profilo autobiografico* stresses, not the Romantic dramatists and poets, but the humorous novelist Jean Paul (Friedrich Richter), who 'certainly had a great influence in forming his taste'. It only vaguely mentions the German classics, Shakespeare in translation, and 'some Russian writers, first and foremost Turgenev'.[53] Svevo's failure to mention Schiller and Goethe seems odd, if not downright misleading. Casual allusions throughout his life and work testify to his familiarity with Goethe at least. But the mention of Jean Paul sounds like a retrospective pointer. The ironic structure of Svevo's novels has a certain kinship with those of Jean Paul, the practitioner of 'Romantic irony' and self-parody, the art of infinite incongruity, of the comic gulf between the ideal and the real, humorously showing the one-sidedness of every rational proposition, annihilating not the single object but finiteness as such, with what Hegel called 'Satanic impertinence'.[54]

German Romantic interpretations of Shakespeare led in the same direction, throwing a suggestive light on Svevo's own work. A. W. Schlegel's famous *Lectures on Dramatic Art* acclaim Shakespeare's genius in making 'each of his principal characters the glass in which the others are reflected'; in laying bare their 'facility of self-deception', their 'half-conscious hypocrisy' in attempting 'to disguise ... selfish motives'; in 'the secret irony' of his characterizations and the 'secret understanding with the select circle of the more intelligent of his readers or spectators'; in his tacit awareness of the insubstantiality of the whole fictive process.[55]

Turgenev and other Russian novelists, also mentioned in *Profilo auto-biografico*, largely shared the same German influences, and can be seen to have led Svevo in a consistent direction: the problematical hero, the Hamlet type, the 'superfluous man', a social and metaphysical misfit, is characteristic of the Russian novel and akin to Svevo's own anti-heroes.

While at Segnitz, Ettore also joined in philosophical discussions with his schoolfellows and wrote a 'short philosophical treatise' in German, now lost.[56] Svevo's wife tells us:

He brought back good memories of the headmaster, a strict and austere but just man, whose authority he had accepted in a filial spirit. He kept in his heart a sweet idyllic memory: the image of the young Anna Herz, the headmaster's niece,* who had preferred him to his brother Adolfo. This was a painful shadow between the two brothers and he would never raise the memory of it. Older than Ettore, there had been a vein of maternal protectiveness in her feeling towards him, which is also visible in the dedication she inscribed on *The Works of Shakespeare*, the book she gave him as a farewell present.[57]

Strangely, Elio never mentions these mutual feelings between Anna and Ettore, but writes, around 1880, that Adolfo and Anna were mutually in love.[58] There is no record of any letters to or from Anna Herz. Adolfo never married.

The juxtaposition of Ettore's filial regard for Spier with his romance with Anna may be casual, as also the fact that Anna should give Ettore the works of the author which Spier had confiscated from him, but it all smacks of Freudian 'family romance'. All Svevo's heroines have names that begin and end in A. Of all the women closely associated with Ettore Schmitz, only his mother Allegra and Anna Herz shared this distinction. Anna's inscription, written in German, translates:

---

* Actually, his wife's niece; both women came from Frankenthal in the Rhineland (Elio says), whereas Spier was a Hessian.

'The poet is the consoler of mankind!' Isn't that so, dear Ettore? You yourself have quickly discovered and felt that. May you always find comfort in it. Here I give you your favourite poet. May God protect you. With blessings and wishes.

Anna Herz.

The book, a good English edition of Shakespeare's works, had been Anna's personal copy and is one of very few books to have escaped the destruction of Svevo's library in 1945. It is the earliest surviving possession of his (other than family photographs). He looked after it carefully, and it shows no trace of rough handling or grubbiness. It does not fall open naturally at any one or few places, but *Hamlet, Romeo and Juliet*, and *Othello* seem to have been most frequented—plays which each have a relevance to specific aspects or phases of Ettore's life.

Of the other places at which the book most readily opens, two are of interest for the history of Ettore Schmitz in view of the suspicions of 'Oedipal' conflict with his father. The first is particularly relevant to Francesco Schmitz from the mid-1880s: this is *The Winter's Tale*, IV. 3, where Polixenes, King of Bohemia, disguised, in testing the loyalty of his son Florizel, who is marrying without his knowledge, describes himself as being old and incapable. The second is *King Henry IV*, Part 2, IV. 4, where the ailing old King Henry tests his son Hal by feigning death and leaving his crown upon his pillow. Hal puts it on his own head and walks out, and the king muses on the son's ingratitude for all his father's labours.

Part III

PUBLIC AND PRIVATE DESTINIES
1878–1886

8

THE WAR IN BOSNIA, AND IRREDENTISM: 1878

The brothers Schmitz ended their schooldays in quiet Segnitz and returned to Trieste on 1 September 1878, to find the city in turmoil. Europe had been perilously close to a general war. Imperial Russia had defeated the Ottoman Empire in the name of Pan-Slavism and had secured the independence of the Slav states of Serbia and Montenegro—near neighbours to Trieste—and had further forced Turkey to concede autonomy to Bulgaria, Rumelia and Macedonia. At the same time, however, Austria-Hungary was given a free hand in the no less Slav territory of Bosnia-Herzegovina, not far south of Trieste. Serbia already had dreams of uniting all the Southern Slavs in a great Yugoslav state. The scene was already being set for the conflagration of the Great War, nearly four decades into the future. The events of 1878 were Ettore Schmitz's first introduction to the complex game of politics both in Trieste and in the wider world, which had subtle implications for the writings of Italo Svevo, culminating in the finale of La coscienza di Zeno.

III. Public and private destinies: 1878–1886

The Great Powers met in Berlin in June 1878 and settled the destinies of Europe for the time being. Austria-Hungary's protectorate over Bosnia-Herzegovina was ratified, sanctioning her penetration into the Balkans. Defeated by Germany in central Europe and expelled from most of Italy during the 1860s, she now turned her attention to Slav Europe. The Habsburg Empire became the combined policeman and nanny whose job it was to preserve the smaller Slav nationalities from the lures of Pan-Slavism and Russian imperialism, or national independence. The Dualist system did this by dividing Czechs from Slovaks and Slovenes from Croats between the Austrian and Hungarian halves of the Empire, and keeping Bosnia-Herzegovina completely separate. Hopes and fears were raised of a new, Trialist system of Austrians, Hungarians and Slavs.

The Italians in Trieste already felt under siege from an increasingly self-conscious and powerful Slav nationalism. When the Bosnians, having already revolted against their Turkish overlords, now rose against the decisions taken for them by the Congress of Berlin and against their new Habsburg masters, the Garibaldians and Irredentists, both in Trieste and in the Kingdom of Italy, condemned Austria and called upon the Italians in Trieste and Istria to refuse the call-up for the campaign against 'our heroic brothers in Herzegovina'.[1] But the Slavs of Carniola (now Slovenia), loyal to the dynasty, held public demonstrations in support of Austria-Hungary's action to suppress the Bosnian uprising and to drag their unwilling brother Slavs into the Empire.[2]

The military occupation of Bosnia-Herzegovina roused political passions in Trieste to a pitch beyond anything the city had ever known before. The year from mid-1878 to mid-1879 saw political demonstrations of every kind, and petards went off almost daily. The police responded with searches and arrests, which exacerbated the agitation. For the first time, on 6 June 1878, the call-up obliged Triestines to fight a war to win new subjects for Austria, and Slav subjects at that. Two-and-a-half thousand men from Trieste were mobilized in the 22nd 'Weber' infantry regiment and sent off in August by sea for the occupation of Bosnia-Herzegovina. Several refused the call-up and were pursued by the authorities as deserters. Among them was a university student called Wilhelm Oberdank, as yet unknown, who was to achieve stark prominence four years later. Military conscription and the Bosnian campaign were thus responsible for turning relatively quiescent anti-Slav feeling into widespread Irredentist militancy in Trieste.

This popular feeling came as a gift to the merchants and financiers who ran the city's politics. For Vienna had decided to abolish Trieste's Free Port, as part of a plan to modernize the Triestine and the Austrian economy from their eighteenth-century mercantilist structure to one more suited to the new dynamic industrialism. Trieste was now to handle Austria's import–export trade, as well as developing industries of its own. Railway and steamship transport was already rapidly transforming and speeding up the European economy, but Trieste had lagged behind the great ports of the Baltic and the North Sea such as Hamburg and Antwerp.

A large section of Trieste's commercial class, feeling their interests threatened, couched the question in the language of nationalism and presented abolition of the Free Port as yet another Habsburg encroachment upon the city's autonomy and its Italian identity. In the turbulent political atmosphere of the spring of 1877, the Triestine Liberal Party organ, *Nuovo Tergesteo*, was suppressed, and in its place was born the mettlesome *Indipendente,* the paper with which Svevo was to be associated for so many years. It was set up by a secret Action Committee composed of the foremost Party leaders and also including the old Garibaldian campaigner Giuseppe Caprin as editor-in-chief. By August 1877 *L'Indipendente* had achieved a daily circulation of 2,000 copies, but it was never to go much above this figure.[3] The newspaper clearly sought its readership among the city's financial and commercial classes and achieved the highest level of Italian-language journalism in Trieste up to the turn of the century, even in cultural terms. It quickly became well known both in Italy and abroad as the mouthpiece of Adriatic Irredentism; the Austrian authorities made regular attempts to smother it with censorship, confiscations, prosecutions, levies of caution-money, fines and even treason trials.[4] But the party's financial resources and the often heroic devotion of the newspaper's editorial staff kept it going in the face of all persecution, until Italy's entry into 'the war of redemption' in 1915.

If the Free Port issue made a large section of the city's commercial class resent control by Vienna, the same effect was produced among other classes by the re-awakening of the Slavs, who had founded their own national organization, Edinost (Unity), in 1875, and their own newspaper, with the same title, early in 1876. The Italians of Austria's Adriatic Littoral therefore looked more eagerly towards Italian rule as the only way of assuring their own dominance. But there was already some division between the Mazzinian or Garibaldian Republicans (mostly among the professional and intellectual class, teachers and artisans) and the patrician capitalist class. The latter were more interested in securing advantages for their own economic activities than in forsaking Austria for Italy. They therefore aimed at exploiting Irredentist feeling so as to extract from Vienna economic privileges and concessions, preferential railway tariffs, subventions for the shipping industry and suchlike. It was not always easy to handle the political issues in such a way as to keep the more uncompromising or high-minded Irredentists in line, and on several critical occasions the double-dealing showed through. There had already been open disagreement between Edgardo Rascovich, president of the Italian nationalist labour organization, Società Operaia Triestina, and Hermet, leader of the National-Liberal majority on the Trieste city council.

The Balkan crisis thus united Italian Triestines at just about the time when Irredentism was so christened. There had been a growing nationalist movement in Italy in 1877, and Vittorio Imbriani coined the phrase 'Italia irredenta' (unredeemed Italy). Early in 1878 specifically Irredentist organizations were formed, such as Imbriani's own L'Italia degli Italiani and Avezzana's Associazione in pro dell'Italia irredenta.

Italy's most forthright national poet, Giosué Carducci, came to see for himself how Italian Trieste was. His leonine mane and flamboyant beard were recognized as he arrived at the Trieste railway station that July, and *L'Indipendente* reported his presence, to the further excitement of the local nationalists. Given the deliberate blurring of Italian nationalist politics in Trieste, those modes of struggle were preferred which did least to clarify the issues: what the Triestine Socialist Angelo Vivante was to call 'the bland terrorism of the petards'; and what we might call a bland cultural terrorism. This cultural terrorism, set against the highly charged political situation, explains the excitement aroused by what would otherwise seem an insignificant enough incident, and defines the atmosphere in which Ettore—not yet seventeen—was to find himself.

Carducci was fêted by the leading lights of Triestine culture and taken on a tour of the Roman and Italian antiquities of Trieste and Istria. Deeply moved by the warmth of this reception, he became a champion of Triestine Irredentism in Italy. His Irredentist poem 'Saluto italico' appeared under various titles and in different versions in clandestine publications during 1879. The nationalist rhetoric of its 'eagle verses' is a fair example of the Carduccian school of poetry, which established itself more firmly in Trieste than in most other places. Being banned by the Austrians, Carducci's works were all the more eagerly read in smuggled copies. This helped to immobilize the local poetic culture, justifying the poet Saba's complaint that 'from the cultural point of view, being born in Trieste in 1883 was like being born anywhere else in 1850.'

Svevo's *Profilo autobiografico* mentions Carducci (then, half a century later, still an obligatory point of reference in Fascist Italy) alongside the great literary critic and historian De Sanctis, as one of his only two contemporary Italian masters.[5] The Carducci that might have interested Ettore Schmitz in particular was the anti-Manzonian, anti-Christian and anti-clerical Carducci who reviled the mawkish latter-day Italian Romantics and the *maudit* Romanticism of the sick self which Svevo was later to treat so distinctively and with the very reverse of self-indulgence. Such was the Jacobin Carducci of the 'Inno a Satana' (Hymn to Satan), but also the Carducci of 'Il canto dell'amore' (Song of Love), the poet of full-blooded paganism, the anti-bourgeois bourgeois. Svevo's most specific Carduccian reference was to the poem of 1880, 'La madre', in which Carducci 'finds himself dreaming of social renewal'.[6] Carducci cherished a strong affection for German writers, including two of Ettore's own idols, Goethe and Heine. Above all, he was a master of Italian, not so much in his magnificently contrived verse as in his vigorous prose. Yet no writer could be less like Carducci than Svevo, and the tribute to the patriot-poet in *Profilo* smacks of lip-service.

Austria-Hungary's occupation of Bosnia-Herzegovina got off to a bad start. The advance on Sarajevo was hampered not only by Bosnian ambushes but by dysentery, sunstroke and marching fatigue. The largely Triestine 'Weber' 22nd Infantry Regiment suffered heavy losses at Banja Luka and in successive battles and when it got back to Trieste on 5 December there was nothing left of it but the fourth battalion led by a captain.[7] More political rows resulted in Trieste, and the Lieutenancy ordered the dissolution of the Italian-dominated city council in November. There were public demonstrations and petards right through till the middle of 1879, though the petards (noisy but fairly harmless bombs) had little more than nuisance value. Veronese records few injuries to persons and none to property,[8] and Bazlen says the *bora* did far more damage.[9]

The war between the Irredentist cloak-and-dagger and the Austrian mailed fist was usually closer to farce or operetta than to high drama, indeed often taking the form of high-spirited jokes and cocking of snooks. Lady Burton catches the tone: 'If an Austrian gave a ball, the Italians threw a bomb into it; and the Imperial family were always received with a chorus of bombs—bombs on the railways, bombs in the gardens, bombs in the sausages...'.[10] These 'bombs' were in fact only petards. Triestine life was pervaded by all sorts of displays of patriotic feeling, such as ingeniously contriving to flaunt the forbidden green, white and red of the Italian tricolour or wearing a daisy (*margherita*) in the buttonhole as a mark of devotion to the Italian Queen Margherita of Savoy.

Culture played a key role in kindling national zeal. The classics of Italian literature became symbols of nationhood to a sometimes comic degree:

The amazement of visitors from 'the Kingdom' during the Irredentist period upon encountering this ardour in Trieste cannot be described. Unforewarned, for instance, lecturers would unthinkingly utter a name, say, Dante Alighieri, to see the entire audience leap to their feet as if thunderstruck, clapping their hands in a frenzy and yelling out 'Viva Dante!' and even burst out singing the anthem of the Lega Nazionale in chorus: 'Long live Dante, great master of the Italian tongue.'[11]

National politics could make an issue of the most trifling and unexpected things. Spaini recollects 'frightful *gaffes* frequently perpetrated by ladies from the Kingdom unaware of the taboo against the yellow and black of the Austrian flag. A black hat with a lovely yellow ribbon innocently worn in the streets of Trieste could give rise to all sorts of trouble.'[12]

The theatre (to which Svevo was so attached) was the favourite scene for the expression of national feeling. Nordio reports a famous and typical incident which took place during the opening season of the imposing Politeama Rossetti opera house in 1878. Verdi's opera *Ernani* has a famous chorus 'Si ridesti il leon di Castiglia' ('let the lion of Castile awake') in which the words 'siamo tutti una sola famiglia' ('we are all but one family') always stirred the audience into a delirious state of patriotic excitement and was the signal for tossing tricolour ribbons, inflammatory leaflets and doves over the auditorium. The words 'Ernani involami all'aborrito amplesso' ('Hernani, save me from his loathsome embrace') had the same effect. 'At the first showing of the opera', Nordio relates, 'as the chorus started, a pigeon with a tricolour round its neck was released from one of the boxes. The bird fluttered this way and that for a few moments and then, by an ironic chance, alighted at the very feet of a police commissioner who caught and confiscated it amid the cries of the audience.'[13] The even more famous, beautiful and moving chorus of the captive Israelites in Verdi's *Nabucco* ('Va pensier ...') was another operatic passage which was taken as a veiled hint at Trieste's Austrian bondage and never failed to excite the audience to fever pitch.

Elio reports the expulsion from Trieste of Felice Cavallotti, a well-known Irredentist member of the Italian parliament, who had come in April 1880 for the showing of his drama *La sposa di Menecle*.[14]

9

HOME LIFE AND LEARNING

The earliest first-hand document of Ettore's life is a manuscript entitled *L'Adotajejojade di Trieste,* an amusing family newspaper whose title combines the names of the three Schmitz brothers (Adolfo, Ettore's pet-name Tajé, Ejo for Elio—who was also nicknamed Mitti). It is hard to tell whether the handwriting is that of the 'editor', Adolfo, or of the deputy editor, Ettore, or—as is most probable—the 'executive editor', Elia (as his name is mis-spelled). Dated 12 october 1879, the four-page newspaper's high-spirited levity is surprising, considering the political tension of 1878-9 and the death of Noemi Schmitz in August 1879: the *Adotajejojade* makes no reference to either.

The front page announces that 'Great discontent reigned at the news that upon their Majesties' departure the realm would be placed under the regency of Archduchess Natalia' (the third of the Schmitz sisters and now the eldest in the house, since the marriages of Paolina and Noemi). Numerous jokes follow about Natalia's lack of skill as a housekeeper and her brothers' resulting starvation. One of these jokes contains the only reference to politics to be found in the Schmitz family gazette, which calls itself 'A Pan-Slav Journal (if dinner is on), a Turcophile one (if not)', implying that the Schmitz household had a Slav cook.

The *Adotajejojade* tells us that Francesco and Allegra had left Trieste on 5 October on something like a second honeymoon combined with a business trip, perhaps taking with them Ortensia and Ottavio, both under ten, and going by way of Venice, Bologna, Florence and Rome to reach Naples presumably on the 14th, since 'On the 14th Prof. Palmieri in the Vesuvius Observatory will discover a new constellation over Naples which will be named the Schmitzes.' This astronomical prediction was the work of 'Reporter Vivante', that is Giuseppe (Beppe, Bepi, Peppi or Pepi) Vivante, who was courting Natalia and was to marry her in June 1881. He describes her in a tongue-in-cheek personal advertisement for a wife: 'Not good-looking, expert concert-performer, light eater (as the young man in question wants to live *very* frugally), no breeding and little or no love.' Vivante also describes himself: 'Well-to-do young man, good-looking, not tall, though with rather a large nose, enjoying *perfect* health, headaches only every other evening...'.

There are also advertisements for Ettore: 'A dog (mongrel) ... rather lazy' who 'dozes in the sun', and for Elio: 'Escape-pole, Transparent lampshade etc.

A young man of preternatural height' who in the capacity of a chimney-sweep 'Sticks one leg down a chimney from the roof-top and uses it as a brush' and can work as 'a Hand-diver owing to the extraordinary length of his arms'. On another page is an account of a blaze in which Elio 'acted as an escape-pole', and saved no less than twenty-three people from the fourth floor.

There is a great deal about the Hotel Schmitz 'Land of Cockaigne' where one can dine free on '*Minestra,* meat, fish, *terrano* wine (six bottles with every meal), sweet wine ($1\frac{1}{2}$), *framboise* ($1\frac{1}{2}$)'. Under the heading 'Mystery' we find the following story: 'A certain A. S. was arrested while trying to cut the Prinz shop-window with a diamond so as to steal some bread. Questioned as to why he attempted the crime, he replied somewhat obscurely in dialect as follows: "Since Mum and Dad bin away, Natalia don't give us much grub and I were 'ungry"', and it subsequently appears that all three Schmitz brothers are ravenous with hunger.

Another article reports a booze-up enjoyed by the four lads (including Vivante) at the Finzis' (that is, the household of Paolina Schmitz), where the amenities included telegraphs and telephones in every room—the former even fitted to the tables and pillows (*sic*). Tucked in between the brain-teasers and the stop press appears the eighteenth instalment of a serialized novel *The Love-life of St Catherine of Siena, or Everyone in his own place.* It opens ' "Oh!" exclaimed Carlo, falling from the third floor, "she loves me!" Fortunately he fell on to a dung-heap and was unhurt. He got up full of love and ... "Oh!" he exclaimed, banging that part of his person which out of sheer force of habit he called his head against a wall which he failed to notice, "what bliss...".'

The light-hearted tone matches that of Ettore's first extant plays (though these also have grave undertones) and shows the Schmitzes as yet far from being thoroughly downcast by deaths and misfortunes in the family.

For, after aunt Peppina's disastrous marriage with Ignazio Tedeschi, uncle Vito had died suddenly in 1877, of an unknown cause, only shortly after his marriage with Sofia Piazza. Elio recalls the lovely May morning when a telegram summoned Adolfo home from Segnitz. His younger brothers, left behind, did not have certain news of Vito's death until two weeks later. They also missed their sister Paolina's wedding to Raimondo Finzi, which was held four days after her uncle's death.[15]

Another beautiful day saw Noemi die of peritonitis shortly after she gave birth to a baby girl. The Schmitzes were at Opicina for the summer. At five o'clock on the morning of 7 August 1879, Francesco, who with Allegra had spent the night at Noemi's, arrived at the door of the Schmitzes' holiday villa to take his children down to town by tram. One at a time they entered the bedroom where, changed beyond recognition, Noemi lay dying, while the two doctors declared that 'up to that point the treatment had gone very well.'

Elio wept over his sister's tomb in the Jewish cemetery nearly every Sunday, frequently accompanied by Ettore, who wrote a poem to Noemi. Dated October 1879, it is now lost.[16]

Paolina, not long married, was already desperately unhappy with her wealthy but boorish husband.[17] She was eventually to return, with her children, to the Schmitz household, of which she had taken over the running by about 1890.

Upon the return of the Schmitz brothers from Segnitz in 1878, Francesco entered Ettore into the newly opened Italian-language Revoltella business school, which he attended until 1880: 'two years' hard work,' says *Profilo autobiografico,* 'which made up Italo's mind that he was not born for business.'[18] Elio studied commerce at the German-language Royal-Imperial Academy.[19]

As late as 1914, the polemical Scipio Slataper believed that Baron Pasquale Revoltella's intention of giving Trieste a whole class of businessmen who shared his own breadth and modernity of outlook had been far from realized: 'the only subject that could fulfil the school's objective—the study of modern societies—is not taught. What I have in mind is the economic geography, the constitution, character, state of culture in the broadest sense, of the various peoples with which Trieste has most dealings.'[20]

The *Profilo autobiografico* goes on to say that Ettore gained his real literary education from the town library, where he spent most of his evenings. It mentions, apart from Carducci and De Sanctis, other writers in the realist or de-mystificatory vein, both Italians (Machiavelli, Guicciardini, Boccaccio, but *not*, it is stressed, Manzoni) and French (plenty of Flaubert, Daudet and Zola, some Stendhal, a great deal of Balzac and of Renan), and then, in culmination, Schopenhauer.[21]

Clues as to what else Ettore read are few and sporadic for every period of his life. Trieste's Biblioteca Civica kept a record of loans up to 1880, in which Ettore's scrawled signature appears a mere six times between 15 November 1878 and 5 March 1879. Four times he took out a book on business (*merciologia*), and once each Boccaccio, the B–Bzo volume of the *Nuova enciclopedia* and the collected works of Shakespeare in an edition by Fink. It is interesting that he still preferred a German to an Italian translation to help him cope with Anna Herz's English Shakespeare. On 7 February 1880 he signed out Giovio's *Storie,* which we may fairly surmise he was consulting for the background of the verse-play *Ariosto governatore* which he was then writing.[22] These loans clearly represent no more than a marginal element in his library readings.

As Umberto Saba described it, the Biblioteca Civica, as late as 1900, still

consisted of a dusty room, with readers few and far between, which you entered by a lobby whose walls were hung with portraits all looking alike, of powdered characters in white wigs. In the reading room you had to fill in and sign a form which you gave to a bizarre attendant who waited beside a window from which he eventually jumped to his death. He was a terrifying, almost spine-chilling figure ... After I had waited about half an hour he fetched me the poetical works of C.[23]

The mysterious 'C.' was probably the forbidden Carducci.

Scipio Slataper was particularly critical of the Biblioteca Civica and of its director for several decades, Attilio Hortis: 'librarian's mania is the vice common to Italian libraries: hence the appalling gaps in sociology, philosophy and religion'. Hortis and his library had inherited the formidable tradition of Domenico Rossetti's historical and literary scholarship, along with his collections of Petrarch and Aeneas Sylvius Piccolomini material, which are the nucleus of the library. 'So, for lack of space, the books are piled up randomly in corners, under tables, in window bays: who's to find them? and, if found, what a state they're in!' Concentration was thwarted by the chatter of schoolchildren clustered round the only copy of their Latin crib.[24]

Yet somehow Ettore acquired a reading so wide and up-to-date that in May 1881 he could read Zola's *Le Naturalisme au théâtre* almost as soon as it was out.[25] That there were long periods in which he visited the Biblioteca Civica daily is clear from the reminiscences he published in *L'Indipendente* in 1887, 'Il sig. Nella e Napoleone', where he dwells affectionately on the memory of an old and infirm retired man, Carlo Nella, with whom he chatted every evening for six months as they left the library together. Nella was a passionate admirer of Napoleon and had seen the great man from close to when very young. He was now following his life in Thiers's biography, exasperating the other readers in the library with his crescendoes of coughing.[26]

From the Acquedotto, where Svevo lived, to the library was an easy half-hour's walk across town, first down the elegant Corso, at the end of which were the Stock Exchange and the Tergesteo gallery (the offices of the Unionbank, where Svevo was soon to start working, were on its second floor), then along one side of the huge Piazza Grande (Piazza Unità), which stretches as far as the harbour-front, and finally taking the long narrow Via Cavana, which even today is bustling and colourful and was then the main (and ill-reputed) thoroughfare of Città Vecchia. Alternatively, he could follow the harbour-front, in those days thickly lined with the rigging of sailing-ships and the smoke-stacks of steamships from every corner of the world, and cluttered with horse-wagons and goods trains. Then he could turn right along the so-called Canal Grande, probably the shortest canal in the world.

The Schmitz business premises were just here, at the inner end of the Canal Grande, beside the church of Sant'Antonio, where ships discharged cargoes of all kinds on to the quay-sides. The architect Camillo Boito, visiting Trieste in 1877, describes the 'hustle and bustle of seamen and dockers shoving ashore sacks and bales and crates and casks and barrels of every kind', the 'din of railway wagons ... the jabber, shrill and uproar of busy people of all lands, wearing the Turkish turban, the Albanian kilt, or the long tunic of the German Jew'.[27]

10

THEATRICAL PASSIONS

Elio's diary marks the gradual darkening of the life of the Schmitz family. At the start of 1880 he wrote: 'We no longer visit any of our relatives', and on 25 February the Jewish Purim festival was 'passed over in silence as papa does not want family festivities which only remind us of our bereavements and our troubles'.[28] So far, however, this mournful atmosphere did not dampen the youthful enthusiasms of Elio and Ettore, and in particular their enthusiasm for the theatre. Trieste had five theatres, of which the Comunale (now called the Verdi), standing between the Tergesteo and the San Carlo pier (now the Audace), enjoyed in Italy a reputation perhaps second only to La Scala in Milan. The grandiose new Politeama Rossetti could seat five thousand and was only a few yards from where the Schmitzes lived on Via dell'Acquedotto, but they hardly ever seemed to go there—perhaps because the cheapest seats cost a florin (two crowns). For the Triestine middle and upper classes who could afford it and who found it a pleasant meeting-place for which they could dress up, the theatre was not only the staple form of entertainment but the main venue and focus for social life. The less well-off had to wait until the beginning of this century for serious theatre at a price they could afford.

Trieste's theatrical culture was severely conditioned by the social function of the theatre as entertainment and fashionable venue. Ettore Schmitz's earliest articles on the theatre bitterly attacked the theatre-going public for smothering creative theatre in Italy by the shallowness and volatility of its taste, its cult of the great actor and the latest vogue and of what we would now call the 'hit', the box-office success. Ettore dismissed Italy's entire theatrical production of the past decade.[29]

The Triestines, obsessed with business, were not much given to the cultural life, except as regards music and opera. Slataper conceded that they were finely receptive to music, which, by 1908, was taught in three conservatories, while 'the musical evenings at the Università popolare *were* a public feast.'[30] Ettore Schmitz too imbibed opera as part of his sensibility. His interest as a writer, though, centred on straight theatre, and in this field, apart from a very limited classical repertoire (Shakespeare and Alfieri) and the medievalistic dramas of the earlier Giacosa, it was the drawing-room theatre of Dumas *fils* and Sardou and of their Italian imitators such as Torelli and Ferrari that predominated. We can get some idea of what the public wanted from the title *Adam and Eve at Montecatini Spa,* a regular favourite for years.[31]

Venetian dialect theatre was most popular in Trieste (although Goldoni's plays did not come back into vogue until the end of the century). Above all others, say Coceani and Pagnini, 'Trieste cherished Giacinto Gallina like an adoptive son.' The Venetian Gallina had first come to Trieste in 1872 for the first-ever showing of his *Una famegia in rovina* (A Family Ruined),[32] and Gallina is the first playwright to be mentioned in Elio's diary, in January 1880, though—and he is a typical Triestine in this—he reserves his enthusiasm not for the playwright but for the child actress Gemma Cuniberti, already famous at eight years of age, whom he watched every evening: 'the enthusiasm! cheers and applause at every few words.' He wrote Gemma a play, *Una congiura a palazzo* (A Palace Conspiracy), but the Cunibertis showed no interest in it.

Ettore too was caught up in the excitement over Gemma Cuniberti and wrote for Elio's diary the first piece we have in his hand. He calls his anecdote 'one of those perfectly ordinary incidents of perfectly commonplace life' which 'nevertheless have a bearing on my own future destiny.' He had written Gemma two letters, 'in which, as full of myself as ever, I gave her some advice on dramatic art.' Then, wishing to meet her in person, he went to the railway station on the day of her departure. He records the fragmentary dialogue which followed, in which, as Elio remarked, 'Ettore never let her finish a sentence.' In it Ettore introduced himself under the pseudonym of Erode (Herod),[33] a name that might well scare a little Nazarene. Elio thought that Ettore was in a state of some excitement as a result of his conversation with Gemma.

The Gemma cult persisted. On 13 March Ettore wrote to tell her that he was going to Barcelona (presumably to see her there), and during Gemma's next Trieste season, Elio hoped that Ettore would write her a play, but dared not suggest it. Gemma drew the two brothers to her like a magnet: they stayed on in the theatre after her last performance and after the rest of the audience had gone out, and they were rewarded by a completely novel experience: 'The curtain rose and in the semi-darkness we made out on the stage the little one in her mother's arms and all the actors scurrying this way and that. In a word, a very striking scene for someone seeing it for the first time.'[34]

The 'Erode' of February 1880 had hinted at his possible theatrical 'destiny'. That is the date of the very first dramatic fragment of his that has survived. But perhaps it was as a result of the profound impression he had received in that theatre on that Saturday evening, 27 February 1881, that Ettore tried to embark on an acting career. In November 1879 the great Tommaso Salvini had been in Trieste for a classical season and had won particular applause for his acting in Giacometti's *Sofocle*. He made frequent visits to Trieste, two in 1882, when he played in *Othello*, *Hamlet* and Alfieri's *Saul*. In 1884 his farewell visit to Trieste included performances of *King Lear*, *Othello* again and modern works such as Soumet's *The Gladiator* and Fournier and Mayer's *The Coastguard*.[35] Salvini, now in his fifties, had won world-wide acclaim and had played Othello and Hamlet triumphantly even on the London stage. He also gave amazing performances in secondary roles—Iago, and, when over sixty, the young David in *Saul,* and Pylades in Alfieri's *Oreste.* It was this performance which Saba recalled in a passage which vividly evokes the style of Italian classical theatre during Svevo's youth:

Pylades, tall and stout, his face half hidden by his cloak, stepped very slowly forward ... to say to his friend Orestes, as yet unaware that he had killed his mother as well as his stepfather: 'Give me that sword.' Oh, how that voice, that step, that look, now directed fearfully around him, now fixed steadfastly on the ground, every part of his impressively virile frame, conveyed the horror of the tidings which he must and could not bring himself to tell to the unhappy Orestes! And those first words really fell upon the spectator like drops of hot blood. No, no one could look more downcast, more full of horror, of pity for his friend and revulsion for the matricide; no one, in a word, could look more like the great tragic actor. I unfortunately never saw, but I heard described, the prodigious bounds across the stage, two and a half metres long, with which as a younger man he enacted the jealousy of Othello the Moor, the roars of a tiger wounded and craving vengeance with which he answered the vile Iago's innuendoes.[36]

Livia Veneziani records that 'Ettore conceived such an enthusiasm for the theatre that he wanted to become an actor. He presented himself to Salvini but was rejected because he couldn't pronounce his Rs properly' in spite of having done 'many elocution exercises'.[37] Silvio Benco confirmed that still in the 1890s 'The theatre was then his passion [*sospiro*]; he was an assiduous theatre-goer ... "The form of forms, is the theatre," he would say; "the only form in which life is conveyed directly and exactly." '[38] Svevo never gave up writing plays; yet, oddly, he never became part of the theatre world, not even as a critic. His articles often discuss the theatre and yet do not include a single review of an actual performance.

In February 1880, at the height of the two brothers' admiration for Gemma Cuniberti, Elio noted that Ettore was writing a verse-play, and wondered how it would end: 'In the fire, perhaps, like everything else. He has begun so much poetry, prose, verses, farces, plays, but *their destiny* [Elio's emphasis] is the flames.' Elio tried to speed things towards completion by making a business deal with Ettore: 'I made him sign an undertaking that he will complete *Ariosto governatore* by 14 March or else pay me 10 *soldi* for every cigarette he smokes in the next three months.' So Ettore's first known literary effort is already bound up with his compulsive smoking, which was to play such a prominent part throughout his life and in *La coscienza di Zeno.* On 28 February Ettore submitted what he had written so far to his brother-in-law Samuel Salmona for judgement. Samuel advised him to write it in prose (and this marks the beginning of Ettore's lifelong aversion to verse), but Elio preserved the fragment.[39]

The opening of the fragment hinges on the contrast between the historical characters of Equicola and Ariosto. Mario Equicola (courtier and author of several courtly works, and comfortably established as secretary to the powerful sixteenth-century ruler Isabella D'este) is bent with almost youthful unconcern, despite his age, on continuing to live an easy life through sycophancy. Ariosto, the great poet, though much the junior of the two, feels prematurely aged, having experienced 'the evil of existence' ('il male/che è la vita') and found 'glory, life itself, and my own heart all chill'. He proffers the maxim: 'Life leaves no space for illusion'—a proposition which can be seen as the linchpin, the presupposition, of Svevo's entire *œuvre,* in which the dialectic between vain reality and vain illusion is central. This early fragment already has a Schopenhauerian ring about it.

The end of the fragment is no less interesting. Here Ariosto appears as governor of the troubled Este possessions in the Tuscan Garfagnana. He is both poet and instrument of power:

> ... I have seen
> great and small, masters and servants, here below. The cries
> of the oppressed touched my heart, made me
> their fellow ... and for them I wept; and when the sound
> of my own lament reached my ears, I thought upon my state
> and found myself among the great, for he who made me
> gave me genius. The injustice is apparent ...

Ettore already airs a bad class conscience, and precisely over the privilege of poetic genius. The bad conscience was never to leave him, though he never again showed his hand or his heart so plainly and henceforth treated the theme of masters and servants more obliquely. But the time-serving conformist Equicola and the doubt-racked, guilt-ridden Ariosto remained stuck together in Ettore's personality.

Ettore dismissed his *Ariosto governatore* in a piece of self-criticism which Livia assigns to 24 February 1881,[40] but which is probably earlier. It reads:

Ariosto governatore. I've thought about this more than I've written and all the necessary overtones seemed to have been so well captured that I forecast a very successful outcome for this first attempt. But how my wish deceived me. I didn't complete the 1st scene because there I recognized the abstruseness of the idea and the ugliness of the verse. Amen.

However, in allowing the fragment to be preserved, the writer implies that it is of special significance.

Ettore's presentation of Equicola, for all its brevity, was entirely original, quite unlike any view of the man current until very recently. It is either a brilliant intuition or else derives from a reading of Equicola's long-neglected *Libro de natura de amore.* The Trieste library held copies of the work, and in 1880 there was no other source for such a characterization.[41] If Svevo read such a recondite and bulky work while still only eighteen, that would emphasize the extraordinary breadth of his reading, about which *Profilo autobiografico* is unduly modest.

On the same sheet of paper preserved by Elio, Ettore likewise dismisses two other dramatic efforts. He says that the scene he had written of *Stuonature d'un cuore* (A Heart out of Tune) had 'conventional phrasing, a stilted movement, prose which tries to sound like poetry but isn't even prose', while the ending which he had projected was logical but an impossible Chinese puzzle like the *Hoei-lan-ki* (the famous *Chalk Circle*). *La rigenerazione* (Regeneration) could have filled one act, but he tried to stretch it over four, of which two had been written.[42]

Poems, stories and plays followed each other uninterruptedly from 1879. In March 1881 a story 'Tre caratteri' (Three Characters) was planned for *L'Indipendente* but threatened to turn into a novel before it followed the same 'destiny' as its predecessors.

I I

THE WRITER'S DESTINY AND THE UNIONBANK

Ettore therefore already seemed set on his literary vocation before he left the Revoltella and joined the Unionbank (or Banca Union). *Profilo autobiografico,* so far uncritically accepted in this regard, presents him as something of a martyr and a hero:

His father, like the gentleman he was, would have allowed him to resume his studies, but suddenly and unexpectedly catastrophe occurred. In order to increase his business his father had bought a large glassware factory which swallowed up his entire capital, and Italo immediately had to seek employment as a correspondence clerk in the Trieste office of the Vienna Unionbank.[43]

All the errors in this account do not necessarily disqualify Svevo for a martyr's halo, which Césari may have given him in all innocence in drafting the *Profilo,* or which Svevo himself may have adopted to save himself and the world from embarrassment over the fact of his having spent little short of twenty years as a bank clerk. In fact, the Loog factory was leased in November 1881, more than a year after Svevo started to work for the Unionbank.[44]

Elio's diary shows hardly a trace of Ettore's secret dream 'of persuading his father to send him to study for a year or two in Florence,' for which the only evidence is his widow Livia's biography. 'He knew, however,' Livia continues,

that this was nothing but a dream and that his destiny was to become a businessman like his brother Adolfo. So his father had decreed. Literature was remote from the mind of the elder Schmitz, and Ettore, despite his burning vocation to be a writer, lacked the strength to oppose his father's will, which ruled the family with unbending authority even now that its prosperity was declining. The young man was unable to stand up to the force of circumstances and of his environment, although he still cherished a timid hope in his heart.[45]

This, not the version in *Profilo*, seems to give us the truer portrait of Ettore Schmitz. He already prefers to 'dream', study into the small hours and write in secret rather than grapple with his father. Whether we see this as the filial obedience expected in a Jewish family or a special case of paternal despotism precluding any independence on Ettore's part, it confirms a pattern already suggested by the Segnitz episode and often to be repeated as time and again Ettore was to bow to what he saw as the force of circumstance. Many times in the course of his life Ettore Schmitz was to come across other young men more adventurous and enterprising than himself who took the path which he did not take, and they left him quite bemused. He was often to show himself well aware that he did not feel up to facing what he called 'the struggle for life'. He was unwilling to give up the comforts and affections of family life and persisted in staking everything on a literary 'success' that would free him from financial dependence. In his own way, Svevo as well as Joyce vowed himself to 'silence, exile and cunning', even though in Svevo's case 'exile' was much less spectacular, a purely mental step and not an act of open defiance. He adapted outwardly to his environment, took on protective colouring, provisionally (that is, for a lifetime) kept up appearances so as subsequently to exact subtle vengeance in his writing. He played Equicola so as to remain Ariosto. Italo Svevo is the name he was to give to this double game.

So he offered no resistance except to safeguard his leisure for reading and writing. It was not Ettore but Elio who in his diary voiced his dream of leaving Trieste. Music and medicine were his two vocations; but, at seventeen, he felt too weak to brave his father, and declared himself 'something of a fatalist, like all those who feel they lack the strength to rule themselves'—a definition that fits Ettore's whole career also. Elio told himself: 'If I leave Trieste, I shall study music, otherwise not.' He contrasted himself to Ettore: 'If, for instance, I were to stay up tonight so as to study—lacking the time during the day—everybody would treat me like a madman, Papa would disapprove and forbid it, as he has done for Ettore. Ettore is strong and steadfast; I am not, I am weak in this and would soon bend under Papà's will.'[46]

While Ettore was at the Revoltella discovering that business was not the life for him, he appears to have shown Elio no sign of rebellion. Perhaps this was when Elio sketched that brief portrait of his brother as having an appearance of apathy and being possessed by the dream of achieving fame as a writer, of which, by May 1881, he had become 'a virtual prisoner'.[47]

In 1880, then, Ettore was making vain attempts at 'Pindaric flights' and seemed quite uninterested in a career. While Elio was trying to persuade his father to let him pursue one of his long-cherished vocations as doctor or musician, Ettore was asking Elio to allow him an extended deadline for the completion of his new play *Il primo amore* (First Love) and signed 'five bills of hand at twenty-day intervals' for the five acts of the projected work, curiously turning writing itself into a kind of business. In May there seemed to be prospects for Ettore in the newly founded bank of Goldschmidt and Nephew.

Ettore was still writing. In June, Francesco quizzed the two brothers about business.[48] In August we hear of three new literary efforts by Ettore whilst he was being considered for a job in a factory in Moravia. This did not distract him from starting a new work, *I due poeti*. A few days later, after Francesco had advertised in *Il Cittadino*, Ettore was invited for interview at the brothers Mettel, 'but after a long time spent in the waiting-room,' wrote Elio, 'nothing came of it as the applicant is an Israelite.' This is the first recorded occasion on which Ettore was the victim of anti-Semitism, and it can be no coincidence that his first published writing, which came a few months after, touches on that very theme.

This is where Elio first mentions his father's financial difficulties:

Papa's business was going badly and these things made him more annoyed. What was to be done? He enrolled Ettore at Latoschynsky's to study for the officers' call-up exam. That evening Ettore's joy was beyond description: four hours of lessons a day and the rest of the time free—for writing plays, that is.

So Ettore did not seem at all bothered about having to serve in the Austrian army, though, for all he knew, there might be another Bosnian campaign, or even a war against Italy. However, a few days later Peppi (Giuseppe) Vivante turned up with an offer of an apprentice-clerk's job for Ettore from his brother Fortunato, the director of the thriving Trieste office of the Viennese Unionbank. 'Papà accepted "with open arms" and Ettore also accepted, even if not with open arms. He started at the bank today and is very happy there,' wrote Elio.[49] The date was 27 September 1880. Ettore was to be a bank clerk for nearly twenty years.

A month later, on 31 October, Elio wrote:

Ettore is now studying for the officers' call-up exam and is fairly happy at the 'Banca Union', though the work doesn't demand much of a head, as he puts it. Naturally, he's writing a play, *I due poeti*, but making little progress as he hasn't much time.

On 12 November, Ettore, tired after having stayed up many nights, was sound asleep.[50]

There was no sign of any overriding financial stringency compelling Ettore to take the bank job. If business was bad in September 1880, it was better again by the new year. That was not the real problem. Elio, now temporarily employed in his father's office, complained: 'My work with Papà grows worse day by day. I rush around town the whole blessed day and get told off for no reason whatsoever, merely because Papà is impatient and bad-tempered, even though business is now tolerably good.' A couple of weeks later, owing to a lack of turnover of goods, the flow of cash had stopped. Francesco, Elio noted, 'has days when he won't eat ot speak'.[51] This was the month, in fact, when the Triestine economy suffered a setback and labourers had their wages cut, whilst *L'Eco del Popolo* was confiscated for commenting: 'Why not cut the emoluments of bank directors and of the parasites of commerce?'[52]. Elio confirms this: 'trade is almost at a standstill and in consequence the lower classes are, one may say, starving to death and businessmen are losing money instead of making it, that is, those who have money to spare, the rest give up either by going bankrupt or in other ways.' The real problem was that Francesco seemed to have lost his nerve and resilience. He tried to diversify his business by entering into partnership with a certain Mayer Rosenthal, who was in critical circumstances and short of capital for his Near and Middle Eastern ventures. But, Elio remarked, Francesco's mood was going from bad to worse. 'If God and Noemi don't help us', he wrote. 'I don't know where we shall end up.'[53]

Yet on 12 June a 'very brilliant' wedding was held in the Schmitz household between Natalia and Giuseppe Vivante, complete with contract, ices and sonnets handed round by the three brothers;[54] and one year later business was going 'tolerably well'. Elio was more worried on account of Papà, whose 'cares' were again 'going from bad to worse' and proving 'the ruin of his life', and who, whether because of 'some illness' or some other reason such as 'Samuel's character', was 'constantly declining in health'. In July 1882 Elio found it impossible to calm his father by pointing out that his business affairs were not in such desperate case as he imagined them to be, for Francesco seemed unable to control himself, as he himself admitted.[55]

Only in October 1884 did Elio finally give a fairly detailed explanation of the reasons for his father's now pitiful condition. The winding up of the glassware factory about a year earlier with a loss of 15,000 florins was only the last blow for the Schmitz firm, which now had to keep going by selling the 20,000 florins' worth of shares belonging to Allegra. The main outlays had gone on the family—an expensive education for the children; around 45,000 florins for the dowries and trousseaux of the three married daughters; and 25,000 and 90,000 florins respectively to Vito's widow Sofia Piazza and to Peppina's good-for-nothing husband Ignazio Tedeschi, 'with his costly oil store'.[56] Family bereavements and disappointments must have demoralized Francesco Schmitz: the disastrous marriages of his sister Peppina and his daughter Paolina; his brother Vito and his daughter Noemi dead before their prime; Ettore and Elio with little aptitude for business or interest in it; and Elio always ailing. A disappointed and broken man, by 1884 he had stopped considering his family altogether. Elio sadly observed that 'he doesn't even know what form Ottavio is in at school.' He went as far as to press the ever-ready Adolfo, 'with his childish character', to marry a large fortune so as to build up his working capital.[57] All in all, a bourgeois tragedy on the theme of money and family which Ettore Schmitz had no need to discover in the pages of Balzac or Zola.

The thirty florins a month which Ettore started receiving as his salary from the beginning of 1881 could make little difference to the Schmitz family finances. Ettore had to work without pay for a couple of months, but then got a New Year bonus of a hundred florins, out of which he tipped Elio five.[58] But Ettore's earnings perhaps gave his father less satisfaction than a little success that came his son's way on 2 December 1880, precisely on Francesco and Allegra's twenty-fifth wedding anniversary. *L'Indipendente* that day carried Ettore's first published work, a modest article dashed off the evening before in a few minutes,[59] entitled 'Shylock' and signed 'E. S.'. This shows no intellectual strength, but combines three important strands of Svevo's sensibility: his Jewishness, his passion for Shakespeare, and his love of the theatre.[60]

The article anticipated the performance of *The Merchant of Venice* on that evening, with a cast headed by the great Ernesto Rossi. E. S. attempts to persuade the spectator that, whatever Shakespeare's prejudices or those of his time may have been, his genius did not see the Jew as someone to be derided, but sensed his inmost suffering essence. Ettore was, among other things, making up to his father for the upsetting Mettel affair.

The opening of the article identifies its author with 'that renegade Heine', concerned 'to reconcile his enthusiasm for Shakespeare with the veneration he still felt for the beliefs of his ancestors'. This always seems to have been the attitude of the renegade Ettore Schmitz also, though he was never to take public issue on behalf of either atheism or Judaism. His family do not seem to have practised their religion very seriously, but always remained part of Trieste's Jewish community. In 1880 Francesco was elected a Hatan Bereshid. All his business partnerships were with Jews, and all the family's in-laws, relatives and friends were Jews. And Ettore, even after marrying a Catholic and being himself baptized, never forgot he was a Jew, though his rare references to the fact were always jocular. Elio, returning from a visit to Vienna in 1885, was more indignant: 'I saw no one but anti-Semites.' These were the years of Schönerer's non-religious anti-Semitism, to be followed in the 1890s by Lueger's Christian Social anti-Semitism. Lueger was eventually installed as Mayor of Vienna after having been repeatedly elected and having had his election repeatedly annulled.

Ettore's 'Shylock' rather awkwardly linked his absolution of Shakespeare from the taint of anti-Semitism with his own championship of the Zolaesque school of theatre, and the article in fact opened his personal eight-year campaign for a Realist theatre in Italy. It contrasted Shakespeare, as 'profound observer and realist tragedian' with the conventions of the contemporary theatre, the *pièce à thèse* or 'play with a message', and the 'happy ending': 'For us (on the stage at least) good must triumph, evil succumb.—But is this axiom true, or just?'

Ettore was obviously well up with the French literary scene and quickly absorbed Zola's *Le Naturalisme au théâtre* when it came out in 1881. Elio reported this uncomprehendingly:

He has changed sides somewhat in art now. He is a Realist [*verista*]. Zola has confirmed his notion that the object and interest of a play should be character rather than plot. Everything should be true and commonplace: climaxes have no right to exist in a play, Zola says in *Le Naturalisme au théâtre,* since they do not exist in life. An actor who rants and goes in for 'les grands bras' makes me laugh, he says. And, thanks to this theory, the public will go to the theatre to look at naturalism and commonplace truth, but they'll realize it, and hiss.[61]

Elio often tried, with his unfailing gentleness, to persuade Ettore to change what he considered to be a mistaken course, but Ettore would reply arrogantly, if not rudely. Perhaps he was beginning to feel the awkwardness and falsity of his situation as reluctant bank-clerk and aspiring writer in his father's house and to realize that strokes of genius and ensuing fame would not come so readily. In June, Elio hinted as much, and 'a little to-do' resulted.[62] Though sharing a room with Ettore, Elio was reduced to writing letters to him in the hope that literary discussions on paper 'will not make you fly off the handle as a verbal discussion does', but Ettore did not reply.[63]

Elio was even more to be commiserated with than Ettore. In 1880 his father had squashed his hopes of attending the five-year medical course at Vienna. Listlessly, Elio went through a succession of commercial jobs, virtually unpaid and often working till ten o'clock at night. Skivvying in his own father's firm was worst of all. Music and his violin became his only solace. In this respect his father was quite indulgent and paid for lessons.

In 1882 his state of health was found to be critical. He cut smoking and followed a treatment of goat's milk, lichens and tar, but was still often bedridden and spent time convalescing in the country air at Lueghi (Predjamski Grad, in Slovenia), which has a spectacular castle built in a huge cave in the mountain-side, and where Francesco had his glassware factory. Now a chronic invalid, Elio took a gloomy view both of Trieste and of family life, being unable to join in the Carnivals and other festivities which the Schmitz family continued to enjoy.[64]

The Trieste Carnival was celebrated in great style. Everyone joined in. There were balls, all-night masques, masquerades and processions in fancy-dress, and the theatres competed in putting on spectacular shows and feasts. In 1879, for instance, the Politeama Rossetti for its first Carnival held thirteen public balls, eight all-night masques and a Masque of the Flowers.[65] (It was at the Politeama, just opposite where the Schmitzes lived, that Elio was so enraptured by Gounod's *Faust* in November 1880, though the Schmitzes were enrolled at the Teatro Comunale.)[66] And Carnival ended no less spectacularly, with the burning of its effigy at Servola on Ash Wednesday and an opulent parade of patrician carriages, showered with violets and bouquets by the ladies' admirers.[67]

There were also other public occasions, an outstanding one being the fiftieth anniversary celebration of the Società Filarmonico-Drammatica in December 1879, which included a Prologue and Cantata with words by Alberto Boccardi, musical arias and a chorus by Verdi, Nino Rota, Rossini, Donizetti, Umlauf and Campana, and Achille Torelli's *Nonna scellerata!* (Dreadful Granny!). The Prologue was recited by Francesco Hermet, the grand old man of Triestine politics. A Festa da Ballo followed on the Saturday.

Boccardi's Prologue gives the flavour of Triestine literature: it describes Art plying its golden-plumed wings from the resplendent shores of Greece to alight at Trieste, whose fiery youths temper their breasts in the contests of Art for the battles of life.[68]

12

THE MARTYR

There was some change in the Schmitz family's life with Natalia's marriage in 1881. Now Francesco and Allegra, left with their three elder sons and the children Ortensia and Ottavio, moved house, only a couple of streets away, to the spacious Corsia Stadion (now Via Cesare Battisti) at the lower end of the Giardino Pubblico, where they took a large and handsome apartment on the second floor.[69] [See Plate 2]. A curious law in Trieste dictated that all house-moves must take place on 24 August, so that on that day the city was full of processions of carts and wagons laden with furniture and boxes.[70] The Schmitzes would have been part of this caravanserai.

The apartment was large enough for them to hold a ball there in 1884 for guests too numerous for the wealthy Finzi house, which indicates that Francesco's business collapse in 1881 was only relative. He and Adolfo remained on the register of the second electoral college, allotted to approved wholesalers or merchants paying over 100 florins a year in tax.

Ettore joined the Associazione Triestina di Ginnastica, the sporting organization of the Italians which fostered national rivalry with the Slav Sokol and the German Turnverein Eintracht, and was probably also already attending the meetings and lectures of the Società di Minerva, which likewise wedded culture and nationalism. Between 1879 and 1882 the lectures ranged from demography and meteorology to religion and 'medicine and the enigma of the world', but the point of view was always strongly positivist and Darwin was the central deity. Literature received generous attention: there were readings by Erminia Bazzocchi of her own poems, one of them on an earthquake, another on 'the mystery of being'; Adele Butti discussed modern Italian poetry under the heading 'Ideal and Faith', as well as 'Female emancipation and the family' and 'George Sand's *Lelia*'; Alberto Boccardi discussed the poetry of Emilio Praga, and Giacosa gave talks on 'Truth in theatre' and 'In praise of puppets', and there was also a lecture on Petöffi.[71]

The year 1882 was greeted by the arrival of a new Italian-language newspaper whose first number appeared just before the New Year. This was *Il Piccolo*, so called because of its handy tabloid format, which, along with its lower price and more easy-going style, enabled it to attract a much wider readership than that of *L'Indipendente*. It was not at first licensed to discuss politics, but aimed to further the spread of Italian national consciousness. It did not for many years sport intellectual or cultural pretensions of any kind until it superseded *L'Indipendente* as the main Liberal-National organ towards the turn of the century. It was owned and run by a lad of twenty, Teodoro Mayer, like Ettore a Jew of Hungarian antecedents who had started work at the canonical age of thirteen to help his needy family and had brought out his own first periodical, *Il Corriere dei francobolli,* when he was sixteen and made a success of it. Almost exactly the same age as Ettore, but in striking contrast with him, he was the very model of the enterprising young man, and he was very soon a member of the caucus of grey eminences who managed Trieste's national and political life from behind the scenes. *Il Piccolo* became, then, according to the favourite quip, the Sancho Panza to *L'Indipendente*'s Don Quixote. If the *Indipendente* was a past master in the art of getting itself censored, *Il Piccolo* cultivated the art of *not* getting itself censored by developing in a different direction *L'Indipendente*'s own skills in letting its readers read between the lines.[72]

The efforts to influence public opinion by the blander methods of *Il Piccolo,* which was competing especially with the less nationalistic and more socially conscious *Il Cittadino* and *L'Eco del Popolo,* betokened the fact that political tensions had by no means completely subsided after the crisis of 1878–9. The abolition of the Free Port, military conscription and Slav nationalism were still live issues, and January 1880 had seen the foundation by seven young men of a secret society, the Circolo Garibaldi, for the production and application of petards and propaganda.[73] This and other secret societies were useful but sometimes unruly tools for the nationalist leaders. The Kingdom of Italy was steering its foreign policy more and more towards rivalry with France in the Mediterranean and over North Africa and consequently towards friendship with Austria. The Irredentist agitation which swept Italy in 1880 and 1881 was suppressed more or less effectively with an increasing degree of co-operation between the Italian and the Austrian police. When King Umberto paid a state visit to Franz Josef in October 1881, the Irredentists saw it as open betrayal, though of course friendship between the two monarchs and their realms suited the interests of high finance and big business in Trieste very well indeed and made it easier for them to get favourable treatment from the Vienna government. Elio commented in March 1882 on the enforced compromise and the prevalent opportunism:

Trieste is going from bad to worse and is in precisely the same case as I am! It has to sacrifice its nationality for the good of its trade and I must sacrifice my violin for gain. Neither of us profits much from our sacrifices, for trade is going from bad to worse and I am earning nothing. Perhaps if we made no sacrifices Trieste would be happy and even trade would be better and I would also be more contented and might even earn more.

... My homeland [i.e. Trieste], which is what I love most after my family, is in a sorry plight. Everything is topsy-turvy, trade, industry, everything is just a game for half a dozen rascals who are after decorations and crosses.

And he added a reflection that must certainly have passed through Ettore's mind also: 'In a while I too will have to serve and perhaps go to war for causes which are not my own.'[74]

Ettore, 'Very frightened', successfully took his officer's examination on 27 January 1881, but was rejected for military service that year 'because one of his shoulders is lower than the other, and it's likely that this defect is due to his hunching with his head bent down over his books for too long.'[75] In 1882, however, his passion for literature no longer saved him from the army and Elio addressed him jocularly in a letter that June as 'one of the Weber mob' (meaning the 22nd Infantry) with whom it might be dangerous to 'discuss politics, the police closure of the Ginnastica, or the recent elections'.[76]

The only way in which Ettore could avoid the call-up (barring physical inadequacy) was by leaving Trieste. Italy demanded no such heroism from him. In this 'period of reaction', as he called it,[77] it laid no claim to Trieste. Indeed, on 20 May 1882 Italy signed the Triple Alliance with the two Germanic Empires and Austria decided to celebrate the five-hundredth anniversary of Trieste's *Dedizione,* or voluntary subjection to the Habsburg crown, by holding a grand international exhibition. Irredentist agitation in Italy and in Trieste grew more intense, still more so upon the death of Garibaldi on 2 June, which led to further demonstrations, the closure of the Associazione Triestina di Ginnastica by the police, repeated censorship and confiscation of *L'Indipendente* and police searches.

Even the brief references in Elio's diary, some of which have been quoted, make it pretty clear where the sympathies of the Schmitz brothers lay, though I have found no trace of direct political involvement on their part. Francesco was a member of the Società Operaia Triestina in 1874,[78] but, whilst the Triestine nationalists called for a total boycott of the Exhibition and all its attendant festivities and functions, he took a stand as agent for the glass-factory of Prince Hugo Windisch-Grätz in Styria.[79] With Prince Windisch-Grätz breathing down his neck, Francesco Schmitz might well feel his hands were tied. His situation was fairly typical of Trieste as a whole. Elio's diary is strangely silent about the Exhibition (unless we take his general remarks about Trieste's plight as oblique reference). Nor does he mention the dramatic events which followed.

The Exhibition was opened on 2 August by Archduke Karl Ludwig. In September the Imperial family, Franz Josef in person, the Empress, Prince Rudolf and Princess Stephanie, were to come and see it. Isabel Burton wrote: 'The city was illuminated at night almost as brilliantly as Venice had been for the Congress, and Trieste illuminated makes a grand effect with its rising mountain background.'[80] During the ceremonial parade down the thronged

Corso on the opening day there was an explosion: not the usual petard but a real bomb, which killed a young spectator who had nothing to do with politics and injured several of the veterans of 1878, some of them gravely. Dr Dorn of the *Triester Zeitung* had his leg shattered.

The Italian press condemned the bomb attack and several Triestine Liberals vacillated over this new turn of events. Furious crowds assaulted the offices of *L'Indipendente* and of the Liberal National Party, of the Ginnastica (which had already been shut down) and of the Società Operaia Triestina and other Italian nationalist premises. On 18 August two more bombs, a petard and thousands of leaflets were discovered on board the Lloyd steamer *Milano* which had arrived from Venice. The King-Emperor was expected in Trieste on 17 September and police searches and arrests reached a climax. Just a day before the Emperor's arrival the deserter of 1878, Wilhelm Oberdank, was held by the police at Ronchi on the border with Italy, and found to be carrying two more bombs. A vast plot to kill Franz Josef was scented.[81] The Tsar had been assassinated only the year before.

The Exhibition was almost deserted. All the foreign visitors had left Trieste and only about two thousand people entered the Exhibition grounds. Lady Burton, when she went, found barely a score of other visitors. On another occasion, her party had to leave the Exhibition because of a riot in the old quarter of town.[82]

The Emperor was welcomed by the whole of official Trieste on 17 September, and for the next day Baron Morpurgo, director of the great Austrian Lloyd shipping company, had prepared a splendid fête on board the *Berenice*.[83] But after the discovery of the bomb on the *Milano* and now the news of the arrest of Oberdank, there were fears of an attempt on the Emperor's life: the Imperial cutter circled the *Berenice* and returned to Miramare. In the remaining thirty-five years of his long reign Emperor Cecco Beppe (as the Italians nicknamed him) never came back to Trieste.

The interrogation and court-martial of Wilhelm Oberdank—or, as he now preferred to call himself, Guglielmo Oberdan—began. The proceedings were secret. Oberdan admitted his intention of blowing up the Emperor and throwing his own body in martyrdom between Austria and Italy, but it could not be proved that he had thrown the bomb of 2 August. On 4 November he was sentenced to be hanged. His mother, Victor Hugo and Giosuè Carducci appealed to the Emperor for clemency, but in vain.

Guglielmo Oberdan, the Martyr of Triestine Irredentism, was executed in his twenty-fifth year on 20 December 1882. As he faced death on the gallows he cried: 'Long live Italy! Long live free Trieste! Out with the foreigners!' It was the day after Ettore Schmitz's twenty-first birthday. Or maybe the same day, if the entry for Ettore's birth in the Jewish register is correct. Might Ettore have moved his birthday because of the execution? There is no knowing.

Neither Ettore's nor Elio's writings ever refer to the Martyr whose silhouette looms starkly over Triestine Irredentism. Sympathy with Oberdan counted as treason. But the coincidence of Oberdan's execution with Svevo's twenty-first birthday signals or symbolizes the invasion of public history into the private sphere, rupturing any flimsy illusion of abstention, absenteeism or neutrality. It forces a juxtaposition of the two men and their respective careers.

It looks like a characteristically Svevian choice, then, that, on 22 November, whilst *L'Indipendente* was braving the censor after the sentencing of Oberdan, Ettore Schmitz, signing himself 'E. S.', had his second article, 'Riduzioni drammatiche' (Dramatizations),[84] published in its pages, two years after his first, 'Shylock'. The article argues that a good play cannot be made by dramatizing a novel. 'True artists feel no need to turn novels into dialogue.' Much better is it to draw directly on nature and enrich the impoverished Italian stage with new works. Oberdan and Irredentism are not even hinted at, but, merely by contributing to *L'Indipendente*, Ettore Schmitz was showing which side he was on.

Before his death, Oberdan refused all religious rites in terms which had a touch of Freemasonry: 'I am a mathematician and a freethinker, and do not believe in the immortality of the soul.' He also refused to see any of his relatives and particularly avoided a last farewell with his mother, whom he adored.[85] We may see in this uncompromising young man another contrast to the all too accommodating Ettore.

13

THE DILETTANTE AND THE PUBLIC

The hanging of Oberdan left Triestine politics in confusion. In October 1882, even before the execution, the nationalist leaders Caprin, Muratti and Felice Venezian had travelled to Italy to work out a *modus vivendi*. The Italian government was engaged in colonial adventures on the Red Sea and was loath to antagonize Austria and thus upset the Triple Alliance. It therefore requested that *L'Indipendente* should moderate its activism and adopt a 'see-saw policy'.[86] In March 1883 the Triple Alliance was ratified by the Italian Parliament.

Triestine feeling over Oberdan's death was exasperated by the harsh vindictiveness of the Austrian authorities. Sabbadini, the coachman who in all innocence had driven Oberdan across the frontier, was sentenced to death, and, though the Emperor commuted this to twelve years' imprisonment, tempers rose again in Trieste, not least as a result of intensified police searches and censorship. Two young journalists on the *Indipendente* staff, Enrico Jurettig and Riccardo Zampieri, spent a year in gaol.

Despite repression both in Austria and in Italy, the secret 'Oberdan societies' had multiplied to seventeen in the two States by 1884 and forty-nine by 1887. Even the older 'Garibaldi Circles' regarded these new organizations as revolutionary or anarchist cells bent on the overthrow of 'the existing social order'.[87]

It was after Oberdan's execution that Ettore's link with *L'Indipendente*—which made no secret of the fact that its sympathies lay with Oberdan and the Irredentist cause—grew closer. His contributions—still signed E. S.—grew numerous and, when Jurettig died at an early age in 1887 as a result of hardships suffered while in prison, Ettore was one of the pall-bearers at his funeral. This was tantamount to public acceptance of Oberdan's political legacy.

Ettore Schmitz never wrote a line openly supporting Irredentism. (This was treasonable and would have been censored anyway.) But Irredentism peeps between the lines of some of his early articles. In 'Il vero paese dei miliardi' (The Real Land of Plutocrats),[88] of 12 June 1883, he springs to the defence of France against the carping criticism of the formidable Max Nordau and, more generically, of 'the reactionary press'—a pinprick at the Triple Alliance, which was largely directed against France. In reviewing Olindo Guerrini's *Brandelli* (Fragments), he makes fun of Prince Metternich, the arch-reactionary Austrian Chancellor of the post-Napoleonic Restoration, and takes up Guerrini's own defence of noble ideals (Irredentism counted as one of these), which cynics dismissed as mere 'rhetoric'.[89] On 29 January 1884 came a translation by Ettore (probably from a German version) of Turgenev's dialogue 'The Worker and the Man with White Hands', in which, E. S. remarks, 'what is really moving is not the death of the man with white hands, but his self-sacrifice on behalf of people who are unable to appreciate it.' In order to free the workers, the man with the white hands braved prison and then the gallows. Triestines could not miss the allusion to Oberdan, which clearly demonstrates the light in which Ettore viewed the matter.[90] The contrast drawn between Turgenev and Alfieri shows Ettore to have been perfectly aware that he was setting himself up as an apostle of national 'redemption' in a city whose population was indifferent or hostile to the cause.

Between 12 June 1883 and 13 May 1885 Ettore published in *L'Indipendente* thirteen articles of literary and dramatic criticism, all signed E. S. Of these, eight appeared in 1884, which therefore marks the high-point of his critical activity. From May 1885 to October 1886 *L'Indipendente* carried nothing by him, probably because Svevo was then doing his military service.[91] The year 1887 saw another concentration of five articles in as many months. After that, his critical contributions to the newspaper fell off for good.

Little is known of Ettore Schmitz's life in these years, and nothing at all of his work and colleagues at the Unionbank. Its director, Cavaliere Fortunato Vivante, was an efficient banker: in 1894 his branch increased its net profit to over 300,000 florins from the 213,250 which it had made in 1893—despite the crisis in the Italian banks. The Unionbank as a whole made a profit of 2,269,947 florins in 1894, after having paid 348,171 florins in salaries and 115,706 in tax. The Board of Directors sported an array of aristocratic titles and had one of the foremost noblemen of the Empire, Count Kinsky, as Acting-Chairman.[92]

What Ettore Schmitz's daily life was like we can only guess from the pages in *Una vita* devoted to Alfonso's experiences as a clerk in the Banca Maller, as the *Profilo* suggests: 'That part is truly autobiographical. And the two hours spent at the Biblioteca Civica every evening are also described.'[93]

On 1 May 1883 another blow descended on the Schmitz household: the illness which had dogged Elio for so long was diagnosed as nephritis—Bright's disease. For three months, from June to August, Elio went to stay at Vittorio Veneto to rest and breathe country air in that small town situated below the mountains at the northern edge of the Venetian plain. He was accompanied and attended by his ever-patient, solicitous sister, Paolina Finzi, who got on his nerves with her 'incessant attentions'.[94] He was further troubled by falling in love against his rather prim better judgement with an emancipated young lady whom he called 'Signorina U'.[95]

Francesco Schmitz's decline was aggravated by Elio's illness. Elio was 'in despair' because his father resented the expense of his harmony lessons and this led to an altercation 'which went beyond all bounds'. Elio felt he would knock his head against a wall 'if only it would get me a job away from here so that I could keep myself ... In the short time which I count as my "future", I want to prove to Papa that I can do something.'[96]

Elio felt that his father had grown as incompetent as his partners—Adolfo and Noemi's widower, Sam. He had lost all his business sense and borrowed money recklessly. Of all the family, only 'the good Allegrina' never lost heart but put up with everything: Francesco's rages as well as Elio's nephritis.

About his doctors and their treatments Elio waxed despairingly sardonic: 'I consign Delfino to his bath, Pimser to beer, Luzzatto to iron, Levi to bed, and Nicolich to milk and arsenic.'[97] Svevo was to fill *La coscienza di Zeno* with caricatures of doctors, and no doubt Elio's long illness led Ettore to acquire that medical knowledge which a few years later impressed Silvio Benco.[98] Certainly he showed a thorough knowledge of his brother's affliction.[99]

Finally Elio had his wish to leave Trieste. A long stay at Levico near Trent in 1885 brought no improvement in his condition. The quarrels with his father continued, and in his 'money-mania' Francesco had reproached Elio for 'enjoying' nephritis while he 'suffered' it by paying for it. Elio therefore made up his mind to go and stay with relatives in Egypt where he might at least be able to 'live by my own work without help from Papa'.[100]

He left Trieste on 23 October 1885 on the *Vorwärts*, bidding farewell to all his family and relations at the pier. Only at that moment did he realize 'all the magnitude, all the enormity, all the meaning of the step I was taking; otherwise I should not have left.'[101] This scene is echoed in the ending of the penultimate section of *La coscienza di Zeno*, where the protagonist waves goodbye to the ailing Ada as she sails away, feeling that now he would never be able to prove his innocence to her. Ettore may well have felt remorse at having neglected his brother.

While the sick Elio left for Egypt, perhaps with the courage of despair, Ettore stayed on at home as foreign correspondence clerk at the bank. In 1883 there had been a changing of the guard on the staff of *L'Indipendente*. Giuseppe Caprin was succeeded as editor by the more retiring Cesare Rossi, a friend of Ettore's, who also did the theatre reviews.[102] This may partly explain Ettore's increased contributions to the newspaper. If there was an opportunity for him to join the staff of the newspaper, he did not take it.

But the humble bank-clerk must have been harassed by feelings of inferiority. He wrote an indignant article, 'Il dilettantismo', in November 1884, in answer to a derisive attack on dilettantism in *La Domenica Letteraria*.[103] We can quickly recognize a self-portrait of the literary dilettante Ettore Schmitz, then trying to write plays, in the 'somebody who gives vent to instincts which are not satisfied by writing letters for a bank' and who 'satisfies, as far as he is able, the desire to reproduce ideas or aesthetic forms which mother nature so unreasonably injected into his blood', but cannot devote to his art sufficient time to achieve originality.

The article goes on to surmise that such a dilettante may go to bed unknown one day to awake the next roused 'by celebrity in person coming to claim her chosen one' and perhaps seat him on 'the vacant throne of the national theatre'. Ettore still had forty years to wait for celebrity. For the time being, 'the dilettante, too, feels the need to keep up with the literary trend. Every week he reads the Sunday papers, Zola's latest novel, lots of literary essays and, if he is one of the best sort, Carducci's books', and plagues all those around him with his fads.

The dilettante Ettore Schmitz in fact read not only *La Domenica Letteraria* but *Nuova Antologia* and *La Domenica del Fracassa*, as well as the Paris newspapers.[104] In 1887 he quoted from *Le Figaro* and *Le Temps*,[105] which he probably had to scan at the bank for financial news. In general, his articles between 1883 and 1885 show him to be well-informed on all aspects of contemporary theatre and the novel, as well as on the European (and especially Italian and German) literary classics. They also show a thorough knowledge of modern thinkers such as Schopenhauer, Taine and Renan. If he was a dilettante, he had already acquired a wider reading than many professional intellectuals and men of letters. This can only have intensified his sense of frustration and failure at not having proved himself as a creative writer and at remaining chained to his clerk's desk. His feeling of frustration must have been coupled with a sense of inferiority in another respect, upon which the engaging Roberto Bazlen, of the generation following Svevo's, throws an interesting light. Bazlen recalls how he too suffered 'mortally' at having to attend a German school in a city so fiercely Italian in sentiment.[106] For Ettore Schmitz, mortification over having had the 'wrong' education must certainly have been aggravated by his difficulties with Italian—real or imagined. His German thoughts and style dogged his entire literary career, especially in Trieste.

Silvio Benco had a great deal to say about Svevo's awkward style,[107] and certainly many passages in Ettore's newspaper articles justify Benco's remarks. Svevo's 'style' may lend itself perfectly to narrative: in fact, when Svevo starts narrating, his language, without losing any of its character, seems to undergo a transfiguration. But it fits none of the canons of style acceptable in late nineteenth-century Italy, let alone in Trieste, whose nationalism made a fetish of literary Italian. Benco said that Svevo could confound his friends and critics by writing a page in perfect Trecento idiom but could never write a natural, easy, everyday Italian. To Svevo, as to Zeno, it was, in effect, a foreign language: Triestine was their mother-tongue.

Yet Ettore Schmitz did feebly try, in 1884, by double proxy, to make his modest mark in the theatre world, during the long and triumphal season given at the Filodrammatico theatre in Trieste by the new star of Italy's theatrical firmament, Eleonora Duse. The whole season was booked out. Cesare Rossi's reviews in *L'Indipendente* chronicled the actress's success in the crowded theatre. On 1 March Meilhac and Halévy's *Frou-frou* brought the house down. So did Sardou's *Fedora* on 2 March. And so it went on with *La femme de Claude* (in Italian, of course) by Dumas *fils*, Sardou's *Odette*, Goldoni's *La locandiera*, and *Adrienne Lecouvreur*. Verga's *Cavalleria rusticana* was a flop on 10 March (Trieste, of all Italian cities, was unique in this) and so was the hitherto sure-fire *La Dame aux camélias*. But Duse's apotheosis came on 2 April with Sardou's *Divorçons*.[108]

That very evening *L'Indipendente* carried an article signed E. S., entitled 'Una commedia in lingua impossibile' (A Play in Impossible Language), on a modest but lively play written by Policarpo Petrocchi in 1881 in a colloquial and contemporary Florentine idiom. This play had never found its way into the theatrical repertoire and Ettore concluded his account of it by asking Duse's company to give it a try.[109] This was the second time that Ettore Schmitz offered Duse someone else's wares. Elio's diary entry for 31 March reads:

Ettore has made the acquaintance of Signora Duse-Checchi and has played one of his tricks. He sent her an Italian translation of *Romeo and Juliet* inscribed as follows: 'The undersigned takes the liberty of offering you for performance this drama which he wrote with you particularly in mind. He asks for no royalties other than those allowed to him by the laws obtaining during his lifetime. W. Shakespeare.'

On 3 April Elio went to the Filodrammatico to see Duse once more. Presumably Ettore went along with him, but no more is mentioned of his dealings with the actress. A writer younger than Svevo, and younger still than Eleonora Duse (who was born in 1858), was, from 1895, to have close dealings with her and write, 'with her particularly in mind', sensationally successful dramas: Gabriele D'Annunzio.

Trieste's failed playwright consoled himself by picking on the audience: 'the [theatre-going] public is corruptive by nature, and the continual contact with each other into which author and spectators are brought especially in our country is bound to be fatal to art.' And: 'On the stage, for our public, morality may be disregarded, but not the semblance of morality.' Ettore had written this in the article 'Il pubblico' on 2 October 1883, in which he also described with cold anger how a theatrical fiasco or success was manufactured, with sneezes, coughs, clatters, then hisses, or indiscriminate and intrusive applause and interminable curtain-calls.[110]

Ettore's article was following the lead given by the critic Costetti, who urged the young playwright who did not wish his talent to be overwhelmed to flee from contact with the monstrous corrupting public. This was a counsel of artistic heroism, but a negative counsel. To the aspiring young writer it represented another setback. Ettore's dislike and contempt for the bourgeois public, that vulgarly capricious arbiter of literary destinies, never altered. In the article on Ohnet, of May 1885,[111] his target was the novel-reading public (not very different from the theatre-going public), and his sarcasm was again directed against 'the public's moral sense or ... the sense so named by the public', and against the class perspective of the bourgeois public mirrored by the best-selling Ohnet in 'the relationship which the author sets up between workers and capital. "We're good, you're good, we love you", they tell Clara and their employer.' And E.S. comments: 'Very reassuring!'

14

APPROACHES TO 'TRUTH'—ZOLA AND SCHOPENHAUER

These articles therefore trace a clear distinction between popular success, which Ettore despised and feared, and true artistic success. If a value emerges from his critical writings, that value is truth. To use the word is, of course, to attempt to appropriate it to the cause one wishes to advance. So, in this most overtly committed phase of Ettore's life, the truth or truths which he repeatedly invokes are polemical, implicitly critical of bourgeois complacency and official optimism. Truth is scientific observation and enquiry; truth is moral judgement. But, in being these things, it is also a quest, a struggle: a continuous struggle against all forms of falsehood, hypocrisy, convention and prejudice; in short, courage against baseness. And, as such, it is political, always implicitly and often explicitly: a struggle against certain social and political, as well as cultural and intellectual, forces. Defeat and disappointment were to force Ettore increasingly to dissimulate his polemical passion; and the bitter experience of the complexities and contradictions embedded in the causes he believed in, and in his own personality, were to drive him into more subtle and supple, more wily and indirect ways of trying to approach his elusive goal. Irony becomes an ever more important element in his writing and in his everyday personality. But even so his most fervent convictions were to surface from time to time—as, for instance, in his first attempt at a draft of a pacifist essay at the end of the Great War, which he then cautiously revised as the pressures of the immediate situation bore down on him again.

This embattled conception of truth was clearly implied in the article on Guerrini in September 1883. In 'La verità', of 14 August 1884, E. S. condemned Renan for discovering the truth about Christ and yet being too fond of its opposite. In March 1885 he invoked Schopenhauer's authority to confirm Giordano Bruno's heroism in braving the stake for the sake of ideas which he felt to be true. In December 1884 he criticized Wagner—despite admiring his music—for his subtle distortions of the truth or for making truth evaporate into a cloud of mysticism. In these last three cases E. S. implicated religion as an agency in subverting truth. Later, in 1887, he expressed his respect for Taine ('his goddess is truth') for never swerving into partisanship away from truth.[112]

'Accademia', another article of 1887, gives no quarter to the French Academicians Leconte de L'Isle and Alexandre Dumas *fils,* exposing their equivocations, their wheedling eloquence, their fawning on each other.[113] This almost makes Ettore Schmitz himself guilty of *parti pris.* Certainly, he was waging his own literary battle in the name of truth (a battle whose political correlatives he did not disguise), and taking the side of Zola and the Naturalists against the Academy. He resumed his attack on the Academy in 1888 in his enthusiastic review of Daudet's ruthlessly satirical novel *L'Immortel.*[114]

Ettore's commitment was clear. Through the apparent jumble of his critical articles he was carrying on a provincial literary campaign of his own which was part of the large-scale campaign pursued by Zola and his school to involve literature more seriously and effectively in live human and social issues. Naturalism was Svevo's real starting-point and the fertile matrix of his entire development as a writer.

Evidence abounds. From his 'reconfirmation' as a Naturalist in 1881, Schmitz–Svevo always held to the premises and aims of Naturalism, even if he showed them to be increasingly problematical. *Profilo autobiografico* is clear about the young Ettore's 'passion for the French novel' and goes so far as to avow that 'Una vita is certainly influenced by the French Naturalists (*veristi*)', pointedly avoiding the captious distinction between Realists and Naturalists.[115] Svevo's oldest friend, Giulio Ventura, questioned as to the writer's literary preferences before 1890, 'answered without hesitating: "Zola was his god; the *roman expérimental,* his credo." '[116]

In 1925 Svevo still admired Zola enough to write:

Les objections qu'on soulève contre Proust ne pourraient pas lui empêcher l'accès au public. Au fond ce sont les mêmes objections qui auraient dû nuire à Zola. Mais celui-ci avait eu la fortune de trouver en Italie un critique de la force et renommée de Francesco De Sanctis.[117]

We may well credit De Sanctis with having introduced Svevo to the world of Zola. The magnificent essays of 'Studio sopra Emilio Zola' were republished in De Sanctis's *Nuovi saggi critici* (New Critical Essays) in 1879 and Treves brought out De Sanctis's pamphlet *Zola e 'L'Assommoir'* in the same year. When E. S. wrote that in Zola 'the scientific notion of heredity has taken the place held by destiny in Greek tragedy',[118] he was echoing De Sanctis: 'There it was a matter of Gods and Goddesses; here it's a matter of kidneys.'[119] Ettore's critical articles are evidence of his familiarity with the writings of De Sanctis who, as it chanced, died on Ettore's twenty-second birthday.

Ettore Schmitz, not yet twenty years old, must have been impressed by the impassioned eloquence with which De Sanctis acclaimed Zola as the great artist of the real, 'a realist in science, an idealist in poetry', equipped with a 'style as sharp, swift and sure as a surgeon's scalpel ... language potent and proper' which made him the greatest French stylist since Proudhon precisely because it was so far removed from the artifice of fine writing.[120] De Sanctis's pages conjure up a Zola incomparably superior to the mannered Italian *veristi,* would-be realists, of the 1870s—a Zola who gave prominence to the ideal by presenting only the real and by this very token proved himself so consummate an artist that 'there is nothing outside the narrative but the narrative, the reader's assent [*fede*] is total, the illusion is perfect.' But Zola was not only an artist. His writing was also a political act, stripping bare the corruption which had become the rule of life in France under the Second Empire. De Sanctis's first three essays on Zola had corruption for their title—political, social and natural corruption respectively. He explicitly compared Louis Philippe's cynical balancing of Right against Left to the no less corrupting *trasformismo* (political transvestism) of the new Italian Kingdom. The Empire of Napoleon III extended the political corruption of Louis Philippe still further into the economic sphere, inviting all classes to 'Get rich!'—a motif that might well interest an inhabitant of Trieste, a city dedicated to Mercury, the god of commerce. De Sanctis's reference to the police-spy apparatus made the parallel with Trieste even more striking: 'It was the reign of the full belly and the empty head.'[121]

Svevo's own writings indeed always have socio-political undertones and implications (conscious and diagnostic ones, not unconscious and symptomatic), but he puts the psychological level uppermost. In this respect also the 'Studio sopra Emilio Zola' has some interesting things to say. De Sanctis saw that Zola went much further than the founder of the psychological novel, Balzac: 'Psychological history has become natural history, which absorbs even the soul. Psychology turns into physiology, character into temperament: virtues and vices are good or bad instincts, natural phenomena stamped in the bumps of the head and the features of the physiognomy.'[122]

Ettore must have also read in the *Nuovi saggi critici* De Sanctis's 'Il principio del realismo' (The Principle of Realism),[123] in which the critic used Kirchmann's philosophical work of the same title to correct and supplement Hartmann's 'philosophy of the unconscious'. Hartmann took up leads from Hegel, Schelling and Schopenhauer to identify the unconscious as the location of the painful clash between will and reason, and argued that this clash could be resolved through consciousness. (De Sanctis's word was *coscienza*, which was to appear in the title of Svevo's third novel, disguised in the English translation as 'confessions'). This consciousness, for Hartmann, is realized in culture—including ethics, aesthetics, religion, philosophy. De Sanctis saw this as an abstract hypothesis that needed testing against the direct experience of reality.[124] There was no more room, he wrote, for pure thought: 'We're in the full swing of realism.'

This argument was part of De Sanctis's conception of literary history as a progressive incarnation of the ideal within the real and must have weighed with Svevo, for throughout his life and his writings he gave absolute priority to the test of reality, of actual experience, of objectivity, and fought off every temptation to decadence, irrationalism, aestheticism or transcendentalism. In this essay De Sanctis urged his Italian readers to acquaint themselves with German thought,[125] and Ettore was among those who took up his call. Hartmann as developed by Kirchmann was a promising starting-point for his pre-Freudian interest in psychology. For the 'realist' Kirchmann the two sources of knowledge were the senses and consciousness. De Sanctis developed the argument:

But since in this way you have knowledge only of your own soul, you have none as to the states of the souls of other men. You can judge of them by their physiognomy, gestures and aptitudes and by a reasoning process, that is, by thought; but you can see no deeper into them than your own experience allows. That is why 'know thyself' is the basis for all these other states of mind.[126]

It would be hard to define more precisely that link between objectivity and subjectivity, between naturalism and psychology, evident in Svevo's novels.

The same passage of De Sanctis adds another point, or rather, indicates a gap: '*Being* in its positive nature eludes knowledge, and its concept is for us purely negative: it is the unknowable in things.' This gap, for Svevo, was to be filled by Schopenhauer's metaphysic, which saw, underlying the phenomena of the physical world, the world of Will.

The *Profilo autobiografico* does not give much prominence to Zola among the other French *veristi*, but does give rather more to De Sanctis: 'Then some sort of order was introduced into his studies through his acquaintance with the works of Francesco De Sanctis'.[127] This implies acceptance of De Sanctis's guiding principles. But Ettore was resolute in defending Zola in 1884 against the charges made in Scarfoglio's *Il libro di Don Chisciotte* (The Book of Don Quixote):

Not a scientist but an artist, Zola describes life in the light of a theory which explains it to him. If this theory were to be supplanted by another, our successors would see in Zola's work a representation of life as it is felt to be by the most highly cultured of our contemporaries.[128]

And he further championed, against Scarfoglio, the originality of the Realist–Naturalist current in literature as compared to its Romantic precedents:

Romanticism shifted the Pillars of Hercules to mark the bounds of the territories which it had enlarged, but it still called those Pillars the furthermost limits of the world, whereas they were not so; to perceive this and go on to discover what had been left out was a revolution and not a mere contribution, as Scarfoglio asserts. Centuries will go by before distance shrinks the difference in the eyes of posterity, which seems to us as great as the difference in ends and means between Benjamin Constant, Madame De Staël, Walter Scott, Victor Hugo and Balzac, Zola, the Goncourt brothers.

The most surprising thing Svevo ever wrote about Zola, and the best mark of his love, even more than admiration, for the great French novelist, is his review of Zola's *La Joie de vivre*.[129] Ettore did not write hack reviews for *L'Indipendente*. His every article was motivated by protest or proposal, praise or blame, or personal experience of life. If he chose this particular novel for his only Zola review, he had his reasons. He dwelt on the character from whom the book gets its title—Pauline: a character endowed with an almost irrational *joie de vivre,* so much so that

A malicious person ... wishing to catch Zola in contradiction with his own theories might consider Pauline to be a personified ideal and it would then clearly appear that the novel has a polemical thesis as its aim.

The truth of the matter, for Ettore, lay both here and elsewhere: Pauline was none other than Zola himself: 'Pauline loves and is engrossed by all that exists, the lovely and the ugly, like Zola himself. Zola evidently wishes to demonstrate that his art was born out of love for life.' Svevo's love of Zola was love for the love of life.

This same article also contains Svevo's first reference to Schopenhauer. One of the characters in the novel is cousin Lazare, a follower of Schopenhauer. He 'shudders and despairs gazing at the stars and thinking of infinity' beside Pauline, while 'she gazes at them with calm curiosity but does not suffer the anguishing sense of her own nullity.' This passage heralds from afar the relationship between Zeno and his wife Augusta:

She knew all about the things that drive one to despair, but they changed their nature when she viewed them. Even if the world did go round, there was no need to be seasick. On the contrary, the world went round, but everything else stayed in its place.[130]

And just before that: 'for her the present was a tangible reality in which we could take shelter and be snug together.' And so on for a couple of pages. This passage in *La coscienza di Zeno* draws closely on a family memoir which Ettore wrote in 1897.[131] Here his wife was described in very much the same terms as

Zeno's wife, summed up in the pointedly Zolaesque phrase: 'it is an absolute and inexplicable *joie de vivre*.' So life corròborates literature and literature develops the dialectic of life.

If Svevo's wife was to be Zolaesque, Svevo himself was Schopenhauerian. His *Profilo autobiografico* affirms: 'However, his favourite author soon became Schopenhauer.' It attributes the pseudonym 'Svevo' to his influence and declares that *Una vita*—on whose cover that pseudonym first appeared—was born under the sign of Schopenhauer's philosophy. Its hero Alfonso 'was to be precisely the Schopenhauerian affirmation of life which is so close to its negation', so much so as to make 'the ending of the novel as abrupt and crude as the member of a syllogism'.*[132]

Ettore did not begin writing the novel until the end of 1887. Before that, there are just four relatively trivial references to Schopenhauer in his articles, from the one on *La Joie de vivre* of 8 March 1884 to the one on Péladan of 20 October 1886. The most telling of these references is in 'Giordano Bruno giudicato da Arturo Schopenhauer'[133] on 20 February 1885, where E. S. showed he had read meticulously *Die Welt als Wille und Vorstellung* (The World as Will and Representation) in the first *Sämtliche Werke* published in 1873. In 1929 Carlo Franellich reported having visited Svevo's house and seen his Schopenhauer collection in the 1877 Leipzig edition.[134] The whole of Svevo's life shows traces of the deep impression left on his mind by the 'philosopher of pessimism', but his application of Schopenhauer was not the usual one. In the last year of his life Svevo wrote of Schopenhauer as 'the first to become aware of us'—that is, us 'sick people', contemplators, 'the sort who think'—regarding them as products of nature, as finished as the 'healthy', the 'fighters', 'the men who act', but of a different species, 'two different animals'.[135] This perspective implies, really, the *superiority* of those who stand aside from the fray of conflicting individual wills and are potentially *au dessus de la mêlée*, closer to the untroubled, undifferentiated, unconditioned universal Will. Yet Svevo never accepted Schopenhauer's philosophy as a justification for renunciation, or for aesthetic escape, as so many did.

It is quite likely that Ettore first learnt about Schopenhauer from De Sanctis's tongue-in-cheek dialogue on ' Schopenhauer e Leopardi', which first appeared as far back as 1858 and was republished in *Saggi critici*. De Sanctis touched lightly but firmly upon Schopenhauer's explicit preference for reactionary politics—which partly explains why Schopenhauer did not find favour until after the collapse of liberal aspirations in Germany in 1848. The 'abyss' that separated Schopenhauer's renunciatory pessimism from the heroic pessimism of the Italian poet, whose thought bears such an uncanny resemblance to

---

* These remarks are not unequivocally clear, but they involve Schopenhauer's notion that suicide is not a rejection of life but only of the terms upon which life is offered. It is therefore an act of individual will rather than a liberation from it and a reunion with universal Will. Some of the key notions of Schopenhauer's ambitious holistic philosophy are touched upon in the following pages in so far as they relate to Svevo.

Schopenhauer's, could be measured by the fact that for Schopenhauer 'the slave differs from the free man more in name than in fact', whilst 'Leopardi produces the effect opposite to the one he intends. He does not believe in progress, and yet makes you long for it: he does not believe in liberty, but makes you love it. Love, glory, virtue, he calls illusions, yet kindles in your heart an inextinguishable ardour for them.'[136]

So the Schopenhauer who emerges right away is a problematic Schopenhauer, who no longer offers 'a philosophy of words', like Schelling or Hegel, but 'a philosophy of things'.[137] Schopenhauer's metaphysic sees the world of phenomena as a veil of Maya spread over and concealing the blind unknowable essence of Will which sustains it. For Ettore, as for Schopenhauer, life was a charade, an act, make-believe. However, both men refused to give up this make-believe for an aesthetic or mystical nirvana. We have seen what E. S. thought of the mysticism of the self-styled Schopenhauerian, Wagner. In *Senilità* also, Wagner stands for Schopenhauerian mysticism. For Schopenhauer, music, the most sublime of the arts, speaks the language of the universal Will, in which individual wills may regain unity. Svevo superbly evokes the music of *Die Walküre*, in which Amalia, desperate in her love for Balli, senses everyone's destiny and her own, which arouses no more tears than other people's destiny, but the same ones, whilst her brother Emilio has drawn from the same music nothing more than 'an interval of peace', only to return to compassion for himself, for Angiolina and for Amalia.[138] But the Schopenhauerian effects of Wagner's music, far from saving brother and sister from their situation, lead them deeper: in Emilio's case, into an ever more sordid love-affair; in Amalia's case, into despair and alcoholism.

Anna Herz's inscription in the Shakespeare volume which she gave to Ettore already contained the tendentially Schopenhauerian notion of poetry as consolation. But for Svevo art serves quite another purpose, for which Schopenhauer's thought provides him first and foremost with a means of critical inquiry enabling him to pick out from the tangle of conscious motivation and rationalization the unconscious motives and the hidden egoism which is always working away in secret. In other words, Svevo uses Schopenhauer's philosophy as a critical and self-critical philosophy and, more, as a critical psychology, which, as Thomas Mann pointed out, largely anticipates Freud. No escapism, then, no aestheticism. Rather—following Hartmann who is in this respect halfway between Schopenhauer and Freud—art is an instrument of knowledge, or better, *coscienza* (consciousness, conscience, awareness). Bringing to the surface the individual's mystificatory rationalizations and the unconscious conflicts which underlie them, it sets him on the road to resolving them.

This use of Schopenhauer by Svevo explains how he could have been at one and the same time both a Schopenhauerian and a Zolian. Darwin's theory might well have appeared to him as an extension of Schopenhauer's thought into the world of zoological phenomena. What is the instinct of self-preservation if not the Schopenhauerian Will as it evolves in the natural world? What is the struggle for life if not Schopenhauer's 'bellum omnium contra omnes'? Scientific positivism could well complement Schopenhauer's metaphysic and his psychology. For this reason it is beside the point to talk of 'the discovery of Schopenhauer and the crisis of naturalism' in Svevo, as does Savarese, in keeping with most Svevo scholars.[139] Svevo's peculiar originality as a writer lies precisely in carrying on both lines of thought together in such a way that they test and supplement one another at the same time as the two of them together subject life itself to a critical experiment through the pages of his narratives. Later on, Marxism extended the metaphysic of the Will and the science of man into the field of social relations. These 'theories' were used not as 'theses' to be demonstrated, but rather as working hypotheses which enabled the writer to extend to the utmost certain possibilities of understanding and explaining to us the world and ourselves. Even in Zola the grafting of a critical psychology of the unconscious or the half-conscious upon 'external' naturalism was clearly not only possible but inevitable: we may think of the finesse with which thirst for justice and egoistic ambition are perceived to be intermingled in the motivation of the hero of *Germinal*, Etienne Lantier. Svevo inverted the proportions as between external and internal realism, more markedly with each succeeding novel.

For Svevo, Schopenhauer throws a problematic light upon the individual. The individualism characteristic of bourgeois society which had triumphed in the French Revolution over the remnants of a feudal society organized according to hierarchy and to caste is indeed elevated by Schopenhauer into an ontological principle: he makes it a fact of nature rather than of history—but only to condemn it as the source of all suffering in the world. To overcome or transcend individualism is therefore as necessary as it is arduous. Svevo dismisses the Schopenhauerian roads beyond individualism through mysticism or aesthetic contemplation, in which individual willing is suspended, but he does not dismiss ethics, as this does not suppress individual willing but consciously and actively allies and identifies one's will with the will of others. He pursues art not as an escape route or a refuge but as a means of communicating knowledge and truth, a means of laying bare the vices of individualism and, by so doing, curing them. Svevo's writing thus combines egoism—thirst for fame, self-aggrandizement—with altruism, mapping out within the inmost recesses of individual awareness a condition which is common to all. His books, however, transcend this contradiction and contain within themselves their own critique: they choose as their targets protagonists who try to get the better of life and of others through literature, through a deemed moral, intellectual or imaginative superiority, through 'success' in any guise.

All this was to mature slowly in the writer's mind. Nowhere does he state this position explicitly. If Svevo was absorbing and coming to terms with Schopenhauer in 1884–5, he was not to begin his 'Schopenhauerian' novel until the end of 1887, and there we still find a gulf between the 'strong'—Maller, Macario, Federico, Francesca, Annetta—and the 'weak', foremost among them the central character, Alfonso Nitti. Such a dichotomy hardly exists in *Senilità* and is completely transcended in the third novel, where all the characters share the same ontological dimension.

15

EARLY PLAYS

In the meantime, in the years preceding *Una vita*, Ettore wrote, apart from his articles, only plays, of uncertain date.[140] Only *Le ire di Giuliano* (The Bad-Tempered Husband) carries a date: 1881. Yet, until the end of 1882 Elio's diary implies that Ettore had not completed a single literary work. Svevo may have written in that date long after he wrote the play and mistaken the year. The play, however, shows the beneficial effects of the theatrical mode of Naturalism which Ettore had re-espoused in that year. Both dramatic *tours de force* (*punte*) and didactic purpose (*tesi*) are avoided. The subject-matter is drawn from everyday life and in fact closely mirrors the Schmitzes' own family situation. Lucia, unhappily married to the wealthy but irascible butcher Giuliano, is rather like Paola Schmitz in her marriage with Raimondo Finzi. There is no strict symmetry in the parallel, as the character Giuliano also has much in common with Francesco Schmitz, and indeed the final scene introduces a touch of sympathy for Giuliano who finds himself left 'alone to improve my character ... in that horrible butcher's shop',[141] which partly counterbalances the dominant theme of the power which he exerts over the whole family through his money. This Naturalist theme *par excellence* of the power of money appears in most of Svevo's plays.

Le ire di Giuliano is certainly no masterpiece, but is dramatically well worked out and displays an exact grasp of reality and a confident treatment—in short, an 'impersonality' in every sense which is quite impressive, and which suggests that Svevo revised the play more than once to streamline it. This he was to do with nearly all his works.

By contrast, the two-act *Le teorie del conte Alberto* (The Theories of Count Alberto)[142], though it calls itself a *scherzo drammatico*, is awkwardly constructed as well as being thin in subject-matter. The protagonist hurriedly abjures his faith in science and in heredity which he finds to have been belied by the girl he loves, who is the pure and honest daughter of an immoral mother. Simplistic categories of virtue and vice are thus identified with particular characters, whereas in everything else Svevo wrote such categories are dissolved by his sceptical and analytical irony. There is a reference to the

Darwinian scientist Lubbock;[143] Ettore probably had in mind his *Ants, Bees and Wasps,* which came out in London in several volumes between 1882 and 1889 and was quickly translated into other languages, including Italian. The fact that the play is signed E. Samigli points to the years 1886–91, which is when Ettore used that pseudonym, but again, this might indicate a later revision.

Another 'scherzo drammatico', the one-acter *Una commedia inedita* (An Unpublished Play),[144] is not much better. Here the autobiographical figure of the failed writer makes its first appearance, interwoven with the standard triangular situation. The playwright, however, is the target of his own irony, in the figure of Adolfo, whose petty reaction of wounded *amour-propre* disappoints Elena, the married woman he admires, when she criticizes his play.[145] The suggestion that Elena is prepared to contemplate an 'immoral' liaison herself but not to read about it in a play follows the lines of E. S.'s articles attacking the hypocritical morality of the public. An allusion to *Postuma,* the poems by Lorenzo Stecchetti (the pseudonym of Olindo Guerrini), which came out in 1877, not only suggests an early date for the work, but, as Elena's husband refers to Stecchetti as brazenly immoral, reinforces the irony at the expense of middle-class respectability.

Il ladro in casa (The Thief in the Family)[146] is the most ambitious piece of Svevo's early period—unless, that is, it was really written in 1895, as was averred by Svevo's friend Piazzetta, to whom Svevo presented the manuscript. The play is a four-acter, as light in tone as the three previous plays, and is signed E. Samigli (which is the main evidence for dating it somewhere between 1886 and 1891). The Triestine world of commerce which provided the background to the previous plays here moves into the foreground. The play revolves around the fraudulent financial dealings of Ignazio Lonelli, a merry scoundrel who weds a large dowry, proceeds to extract huge loans on business pretexts from his brother-in-law and his uncle, and finally attempts to run off with stolen gold and jewels and someone else's wealthy wife. The denouement is the most boisterous thing that Svevo ever wrote—the 'thief in the family' falls to his death from a roof-top and 'It will take a broom to get all those bits and pieces into the coffin.'[147]

This play then shows Svevo almost anticipating the *teatro del grottesco* or absurdist drama. All his plays, while rooted in the objectivist mode of naturalist theatre, incline in varying degrees to an expressionistic distortion of reality, and the negation of reality through parody. Yet, once again, family history provides the germ of this play. It is not hard to see in the career of Ignazio Lonelli an elaborated and transposed version of that of Ignazio Tedeschi, who had married Ettore's aunt Peppina and abandoned her after her wedding, making off to Egypt with all their money and valuables. Carla and Carlo in the play correspond pretty closely to Peppina and Francesco Schmitz, and Carlo's wife Fortunata corresponds even in name to Allegra Schmitz, though the parallelism need not be overdone. Anna Maria Famà reports that the play's denouement was based on events which actually took place in Trieste at the time.[148]

It is hard to understand why this play has never been staged (as far as I know) either during Svevo's lifetime or since. Its caustic critique of Triestine and generally bourgeois economism as well as of middle-class gullibility is masked by its comic and theatrical gusto and by the sly irony which enables the tragic end of Ignazio Lonelli (which also confirms his victims' ruin) to appear as a conventionally moral 'happy ending' in which evil is defeated. Lonelli is perhaps too openly the brazen opportunist, but is otherwise no mean predecessor of Zeno Cosini and is in fact the first real 'character' that Svevo created.

Svevo's articles of theatre criticism show that he was well aware that the eighties were the worst possible decade in which to write for the theatre. He did not manage to bring off what the still unknown Ibsen was at that very moment doing—revolutionizing the theatre from a Naturalistic starting-point. The renewal through Naturalism of Italian theatre was yet to come. Verga's *Cavalleria rusticana* (Rustic Chivalry) indeed appeared in 1884, but for the urban public it could be served up as an exotic dish of picturesque rusticity. The real challenge did not come until the nineties, largely thanks to the impetus provided by Ibsen. Giacosa's first masterpiece in a naturalistic vein was *Tristi amori* (Sad Loves) in 1888; Rovetta achieved his first real success with *I disonesti* (Those without Honour) in 1892. Marco Praga's plays began appearing from 1886, but his first success, *La moglie ideale* (The Ideal Wife), came in 1890. Bracco too started in 1886.

Things were not much different in Venetian dialect theatre. There was the partial but telling exception of Gallina. Trieste was the first town to see nine of his plays. From 1881 to 1913, Ferruccio Benini, the Gallina actor *par excellence*, gave no less than 750 performances in twenty-eight Triestine theatrical seasons.[149] Svevo only once tried dialect theatre, and then only in a 'minor' work (*Atto unico*). Nor did he ever closely echo Gallina's plotting or stage style. Nevertheless, Gallina was almost the only tolerable Italian playwright through most of the eighties, and this might partly explain the limitations of Svevo's attempts at a new theatre. Another possible guiding light was Goldoni, who in the eighties began to enjoy a very gradual revival, largely due to another great Venetian dialect actor, Emilio Zago.[150]

The quality and depth of Goldoni and Gallina are not to be underrated, and Svevo was to remain a devotee of Venetian dialect theatre all his life. But if it could teach him deftness of composition and comic verve, it could not offer him the means of expressing his highly problematical *fin de siècle* sensibility in terms of the advanced culture of contemporary Europe. Above all, what eluded him was the means of matching external objectivity to the character's subjectivity, his inner world. Both the canons of Naturalism and the theatre of Goldoni and Gallina led him to set all his characters on the same unrelieved plane. This promoted the analytical presentation of milieu and the disciplined exclusion of every kind of arbitrary subjectivism. But it hampered any development of the theme that we now recognize (in the light of the novels) as most characteristically Svevian: the urge to integrate individual and society, 'subjectivity' and 'objectivity'.

16

LITERARY CULTURE IN THE 1880s: ITALY AND TRIESTE

Italian narrative literature had hardly anything better than Italian drama to offer a writer of Svevo's inclinations. The greater *verismo* of Verga's 'second period', or that of such writers as Matilde Serao, characteristically dealt with the archaic South and was not an appropriate import for a large mercantile city cut off from its rural hinterland as Trieste was. It was better to return to the French source from which the South Italian *veristi* had themselves drawn inspiration. In any case, *verismo* had to fight for survival in Italy, and it may be argued that it never took firm root. Svevo was to praise Crémieux for emphasizing the influence of Verga's 'first period':

It appears to us as a discovery that one should attach some importance to Verga's pre-'veristic' novels. They obviously were important. They created a school. And besides, we know that they still find passionate readers whom Verga himself did not manage to persuade to turn to other reading.[151]

Verga's *Storia di una capinera* (The Caged Bird) remained his most widely read book till long after he died in 1922, and his other early novels found scores of imitators, not least in Trieste. Their titles indicate their content: *Una peccatrice* (A Sinful Woman), *Eva, Eros, Tigre reale* (Royal Tigress). They are in the line of Sainte-Beuve's *Volupté* and Tommaseo's *Fede e bellezza* (Faith and Beauty), whose theme is sin, the sinner caught between passion and religiosity. This literary current was to re-emerge prestigiously with D'Annunzio, who dwelt on the first of the two terms, and Fogazzaro, who emphasized the second. Svevo parodied, satirized and corrected this sort of 'literature' in *Senilità*. He shows Emilo Brentani trying to write a novel out of his love-affair with Angiolina, and drawing on his youthful novel: 'the story of a young artist who was ruined in mind and health by a woman. He had portrayed himself in the hero, his own innocence and gentleness of nature. His heroine he had imagined after the fashion of the time: a mixture of woman and tigress . . .'[152]

If Italian culture, then, had little to offer Svevo, Triestine culture had still

less. The town at this time was enjoying a state of cultural repose barely
disturbed by the arrival of Wagner's *Der Ring* cycle, which was performed in
its entirety at the Politeama Rossetti in 1883. Ettore Schmitz must have heard
that strange new music on the evenings of 18 to 21 May, its effect mingling in
his mind with anxiety over his brother Elio, such a passionate lover of music,
who was now confined to bed, his nephritis having only been diagnosed at the
beginning of that month. The pages about the performance of *Die Walküre* in
Senilità may well be a reminiscence of this occasion, though the chronology of
the novel relates to another performance in 1893.[153]

The cultural repose persisted despite a wholesale changing of the guard. The
Società di Minerva, under its new statute, was now run by Boccardi, Hortis
and Lorenzutti. Membership cost 18 florins per annum. In 1884 there were 228
members and the Friday evening lectures were always packed out. The subjects
treated were extremely varied. Among the literary ones were two talks by
Boccardi, 'The public and the novel' and '*La Favilla*' (the Triestine journal of
1836–46); also 'Rousseau's *Emile*' by the poetess Adele Butti, and a satire,
'The criticism of criticism', by another poetess, Erminia Bazzocchi, and G. C.
Bottura's 'On Italian satire'. Talks on social and scientific subjects included
'Suicide' and 'Thought and the brain' in 1883, 'On nervousness' and 'The social
doctrines of naturalism compared to the social philosophy of Christianity' in
1886. And there was Lorenzutti's talk on tobacco of 5 January 1888, mentioned
in Svevo's humorous article on smoking which appeared in *L'Indipendente*'s
social column 'Echi mondani' on 17 November 1890.[154]

Hortis and Boccardi were now, with the possible addition of Pítteri, Trieste's
leading literary lights. Attilio Hortis, the librarian at the Biblioteca Civica and
already a man of some renown as a scholar and patriot, engaged in just the
sort of purely abstract erudition of 'learned monographs and commentaries on
ancient works' referred to in one of Svevo's articles.[155] His work has been
criticized for its lack of method and of intellectual control and for its total
subordination to his passionate nationalist concerns.[156] He belonged to the
inner circle of politicians who controlled Triestine affairs.

Alberto Boccardi published his first novel, *Ebbrezza morale* (Moral Elation),
in 1880. In ten years it ran to five editions. Boccardi's copious writings included
two more novels: *Morgana*, published in 1884, and *Il punto di mira* (The Goal),
published in 1896. These novels won, at the provincial Triestine level, the
popular success which Ohnet achieved in France at a national and international
level (remarked upon by Ettore in his review of Ohnet), and by roughly the
same means—a skilful blend of social climbing, romantic passion and a high
moral tone conveyed with a certain deftness of style that could hold its own
until it was eclipsed by the far more prestigious prose of D'Annunzio and
Fogazzaro. Of Boccardi's verse, some idea has been given at the end of Chapter
11.[157] This was another of the forceful young men who achieved quick prominence and with whom Ettore could hardly have helped comparing his own
ineffectuality.

The other Triestine poets of the late nineteenth century were not very different from Boccardi in thematic and stylistic range. One of them, Elisa Tagliapietra-Cambon, held weekly gatherings of all the town's literary and intellectual personalities in her salon, flippantly dubbed 'the Triestine Parnassus'. Coceani and Pagnini list among the members of this Parnassus everybody except Ettore Schmitz. Nothing could more eloquently testify to the latter's isolation. If he frequented the salon, he made no mark, or was deliberately cold-shouldered. At these gatherings 'Attilio Hortis poured out an inexhaustible stream of anecdotes', whilst 'the cult of the national literature always held a high place in the conversation.' Most members of the group were born in the early fifties, which may be another reason why the younger Ettore Schmitz was not prominent in it.

Patriotic feeling led the Triestines to admire poets like Giuseppe Revere and Filippo Zamboni. Revere was Jewish, born in 1812, and had left Trieste as a young man, 'not taking to the humdrum life of a business office while a thousand dreams of love and glory filled his heart'.[158] Another of Ettore's opposites, the high-minded Revere plunged into the battles of the Risorgimento, and his poetic works were themselves part of that struggle. Zamboni, born in 1826, had also fought with Garibaldi. In 1885 there appeared what even Stefani, the chronicler of Irredentist poetry, calls one of his 'mastodontic epics', *Sotto i Flavi* (Under the Flavians).[159] 'Obscure and plethoric' as it is, Ettore, it seems, read it: Zeno refers to 'the kiss that the poet Zamboni thought he had seen in the moon'.[160]

Riccardo Pítteri, whose poetry has an easy flow, whether idyllic or humorous or civic and exhortatory, not only frequented Elisa Tagliapietra-Cambon's gatherings but was a moving spirit in Trieste's cultivated social life, particularly in the Circolo Artistico. This was founded in 1884 largely through the initiative of Riccardo Zampieri, who had just come out of prison and who envisaged it as 'a new hotbed of Irredentism'.[161] Once again, the chronicles of the Circolo Artistico mention every name but that of the self-effacing Ettore Schmitz.

The Circolo Artistico not only organized nude and costume studies and art exhibitions, but also brought to the pursuit of the figurative and musical arts a carefree, colourful, fanciful and whimsical gaiety and bohemianism. Coceani and Pagnini mention 'Concerts, lectures, feasts, fancy-dress balls', historical pageants in ancient Egyptian costume or medieval dress with décor to match. 'Then their Saturday nights [*sabatine*] were famous. Riccardo Pítteri never missed those gay Saturday get-togethers. As yet unmarried, enormously entertaining, he had an inexhaustible fund of witticisms, anecdotes, epigrams.' Pítteri was also behind the Circolo's most hilarious events: the stagings of burlesque versions of grand operas such as *Otello* and *Cavalleria rusticana* 'with librettos rearranged by Pítteri' in which all the roles were taken by men.[162]

Ettore may have been implicitly contrasting his own lack of social ease with Pítteri or his like when he referred in 1883 to some modern gentleman who has been accustomed from youth to mix in society and who experiences no embarrassment or emotion upon meeting new people, who readily talks on any subject with wit, who behaves in such a way as to show that he knows all the rules of etiquette even though he follows none of them precisely ...[163]

and there is an autobiographical ring about the page in *Una vita* which describes Alfonso Nitti's awkwardness upon entering for the first time into the pretentious Maller household where Annetta holds her literary meetings, whose smug superficiality is particularly personified by the glib Macario.

17

DEATH AND INDIVIDUALISM

Before Elio left for Egypt in October 1885, he had rested through the three summer months in Gorizia. Ettore visited him there, and was to show his knowledge of the area in *La coscienza di Zeno,* where the narrator is surprised by the outbreak of hostilities at Lucinico, just outside Gorizia. Ettore's earliest extant letter, addressed to relatives there, recalls 'the green of your countryside and the white of your milk'. By contrast to Gorizia, the summer in Trieste was scarcely bearable: 'It's horribly hot, the sea is as warm as the liquid which Elio took to ennobling with albumen ... I no longer study in the evenings because I sweat and if I sweat ... I yawn with every part of my body like the woman described by my friend Lamberti...'. Apart from the relaxing diversion of taking a boat to the swimming baths, Ettore's life was compounded of stomach-ache, bank correspondence and, *schrecklichste der Schrecken,* dialogues which he had promised to write as a surprise for the thirteenth birthday of Fortunato Cohen, nephew of Fortunato and Giuseppe Vivante. 'I've done my best to heartily bore the audience and I don't doubt that the actors [presumably the Cohen children] will do all they can to help me achieve that goal.'[164]

In Egypt, Elio's health still did not improve, and he took care not to send home precise reports. Ettore was now doing his military service and had to spend some nights on guard duty.[165] In later years he used to tell a story about an overbearing Austrian baron who was one of his superior officers. This man was climbing up a bank on exercises just ahead of Svevo and warned him: 'See you don't bite me in the behind.' To which corporal Schmitz replied: 'Don't you know Jews don't eat pork?' One of his fellow-conscripts, Hermannstorfer, was nicknamed 'lard-licker'.[166] Many years later, as Giani Stuparich records, 'Italo Svevo, thundering out his story as he got carried away by it, would jump up from his wicker armchair and go through the motions of marching as one of "Franz Josef's conscripts".[167]

Elio returned to Trieste more ill than he left it and died a few weeks before his twenty-third birthday, on 26 September 1886. His family's grief can only have been deepened when they opened his padlocked 'memory-chest', which 'Mama wanted me to take as my trunk' on his journey to Egypt, to find in it the book of memoirs to which, rather than to his own family, Elio confided his most private thoughts and feelings. Elio's smothered life haunts the pages of his diary like a ghost. Ettore must have been particularly moved and shaken to find himself admired, and his doings followed even more closely than Napoleon's.[168] He accused himself of having been too little moved by Elio's death.[169] The follower of Zola, moreover, could hardly fail to be amazed at this all too authentic *document humain* in his own home and to be struck by the whole internal *verismo* of Elio's account of his own life, in which the subjective and the objective coincide—a model of autobiographical writing* for the future Italo Svevo, with an added motif which was to recur several times in Svevo's own life—that of 'salvaging the past' by writing one's memoirs.[170]

Elio's diary shows the young idealist disappointed in all his ideals and in all his hopes,[171] partly by the Triestine milieu which he simultaneously loved and despised, but most of all by his own weakness, which inclined him merely to dream of success—say, of putting Verdi in the shade with his own never-written *Marceau*.[172] This developed in Elio a fine analytical sensibility which he turned mostly against himself, with touches of irony which were also to appear in his brother's novels. Elio himself became aware of a link between his illness and the growing sharpness of his irony and came to attribute his illness itself to his disappointments and frustrations.[173] The figure of his father loomed large in all this, a tyrant, even if made of clay, benevolent only as long as his wishes were not opposed.

Elio described his own posturing as a superior individual, remarking that 'when in society one puts on a forced ease, one makes a fool of oneself',[174] and he had occasion to contrast his own affected manner with the straight-forwardness in word and gesture of his questionable but adored Miss U:

She says little, and her words contrast sharply with mine. In hers there is no affectation, just plain unpretentious things, good sense and nothing else; while mine are all rhetoric, figures of speech, would-be philosophizing and eccentricity, a complete, jumbled display of all my superficial knowledge in every field, the desire to impress. Imagine that music is debased by me so far as to be nothing but a means of impressing...[175]

The diary relates his love-affair with Miss U.—a love so one-sided as to remain undeclared, let alone shared or fulfilled, while Miss U. 'lives her dazzling life

---

* Elio's introspective tragedy of frustration and despair was paralleled at a higher intellectual and literary level by the *Journal intime* of the Swiss Henri-Frédéric Amiel, large parts of which had been published in 1882–4 after the author's death, and had made a considerable impression.

without even thinking that I think about her'.[176] Some aspects of it are related in fine detail. The character of Miss U. and her beauty frequently come to life on the page, and Elio's doubts and hesitations are expressed with vigour. Too late he realized he had been 'a fool not to court the young lady. Devil take it! you mustn't trespass on the time of a girl who's looking for a husband!' But the future lay with her, not with him: 'the future belongs to those who don't give it a thought and enjoy themselves today, which is after all the future of yesterday'.

Here, then, in his own brother, Ettore met a *coscienza* which, impotent to fulfil itself in the world, could only turn into malady, confession, life as literature (or writing) and literature (or writing) as life. But, at the same time, this *coscienza* threatened to invert its relationship with the world, with 'health', to show up that world and its health as being themselves diseased. This was Elio's real literary 'influence' on his brother, an influence which helped drive the latter to 'shift the pillars of Hercules' left by French Naturalism to 'mark the bounds' of the world, moving them in the direction of an enquiry, still 'objective', into the self, the territory of Romanticism, a forbidden territory fraught with unknown perils. Elio also left behind him more structured literary works— sonnets on friendship, the play he wrote for Gemma Cuniberti, *Una congiura a palazzo* (A Palace Conspiracy), librettos—which hardly rise above the level of schoolboy exercises and certainly do not compare with the literature of life which is his diary.[177]

On 20 October 1886, after Elio's death, and after a silence of over a year, an article by Ettore appeared in *L'Indipendente*, signed with the pseudonym E. Samigli. The article, 'Un individualista',[178] was a condemnation of the theoretically based egoism and the intrusive autobiographism of the novelist Joséphin Péladan 'which disrupts the objective view'. Like Elio Schmitz, Péladan was an 'individualist' who had escaped the 'irresistible current' of collectivism because he was 'segregated by his sickly organism sometimes for months at a time in bed with a book as his sole companion'. The critic who signs himself Samigli admits and avows that all institutions are designed to subdue individuality—school ('just like a regiment, with one single system for a thousand characters and more'), commerce, science, art—and concludes: 'we in the last three decades thought we were only doing our duty in allowing ourselves to be uniformed and drilled in the most ferocious of collectivities.' Ettore seems to have military service in mind, as he goes on to relate an episode in Péladan's life in which the Frenchman suffered a three months' illness as a result of being gaoled 'for having failed to comply with instructions to attend for a military check-up', and he devotes three paragraphs to Péladan's anti-militarism.

Just for a moment Ettore seems to be on the point of agreeing with Péladan's pure individualism and to border on an anarchistic position:

In this way, at a given age none of us is any longer what mother nature intended him to be; we find our character bent like a tree which would have liked to follow the direction indicated by its root, but which changed direction in order to find its way through stones that were blocking its passage.

The argument is complicated by the mention of Péladan's dead brother with its analogy with Elio Schmitz. Péladan addresses his brother:

Tu as été repoussé et vilipendé par les facultés, je nierai toute collectivité; un chef d'œuvre, une loi se signent d'un seul nom. Tu as été torturé par le Récrutement, je nierai le devoir du sang, je nierai la nationalité. Tu as été trahi et vendu par les monarchistes; je nierai l'hérédité du pouvoir et des titres.

This quotation marks a transition from the personal analogy with the brothers Schmitz (Elio, already ill, having been dispensed from military service, Ettore having just sampled its delights) to the analogy with Trieste, whose cause had been betrayed by the Triple Alliance of the monarchies.

How, then, are we to take Ettore's comment: 'To judge from this extract, Péladan's entire political programme is dictated by his brother's fate'? One is tempted to retort: Why not? is it not valid to judge a system by its effects upon individuals? But perhaps Ettore's objection here is to be taken at face value.

It is still possible to take Schmitz-Samigli at face value a little further on when he continues:

[Péladan] argues still more haplessly when he attempts to base his judgements more broadly: 'Les Prussiens sont des scélérats de s'annexer l'Alsace–Lorraine qui voudrait rester française; mais les Français sont aussi des scélérats de s'annexer l'Algérie qui voudrait rester arabe.'

But the analogy with Italian Trieste under the Austrian yoke could not be more obvious, so is this an ironic hint of the kind that Triestines were well accustomed to picking up between the lines of *L'Indipendente*? And is the following paragraph also ironic?—

It would be easy to defend the State against his attacks as he [Péladan] sees in the State nothing but a monstrous entity that prostitutes women to pleasure and men to death. The argument would be mere enumeration; the enumeration of the services which the collectivity renders to the individual and it is only because it would take too long that I do not undertake it.

Two interpretations are possible. Either Ettore, veiling himself in irony, is making a mockery of militarism, imperialism and colonialism, the State, schools, and all institutions. Or else, in all seriousness, he defends them all, winding up with a concluding tirade of typically Irredentist dye:

The highest Latin glory derived from military valour, from battles, from conquests, from a powerful organization. Latin virtue did not know that five well-turned lines of poetry are worth a victory like Marengo. Had it known this, it would have leapt across the centuries and the seas to cross over from Rome to Byzantium.

My view is that he is serious. He accepts the State and war as harsh necessities of life. He resigns himself to finding that he too has a 'bent character', to being a bank clerk and a conscript in Franz Josef's army instead of choosing the path of exile and action, even martyrdom, like the heroes of Irredentism, Revere and Oberdan. However, even as he resigns himself to these necessities and to their 'discipline', he is only half convinced. Individualism, with its values and its problems, still claims his attention. In the light of *Una vita,* the novel upon which Svevo was to embark little more than a year after this article, I would suggest that he is drawn by the problem of integrating the individual into the collective—a process which is nullified by the fact that both terms, the individual and the collective, are found to be themselves null. In this article, Ettore Schmitz, in his new personality as E. Samigli, has begun to stake everything on ambiguity, on a hesitation between two positions both of which are sensed to be negative. The solution is therefore displaced from the level of immediate reality to the mediated reality of art, of writing. The article on Péladan contains, in fact, in addition to the two hypotheses which I have outlined, a third one:

Taine holds that the only lasting happiness is that reserved to the individual in collective work. Man must be kept alive by his devotion to something which seems to him immortal; in this way he feels he is actually creating immortality for himself. The artist, the scientist need no other collectivity; art, science are the supreme collectivities; they embrace human intercourse in its entirety, and it is wrong to sign a masterpiece, a discovery with a single name; a date would be better; its true authors are the author's predecessors and contemporaries.

So the writer transcends—or sidesteps—his argument with Péladan on militarism, on nationalism, on the State, on institutions: an argument which he now shows as irrelevant. The supreme institution is that of art and science, the supreme collectivity is that of human intercourse in its entirety, supreme individuality is the immortality conferred upon the individual by the collectivity of human intercourse and by the institution of universal art and science in collective labour. Once again it is the hope of literary fame (immortality) that offers Ettore Schmitz hope of redemption from all the frustrations and disabilities of his condition, from his passivity or his impotence.

When Europe was savaging itself in the Great War Svevo was to relate that 'Papà used to tell me that I would come to my senses when I was forty...'. Now, at twenty-five, he was a long way from 'coming to his senses'. He had given up the initials E. S. and joked about the impeccably Italian pseudonym, E. Samigli, which he kept until *Una vita* came out in 1892. He told his friend Giulio Piazza (the dialect poet Piazzetta) 'I'm sorry for that poor 'i' in Schmitz bashed about by so many consonants.'[179] The pseudonym was the phonetic equivalent of his protective new literary persona.

Part IV

DISILLUSION
The years of *Una Vita*
1887–1895

18

UN INETTO

Ettore's last contributions to *L'Indipendente*, which appeared in the years 1887–9, show a marked chronological pattern. Five articles came in the five months from February to June 1887; then there was nothing until 12 December, which is the date shown on a long (unpublished) essay: 'Del sentimento in arte' (Artistic Sensibility). A week later, on his twenty-sixth birthday, Ettore started writing his first novel, and immediately after that his short story 'Una lotta' (A Contest) was serialized in *L'Indipendente* from 6 to 8 January 1888. Then there was another gap until the appearance of his reviews of two novels, Cherbuliez's *Ghislain* and Daudet's *L'Immortel*, in June and July. Ettore had previously reviewed only two other novels, Zola's *La Joie de vivre* and Ohnet's *La Grande Marnière*. Nearly the whole of 1888 must have been given over to the writing of his own novel, for the only other things we have of that year are a very brief silver wedding valediction, of 15 August, in which he was gently ironic at Kant's expense on the subject of the objective reality of the passing of time,[1] and the article 'Critica negativa' (Negative Criticism), which appeared on 15 December.[2] He seems to have published nothing at all in 1889 until his review of another novel, Verga's *Mastro-Don Gesualdo*, on 17 December. During that last year, his own novel had already been completed, and rejected by a publisher and, from 12 June or shortly after, he was giving up much of his time to help keep the newspaper going after the police had arrested most of its staff.

This pattern reveals Ettore's gradual withdrawal from dramatic writing, in contrast to his urgent concern between 1882 and 1884 at the parlous state of the theatre, especially in Italy. Now he defended only a sixteenth-century play, Machiavelli's *La Mandragola*.[3] In another article, 'Accademia', he referred sardonically to 'that art practised *by leave of the authorities* which is the dramatic' (his italics).[4] His interest had clearly shifted to the novel. 'Critica negativa' was virtually an obituary on the Italian theatre, which the author pronounced finally murdered by the critics.

In 1888 that might well have seemed to be the case. It is significant that this article contains Ettore's first reference to Ibsen, and that he equates the 'tirades' (*retoricate*) of the latter with those of Sardou, Arronge, Ferrari and Torelli. Ettore must have just got wind of Ibsen's belated celebrity and hastily read through some early work of his which he had ferreted out of the library or a bookshop and which would have given him no inkling of the author of *A Doll's House*, a play which he was soon to admire. The 'discovery' of Ibsen ushered in the great tide of naturalistic drama, which Zola's circle had attempted with scant success and which had first been truly realized by Ibsen himself, followed later by Strindberg, Hauptmann and, progressively, by dramatists right round Europe, up to Chekhov. The Italians made no mean contribution to the great theatrical revival carried out in the name and style of Naturalism. Marco Praga and Bracco were followed by Rovetta, Antona-Traversi, Giacometti, Lopez, Bertolazzi and Di Giacomo. The themes which predominate in this theatre are those of family life being undermined by financial interest and of ideals crumbling upon exposure to reality, a reality which is no longer presented as an unexpected and arbitrary *coup de théâtre* but shown concretely in social and even in material terms. This new theatrical climate was one in which Ettore could breathe freely, but in 1888 he was not yet aware of it, and, as Ruggero Rimini remarked, it was to be around 1900 that he undertook his second theatrical apprenticeship in order to master the new conception of theatre.[5] Missing the Naturalist tide was the price of his dilettantism.

So, in 1888 and 1889, Ettore Schmitz was no longer concerned with writing plays, but with the novel. The articles which he wrote at this time show that his approach to writing had not changed. As in his earliest articles, so in 'Per un critico' (A Critic), on Taine,[6] and in 'Accademia', on the French Académie,[7] what counted for Ettore was 'truth' in the sense we have already established, including its most empirical sense of observation of milieu and character. This is clear from his reviews of novels and of the Goncourts' *Mémoirs*. In 'Una frase sulla *Mandragola*' (About Machiavelli's *La Mandragola*), art and truth are linked in a manner which takes us right back to Ettore's very first article, the one on Shylock: the two things are one, he argues, in a great writer's profound understanding of the human heart and of circumambient society; art perishes without truth and neither can be forced to yield a thesis within a literary work. Svevo was so emphatic as to overstate this point with respect to *La Mandragola*.[8] He was here again defining his own kind of naturalism. Like all great naturalism, this is no mere matter of 'surface' realism, of 'externals', but is a 'deep' naturalism which admits no bounds to its investigations and which will lead in an unbroken development towards the complex and open-ended Freudianism of the writer's later years. This drive towards truth in art brushes aside the glib morality which seeks to reassure the conventionally minded consumers of literature. Ettore had stressed this point in writing about Ohnet in 1885 and he reiterated it now in contrasting Machiavelli with Sardou, and in his remarks on Dumas *fils* in 'Accademia'.[9] Truth also brushes aside preconceived notions of form and style: the same articles speak of Machiavelli revolutionizing the literary form of his age simply by pursuing his own 'idea'; and, conversely, of the 'immortals' of the French Académie, in whose speeches it is impossible to distinguish eloquence from deceit. Ettore here was saying nothing very original, to be sure, but rather making a resolute, even a naïve, stand against the ever-recurring incursions of falsity in language and thought, the all-too common perversion of a meretricious culture.

There is one marked change between the articles up to the one on Ohnet in 1885 and those which came later. Up to 1885 Ettore frequently berated the corrupt taste of the public and sought to improve it without concealing his contempt for vulgar success on stage or in print, as typified by Ohnet. After 1885, he toned down his contempt for the public. In reviewing a novel by the highly popular Cherbuliez he granted all that could possibly be granted. In 'Critica negativa' it is the carping critics, not the public, who are blamed for the demise of the Italian theatre. Schmitz-Samigli had realized that literature cannot do without a public, however corrupt. He wanted to make his name as a writer: he needed a public. He was writing a novel: it did not help to reject those who read novels. It was much better to give them good novels.

This seems to be obscurely argued in 'Del sentimento in arte',[10] just before he embarked on the novel. He inquires into the artistic sensibilities of those who have no training in a particular art, contending that art has wide powers of communication, that it is essentially democratic, because the artistic faculty, imaginative sympathy or *sentimento*, is universal and inborn. Art emerges as the *maximal* communication, available to the emotional experience or *sentimento* of all. As he took up his pen to write his first novel, the new writer Svevo wanted to feel that everybody could read him, wanted to speak to everybody.

He also returned to his earlier notion of a dilettante as someone who could devote only a part of his time to literary or artistic production, but this time he suggested a connexion between dilettantism and anarchism and put himself on his guard against 'extremes in art as in politics', against 'excess', 'quirkiness', 'exaggeration'. Yet again, this moderate Samigli was counterbalanced by Samigli the megalomaniac dreamer. He posits daydreaming as a paramount artistic and creative faculty which more than compensates for 'lack of practice'.[11]

All this seems to point to the autobiographical heart of the novel that Svevo was soon to write. Its protagonist, Alfonso Nitti, constantly loses himself in dreams and 'A well-written book gave him megalomaniac dreams.'[12] The individual's daydreams and fantasies remain at the centre of Svevo's writing, especially his narratives, up to *Senilità*, which is his most systematic articulation of the theme. Even before the publication of *Una vita* he made two *divertissements* out of the theme in 'Sogni di Natale' and 'Il fumo'. In the second of these, fantasy-activity (*sogno*) goes hand in hand with smoking. Svevo himself never gave up either of these twin compulsions.

Samigli's articles give tantalizingly sporadic evidence of what he read. He shows himself thoroughly grounded in the works of Taine, Renan and Thiers. He is well informed on French and Italian dramatic criticism. He has read popular novelists like Ohnet, Feuillet, Cherbuliez, Paul De Kock and Gutzkow. He has read the latest biography of Darwin and all the reviews of Verdi's *Otello*. He is familiar with the debate between Kant and Richter on the role played by inspiration in art and science respectively. He has read works of phrenology and Arab fairy-tales. Yet in 1892 Svevo gave his novel the title of a masterpiece by Maupassant which had appeared in 1883, *Une vie*, but which he claimed not to have known about at the time.[13] Nor is Schopenhauer, so crucial to the novel, mentioned in these articles.

Another suprise is that Ettore showed little interest in Stendhal, though Zola acclaimed him as a predecessor in *Les Romanciers naturalistes*. Stendhal was also strongly in favour of Italian independence, and had even spent a few months in Trieste as French consul in 1830. Moreover, Stendhal's Napoleon-cult foreshadowed Svevo's, which is evident in many of his writings, especially in the story 'Il malocchio' (The Evil Eye) and in Zeno Cosini's self-portrait. Svevo, shortly after completing his own novel, referred to Stendhal as 'a Frenchman turned Milanese by adoption' with a predilection for Italian blood.[14] Yet he did not read *La Chartreuse de Parme* until 1913, when he wrote to his wife that he liked it much more than the 'other novel', meaning presumably *Le Rouge et le Noir*, which he appears to have read in the 1880s.[15] We can only surmise that he felt Stendhal had not sufficiently distanced himself from his hero, Julien Sorel.

It is even more dangerous to try to extract a reliable profile of Svevo's reading habits at this time from the cultural references which are so liberally sprinkled in the pages of the novel itself, for there they are strictly functional to characterizations quite distinct from the author. Culture, in fact, marks the greatest difference between Alfonso Nitti and his creator. Each frequents the Biblioteca Civica, 'saving on his meagre budget', and each reads German philosophy, but Alfonso, unlike Ettore Schmitz, knows no German and has to read French translations; nor has he ever read an Italian classic right through. The character's education is based on the Latin classics, very different from Svevo's, and it is the German Idealists that he reads, rather than Schopenhauer.[16]

Possibly the title of the treatise which Alfonso dreams of writing, *The Idea of Morality in the Modern World*, carries echoes of Schopenhauer and Nietzsche, as well as Hegel. Nietzsche is in fact the great absentee in Svevo's writings: only in his later years does Svevo seem to notice him.[17] Yet it is unthinkable that Svevo had not read him by the late eighties, when Nietzsche's fame was secure. The 'individualist' Alfonso Nitti may well be seen as a failed 'Nietzschean' unable to create his own values.[18]

As puzzling as Svevo's silence on Nietzsche is his lack of reference to Paul Bourget's *Essais de psychologie contemporaine*. These had appeared in two volumes in 1883 and 1885 and examined all the writers in whom Svevo might be expected to be most interested, diagnosing in them the modern disease of analytical excess. Bourget described Stendhal's narrative procedure in words which—apart from the concluding judgement—apply equally to Svevo: 'En dix phrases, il y a dix voltes-faces de ces questions angoissantes.' He recalls all the 'Fabrice se dit ... Fabrice se demanda ... Fabrice comprit ...' and concludes: 'Et lorsque le drame arrive, lorsque l'homme agit ... c'est à la suite d'un examen de conscience si minutieux que, pour beaucoup de lecteurs, l'illusion de la réalité devient impossible.'[19] It is hard to believe that Svevo did not read the

Essais, but he never mentions them, though he did read Bourget's novel *Crime d'amour* of 1886.[20]

If Alfonso Nitti's culture is not Svevo's, being more limited and outdated, a culture of Latin commentaries and pure thought, Alfonso's rival Macario exhibits a no less limited positivist culture based on Darwinism and Naturalism;[21] but Macario also makes some remarks on objectivity in novels which slip the reader a sly clue as to how Svevo's novel is to be read. He offers an ingenious thesis on Balzac's *Louis Lambert*:

'Do you know why it's such a fine book? It's the only one of Balzac's that is really impersonal, and it became so by chance. Louis Lambert is mad, all those around him are mad, and the author was pleased on this occasion to show himself as mad too. So it's a little world which presents itself intact, completely free from outside interference.'[22]

Svevo, through Macario, seems to be hinting that his own novel is the product of 'mad' characters, so that its objectivity and impersonality derive precisely from the exact rendering of their diverse subjectivity, as on the stage. Thus the realist or naturalist novelist Svevo becomes the invisible god who hides within his own creation.

In 'Del sentimento in arte', written just before he started on his novel, Svevo spoke of 'that little gem of modern drama' *La Visite des noces* by Dumas *fils*, in which a young man, just married, is tempted to go back to his mistress who has made him believe she has had several other lovers. On discovering, however, that she has always been true to him, he decides to stay with his wife. Svevo suggested a better ending, which he said came from Zola.

It is not true-to-life ... that he [the young man] will speak as Dumas has him speak. It is not true-to-life that he should be aware of these emotions and that he should be able to formulate them. He will be beset by scruples, by remorse, and he will go back to his wife in the belief that he has been saved by a sudden reawakening of his moral sense.[23]

Now Gennaro Savarese has established that Zola's critique said nothing of 'scruples' or 'remorse' but spoke only of the need to round off the play less abruptly and with greater verisimilitude.[24] Svevo, it seems, invented his own ending, an ending which would face the spectator with an insoluble puzzle. No one-sided interpretation would then be possible, and the public would not, any more than the protagonist himself, be able to determine the latter's true motives, the authenticity or otherwise of his scruples, his remorse and his moral sense. In other words we have here an impersonality based on the psychology of the unconscious and sustained by the Schopenhauerian principle that every reason is a rationalization by which the will justifies and asserts itself, and the individual pulls the wool over his own eyes and other people's. The illusion of morality is therefore a typical product, as in this case, both of the individual and of the collectivity.

All Svevo's novels in fact end with a more or less indecipherable self-justification on the part of the protagonist, but it is in *Una vita* that the author most readily shows his hand by continually laying bare the inner machinations of his protagonist, and he can go so far as to say: 'As always, his reasoning was nothing but dressed-up emotion.'[25]

There is no significant factual autobiography in the novel, which was originally entitled *Un inetto* (One of the Unfit). Alfonso's difficulties at the bank must partly reflect Ettore Schmitz's experiences in the Unionbank; Annetta's literary evenings may owe something to Elisa Tagliapietra-Cambon's 'Triestine Parnassus'; Ettore, like Alfonso, used to go for long walks in the hills around the city and visit the public library. And that is about all.

Likewise, the novel offers only a selective picture of the town. It is set in Trieste and is topographically faithful and precise. The Lanuccis' house in Città Vecchia, the Mallers' in Via de' Forni, the Biblioteca Civica and its surrounding streets the sea-front, the pier, the Corso, Piazza Ponterosso, the bay, the lighthouse, the railway station and the line out of Trieste: everything is in the right place. Yet the town is never named as Trieste and has no Slavs or Austrians, no petards, no *Indipendente*, no Irredentism and no Oberdan. The action is very vaguely dated. It begins between 1881 and 1883, for the fourth chapter mentions the imminent Paris première of Sardou's *Odette*, which took place in 1881; and Gambetta's pistol-wound, which he got on 27 November 1882, as the previous winter's talk of the town. The novel is therefore set right at the time of the Oberdan crisis, and yet completely ignores it, as though it had never happened or had nothing to do with Trieste, the city of banking and commerce, of the *grande bourgeoisie* of high finance and the *petite bourgeoisie* of clerks and salesmen struggling to climb upwards or not to slither back down into penury, in a climate of economic stagnation which closely matches that of the 1880s. Marriage is regarded and felt as a money-arrangement designed to improve or safeguard the social status of the contracting parties. The world of banking can be seen as Svevo's original contribution to the naturalist novel— a new 'milieu' for literature—but the writer does not explore or seem to grasp the central role which high finance plays in economic life: the Bank in the novel appears as a business institution just like any other apart from its specific working conditions, though the abstractness of money as a commodity is a correlative to the abstractness of Alfonso's life and his particular alienation. Even as a 'social document' of Triestine life, the novel limits itself to depicting only the social circles represented by the Mallers, the Lanuccis and Alfonso and his fellow-clerks. Certainly, a naturalist novelist who wished to explore the town's proletarian life would have found plenty to show his readers.

A study on *Le condizioni delle abitazioni a Trieste nel 1890* by Attilio Frühbauer shows that a third of the population lived in one- or two-roomed apartments, of which half were overcrowded. More than two thousand dwellings lacked a kitchen. In the working-class districts of Città Vecchia and Barriera Vecchia houses were without water or gas. Sanitation was appallingly bad. Only half of those infants born alive reached the age of five. Alcoholism and prostitution, including child prostitution, were rampant. Death through starvation was not uncommon, and suicide a frequent occurrence, though not always the result of poverty.[26] As late as 1903–5 (when economic conditions were improving) Trieste still had 201 suicides and 188 suicide attempts. Of these, two-thirds involved males, and the majority unmarried people between twenty and thirty years of age; the suicide rate reached a peak in springtime.[27] In 1883, when Sir Richard Burton's fencing-master, Reich, killed himself, Lady Burton remarked: 'Suicide is the commonest thing in Trieste; nobody takes any account of it.'[28] Césari records the suicide in 1886 of the Secretary of the Banca Popolare (associated with the Società Operaia) after the treasurer Pescatore had absconded.[29]* Russell's readings in *Il Piccolo* confirm the frequency of the phenomenon,[31] and Bazlen, writing about the years preceding the First World War, says that 'Trieste had ... one of the highest rates of tuberculosis ... insanity and suicide in Europe.'[32] Svevo's Zeno Cosini also remarks on Trieste's high suicide rate.[33] Alfonso's suicide in *Una vita* can be usefully viewed as an instance of this social phenomenon.

This novel's 'realism', however, is mostly not of the specific and documentary kind. It revolves around the notion and the fact of competition. *Lotta*, or 'struggle', is displayed almost programmatically, most insistently in the competitive careerism and status-seeking of Alfonso's colleagues in the bank. Alfonso's own behaviour falls into this pattern: his affair with Annetta carries the implication of social promotion, as all concerned are well aware. His first encounter with the girl has all the characteristics of social as well as sexual and personal antagonism, and the whole book can be read as an account of Alfonso's attempt to avenge that first slight. The issue is complicated by Alfonso's psychological as well as cultural infantilism. He has entered the social and economic rat-race whilst claiming immunity from its motives and values. All the figures in the novel are presented as winners or losers in a continually varying situation, though any victory is flawed and largely hollow.

The losers, the Lanuccis, do not represent moral superiority but merely ineffectuality. Failure is no virtue. Bourgeois competition excludes class struggle, and the figure of Gustavo Lanucci (a petit bourgeois, if we like, who has slipped into the sub-proletariat) indicates how far Svevo is from showing any class dialectic. He seems unaware of the proletariat as a historic force offering any ethical alternative to the prevailing norms. This unawareness on Svevo's part was of a piece with contemporary Triestine politics, in which the issue of nationalism for the time being overshadowed that of class.

Bourgeois individualism—the competitive struggle between individuals, even on a supposedly 'spiritual' level—is thus the subject of the novel. Svevo's focus is on the actions of his characters: although undisclosed or even unconscious motivation plays a large part in their relations and communications with one another and gives the novel a powerful appeal, it does not assume the prominence which it is to have in *Senilità*, where the whole narrative is conducted

---

* In *Senilità*, Emilio learns that Angiolina has absconded with a dishonest bank treasurer and that the affair had caused a public scandal.[30]

in terms of the characters' *mis*apprehensions of one another and of their *mis*leading of one another; where human intercourse seems to consist of nothing but deceit or mystification; so that, in consequence, the sense of a solid reality which still prevails in *Una vita* turns in *Senilità* into a sense of the elusiveness of even the most immediate and inescapable of realities.

In *Una vita*, Alfonso is the figure in which the contradictions of his society and its culture—the competitive drive and the abstract idealist ethic—come together: he lives and dies by the individualistic fallacy, both socio-economic and intellectual or ethical, of his age.

19

ETTORE'S 'HEROIC' 1889

It was only in 1888 that Socialism made its first really determined attempt to establish itself in Trieste, an attempt contested by the nationalist friendly society for Italian workers, the Società Operaia Triestina. In the major dispute of 1889 the Società Operaia intervened firmly against the newly formed Confederazione Operaia, whose ideals were those of international Socialism, and against the 1,500 workers in the great Lloyd shipyard, who were striking against the extension of their working day by one hour without extra pay as from 1 April. (This gave them eleven hours' work a day for a wage varying between 1 florin and 1.50.)[34]

The striking workers were defeated on this occasion, but the episode formed part of the intricate and obscure crisis which *L'Indipendente* underwent during that year, for not only did *L'Indipendente* join *Il Piccolo*, the Società Operaia and the other Italian nationalist bodies in a determined campaign to defeat the strike, but also dismissed one of its own typographers, Gerin, who was a member of the Committee of the Confederazione Operaia.[35] This coincided with Svevo's most exposed and least sincere political involvement.

For the time being the Confederazione Operaia had been checked. But the dispute had cleared the air and shown the workers that only the Socialists were ready to fight in earnest on their behalf. This year in fact marked the beginning of the rise of Socialism in Trieste, and it was in the 1890s that Svevo showed most overt (though ineffectual) 'Socialist' leanings. On 22 February 1889 the Confederazione Operaia had brought out its 'Programme', which illustrates the political climate in Svevo's Trieste and uses language very similar to that occasionally used by Svevo himself. It also throws some light on Svevo's 'Socialism'. Socialism might at the very least stand in Svevo's eyes, among his numerous other dreams, for the grandest and most alluring dream of all, a dream woven of economic justice and human solidarity and—what counted for most in a city torn by national strife—harmony among all peoples, the only conceivable way of reconciling all that was irreconcilable. Part of the programme ran:

Is anybody unaware how vigorous is the struggle for existence today? how it encourages the growth of egoism, which overwhelms and smothers all the other noble and humane sentiments and is the main cause of the growing misery? Is anybody unaware of the way in which this egoism often disguises itself the better to exploit the productive capacity of the trustful worker and, having made of him its instrument, forgets him when he is no longer of use, to lavish upon him attentions and words that cost very little whenever new needs arise which require that he be yoked to the wagon anew?

Against 'the worker's false friends', the Confederation 'aims first and foremost to promote the general education of its members . . . in their respective mother-tongues', but recognizes Italian as 'the business language of the Directorate, the Council and the Assemblies', that being the tongue 'of the majority of the membership and of the territory'.[36]

The year 1889 in fact saw Austria's first Socialist congress, at which Viktor Adler rallied the Socialists of the Empire's various nationalities with a programme of internationalism, universal suffrage, free secular education, and separation of Church and State. Socialism thus became accessible—indeed, an inescapable presence—and these political objectives of 'Austro-Marxism' must also have made it attractive to Svevo, especially at a time when he was disillusioned with nationalist politics.

The 1880s were the years of virtually unchallenged Liberal control in Triestine municipal politics. The city's Italian character was strengthened and Slav consciousness retarded by measures which favoured the Italian language in schooling and public business. The most impressive of many public demonstrations of Italian nationalism was the funeral of Enrico Jurettig in October 1887, accompanied by *L'Indipendente*'s entire staff—including, as we have seen, Ettore Schmitz as one of the pall-bearers (though Veronese, chronicler of *L'Indipendente*, did not think his name worth recording).[37]

Jurettig's funeral, together with the salvage operation on *L'Indipendente* two years later, constituted Ettore's most active commitment to the Irredentist cause—precisely when he was omitting all mention of Irredentism in his novel. The events of 1889 caused a crisis in Triestine Irredentism and in Svevo's, and consequently also in Svevo's sense of identity.

Italian nationalism in Trieste was being directed more and more against the Slavs than against Vienna, the Germans and the Habsburg regime. So a branch of the Italian national Pro Patria organization was set up in Trieste in 1886. It collected two thousand members within a few days.[38] Felice Venezian rose to prominence by playing the anti-Slav card more forcefully and consistently than ever before. At the first congress of the Pro Patria organization of the Austrian

Littoral in 1886, he dwelt on 'the Slav peril' and on 'saving for the future the lands which Rome and God entrusted to our keeping'.[39] It was Venezian who had refused to give the Slovenes a school which used their language, and thus further embittered national antagonisms and hastened the foundation in 1885 of the Slav educational association named after saints Cyril and Methodius.[40]

The rise to the Italian premiership of Crispi, a former lieutenant of Garibaldi's, encouraged in 1887 fresh Irredentist expectations. Crispi, however, strengthened Italy's bonds with Austria-Hungary within the Triple Alliance and directed Italy's foreign policy towards economic and colonial rivalry with France and colonialist expansion along the Red Sea. But in Trieste agitation for union with Italy kept mounting, and in November 1888 there were mass demonstrations on two successive Sundays under the patronage of Pro Patria. The leadership sometimes emphasized and sometimes obscured the distinction between the peaceful and lawful defence of Italian national rights, and a direct challenge to the Austrian authorities. Every other political issue was laid aside or completely forgotten in the overriding concern to 'redeem' the Italians who were still under Austrian rule: 'there was never, in Julian Venetia at that time, any argument over monarchy or republic, liberalism or clericalism, conservatism or radicalism.' Crispi's increasingly harsh measures against Irredentism, however, tended to drive the movement towards radical, republican and extreme left circles. One of the conspiratorial agitators, a twenty-year-old student called Camillo De Franceschi, typically, blamed not the Liberals, but the 'basso popolo' of Trieste for failing to rise up against the Austrians out of concern for their own economic interests. 'It was the doughty *Indipendente* which almost openly supported the activity of the Circolo Garibaldi and its action groups.'[41]

De Franceschi described a rising tension as the anniversary of Oberdan's death came round in December 1888. In Italy, Andrea Costa, the left-wing Irredentist Parliamentarian, was sentenced to three years in goal for participating in a demonstration commemorating Oberdan. The centenary of the French Revolution in 1889 aroused expectations that there would be an Italian Revolution. Camillo De Franceschi, with another young man, Alfieri Rascovich, was virtually in command of the Circolo Garibaldi, and they even considered seizing the Castle of San Giusto.[42]

The Italian consul in Trieste, Cesare Durando, secretly instructed by Crispi to do all in his power to quell Irredentism in Trieste, was publicly accused of conniving with the Lieutenancy, and there followed a sharp debate in the Italian Parliament in which Cavallotti attacked Crispi and his entire foreign policy. Crispi defended Durando. On 9 June, Alfieri Rascovich set off a petard at the Italian consul's residence, and this explosion was the immediate occasion for the police action against the *Indipendente*. The general editor Cesare Rossi, the sub-editors Ferdinando Ullmann and Riccardo Zampieri, the manager Bartolomeo Apollonio, and two typographers were arrested. The police hoped that these arrests would finish off the paper once and for all. The result was the opposite. *L'Indipendente* became more than ever the focal point of Italian

nationalism in Trieste and was kept going by a group of young men of whom
the oldest was Ettore Schmitz.

Ettore came to the newspaper's office every morning to dash off a regular
column on foreign politics with the help of the German newspapers before he
started his work at the bank at nine o'clock in the morning. There is a first-
hand account of him at this time:

He was a conscientious worker, precise and quick, too, though he sometimes had second
thoughts; but from time to time, as if in boredom, he would raise his head from the
sheets and, with his fine, deep drawling voice, deliver himself of some witticism about
the day's events. Then he would again pick up his cigarette and his pen and return to
work with a patient smile ... We were two or three lads, or little more than lads,
running *L'Indipendente*: a man of thirty, Ettore Schmitz ... represented amongst us the
other face of life, maturity. He did not make us feel this. His courtesy—a combination
of nature and breeding—would not allow him to let boys like us feel they were any
different from him, even in experience. He could not converse with a human being
without putting him on the same level ... he talked a lot and enjoyed having an audience
... humour was for him the natural tone of conciliation.[43]

Ettore recorded his own feelings in those same circumstances in a private
memorandum of 19 December 1889:

This is my twenty-eighth birthday. My discontent with myself and with others could
not be greater. I note down this impression of mine because maybe a few years from
now I might call myself an idiot yet again, finding myself even worse off, or I might be
consoled, finding my condition improved. The money question is becoming more and
more acute, I am not content with my health, or my work or all the people that
surround me. It stands to reason that since I myself am not satisfied with my work I
cannot expect anyone else to be so. But, with the unbounded ambitions which you
cherished in your time, not to have found anybody, *not anybody*, who takes an interest
in what you think and what you do, to find yourself forever obliged to behave as though
you took an interest in other people's concerns that being the only way to attract just
a little of the consideration which you yearn by hook or by crook to have. Two years
ago precisely I started on that novel which was supposed to be God knows what. Instead
of which, it's a mess which in the end I shan't be able to digest. My strength always
lay in hoping and the trouble is that even that is fading.[44]

The 'courtesy' mentioned by Benco, then, is systematically put on. The real
Ettore Schmitz is invisible to 'all the people that surround' him. It is clear too
how unimportant to him are the Irredentist politics which he must have been
including among the 'other people's concerns' towards which he was 'obliged to
behave as if he took an interest' in them. This need not prevent us from seeing
his commitment to *L'Indipendente* in the heroic light in which it is presented
in *Profilo autobiografico*: but it is clearly an act, lacking conviction—perhaps
not as far as the cause itself is concerned, but as regards the people in charge.
The identity of Ettore Schmitz can be seen split into an inside and an outside.

There was good reason for him to be disillusioned with Irredentist politics.

Malodorous underhand dealings were defiling the gallant efforts to save *L'In-dipendente*, and staining the Irredentist cause with at least a suspicion of cynical opportunism. The National Liberal party appears to have been playing a double game of posing as the champion of Irredentism while actually attempting to stifle any serious Irredentist impulses, in an episode which the historians of Irredentism have hushed up and which appears to have been forgotten. It throws some light on the obscure circumstances in which Svevo made, with such scant conviction, his greatest contribution to Irredentism.

A man called Giovanni Clarizza, born in Zara (Zadar) in 1863, after three months in prison awaiting trial on a charge of distributing Irredentist propaganda in Zadar and Split had been acquitted and had just come to Trieste, where one of the Liberal leaders asked him to take over responsibility for *L'Indipendente* after the newspaper's staff had been arrested on 12 June. He agreed to do so, and ran the newspaper in collaboration with Giulio Césari, a twenty-year-old member of the Circolo Garibaldi, and under the supervision first of Professor Abramo Jona and subsequently of Dr Isidoro Reggio. Clarizza and Césari soon realized, however, that Reggio was losing readership and ruining the newspaper by denying it any independence of outlook and reducing it to little more than a survey or summary of the foreign press (which was precisely Schmitz's job). Clarizza wrote a pamphlet in his own defence. It makes no mention of Ettore Schmitz, who must however have realized that he was a tool in the Party's design to abate Irredentist fervour.

The six *Indipendente* staff who had been arrested were taken to Innsbruck to stand trial, but the proceedings against them were dismissed, despite Zampieri's insistence that the trial should go ahead. On 17 November the freed journalists returned to Trieste to an enthusiastic welcome from their friends and sympathizers. According to Veronese,[45] the rumour was encouraged that Crispi had secured their release from the King-Emperor Franz Josef during the latter's visit to the Italian royal family at Monza, and that this was part of a deal involving the forthcoming elections which had been agreed between Baron Rinaldini, Austria's Lieutenant in Trieste, and the Liberal National leadership. All the Irredentist historians agree that this electoral 'compromise' took place. Only De Franceschi, however, bothers to record that, while the journalists were let off scot-free, the business manager of the *Indipendente*, Apollonio, and the two typographers had to serve a short sentence.[46]

I offer my own interpretation of the events of 1889, though it is impossible to say how far Svevo would have shared it. Italian and Austrian interests under the Triple Alliance involved suppressing the wave of Irredentism, which was an embarrassment to relations between the two countries. Also, given the political context in both countries, Irredentism was radical and even insurrectionary in character. In return for discouraging Irredentism Italy secured favourable terms of trade both for itself and for Italians living within the Empire. This meant that the Triestine Liberals had hopes that Vienna would compensate them for the impending abolition of the Free Port by granting them new economic privileges such as protective tariffs and state subventions. So they first used Irredentist agitation, conspiracy and petards in order to extract the greatest possible concessions from Vienna against a promise that they would call off the Irredentist onslaught. It would then suit the Liberals to let the pro-Vienna party hold the majority on the Triestine Diet at the time of the abolition of the Free Port, which was scheduled for 1 July 1891. Thus they could avoid bearing any responsibility for the measure and even maintain the fiction that they bitterly opposed it, so as to retain the support of the Italian-speaking Triestines. This plan also suited Austria's aim of carrying through the modernization of the port and city of Trieste as the Empire's great outlet to the sea and as a large new industrial centre to scale with Europe's new mass-production economy. The electoral compromise between the Liberals and the acting-Lieutenant, Rinaldini, saved the former from a double embarrassment: either losing control of the young conspirators of the Circolo Garibaldi, or giving ground to the emerging challenge of Socialism. Either way, the Liberals' 'phoney left wing' threatened to become quite real, and it was high time for the circles who controlled finance, commerce and industry in Trieste, whether pro-Italian or pro-Austrian, to close their ranks against the real enemy.

If I am right in this analysis of National Liberal policy, it seems likely that Reggio was trying to muffle *L'Indipendente*'s voice and produce the acquiescence necessary for the abolition of the Free Port to go through smoothly. Clarizza now entrusted Césari with the task of complaining about Reggio's interference and virtual gagging of the newspaper to the previous editor, Cesare Rossi, who had just returned from Innsbruck, and to the political committee which controlled *L'Indipendente* behind the scenes. But Césari changed sides and backed Reggio, who, according to Clarizza, won him over by promising him the editorship then held by Clarizza. The party's political committee decided in favour of Reggio and Césari, and Clarizza was forced to resign. In his history of *L'Indipendente*, Leone Veronese lists Clarizza among the editors-in-chief of the newspaper for the period 12 June 1889 to 4 September 1890, when Edgardo Rascovich, Chairman of the Società Operaia, took over; but his account of the years 1889–90 skips the incident of the quarrel between the party and Clarizza, and the latter is not even mentioned.[47] The year 1889 is presented as the heroic year of the newspaper. Clarizza emigrated to America with a libel action pending against him.[48]

Giulio Césari writes that behind the scenes were 'the newspaper's political committee (Moisè Luzzatto, Felice Venezian, Guido D'Angeli, Edgardo Rascovich, Jacopo Liebmann, Lorenzo Bernardini) and the other leaders of the political party', and that Rinaldini, 'acting-Lieutenant of Trieste and aspiring to the permanent office', proposed an electoral pact to the Liberals, leaving them twenty out of the fifty-five seats on the provincial Diet, and threatening a big political trial if they refused. So in October–November 'the elections took place amid palpable demoralization.'[49]

This is Pagnini's account:

After a short spell under the care of Prof. Abramo Jona, the direction of the newspaper was entrusted to Isidoro Reggio, an able journalist from Gorizia, who, on the instructions of the party, maintained a more subdued tone, though always holding an intransigent position towards Austria. Confiscations [by the censor] continued as before ... The extreme wing of the party could not countenance *L'Indipendente*'s putting on kid gloves and Zampieri himself left it to found, on 2 October 1894, a dissident daily, *Il Paese* ...[50]

As for Svevo, my best guess is that he half-heartedly accepted the change of tactics as being dictated by political necessity and continued for the time being to play his part in preserving *L'Indipendente*. With what good faith he played his part in the confidence trick which presented 1889 as the heroic year of *L'Indipendente*, I need hardly conjecture.

His biggest disappointment clearly concerned the collapse of his 'unbounded ambitions', and especially 'that novel which was supposed to be God knows what' but which on the contrary was 'a mess which in the end I shan't be able to digest'. He had sent the manuscript to Emilio Treves, a Triestine Jew who had left his native town as an enterprising young man and in 1861 founded in Milan his own publishing house. It quickly became one of the most important in the Kingdom of Italy, and published works by many young writers who were to rise rapidly to celebrity, among them Verga, D'Annunzio and Pirandello. Treves was associated in particular with the rise of *verismo* and to some extent with Irredentism, and his extremely popular weekly *L'Illustrazione Italiana* was often banned by the Austrians.

It was not until many years later that Svevo heard what had happened to his manuscript. He then met Dall'Oro, who as a young man had been a reader for Treves and remembered having received in around 1899 a heavy bundle of manuscript, a novel entitled *Un inetto*, by Italo Svevo. He read the novel and liked it, and said so to Treves. The latter replied, however: 'Oh, come on, there are already too many unfit people in life: do you want to bring them into art as well? No, no, better send it back.' Svevo changed the title to *Una vita* and quite forgot the original title.[51] His contribution to the Irredentist cause had not won him favour with a patriotic publisher from Trieste.

Ettore's twenty-eighth birthday memo expressed profound dissatisfaction not only over the rejection of *Un inetto*, but also with his health and money problems. His health may already have been affected by his now well-established vice of smoking, or possibly by the extra hour's work he was doing for *L'Indipendente*, which may have meant giving up his long walks outside town. As for the money problems, it is even harder to guess their cause: perhaps it was that around 1885 Francesco Schmitz had begun gambling disastrously with stocks and shares.

Svevo, as ever, is largely invisible. It is even possible that some of his lesser writings of the early 1890s are yet to be found, if a remark of Benco's is anything to go by: 'The little tales, monologues, fables which he published labelled him an eccentric rather than revealing the profound seriousness with which he observed life.[52] We have but one monologue, *Prima del ballo*,[53] and the stories 'Una lotta' and 'L'assassinio di Via Belpoggio'. The two *divertissements* 'Sogni di Natale' and 'Il fumo' are more easily labelled 'eccentric'. We have no fables until 'L'asino e il pappagallo' in 1891.[54] 'Una lotta' remained buried in the pages of *L'Indipendente* until 1972, and other pieces by Svevo may have escaped attention. My own searches through Triestine literary periodicals of the period have revealed only two tiny pieces which might correspond to the 'fables' mentioned by Benco.

The pieces in question are two *favole* which appear on page 87 of the Charivari *Strenna del Circolo Artistico* for New Year 1888. They are signed 'Collimaco', and their manner is quite Svevian and quite unlike that of any other known Triestine. They run as follows:

An assembly of beasts determined to elect a king; they decided to choose the strongest. The strong ones proposed the lion, while the weak ones, who did not even know what strength looked like, cried out: 'We want proof.'

An ant lay dying. In her little body the spark of life was burning itself out. In her disintegrating eye the sun was vanishing, the earth shook to its very foundations within her disturbed organism. 'The world is dying,' murmured the little creature as she died.

The date of these *favole* neatly matches that of 'Una lotta', Svevo's first published fictional narrative, which was serialized in *L'Indipendente* on 6, 7 and 8 January, signed E. Samigli.[55] A paradigm of Svevian narrative, this rather wooden story recounts a 'lesson' inflicted by reality upon the literary man Arturo Marchetti, who is a rival of the athlete Ariodante Chigi for the affections of an attractive blonde called Rosina. Arturo's faith in the power of language is belied by the 'struggle' or 'contest' in which Ariodante's strength simply brushes him aside and leaves him in a fever dreaming of impossible revenge. The author offloads on to his protagonist all his own besetting vices—rhetoric, self-delusion, pretentiousness and impotence. Writing is self-chastisement, a masochistic recognition that strength is superior, as 'scientifically' proved from the experience delineated, and that its superiority is not merely physical but moral also, for strength is serene, innocent, without malice, whereas literature shows itself to be the instrument of a mean mind, and almost a fault in itself.

On Christmas Day 1889, just six days after the birthday memo recording Ettore's 'discontent', in 'Sogni di Natale' (Christmas Dreams), the twenty-eight-year-old Schmitz pretended to be a sixty-year-old Samigli. This anticipated senility reinforces the sense of futility and frustration of which his daydreams are a symptom, as they are its compensation: 'I was born, I grew up, I grew old, but I have done nothing else, nor has anything happened to me. I don't count my everyday work and I recollect neither its toil nor its meagre joys.[56]

20

SOME COMPANIONS

In 1890 a lad of sixteen called Silvio Benco joined *L'Indipendente*. No doubt the Nationalist politicians thought they could handle this stripling, but within a few months he had managed to enrage the Italian government with a leading article entitled 'Demolendosi', which was a root-and-branch indictment of Crispi's policy of strengthening the Triple Alliance and combating Irredentism. Isidoro Reggio had to apologize abjectly on behalf of the newspaper, and from then on Benco carefully minded his political manners. It is to Benco that we owe most of what we know about Svevo in the early 1890s.

With his voluminous reading and his prodigious output in journalism, historiography, narrative fiction, dramas, librettos and literary criticism, Benco was quickly to become Trieste's outstanding intellectual and literary figure. In intellect, sensibility and style he was far superior to Hortis, Caprin, Pítteri or Boccardi, though, like them, all too ready to indulge in frothy rhetoric or the aesthete's purple prose. Here, then, was yet another young man effortlessly eclipsing Ettore Schmitz in Trieste's literary and intellectual firmament and plunging straight into a brilliant career. Before the 1890s were out, Benco was to become a close friend of the composer Antonio Smareglia and of the great actress Eleonora Duse, and to meet D'Annunzio.[57] The three novels he wrote after the turn of the century were regarded by Svevo himself as being worthy of serious attention, though saturated with D'Annunzian aestheticism. Scipio Slataper was to write in 1909 that Benco's work as sub-editor for *Il Piccolo* (to which he had moved in 1903) ruined him for the cultural articles he wrote for *Il Piccolo della sera*.

Silvio Benco, a genuine art critic, almost the perfect soul of critical journalism, unconsciously, and even against his own grain, slips into shallowness of thought ... his is not an abundantly fertile intellect: a self-taught artist, indeed, such as Trieste has never before thrown up, a man who learnt English so as to read Shakespeare; who never gives a lecture unless he has something to say and has enquired thoroughly into it ...[58]

Benco is the only source of information on Svevo in the early 1890s, when Ettore had a 'smarting disappointment' (Benco's phrase) about which tantalizingly little is known. He was courting the tall, good-looking and elegant Giulia Babersi, but her father, a Catholic, heard that Ettore was a Jew and forbade Giulia to see him again.[59]

Benco saw in Svevo:

an excitable temperament, a curiosity for adventure which entangled him in passion and its fevers, a philosophical detachment which covered like a palliative his smarting disappointments in love ... And dreams ... a young man's dreams of finding a heaven on earth, of conquering the world. And the dread of not succeeding ...[60]

Benco also remarked that Svevo was not 'a seeker-out of new writers' but 'discovered many books by chance...'. The Norwegian Naturalist Arne Garborg's novel *Traette Mœnd* (Tired Souls), which came out in Norwegian and German in 1891, fascinated Svevo by 'its unvarying flat, grey tone, its pessimism which allowed no glimmer of either tragedy or action, much less well-being or joy'.[61] There is no better illustration of Svevo's isolation than the inability to understand him betrayed even by Benco, who was Trieste's best literary mind and yet could be so wide of the mark as to write: 'Basically he read what the young men of his time read; nothing esoteric; he could be called an orthodox follower of the literary religion then dominant.'[62] Svevo was in fact far removed from Benco's aestheticism. Benco himself emphasized the extraordinary interest which Svevo took in the social and economic sciences, in the natural sciences and in medicine: 'A perpetual tendency to be carried away by his interests, and a smile which asked you to commiserate with his faith in the magic of science.'[63] There is a hollow ring in Benco's assurance that men like Giulio Ventura, Giulio Césari, Isidoro Reggio 'were well aware of a mind of superior quality' in Svevo.[64] There was no real intellectual fellowship between Svevo and any of these men.

Benco himself, thirteen years younger, showed himself to be in some respects the most acute of his colleague's acquaintants when he observed that:

Svevo had always had a humorous bent; he had found humour to be a seemly and pleasant mask behind which to hide his embarrassment as an onlooker and a thinker, secretly plagued by painful love-affairs and by his failure to win recognition as an artist, but surrounded by more casual and practical men

and that Svevo 'realized his negative feelings in fictional characters to whom he did not allow his own vigour as balancing counterweight'.[65]

Giulio Ventura, an expert fencer, was one of these more casual and practical men who remained a good friend of Svevo's all his life. One of the young men who rallied round *L'Indipendente* in 1889, he was 'the son of a rich Jewish merchant who provided him with the means to live extravagantly'. He wrote mediocre verse, including the epic poem *La Terza Roma* (The Third Rome), and the historical novel *La caduta di Napoleone IV* (The Fall of Napoleon IV).[66] In intellectual calibre he had little in common with Svevo, as appears from another novel of Ventura's, *Dora Tyrr*, published in 1889. This is set in a fabulous epoch, among a fabulous aristocracy, with characters who have fabulous names—Damaso and Dora Tyrr, Jehane de Castelbraquemart, Armando di Pontormeiul—and everything unfolds in a fabulous atmosphere without anything actually happening: in short, a pure escapist fantasy.[67]

Giulio Césari, who also joined *L'Indipendente* in 1889 and remained a lifelong friend of Svevo's, was twenty when Svevo met him: yet another of the enterprising young men who punctuate Svevo's life and mark out his otherness. Césari not only came immediately into close contact with Trieste's ruling political inner circle, but also took literature by storm. His one and only novel, *Vigliaccherie femminili* (Female Dastardliness), came out in 1892, was to be far more popular than *Una vita*, and reached its third edition in 1895. It is partly set in the offices of what is clearly *L'Indipendente*. The narrator and protagonist, the autobiographically fictitious Giorgio Venturini, makes the most (by implication) of the heroic myth of Irredentism:

Yes, glorious! My desk had felt the thrill of the word of fire that flashed like lightning to fall into line upon the page, burning with the fever of the writer whom that fire embodied, as he himself was fire, and who quenched the phosphorus of his patriotism in the powerful spear-thrusts of his polemicizing and his annihiliating onslaught.[68]

Venturini sweeps on in his quest to realize an impossible artistic dream and falls in love by correspondence with one Serafina (a name reminiscent of Svevo's Angiolina). This lady not only turns out to have a limp, but is also ungracious enough to write a best-selling novel, goes on to win sensational acclaim as an actress, marries another man, and only then confesses to poor Giorgio that all along she has loved no one but him. The cover of the first edition shows by enchanted moonlight a hovering, alluringly underdressed female figure flanked by two newspapers, entitled respectively *Patria* and *Amore*.[69]

A more interesting character is Venturini's friend Mandelli, a man in his twenties. Venturini warns Mandelli that the girl he is in love with is a trollop, and then sketches a portrait of his young friend:

Mandelli was kindly, an idealist and an enthusiast in everything. He had, however, taken to posing as a sceptic, as one disillusioned and weary of living. He would break into declamations against the imaginary poetry of that youthful life of ours … But he had risen up many a time to revolt against that melancholy that ruled him. In vain, for in those inward battles gloom prevailed. It was during one of these moments of struggle that he saw, like a sudden fantastic apparition, the white maiden* of our print-room.[70]

That remark about 'the imaginary poetry of that youthful life of ours', like the portrait of Mandelli in general, fits in perfectly with the self-portrait which Svevo penned on his twenty-eighth birthday, and it convincingly extends our picture of his relations with those around him. I believe that in Mandelli we have an unmistakable, if sublimated, portrait of Ettore Schmitz, as he was seen through the eyes of his Irredentist friends and associates.

Far more sober in temperament than either Ventura or Césari was Cesare Rossi. Rossi had been with *L'Indipendente* since 1880, and Ettore must have made friends with him by 1884, when Rossi became editor and Ettore's articles became frequent. This friendship seems to have been closer or deeper than any

---

* This 'white maiden' may be a clue to the adventure which provides the plot of *Senilità*, or to another of Svevo's 'passionate little love-affairs' mentioned by Benco.

other Svevo made up to this time. Rossi was no mean poet, anticipating much of the register of Pascoli and Saba, with distinctively Triestine touches. His *Rime* went through three editions from 1890 to 1893. He was to write the verses for Ettore Schmitz's wedding.[71] The first and second of the three ten-line stanzas of Pascolian tercets open with reminiscences: 'Do you remember how in our youthful years,/following in flight a gleaming idea/like brothers along our native shore,/whilst your impetuous blood was surging/and my verse flashed indignation,/I called you one of life's castaways?' And: 'And one day, Ettore, when upon your registers/your head sank down, desolate and weary,/oppressed by sinister imaginings. . .'. Rossi urges upon him the compensating satisfactions of 'the quiet/serenity of humble work' and especially—since 'Vain is our every love whose cares/are not lightened by dear offspring'—of starting a family: 'and hark! from the snow-white cradle/comes an infant's cry.' With this verse the nuptial poem ends. We see that Ettore Schmitz could confide in Rossi but could not expect from him the encouragement he needed to make the creative effort for which he mainly lived. This encouragement came from the man whose friendship was to be the most important in Svevo's life, the painter Umberto Veruda.

21

A BROTHER IN ART—VERUDA

Ettore's memo of 19 December 1889 records his utter isolation, his lack of any kindred spirit with whom he could share his aspirations, his ideas, his problems. This need was soon to be spectacularly satisfied.

Ettore first met Veruda in 1888, when the painter was nineteen.[72] But Livia Veneziani is surely right in suggesting that the friendship between the two men began in real earnest in 1890, when Veruda was back in Trieste after his trips to Rome and Paris:

Ettore's inner solitude was broken towards 1890 by his meeting with Umberto Veruda, a young painter full of talent who was revolutionizing nineteenth-century Triestine painting, but ... his native town ... did not comprehend the new painting of light. In Ettore, who was his elder, Veruda found a fraternal spirit. Their mental affinity was complete and for a long period of years there was a deep mutual understanding between them. Whenever Veruda was back from his frequent visits to Munich, Vienna, Paris or Berlin, they would meet two or three times a day. In the evenings Veruda would wait for Ettore in his office at the Banca Union and would while away the time sketching the people who came and went. They would stroll along the Corso and spend much of the night together at the café of the Portici di Chiozza, where all Trieste's cultured set would be gathered. Each confided his hopes to the other, and each encouraged the other. Feeling that he was understood, Veruda was able to go into the exciting problems of painting with Ettore. Ettore spent many hours in his friend's studio in the old Via degli Artisti where Veruda painted with his faithful and enthusiastic disciple Ugo Flumiani ... Both Svevo and Veruda were swimming against the current and suffered from deep depression, which the painter tried to dispel by abandoning himself at the Saturday evening gatherings of the Circolo Artistico to wild gaiety ... Ettore tempered the boisterousness of Veruda's eccentric character with his own mild good humour and restrained his lashing tongue ...'[73]

Veruda had studied under Max Liebermann at the Munich Academy, as well as in Paris and Rome, and he had brought back to Trieste a vivid but controlled freedom of colour. The painters and critics of the old school charged him with a total deficiency in draughtsmanship and perspective, which Veruda deliberately ignored until in 1897 he undertook a visit to Paris for the exclusive purpose, as he told Ettore, of perfecting his draughtsmanship, never once touching oils during his stay there. Veruda's most celebrated painting was *Sii onesta* (Be a good girl), which had already been acquired by the Galleria d'Arte Moderna in Rome in 1890. With pathetic irony, it shows a girl who has collapsed in grief beside the death-bed of her poverty-stricken mother, who pleads with her to keep her virtue, while the girl's appearance makes it clear that the plea has come too late. This image of prostitution as the curse of poverty perhaps not only directly expresses Veruda's social ethic but also, symbolically, an awareness of his own plight as an impecunious artist.

Veruda took his personal independence of mind to the point of barefaced impudence. As a young art student he once retorted to a teacher who was over-insistent in attempting to discipline his style: 'I beg your pardon, professor, but I don't recognize your competence.' He told Giulio Césari: 'It's all very fine for the critics to say "You've got to do this, that or the other"; but do the critics ever really "do" anything?' Veruda used to tell Svevo: 'You're original because nobody bound you.'[74] Svevo had always instinctively followed a maxim of Veruda's, namely, that: 'The best schooling is to work without respite and study oneself.'[75]

Svevo met in Veruda for the first time the spirit of the artist made flesh: a man who lived for art and through art, uncompromisingly, and who stood up for his art and for himself as an artist, in the teeth of an uncomprehending bourgeois Trieste, towards which, unlike Ettore, he showed utter disrespect. It is clear that he made it his point and practice to *épater les bourgeois*, mocking their politics along with their other attitudes. In 1899 he wrote in a letter to Ettore of 'you poor wretches who live in a noisome place which was and is my home by sheer chance'.[76] In a word, Veruda was for Ettore a dream come true, the glamorous and slightly suspect figure of the successful artist who could afford to bait the public who bought his paintings. He stood for the individualism of art, the sublime exemplar of bourgeois individualism, which he might pretend to rebel against but which his art really sanctioned. Veruda lived out his role as artist with consistency and courage; as Svevo lived out his in his own different way but no less completely.

Benco gave Veruda credit for being 'the first person to understand [Svevo] completely and courageously, with the gifted artist's breadth and sureness of outlook',[77] and suggested that it was he who instilled in Svevo the chromatic and painterly sensibility which distinguished the landscapes, interiors and portraiture of *Senilità*.[78] Svevo was to translate into literary terms Veruda's pictorial freedom and fluidity of composition. Benco also saw in the sculptor Balli in *Senilità* a portrait of Veruda, 'marvellously alive, capturing the man in his bearing, his make-up, his way of thinking and behaving, and in his character', but 'without his external eccentricities'.[79] Privately, Svevo was to limit the extent to which Balli was modelled on Veruda: 'Veruda's character is . . . radically different from Balli's.' Unlike Balli, Veruda had enjoyed artistic success from the start, and also success with women. But he had his parents to support, and treated women with caution. 'There was no talk of love with Veruda,' wrote Svevo, 'and for years and years there were no women with us.' Then Veruda did have one passionate relationship, 'but that ended with his departure for Vienna without any regrets'. He once slapped his lover in public at the Politeama, 'which she boasted about for some time after'. He did laughingly consider marrying a fortune, counting the millions he had lost at every wealthy marriage. Svevo urged him to cultivate the friendship of the rich, 'but he preferred the company of literary nonentities like myself, a scatter-brained doctor of genius, a crankish clerk, to wealthy people who could have commissioned paintings from him.'[80]

There is more than a whiff of flamboyant and cheeky socialism about the bohemianism of the Veruda circle. Svevo was always to be seen with Veruda, wrote Benco, 'promenading and discussing women, or in the haunts of high society, which they both loved greatly: Svevo always the soul of middle-class propriety, with the air of a fashionable bank-clerk; Veruda gigantic and spectacular, wearing extravagant clothes, imperturbable among the tittering ladies, who would eventually all fall for him.'[81] But they clearly also enjoyed low haunts as do Emilio Brentani and Stefano Balli, and it was not for nothing that Ettore chose to be married in the working-class district of San Giacomo, in neither his bride's nor his own part of town.

The Circolo Artistico, which Svevo and Veruda frequented, held a contest of popular songs in December 1890 in readiness for the coming Carnival. The second prize was taken by Ugo Urbanis's 'Fazzo l'amor, xe vero' (What if I do make love?) which Zeno hears upon the lips of his mistress Carla Gerco.[82] If there were any 'passionate little love-affairs' at this period, Ettore must have given them second place to the friendship with Veruda, or at least kept his different relationships apart. Veruda shared some 'unforgettable' weeks with Ettore and his sister Ortensia one summer at the quiet village of Tricesimo near Udine.[83] All in all, it seems beyond question that in Veruda Ettore had at last found a friend with whom he could really be himself, without pretence or reserve.

22

LAST WRITINGS OF E. SAMIGLI

This life stimulated Ettore into a considerable burst of fresh literary activity, even as he was looking for a publisher for his novel (and perhaps revising it). From 4 to 13 October 1890, *L'Indipendente* serialized his longish story, 'L'assassinio di Via Belpoggio' (The Murder on Via Belpoggio), and it was followed on 17 November by the piece called 'Il fumo' (Tobacco) in the newspaper's social column 'Echi mondani', and by the dramatic monologue *Prima del ballo* (Before the Ball) in the newspaper's *Befana*, or New Year supplement, for 1891. All were signed E. Samigli.

'L'assassinio di Via Belpoggio' must be the 'long story' dismissed in *Profilo autobiografico* as being 'of scant interest',[84] but it is not at all to be despised and is indeed Svevo's first considerable published work.[85] Like Alfonso Nitti in *Una vita*, the central character acts but is then unable to carry through the consequences of his act. Upon a sudden, almost physical, impulse, he kills and robs a man only to be overcome by a paralysis of the will. The murderer, Giorgio, is an impoverished *petit bourgeois* whose act of robbery would mend his social disadvantage, and he tries to justify it to himself with the thought that he can now support his mother, whom he has in fact long neglected. The story opens the moment after the crime has been committed and, like all Svevo's narratives, is conducted entirely from within the character's mind, following the web of his rationalizations. Giorgio disguises his fear as an argument[86] just as Alfonso Nitti dresses up his every emotional impulse. The sober character-study is impressive, and carries far deeper overtones than 'Una lotta'. The story gains solidity from its Trieste setting: as in *Una vita*, the town is not named but its topography is clearly recognizable and milieu is sensed as an active, even deterministic, force in the drama. Social redress is still viewed in individualistic terms.

'Il fumo'[87] shows Svevo's remarkable knowledge about everything to do with smoking, and especially about the attitudes to smoking of writers and scientists. (Benco confirms that by this time Svevo's complex about smoking was already well established: 'He gave it up daily, and he never gave it up.')[88] Still signing himself 'E. Samigli', Svevo develops the connexions between smoking and disease and between smoking and daydreams, and goes on to suggest the artistic advantage of experiencing abnormal states of mind induced by smoking. So he demolishes the motto of the Unione Ginnastica, of whose governing board he was shortly to become a member: 'Healthy mind in healthy body'.

We can already trace here the roots of *La coscienza di Zeno*, and not merely in the preoccupation with smoking. The relationship between health and disease has already become problematical to the point of paradox. Svevo's strongly held positivism is no longer a simple faith. The 'scientific' study of the morbid and the abnormal is leading to the reversal or the transcending of axiomatic notions of 'health', 'normality' and 'reality'. But the scientific method as such is not challenged. The notion of the experiment on oneself, which this article takes seriously despite its flippant tone, is a crucial way of extending scientific method without shattering it, annihilating the distance between subject and object, as Svevo was to do in all his subsequent works, while preserving the precarious objectivity of art. 'Il fumo' argues:

The smoker is first and foremost a dreamer... The dreamer is never consistent because dream carries you far away and not in a straight line ... The true dreamer ... always leads a double life and both his lives are equal in intensity... Thus his inspiration has two sources: Pure observation and dream, dream which is distorted by corrupted nerves.

All Svevo's narratives centre on indefatigable dreamers and the primary characteristic of those narratives is precisely the constant swinging back and forth between 'dream' and 'reality'.

Among the writers and scientists mentioned pell-mell in 'Il fumo' is the celebrated George Miller Beard who pioneered the use of electricity for psycho-therapy (and Ettore himself tried it). Beard was among the first to subject psychic phenomena to scientific attention and to link neurosis to social conditions, and to industrialization in particular. His books, most signally *American Nervousness: Its Causes and Consequences*, won him world-wide renown. Beard can be said to have developed clinical psychology along the lines suggested by Balzac's Louis Lambert in the novel referred to in *Una vita*, that thought itself is something physical and material.[89] For Beard, neurasthenia was produced by civilization and was an illness which prolonged life. Reviewing the Italian translation of *American Nervousness* in 1892, Guglielmo Ferrero described nervousness as 'a foretaste of times to come, which, like any foretaste, must be considered morbid'.[90] This paradoxical equation of disease with progress lends itself very well to the play of Svevo's irony. Beard's *Practical Treatise* also offers the idea, used in Svevo's third novel, of maladies as treasured possessions.[91] Though historically interesting, Beard now looks irremediably gauche and pseudoscientific and is not unfairly spoofed in *La coscienza di Zeno*.[92]

Svevo's brief *Prima del ballo*[93] gives a caustic perspective on Triestine polite society in the form of a monologue by a young lady who is a sort of embryonic Hedda Gabler or a new Annetta Maller. As she prepares to go to her second ball, she demolishes with ruthless scorn everybody she is likely to meet there. The monologue form provides Svevo with a promising new way of ironically relating the subjective and the objective, and the chosen viewpoint interestingly extends his range.

New possibilities were now arising in the theatre, thanks largely to the discovery of Ibsen. Trieste had its first Ibsen performance (*The Wild Duck*) in 1891, the year of G. B. Shaw's *The Quintessence of Ibsenism*, when the Ibsen controversy had brought the Norwegian playwright to stay on the European stage. The next two years saw performances in Trieste of *A Doll's House* and *Ghosts*, with Eleonora Duse. By then Ibsen had come to stay for Trieste and for Svevo also, though Trieste had its own miniature Ibsen controversy in the pages of *L'Indipendente* in 1892. One reviewer, signing himself *I.*, praised *A Doll's House*, speculating vaguely in Schopenhauerian terms ('the sad veil of the world as it is and not as it should be') and in terms more sharply Socialist: the redemption, not of a nationality, but of the whole of humanity, through total revolution. Another reviewer, *b* (possibly Benco?), at first failed utterly to understand Ibsen's play, but, after seeing *Hedda Gabler*, came to acclaim Ibsen as the leader of the great revolution in European theatre, displacing Ibsen's revolution, however, from the social and political plane to that of pure art by defining his dramatic work as 'the real representation of an ideal truth'. *L'Indipendente* was soon to enshrine the Norwegian as the greatest living playwright.[94]

During 1891 and 1892—up to the publication of *Una vita*—Svevo seems to have written only two small pieces. The first is a nuptial offering in his own name to his fencing-master, G. B. Angelini. It takes its place in a little miscellany of literary offerings by Triestines as eminent as Felice Venezian, Elda Gianelli, Riccardo Pítteri and Giuseppe Caprin, published for Angelini's wedding on 6 April 1891. Schmitz's piece, 'Conseguenze di un traversone' (Consequences of a Cross-thrust),[95] makes fun of fencing: first of all, of his own incompetence at it, his comic *fear*. But he turns the tables on his betters (that is, everybody else) by hinting that their skill, no less than his fear, is also an instinct, not really superior to the instinctive fighting prowess of uncouth peasants, or of beasts. He thus implies his own superior evolution. True enough, he opens his piece with a rueful joke about his own difficulties with the pen, but such self-deprecation cannot quite conceal the tongue in his cheek. He ends in a typically ambiguous way, mocking the heroic myth of the duel between Hildebrand and Hadubrand so as at one and the same time to please his nationalist friends with a mildly anti-German gibe and annoy them by refusing to take the noble sport quite seriously.

His other surviving piece from these two years is the tiny fable 'L'asino e il pappagallo' (The Donkey and the Parrot), dated 16 July 1891, which he did not publish. It is similar in style and tone to the two fables by 'Collimaco'. The parrot of the title is the useless artist or writer who has fine plumes and knows how to say 'Poor Charlie!' and hails his master whenever he goes by; while the ass does nothing but make the mill-wheel go round. Yet when they fall sick the doctor cures the ass and lets the parrot die, so that 'it is a wonder that the grey of the ass's hide doesn't cover the whole of the earth and that the gay coloured feathers don't disappear altogether.'[96] As usual, Svevo dealt out his irony impartially to himself and to others.

Just as Svevo was about to publish his first novel, his chances of success were not improved by the change that was now swiftly overtaking the Italian novel. While drama was moving towards naturalism, narrative literature was moving away from it. In 1889 D'Annunzio's novel *Il piacere* (Pleasure) blazed across the sky. Until then D'Annunzio could be taken for one of the better poets of the Carduccian school or for one of the better writers of 'veristic' tales. But in this novel D'Annunzio's sensuality took on the glitter and glamour of high society: *Il piacere* thus raised a hullabaloo that ensured its literary success.

A critic from Messina, Pietro Bianco, took 'the critics of *Il piacere*' to task in the Triestine journal *Pro Patria Nostra* in 1889: whilst he had 'excommunicated' the novel, he found all the other critics enthusiastic in its favour.[97] He quoted passages from the novel which other critics (including Nencioni) had picked out as examples of D'Annunzio's stylistic artistry, and asked what on earth they *meant*—just as Svevo was to do a score of years later in discussing D'Annunzio with James Joyce.

But despite Bianco's objections, *Il piacere* remained Italy's great literary success of 1889. A few years later, D'Annunzio discovered Nietzsche and found in him a Superman made in his own image with whose help D'Annunzio completed his conquest of Italian letters with *Il trionfo della morta* (Triumph of Death) in 1894 and *Le vergini della rocce* (Virgins of the Rocks) in 1895. Svevo's contempt for the D'Annunzio vogue that swept Italy and spilled beyond its frontiers was shared by few: among those few was *Critica Sociale*. Its attitude was well represented by the ending of Amedeo Morandotti's review of *Le vergini delle rocce*:

The terribleness, the Superman status of Claudio Cantelmo [hero of *Le vergini*] is nothing but words; where is the man, let alone the Superman? When does his experiment of dominating the three girls begin? You don't even find the male.[98]

23

IRREDENTISM IN THE DOLDRUMS

Trieste's Free Port was abolished on 1 July 1891, and the Triestine economy, after stagnating from about 1880 onwards, did indeed start getting under way again towards the end of the century and expanded steadily until the outbreak of the Great War. Benco was to write of 'fierce and spasmodic building speculation' and of 'maritime subventions' from the government 'which balance the accounts of the shipping companies who are ever ready to declare themselves bankrupt . . .'.[99]

With this economic change in Trieste, and after the dissolution of the Società del Progresso and Pro Patria, the main instrument of struggle in the 'unredeemed' lands, especially over schooling, was the Lega Nazionale, founded in 1891. This already counted fifty branches, with a total of ten thousand members, by the time it held its first congress in the November of that year. Its task was to carry out the policy of 'national defence' conceived by Felice Venezian, who was by this time orchestrating Triestine politics from the 'little red room' where the leaders in the national struggle used to meet almost every evening and take the policy decisions which were then passed on to the Party.[100] Felice Venezian rose to the highest rank in Freemasonry, a '33':

In the organization of Venezian's time there was no longer a secret committee working alongside and in apparent or real independence from the public and official organization, with the Masonic Lodge sanctioning and co-ordinating the activities of individuals; rather it was a section of the party leadership that had constituted itself into a Lodge, which was thus directly integrated into Trieste's political organization in immediate liaison with the Grand Orient of Italy.

In 1894 Venezian, Caprin, Giulio Cambon and Mayer along with Jacopo Liebmann and others formed a new Lodge named Alpi Giulie: 'Everything done by the Italian side from its foundation up to the First World War is associated with it.' The Lodge never comprised more than about a score of members. Lists are incomplete. No Schmitz appears on them.[101] Not that this is very surprising. Relations between Ettore Schmitz and Felice Venezian, despite a family connection through marriage, were not close. When the latter was dying in 1908, Svevo remarked, using Venezian's popular nickname, 'Poor Windbag!'[102]

It was just when nationalist morale was at its lowest ebb that Ettore Schmitz accepted an office which denoted some commitment to Italian nationalist politics. He became one of the sixteen directors of the Unione Ginnastica for the biennium from 25 January 1892 to 22 January 1894.[103] Like most other Italian organs in Trieste in the early nineties, the Ginnastica was languishing, perhaps because of the political compromise which had accompanied the abolition of the Free Port:

It was not so much on account of a falling-off of membership and the absence of certain kinds of initiative that the years around 1894 are among the least happy in the history of the Unione Ginnastica, as because of a certain scepticism, a despondency almost, which set in.

Presel attributes this despondency to continual police harassment and shortage of funds. It was probably part of the political bargain struck in 1889 between the National Party and the Austrian Lieutenancy that the men of wealth who were behind the National Party should no longer subsidize such a breeding-ground of activism as the Unione Ginnastica. The low morale of the Ginnastica at this time is amply demonstrated by Presel's description of its poky and neglected premises and 'the feeling of oppression that came over you as you entered that low, cramped lobby, black with dust and with the grime left by the flickering and smoky gas jets with which it was feebly illuminated'.[104] While Svevo was a director, the shooting gallery and the reading room were closed down for lack of support, and there was an obscure quarrel about the cycling section.[105]

After flourishing in the 1880s, the learned Società di Minerva was now also overcome by lethargy. Between 1893 and 1899 membership dropped to 129 (a hundred fewer than in 1884) and lectures dwindled to seven a year by 1896 and as few as four in 1899.[106]

L'Indipendente, like every other organ associated with Irredentist activism, underwent a serious crisis which was, according to Gentile, largely due to Isidoro Reggio's administrative incompetence. In fact Giulio Césari went over to *Il Piccolo* towards the end of 1892 and Reggio himself resigned a year later. Zampieri founded a rival daily, *Il Paese*, in 1894, but rejoined *L'Indipendente* in 1896.

Italian national culture in Trieste gave its best, if modest, fruits in a stream of books by Giuseppe Caprin, who had been editor-in-chief on *L'Indipendente* and was still one of the Party's grey eminences. They are appealing works of local geography or affectionate evocations of the past of Trieste and its surrounding region of Julian Venetia. *I nostri nonni* (Our Grandfathers) of 1888 and *Tempi andati* (Times Gone By) of 1891, respectively describing Triestine life from 1800 to 1830 and from 1830 to 1848, are still read in Trieste. But the others too were popular: *Marine istriane* (Maritime Istria, 1889), *Lagune di Grado* (The Grado Lagoons, 1890), *Pianure friulane* (The Plains of Friuli, 1892), *Alpi Giulie* (The Julian Alps, 1895), *Il Trecento a Trieste* (Fourteenth-Century Trieste, 1897), and *Istria nobilissima* (1905–7). Between them, these books amount to nineteenth-century Trieste's most substantial literary achievement (saving, of course, that of the neglected Italo Svevo). Their appeal also acted as the mortar which cemented the solidarity of the Italians of Trieste, especially those of the middle classes. Caprin's position as darling of the Triestine reading public helped to keep in the shade a writer like Svevo whose tone was so much less convivial and conducive to collective self-congratulation.

24

ITALO SVEVO, NOVELIST: *UNA VITA*

It must have been in 1891–2, when Veruda was in Venice and he and Ettore were unable to see each other very often, that Ettore fell in love with his working-class *femme fatale*, Giuseppina Zergol. One evening at the theatre, between the second and third acts of—appropriately—*Carmen*, he told Benco the story of 'a youthful passion of his, the winter nights he spent out in the frost and the *bora* jealously watching the front door of a humble dwelling where there may or may not have been the faithless creature who was not worth the torment she caused him': the adventure—about which so little is known—that was to make *Senilità*.[107] *Profilo autobiografico* says that many chapters of Svevo's second novel were written around 1892 'as a preparation for Angiolina's education',[108] so the affair must have been well advanced by then. Giuseppina, who was to end as a circus equestrienne, was 'the first to be acquainted with part of the novel which dealt with her'.[109] Nothing more is known of Zergol except what can be divined from the pages of *Senilità*.

The affair with Giuseppina must have been at its height when Ettore's father died. *Il Piccolo* of 2 April 1892 carried the announcement of Francesco's death the previous morning at four o'clock 'after protracted sufferings'.[110] His death-bed was attended by all his relatives, among whom bonds of family affection were very strong, according to Livia Veneziani, then eighteen, who was one of their number. It was from that time that Livia took to visiting the Schmitz household twice a week. Having lived in Marseilles until the age of eleven, she was fluent in French, which was the language she used in correspondence, and she came to give French lessons to Paolina's daughter, Sarah Finzi.

At the Schmitz apartment Livia would find, in addition to Paolina and her children and Allegra, only Adolfo, Ettore and Ortensia. Ottavio had already left home for Vienna in 1890 at the age of eighteen to embark upon a highly successful career in banking. Ettore used to get home from his bank in the early afternoon for lunch. Livia saw him as 'a tall, spare young man with raven-black hair and a clear velvety voice, of simple attire and lively humour' and had 'great conversations with him, within the bounds dictated by their difference in age'. With Livia 'his manner was full of delicacy and respect and he immediately confided to her his firm resolve to give up smoking as this great obsession of his life was damaging his lungs'.[111]

Svevo did not get his first novel published in time for his father to see. He eventually had a standard thousand-copy edition brought out at his own expense by the Triestine publisher Ettore Vram. He had started teaching at the Revoltella Institute to help pay for it. The book carried the date 1893, but actually appeared late in 1892. Svevo little by little got through his thousand copies by giving them away to friends and acquaintances.[112] The cover of *Una vita* carried the new pseudonym Italo Svevo, which from the first puzzled readers and critics. Despite embarrassment, the author kept this pseudonym for the rest of his life.

In explaining this pseudonym we may count both the reason which Svevo denies in *Profilo autobiografico*—his Germanic antecedents—and those which he admits—his German schooling and the influence of Schopenhauer. To these reasons we can add others. One is the family link with the Schwabenland in what was then Hungarian Transylvania, where lies the small town of Köpchen, home of Ettore's paternal grandfather. It took some courage, no less in 1892 than in 1928, for an Italian of Trieste to adopt 'a pseudonym which suggests a brotherhood between the Italian race and the German', as the *Profilo auto-biografico* puts it,[113] then going on to explain the pseudonym in terms of Trieste's function of mediating between Italy and Germany. This must surely have been the intention of Ettore Schmitz. In fact the pseudonym suggests a kinship of the peoples but not of the dynasties of the Triple Alliance. The latter were the Hohenzollern, the Habsburg and the Savoy, while the Swabian Hohenstaufen were the rivals of the first two. In the thirteenth century, more-over, in the person of the Holy Roman Emperor Frederick II, they initiated Italy's first vernacular culture (the so-called Sicilian School), as well as the truly international culture of the imperial court in Palermo. Svevo also chose his pseudonym as a joke about his Italian style, on account of which his friends used to call him the 'Ostrogoth': 'Hence my pseudonym of Italo Svevo.'[114]

Una vita was reviewed on 27 November 1892 in *Il Piccolo* and *L'Indipendente*. The latter remarked that the 'queer' pseudonym Italo Svevo concealed a Triestine who was well known to the newspaper and mentioned his articles whose 'form' was 'slightly stiff, but his own'; it dwelt upon his unflinching philosophy and praised the novel for its Zolaesque study of environment and its thorough 'dissection of a soul' which left no room for either 'the demure dewdrops of the old romantics whose sun has now set nor the indecent sensuality of the present-day naturalists'. The influence of Paul de Kock was detected in the presentation of the Lanucci household.

Il Piccolo likewise declared as an outstanding merit the fact that '*Una vita* is a book neither wordy, nor inflated, nor empty', but concluded lukewarmly that the novel gave promise of a 'full achievement'. It criticized the study of both psychology and milieu in the novel, finding both too minutely detailed, and particularly found fault with what the reviewer saw as the awkwardness and impurity of Svevo's style. The author was also taken to task for failing to explain the freedom, rather unusual for a Triestine woman, enjoyed by Annetta Maller.

On 12 December *Il Piccolo* reprinted the review of *Una vita* by Domenico Oliva which had come out the previous day in Italy's leading newspaper, *Il Corriere della Sera*. Svevo remained all his life pathetically grateful for his review,[115] and it is not easy to see why. For all Oliva's repute, his review contains nothing original or interesting or even particularly apt, and while he is free with his criticisms his praise is confined to two sentences which bristle with reservations:

> though of scant interest, though of very limited technical virtue, this novel does reveal an artist's sensibility and a clear-eyed observer.... You can see and understand this Alfonso Nitti. You cannot understand his suicide, but the author was concerned to find an ending of some sort for his novel. Which, basically, for all its flaws, is not the work of a tyro.

It is not surprising that these few half-hearted reviews were soon forgotten and that 'then an inexplicable silence surrounded the book'; nor that 'Ettore's flop threw him into a state of despondency.'[116] What *is* surprising is that Svevo never realized that literary 'success' is produced in literary circles; that a writer had to go to Rome or Florence to seek success by cultivating celebrated or influential men of letters. Svevo's courage lay in his dim and even unconscious sense that Trieste was his inspiration, which he could not get by sallying out to seek his fortune, leaving home and staking everything on his genius like a Veruda and later a Joyce. The *Profilo autobiografico* insists on Svevo's need for encouragement in his lonely literary vocation: 'There is no doubt that if *Una vita* had been better received Svevo would immediately have been able to give up his badly paid job and mend his badly neglected literary education a little.'[117] We may be glad *Una vita* was not a success, if Svevo really understood himself so little. But perhaps he was only pretending not to understand himself for the benefit of the linguistic purists of Italy and of Trieste.

Some of the difficulties encountered by *Una vita* were shared by Triestine writers in general. Scipio Slataper wrote of the unwarranted but all too real literary inferiority complex which Trieste felt with regard to Italy: 'A book printed in Trieste is taken for an Italian publisher's reject.'[118]

Meanwhile, as *Una vita* was slipping away into oblivion, Trieste was changing and with Trieste Svevo was changing too, at least in his manner of articulating his ideas. Socialism was coming in.

25

SOCIALISM AND THE WRITER

In 1890 the Socialists won their first political success at the municipal elections in Muggia, the small fishing town adjoining Trieste to the south, and the workers' May Day festivities were quite a success even in Trieste. Only *Il Piccolo* and *L'Operaio* (organ of the Società Operaia) continued to spit fire at the Socialists. The Socialist Confederazione Operaia was, however, abruptly suppressed by the Lieutenancy in 1891 and that year's May Day celebrations banned. Harassment by police and employers continued for another three years and more, and it was not until late in 1894 that it was possible to found another Socialist organization in Trieste, the Lega Social-Democratica.[119]

Socialism in the early nineties had thus filched from Irredentism the role of persecuted victim. Freedom and justice were trampled underfoot, but struggled on steadfastly and uncompromisingly.

This forced the nationalist Società Operaia into vying with the Socialists:

with economic depression, working-class pressure increased as in 1895 the Società Operaia finally opted in favour of the May Day festival, even if *L'Operaio* stressed once more that 'There are antagonisms of race that no humanitarian idea will ever manage to destroy.'[120]

In 1892 *L'Indipendente* was very critical of the authoritarian measures taken in Italy to repress the swelling Socialist movement there and spoke of a 'tacit proclamation of a state of siege' by Baron Nicotera's government, intended to prevent the workers from demonstrating on May Day.[121] In general the paper displayed an open attitude. It deplored the conversion to Socialism of De Amicis, a champion of Irredentism, and his rejection of paternalistic liberal reform.[122] But it was not immune to the spell of the somewhat Utopian or Platonic Socialism preached by Zola and Tolstoy.[123] Their Arcadian visions were akin to that of Morris's *News from Nowhere* which had come out in 1891 in a cheap Italian translation, and Svevo's story 'La tribù' (The Tribe) shows a weakness for this rather literary brand of Socialism.[124]

The foundation of the Lega Social-Democratica came at the time of the gestation of *Senilità*. The purely imaginary and escapist 'Socialism' of the novel's protagonist Emilio Brentani echoes the Social Democrat manifesto of 22 September 1894: 'In the struggle which the proletariat of the whole world has engaged for its own emancipation, the need for the organization of all workers in a strong party is spectacularly proven.'[125]

Conditions in Trieste had deteriorated since the dissolution of the Confederazione Operaia. The new Lega therefore picked up considerable support and in February 1895 was able to launch its own periodical, *Il Lavoratore*. Gianni Pinguentini records many working-class grievances of the time. In five years the price of meat had risen by 50 per cent, and there had been similar or greater rises in the price of coal and paraffin, 'the poor man's lighting'. At Barcola, where the Triestines today still go for their sea-bathing, the fisher-folk were protesting 'because after the great square of their district had been turned into public gardens they no longer had enough space to mend or dry out their nets.' In a letter to a newspaper 'a female citizen protested against the abolition of free tickets for entry into the baths at the Central Hospital which had up to then been allowed to poor people.'[126]

Trieste was suffering not only from the dislocation caused by the abolition of the Free Port in 1891, but also from the effects of the ills then afflicting Italy, especially as a result of the trade war with France, which led to the collapse of many Italian banks and helped to spark off the serious Sicilian revolt of 1892–3. Rivalry with France clinched the renewal of the Triple Alliance in 1891, almost simultaneously with the abolition of Trieste's Free Port, and trade links between Italy and Austria were strengthened.

Irredentism was now being pushed towards the Right, especially after the formation in Italy of the nationalistic Società Dante Alighieri. (The political Left was more and more being taken over by the Socialists.) In 1893–4, with Crispi's return to power, Italian politics took an authoritarian turn: the franchise was further restricted, the parliamentary deputy De Felice was imprisoned, the Socialist Party suppressed, and its leaders put on trial. The groups of the Left met in Milan and joined together in the League for the Defence of Liberty. But Crispi simply hushed up the bank scandal which had recently come to light, dissolved Parliament and rigged himself a solid majority in the elections of May 1895. However, he was once more forced to resign when the Ethiopians wiped out the Italian expeditionary force at Adowa towards the end of 1895, checking Crispi's schemes for Italian colonial expansion.

Socialism began to gain ground in Italy. Pope Leo XIII, who had condemned it in 1878, issued the encyclical *Rerum Novarum* in 1891, urging a measure of social justice and a living wage for all workers. The International Socialist Congress held at Reggio Emilia in 1893 saw the spectacular conversion to Socialism of the Republican Enrico Ferri, while in the countryside the Socialist Leghe were also winning support.

Many intellectuals were to be attracted to Socialism, which might well appear to them the natural and necessary development of classical nineteenth-century liberalism or Mazzinianism. A poll of intellectuals in 1893 showed 163 in favour of Socialism and only thirty against. One of these latter, the novelist Matilde Serao, foresaw as the effect of Socialism 'the death of art, poetry, glory and all the most beautiful Italian chimaeras'.[127] Among the many Italian writers who supported Socialism was Edmondo De Amicis, who had been fêted by Caprin,

Hortis, Teodoro Mayer, Felice Venezian and others when he had visited Trieste in 1887 in the full flush of the phenomenal popularity of his *Cuore* (Heart). His conversion to Socialism was bound to influence the more thoughtful Irredentists in the direction of a 'Socialism of the heart'.

Intellectuals of the positivist mould were liable to be drawn towards Socialism, but on the other hand many Mazzinian radicals and republicans were still able to remain hostile to it. Such was a writer for whom Svevo had expressed admiration, Olindo Guerrini. His outlook was suggestively summarized in *Critica Sociale*: 'Convinced by its own experience, humanity must march towards extinction, the only release from its torments.'[128] Here we may detect a very early anticipation of the apocalyptic finale of Zeno's diary, where also Socialism and annihilation are presented as alternatives. Arturo Graf, an eminent poet and professor of literature at Turin University, also accepted Socialism as 'something absolutely inevitable, determined by the law of evolution', and declared himself a Socialist, but only 'in so far as my inveterate and incurable pessimism allows me to be one'.[129]

Svevo too became a curious Schopenhauerian Socialist, juggling with the opposed hypotheses of pessimism and Utopianism. He was to present his wife with one of Schopenhauer's books, one of Marx's (which could only be *The Communist Manifesto*) and August Bebel's *Woman and Socialism*.[130] He subscribed to the leading Socialist periodical, the fortnightly *Critica Sociale*, to which he contributed 'La tribù' in 1897. His adopting the pseudonym Italo Svevo was bound to be seen in Trieste as provocatively internationalist. But the main outcome of his highly problematical 'Socialism' lay in further sensitizing his writing to the ethics of social relations. It is not hard to guess that Veruda supplied much of the dynamism for Svevo's Socialism.

Critica Sociale offers some interesting leads to the reader of Svevo, in much of whose writing may be sensed an often problematical synthesis of Darwinism with Marxism. Already in *Una vita* competitive struggle is transposed from the zoological to the social and sexual sphere, and the original title *Un inetto* is explicitly Darwinist. *Critica Sociale* opened its pages to a controversy on this issue between Guglielmo Ferrero and Umberto Boffino. Neither was a Socialist: Boffino called Socialism 'the malady of the age' and Ferrero declared that Marxian sociology had been outstripped by the Darwinian school. The editor, Turati, intervened to remark that 'Marx is precisely the Darwin of social science.'[131] This is of course the Marxist position *par excellence*, and when Enrico Ferri published his *Socialismo e scienza positiva* in 1894 he entitled the second chapter of Part III: 'Karl Marx completes the scientific revolution begun by Darwin and Spencer.'

Critica Sociale also plunged into a favourite topic for both positivists and decadents—disease, understood in its broadest sense. Not unexpectedly, Marxism identified disease with individualism—that is, egoism conceived as bourgeois individualism: not a physiological category, nor a moral one, but a strictly socio-economic one. So, for 'A. L.' in 'Individualismo e socialismo',[132]

'Socialism is nothing but a higher evolutionary stage of individualism', a 'rational individualism' contrasted to 'that wild and insane form of individualism' which he calls 'morbid, anti-scientific and anti-social [*anticivile*]', 'the most rigid egoism', 'the assertion of self in despite of all and against all, the war of each against all'. (These terms of discourse are very close to those in which Svevo had rejected Péladan's 'individualism' in 1886. Socialism might well have appeared to him as a 'dream' of transcending that very ontological individualism which Schopenhauer had theorized). A. L. went on to quote approvingly Herbert Spencer's dictum (also Marx's) that the freedom of any one person depends on the freedom of every other person. He rejected the constructs of the old-fashioned communism of Cabet, Fourier and Owen 'in which in reality all individual spontaneity was suffocated by the severe harmony of the whole.'

Thus the Socialists contested the identification of 'Social Darwinism' with bourgeois individualistic competition. Edward Bernstein wrote that: 'Ray Lankester ... in his *Degeneration: A Chapter in Darwinism* showed how often the *fittest*, the victors in the struggle, are also the least developed and the most degenerate. History confirms this remark.'[133] It is not hard to see here a first germ of the fantastic pseudo-Darwinian theories that Svevo was to sketch out in 'L'uomo e la teoria darwiniana' (Mankind and Darwinian Theory) and 'La corruzione dell'anima' (The Corruption of the Soul) and that were later to be echoed in the ending of *La coscienza di Zeno*. This link becomes clearer still when we find, in the same volume of *Critica Sociale*, articles by G. Massart and E. Vandervelde on parasitism, which compare animal and human parasitism to organic and social parasitism, a connexion which Svevo was also to suggest in his essays and which is implicit in the figure of Zeno. Social Darwinism was critized from within by the non-Socialist A. Loria:

the human struggle for existence presents features that are sharply opposed to that among animals ... it is always the case that human conflict, far from favouring the strong, favours the weak, far from being a factor for progress like struggle among animals, is an element of regression and degeneration.[134]

The theme of 'degeneration' was brought into the limelight by Max Nordau's vastly influential book of that title, reviewed in *Critica Sociale* in 1893.[135] The review stressed among other things that while positivists like Lombroso, Ferrero and Bianchi 'object that genius is always a morbid product, that there is no such thing as a healthy genius ..., Nordau says: the products of unhealthy minds are confused and false, they do not correspond to the reality of nature.' Thus Nordau severely criticized the tendency towards making a cult of 'disease' and 'mysticism'. For him, as for Svevo, disease could be taken as a subject but writing should be a cure and the cure consisted in re-establishing contact with reality; though Svevo could not have gone all the way with Nordau in dismissing the late Tolstoy, Ibsen and Zola as 'degenerates', nor could he accept Nordau's over-rigid positivism.

Nordau applied his conception of healthy literature in his own narrative fiction, mostly short stories. *Critica Sociale* enthusiastically reviewed his *Commedia del sentimento* (Plays of Sentiment) in terms which might throw light upon and enhance the relationship between the writer and society for Svevo himself:

The plot is slight, the action brief and the characters in the story few, but as one reads one cannot miss the whole blatant absurdity of the criteria which in bourgeois society distort and pervert the very basis of love and family and bring in calculation, a mercenary spirit, and pretence where there should be only a meeting of souls and the sincere fulfilment of lofty natural impulses. Some might feel that a message is being preached and turn up their noses; ... suffice it to say that no one will read without interest or profit a depiction of *mores* which touch us so closely and which constitute so large a part of present-day society. To have shown them up yet again amounts to a good deed.[136]

If writing is health, as against the 'ailments' of society, it follows that even to depict corrupt *mores* is a good deed. This maps out, however crudely and ingenuously, a role for the writer Svevo in the changed circumstances of the new decade which is only an extension of the role which he had learnt from De Sanctis and Zola.

In a lecture on 'the social function of art' in 1897, Nordau held forth against art conceived as a class privilege, using terms which recall those in which Svevo had appealed to the 'collectivity of art' in his argument against Péladan in 1886. Nordau writes:

By means of art, man, who is cut off and imprisoned by his daily toil, enters into communion with his entire species ... Man, held in slavery by the machine and by the tools of his own work, recovers his liberty and his universality, man comes into his own again, rejoicing in earth and heaven and in the full greatness of the loftiest souls and hearts.

The equation of art with the religion of the future, an equation whose Socialist credentials are very doubtful, becomes explicit in Nordau's finale:

The art of the future will be no paltry chapel, but an immense cathedral which will hold the whole of mankind. The art of progress will not be the art of the trivial pleasures of an affected high life ... The sweaty toil of sublime endeavour, the precious tear of pity for the sufferings of others, the sacred blood of the martyrs of thought—these are the holy chrism of progress.[137]

This is an ambiguity which, trimmed of its rhetoric, was to run through not only the entire work of James Joyce, but, more unobtrusively, Svevo's as well. It is the ambiguity of 'democratic art' which is on the one hand a battle for the conscience of humanity and on the other an attempt at escape and redress on the purely aesthetic level, an aesthetic level which in order to be effective must appear anti-aesthetic.

This theme was developed by Claudio Treves, who defined aesthetes as 'the alienated who simulate alienation ... , the aristocratic lunacies of degenerates';

bourgeois artists or writers who 'ape a superior refinement and pose as the *non plus ultra* of ... the anti-bourgeois!' This is the pseudo-culture which Svevo was to make his target in the Emilio Brentani of *Senilità*, the inauthentic part of himself which his writing worked to expunge. Treves's sketch of the aesthete must have quite closely fitted the bohemian Svevo of this period:

I have met several of these young men, both kind and clever, of the truly refined temper of the artist and dreamer—a little subject to *mal du siècle*, if you like,—but plainly Socialist at heart, who have had to get over a keenly and deeply felt repugnance before they could bring themselves to accept our tactics of coming to power through electoral suffrage.

Treves concluded by saying that there was no poetry comparable to that of the struggle for Socialist freedom.[138]

Likewise, in 1894, E. Vandervelde opened his article on 'Capitalism and intellectual labour' with the words:

To pursue art or science under a capitalist regime without the risk of ending up in hospital one must satisfy one of these two conditions: either have independent means or do work that affords pleasure or utility to those that do.[139]

Svevo too had turned his irony in 'Accademia' upon Dumas, who worked for the stage 'by permission of his superiors'.

Socialism in fact carried further the conception of literature which was held by Zola, and using similar physiological terminology. So Giuseppe Rensi in 'The contribution of literature to social critique':

We are led to high esteem for the effect of 'immoral' literature precisely as an antidote to any optimistic illusion. [The novel] may inspire more disgust at the cankerous civilization that it portrays than the most stirring invectives of the 'subversive' press.[140]

Literature becomes 'immoral' in reproducing an immoral society of which it is a living condemnation, and by this means it smooths the path towards Socialism. For Rensi, society is 'one huge Augean stable' and 'the pages of almost the whole of contemporary literature perform the rite of registering the evils, perturbations and deformities that afflict capitalist society from its base to its summit.'

Critica Sociale offers one particular Svevian curiosity. An article entitled 'Cooperazione socialista' on 16 October 1896[141] ascribed to the Socialist Brentano the view that Socialist co-operatives 'demonstrate much more than a mere commercial success; they signify the achievement of a new social organization.' The article was signed 'EMILIO' (possibly Emilio Sartori). Svevo gave the name Emilio Brentani to the protagonist of the novel which he was then writing.[142]

Alongside Socialism, feminism was also gaining ground, the two sometimes walking hand in hand but feminism sometimes making its own separate way, with the encouragement of Ibsen's works. As far back as 1879 Ibsen had given a public speech in Rome on women's rights; then, it had passed unnoticed. But now things were on the move. On 22 May 1890 *L'Indipendente* had summarized

Parassitismo della donna by Anna Kuliscioff, Turati's companion, in the words: 'Woman is basically what man has made her ...'. In its issue of 16 January 1892 *Critica Sociale* advertised cut-price books including an Italian translation of August Bebel's *Woman and Socialism*. In 1893 there was a review by Adolfo Zerboglio of Cesare Lombroso and Guglielmo Ferrero's *La donna delinquente, la prostituzione e la donna normale*, accepting the remarks of the two positivist savants on woman's character as being deceitful, simple and incapable of analysis: as so often, it was the editor Turati who felt duty bound to intervene and contest some of their conclusions with the arguments used by Kuliscioff and Bebel.[143] An important theme of *Senilità* had thus been already outlined during the years when the novel was taking shape.

Direct and incontrovertible connections between Svevo and his milieu in the early 1890s are hard to make. There is little information about the writer in the years 1893 and 1894. On 27 November 1893 there was a contribution signed 'Italo Svevo' to *La Famiglia*, a Golden Wedding offering to the Levis (presumably relatives or friends). For such a unpromising occasion, Svevo managed to be quite witty. The elderly Levi's numerous offspring, 'all those pairs of boots to re-sole at the year's end', would make him think warmly 'of Buddha, who was such a pessimist even though he had no children and went barefoot himself'. This gentle Schopenhauerian irony was accompanied by an equally gentle (and veiled) Socialist satire of 'the joy which is the struggle for life' and of 'work, which he says is not enslavement but the foremost mark of the free man'. But this Thersites (as Svevo dubs himself in his concluding remark) also made an autobiographical confession: 'It would be so easy to gather from our [that is, the younger generation's] past that our destiny will be that of studying life without understanding it because we shall not have known how to live it.'[144] Veruda had clearly not removed Svevo's pessimism.

Veruda and Socialism apart, Svevo's life generally does not seem to have much changed. The *Guida generale* to Trieste for 1894 listed Ettore Schmitz as a temporary teacher at the Revoltella Institute in Via Giotto, alongside two permanent and ten other temporary instructors. He appeared also as one of the sixteen correspondence clerks at the Banca Union, which then employed about sixty office staff and fifteen attendants, and among the sixteen governors of the Unione Ginnastica.[145] The *Guida* for 1895 no longer listed him on the board of the Unione Ginnastica, but he now appeared as a *docente* at the Revoltella, with the further appellation '(Italo Svevo) writer.' His address was always shown as Via Canale, 7, (3rd floor), which was also the Schmitz firm's business address.[146]

On 12 October 1894 Ettore made one of his wagers: he got his cousin Livia Veneziani to promise that if he gave up smoking for three months she would give him a kiss. 'When the three months had gone by', writes Livia, 'he demanded the reward for his determination and kissd me on the cheek.' In fact, Livia had been duped, with the connivance of Ettore's sisters Paola and

Ortensia, and the following day Ettore sent her 'the works of Manzoni in a magnificent binding' in which Livia found the following inscription:

To cousin Livia, this commemoration of her kind-hearted though fruitless attempt to aid me in my struggle against vice; but also of my deception, which, of the two deeds, was the better one. Trieste, 13–1–1895.

At this time neither Ettore nor Livia had any inkling of anything more than friendly affection for the other. 'He was a frequent visitor at our ever hospitable house, joined in our grand Christmas dinner, and appeared, along with Veruda, at our open receptions on Sunday afternoons.'[147]

The Veneziani house then contained four girls, like the Malfenti household in *La coscienza di Zeno*. Nella was twenty-one, Livia twenty, Fausta eleven, and Dora nine. The only boy, Bruno, was four. And not far from the Venezianis in the district of Servola lived the Wieselbergers, who also had four girls in the family, but no boys. Of these the first three had names beginning with A— Alice, Alba and Adele—as did all four Malfenti sisters. So this point of Svevo's fiction is rooted in fact. Ettore once danced with the fourth Wieselberger sister, Elsa. Little dreaming that he was destined for world renown, she did not pay him 'overmuch attention or consideration as he was not, as she was, young and good-looking; he was just "very, very nice" and "such a high-minded person".' Soon this 'high-minded person' was to reveal himself rather more fully to another young lady of Elsa's own age.

Part V

THE FAMILY MAN
1895–1902

26

A KATZENJAMMER

On 4 October 1895 Allegra Schmitz died. Ettore described her last days and hours in a long letter to his younger brother Ottavio, who was twenty-three, already married to an accomplished pianist, Fritzi (or Frizzi) Freiberger, and well set on a banking career in Vienna.[1] Relations between Ettore and Ottavio, as among all the Schmitzes, were warm, and Ettore told Ottavio that he was writing to him 'precisely so as to cheer myself up'.

Allegra was sixty-two and still physically a strong woman, but for at least ten years she had been troubled by diabetes. This probably encouraged the outbreak of boils which gave her severe pains under her rib-cage. Ettore let the doctor persuade him to put off giving her morphine, but, through thirty-six hours of pointless suffering, Allegra never ceased to display her affection to all those around her. Ettore endeavoured to conceal the gravity of her condition: 'my main task was to deceive her.' Equally, he tried to keep his sisters in the dark. (Ortensia was away on honeymoon.)

Allegra's condition was aggravated by pleurisy. After a brief, deceptive improvement, she died at seven minutes past four in the afternoon—a moment which Ettore was to commemorate with innumerable last cigarettes and iron resolves, maybe because he felt he had not really mourned her.[2] (He had already accused himself of not having felt deeply enough about Elio's death.)[3]

Among the family mourners at Allegra's bedside was Livia Veneziani. Seeing Ettore close to collapse, she handed him a glass of Marsala. This affectionate gesture, Livia relates, made him see her in a new light. 'A few weeks later, he, who was usually so indecisive, discussed the matter with my mother.' Olga Veneziani took a dim view of a needy bank clerk thirteen years older than Livia as a suitor for the hand of her favourite daughter. Ettore was indeed closer in age to Olga, who was born in 1852. She forbade him to raise the matter with Livia. Here is Livia's account of what followed:

The secret, however, was disclosed to me by my cousin Bianca Veneziani. Being apprised of Ettore's feelings towards me, I too set my thoughts on him and meeting him would throw me into confusion. He guessed my state and tried to meet me whenever he could. I still kept visiting his house, where his sweet-natured sister Paolina had taken her mother's place, and there we spoke of our love. As soon as I was sure of my own feelings, I raised the matter firmly with my parents and after some heated debate I gained my point; we were engaged on 20 December 1895.[4]

As late as 29 November, Ettore was writing to Ottavio to let him know that Olga and Livia were visiting Vienna and to ask him to look after them well,

adding: 'All is definitely over between me and them.' He was suffering from
what he called a *Katzenjammer*, an emotional hangover resulting from his
discomfiture as a suitor at Olga's hands. He was even considering moving away
from Trieste and trying his luck in Vienna with Ottavio. However, in Trieste
he could live cheaply at home, which he could not do in Vienna. And money
was very very short. He had apparently borrowed from the Unionbank, possibly
to pay for the publication of *Una vita* or maybe to cover his losses on the
Trieste Stock Exchange. This meant that the bank kept 70 florins a month out
of his salary, leaving him just 50, with another 50 which he earned by night-
work scanning the foreign newspapers for *Il Piccolo* and by his part-time
teaching at the Revoltella Institute, which he had taken up in 1893 (there too
his work concerned foreign correspondence).* Ettore wanted to know from
Ottavio whether he could count on exceeding this meagre income by adding
to his expected bank salary in Vienna the proceeds of occasional literary or
journalistic work in the imperial capital.

In subsequent letters he was quite sheepish about the *Katzenjammer*—the
'result of the sort of love one experiences at twenty-two'. He no longer wanted
to go to Vienna and disturb Ottavio's sleep, as he had done in the past.
(Ottavio was always in delicate health, yet lived to be eighty-three.) Ettore was
extraordinarily indecisive. He was swayed not only by his brother Adolfo, but
by his principal at the bank, Fortunato Vivante, who proved quite sympathetic
and sensible. Ettore readily accepted Vivante's argument that it would be silly
to change his life so drastically merely because he had burnt his fingers in a
transient infatuation, and by 5 December had sufficiently changed his mind to
write to Ottavio that he would simply come to Vienna for the Christmas week.

So one of Svevo's few serious plans (that we know of) to leave Trieste and
seek his fortune, especially his literary fortune, in the wider world, fizzled out.
On 29 November he had written: 'When I think of Vienna I see the world lie
open, literature, journalism.' But he went on to express to Ottavio his raging
terror of indigence: 'If it means my getting even *thinner*, physically and morally,
I'll stay put, because over there I'd go into a raging, rabid fury and you'd
hanker to be back in sweet solitude.'[6] This self-portrait of an 'Ettore Furioso'
is by no means an imaginary one. There is lots of evidence in later letters that
he was capable of throwing a fine tantrum. What is harder to determine is
whether material well-being was his main motive for staying in Trieste. When
he announced his decision to stay, on 6 December, there was still no mention
of a *rapprochement* between him and Livia. Yet a fortnight later the couple
were formally engaged. In those intervening two weeks Livia resolved the
matter for him.

Livia's mother, Olga, was Ettore's first cousin, being the daughter of Allegra's
brother, Giuseppe Moravia. Her parents had had a strange matrimonial adventure. Her mother was Fanny Wolf, a German Austrian from Klagenfurt, and a

---

* In 1895 the Austrian florin was worth just over two Italian lire or French francs, nearly half a
US dollar, 1.7 German marks, or about 1s 7d sterling.[5]

fervent Catholic. Born in 1822 of humble parents, when only nineteen she came to earn her living in Trieste as a seamstress. Very soon she met Giuseppe Moravia, Jewish and three years her junior. They fell in love and by 1842 were living together. There followed three children born out of wedlock, for mixed marriages were as yet not permitted under Austrian law and neither Giuseppe nor Fanny was willing to change creed, despite their deep attachment to one another. It was only by adopting Italian citizenship in 1867 that they were able to contract a civil marriage at the Italian Consulate in Trieste.

But this caused a political storm behind the scenes. The Bishop of Trieste protested to the civil authorities that civil marriages were still against Austrian law. There were interminable administrative and diplomatic wranglings. Fanny had to go through countless interrogations, produce countless documents and sign countless statements. Finally the marriage was declared null and void. But Giuseppe and Fanny refused to give up. They went on submitting petitions and producing documents until at last in 1872, after having lived together for thirty years, they managed to get themselves a legal civil marriage.[7]

Elio Schmitz entered in his diary at the beginning of 1880: 'Aunt Fanny is a kind woman, but though she is married to a Jew (uncle Giuseppe) she is a good Catholic. We're still on good terms with them ... Uncle Peppi is a capable man but has always taken more trouble on behalf of other people than for himself.'[8] Giuseppe Moravia consented to having his children brought up as devout Catholics and sent to religious boarding schools. Olga spent a few years at the convent school of the Ursuline Sisters at Gorizia. She and Gioachino Veneziani were already in love and he had to get his love-letters smuggled into the convent. They married, after several years' courtship, just after Olga's own parents, in 1872.[9]

In Trieste in the 1870s Olga and Gioachino had a hard time of it. Giuseppe and Fanny Moravia had a paraffin factory and a factory which produced axle-grease for the huge horse-drawn wagons which still carried most goods traffic. The Moravias did plenty of business but were not very good at balancing their books and sold too cheaply. The business could not give Olga and Gioachino a decent living so, some time around 1880, they moved to Marseilles. There, however, they fared little better. Gioachino worked mother-of-pearl and manufactured beads and decorations for—among other things—funeral wreaths; but it was not a profitable business, especially as he was swindled by his partner.[10]

Giuseppe Moravia died in 1885, leaving all his property to his widow, including a mysterious secret formula for a paint for ships' hulls which he had never actually merchandized. He left his paraffin and axle-grease business burdened with debts, but Fanny Wolf showed her characteristic energy. Only three months after her husband's death she took out a lease of 650 florins a year on a factory at Chiarbola, on the southern outskirts of Trieste, close to the sea between the great Lloyd shipyard (Arsenale) and the small village of Servola.[11]

Olga and Gioachino returned to Trieste as quickly as they could. By the end of 1885 Gioachino had signed a contract with Fanny which put the running of the Moravia business into his hands but left all ownership rights to Fanny. He had had some experience of chemistry in his trade dealings in Marseilles and he set to work on turning to account Giuseppe Moravia's formula to produce a paint which would protect the iron of ships' hulls from corrosion and keep them clear of barnacles and seaweed and other marine growth which cut down the vessel's speed. He devised a soap-based paint which had to be applied hot and then hardened on the hull as it cooled. This 'hot green paint' proved far more successful than any competing product. Even though four times the quantity was needed, it reduced the frequency with which ships needed to be overhauled to such an extent as to represent a huge saving. Gioachino's first great success with this new paint came in 1887: the Austrian-Hungarian Lloyd shipping line agreed to use the 'Moravia anti-fouling compound' on all its ships and issued Gioachino a certificate to this effect which enabled him to attract a fast-growing business. As years went by, he collected more and more of these testimonials to the superlative quality of his paint from admirals and aristocratic yacht-owners and shipping-lines of practically every nation on earth. The Veneziani family fortune was made.[12]

Gioachino Veneziani came from a Jewish family of Ferrara, but he had turned Catholic, unlike his cousins (including the leader of the Italian nationalist party in Trieste, Felice Venezian) who had modified neither their surname nor their creed. Among these other cousins were the two Giacomo Venezians, the elder of whom had died fighting for the Roman Republic alongside Garibaldi in 1849; the younger was to volunteer for the Italian army when already over fifty and die in the first few months of fighting in 1915 in the war to redeem Trieste for Italy. The Veneziani were *italianissimi*: Gioachino and Olga were both dyed-in-the-wool Irredentists and Felice Venezian was their family and business lawyer. A legendary story had it that once when the police were searching the houses of known Irredentists, Olga disposed of some petards in her possession by putting on the oldest clothes of one of her servants and carrying the forbidden goods underneath them as far as the waterfront, where she dropped them quietly into the sea.[13]

With success came trouble between Fanny Wolf-Moravia and the Venezianis, which ended in 1894 with Fanny's having to bow to the forensic skills of Felice Venezian and effectively surrender her rights in the firm. During this dispute Fanny left the house beside the factory which she had been sharing with her daughter's family. She returned once the dispute had been settled, but did not have much longer to live. She died at the age of seventy-three, on 27 October 1895 exclaiming in her delirium: 'Bitte, bitte, nur frische Kirschen.' Earlier that same month her sister-in-law, Allegra Schmitz, *née* Moravia, had died. A month later Ettore Schmitz was going through his *Katzenjammer* over his apparently doomed passion for Livia Veneziani. The sight of her grand-daughter's grief, or perhaps the thought of the Veneziani inheritance, may have made Fanny's death-bed a turning-point in the progress of Ettore's passion.[14]

Another matter also engaged his attention at this time. On 23 November there was an exchange of letters between him and Silvio Benco.[15] Italo Svevo, then nearly thirty-four, was asking the twenty-one-year-old Benco for advice on how to improve his play *Un marito* (A Husband). Perhaps he was still hoping for a literary success which would give him some sort of independence, perhaps even financial independence, and thus strengthen his suit for the hand of Livia Veneziani. Even after they were married, before he finally joined the Veneziani firm, he was to make other bids for independence and for literary success and to send a play of his—probably the same one—to a leading Italian playwright, unnamed, asking him for the advice he had sought from Benco,[16] but this time getting no reply.

Svevo assured Benco that, despite appearances, he always worked slowly and laboriously, going over and over the same thing repeatedly, altering and revising. In fact he did not complete *Un marito* until 1903. He confessed to two 'ailments' (*malattie*) as a writer: his 'inability to achieve the direct representation of something real in the form which other people sense as belonging to that thing'; and 'my terror of my own idea which makes it almost impossible for me to stay with it for long. I go over it time and again but basically I simply reproduce the same development and even the same words, because I am unable to rethink intensely.'

Un marito is the first of Svevo's theatrical works which is gravely, even grimly, dramatic in tone, catching the mood of European theatre since the discovery of Ibsen. It is probably also the first play he wrote since the mid-1880s. It was, therefore, Svevo's most important effort to change course somewhat and catch up with developments in the theatre. However, the play's frankly polemical 'social' theme of the husband's supposed right to kill his unfaithful wife seems almost a return to the *pièce à thèse* of the time of Dumas *fils* and the play has more of Ibsenism than of Ibsen in it. Benco found the subject too abstract and the setting too vague and advised Svevo to amplify the plot and the characterizations.

So in *Un marito* Svevo explored the theme of marriage before himself experiencing the state, and the jealousy which was to mark his married life does not find a place in the play, which is rather about the husband's supposed right of ownership over his wife, his right to kill for 'honour'.

But for the time being, the love-affair with Livia interrupted the labours of the playwright. Ettore gave up his planned Christmas visit to Vienna and, having declared himself on 11 December, he became engaged to Livia on 20 December 1895.

27

THE BETROTHED

It is surprising that two families so devoted to Irredentism should have chosen the thirteenth anniversary of Oberdan's execution for a betrothal. The day before was Svevo's thirty-fourth birthday, and Livia had just turned twenty-one on 7 December, which no doubt had something to do with the new twist to events. On the day of his engagement Svevo added to his inscription in the Manzoni volume which he had presented to her after having tricked a kiss out of her the title of a comedy by De Renzis: 'A kiss is never wasted.'

The engagement celebration was an intimate family affair, and no doubt five days later Ettore joined in the Venezianis' great Christmas dinner. The custom of the family was that at precisely five o'clock in the afternoon the children were let into the drawing-room where the baby Jesus had left their presents and, before being allowed to rush to open them, they were made to spend one endless minute admiring the Christmas tree, which went right up to the ceiling and was lit with candles.[17]

Two days before Christmas, Ettore sent his bride a letter telling her of his delight at her inspired present: a betrothal diary in which 'I can set down on paper my pure dream!'[18] She also gave him a gold pen.[19] Ettore's dream was so pure as to alarm him: 'So pure that I sometimes truly doubt whether this is love for I have known love to wear quite a different countenance.' So pure that he was amazed that he, a worthless 'latest product of the ferment of a century', should 'feel the need, as I kiss you, to utter a word that made you marvel too: "Sister!".' It was not to be the last time that Ettore Schmitz, not content with having married his cousin, called her sister. The word 'lover' awakened hateful memories in his mind of affairs about which he was careful to divulge little or nothing.

The writer who had endured such loneliness for so long could hardly believe his luck in now being offered the opportunity of baring his soul in ink and we thus have Livia to thank for Svevo's most intimate autobiographical document, the first since that despairing memo of his twenty-eighth birthday. The diary he wrote for her in early 1896 and the letters he wrote his wife in future years during their several enforced separations, are the most valuable direct evidence we have about the mind and feelings and character of Italo Svevo.

For the time being, Ettore Schmitz could hardly believe that his happiness could be real or lasting. An unlooked-for, fugitive springtime warmed his soul:

'the still wintry landscape warmed to a sun which wasn't known to exist.' Livia was a St Anthony who was not concerned to rid the doubting Thomas who was Ettore of his doubts, and doubting Thomas was enchanted. He confessed his sadistic delight in his 'victory' of bringing Livia to tears. 'I managed to be so cool and calm during those weeks of trial principally because I knew you to be suffering and I spent hours of unforced gaiety upon hearing that you'd been crying ... There is no relationship more intimate than that between one who suffers and one who causes suffering.'

Ettore had been working on this letter since his engagement day and he recorded the progress marked by his first three kisses, from the coldness 'with which I might have signed my name to a contract' to 'an enormous curiosity to analyse both you and me' to the simple 'desire for what is left of my youth'. His love was serious enough, but he turned it into an emotional and literary adventure. Certainly, Livia and Ettore would always remember, even sixteen or eighteen years later, their third kiss, which took place on their engagement day in the Venezianis' brougham, which was later, 'naturally', Ettore wrote, to catch fire.[20] For Ettore the first kiss, the most chaste, was the most important. He was to write to Livia in 1898: 'I can still feel that warm warm joy—my first after many long sad years—when you let my lips touch your cheek'.[21]

Livia relates that during their engagement Ettore tried to smoke away his emotional turmoil, which ruined his sleep. 'He once went so far as to say to me: "Remember that a single word out of place would finish everything." '[22] The lovers spent several delightful hours together every day in the spacious garden of the villa beside the factory which the Venezianis had inherited from Livia's grandmother Fanny. Ettore, profoundly happy, entertained Livia with his witticisms and often played *quattro cantoni* and *barre* with her and her female cousins.[23]

Svevo's betrothal diary opened in the New Year of 1896 with the *bora*, which prevented him from going to spend the evening with Livia. He analysed his feelings and concluded that he was 'an incorrigible egoist'. His tone throughout the diary remained light-hearted but he did not miss the opportunity to set up an understanding with his wife-to-be and prefaced the diary with an epigraph from the Hungarian writer Joseph von Eötvös on the need for close mental communion in marriage.

Svevo's first reflection in the diary was characteristic: 'A man can only have two sorts of great good fortune in this world: that of loving greatly or that of contending victoriously in the struggle for life.' As, he said, the two seldom came together, he found it 'strange that when I think of my Livia I see both love and victory'.[24] And a few days later he turned his irony on his new-found role as bourgeois owner-husband: 'I feel you fully belong to me even when you're away and there descends upon my soul the serene assurance granted me by this dastardly bourgeois world. I win you now but *it* will see to it that you are bound to me by unbreakable bonds and quite right too. Oh! our dear kindly bourgeoisie!'[25]

Svevo's sceptical irony led to the first small crisis between the betrothed couple on 11 January. Ettore's Schopenhauerian cast of mind was always to be the great gulf between them. He wrote on 12 January:

I've thought it over a great deal since yesterday. At the [tram] station I uttered a *bon mot* which hurt you: I expressed my indifference towards everything but the cigarette. I then excused myself by saying that it was meant as a joke, but the matter remains more serious than I wished to admit or than you can believe. My indifference towards life still stands: even when I enjoy life at your side something still remains in my soul which does not share my enjoyment and which warns me: Take care! All is not as you think, everything's still a make-believe, for in the end the curtain will fall. Besides, indifference towards life is the essence of my intellectual life. In so far as what I say is witty and forceful, it is nothing but irony, and I fear that on the day when you succeed in making me believe in life (which is quite impossible) I would find myself greatly diminished. I would almost beg you to let me stay as I am. I greatly dread that happiness would make me stupid, while I am happy (how pitiful you must find me) only when I can find, moving inside this large head of mine, ideas which I think do not move in many other heads. But that it is my sincere wish not to hurt you is proved by the very fact that for your sake (really for your sake) I want or would like to renounce the cigarette I dared to make your rival.[26]

While still betrothed, Ettore vowed to stop smoking so as to 'use my cigarette money for the dowries of our numerous daughters'[27] or at least for the first, whom he had already named Letizia.[28] His smoking had affected his nerves and his heart and therefore his aptitude for love: so he would cure his vice for love's sake and not merely his own.[29] But his last cigarette went on for ever. He made Livia all sorts of vows to give up the vice and conjured a sort of numerological magic out of dates to help him, but he never failed to break those vows, to confess, get himself absolved and start all over again.

Though Ettore's diary began light-heartedly, the tone sharpened little by little. At first he exclaimed gaily 'how splendid is violence in love'; and 'more than ever I feel you are in my clutches ... and I don't yet know whether to eat you or to kiss you'—but in any case 'for me a kiss tastes like a bite.' His sensual appetite did not slacken during the engagement, though it was held in check by polite convention and by his own 'pure dream'. But psychological and emotional harmony between himself and Livia did not come effortlessly. On 6 January Ettore telephoned Livia simply so as to hear her voice, whose colour for him was like that of her lilac dress; but five days later he confessed that telephone conversations with her always left him feeling upset: the presence of his fellow bank-clerks meant that he could only speak non-committally and Livia for her part sounded so chilly that Ettore called her 'a world-weary little English monster'. On 14 January, however, her 'transparency' sent him into raptures:

In the open air I saw your eyes so transparent that I seemed to be looking straight into your soul. You were totally transparent, your skin too, even the red of your lips and all of you was smiling, smiling at me. That—that is how I want you. Oh! if I could be allowed to make your whole life as gently serene as that.[30]

But this was just the moment when Livia was being racked by doubt. On the 15th Ettore was hard put to it to convince her that what he wrote in his diary was profoundly serious: 'You told me that this whole book strikes you as very *fin de siècle*. It would be sad, very very sad, if you missed the passion in my words. In that case we would really be parted.'[31] Livia may have been upset by the macabre fantasy in which Ettore, after having seen the body of an acquaintance, imagined Livia mourning over his own death: 'And, with the energy which I love in you, you were in intense thought rather than intense grief.'[32] He developed this idea in a narrative fragment entitled 'Livia'.[33] After Ettore's death Livia accepts another suitor, Ettore's antithesis: 'a handsome man, tall, straight, strong, with splendid teeth and a far from *fin de siècle* moustache; *last but least* [sic: Svevo's English] he was rich.' This last merit is the one which Olga uses to secure Livia's consent, while Ettore's ghost rattles the door. But this new suitor doesn't even care to know about Ettore: 'Your mother', he tells Livia, 'has already told me that you accepted him out of pity'— words which make poor Ettore die a second death.

Perhaps, too, Livia was upset because Ettore's jealousy and ironic remarks about a previous admirer of Livia's, darkly referred to as 'M',[34] had made her realize how demanding Ettore's passion was, that it threatened to take over her freedom completely. When Olga telephoned Ettore on the afternoon of 15 January to tell him that Livia was 'indisposed, slightly indisposed, or rather, more upset than indisposed', he promptly imagined her to be gravely ill and himself as her nurse. In fact, though Livia at twenty-one was for him a symbol of health as opposed to his own 'decadence' or 'old age', she was the one, not he, who suffered constant colds and other ailments. On 25 January she had to spend a day in bed and when she went to Vienna a week later with her mother Ettore warned her in his letter to keep out of the cold: 'I wouldn't be too pleased to see you shut up for repairs again and obliged to enter the chest' (he was referring to a heat-chest which the Venezianis used for treating chills).[35]

On 15 January, however, Livia did not have a cold: 'You were indisposed through lack of faith in your own love! So my wife is more *fin de siècle* than I am, because I, so far, have had doubts about your affection, never about my own.' He was worried by Livia's need to re-read *Una vita* so as to feel closer to him, and even more so by her telling him that even if she did not love him she would not leave him, so that he could never be sure she loved him. So it was the simple, transparent Livia that introduced deception and doubt.

If *he* discovered he no longer loved her, he declared, he knew exactly what he would do:

I would leave you as calmly as I sought you out. One evening I would go away whistling, after giving you a last kiss ... I would walk on and on, all night long, until I came to a station where no one could recognize me and I would at last be able to run away from

you by a means of transport swifter than my legs. I would go into the empty world
without a qualm, knowing that I was being more honest than ever. And in the very
instant when I have to admit that you married me without loving me I would think:
Strange, how amid so much religion there can be so much dishonesty.

And there was worse to come:

You told me that I wasn't worth my salt if I couldn't win you back. I am no good at
winning anything. I want to have and to hold without effort. Otherwise life becomes
disagreeable to me, full of responsibilities and threats. If I cannot have and hold without
effort, I willingly relinquish, I unhesitatingly relinquish ... I have done nothing to
win your love. That would have been seduction, and I don't want to seduce a living
soul. In fact I piled up obstacles between us so as to see if you could sweep them
aside.

And his diatribe ended:

You don't know how to love, you *Knospe* [blossom]! ... I am offering you a love that
you cannot even understand. And who knows what surprises lie in store for us! After
this latest adventure, I grant that anything might happen. The least probable eventuality
is happiness![36]

Now began the real test of love for the betrothed couple. Ettore's 'frogs' (his
word for bugbears) began to croak, the loudest being the money frogs. On 20
January he asked Livia for the loan of 1,500 florins to help Adolfo's ever-ailing
business. Ettore was bothered by the fact that he was not a 'minting machine'
and would not be able to satisfy his future wife's taste for finery.[37] He and Livia
had fallen into commemorating their engagement each month by exchanging
presents and on 20 January he had nothing better to offer her than a personal
copy of *Una Vita* which he inscribed apologetically: 'An ugly binding and ugly
book. But still, an unusual gift for a bride. For this reason and this alone I am
glad to have suffered so much for the sake of producing and publishing it.'[38]
'Oh! *bon-bon*!' he exclaimed a month later, 'Why aren't I rich so that I can
twine a new gem into your hair every month?'[39]

The engagement went more evenly and uneventfully for a while; then it was
Svevo's turn to doubt his own love: 'Really a decadent fellow like myself cannot
love well.' If Livia looked him in the eye after they had kissed he would feel
unworthy of her and fear that he was only after the woman in her, 'that is, a
creature with no soul but formed in such and such a way!'—even though
he so well understood 'all the deeply-rooted delicacy of your somewhat
rough-and-ready kindly girl's soul, your head not only full of hair but
also of conventish categorical imperatives.'[40] Like her grandmother Fanny
Wolf, whose affectionate character hers so resembled,[41] Livia was in fact a
devout Catholic, educated by the nuns of the Notre Dame de Sion convent in
Trieste.

Livia's cousin Bianca Veneziani must have been acting as chaperone, and
this whetted the pleasure of the decadent Italo Svevo for whom every stolen

endearment felt like 'something I'm not entitled to and which I've won by fraud against all society's rules'. And more:

I reflect: What would everyone—especially female—who knew her have to say about Livia Veneziani's letting her cousin kiss her and embrace her? How shocking! And the shockingness pleases me as much as the lass. Oh! how lovely to have something forbidden! This is the emotion that makes me fear both for my future and yours.[42]

Conscience is the one redeeming feature of this decadent lover with his little boy's vices. As for marrying close blood relations, Catholics did need to ask special permission. For Jews it was different: Ettore's own sister Ortensia had just married a maternal first cousin. But the matter of religion was to become really troublesome to Livia only about a year after she had married Ettore.

Ettore, plagued by jealousy and sleepless nights, tried to calm himself by weight-lifting exercises which he chattered about incessantly and entertainingly to Livia.[43] On 29 January a sea-captain, a family friend, was paying court to Livia 'in the cheerful manner of his calling'; the next day an officer was making eyes at her quite brazenly in a café. What really infuriated and humiliated Ettore was that Livia appeared openly gratified by these attentions.[44] He told her off sharply, even brutally, even in the presence of 'that imbecile Schreiber', the Venezianis' clerk. Livia seemed not to mind these outbursts and may simply have been testing his feelings for her.

On 2 February Livia and Olga went on their brief trip to Vienna, where they looked up Ottavio and Frizzi Schmitz. Ettore got up early to accompany Livia by train as far as Sesanna on the Carso, and complained that there weren't enough tunnels. When Livia finally left him she gave him a rather desultory wave. As a result—

On my way back I had a last smoke, puffing like a Turk, and travelled with the Sesanna postal inspector who urged me not to marry. He was most insistent and in the end I had to promise him that I would not marry. So we parted good friends.[45]

In writing a letter to Livia the same day, Ettore of course took good care to say only that he promised the postal inspector that he 'would think it over'.[46] It was his usual way of making everybody like him.

Receiving Livia's letter from Vienna, Ettore was struck by the difference between his letters and hers, and shamed to tears by comparing her unaffected expression of love with the 'terrible rhetorician' and the egoist in himself: 'I love in the same way as I used to play when I was 12: that is, in terrible fear of being called childish!'[47]

After Livia's return from Vienna, Ettore discovered in himself the urge to change Livia's character and risk forcing her into dissimulation, against the principle, on which he had always prided himself, of encouraging 'the characters of all those around me to display themselves and develop naturally'.[48] He was really in no danger either of not properly knowing Livia's simple and straightforward character or of forcing his own upon her, but a certain disaffection between the two was growing. On 10 February Ettore noted: 'I won't forget in a hurry that ride from the Tergesteo to your house during which I wished I was under the coach instead of inside it' on account of some 'disastrous words' of Livia's over which he agonized for many days. She had ill-advisedly shown him a letter which she said had been meant for him about a couple of months earlier—that is, just before their engagement—but in which Ettore, to his own initial disbelief, made out a crossed-out 'K'. This turned out to be the initial of one of Livia's previous admirers, a Bulgarian, and there was quite a hullabaloo. Ettore went to great lengths not to appear jealous, writing a long letter to Livia and another to her sister Nella who was then in Bulgaria with her husband. He advised Livia to return to K. all the gifts he had given her and for some obscure reason seemed very concerned that he might have made a laughing-stock of himself by keeping so quiet about his engagement to Livia.[49]

Olga Veneziani set more frogs croaking on 18 February. Her husband Gioachino was regarded in the family as a sort of 'Master-Builder' because of his grand projects—'the villa, the garden, the frigate'—which kept his wife 'in a state of dependence, anxiety and hectic and partly pointless flurry', so that she had come to conceive of him with 'a sort of loathing, as towards an enemy' to whom ill luck had bound her. Olga's panic roused fears in Ettore that Livia would turn out to be a second Gioachino and steamroll him as Gioachino steamrolled Olga; so much so that he trudged the streets 'not even noticing the Carnival costumes'. He managed to calm himself down by persuading himself that 'I'm really the one with the master-builder's character and you the restrainer'.[50]

This quarrel between Olga and Gioachino must have had something to do with Gioachino's negotiations to raise a huge loan in order to buy outright the Servola factory, which until now had been under lease. He was also buying a second factory on the Venetian lagoon for the tidy sum of 180,000 lire. Repayments on the first loan were to continue until 1904. These large-scale undertakings might well have shaken Olga, who was a frantic worker and often got into a state of nerves. She frequently herself prepared the secret mixture to go into the paint, locking herself up in the factory's private workshop, and would then supervise the composition of the paint, directing the workers and checking quantities and temperatures, which were also secret and required the use of doctored scales and thermometers. Olga saw to most of the rest of the firm's business too—ordering and despatching, hiring and firing. As her husband went in for ever more ambitious projects and huge outlays, she kept an ever stricter watch on the firm's running expenses, down to the smallest details. So she was beside herself when he returned from a business trip to Russia with two pairs of splendid horses or a consignment of stags' antlers for use as candelabra, or when he had a large aviary for rearing pheasants built beside their factory in the countryside near Dolina south of Muggia, where the toxic verdigris for the copper-based Moravia hot green paint was manufactured. These things strained relations between Olga and Gioachino, and the latter turned into a womanizer. Olga was careful to take on only old or ugly servants, but Gioachino was 'more interested in quantity than quality' and indiscriminately pursued his serving-women at home and the peasant girls in the country.[51] Ettore felt his own conjugal serenity threatened by the 'dragon', as he called Livia's mother. He foresaw the disadvantages of setting up house with the Venezianis: 'I'd rather put up with poverty than a surly display of continual rancour.'[52]

Ettore and Livia's Carnival went by with Ettore racked with jealousy and with guilt that he, with his 'foul past', should be jealous of the 'pure' Livia.[53] Then his diary sprang one last surprise. The Italians suffered a disastrous defeat in their colonial adventure at Adowa at the hands of the Ethiopians. On hearing the news on 3 March, Ettore wrote:

The news of the Italian defeat in Africa has upset me very, very much ... I'd have done better to spend what little remains of my youth out there instead of devoting it to robbing you of your peace and quiet and making you cry.[54]

This daydream of going out to rob the Ethiopians of their peace and quiet shows that Socialism had not budged him from the imperialistic nationalism which he had expressed ten years earlier in 'Un individualista', referring to the conquests of Rome. Many other woolly-minded Socialists indeed saw colonialism as a more attractive alternative to revolution.

As an epilogue to his diary, Ettore added a prose poem about Livia Veneziani, born for Schmitz with her hair so abundant that 'sometimes her entire person is tilted over by it like a pagoda', with her green eyes and her contralto voice, 'low, deep, menacing', which 'stays mild and gentle so often and one can't understand how ... harmonious, but not harmonizing with the colour of her face and hair ... Oh! so blonde in sentiment dear Livia!'[55]

As the fine weather set in, this emotional warmth and enjoyment gained ground in their relationship and Ettore was able to cycle over with iced coffee for Livia to sip in the garden, pedalling his way along the sweeping curve of the promenade of Passeggio Sant'Andrea where he could enjoy the southward view over the broad bay towards Istria. The courting couple revelled also in the warm and sly sensuality of Goethe's most unelegiac *Roman Elegies* (just translated into Italian by the as yet unknown Luigi Pirandello).[56] In May there was a trip to the newly acquired Veneziani establishment at Murano, the island next to Venice. In June, Ettore expressed his regret that he hadn't recorded an emotional avowal by Livia, 'half words, half sobs', on the phonograph.[57]

28

ETTORE AND LIVIA'S FIRST WEDDING

Ettore and Livia were married at the public registry on 30 July 1896, exactly sixty-eight years after the marriage of Ettore's paternal grandparents and exactly sixty-one years before the day Livia died. For a deeply religious Catholic like Livia civil marriage was not something to be undertaken lightly (her grandmother Fanny had done so only after many years of common-law marriage). The Church still did not recognize it, even if recent Austrian legislation allowed it and a modern-minded man like Ettore Schmitz approved of it. Many Jews towards the turn of the century were undertaking civil marriage and 'nearly all civil marriages were mixed.'[58] For an atheist like Ettore it was an easy matter.

The marriage was an emancipated one also in the sense that Livia brought no dowry.[59] On the other hand, her parents did not keep her penniless and, besides, they had the Schmitzes to live in with them on easy terms in their spacious villa next to the factory, in a second-floor apartment.

It was Olga, dictatorial as always, who decreed that her favourite daughter should stay at home, and also that the wedding should be celebrated 'with some style, with all our numerous relations present'. But at least during their month's honeymoon Ettore and Livia were free. They travelled (by rail) entirely in German territory—probably avoiding the Mediterranean summer heat.

They stopped first at the Alla Posta inn at Gorizia, where Ettore woke up 'to the two effs—felicità and fumo',[60] though he did not come wide awake, being 'overcome with sleep for four days'.[61] After Gorizia, Livia and her sleepy-headed husband crossed the Carnic Alps and spent a night at Pontebba,[62] then descended into Austria as far as Annenheim, their first stop. They crossed over to Germany, passing by way of Mittenwald in the Bavarian Alps near Garmisch and Partenkirchen.[63]

So they continued on their long railway tour of central Europe with several brief stops in towns or holiday resorts, possibly including Salzburg and Munich. There was another stop at Weissenfels, on the Saale between Weimar and Leipzig, but there is no record as to whether they had time to see Leipzig or go on to Berlin (where they might possibly have found Veruda) or stop in Prague on their way back towards Vienna. In Vienna, where they saw Ottavio and Frizzi, they stayed at the Hotel Residenz and then spent 'an unforgettable day' in the mountains at Semmering, on the way to Graz, before returning to Trieste by way of Fiume (Rijeka).[64]

It must have been a queer experience for Livia to have the first three chapters of *Senilità* read out to her on her honeymoon, given that the book was based on a fairly recent and (on the evidence of the book itself and of occasional dark references by Ettore) somewhat sordid love-affair of her husband's.[65] This chronicle of indirections and misunderstandings, illusion, cowardice and falsehood, first written to educate Ettore's mistress, now inaugurates the education of his wife and signals his own confession and absolution from his past.

Returning to Trieste and his work at the bank, Ettore penned a final entry in his betrothal diary: 'Strange! I have been married for a month and over and I find myself exactly the same with all my vices';[66] this was at 10 a.m. Two hours later he was smoking a last cigarette,[67] of which there were to be countless others, many of them recorded on paper with new variations of dates and circumstances and usually dedicated to his *bon-bon* or his *capra* (giddy-goat). On 11 October, the wedding photographs arrived, showing a demure and apprehensive Livia and a slouchy Ettore (Plate 8) who captioned the one showing the bridal pair pretty accurately:

She virginally composed but though fair and white youthful and fresh. He on the other hand like the old *marcheur* that he is, looking brutish from the traces of his every single thought which adds another vice and loses him another hair.[68]

Ettore had removed his goatee beard in 1892 after Veruda had painted the magnificent portrait of him with his handsome fair-headed sister Ortensia amid clouds of flowers—the portrait which the painter had dedicated 'To Ettore Schmitz—more than a friend, a brother'[69] (Plate 5). He now wore thick moustaches and only briefly around 1900 again tried a beard, full but close-cropped.

From their second-floor apartment in the parental villa the Schmitzes had a view of the sea. The Venezianis occupied the floor below them. The villa was the only bourgeois dwelling in the immediate neighbourhood. It was near the timber docks, on the edge of the industrial area next to open country. It was convenient to have the house next door to the factory and promoted both security and friendly relations with the workforce. A wistaria adorned the front of the villa and two huge and shady horse-chestnuts which stood in front of it provided shelter for the throngs of sparrows about which Svevo wrote so many little fables. In the large rear garden were Gioachino's bowling-green and the cork cool-house where he pursued his hobby of mother-of-pearl marquetry and inlay work. The house had spacious reception rooms with grand pianos—one room all in white eighteenth-century Venetian style. Gioachino kept extending, improving and decorating the house over the years and in 1903 it was valued at a quarter of a million crowns—a huge sum for those days.[70]

From the villa could be seen the little village church of Servola on its small hill. Servola was where the Carnival came to its end, to be burnt in effigy on Shrove Tuesday, while the following day the parade of carriages would take place along the Passeggio Sant'Andrea, a little way on the Trieste side of the villa. A tramway ran from the centre of town to Servola, and Ettore generally travelled on it, except in fine weather when he might cycle to work.

Livia and Ettore spent five extremely happy years in their three-room apartment. Ettore made it a point of honour not to be financially dependent on the Venezianis. He had had to give up his night work at *Il Piccolo*, but still carried on his part-time work at the Revoltella Institute as well as his bank job, while Livia helped to make ends meet by doing some secretarial work for the family firm. Ettore was helping out his brother Adolfo as well as a bank colleague, Halperson, for whom he had apparently stood guarantor. He tried to recoup by gambling, disastrously, on the stock market. In the three years up to March 1898 he had lost about a thousand florins in this way.[71] On 8 January 1897, when Livia's pregnancy was confirmed, the first thought of the expectant parents was that now their debts would certainly not be paid.

In the meantime, in spite of his philosophy of impassivity, Svevo marvelled at his own changed circumstances and at his wife's unchanged and unchangeable character and attitudes. He wrote a 'Cronaca della famiglia' (Family Chronicle) about his first year of marriage;[72] in it he described his failure to influence Livia:

I, created for rebellion, indifference, corruption, always entranced with what might be and never acquiescent towards what is, married with the conviction that this was a highly novel experiment in sociology, the union of two equals bound together by an inclination which might be merely momentary, a union from which jealousy was to be ousted by science, that is by resignation to actual emotions and things, a union which imposed no alteration on either party for after all in order to stay together people do not need to be alike! I married feeling certain that if either of us had to change it certainly wouldn't be me! Rather I wanted to change my wife slightly in the sense of giving her more freedom and teaching her to know herself. I bought some books by Schopenhauer, Marx, Bebel (*Woman*)* intending not to impose them but to insinuate them little by little. Instead, literature, at least the sort I particularly had in mind, vanished from our relationship. Only once did we discuss my ideas and that was with regard to Heine. Blow that Romantic whom I proclaimed—just once in my life, in the heat of discussion—my God! After that I was left to my ideas and with the gentlest and most skilful diplomacy never again excited by having them mentioned. After all, for that *bourgeoise* the essential thing is to live in peace and harmony with all and sundry and keep her ideas inside her little head protected by all that hair; she is not concerned to convince anyone. Whilst we are all apostles of some ideas or of *nothingness*!

No doubt Svevo had seen himself in the terms suggested by Goethe in *Dichtung und Wahrheit*, as a new Abelard introducing his Heloise to the life of the mind in a delightful pedagogical relationship which would generate the most powerful passions and the most intense joys and sorrows.[73] But, despite some further competing efforts on both sides, intellectual communion was not to be a part of Svevo's marriage. Livia tolerated his literary and philosophical interests as a more or less harmless and rather superior pastime.

In moving towards Livia, Ettore had drifted away from Veruda. Relations

---

*i.e. *Die Frau und der Sozialismus*, which Ettore must have given to Livia in the Italian translation.

between the two men were already strained by 1897. Ettore was well aware that his marriage and, even more, living in his wife's parents' house, meant embracing the loved and despised bourgeoisie. 'Cronaca della famiglia' describes the relationship between Ettore and Livia in terms close to those in which Zeno in *La coscienza* was to describe his marriage with Augusta. For Livia, everything has its proper place and time—meals and clothes and prayers. 'She takes everything seriously: the cook Maria, her own husband, life ... She takes every degree of relationship seriously.' Maria the cook was a colourful character, the overbearing servant. Disliking meat, 'she eats all the bread she can find in the house and, if she could find any, she would drink all the wine.' The Schmitzes kept leaving the dishes she prepared for them to go cold: instead of sitting down to dinner, they would go off to have a look round their new apartment and all the other new things.

Maria is brought into 'Cronaca della famiglia', however, simply to help illustrate Livia's character. For Livia, 'everyone has his place'; there has never been any social evolution, because, 'though individuals might change, the places they occupy do not'. In this respect she seems not yet to have reached the French Revolution. Ettore just couldn't understand her 'absolute and inexplicable *joie de vivre*', which he had admired in Zola's Pauline and which was to typify Svevo's very 'Livian' character of Augusta in *La coscienza di Zeno*.

Ettore was astonished at the way things had gone. He found he was just what he didn't want to be—'the real head of the household': merely out of curiosity, for experiment, he rejected his wife's suggestion of buying gas heaters for their apartment, as 'gas here costs as much as if it were extracted from gold instead of coal', and was 'absolutely amazed' to find his veto taken seriously. Livia had trapped him by her very submissiveness. Only his vices of smoking (the only real source 'of great and profound disagreement in our family')[74] and of writing (which Livia tolerated) marked out some freedom for him from his 'beastly giddy-goat'[75] of a wife. For the rest, the two of them were linked by affection and physical attachment, by *joie de vivre*, by their emotional interdependence and by the creature comforts and security of bourgeois living. So, what Ettore had approached as 'a highly novel experiment in sociology' turned out to be a fairly ordinary marriage.

At the beginning of 1897 Livia announced that she was going to be a mother. Ettore immediately reflected that the just-conceived Francesco Schmitz, 'akin to me in mind, would start by dreaming of having the destiny of a Napoleon and perhaps—following the same kinship—would end by having that of Travetti' (the proverbial nondescript clerk).[76] Despite disappointments and difficulties, Ettore kept up his good humour, kept repeating his 'iron resolves'.

In March his mother-in-law Olga persuaded him to skip two days' work at the bank to go to Vienna on behalf of the firm. The business could just as easily have been carried out by post, and Ettore did not even find Ottavio in Vienna. But he did at least see Veruda and spend a couple of hours strolling along the Graben with him. The train journey to Vienna was enlivened by a conversation with a fashion buyer called Signorina Ukmar and with some Germans. Ettore pretended to be Milanese, probably in order to avoid acrimony over the results of the recent Parliamentary elections—the first ever in Austria to include an element of manhood suffrage[77]—in which he had figured publicly (though to a minimal extent, as we shall see).

The Italian Nationalists had made a clean sweep in these historic elections—the first to the Vienna Parliament which they had contested. The electoral reform of 1896 had added a fifth category of voters—that of all adult males. The Nationalists needed to show they had the support of this new mass electorate and spared no effort to mobilize opinion on their side against Germans, Slavs and Socialists. Their victory in the so-called universal suffrage category was a personal triumph for their candidate, Attilio Hortis, but they also won the town seats in all the other four categories as well, and all forty-eight town seats in the municipal elections (in which the suffrage remained restricted).

This was the first time Ettore Schmitz had been given the right to vote, and his name appeared on the nomination list for Attilio Hortis's candidature.[78] The fifth category in which he was entitled to vote also gave a second vote to the electors of the other four privileged categories. This represented an epoch-making advance in Austrian electoral history. The total discomfiture of the pro-Vienna parties in these elections may well explain why Ettore may not have cared to be identified as a Triestine Italian by a party of Germans.

Svevo was at this time busy with *Senilità*—or rather, *Il carnevale di Emilio*, as he was thinking of calling the novel; but there were moments when everything seemed to be going against him—his writing, a scene with his wife, his losses to Gioachino at the card-table, Olga's 'instructions', the presence of the Venezianis' clerk Schreiber, even the weather.[79] He received some slight literary encouragement in June in the shape of a letter from the eminent German writer Paul Heyse, who was also an Italian scholar. The publication of Heyse's *Gesammelte Werke* in twenty-four volumes had been remarked in the prestigious new Italian literary magazine *Il Marzocco* in February 1896. Svevo sent him a copy of *Una vita*. Heyse read it and recognized that it was above the common run of novels sent to him by unknown Italians, but he found it too much like Zola, giving too little prominence to the central characters and, like most Italian novels, twice as long as it ought to be. Worst of all, he thought that minute analysis was thrown away on a hero who was far too insignificant, not to say repellent. Heyse did praise Svevo's pursuit of psychological truth, but did not offer Svevo any practical help in getting known as a novelist, nor any sustained literary intercourse. Heyse (who won a Nobel prize in 1910) did not have much in common with Svevo as a writer, but his letter seems to have encouraged Svevo to keep on writing and publishing.

When Ettore began 'Cronaca della famiglia' on 12 August 1897, he had just seen the photographs of his and Livia's first wedding anniversary and he joked about Livia's refusal to be photographed with Roentgen rays to show the child in her womb[80] (see Plate 9). What he did not mention was that the issue of religion had arisen between himself and Livia.

29

ETTORE AND LIVIA'S SECOND WEDDING

Livia describes how Ettore was 'converted' to Christianity:

Ettore and Livia discussed religion before their engagement ... The discussions went on through the engagement and delayed the wedding. But one day everything was resolved in the most unexpected manner: when Livia, seeing no other way out, had resigned herself to Ettore's will, that is, to a civil marriage, he said: 'So you agree to attach yourself to a Jew?' 'Yes,' replied Livia, earnestly and resolutely. Whereupon Ettore exclaimed cheerfully: 'Well, then, I'll be baptized!' The baptism took place in the church of S. Giacomo, in the workers' quarter, and so did the marriage.[81]

This account carefully conceals the fact that the religious ceremony came a year after the civic wedding. Furbank's account is not quite accurate either:

As a result of the birth [of Letizia] Livia fell seriously ill and with the thought of an early death in her mind she became more and more disturbed at her sin in having married a Jew. Finally, Svevo, on an impulse (or, according to another account,[82] at the suggestion of their family doctor) said to her: 'You accept the idea of having a Jewish husband? Well then, I'll make you a present in return. I'll get baptized!' Livia began to recover almost at once. 'My poor wife, still suffering from fever, received the news with such joy,' Svevo told Marie-Anne Comnène, that 'I have never troubled to decide whether it was the Jewish God or the Christian who performed the miracle.'

Furbank adds a detail which he heard from Svevo's daughter:

He went along to a priest and began his religious instruction, but finding it impossible to learn the catechism he gave the priest an ultimatum: 'Either I get baptized without learning from memory or I don't get baptized.' The priest baptized him on his own terms, and when Livia was sufficiently recovered she and Svevo had a church wedding.[83]

Comnène reports that Svevo also told her: 'She [Livia] really thought she had made a convert.' If Livia's account safeguards the religious credentials of her marriage, Svevo's sought to justify his false position by dramatizing the circumstances of his 'conversion'. It is characteristic of Svevo that the circumstances of his baptism, like those of every important decision of his life, should be so obscure. Livia's scruples are fully understandable, for in the eyes of the Church civil marriage meant living in a state of mortal sin, so that she could not fulfil her religious duties and was risking damnation. However, the records of the parish church of San Giacomo in Monte show that Ettore Schmitz was baptized and married as a Catholic on 25 August, whereas Letizia was not born until 20 September.[84]

Ettore, now a 'Christian' was thus more than ever living an inauthentic fiction, divided between several false alternatives. He never forgot he was a Jew and often joked about it, as about his conversion. In 1903 his letters to Livia often referred to his religion, especially in connection with his daughter, who was brought up a Catholic by her mother. On 7 August 1903, it was Livia who he said was 'as rueful as a Jew being baptized', a simile which he used several times. On 21 November he wrote from London: 'Kiss my Titina [Letizia] and remind her of her father who may—as she says—no longer be a Jew but is more wandering than ever.' A fortnight later he caught a glimpse of the English winter sun, who asked him: 'You descendant of the Orientals, how did you get here?' To which he replied: 'Titina says I *descended* from the Orientals but I don't any more.' And another week later, letting slip the expression 'Thank Heaven', he hastened to explain: 'I mean the starry or cloudy sort, so don't tax me with religiosity.' In 1906 it amused him that a lady tried to convert him (probably to Protestantism) on the train from Dover to London, and, the same evening, fearing that there were thieves in the London house, he backed away from the front door 'with the prudence which Marco ascribes to my race.'[85]

A good deal has been written about Svevo's crypto-Jewishness. We can accept with Carlo Fonda that to be a Jew in Italy was not felt as a problem as it was in Germany or Austria.[86] In Italy Jews were quite free to rise to the highest position, political or military. One Jew, Sidney Sonnino, became Prime Minister; another, Luzzatti, was several times Finance Minister. Italy had for centuries had no tradition of popular anti-Semitism. In Trieste, Jews were well integrated into the nationalist movement, right up to the leadership level, but they were also part of the Habsburg establishment, with a Baron Morpurgo at the head of Austro-Hungarian Lloyd and other Jewish families well established in banking and insurance. Anti-Semitism rarely showed its face in Trieste and never took strong root. But in the Empire of Austria-Hungary to which Trieste belonged it was a very different matter. Eighteen ninety-seven happened to be the very year in which the most anti-Semitic political party, Lueger's Christian Social Party, emerged as a powerful popular force, soon to become the strongest party in the Vienna Parliament. The prominence of Jews in the Empire's finance, commerce, industry and publishing made them targets and scapegoats for any discontent arising from all the ills of the realm, political, social and economic, although in fact the Jews were never fully integrated into the Monarchic System and always formed a large part of the urban proletariat. In Vienna there had been relatively few Jews until the middle of the nineteenth century—just when Adolfo Schmitz had moved there. Till then there were as many Greeks as Jews in Vienna, and considerably more Italians. By the end of the century Vienna had about 170,000 Jews, largely as a result of the massive immigration of poor

Jews of strict observance from Galicia. Most of these lived in the Leopoldstadt district (2nd Bezirk), which was 70 per cent Jewish, and, in keeping with the prevalent nationalism, their politics were usually Zionist.

Towards the end of the century the 'Jewish question' had become one of the issues of the day, and was widely debated even in Italy and largely by Jews. It cropped up regularly in the pages of *Critica Sociale*. In 1896 Felice Momigliano rejected Lombroso's theory 'explaining the prevalence of madmen and neuropaths among Jews by their greater production of geniuses', preferring to explain the phenomenon in terms of the Jews' precarious and anxiety-ridden social position, debarred as they had been for centuries from acquiring real estate and forced into high-risk trade and finance.[87] In France, anti-Semitism was not a matter for academic debate, as it was in Italy, but a fiercely political issue, as in Austria. In 1894 the French Right picked on the Jewish army captain Dreyfus, who was accused of passing military secrets to the Germans and charged with high treason. There was no real evidence against him, but, before he was finally proved innocent, the Dreyfus affair split France in two. On 13 January 1898 Emile Zola published his famous letter to the French President in *L'Aurore*, which gave its opening words 'J'accuse' banner headlines. Both Zola and the editor of *L'Aurore* were themselves indicted for this, and Zola had to seek temporary refuge in England.

There were two implicitly anti-Semitic attempts to break the National Liberal hold on Trieste in 1898. A Jesuit called Pavissich came to give a series of public talks in S. Antonio Nuovo. Such was the popular feeling, led by the National Liberals and by the Socialists, that his meetings had to be kept clear of demonstrators by the bayonets of the 97th Infantry for three successive days, until they were abandoned on 15 April. However, the Socialists challenged Pavissich to a public debate which was held on 24 April and lasted five hours, exciting great public interest. That same summer Karl Lueger came to Trieste to launch his Christian Social Party there: his visit was a total failure.[88] The most fetid sort of anti-Semitism was occasionally voiced in Trieste: one instance was a feature entitled 'The Jew and his portrait (two splendid photographs)' and signed *Antisemita*, which appeared in the 'Christian Social periodical' *L'Avvenire* on 27 January 1899, and showed a monstrously deformed Jewish stereotype picture.

Otto Weininger's *Geschlecht und Charakter* (Sex and Character), which appeared in 1903, just before its twenty-three-year-old author shot himself, attracted immediate and widespread attention. A convert from Judaism to Protestantism, Weininger combined anti-Semitism with anti-feminism, attributing to both Jews and women the same characteristics of parasitism, passivity, deceit and neurosis. The book remained part of Europe's cultural consciousness until Hitler's time, and Zeno Cosini was to deride his rival Guido Speier for taking it seriously.[89] But this was just one outcome of a whole complex of attitudes which were in the air at the turn of the century and which regarded the Jews as a special case, outside the common run of ferocious national

antagonisms which then flourished. Pogroms were increasingly frequent from
the 1870s, especially in the parts of Eastern Europe ruled by the Hungarians
and the Tsar. They reached as far as Bratislava (Pressburg), not far down the
Danube from Vienna itself. Given all these circumstances, Svevo was bound to
feel that his 'conversion' might seem like a betrayal, even if he had not
undertaken it out of fear of conformism.

But despite and *after* his 'conversion' Livia fell gravely ill after giving birth
to her daughter on 20 September 1897. She wrote:

My family were in anguish. I had to stay forty days in bed, during which time Ettore's
younger sister, dear Ortensia, died of a sudden attack of peritonitis. This blow was
concealed from me so as not to worsen my own condition. Ettore too masked his grief.
Before entering my room he would change his black tie for a coloured one. One day
he forgot to do this and when I remarked on his mourning tie he replied instantly that
he had an ink-stain on his red tie and had bought a new one.[90]

The birth itself took place happily enough. The child was a girl, dark-haired
and dark-eyed like her father. She was named Letizia (a synonym for her
grandmother's name, Allegra), Fausta after Livia's sister, who was godmother,
and Pia, as she was born on the 'sacred day' when the Italian Army had entered
Rome after storming the Porta Pia in 1870.

During Livia's illness, Svevo completed his fable 'La tribù',[91] which was
published in the Milanese *Critica Sociale* on 1 November. Publishing something
in Turati's Socialist periodical might be seen as a gesture of independence if
not defiance towards Svevo's parents-in-law, although *Critica Sociale* often
published non-Socialist pieces. If Svevo showed some degree of commitment
towards Socialism by the very act of contributing to *Critica Sociale*, and if he
showed a good understanding of class theory and accepted it in principle, the
nostalgia for tribal society which his story expressed, and its rejection of
capitalist progress and therefore of the proletarian revolution against capitalism, are not exactly Marxist perspectives. As usual, Svevo preferred to dream
of impossible happiness rather than to struggle in hope. The prospect of class
war clearly appalled him. Yet his works show him to be a convinced Darwinian.
He accepted the struggle for life, much as he disliked it, just as the nationalist
and Irredentist in him, for the time being (quite a long time), accepted the
necessity of national struggle and even of colonial conquest. And again, as an
admirer of the achievements of modern science, he could not simply and
straightforwardly reject scientific and technical progress as he seemed to do in
'La tribù'. There is an oscillation here, an ambiguity, which will remain evident
up to the finale of *La coscienza di Zeno*. Svevo's Socialism, then, was not yet
(if ever) a coherent construct but an instrument for the understanding and the
critique of his society, an ironic image of 'what might be', in a word, a facet
of *his* 'coscienza' (conscience, consciousness, awareness).

That December he wrote five brief fables,[92] perhaps as Christmas or New
Year crackers, and they are pointed in their critique. Selection is no longer

1. Ettore Schmitz, aged 12, in the uniform of the boarding-school
he attended in Bavaria.

2. The street in Trieste where Svevo lived from 1881 to 1896, Corsia Stadion (now Via Cesare Battisti). The Giardino Pubblico can be seen at the end of the street, with the Carso plateau beyond. (From an old photograph)

3. Trieste's Canal Grande, looking towards the façade of Sant'Antonio Taumaturgo. The Schmitz business premises were in the four-storey building just in front. (From an old photograph)

4. Svevo and Veruda in the early 1890s.

5. Veruda's painting of Svevo and Ortensia Schmitz, dated 2–4–1890 and inscribed 'To Ettore Schmitz: more than a friend—a brother'.

7. Livia Veneziani during her engagement (aged 21).

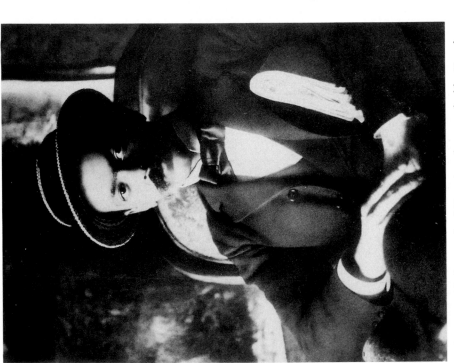

6. Svevo with the proofs of *Una vita*, photographed by Veruda.

9. Ettore and Livia (hiding her pregnancy) on their first wedding anniversary.

8. Ettore and Livia on their first wedding day, 30 July 1896.

11. No. 67 Church Lane, Charlton, in 1986. (Photo: John Gatt-Rutter)

10. The converted convent (now modernized) on Murano, where the Veneziani paint-factory was situated. (Photo: John Gatt-Rutter)

13. Olga Veneziani after the Great War.

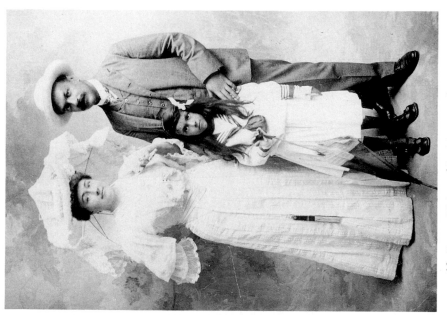

12. Ettore, Livia and Letizia around 1904.

14. James Joyce, about 1917.

15. Svevo smoking a 'last' cigarette, watching the landing of Italian troops in Trieste on 3 November 1918. An Italian soldier can be seen standing behind him.

natural: among men as among tumbling pigeons 'it is not the best that survive but those that are best at performing somersaults.' Another fable argues, against the preachers, that the poor and the weak are temptations to crime and exploitation rather than opportunities for the exercise of charity. In a third, God becomes a Socialist and abolishes Hell and Purgatory: consequently, a Croesus finds himself in Paradise; but, seeing no one suffering there, he opts to go back to earth. A Hero asks a good fairy by turns for glory, love and quiet happiness, but each time she advises him to accept gold, without which he cannot have any of these or anything else. While an old businessman who has survived financial ruin takes his own life once Herbert Spencer has explained to him the rightness of the natural law which eliminates the unfit.

Svevo also wrote for his small brother-in-law Bruno (born in 1890) the almost finished story 'La morte del gatto' (How the Cat Died).[93] This cat died in the same fire that destroyed the brougham inside which Ettore and Livia had exchanged their famous engagement kiss. The story is the first in which Svevo goes outside his quasi-autobiographical character to identify with another subjectivity, but he was never to complete anything of this kind on any scale. In this first of Svevo's animal stories, the cat shares two characteristics which Svevo constantly finds in himself: egoism, and fantasy (*sogno*: dreams, or daydreams). He assumes and dreams that the world was made for cats and that the carriage in which he shelters from the chill *bora* was left in the coach-house for his especial use and it is just as he is dreaming his 'sweet dreams' of an earthly paradise for cats that reality in the shape of choking fumes cruelly interrupts him.

The story gives us a glimpse of life at the Veneziani villa, with its three dogs, including the great Dane, Tyras, its summer and winter carriages, the coachman Giusto, whom *sior* Gioachino instantly dismissed for having left the coach-house door open, and the new and more conscientious coachman Toni, who shut the cat inside.

During the first few months of 1898 Ettore's good humour was showing signs of strain. Money was still the main problem, and getting worse. Without Ettore's night work for *Il Piccolo* and Livia's secretarial work for the Venezianis, there was less money coming in just when the child had added to their expenditure. The Halperson debt was perturbing Ettore more and more, and his 'last cigarettes' took on an increasingly financial aspect, as money was now a more pressing problem than health. He still managed to joke about them, however: he declared himself a Lenten Ettore even though Carnival was in full swing. But less than a week later his smile was close to despair:

Everybody is setting upon me and stamping on me: for my part I do stupid things, I lose money on the stockmarket—I smoke, in other words I'm ruining myself in health, in pocket, as husband, father, bank-clerk and writer. That is why it is time to have done. At the very pitch of despair I vow that this day 4 p.m. 27 February 1898 I give up smoking once and for all. At least I don't want my impending ruin to be my own fault.[94]

On 7 March he resolved to make good his stock exchange losses by giving up for ten years not only cigarettes but wine and coffee as well, and three days later, again at 4 p.m. (the time of his mother's death), he renewed this resolution and regarded himself as having already as good as saved his thousand florins, 'which I shall spend right away on sending my GIDDY-GOAT to Salsomaggiore to set all her ruffled fleece to rights.'[95]

30

ETTORE THE REACTIONARY:
SALSOMAGGIORE, 1898

Livia's health did not improve after the birth of her daughter Letizia. Despite the new expenses which this entailed, it was decided that Livia should take the waters for a month at Salsomaggiore near Parma, and she set off by train on Sunday, 8 May. The evening before she left, however, Ettore blew up. He wrote an amusing letter to Livia the day after her departure[96] to apologize and clear the air and cheer her up: 'in an angry moment I was driven to be rude, for which I am now sorry, and I wish I had not spoken so.' His outburst made Livia poorly, and clearly the whole question of going to Salsomaggiore had stretched their nerves, more on account of their forced separation than the money. Ettore's letter of 9 May attempted to soothe the tension and reassure Livia: 'It's not at all easy to make me as happy as I am (or rather have been and will be), and you have done so. I'm grateful for it.'

The cause of the argument was Livia's apparent intention of cutting a dash at Salso. She crammed her suitcase with dresses and jewellery which Ettore considered unbecoming to her condition and which roused jealous fears in him over the imagined perils of spa society for the virtue of a pretty young wife and mother[97]—this despite the fact that Livia was chaperoned by the totally respectable Rosely, wife of the lawyer Graziadio Luzzatto.

But it wasn't just a matter of jealousy. Indeed, Ettore was anxious to convince himself, as well as Livia, that he was not playing the bourgeois proprietary husband: he was acutely sensitive to his own poverty and tried to win Livia's sympathy: 'In other countries luckier than our own a princess may marry a slave and she remain a princess, he a slave. Not so here, for the poor husband of a rich wife is subjected to ridicule.[98] He wanted Livia to tell him what she was doing, whom she was meeting, so that he could, in his daydreams, 'share even this short spell' with her. He had, in fact, already dreamt about her:

Last night I dreamt of riots at Salsomaggiore. You—exploiter of the people that you are—were plunged into some kind of boiling spring, whilst the *avvocato* Luzzatto harangued the populace, telling them that now they had exercised justice upon you they might let *his* wife go.

As to how Svevo imagined spa society, we may glean some notion from a few fragments for a play *Degenerazione* which he seems to have planned some time before October 1899. There is, however, a surprising transposition of Ettore and Livia's situation, for the worldly-wise or 'degenerate' protagonist is none other than a counterpart of Svevo himself and a distant but easily recognizable predecessor Zeno Cosini, quite distinct from the Emilio Brentani of the novel which Svevo was just completing. And what is more, the theme of neurasthenia, which Svevo had first studied in Beard's writings and which he was to follow up a decade later in the far more absorbing and rigorous work in Freud, is here already in the forefront. On this occasion, Svevo's tutelary medical deity is the rather unpromising Kneipp, the humble Bavarian parson who had died in 1897, having convinced first his own parishioners and then the world of the health-giving virtues of mineral water.[99]

Badly shaken by the quarrel, Livia caught the train for Italy on the morning of 8 May. Ettore saw her as far as the frontier station of Gorizia. Having alighted there, 'in order to masticate my feelings' he busied himself by cabling a greeting for her arrival at Salso. This cost him 1.90 florins, leaving only 1.05 florins in his pocket and when he came to the ticket-collector he discovered that for once Livia had been more absent-minded than himself and had given him only his outward ticket. He was now short of money for the journey back to Trieste. 'I left the station humming "Oh! mein lieber Augustin, Hut ist weg, Stock ist weg, Augustin liegt im ... " '[100] Both the situation and the words find an echo in the last section of *La coscienza di Zeno*, when the outbreak of war divides Zeno from his hat, his jacket, his *café au lait* and his wife. Stranded in Gorizia, he gets on to the last train to Trieste without stopping for a coffee or a snack.[101]

Ettore described to Livia how he had trudged to the inn Alla Posta, where he had stopped with her on their honeymoon. On the way there he tried without success to pawn his diamond ring. So he spent what little money he had on a goulash with three bread-rolls and another roll with some Roquefort cheese (or 'Rockford' as he called it); and 'I washed down the lot with two glasses of beer as if I were a millionaire.' He now thought of looking up his acquaintances the Sinigaglias so as to borrow some money to see him back to Trieste. No one could tell him where they lived. Finally he accosted, in French, a customer 'who spoke Friulan dialect with a pronounced French accent'. The Frenchman, believing he was talking to a fellow-countryman, was so delighted that Ettore tried to keep up the illusion by also 'prudently' speaking Friulan with a French accent. This pantomime earned him a useful lead, and he spent his last 30 *soldi* on a cab which took him to the Sinigaglias. Here another protracted comedy ensued, until Ettore was finally recognized from his somewhat slender resemblance to Ottavio. He stayed to lunch and eventually returned 'in triumph to the station with 5 flor. in my pocket, a cigarette stuck in my mouth and altogether the air of a millionaire'.

Ettore's dream about Livia the exploiter of the people being plunged into a boiling spring was, as dreams go, not far from reality. For Ettore as for Zeno private life got caught up in public events—or nearly. Popular unrest was indeed seething. Italy over the past few years might have served as a perfect model to illustrate the Marxist theory of the increasing misery of the proletariat under capitalism. Political repression kept wages down while the punitive excise duty on imported wheat kept the prices of staple foodstuffs high just when a series of bad harvests had cut down the supply of home-grown grain. Worse still was the hated grist-tax (in effect, a tax on flour). Workers and peasants in Italy were convinced that the rich who ruled the land were starving the poor in order to make themselves richer still. Pressed beyond endurance, they had already started in 1897 to express their anger in sporadic riots, demonstrations, small local *jacqueries* and strikes. The Socialists aimed at 'winning public office' by electoral and parliamentary means and had not the slightest inclination to undertake a violent class struggle or a frontal assault upon the bourgeois monarchic State. They strove to stem the alarming spontaneous action of the masses and channel it into their own legalitarian movement.

Nevertheless, the rage of the people grew in proportion with their misery in the early part of 1898. The government decided to quell the unrest not by such economic redress as abolishing the excise on wheat and the grist-tax, but by expanding the army. It didn't work. North and South, town and country, the whole of Italy experienced increasing turmoil. There were strikes here, attacks on law-courts and tax-offices there. Great landowners had their mansions pillaged, and some magnates and public officials were lynched. Government and Court circles insisted that there was a Socialist plot to spring a revolution on the country on May Day. In fact, the May Day marches, carefully organized and supervised by the Socialists, went off rather quietly and uneventfully. This was also true of Trieste, which saw its first May Day rally on a mass scale at the Montebello racecourse instead of in an outlying street as hitherto.

The days that followed, however, saw violent clashes in Italy which appear to have been deliberately provoked by the forces of law and order. In Milan the soldiers fired machine-guns and cannon at the crowd, killing at least four hundred; the wounded were not counted. Virtually all the casualties were civilians. The two or three police and military men who died throughout Italy had all been caught in their own crossfire. The government declared a state of siege in Milan. A similar sequence of events took place on a smaller scale in other towns and rural areas of Italy. The crisis of post-Unification Italy had come to a head.

Svevo shared the expectations of a well-planned Socialist revolution which the moderate and right-wing press had fostered, and on 10 May, hearing that there had been trouble in Parma, and not having yet heard from Livia, he was seriously worried about her safety. 'I assure you that I have never felt less of a Socialist than at this moment. Scum; they're wrecking Italy to no purpose.'[102] He was not reassured the next day, as the news from Italy was censored, but a letter from Livia at last 'lightened *his* stomach'. A promise from Olga to send Livia money also made him breathe more freely. He was so busy acting as interpreter for a Scottish sea-captain, whose ship was getting a coat of the Moravia compound, that he could not devote a single moment to the project for an Italian language lower high school (*ginnasio*) for the girls of Trieste.

The situation in Italy contined to worry Ettore for a while. He wrote to his wife advising her, in case of danger, to summon him and Gioachino by cabling 'Send clothes' (so as to elude censorship) and asked the journalists at *Il Piccolo* and the Veneziani representatives in Lombardy to let him know if there was an uprising in Salsomaggiore. On 17 May, discussing the recent events in Italy with his brother and sisters and brothers-in-law, he was surprised to discover that he was the only one on the side of the authorities.[103] In Trieste even *L'Indipendente* on 15 May affirmed that the riots had not been instigated by the Socialists but were a spontaneous outburst of popular feeling against dear bread, poverty and oppressive government.

The Italian government now closed down all the left-wing newspapers and arrested all the Socialist parliamentary deputies. Among these was Turati, who was sentenced to twelve years' imprisonment for Socialist propaganda. His *Critica Sociale* thus did not appear again until 1 July 1899. The Di Rudiní government was followed by the far more purposeful Pelloux government, which systematically set about what has been called 'the *coup d'état* of the bourgeoisie'.[104] In February 1899 Pelloux presented a bill which banned public meetings and provided for sending political prisoners into internal exile, and in June he announced the 'return to the Statute' and government by Royal decree, regardless of parliamentary consent. It was an improvement on Crispi's bid of a few years earlier to establish dictatorial rule. It also foreshadowed the totalitarian success of Mussolini and Fascism a quarter of a century later. However, in February 1900 the Court of Appeal declared that government by decree was unconstitutional. Pelloux went to the country, but the Left gained ground in the elections and he was defeated.

Ettore could not foresee all this in May 1898, and once the crisis was over he resumed his democratic and Socialist sympathies. In 1903 he was eagerly to follow the accounts in the Socialist press of the trial of Admiral Bettolo who was involved in a corruption scandal over naval contracts. But at this juncture he appeared astonishingly prone, for a *fin de siècle* Socialist, to authoritarian sympathies, and he was often in future to teeter between bourgeois class attitudes and aspirations to a classless society.

31

'THINGS OR BEINGS GREATER THAN MYSELF'

At this historic moment for Italy, Ettore Schmitz was absorbed in petty matrimonial politics. He made an issue of principle out of the matter of Livia's finery, even though none of his family or friends agreed with him. He found his father-in-law Gioachino the best person with whom to discuss his conjugal wrangles. They often played cards or dominoes or bowls together, and Gioachino's calmness did Ettore good, though he suspected a touch of irony in it. Gioachino maintained a sagely neutral stance towards his daughter and son-in-law: 'He reflected quite a while, then said that women took a childish delight in their dresses and jewellery. Finally he remarked, "I'm content as long as they leave me in peace."' Ettore in his turn remarked to Livia: 'I feel pretty superior to him as a husband and I wish both of us never to hear any such utterance.' As far as he was concerned, his wife must be above suspicion: 'Were it otherwise, your absence would be irremediable.'[105]

Ettore was for imposing upon Livia a freedom of his own devising: 'My family, root and branch, *must* be regulated according to my tastes in so far as that is compatible with your personal freedom of character and beliefs, which I want you to retain, so much so that I have set out to free you from scruples of any kind.' Livia was to be free, then, as long as she became more like her husband:

Yet I stay the way I am because the only means of holding you is to make you as like me as possible. I believe that already you resemble me more than you think, and every time I perceive that, I rejoice; I suffer intensely when I come up against the ideas in you which I do not love. I suffer like an artist who has let himself be carried away into making vulgar brushstrokes in false colours.[106]

Livia immediately replied—for they exchanged letters every day—agreeing that husband and wife should grow ever more alike. This amounted to a tacit reaffirmation of her own rights, as she was not conceding that it was solely up to her to move towards him. But she added the conciliatory observation that her ideas had already come much closer to Ettore's. This battle between their two characters was never to result either in a victory of one over the other or in a complete understanding between them.

On this occasion both Ettore and Livia underwent a veritable nervous crisis—their strong mutual attachment made painful by separation and acrimonious by shortage of money.

Ettore's letters were far less affectionate than Livia's, though concern for her well-being was apparent in every letter he wrote her and whenever her letters were late in arriving he quickly grew agitated. On 21 May he wrote that Livia's sister Nella had sent her (from Bulgaria) a present of 'such a fine pair of boots that I flushed to think that she had intended them as a present to me too', and continued: 'The trouble is that I don't care for the boots on their own. I need the foot inside them and everything else all the way up.'[107]

On 25 May a letter from Livia brought tears to his eyes.[108] Only a few days later did he confess the resentment he had been feeling towards her. He had even thought to vent this resentment and his 'by then already pent-up desires' by resorting to another woman whom he knew, from whom he was not likely to pick up any diseases. He felt fully justified in so chastising his wife. The only reason for his having held back from doing so was repugnance.

Livia was by now herself exasperated and resentful at Ettore's jealousy and at his complaints that she was a frigid lover and indifferent towards him. She vented her own feelings of jealousy, and mentioned that as a bride she had been warned to beware of still waters. Woe betide Ettore if she discovered that he had transgressed just once. So when she received his letter, though she managed to control her feelings to the point of addressing him as 'Mon très cher Ettore', her bitter reaction left him in no doubt about the consequences if he carried out his threat. If Ettore thought he had shown extraordinary frankness, the unaffected and outraged love expressed in Livia's reply made him look mean and nasty, and he had to face her reproach for having jeopardized her recovery by tormenting her with his monstrous egoism. As it was Pentecost, she turned for comfort to the Holy Spirit.

Ettore now changed his defence from 'repugnance' to 'heroism'. He tried to smooth the matter out by appealing to the sexual double standard: a dodge hardly worthy of the man who had tried to make his wife read Bebel's *Woman and Socialism*. He was also forgetting that a few days earlier he had told Livia that his depression was 'taking away my (physical) need if not my desire', so that 'I resemble the queen who was fitted with a chastity belt.' He even doubted whether his 'heroism' was well-advised, but he tried to correct the word 'desire' which he had incautiously used, and he warmly avowed to Livia that he would always remain faithful.[109]

This exchange of letters shows Livia as being in some degree the conscience of Ettore Schmitz. On the other hand, Ettore caught Livia out in keeping quiet about the 'jeunes gens' at Salsomaggiore. She and the Venezianis had avoided mentioning them so as not to arouse his jealousies, for which Ettore acknowledged himself at fault. By way of partial compensation, he embarked on yet another fantasy about his own death and Livia's remarriage to a husband younger and wealthier than he, but one who would never write her such letters.[110]

So Ettore, in almost childish fear of losing the love of his *bon-bon*, dreamt of punishing her by going with another woman and actually did punish her by mentioning it: only Livia's threat really to withdraw her love brought him around. A great deal of Ettore's trouble however, was undoubtedly due to that highly sensitive part of his ego—his wallet.

Livia's visit to Salsomaggiore had not been Ettore's idea, nor her own, nor even her doctor's, but Olga's. Ettore and Livia had pretended to be undecided, so as to encourage Olga to help them out financially and so avoid taking out any more loans at 8 per cent.[111] Wishing to save further expense, Livia had dissuaded Ettore from seeing her all the way to Salsomaggiore, only to blame him later when the same consideration led him to turn down her plea that he should somehow borrow enough money, from anybody except Olga, to come and visit her. This squabble reduced the two of them to the verge of despair, and went on almost to the end of Livia's stay at Salso. In the end, fearing that she might stay on there longer, Ettore threatened that if she did not return home on the agreed date he would go and live with Ottavio in Vienna or even in Berlin with Veruda.[112]

Livia's medical treatment was not Ettore's only financial burden. Since his marriage he had gambled away 600 florins on the stock market and now formally promised Livia to stop: his father had caught stock market fever after twenty years' abstinence, and it had completed his ruin.[113] Ettore was also worried about having stood guarantor for the debt incurred by his bank colleague Halperson: 'It would be a good idea for me to punish myself by bashing my head against a wall until my doltish brain, which led me do such a daft thing, spills out.' He was almost less worried about the money than the possibility of being let down by a trusted friend. If this happened it would 'paralyse my every activity and all my faith in human character.' But perhaps Ettore was once again trying to make Livia feel sorry for him. Or was it, on the contrary, to save her anxiety that he subsequently made light of the Halperson business?[114] He was still floundering in his attempts to pay off the last 120 florins of the debt in 1900.[115]

Money would have been short even without that extra blow. Livia quickly wrote to Ettore telling him to send on 100 lire which her mother owed her and 150 florins from Adolfo: Ettore sent her his month's pay of 200 lire. He said that Olga would send her 100 lire herself, and encouraged Livia to ask for more. As for Adolfo, his business affairs were still going badly and he was having to borrow 600 florins from Olga. Ettore was so badly off that he contrived to get himself invited to free meals with his sister Paola, whilst finding excuses for not going with her to the theatre. He couldn't afford to pay right away for the nineteen volumes of Dumas père's Les Mohicans de Paris, which Livia asked him to send her, and he could not even spare 1.20 florins to buy frames for the photographs which she had taken to Salso. Nella's expensive presents, 'a magnificent pair of shoes and a magnificent silver cup' for Letizia and the boots for Livia, put him to shame. One day he was caught in a downpour in the working-class district of San Giacomo: he couldn't afford a cab and there wasn't a tram in sight, so his new suit was soaked and ruined.

On one occasion, poverty proved a blessing for Ettore. Deeply engrossed in reading Livia's latest letter in the street, he collided with a passer-by (he said that the passer-by collided with him). Ettore ran after the fellow, who turned out to be a white-bearded, craggy-faced Englishman. Being unable to understand what he said, Ettore did not give him the intended caning but exchanged cards with him and went to look for a second for the duel. Fortunately his cousin Ziffer established that the Englishman had meant no offence. Ettore could never in any case have afforded the 200 florins which the duel would have cost him. Livia could hardly believe that he had really meant to fight one.[116] Perhaps Ettore felt inspired by the example of Felice Cavallotti, the Italian radical leader and an unswerving Irredentist, who had died just two months earlier fighting his thirty-second duel. Even a year after this incident, Ettore expressed disdain for a friend of his who seemed far too careful in avoiding a duel.[117]

Money was so short that Ettore was considering leaving his job at the bank (or so at least he said), even if it meant giving up his pension, and going into partnership with Adolfo with 30,000 florins of fresh capital to broaden the base of the business, if only he could raise the money. He wanted to be financially independent so that he could go on writing. He was also torn, he said, between his calling as a writer and his family responsibilities. He wouldn't mind leaving the bank, especially as the manager, Fortunato Vivante, behaved unpleasantly towards him.

Livia tactfully reminded him that he might be able to join the Veneziani firm. Here, too, Ettore seemed divided, or equivocal. He thought he had practically no such chance and that even if he did join Gioachino he would not be much better off; but on the other hand he empowered his friend Pietro Sandrini to ask Olga straight out what his chances were.[118] The curious thing is that throughout this month's correspondence there was never a mention of the imminent publication of *Senilità*, whose serialization in *L'Indipendente* began on 15 June and which appeared in book form a few weeks after the final instalment of 16 September. Svevo always made out that he was counting on a literary success to encourage or enable him to devote himself more fully to writing. Yet on 26 May he already despairingly took the 'demise' of his 'aesthetic dreams' for granted.

In his state of disarray during Livia's absence, and on her advice, Ettore took some bromide powder every day. It didn't work:

It is a long-standing vice of mine that when things happen in my life which may mean the start of a new period, what I might call a break in my life, I withdraw into myself and review the whole of my past life and its immense nullity in itself as well as the total vanity of every effort I have made in 38 years' existence.[119]*

His condition grew worse: 'I have a depression which makes me feel like a

* It may be thought suggestive that Ettore, who was not yet thirty-seven when he wrote this, should add a full eighteen months to his 'existence'.

powerful steam engine which is completely run down, in fact rusty and abandoned.' He couldn't write to Livia without getting into a rage and would tear
up three or four letters before he managed to produce one that was a little
milder. At night he was plagued by mosquitoes. He got little sleep, but when
he did sleep there was no waking him, even for the wet-nurse, whom he could
not get on with ('Either she goes or I do'). He tried sleeping in the afternoon
but wandered 'from fantasy to fantasy, getting irritated and agitated like a
raving lunatic'.

On Sunday 22 May he awoke to 'a sort of tap on the nose': it was a fledgling,
which after a bit of panic found its way out of the window and was immediately
'snatched up by its mother and carried on to the coach-house roof': Svevo
cheered up in relating this incident to his wife and concluded: 'It's not easy for
every bird to find its hole', with a *double-entendre* which in Italian cannot be
missed. Apart from bromide and fledglings, he found that weight-lifting also
calmed him down: 'If anyone enters my room, I am to be found hunched down
on my knees or stretching up on tiptoe holding the bar up high over my head
or possibly lying on the floor and holding the weights straight up in line with
my stomach.' But he remained in a state of stress:

Every day there are periods, by no means short, when I feel profoundly ill. A trifle will
set off my turbulent fantasies and I have images of you which you would never forgive
me for if I disclosed them. I sat down to dinner yesterday in excellent humour and with
a good appetite. Someone made a perfectly harmless joke which made me laugh too;
but shortly after I felt as it were a noose closing round my throat, I left my food and
flung myself on the sofa exhausted as though by a struggle with things or beings greater
than myself. Paola laughed at me and I denied that you might have been the cause of
my distress, as I always do. I had already somewhat recovered when Pepi related that
his doctor had prescribed Roncegno [a health resort] but that Natalia wouldn't go on
her own to Carlsbad [the famous Bohemian spa] and that therefore he was giving up
Roncegno, seeing that he couldn't take two months off. It made me ill and it took me
an effort not to write some very sharp words in my letter to you yesterday. By evening
I was choking. I saw our carriage in town but preferred to walk home.[120]

That 'struggle with things or beings greater than myself', of which he always
denied Livia to be the cause, though knowing her to be so, suggestively bears
out a sense of trauma of which Ettore himself, clearly the prototype of Zeno
Cosini, was at least half aware. There is more than enough to explain this
trauma: emotional and financial insecurity and his sense of being at a social
disadvantage; his difficulties in living up to his own idea of himself as an
emancipated man embarking on marriage as 'a free Socialist union'; his feeling
that he had failed as a writer.

But he was not alone in his troubles. Ettore was surrounded by invalids.
Everybody was undertaking treatment and going off to health resorts. He was
the only imaginary invalid, whose afflictions the doctors were incapable—and
would not dream—of treating. He was an imaginary invalid especially by
contrast to his wife—or so at least it appears at first sight. Livia displayed

moral health, steadfastness, good sense. But, as Zeno Cosini observes of his wife Augusta, to analyse health is to convert it into a malady. And what was Livia's mysterious malady? What was the pain in her leg which tormented her upon her arrival at Salso? What about the faintness which made her put off some of her immersions there? And the cramps and pains in her stomach, viscera, chest and back?[121] She consulted the gynaecologist De Bassini in Padua, on her way back from Salsomaggiore. Whatever his verdict, Livia never had another child after Letizia but kept Ettore in hope of one until at least 1912. Her gynaecological problems kept taking her back to Salsomaggiore. And why was she to order Ettore to burn all her letters to him? There is no need to psychoanalyse Livia, but much that remains unexplained about her behaviour seems to be obscurely bound up with her relationship with Ettore—perhaps because of their difference in outlook and intellect, age, experience and religion. Perhaps Livia was torn between desire and guilt in marrying an atheistical Jewish cousin with a 'foul past', a brilliant and ineffectual dreamer, in the teeth of her mother's disapproval. Perhaps she regretted the loss of her youthful freedom, or she was trying to come to terms with motherhood. Perhaps something eluded her: a side of Ettore which she never fathomed.

Ettore and Livia both independently agreed that she had come a good bit closer to him in her thinking. Their letters during this first separation and successive ones shed some light on Svevo's tutorship and on his intellectual interests and activities. Ettore betrayed a certain impatience with his wife's mental rigidity, but also a rather comic patriarchal puritanism which led him to try to shield her, as if that were necessary, from corrupting influences, such as Bourget's novel Crime d'amour, or Meilhac and Halévy's Frou-frou.[122]

Livia also read Zola's La Faute de l'abbé Mouret, 'en Italien, malheureusement', and later Fogazzaro's Piccolo mondo antico, which she found 'très bien écrit'. (Svevo, of course, was always dismissed in Trieste as a poor writer).[123] Ettore, for his part, was reading Darwin and made a joke of his theory on crossbred horses at the expenses of his friend and fellow bank-clerk Max Ehrlich, nicknamed Spofford on account of his supposed resemblance to a famous racehorse. A remark about calling Livia from afar reveals that he had at some time read Jane Eyre.[124] Lack of money made him miss the showing of Langmann's play Bartel Turaser, but on Saturday 21 May he borrowed two florins from the Venezianis' clerk, Schreiber, and accompanied Paola and her daughter Sara to the Fenice theatre to see two one-act plays: La guerra by Sabatino Lopez and Before Death by 'my friend Strindberg'. The former, he said, 'although not up to much, shook me profoundly, first of all on account of Zaccone's [Ermete Zacconi's] masterly performance and secondly because of my receptivity to certain emotions and heartaches.' Svevo was very much alive to the weaknesses of Lopez's stagecraft and the aisance with which Zacconi overcame them. As for Strindberg's play, he merely gave a synopsis and drew a jocularly anti-feminist conclusion.[125]

Ettore was also attending—in his rare free moments—to the Banco Modello, the art school founded by Revoltella on whose board he served, and to the plans for the Italian-language Trieste girls' school, whose aims were of course nationalistic as well as educational.[126] For the rest, the letters gave some idea of the ordinary run of his life among family, friends and working colleagues. His friend Giulio Ventura took a surprise photograph of him in the street; Olga (when she was not at the factory at Murano, near Venice) whirled around him in her factory clothes while he wrote his letters to Livia, or else she played the piano with her daughter Fausta; Ettore went to see his sister Paola in town or his other sister Natalia Vivante, out of town; he played with his daughter Titina, not yet one year old but already bent on walking, or rather running, in an attempt to race the Great Dane, Tyras. Titina was happiest spouting water in her bath. She already had four teeth and was jealous of her baby cousin Nico Bliznakoff, who was staying at the Venezianis while his parents were in Bulgaria. Whilst Livia was away, Ettore and his daughter had the opportunity to get used to each other, and Ettore had her in bed with him every morning.

At last, on 7 June, Livia returned to Trieste. Summer had brought the good weather at last. On 16 June Ettore had to start conducting examinations at the Revoltella Institute at 7 a.m.[127] Then for two months he was free from his tiresome teaching job. He would have more time to spend with his wife and daughter and perhaps to write.

32

AS A MAN GROWS OLDER: THE PUBLICATION OF *SENILITÀ*

The day before the examinations, the first instalment of Svevo's new novel, *Senilità*, appeared in *L'Indipendente*. Circumstances—political and literary, locally and in Italy—were unpropitious. People in Italy, as we have seen, had other things besides literature on their minds in 1898, and, of course, so did people in Trieste. Before the last instalment of the novel appeared, on 16 September (followed by its publication in book form and a few reviews), there was some political trouble. On 2 August, the shipyard workers came out on strike in response to the arrest of one of their leaders. On 6 August, Giuseppe Garibaldi's son Menotti visited Trieste amid the excitement of the nationalists. On Sunday 10 September, the Empress Elizabeth of Austria was assassinated at Geneva by the Italian anarchist Luccheni. When the news reached Trieste, violent demonstrations against the Italian nationalists broke out. On the Sunday, while the wealthy Italians, disregarding the official mourning for the

Empress's death, were sitting outside the cafés of Piazza Grande, the mob swarmed upon them, drove them away and finished off their abandoned coffees and ice-creams. This episode became legendary and earned the Austrian sympathizers the derisive nickname of *leccapiattini*, or 'lickers-up'.[128] Though they disclaimed any part in the affair, Svevo is said to have applied that nickname to the Triestine Socialists, whom the Irredentists saw as being stooges of Vienna.[129]

In the years 1896–9 the literary world of Trieste found a platform in the little journal *Trieste Letteraria*. It was not Svevo's scene. His name or pseudonym does not appear among all the other literary names of the city: Silvio Benco, Alberto Boccardi, G. Italo Boxich, Adele Butti, Nella Cambon-Doria, Willy Dias, Elda Gianelli, Haydée, Dr Gian-Giacomo Manzutto, Riccardo Pítteri, Cesare Rossi, Elisa Tagliapietra-Cambon. There were two contributors from Italy: Camillo Antona-Traversi and Mario Rapisardi.

The Italian literary climate was inclining more and more towards Decadence. The Florentine *Il Marzocco*, which in 1896 joined the aestheticizing Roman journals *Cronache bizantine* and *Convito*, paid little or no attention to Darwin, Comte, Spencer, Lombroso or Nordau, nor to Baudelaire, Nietzsche or Weininger, much less to Marx, Labriola, Morris or Turati. Even Shakespeare, Shelley, Shaw and Turgenev were virtually ignored. Zola received some attention; Tolstoy slightly more, after 1900; there was some Chekhov and, from 1897, the occasional short story by Gide, and also some pieces by Gaio (Adolfo Orvieto), Neera (Anna Radius) and Gargano. But the forefront was held by Croce and D'Annunzio, Pascoli, Conti and Ojetti, Vittoria Aganoor-Pompilj and Adolfo Albertazzi, Diego Angeli and Enrico Corradini. The journal was very markedly aesthetic and the 'Prologo' to the first number on 2 February 1896 positively rejected the patriotic themes as well as the scientific, historical and documentary approach of the older generation of writers in favour of a new Idealism in art. The journal, in other words, championed that very cult of art for art's sake for which Svevo had always shown so little sympathy. That this prestigious journal reviewed *Senilità*, though negatively, itself constituted a minor success. For no apparent reason except the unlikely one that he may simply have been unaware of them, Svevo never mentioned either this or other reviews of the first edition of *Senilità*. 'No Italian periodical paid any attention to it, except *L'Indipendente* which had serialized it', reads *Profilo autobiografico*, more than usually wide of the mark.[130]

Incidentally, and interestingly, a piece in *Il Marzocco* points to one of the possible genealogies of *La coscienza di Zeno* and its hero. On 12 February 1898 Enrico Corradini reviewed Ugo Ojetti's best-selling novel *Il vecchio* (The Old Man). The anti-hero of this book is an old egoist called Alessandro Zeno who fantasizes about the destruction of the world: 'He, the last, will be the supreme winner, because all other men, all his enemies, will have died before his eyes, before him. He, the Last!' In the finale of *La coscienza di Zeno*, Svevo was to shift the theme of the end of the world suggestively to the very height of the

Great War. He found his raw materials not only in life but in literature, which is part of life.

L'Indipendente was the first to review *Senilità*, on 12 October 1898. The review, by the twenty-four-year-old Benco, reproved the thirty-seven-year-old Svevo for his youthful naivety of language and style and found the title baffling and inappropriate, but appreciated Svevo's observation of the inner workings of the mind, his humour and the delineation of Amalia, dwelling on the autobiographical basis of the novel.

Two other Irredentist newspapers reviewed the novel. On 15 October, *L'Idea Italiana*, of Rovigno in Istria, found the title strange and the contents repugnant. On closing the book, the reviewer wanted to drive Angiolina from his memory. For all its moral indignation, this is the most interesting review of any of Svevo's novels, not only as a typical response from one of its earliest readers in 1898, but also because it showed a great deal of perception. It precisely caught the 'common and vulgar' quality (which makes Svevo's work so profoundly and bravely representative), though finding the novel inartistic because of it. It condemned Emilio Brentani and deplored not only Angiolina's vices, but her obtuseness; it expressed disapproving horror at Amalia's fate. But the reviewer completely failed to realize that the author intended to produce these moral reactions not against the book and its characters, but against the world of which the reviewer himself acknowledged the book to be an authentic portrayal. Readers (especially in Italy) looked for what they insisted on calling 'the ideal', or 'ideals' in the plural. In this respect the provincial reviewer of Rovigno was no more naïve than the exquisitely cultured reviewer of *Il Marzocco* or the celebrated Paul Heyse. They all sang the same refrain. A pity, because the reviewer for *L'Idea Italiana* was almost unique in recognizing the 'truth' of *Senilità*, its 'lived sensations' and even the power of its style despite the occasional clumsiness or dialectism.

Ferdinando Busoni wrote in *Il Corriere di Gorizia* on 18 October, warmly praising *Senilità* as an advance on *Una vita*, its 'love of the intimate analysis of the human psyche, scrupulously truthful though with a slight tinge of pessimism'; but he too turned his moral critique against the central character rather than against the state of reality which he embodies, denoted by the title. Busoni makes no mention of the novel's supposed stylistic shortcomings. In fact, of the six reviews of this first edition of *Senilità*, Benco's, apparently so magnanimous in conceding praise, was the least forthright, the least generous, and the least perceptive, with the exception of an outright condemnation of *Senilità* which came on 12 November in the Milan Socialist newspaper *Il Sole*. This consisted of a single sentence: 'Italo Svevo's analytical novel of passion, which indulges in the details of the psychology of love, would gain from greater attention to form and from reducing its largesse of striking phrases.' The reviewer, F. Cameroni, seems to have got Svevo mixed up with D'Annunzio and the Decadents. *Il Corriere della Sera*, this time, ignored Svevo completely; while Paul Heyse, in a letter to Svevo of 26 November, expressed some impatience: Svevo had squandered his undeniable talents as a psychological analyst and an acute observer on a subject unworthy of him which had already received a masterly treatment in Turgenev's *Petrushka*.[131]

Svevo's friend Haydée (Ida Finzi) brought out her review of the novel on 11 February 1899 in the influential Genoa *Supplemento del Caffaro*. She took Svevo's pseudonym as her cue for pointing out the effects of his German education, excusing the occasional woodenness of his style and praising his 'depth of thought and implacable sureness of analysis . . . which are foreign to us Latins'. With warmth and intelligence (and also with generosity, considering that she was no mean novelist in her own right and therefore in some sort a Triestine rival of Svevo's), she went on to summarize the various aspects of the novel's plot and characterization and particularly praised Svevo's 'impersonality tinged with irony' and his impressively un-literary, 'anti-aesthetic' treatment of Amalia's death.

But aestheticism, not impersonality or irony, was now the vogue. The review most significant of the cultural climate was therefore the last of the reviews of *Senilità*, which appeared in *Il Marzocco* on 12 March 1899 and was signed 'A. C.':

If the audacity of the plot and the power of some naturalistic scenes—by which the author chose to cast a murky glow over this second novel—were matched by nobility and power of form, I would be glad to call this a successful work confirming his gifts as a good story-teller—which we had already perceived when we were given his other novel *Una vita* to read—and adding new ones. The observation of life and the naturalistic representation in some scenes and passages, though they frequently recur in life, do not render the writer perfect unless he is able to lend them the light of poetry, depth of observation and harmony of line: in portraying pure reality, one sole aspect of life is manifested to the reader, while there are so many, such various and manifold faces to things which the poet is vouchsafed to illumine by his art!

While *Il Sole* criticized Svevo for being too D'Annunzian, *Il Marzocco* criticized him for not being D'Annunzian enough!

Six reviews are not much. But they are not total silence. Why then does *Profilo autobiografico* ignore them and remark: 'The silence which greeted his work was too eloquent'?[132] Svevo protests too much in justifying his quarter of a century's failure to publish. Looking back in 1928, when he wrote the *Profilo*, he needed to satisfy himself even before anyone else. A quarter of a century wasted! What a betrayal of his inmost nature as a writer! So he built up his already prepared myth of heroic self-denial: 'It was an iron resolve.' Literature had to be sacrificed to life. The *Profilo* dwells lengthily upon the dejection ensuing from his lack of success, and the 1927 preface to *Senilità* also contains an unhappy attempt to justify having given up his literary ambitions, and even attributes the failure of *Senilità* to its 'plain binding'.[133] Svevo must have realized that was a pretty feeble excuse, and did not repeat it when he wrote the *Profilo* the following year.

On 24 May 1899, when *Senilità* was still far from having sunk into oblivion,

Ettore accepted Olga Veneziani's invitation to enter the underwater paint business. He must have hoped that he would still have enough spare time to go on writing. And in fact, even after 1899, there was hardly a year in which Svevo did not produce some substantial literary work.

The *Profilo autobiografico* does all it can to play down *Senilità*'s literary pretensions: 'This novel was not originally conceived for publication ... Here are no philosophic intentions, nor are human weaknesses, first and foremost those of Brentani, sublimated by a theorem.'[134] Svevo seems here to want to stress that *Senilità* is more spontaneous and unaffected than *Una vita*; and in fact *Senilità* does lack the heavy, four-square structure that could be sensed in *Una vita*, particularly in the way in which the various milieu were juxtaposed. Here everything seems more fluid, the passing of time seems of itself to articulate the developing relationships between the main characters in their banal and fatal quadrille. Trieste's various locations appear to pre-exist the novel in their matter-of-factness, rather than to have been built up by the novel, as in *Una vita*. Svevo's very syntax has a new freedom and effortlessness. The play of colour in *Senilità*, ranging from Angiolina's golden glow to Amalia's and Emilio's shades of grey, is only the final mark of Veruda's artistic influence on Svevo, for Veruda it was who, with sublime unconcern, had dispensed with outline as an element or method of composition. *Una vita* was a good, solid novel, at once austere and subtly penetrating despite its heavier structure. If *Senilità* is a masterpiece, that is partly due to Umberto Veruda. Beyond that, it is a development of Svevo's characteristic method and language. The counterpoint between real events and the protagonist's fantasies has now become organic to the narration, part of its texture, no longer of demonstrative intent but, as it were, axiomatic—though continually taking the protagonist by surprise. As a result of this, or rather, dialectically related to it, the actual language of narration, whether in description or in introspection, objectivity and subjectivity, is pervaded throughout by the 'impersonal' language of analytical record. It impassively, scientifically, registers that counterpoint between actual facts, truth, reality and what is variously called 'dream', 'sentiment', 'falsehood'. This latter is articulated through the pretence and distrust that prevail between the characters in their relationships with one another, through their simulations and dissimulations, through the misunderstandings between their various egoisms and their various delusions, through their continual surprises at the revealing of the 'reality' of others which has previously been suppressed or disguised. It is a language which strives to present the most elusive motivation with the greatest possible clarity, a sounding-board of every level of consciousness and of the unconscious level also, which, in Amalia's delirium, draws on dream-activity with marvellous sobriety and insight. This portrayal of conflicting individual wills brings to the forefront—though without heavy-handed insistence—the actual power-relationships, whether psychological, sexual or social, which for Svevo are the key to the understanding of human reality and were for his earliest readers the real reason for their inability to accept him. The title *Senilità*, which literally indicates sexual impotence, more broadly indicates an impotence to realize new human relationships based on affection rather than domination. Even though the title baffled and put off readers and critics both in 1898 and after 1925, Svevo stuck to it, on 'very strong grounds', as he wrote in the preface to the second edition. 'I would feel I were mutilating the book if I deprived it of its title which I think may explain and excuse a little. That title was my guide and I lived by it.'[135] I would guess that *Senilità* indicated for Svevo that period of his life before he established what he felt to be the fully human relationship with Livia.

As in *Una vita*, the autobiographical element is developed in *Senilità* without the slightest concession to naïve self-gratification. Emilio Brentani is and is not Ettore Schmitz. He is certainly not Italo Svevo. He is that part of Ettore Schmitz that Ettore Schmitz must expunge in order to become Italo Svevo and view himself from above. Comparison between the novel and the letters which Ettore Schmitz sent to Livia at Salsomaggiore, with their prevarications and fantasies, their attempts at bullying and self-justification, enables us to judge how far Emilio Brentani was Ettore Schmitz, whom Italo Svevo impassively unmasks and condemns. As Svevo was never to tire of affirming, he succeeded in being himself only in his books. This is what writing meant for Italo Svevo.

33

DOMESTICITY

Giulio Césari was to claim that *Senilità* won and held a considerable readership in Trieste's circulating libraries.[136] Again Svevo gave away most of the copies: one signed copy was traded to the writer Giuseppe Cassieri in 1938 by a ship-caulker's daughter in Trieste in exchange for an armful of carobs.[137]

The four main characters were based on people who were known in Trieste. (Amalia, the fourth, was based on the sister of Svevo's friend Cesare Rossi, Maria.)[138] The Venezianis, and Olga in particular, with her social ambitions and churchy respectability, were pretty embarrassed by the novelist in the family who had published an autobiographical novel about a luridly bohemian love-affair which even a sophisticated writer like Heyse regarded almost as filth.[139] They did all they could, upon stylistic pretexts, to discourage anyone from reading the book. Years later, Svevo confided to Umberto Saba that as a writer he certainly did not feel at home with the Venezianis, and to Guido Voghera that even his wife and daughter, though strongly attached to him, simply did not understand his mania 'for persisting in trying to be a writer without being able to write Italian'.[140] Livia writes that 'He kept his disappointment bottled up and only rarely let it break out,' but that he still read every night, his preferences now going to Ibsen, Dostoevsky, Tolstoy.[141]

So Svevo really seemed to have given up his 'sogni estetici', dreams of literary success. The names of Ibsen, Dostoevsky and Tolstoy illustrate the difficulties of mapping the extent of his reading. For the turn of the century, they are not at all surprising authors for anyone to read, yet Svevo's *Profilo* does not mention them, whilst in all his other writings he barely gives a casual mention to Ibsen and Tolstoy and none at all to Dostoevsky. He struggled to accept his failure as a writer: 'It means people don't understand. There's no point in my writing or publishing.'[142]

In May 1899 Livia paid another visit to Salsomaggiore. Ettore did not repeat the scenes of the previous year. He was looked after almost too well by his sister-in-law Nella, who had returned from Bulgaria with her husband Marco. Their children Vela, Nico and Olga were now all at Villa Veneziani. Ettore reciprocated Nella's attentions after dinner by offering to play her favourite game of dominoes. With Marco he carefully concealed his true feelings, which was 'neither pleasant nor easy'. He regarded Marco as a 'boy' and reported that he thrashed little Olga 'well and truly, that is quite differently from the way I thrash Titina'. Marco appears to have outraged the Venezianis by his treatment of Nella, but Ettore did not witness any rows between them, and found Marco 'a good devil all in all and pretty harmless if you know how to handle him', though there were 'a few gaps in his intelligence'.[143]

There were the usual scenes between Gioachino and Olga. The former had planned a new factory near Servola for about 10,000 florins, but after detailed drawings completed with Marco's help the projected expenditure shot up to 20,000 or 25,000 florins. This amount alarmed Ettore almost as much as it did Olga, but he managed to pacify her by suggesting that it could be amortized over a few years' trading.[144]

In yet another wrangle, Ettore took the part of two maids whom Nella and Olga wanted to dismiss. His trump card in his arguments was that Titina shouldn't be entrusted to strangers during her mother's absence, but when he pooh-poohed Nella and Olga's complaints against the maids his motives were doubted:

I. They were seen in the sun with their hats on, while the children were without them. II. They were both in Gigia's room the other night making a shindy. III. Antonia was heard exchanging some bold words with the coachman. From the way Olga looked when I declared that I think Antonia—the only one I have anything to do with—seems well-mannered enough, I gathered that there were fears for my virtue. I must say that so far I have found her perfectly reserved and have not caught a single glance inviting me to take liberties with her. As for myself, I need hardly say anything. IV. Nella suspects that when Nico doesn't want his milk Antonia or the other girl drinks it up.[145]

The following day Ettore reported that 'Nella saw with her own eyes some meat which had just been cooked set aside by Luzia to take home with her', but this time Nella showed herself to be as humane as Ettore:

Nella didn't let Luzia know she'd been found out and quite rightly. It's only natural that a poor devil like her, whose daughter is virtually starving to death, should steal. She ought to get a thrashing if she didn't.[146]

The servants went on giving trouble for years. A year later Ettore felt obliged to give Maria a dressing-down in Olga's presence whilst hoping that the maid 'realized I had nothing against her'.[147] Olga's persecution of the servants became legendary and in 1913 Svevo parodied her in the character of Amelia in the play *Atto unico*.

Farcical mishaps kept befalling Ettore. One day one of his bootlaces snapped as he was striding down the Corso, to reveal his not-so-white stocking beneath. He immediately got himself new bootlaces and 'a pair of canary-yellow boots which match my face magnificently' and cost him eight florins. He now felt 'unbalanced with so much black on top' (hat or beard, his head being now nearly bald) and light colours below, and the next day went 'to pick up my usual panama which will give my appearance real harmony', only to find when he got home that evening, having spent so much of his scant income, that another pair of new boots (which, apparently, he did not remember ordering) had arrived for him.[148]

A few nights earlier, he was fast asleep when his bed collapsed beneath him. He moved into Livia's empty bed: 'I dreamt ... that the other bed started dancing for joy at having got rid of me. In the morning I laughed when I thought that the misadventure might have happened during our intimate leave-taking.' On 25 May he awoke with a headache after vying the evening before, out of 'national pride', with his German hosts, the Maiers, in drinking 'a certain Moselle wine with strawberries in a sort of glass barrel'. Another time, Ettore acted 'the role which is most alien to me' in an incident in which he advised a friend as to how he could, without risking a duel, issue a challenge to someone who had insulted him, and expressed his contempt towards his friend for not even daring so far.[149]

Family feeling, however, dominated Ettore's letters. He delighted in listening to his brother-in-law, Bruno, who, at the age of nine, already played the piano brilliantly. Adolfo Schmitz, not yet forty, was nearly always beset by ailments and couldn't start sea-bathing, despite the stifling hot weather. Ortensia's orphaned son, Umberto Ancona, born just after Titina, was departing with his father and stepmother. The saddest case of all was that of Ettore's paternal aunt, Peppina Tedeschi, now mercifully widowed, who had remarkably survived an attack of peritonitis. The poverty-stricken woman hadn't had a proper meal for a year, and the family clubbed together to help her: Ettore's share was two florins a month. While this was being arranged, Peppina's daughter Rita appeared. The ensuing scene was so distressing that, Ettore wrote, 'I went up to the window and looked outside so that she couldn't see me weeping like a calf.'[150]

Ettore gave Livia frequent reports on Letizia, that little egoist eager for Livia to get her some bon-bons, a flagellum Dei who hit, scratched and chased even her elder cousins, threw terrible tantrums and terrorized all and sundry, young and old, family and servants, beasts and humans.[151]

Ettore was doing his best to endure Livia's absence. He found that a machine which he had just bought for fifteen florins and with which he 'electrized' himself assiduously every morning to calm his nerves, was no substitute. 'You know how, after possessing you for three years, my desire has kept on increasing.' At first Livia did little to help him through: whilst his letters were nearly always pretty long, hers seemed to be the work of ten minutes so that Ettore took to calling them brevi—'briefs'. When at last Livia provided something by way of description of her life at Salsomaggiore, Ettore found that the local newspapers painted quite a different picture: the place was thronged with infantry officers and high society. Livia complained about the snobbish behaviour which she and her companion, Rosely Luzzato, had to endure from two countesses staying in the same hotel. This took her husband's mind off jealous thoughts. He gave her meticulous instructions on how to deal with the obnoxious ladies and railed against the petty nobility.

But his jealousy flared up when he heard that the mayor of Salsomaggiore had accompanied Livia to Milan, and then again on hearing that she had, without apparent necessity, spent two nights there. He complained that her family was the only one which allowed married women to travel without a suitable companion.[152]

Livia's medical consultation in Milan threw just enough light on her condition to make it even more puzzling. Her family doctor, Zeno Zencovich, believed that Livia could bear no more children, whilst Porro in Milan suggested 'drastic treatment' involving a second pregnancy, which would be very painful.[153]

Distracted by his own and other people's business and overcome by the heat, Ettore was looking for a cheap and quiet holiday for himself and Livia. The country house beside the verdigris factory at Dolina was in disrepair, so Gioachino said. At Murano they would be continually beset by the frenetic Olga, or else would have to spend every day at the Venice Lido. Three weeks at Levico, near Trento, at three and a half florins per day seemed preferable, for the sake of Ettore's health, even if it involved them in some little debt.[154]

34

ETTORE SCHMITZ THROWS IN HIS LOT WITH CAPITALISM

Ettore's money worries had diminished by 1899, but he was still looking for another job, or at least hoping to get a pay rise by bluffing the director of the Revoltella with a threat of resignation. The Institute was involved in an obscure political deal (which would have flown in the face of the avowed policy of the Liberal-National party and did not in fact come off) whereby the Vienna government would take it over from the Trieste Council. (Perhaps this was an early attempt to solve the problem of a national university for Austria's Italians.) Ettore would then be a State employee and might find himself politically shackled. He might also find his teaching hours incompatible with his working hours at the bank.[155]

He was not happy at the bank either, mostly because of his boss. Fortunato Vivante had made good at an early age and in spectacular fashion. He had joined the Vienna Unionbank as an ordinary clerk and in 1870 had already set up a branch in Trieste. He made this a major branch of a minor bank, largely by financing the huge Austro-Hungarian Lloyd shipping company and the construction of new port facilities. He later received the title of Count Villabella and was one of Trieste's wealthiest and most influential men, with a fortune of millions of crowns and one of the finest palaces in town.[156]

In 1899 he was courting. Ettore heard all about the courtship and Fortunato's magnificent presents, which contrasted all too forcefully with the engagement gifts which Livia had received from Ettore. Ettore's envy turned to resentment at being treated as Fortunato's errand-boy, and at the same time he felt he was being passed over as a candidate to join the Veneziani firm.[157]

Marco Bliznakoff, in fact, had been invited to do so, but could not make up his mind. Ettore complained about the life he was leading: up to work on the bank's business (which he brought home)[158] at seven; to the office at 8.30, and after that to the Revoltella; 'and then, devil take it, all my friends want favours, help and even money out of me.' He was tempted by the prospect of a job elsewhere. He wrote to Livia at Salsomaggiore:

In Milan a wealthy company is founding a school in two sections, a theoretical one and a practical one. I'm being offered the headship of the latter with a salary of 5,000 lire.— It's not much and it's not likely to be augmented but it represents only a few hours' work a week. Why not take a chance? In Milan I am much more likely to find some intelligent work to make up my livelihood than I am over here ...

I would like you to turn your mind right away to this proposition, the one that suits me best of any I have been made, because it is very likely that at the decisive moment I shall demand every sacrifice of you so as to help in liberating me.[159]

Indeed, if Svevo desired the freedom to write, this seems to have been the best opportunity that he had ever been offered. With her characteristic energy, Livia telegraphed straight back to Ettore suggesting a meeting in Milan where she had to go for her medical examination, and clearly hoping to discuss the post on the spot.

Ettore failed even to understand her telegram, and wired back to say that he could not leave work. Livia could hardly believe it: 'I'm dismayed that you wouldn't come to Milan. For it was you that wouldn't, wicked.'[160]

Ettore's ensuing letters were full of excuses: he was too worn out for a long journey, he should have applied for leave from the bank a fortnight in advance, and besides the matter wouldn't be decided till September, and then in Trieste not in Milan. Meanwhile: 'My last word was: I'd consider it at 6,000 lire.'[161]

Instead of Ettore, it was Olga who rushed to Milan on 19 May to see Livia. Mother and daughter must have exchanged notes about the possibility that the Schmitzes might move to Milan. Olga—presumably—did not want to be separated from her favourite daughter and now had proof that Ettore had not simply tried to marry into the family firm. Only two days earlier a letter had arrived from Gioachino's nephew Silvio Veneziani in Basle. Gioachino had lent him money to enable him to go to university, but now that he had got his degree Silvio claimed that the money was not a loan but a gift and politely refused to repay capital or interest.[162] Maybe Gioachino had financed Silvio through university on the understanding that he would join the firm after graduating, but Silvio now proposed to marry an heiress from Zurich and had already found himself a good position setting up a silk factory in Germany.

Marco Bliznakoff was still dithering. Not Olga. On 24 May, after her *tête-à-tête* with Livia in Milan, Ettore wrote to his wife: 'Olga has ordered me to hand in my resignation from the bank.' He calculated that his annual income would now be 3,230 florins (equivalent to 6,700 lire or around £260 or $1,500), including bonuses and his earnings from teaching at the Revoltella Institute. The Venezianis did not provide a pension,[163] and he was unwilling to get himself 'dismissed' so as to retain his pension rights.* He agreed to work at the bank for a couple of hours every day on full pay for a month or two longer, so as to obviate a hiatus in the bank's foreign correspondence.[165]

Marco followed Ettore into the firm within a few months, so that Ettore found himself, to his regret, ousted from the factory and driven back into office work or else into travelling about to deal with customers and supervise the application of paint in various maritime or lakeside ports.[166] The constant

---

* Later letters of Ettore's suggest that he was drawing some sort of pension.[164]

travelling was now Svevo's main bugbear: 'I'll surely be in for those frightful trips to Venice and of course—given Olga's character—she's hardly likely to let me take you with me.' He could never decide whether to cut down the travelling by spending a full week in Murano every month or go there for a couple of days each week in order not to be away from Livia for too long at once.[167] It did not as yet cross his mind that literature had to be sacrificed to paint, nor did that drastic proposition appear in his letters or other writings until *La coscienza di Zeno* had won him celebrity. It appears to be, therefore, a retrospective rationalization or myth promulgated most signally in his *Profilo autobiografico*. Svevo's 'silence' between the appearance of *Senilità* in 1898 and that of *La coscienza di Zeno* in 1923 applied to publication but not really to writing. Indeed not a year went past without something being written. Svevo lost, not faith in himself, but hope of reaching a public.

Veruda, on the other hand, saw immediately that in joining the family business the writer was capitulating. In a letter written from Vienna and imprecisely dated '1899', Veruda wrote:

Dear Ettore
I hear with real pleasure that you are exchanging your present position for another. But I do assure you that despite my not so much uncommon as unique intelligence I cannot conceive what it might be. I do appreciate that as far as money goes you would be very wise to leave the bank and devote yourself entirely to literature and I believe that to be your own intention; naturally, I enthusiastically endorse this notion of yours and believe that Livia will make a third in finding this notion of ours an excellent one ... what chapter are you up to? When do you go to press? ... You poor wretches who live in that noisome place which was and is my home by the merest chance, receive my most affectionate greetings,

ciao
Veruda.[168]

Livia's account of this important turning-point in Svevo's life fudges several points.[169] The firm did not pay him three hundred florins a month, nor did it at last give him financial independence, as she asserts: at least, certainly not for the first two years. Only in 1901 did Ettore give up his teaching at the Revoltella, and then only because the firm sent him on missions to distant parts. In June 1900 he was still struggling to pay off the Halperson debt.[170] During that same month he repeatedly hinted that he would like a holiday at Levico if only he were not so heavily in debt. In 1903 he was still complaining that it was too expensive to take Livia to Murano, where he had to work in the Veneziani factory.[171] As late as 1910 he felt unable to afford to take Livia and Letizia to visit Ottavio and his family in Vienna and in that same year it was still Olga who footed the bill for another of Livia's visits to Salsomaggiore.[172] He was no less 'enslaved' than he had been at the bank.

On the other hand, Livia's picture of the Schmitzes' family life is convincing:

he devoted himself entirely to his new job, dividing his day between factory and office. He rose at half-past six, went into the factory at seven and came home for lunch at midday. After lunch he treated himself to two hours' rest in the bosom of his family. A comfortable armchair and a good cigar were his sole desires. We often spent the evening at the theatre, which he adored. We were regular opera-goers and followed the straight theatre seasons at the 'Verdi'. His new job gave him a feeling of satisfaction because it brought him into contact with the factory workers in Trieste and Murano, among whom he liked to spend many hours, and it rescued him from the sedentary tedium of working in the bank. Literature was set aside, but not renounced. On one of the slips of paper on which his perpetual stream of thought took shape, in that same year he was still analysing his literary method.[173]

Here Livia quotes the well-known jotting of 2 October 1899, which begins: 'I believe, I sincerely believe, that there is no better way to learn to write seriously than to scribble something every day'; and which significantly goes on—a year after the appearance of *Senilità*—to discuss the making of a novel and to proclaim that 'there is no salvation outside the pen'.[174]

Livia confirms that Svevo had given up trying to share his literary aspirations and concerns with her. He deliberately spared her his own inner torments and showed her only a 'jovial face', hoping perhaps to draw strength from her uncomplicated buoyancy.[175]

In the early years, though, the Socialist, and perhaps the moralist in Svevo may have felt more ill-at-ease than the writer in such an archetypically capitalist household. Though diehard Irredentists, the Venezianis did not scruple to sell all the paint they could to the Austrian Navy. Admittedly, Austria remained until 1914 Italy's ally, but this very alliance was one of the prime targets of Irredentist indignation. The years to come were to see intense rivalry between the navies of many Powers, particularly Britain and Germany, and the Venezianis supplied paint to most of them. The Russo-Japanese war of 1904–5 was fought largely at sea and culminated in the destruction of the Russian fleet at Tsushima after its epic journey half-way round the world. The Great War must have brought considerations of this sort to a head for Svevo, though he made no explicit reference to them. His pacifist writings of 1918–19 do not address his immediate personal concerns.

Furthermore, it is quite possible that the Venezianis occasionally used under-hand methods to promote business, and thus contributed to the corruption which was especially prevalent in Italy. Gioachino's brother Carlo, who represented the firm in Italy, in 1896 paid over to Francesco Cucchi, Senator of the Kingdom of Italy, who had fought with Garibaldi, the sum of 200 lire in return for his help with a transaction in Genoa.[176] Perhaps this is to scent corruption where there was none: there is no evidence of any further instances of this kind, and in any case Ettore may have known nothing about such matters, which were handled by Olga and Gioachino. The firm did deal with the Italian Navy and it would seem that in 1900 the government was favouring a rival firm, Leoni. On 2 June Ettore's factory-hands in Murano were trying to get him out of bed by knocking at his window-shutters with their oars. He awoke out of a nightmare: 'Fast asleep as I was, I thought that Leoni was shelling the house under authority from Bettolo.'[177] The Genoese Admiral Bettolo was several times Navy Minister and came under suspicion of collusion with several firms, including the Terni steelworks, which drew huge profits from naval contracts around this time. In 1903 the trial involving Bettolo and Enrico Ferri, editor of the Socialist daily *Avanti!*, was the focus of national attention. Ferri had accused Bettolo of extortion and corruption, but Bettolo was acquitted and Ferri convicted for libel. Ettore eagerly followed the trial of 'that rascal Bettolo' in the pages of *Avanti!*[178] It is not wholly clear whether his hostility towards Bettolo was politically or commercially motivated.

For the time being the practical demands of his new occupation weighed more heavily upon him than its political or social morality. He was entrusted with the secret of the famous 'Moravia anti-fouling compound' and had to supervise all the stages of the 'brew', sometimes at Servola, sometimes at Murano. He was in charge of the workforce, had to keep the factory supplied with raw materials and despatch the finished product to the customers. He often had to deal directly with customers old and new, supervise and advise them in painting of hulls, and take charge of the relevent office work. All this under the watchful eye of Olga, who insisted on tight economy.

35

ETTORE AND LIVIA REJECT FREEDOM

Much as Svevo enjoyed dealing with his workmen, his unfinished stories 'Cimutti' and 'In Serenella',[179] set in Murano, express the awkwardness of his position: on the one hand, his bad conscience towards the workers as their boss; and on the other hand his sense of inferiority and dependence amounting to impotence *vis-à-vis* the owners of the firm. Ettore's letters from Murano, as well as the stories, mention the drinking sprees which meant that only half his workforce turned up on a Monday morning or following a feast-day: very upsetting for Ettore Schmitz, who was eager to turn out the required quantity of paint as quickly as possible so as to be able to get back to his home and family in Trieste. The letters often dwell on the toil and the hardships and hazards involved in manufacturing the paint. In the summer heat it was particularly sapping to stand near the boilers and cauldrons, and even though Ettore did not have to stay there continuously, as the workers did, he suffered considerably and was exhausted by the end of the day. The process involved the use of toxic elements such as verdigris and arsenic, and workers occasionally complained of poisoning. On one occasion Ettore cut a pretty sorry figure. It was in 1911, when there was cholera in Murano:

Zuccotto's throat is swollen. He says it's poison from the factory and is staying at home and drawing his daily wage of 4 lire.—Now I've sent for Dr Pasqualigo to pay him a visit, as Zuccotto's a crafty old lag and might expect to get paid for God knows how long.[180]

He may, however, have been diplomatically covering his own kind-heartedness against possible recriminations from Olga about the expense.

And indeed his difficulties with his workmen were trifling compared to those with Olga. Ettore complained repeatedly that Olga created chaos. She sent contradictory instructions, made a complete muddle of the order-book, sent Ettore off to Murano to manufacture paint without any raw materials. He said she suffered from a nervous condition, 'hysterical agitation', 'convulsions', and talked of her 'relapsing into her demented condition'. In 1906 at the Gare du Nord in Paris Ettore was reduced to tears when he discovered that Olga had given him the wrong tickets. He partly blamed her daughters for making her feel that she could not confide in them, and hinted that her condition was largely due to Gioachino's behaviour towards her.[181]

Olga carried business economy well beyond the point of niggardliness. Ettore often had to wrangle with her over his travelling expenses and had to pay heavily whenever he took Livia to Murano with him on his longer spells of duty. He would joke about Olga's tight-fistedness. Once he wrote to Livia about a great family dinner: 'We're contributing the smoked meats (5 fl.) the wine (50fl.) and dessert (30 fl.) and she's paying for the rest (1000 fl.) You see, we'll dine well.' Then, fearing that those figures (5, 50 and 30!) might stop Livia's heart, confessed that it was all a leg-pull. On another occasion he wrote from England: 'Ask Olga if she'd like me to send her a case of champagne which costs 3s. 6d. over here' (that is, 2 florins or just over 4 lire).[182]

Olga had devised an ingenious telegraphic code to transmit the most diverse and intricate instructions by a single word. ARRIGO meant: 'I'm arriving by boat. Send Nicoletto or a substitute to the dock at 6 a.m. in summer and at 7 a.m. in winter. The *sandalo* [large lagoon punt] should wait for me at the Riva di Santa Maria beside the station.' BRUNO was: 'hire three workmen for my arrival' and BIFOLCO asked for four. PARODIA: 'go on board at once to pick up an important parcel from the chief steward'; and PETRARCA: 'send for the letter which is due to arrive by the first post on Saturday at 8 a.m.'[183] Such economy must have greatly increased the opportunities for error and for muddled instructions.

The worst trials for Ettore were the innumerable trips between Trieste and Venice. He tried every means of transport and never came to terms with any of them—not the night boat on which he often lost sleep either because of the stuffiness or the din or rough sea; nor the day boat which cost him either a day's work or a rest day at home with Livia; nor the *Bummelzug*, the 'eternal' train that rounded the top of the Adriatic. In 1901 he was at the end of his tether after having paid no less than thirteen visits to Murano between January and May. The year before, when he had made a business trip to Vienna, he had written: 'I do confess that I am miserable while travelling', and on another occasion he wrote: 'My hair turns white at the thought of a continually roving life.' And again in 1901: 'it has nothing to do with age in my case ... because I remember that even as a boy I hated chasing from pillar to post and seeing all those new faces.' Yet right from the start he had to chase from pillar to post as far as Pola or Fiume or Peschiera on Lake Garda and soon he was to become a regular traveller on the line to London. Even so, in 1900 he would have liked the firm to pay for him to see Russia.[184]

When Ettore first joined the firm in 1899 it was Marco the engineer who went to supervise the factory in Murano, while Ettore the linguist had to deal with customers and supervise the painting of ships in various harbour towns, as well as run the Servola office. At home, at least, he was comfortable, as Livia had arranged him a private study where he could write and smoke without being disturbed and without disturbing her.

He commemorated taking possession of the new study with his 'Schri-bacchiature' (Jottings) of 30 September. Woman, he mused whimsically, must have been destined by nature for the role of wife. The second of October saw the short piece about scribbling and novel-making, the tenth of October his reflections about 'life being buried in the body before the body is buried within the earth' (the germ of the science-fiction tale 'Lo specifico del dottor Menghi', and on the twelfth came the idea for a play to which he gave the title *Degener-azione*, borrowed from Nordau, and for which he vaguely remembered having already written something (probably the fragment already discussed).[185] After that, there is no datable writing until 17–20 March 1900 when he drafted the three-page fragment 'Diario di bordo' (Ship's Log-book), Svevo's only literary foray into exotic adventure, inspired by the polar explorations of Amundsen, Byrd and Scott.[186] This does not amount to much writing, though of course he may have started or completed, and torn up, other pieces. On his thirty-ninth birthday, 19 December 1900, he was despondent about his prospects as a writer, 'the only business in which I can take pleasure. You have no idea how much I brood over this upon this 39th anniversary of my pointless life.'[187]

So in the two years following the appearance of *Senilità*, Svevo had written next to nothing and was once again close to despair over his literary vocation. These were indeed the two most barren years in his life. In 1901 he was to embark on 'a little play in just one act, very light-hearted', almost certainly *La verità* (The Truth), signed Ettore Muranese, later recast as *La parola* (The Power of the Word).[188] On 14 June 1903, he was at last to finish *Un marito*, at least eight years after his first draft.[189] Not a year went by from 1901 onwards without some tangible literary achievement.

He did not divulge this modest but continuing output. The sympathetic

Haydée, whom he described in 1899 as 'more decadent-looking than ever', pressed him about his writing, but he would reply with a smile that did not quite hide his wistfulness: 'Oh, I'm deep in underwater paint.' Svevo had put on his jovial mask. It was Haydée also who told Pier Antonio Quarantotti Gambini how Ettore and Livia once appeared at a Carnival parade at the Teatro Verdi dressed up as Othello and Desdemona—a joke about his obsessive jealousy. Ettore, his face blackened, looked like 'a parody of himself'.[190]

Ettore's letter of 1900 to his sister-in-law Frizzi Freiberger (Ottavio's wife), written in German, gives a good idea of the light-hearted affection between the two couples. He tossed off quip after quip about the respective merits of Livia's *crema fritta* (a sweet dish) and her other wifely attributes and was rewarded by a series of playful slaps from her. Livia and Ettore were hoping to take advantage of a business trip to pay a visit to Frizzi and Ottavio in Vienna, but Livia had to go to Salsomaggiore yet again while Ettore stayed briefly in Vienna.[191] Another time business took Ettore to Peschiera and Milan. 'Yesterday evening', wrote Livia, 'I cried out: "How dull things are without Ettore." Everyone exclaimed: "Thanks for the compliment", so from now on I shall confine myself to thinking it!'[192]

But, as Livia admits in her memoirs, she did not share the concerns of the writer Italo Svevo. Once in 1899, upon reading Ohnet's *Le Droit de l'enfant*, he remarked to her: 'comme c'est bête!' only to hear to his chagrin that Livia admired the book. In 1901 she was reading Ohnet's *Au fond du gouffre* and then went on to Masson's *Napoléon et les femmes*. She did however sometimes read books which were of greater interest to Svevo: Hugo's tragedies, Maupassant's *Mont-Oriol*, Cherbuliez's *Samuel Brohle* (though this was of similar cloth to Ohnet), *En ménage* by Huysmans, and Rovetta's *La signorina*. For his part, Svevo in 1901 was reading D'Annunzio's *Il fuoco* with great interest and distaste.[193]

In June 1900, Livia, then in Salsomaggiore with Letizia, took the initiative in relating literature to life in a very concrete way. She had complained to Ettore about the brevity and coolness of his letters and begged him to 'sugar the strawberries'. Poor Ettore, working at Murano, was too tired in the evenings even to make the short boat-trip into Venice to meet Veruda, and had to content himself with the society of his cousin Gilda Moravia who acted as secretary-housekeeper at Murano and 'keeps me company as best she can'. But Livia's appeal drew from him a long and warm letter which ended with the promise of another child. Livia replied: 'Your own idea coincides with my secret intentions, inspired by Zola's *Fécondité*. Read it, and then we'll discuss it.[194]

Livia and Ettore returned to this subject frequently, and not only in letters and conversation: in February–March 1901, twice in 1903 and twice in 1908, as well as, no doubt, on further unrecorded occasions, their hopes of second parenthood were raised only to be disappointed, so that Ettore called miscarrying 'the family affliction' and tried to outface it with pathetic humour.[195]

At Salsomaggiore again in 1900, after chiding Ettore for the lack of affection in his letters, Livia went on to complain once more about his groundless jealousy on her account: 'The fault lies with the beautiful women of pleasure whom you knew before your marriage.' She recalled with nostalgic regret 'our sweet and light-hearted engagement which lasted all too briefly'. She half seriously uttered a 'sentimental outburst'. 'In your *fin-de-siècle* love', she complained, 'there's no trace of the chivalrous love of old which demanded either the beauty's heart or death.' But she conceded: 'All that does not prevent you from being kinder than any husband can be or me from loving you with all my heart.' Tears sprang to her eyes on account of her sense of being unable to express all she felt towards Ettore, and she implored: 'Read in my heart, my dearest, if you can.'[196]

Ettore's real reply to this letter came several days later, after he had had a dream:

My dear my kind my sweet fair-haired Livia. I have just got out of bed perfectly rested after a long sleep. I dreamt you were dead and laid in your coffin upon my bed. You have no idea of the happiness I felt this morning when I found the sun shining brightly and the conviction, the certainty, that you were indeed at Salsomaggiore, but alive. The dream must have been very brief. The merest instant. The coffin was dark and you inside it were bright all over. In the room there was no one but you, dead and still, your eyes closed and your mouth shut tight with a stubborn expression, your mother rushing to and fro (even in a dream she can't keep still) bringing flowers to adorn you, and I pensively studying your physiognomy where I perceived a marked expression of reproof, I believe actually a reproof for my not having succeeded in bringing enough joy into the life which you had entrusted to my care. Your mother was working away in a hurry as she does in the office. She was never weary of arranging your long hair around your composed body like a golden river. I thought: For what purpose? But she rejoiced over you as though you were still alive ... I think I've already imagined you dead on other occasions. You know how the thought of death never leaves me. But never as vividly as this. I rejoice at the dream now as I do over everything that makes me feel more keenly the joy of possessing you. Possessing you lawfully, but honourably? It's clear that I shouldn't have married you. Today precisely now that I feel morally so close to you I realize that this remnant of youth which I have been able to dedicate to you can't sustain such intense feeling. During the first few days of your absence I experienced anew the old desire to seize you when you returned, lie beside you and exhaust all my strength, my whole life, in you. But today I'd like to have you with me, hold your hand and let you sleep without letting go your hand and wishing with the utmost intensity that it might help you sleep and rest and get better once and for all. I think with Tolstoy (who also reached this conclusion as an old man) that the easiest relationship is that between brother and sister . . . . . . conversely, when in my physical being it is the jealous husband who triumphs I feel like fulminating you. It is the husband in me that is your enemy ... All in all, I'm a neurotic little delinquent and it sometimes makes me feel more unhappy than you can imagine. When you come back I would like to control myself. I do not hope to do so, nor should you hope so, as far as jealousy goes. I let slip this phrase because it was precisely in that respect that I wanted to control myself. It's impossible.... But accept instead this formal promise from me ... I promise you formally that if in your life you were presented with the possibility of a great happiness, of the kind that to a young woman is worth life, tranquillity, virtue, conscience, in a word, everything, I would be able, following an explicit confession on your part (you know that I will tolerate everything except lies), to act in such a way that you could achieve that happiness. After making you this declaration which should make you feel freer, I feel my conscience more at ease ... I think that in this way, and only in this way, can our union be considered a free socialist union ... Thus, and only thus is it permissible to keep for oneself a woman as young as you are.

In the meantime, however, I kiss you and embrace you with my old affection, pure and impure. I don't feel the need to claim for myself the freedom which I grant you. Yours as long as you want him.

Ettore.[197]

If the years 1899 and 1900 were the most barren for the writer Italo Svevo, the the husband Ettore Schmitz demonstrates here that one can still 'write seriously' by 'scribbling something every day', not for the sake of 'making a novel' but to live. For Italo Svevo the distance between literature and life was always very small: so was that between life and literature for Ettore Schmitz, as in this letter of 17 June 1900. And we may recollect in passing that the 'neurotic little delinquent' aspiring to a 'free socialist union' picked up the very word (Tolstoy's) with which, to Livia's amazement, he had inaugurated their engagement in 1895: 'Sister!'

Livia's reply could not have been warmer: 'I refuse absolutely the freedom which you so generously allow me ... If I am beautiful, I want to be so for you, for you alone.'[198]

Ettore was now studiously giving Livia the impression that he had cooled towards Veruda. On one evening he was too tired to go and see his painter friend; next time it was Veruda who didn't turn up. Finally, on 30 May, they did meet: 'Veruda was delighted to see me,' Ettore reported; but he added only that they had sat at Florian's café on St Mark's Square to hear the splendid town band.

They also saw each other back in Trieste, but a brush between Veruda and Olga led Ettore to announce that he was going to give up his old friend, though he held Olga partly to blame. Livia indignantly retorted that Veruda had repeatedly offended both Olga and herself with his impertinence and 'the great airs which he gives himself', and urged Ettore to break off the friendship completely. Ettore made uneasy and undignified attempts to keep in with both Livia and Veruda. Perhaps he was also nettled by the latter's recriminations that he had capitulated as a writer, and he relished having the advantage, for once, of his flamboyant friend.[199]

One Sunday, 24 June, a chat with Veruda and other artist friends inspired him to set up a curious comparison between Livia and art:

I chatted or rather listened to chat once more about art and I found it as refreshing as a cool drink at the height of summer. But I feel so far away from them. They laughed at my nickname of frogman. Goodbye, dear Livia, you yourself are the most refreshing drink of all.[200]

Ettore's visits to Murano brought him face to face with the frequent deaths among the families of the workers. The first was that of Totoio, the child of the factory foreman, Nane Bravin. Ettore wrote on 6 March 1901: 'They're all ill. Totoio's unlikely to recover. He's had a fever for a long time and Nane showed me his pathetic little legs.' The child was probably undernourished and suffering from rickets, then widespread among the Italian labouring classes. On 31 March, Ettore was at his funeral: 'I was moved by Totoio's death. I saw his tiny corpse with a wreath of flowers on his head which looked so drawn, a seeming irony, flowers all over the bier, the usual vain attempt to diminish death.' He described the wretched funeral for Livia—not omitting mention of the priest's meaningless Latin litany and the dog barking so much that 'I had to give him a kick to shut him up', or the workman Cimutti grumbling at the exertion of having to stand in for the sexton, who was also laid up.[201]

The winters at Murano were often severe, and in 1905 'everything in the factory, including the gas, had frozen over.' When it snowed, the skylights had to be shut and heating up the paint became an ordeal. The summer heat made things even worse, whether at Murano or in Trieste: Ettore's socks perished with sweat and even if the furnaces were not lit it was still too hot either to play the violin or to write. After a day's work, 'full of poison' or with his 'nose full of arsenic', Ettore's great delight was his bath. In 1913, when the old one sprang a leak, he bought a new one for 60 lire and had to answer to Livia for not having chosen a smarter model.[202]

Worst of all were the mosquitoes. Trieste had enough of them, but in Murano they made life a torture. At night, Ettore would fight a losing battle for sleep, and grimly paid a hundred francs for an impregnable mosquito-net.[203] The insects put his good humour to a hard test. In 1903 he wrote:

We're thoroughly infested with mosquitoes. There are several sorts: some sing, others don't; some sting, others don't. Each strain prefers a special part of the body, so my flab is in a deplorable state. So I work all day but in the evening I look forward to *not* going to bed because the moment I shut myself up all alone in my room I find I am much less on my own than I should like to be. When I say: 'Bed-time!' the mosquitoes wail: 'Dinner-time!'... Just think, when I'm having a bath, if I stick my finger out of the water, right away I find a winged monster biting it.[204]

Still, conditions must often have been very pleasant at Murano, for he once urged Ottavio and Frizzi to visit there, calling it 'always a real paradise'.[205]

On one of his numerous boat-journeys from Trieste to Venice in 1901 Ettore overslept and, when he at last came out on deck, discovered that the vessel had already been so long at anchor that there were no more gondolas alongside to ferry passengers ashore:

I shouted, we all shouted, but no one came. At last a big six-oared craft took me and my little suitcase to St Mark's. Everybody was laughing, which did not in the least surprise me as I bring merriment wherever I go. That is why I'm sorry not to be in Trieste more often. I feel it's unpatriotic.[206]

On another occasion, in 1905, he thought they had already reached Venice, got dressed and went up on deck, only to find that the ship was stationary in a fog out at sea, and that it was still three in the morning: 'out of indolence I went back to bed in my clothes and finished off my sleep.'[207]

In later years Ettore sometimes kept down the number of his visits without Livia to one or two a year, as in 1906, 1907 and 1912; but sometimes they amounted to nine or ten in a year, as in 1911 and 1913. It is impossible to ascertain the number and duration of the periods which Ettore and Livia spent together at Murano, or how often Olga or Gioachino or Livia's sisters or their husbands were there with them. The Schmitzes had to pay for Livia's keep at Murano (for which Olga raised her charges in 1903), as well as their share of the expenses of Villa Veneziani in Trieste.

Gilda Moravia kept house and ran the office at Murano. The dressmaker Italia De Luca also lived in. Very likely, a cook and a housemaid came in to attend the regular occupants and the various members of the Veneziani clan who sometimes paid lengthy visits there, whether for business or for pleasure. When Livia came, she brought a maid with her.[208] Gilda and Ettore did not have much in common beyond cousinly warmth. In June 1903, Ettore defended Gilda against unspecified complaints by Bravin's wife, Luzietta. That November, Gilda was blaming the Schmitzes for a backlog of several months in the book-keeping, but the trouble seems to have been due to a love-affair of hers with a younger man.[209]

There was little entertainment in Murano itself, whose only distinction is that it is the home of Venetian glassware. Olga and Marco sometimes visited, but Ettore came to prefer the company of Dora's husband, Giuseppe (Bepi) Oberti, a keen musician who was to organize the family string quartet. From at least as early as 1902 the violin was a favourite solace for Svevo, and by no means solely as an escape from writing. He never mastered tempo, but still practised keenly unless there were other visitors. He feared he was 'so tormenting the ear-drums of the peaceful Venetians that I think they're contemplating an appeal to the Government to have me expelled'.[210] He came to refer to his Murano station as 'the house of sleep' or 'the kingdom of sleep, silence and toil'.

He was often bored, kept idle by Olga's muddling of despatches or by the unpredictable behaviour of suppliers or customers. This left him time to think and write and energy enough at the end of the day to cross over to Venice or drop into Pieretto's *osteria* in Murano. It was here that a conjuror once kept him on tenterhooks by borrowing from him a ten-lire note which he did not return until nearly midnight. On another occasion he stood a glass of wine and gave a two-lire tip to Angelo the gondolier who had named his new boat *Letizia*. Or he would play a sort of shove-ha'penny with the young son of one of his workers.[211]

Usually, though, he worked hard, sometimes up to ten o'clock at night, and even on Sundays, especially if Olga was there. He would have to dash back and forth between the factory and the office, changing in and out of his clothes each time with the help of the womenfolk, so that he compared himself to the quick-change artist Frégoli.[212]

For the workers it was even harder. Marco's designs increasingly mechanized the process over the years, but at first they had to stand at the huge tubs of boiling paint to stir it with long ladles.[213] There were eight regular workers at Murano, who worked every day except Sundays and the twenty or so annual feast days, from seven till noon and from 12.45 to five o'clock. Two of them could also be called upon to work on Sunday mornings. In a busy month, with hourly pay and piece-work, a man could get 120 or 130 lire, or about 60 florins.[214]

Ettore often complained of slacking, especially when the work became more mechanized, so it seems that it suited the workers to stretch out the work, as demand would not necessarily expand with faster production to increase their piece-work bonuses. Wages were barely sufficient for subsistence, yet some workers, like Cimutti, who figures prominently in two of Svevo's Murano narratives, spent a quarter or a third of their pay on drink.[215]

The inflammable materials used for paint meant that there was always a risk of fire in the factory. In 1901, while he was in Murano, Ettore heard that there had been a blaze in the Trieste factory and that Marco had suffered slight burns. He wrote back to Livia: 'I don't know how I shall sleep tonight. Just think, we're not insured for Murano and we haven't a drop of water as everything is iced up.'[216]

Venice was the great compensation for being in Murano. Its historic, artistic and scenic appeal hardly needs dwelling on. Ettore already knew the city quite well, loved wandering around in it, and was linguistically at home with its dialect, which is close to that of Trieste. Veruda must have extended Ettore's knowledge and appreciation of Venetian artists, both ancients and moderns such as the painters Luigi Nono and Enrico Fonda and the sculptor Medardo Rosso, whose works are held in the Venice Modern Art Gallery in Palazzo Pesaro. Veruda had introduced Ettore to Nono's brother, the sculptor Urbano, in Trieste in 1900.[217] Luigi, who was born in 1850, painted many rustic genre pictures, including one which may have helped to inspire Svevo's story 'La madre': it shows, larger than life-size, a hen in a basket surrounded by her chicks, one of whom is dead. The works of Medardo Rosso (also born in 1850) bring irresistibly to mind the aesthetic notions of the sculptor Balli in *Senilità*: the figures are rough-cast and almost scaly in texture, in a style well ahead of their time and very similar to some of Epstein's. Palazzo Pesaro also has a

landscape genre painting by Ettore Tito (born in 1859), entitled *The Lagoon*.
It shows a boatman vigorously punting a *sandolo* which is almost swallowed
up by the pale luminosity of the lagoon. Its colour sensibility closely matches
that of the narrative fragments which Svevo wrote during the years after 1900,
when he spent much of his time at Murano on the lagoon.

From Murano one has a good close view of the cypresses and campanile of
the island cemetery of San Micel and, a little beyond, the much taller campanile
of St Mark's, which, on the night of 14 July 1902, suddenly and silently
collapsed, its mortar-work apparently dissolved by pigeon droppings. Its
rebuilding was not completed until 1912.[218] When a new Pope was elected in
1903 Svevo remarked: 'If you knew what a ringing of bells there was for Pius
X! A real test for the palaces, which did not collapse.'[219]

Ettore's wisecracks often had an irreligious tinge, though religion engrossed
him as a phenomenon and he often attended church services and sermons as a
diversion. A sermon he listened to in St Mark's in 1901 aroused his contempt
by its 'phenomenal banalities' and declamatory style.[220]

Livia's health remained parlous, complicated by her abortive pregnancies.
She kept insisting that Ettore should destroy the letters which she wrote him.
He never quite understood her reasons for this bashfulness: 'Why are you so
scared that *other people* might read your writings! I who have published novels
know that *other people* are extremely discreet.'[221]

As ever, Livia's health was not what most worried her husband when they
were apart. Ettore's jealousies were now centred on the mountaineer and
musician Julius Kugy (older than he was) on account of Livia's frequent
rehearsals with his choir, in which she had a solo part:

I have nothing against your singing in the choir. I would like you always to go with
someone either of my family or yours. In principle—without in the least wishing to
object to such an innocent desire on your part—I find it strange that you should want
to sing in a Mass which will be performed whilst you are away from Trieste. And I do
insist that you don't let Kugy treat you as a *Liebes Kind*.[222]

Ettore did not seem to appreciate the cultural contribution of Kugy's choir in
bringing to Trieste the music of Palestrina.[223]

Svevo was still making wagers about smoking, and almost managed to turn
Gioachino and Nella into habitual smokers (possibly by getting them to smoke
ritual 'last cigarettes' with him).[224] He waged epic struggles with his digestion
that went on to the end of his life and very likely contributed to James Joyce's
portrait of Bloom. He kept alternating between gourmandizing and fasting.
He was perturbed in 1900 when he found his purgative was having no effect,
then discovered that he had absent-mindedly been giving himself saccharin
instead.[225] An easy spell at work combined with travelling by tram instead of
by bicycle or on foot had increased his weight, so he took to eating nothing
but greens 'as if I were at pasture'.[226] His life, in short, seemed to be composed

of the same 'microscopic epic' which critics were later to discover in his novels.

He still dreamt at night. He described one of many dreams in a letter of May Day 1901:

I've had a bad dream about Adolfo. I dreamt he'd been attacked by a swarm of wasps and Catina, the maid we had in our childhood, called to me: 'Come, come and see. He's got a lip at the back of his neck just like the one on his mouth.' I have nothing but dreams to tell you about.[227]

He often had trouble sleeping when he was away from Livia. But he was a daydreamer as well as a night-dreamer, and his daydreams were far more pleasant:

You know that even though I'm dead set on becoming a good industrialist and a good businessman as quickly as possible there's nothing practical about me except my ambitions. Faced with my new objective, I'm still the same old dreamer. When I conceive of a business project, if only I were down-to-earth enough to consider it and daydream about it in the form and terms in which it actually presents itself. Oh, I go so far beyond it that the actual project becomes a pitiful trifle, merely the starting-point for fantasies so mighty that they make me quite absent-minded and one of these days I'll walk straight over the side of a dry-dock. I'm reading a book about the distilling of turpentine. I suggested to Gioachino that we should lay aside a few barrels of the raw material and see whether it might not suit us to do our own refining. Very soon that was no longer enough for me, though Gioachino hadn't agreed even to that experiment. I daydreamed all day long—just think—that when it came to setting up our factory in France my idea was borne in mind and that the factory was sited in a turpentine-producing area. And the quality of that French turpentine! The purest there is, an enormously effective solvent, odourless and with the lowest specific gravity. Naturally, I was put in charge of the factory and bit by bit, without informing the firm, by dint of economizing on the factory overheads, I bought up plantations of maritime pine which gave an enormous yield, which in turn enabled me to keep on buying more.

Svevo embroidered on this fantasy with allusions to Zola, Millet and Goethe's *Faust* and realized that it was the creative writer in him refusing to die:

Inside my brain there must be a cog that won't stop churning out those novels that no one would read, and rebels and goes on spinning crazily whether you're there or not. Don't you remember how many times you had to bring me back to reality because you realized I was daydreaming about linseed oil? You must consider the violence I did myself in making such a clean leap into this new line of business. I must be deeply shaken by it and when a fiction [*romanzo*] takes shape unbidden in my mind, I, who have always loved everything I've done, am entranced by my own vivid imaginings and forget the whole world. It isn't business that makes me so lively, it's my dreams. I've tried to give you an exact account of my present emotional life and I hope you won't be displeased.[228]

He was to champion his own daydreams again in 1903 even more defiantly:

My habit of daydreaming is really what keeps me almost continuously serene; without it I'd live like Marco amid the constant troubles of reality which rob him of sleep and of the will to live. And besides, you don't know how I dress you up in my daydreams. I've never told you and never will, my dear wife.[229]

36

BLOOD ON THE STREETS: FEBRUARY 1902

Triestine politics, after the relative calm of the 1890s, entered, with the new century, upon a more confused and violent period, though no one could have predicted the bloodshed that made February 1902 the most tragic moment in Triestine history between the Napoleonic Wars and the Great War.

Liberal supremacy had been apparently assured by the victory of Attilio Hortis in the manhood suffrage election in 1897, but almost immediately began to disintegrate. Felice Venezian and his closest allies—particularly Camillo Ara and Teodoro Mayer—had established a virtual 'dictatorship' which was not to the liking of all their own followers.[230] In the 1930 edition—that is, the one published in the heyday of Fascism—of his history of Trieste, Tamaro bragged of the Liberal-National pre-Fascist 'squads':

the Liberal-National Party, though its leaders often displayed a democratic outlook ... now [i.e. from the eighties onward] went through a phase which, in many respects, can be said to have truly anticipated Fascism ... as it aimed to bind the entire population into a single band [*fascio*]. Alongside the general organization it had genuine action 'squads' or 'committees', mainly composed of young men, who carried out the more radical actions, attacked the Slavs, beat up the Socialists or pro-Austrians, stuck up wall-posters ...[231]*

The Italian nationalists did indeed attack and disrupt a Socialist meeting at Pirano on 30 July 1899 (Ettore's third wedding anniversary). The Liberal-National press crowed 'Pirano docet'. But a twofold split now divided the Irredentists. Edgardo Rascovich led his supporters of the Società Operaia and among the Italian working and lower middle class generally to form a new Associazione Democratica, while a former mayor, Dompieri, tried to challenge Venezian's leadership and led his own independent faction. Still things did not go badly for the official party in the 1900 local elections (where voting as yet went by privileged categories and there was not even a token element of manhood suffrage): Venezian's party made a clean sweep in the first three

---

* This passage did not appear in the 1946 edition but came back in the 1976 edition with an even more overbearing tone.[232]

categories and that of Rascovich in the fourth (comprising small tradesmen).[233] From 1900, Ettore Schmitz was entitled as a businessman to vote in the fourth category. He was again one of the directors of the Unione Ginnastica in 1900,[234] when the police closed it down, and of what was now re-christened the Società Ginnastica in 1902, when Felice Venezian was President. This too was closed down in 1904.[235]

Clearly, then, when parliamentary elections were held in January 1901, in a highly charged atmosphere, Svevo was closely associated with Venezian. Attilio Hortis again won the seat in the manhood suffrage category, but this time only after a second poll against the Slav Nationalists and the Socialists. As he stood as combined Liberal and Democrat candidate, we may guess that the split between those two factions was somewhat spurious, probably designed to win working-class or republican votes from the Socialists.[236]

Nationalistic rivalries in Trieste expressed themselves very strongly in the field of education. This, coupled with the Austrian government's encouragement of modern education, produced good schooling in Trieste and the surrounding area and the illiteracy rate in the town had been brought down from 43 to 14 per cent.[237] The Socialists also contributed to popular education. In 1899 they opened a 'Circolo di Studi Sociali' with its own library and reading rooms open to the public at large. The 'Circolo' also arranged lectures by local and visiting authorities whose appeal went well beyond those of the venerable Società di Minerva. Scipio Slataper admired the Triestine Socialists' cultural and educational efforts, which he said could not be matched in the whole of Italy, whilst their library was the only one in Trieste which served the study of economics and sociology. It was through the 'Circolo', he remarked, that Trieste heard Lombroso, Ferrero, Salvemini, Labriola and Zerboglio, and heard Mazzini and Garibaldi discussed by Salvemini and Ferri—who placed them in a very different perspective from that of the rhetorical myth of the Risorgimento of which Irredentism had made such great play.[238]

The question of a national university for the Italians in Austria had now become the focus of Irredentist politics. Austria had lost its last Italian universities, Padua and Venice, in 1866, and feared that a new Italian university would prove a hotbed of nationalism. Yet the Austrian constitution guaranteed all nationalities the right to instruction in their own mother tongue at every level. The Austrians initiated an improbable solution to this political problem by opening an Italian-language law faculty as an annexe to the university of Innsbruck at Wilten, in the heart of German territory. Its opening in October 1901 was marked by a violent clash between German and Italian students and on Sunday 15 November the Triestines held a huge protest meeting at the Politeama Rossetti to denounce the situation and demand the setting up of a university in their own town. 'Venezian and his friends', writes Tamaro,

thought it useful never to win that concession and thus have—through incessant agitation and the impact in Italy both of the agitation itself and of the denial of so self-evident a right—an excellent means of carrying on an all-out fight against the Austrian government and of preparing Italian opinion for the ineluctable.[239]

Slataper was disgusted: 'this great issue is simply being exploited in a game of party politics.'[240] Bazlen found it amusing:

So the town fights to be Italian. But Austria, undaunted, grants its every demand. Trieste gets all it needs, so much so that, as I've been told, one of the greatest skills of Irredentist policy consisted precisely in demanding and simultaneously being denied an Italian university in Trieste. Had they got it, they'd have run out of issues.[241]

In Italy, Irredentism was moving gradually to the political Right and finding increasing favour with those in government. The Socialists in *Critica Sociale* argued that throughout the Risorgimento the cause of Italian unification had been used as a pretext to fend off democratic reforms within the monarchic State and to strengthen the military. They argued that the Irredentists in Trieste were equally reactionary and that any Triestine worker would prefer the restricted but secure rights enjoyed under Austrian rule to an Italy that used artillery against its own people.[242] A few years later Slataper too was to remark: 'I don't hold forth quite so much against the Austrian police since I've got to know the Italian.'[243]

For a smoker like Ettore, political issues became inescapably acute in 1902 when matchbox labels became the battleground of fanatical nationalism in Trieste. The Pan-Germanist 'Südmark' association brought out matchboxes bearing their symbol and slogans expressing out-and-out German nationalist sentiments, vying with the Irredentist matchboxes of the Lega Nazionale. *Il Lavoratore* joined this sulphurous fray, selling matchboxes which displayed the red flag and the slogan 'Proletarians of all countries, unite!' against the blazing sun of the dawning socialist future. The Slavs were not to be outdone either. Only the pro-Austrian party contented themselves with using matches labelled, in Swedish, 'Swedish safety matches'. Piemontese relates that, the moment someone drew a box of matches to light up, his interlocutor would train hawk-like eyes upon them to identify the brand.[244] Enmeshed as he was in Irredentist circles, Svevo presumably always lit up with Irredentist matches and added patriotism to his reasons for smoking.

Piemontese describes how Trieste in the first decade of the century was uniquely gripped by fiercely exclusive political passions and allegiances. A Socialist would never step into an Irredentist café or hotel, while no Irredentist (National-Liberal) would show himself in a Socialist, Slav or Austrian milieu. People lived in almost watertight social compartments, signalling their allegiance by their matchbox labels. 'Tell me what matches you use, and I will tell you who you are'.[245]

The perils of this tense political deadlock in Triestine society suddenly turned from farce into tragedy in February 1902. The Imperial authorities, not smokers striking matches, were responsible. The trouble began at Austro-Hungarian

Lloyd, whose ships Ettore Schmitz supplied with paint and carried him free of charge to Venice and back. The management of the Lloyd shipyard in December 1901 rejected an appeal by their stokers against a further deterioration in working conditions, pay and working hours. The Lieutenant, Count Goess, gave the employers his full support. When a strike was called and idle ships began to choke the harbours, the stokers were replaced from as far afield as the Levant. When the new hands also refused to work, naval stokers were sent in. This provoked a general strike. Even the shops, including bakeries, were shut, and transport came to a standstill. By Thursday 13 February, writes Piemontese, 'the city seemed dead. A violent, icy *bora* made the streets look even more sinister.' Extra troops from Gorizia and Pola thronged the city. Lloyd's now agreed to arbitration. The Socialists held a vast but orderly meeting at the Politeama Rossetti, then marched across town towards the city hall, only to be stopped in the Piazza della Borsa by the soldiery, who charged the unarmed crowd with fixed bayonets. Fleeing in panic from that confined space, the people ran into detachments of soldiers who had been posted at the exits and who, thinking they were being rushed at, opened fire. The chaos and slaughter went on into the following day. When it was all over, fourteen dead, including a policeman, were counted, and fifty wounded, including some women. On Saturday 15 February the arbitrators sustained most of the stokers' claims and postponed a decision on the remainder. In the meantime, by request of Goess, the Vienna government had declared a state of siege in Trieste which was not lifted until April. The 'February days' won the Socialists considerable support in Trieste, though the Liberals presented the affair as a purely nationalistic battle.[246]

On 28 June the Triple Alliance between Italy, Austria and Germany was renewed.

Part VI

ULYSSES SCHMITZ
1901–1907

37

SCHMITZ ON THE FRENCH RIVIERA

In 1899, Lord Muskerry had the Veneziani paint applied to his yacht *Rita* in Malta and wrote Gioachino an enthusiastic testimonial, declaring it the *only* effective compound against seaweed that he knew. Muskerry must have carried out a very effective advertising campaign with his Navy friends in Malta, for a family story goes that a British admiral in Malta saw a vessel of the Austrian navy which he thought had been freshly painted but had actually been covered with 'Moravia's anti-fouling compound' several months before.[1]

This was the beginning of the British Admiralty's interest in the Veneziani product. It may not be pure coincidence that Ettore complained in 1900 of wasting a morning exchanging inconsequential pleasantries with the Venezianis' Malta agent, A. Kohen.[2] A couple of weeks earlier he had been absorbed in his commercial daydreams about vast resin plantations in France and now seemed to catch no whiff of the huge business prospects that were to change his life. The firm had already decided to send him to England, for early in 1900 he was taking English lessons from a certain Cautley on Saturdays.[3]

At the end of May 1901 he set off on his first long business trip, which was to take him first to Toulon and Marseilles and then on to London, Plymouth and all the way to Ireland. He travelled as far as Milan with Dora Veneziani, now sixteen, who was 'close to fainting with the heat and exhaustion' when she arrived there. Ettore dashed out for his first glimpse of the cathedral, then carried on via Genoa, sharing a compartment with two students who grew so heated in discussing aesthetics 'that I was afraid they'd overturn the train'. Ettore proclaimed that 'it took a good dose of civilization to produce a masterpiece and an even bigger dose of barbarism to believe in it', but refused to give his name, explaining to Livia that he was so filthy that even his hair looked black all over.

Exhausted and dejected, convinced of the futility of his mission, he reached Toulon at four o'clock in the morning. He was shocked to find he spent four and a half francs on transport alone that day, but delighted to get a copious dinner for two francs, and he gave Livia a minute description of the menu. This was his first experience of France, and right away he ran up against French militarism, mistaking a naval officer without his sword for the *maître d'hotel*. The officer took offence, and Ettore had to get out of trouble by pretending not to understand French.

As Livia had visions of 'millions de cocottes' thronging around her husband in France, he took care to inform her that his landlady was 'pretty plain' and that 'While I've been travelling, as I've had to sit in the smokers, I've never or very rarely travelled with ladies.' He repeatedly mentioned how he was missing his wife and daughter.[4] During all their separations, Ettore wrote to her at least once a day, usually at some length. Livia replied that she read his letters 'over and over' but that 'Papa, contrariwise, grumbled about the length of your letter. He said: "See what it means to send a novelist on a journey!" '[5]

Ettore felt rather lonely amid the fashionable night-life of the Boulevard Strasbourg. 'Women who give you looks' served in the cafés, there were women musicians, even an entire women's band. Ettore spent 10 centimes on the automatic 'cinematograph', where he saw *Wedding Night*. He gave Livia a full description of the scene in which the bridegroom discovered he hadn't married a virgin. 'Beside me, an extremely elegant young lady was laughing as she gazed from her booth. I blushed on behalf of your sex and left,' he remarked, with a touch of humbug. He then went in search of a new panama and topper to fit his outsize dome. In one hat shop he was offered a hat that 'rested on the tip of my nose' and was shown out 'with not very benevolent amazement and with—as I thought—a look at my feet as well to see what they were like'.[6] This was one of several little incidents that roused in Ettore a strong dislike of the French. Two days later, when ordering a hat to measure, he caused great merriment by his misunderstanding of a French word (he didn't say which).[7]

The next day, rising at five, he wandered around the harbour and the market, where the women vendors held forth in a vigorous dialect 'which it would have been most interesting to understand'. He was also delighted to find women sweeping the streets, 'great heavy women with hats made of soft black straw'. He took the boat across the 'huge anchorage ringed all round by green islands' on his way to the citadel of La Seyne 'smoked up' by the port industries and swooning in the heat; but he was unable to find the commander of the Russian vessels on which the paint was to be tested, and Lambert, the agent, wasted half his day through having failed to obtain an entry permit to the naval dockyard.

During this enforced leisure, his 'crazy laugh' rang out through the streets of Toulon. Those he spoke to were intrigued by his French and thought perhaps he was from Indo-China. A coachman sold him a cigarette which he found so exquisite that he spent all his time trying to find the same sort of cigarettes or the same coachman again, but in vain. Then a student recommended him to buy, at a reduced price, a brand called 'La fusée', which resembled the coachman's. Ettore lit up and the cigarette started 'smoking on its own and exploding in my mouth crackling pretty loudly'.[8]

He found the language maddeningly difficult to speak: 'Do you think it's nice to have to mould the corners of your mouth and the mucous membrane in your nose in such an outlandish fashion every time you need the simplest thing?' So when he came across five Tuscan workers in the hat shop 'they were astonished by my delight in talking and hearing them talk'. He declined their invitation, however, to go and have a drink with them that evening, though he found them such 'good fellows' and 'almost wept to hear them relate the bitter years they had spent here at the time when the Italians were hated'.* Instead, as was his wont, he relaxed by reading the newspapers: 'I'm full of them, as you can well imagine.'[9]

On Sunday a severe stomach-ache prevented him from having his sea-bathe. He felt better the next day, though still depressed by doubts about his ability to stand that sort of life. The French motor traffic terrified him, too: 'They speed like lunatics ... In Austria half the town would get fined.' A leading article in *Libre Parole* blamed the bad driving on the Jews.[10] Ettore found himself 'flying into a rage' over trifles, especially over the chauvinism of the French: 'so much stupid *Patrie Française* that it lowers this nation to the level of the most stupid of African peoples ...'.[11] At Toulon, where he was supervising the painting of the French warship *Chanzy*, the German name of Schmitz must have made every French naval officer stiffen, whilst for his part Ettore must have been fully aware not only of the right-wing political reaction but also of the anti-Semitism which the French military caste had aroused in the storm over Dreyfus. The ambiguous verdict which the Court of Appeal had given in 1899 still stood: Dreyfus was still held guilty of high treason, but was allowed extenuating circumstances and had been moved from Devil's Island, where he had already served four years' hard labour.

Between visits to the *Chanzy* under police supervision and to the Russian vessels, including a torpedo boat, Ettore started on a play—'a *commediola* in one act, just one, as merry as you could wish'—which must have been *La parola*. 'Don't tell your parents,' he warned Livia. Clad in his beach clothes, he encountered, to his embarrassment, the Veneziani agent Lambert with his entire family, returning from the confirmation of one of their children, and immaculately dressed. He found Madame Lambert a social climber and 'very religious, very likely in part because in France it's a matter of *bon ton*'. Ettore, for his part, enjoyed eating cheaply and well in a plebeian *gargote*, where he would play a *carambole*, or snooker, with the regulars, and spend the rest of the evening reading the papers in the open air.[12]

He then spent three days in Marseilles, studying French customs tariffs, drafting the first scene of his play, and trying to find Livia a run of the magazine *Vie Parisienne*, 'a work of the higher immorality' which he hoped would open his wife's eyes so that she would not go through the same experiences as Olga, whom Gioachino had carefully kept in ignorance. He wrote to her of his little fantasies of Livia in her corset, of 'kissing and biting your white arms', of making meatballs of her, and of kissing her 'guess where'. His only diversion consisted of getting his associate Baronio to show him round the vicinity where Livia had lived and played as a little girl, though he also admitted staying at the Baronios' until midnight, drinking excellent beer and enjoying the household

---

* Italian immigrants in France were frequently subjected to violence: the worst took place in 1893 at Aigues-Mortes, where four hundred Italians were attacked, thirty of them being killed and the rest tossed into the lagoon.

chatter in Venetian dialect. Baronio was to vouch to Livia for Ettore's good behaviour. The latter never tired of repeating that he lacked opportunity or desire to be unfaithful to her.[13]

38

BRITISH ODYSSEY

On 11 June, Svevo received cabled instructions from Trieste to proceed immediately to Chatham, the important naval town on the Medway, between Dover and London, where accommodation had been booked for him at the Sun Hotel.[14] He arrived in Chatham the following day 'full of misgivings'—'There's nothing else inside me, as the Channel has completely cleaned me out.' It was pouring with rain and, after the heat of the French Riviera, he found he was cold in his lightweight coat and needed two blankets on his bed. 'My English is doing poorly, you know,' he wrote. 'Not only do I not understand them, but they don't understand me.' And in a second letter on the same day he went on: 'The simplest word I utter in English causes doubts and misunderstandings. And if I say anything more complicated, they stop trying to understand and give me up.' He found prices shocking too: 'dinner here costs as much as breakfast, dinner, supper, bed and newspapers, coffee and absinthe in Toulon'. So abandoned did he feel that it brought tears to his eyes to receive a telegram from Livia, giving Frantzen, the Veneziani representative in England, a good laugh.

Livia was now at Salsomaggiore again and, though she had the company of Gilda Moravia and of the Vivantes, she too was continually close to tears.[15] Ettore was disheartened to find himself 'so weak and nervous'. To bring out his own unadventurousness he told Livia an interesting little anecdote:

In Marseilles I met a Triestine deserter who is an itinerant corn-curer. He arrives in town without a penny or a friend. He gets himself known about the place and the money comes in. In the end he had 2000 francs and needed 5000. So off he goes to Monaco to *nearly* triple the sum, as he puts it—instead of which he is reduced to cutting corns again in Monaco. Yet he was more cheerful in Marseilles than I was.[16]

That contrast, so consciously drawn by Ettore, between his own feebleness and the self-reliance of others, commands attention. Ettore Schmitz, one is bound to surmise, suffered his keenest feelings of inferiority with respect to the enterprising young men of his time, from Giuseppe Revere and Emilio Treves to Teodoro Mayer, Guglielmo Oberdan, Giulio Césari, Silvio Benco and, especially, the real artists among them like Veruda and, later, Joyce: in other words, all those who plunged adventurously into the fray and braved 'the struggle for life'. The contrast between himself and them must have aggravated his neurotic sense of failure over his abandonment of literature.

But now his abilities at writing impromptu were put to the test by his amazed first impressions of England:

This little town (from one moment to the next I find myself in the very heart of England) is so English that you couldn't imagine. I've never seen anything like it. Solid little houses whose comfort you can gauge from the exterior and everything a grey colour that rises to black in the slate roofs.... This England is so different from what we imagine it to be like that it's impossible for me to give you any idea ... You've never seen such a difference between two neighbouring peoples as between the French and the English. I'm talking about outward appearances, as that's all I know. For a start, the emblematic hat which is taken off only on the rarest occasions! The pomposity of pretending you can't see people you haven't been introduced to! And then, I've just come from the land of by-your-leave, and I find it terribly hard to keep my great crown stuck eternally to my big head.... Everything here is done in a rather unfriendly manner. If you enter a bar to have a whisky, you have to pay for it before you raise the glass to your lips. Otherwise, once you've had your drink, you're making the other party rely on credit ... All in all, *tout-à-fait embêtant* and up to now I prefer the French and their gendarmes.[17]

It was the differences in manners that were most *embêtantes*. On his first night in England Ettore did not sleep a wink, after going to the naval dockyard and then to naval headquarters in Chatham and committing first a breach of propriety and then a commercial error, albeit both without consequence to the company interest. Over his difficulties with English he was utterly dejected: 'I don't think I'll get on top of it even if I'm left here for two or three months.'[18] There was some consolation: 'Frantzen says that this year England will give us orders worth 750,000 francs.'

He spent Sunday 16 June by himself. Frantzen was in Portsmouth and, to make things worse, he had booked Ettore into the Sun as a coffee-room customer, which meant that he paid more and ate his meals privately and was unable 'to make any acquaintances because a well-bred person here doesn't know anybody until they've been introduced'. He found it too cold to take a boat-trip along the Medway. The town was empty, so he walked up to a hill-top from which he could see Rochester close by. He described the view to Livia:

Across the river, work had not completely ceased for Sunday, for fifty or so tall chimneys were smoking away as if it weren't Sunday at all. The town lies among hills; the houses are all down on the level, tightly packed, small and regular, nobly blackened rather than smoke-stained, arranged in straight rows with a slight, regular slant, like our workers' houses ... The only thing which wasn't regular in that wide landscape was the river, yellow and filthy but quite majestic with the steel monsters which it bears and those shipyards—so many miniature towns—which it sustains. Otherwise order reigns supreme in those little houses and in their layout. True enough, there's plenty of greenery in the town gardens but this rather increases than diminishes the feeling one has of something manufactured. Perhaps I'm biased in seeing things this way and I'm trying to make fun of the English who don't want to have anything to do with me. When I arrived in Dover I was impressed by the hugeness and solidity of construction in England. I felt as if I were in a dream inside some plaything. The railway between Dover and Chatham runs wholly atop the hills which are linked together by bridges and viaducts, the whole thing up in the air, starting from the station at Dover. And the speed—they know about speed here! Yet it's like going along a smooth plane, without any jerking or rattling. I who am so irritable managed to read English.[19]

That Sunday afternoon Svevo, bored to death, unexpectedly had his 'most important adventure' in Chatham. He was sitting alone under a trellis in the hotel garden, drowsily gazing at 'the dull river':

All of a sudden I feel something very alive but very light climb up the chair behind me: a cat, maybe. I turn round and see beside me the most beautiful chubby, rosy, fresh face you could imagine. It was a face made to be kissed: the most beautiful English boy you could imagine. He had taken up that posture so as to watch more closely how the smoke came out of my nose. We were friends at once. He must have been 5 or 6 years old and spoke perfect English.

Livia's jealousies thus disarmed, Ettore described his tête-à-tête with the small boy. They talked about Letizia, about the three dogs which the boy had in London, and about English words. But the idyll was rudely interrupted. The boy's father suddenly appeared and, without a word to Ettore, muttered something to the boy. Affronted, Ettore gently bade young Philip goodbye. 'Now he runs off when he sees me,' he added. 'He must have been told off.'

The boredom of the English Sunday at least advanced Svevo's new play: 'As I was writing it I laughed to myself like a lunatic.'[20] In *La parola*, rewritten after the war as *La verità*,[21] Silvio Arcetri's wife finds him in bed with another woman, but he manages to explain the whole business away. Svevo shows how easily fictions can supplant reality (as in Goldoni's *The Liar*) and, more subtly, how all parties concerned—husband, wife and both families—clutch at the most transparent fiction in order to salvage an empty marriage for the sake of appearances and a comfortable set pattern of life. Bourgeois living is itself the protagonist and the real subject of this downbeat play.

Sunday over, Ettore had plenty to do in Chatham both in the docks and at naval headquarters. He began to strike up a closer acquaintance with England. 'Here is liberty, real liberty.' His enthusiasm ran high. In the land which had produced Disraeli he had far less to fear in the way of anti-Semitism than in the land which was persecuting Dreyfus. England also offered an important neutrality: whereas Marseilles was Veneziani territory, here Ettore was completely free to be himself with Livia on an equal footing. He already preferred England to France: 'British militarism is certainly far more attractive than the odious militarism of the French.'[22]

He went to a Chatham *café chantant* which somewhat reminded him of the Ronacher in Vienna, and picked up a friend. 'He's a poor chap and—with all due form of courtesy—I stood him his seat and his drink.' But Ettore's generosity was well repaid: his new friend was a tobacconist and gave him 'a cigar the like of which I have never smoked'. He also helped Ettore with his English.[23]

The twentieth of June was Ettore's epic day. He sent Livia a hurried note in the morning as he was engaged in his usual hopeless battle to pack his bags. He was off to London. It was a short ride, but he did not write to Livia again until midnight:

Arriving with my heart beating with intense curiosity, I saw two or three streets so thickly crowded that it must be quite a job to walk along them! Then I got to this lodging-house, which Frantzen found me. I dined at a kind of family table, pretty well. There are lots of Frenchmen and Germans all of whom speak English to whom I was introduced. Prices here are fixed in advance. At Chatham I was fleeced.

In Chatham he had paid 7s. a day just for bed and breakfast, while in London, at G. Turner's guest house at 46 Woburn Place, Russell Square, he paid 10s. a day for 'a splendid room, an excellent lunch and an exquisite dinner'.

The decision had already been reached on the following morning: 'Must have factory in England.' The same evening he wrote: 'I was given a magnificent reception at the Admiralty; everything's fine but we must have a factory.'[24] This must have been the famous event which he was later to relate to the poet Saba. Saba recounts that Svevo 'went up the stairs to the austere building all of a flutter' and was shown into 'a bare little room, more of a cubby-hole than an office', furnished with nothing but a table and a chair, by a young man in civvies who offered the seat to Svevo and himself perched on the table, crossing his long legs:

he offered and lit a cigarette for his guest and himself, a very fragrant one, showed himself to be well informed about the business in hand, asked two or three questions, said that everything was fine and that the deal was virtually settled. Italo Svevo thought he was dreaming.

He had expected interminable negotiations, instead of which a matter that in France or Italy would have taken five years was settled in five minutes. Svevo left the Admiralty building with 'a vague feeling of guilt' and at the same time with 'the sensation of floating on air'.[25]

There had just been a change of guard at the British Admiralty. Admiral Sir John Fisher, an expert in naval technology and construction, was now Third Sea Lord, and was to become Second in 1902 and First in 1904. It may well have been he who decided in favour of the Veneziani paint while Commander-in-Chief of the Malta-based Mediterranean Fleet in 1899–1900. His decision in 1901 to paint the entire British Navy grey helped to make the fortune of the Venezianis.

This was the biggest business deal in the life of Ettore Schmitz. It cost him virtually no effort other than a linguistic one. Yet his main concern was that he had spent 'the trifling sum of 12 shillings' on cabs: 'I think no traveller on behalf of our firm has ever spent as much as I have done since I've been in England'; and he railed on about 'that bandit stronghold, the Sun Hotel at

Chatham' and sought to justify his expenses in England by his economies in France.

In order to make Livia feel less far away, he painted a detailed picture of the Turners' lodging-house and its assorted guests. There was an elderly German widower who wrung Ettore's heart with his grief over his wife's death, and consoled himself with colossal beefsteaks. Ettore reassured Livia that in the evenings the drawing-room was thronged with 'old or middle-aged ladies only', apart from Turner's niece, who had a young man in tow. There was old Mrs Clarke. Miss Pains was 'no beauty, but extremely pleasant and talks to me very readily and corrects me when I make mistakes: she said I should spend the evening in the drawing-room.' He listed another 'Miss': 'tall and stiff and scraggy, but she plays the piano with some grace.' He added, with an inter-lingual pun: 'Miss Pains sang!! It was an unutterable pain.' And mentioned that 'The poor girl has two brothers fighting in the South African war.' There were besides 'a husband and wife from Hindustan, black as chocolate with a dash of milk', the woman wearing a spectacular sari all of 'silver, gold, diamonds and pearls that would make your mouth water', but 'revoltingly fat'.

That evening, 20 June, Svevo was his usual garrulous self. The conversation turned to Kubelik, then visiting London, and violin-playing. Someone produced a violin and some music, and there was Ettore showing himself up as a violinist 'in the presence of my motley audience' and thinking to himself: 'I don't understand what Kubelik has come to London for when I'm around.'

The pace of Ettore's work was still busy. Many details still had to be settled, and he spent much of Sunday 23 June working out his sums. There was also plenty of work in dry-dock, both in London and in Chatham, where he was obliged to spend the day on the 25th—much to his disgruntlement, as he had planned to see Sarah Bernhardt and Constant Coquelin in the Comédie Française.

The Admiralty was thirsty for ship's paint: 'Cold, reserved, malevolent-eyed, the English are demanding that 120 tons of paint be sent here as soon as possible.' Ettore was again complaining about his nerves and sleeplessness, which were aggravated by the language and manners of the English. One visit to the Admiralty made him 'almost poorly':

If you did but know of my agitation over all the other divergences in character between myself and the English. It seems that in this country I am quite ridiculous on account of my mode of gesticulation. I observed that when I once—just once—spoke *my* English at the Admiralty, the Sea-Lords stared at my hands which seemed to dance about the room. My halting speech made me gesticulate even more than usual. Stick your hands in your pockets and then alone will you be able to speak English. And I have such bad luck! In expressing my dismay at not having grasped a word, I swung my arms apart self-deprecatingly and managed to punch a Chief Constructor in the belly. I've had to buy myself a shaving machine like Marco's. Here it's more acceptable to be drunk than to have one bristle on your snout.

The English carried out real business in the City's innumerable pubs, as he learnt from his dining companion, Wickland, who represented the huge Marconi empire, no less, was always brimful of beer, brandy and whisky and yet remained impeccably well-mannered and clean-shaven.

Ettore still found time to enjoy London. He paid a fleeting visit to the British Museum and a more thorough one to London Zoo, which he described with great zest: 'at every spot I could hear Titina cry out in admiration'. He admiringly described the comfortable houses in Bloomsbury where the residents sat out on their front terraces for a peaceful smoke in the warm evenings. On his first Sunday in London he sauntered through Hyde Park with Frantzen and two young Frenchmen who made a very debonair party: 'At a certain point I realized that their intentions with regard to women were of a buccaneering kind. I wanted to withdraw, but they wouldn't let me.' On the following Sunday he went on a boat-trip along the Thames and saw the great tunnel under the river at Greenwich. In the evenings he went to hear the orchestras in London's many 'magnificent cafés' (*sic*) and admired the ladies of the aristocracy in their evening dress. Most Sundays he attended Mass, as he called it, like the pseudo-Catholic that he was, whether it was at St Paul's or at Westminster Abbey. His lack of English proved a handicap both in church and at the café. So, while, at the latter, 'the act which I best appreciated and understood was that of a performing dog', the Protestant sermons in the churches failed to convert him into a pseudo-Protestant. Rather, he found St Paul's pseudo-Protestant, with its 'show of austerity, which is quite different from real austerity'.[26]

He wrote in later years that he never ceased to be amazed, as a younger man might have, at the English, their achievements and their follies: 'I admired the policemen, who were so respected and respectable, the numerous and luxurious music-halls, the luxury of the conquerors of India at Covent Garden and then the perfect order on the busy streets.' Motor traffic was still virtually non-existent in Britain, and the busiest London streets resembled a majestic and orderly two-way procession of horse-drawn cabs, so that it was safer to cross the square in front of the Bank of England than Trieste's main street, the Corso. Coming to England from a France that was already infested with the 'tœuf-tœuf' of the motor-car was like suddenly stepping back a few centuries, and Svevo recollected the brightly painted cabs of Chatham and Devonport, made of wood and iron, four-square, which seemed to have come straight out of the illustrations to Thackeray. He regretted only his failure to keep up conversation with the loquacious cabbies.[27]

Transport was to become an obsession with Svevo. He had already travelled hard for the firm, but the topic seems to have gripped him on the occasion of this first visit to France and England, and was to figure largely in his post-war articles about London.[28] One of these, entitled 'Kindness', reflects, evidently from first-hand experience, on the good manners of the English when using public transport, so different from those of the foreigner, who 'without noticing it, obstructs two seats' and 'is quite capable of staring at women'.

He was careful on this first visit to allay Livia's suspicions of him on that account, writing from Plymouth: 'I'd have an opportunity to betray you at every turn in this place and I feel so pure, so distant from any desire that I cannot suppose you are any different.' All he admitted was: 'I eye the women as I eye them in Trieste and that's all'; he continued:

Last night I dreamt I had betrayed you and felt such grief at not being able to tell you all about it and at realizing that our relationship was bound to change that I wept in my dream. You will gather that you too can set your mind at rest.[29]

Then: 'I shut my eyes and think of a certain nightdress which I can't remember without a thrill and I say to myself: "Patience!" And I go on smoking . . .'.

In Chatham he had already had enough of ships' hulls and had dreamt of 'having a closer look at the hulls that I'm most interested in, and without having to await a permit', at Levico, where Livia was going for a holiday after Salsomaggiore. His letters were full of affection, as well as physical longing, for Livia, and turned increasingly towards uncontrollable jealousy. Olga had described the Hotel Eden, where they were staying, as a 'hermitage', but Ettore discovered it was thronged with officers. He wrote Livia two furious letters, and it was not until 13 July, after the now habitual exchange of recriminations, that he regained his composure.

While still in France, he had suggested that Livia follow him to England. By now she was quite distraught by the separation, and would gladly have done so. But Ettore made all sorts of difficulties, not least over the travelling expenses, which he thought should be borne by the firm. He also discouraged her from scurrying with him round the English ports, and urged her to complete her rest cure at Levico. He made a curious point of not permitting Livia to stay at the Turners', where he himself had apparently been so comfortable. He said it was a *Klatschhaus*, or chatter-house, full of young men, French, German and English, perfectly well-bred, of course, but loose talkers. He was not having Livia hobnobbing with any young jackanapes, and besides, a Chief of Navy Contracts had shown his surprise that a member of the firm should share the same boarding-house as his agent.

All this could be simply the usual jealousy of the now nearly forty-year-old husband Ettore for his twenty-six-year-old wife. However, Svevo was in later years to entertain the Triestine dialect poet Virgilio Giotti and his circle with hilarious stories about his adventures in London with an English girl-friend. He was quite capable of adding spice to his tales by inventing a girl-friend in place of his wife, daughter or niece, to accompany him on the frequent visits which he paid to London right up to 1926.[30] Now Ettore declared to Livia that he had no intention of 'soiling' himself by joining in the libertine exploits of Frantzen and his fellow young blades from France who had shown him the sights of London: but there is a possibility that it was not so much Livia as himself that he wished to protect from their gossip. (He refused to wear a wedding-ring, saying that it 'throttled' him.)[31] However, Livia was to remark in 1906: 'Isn't each of our trips to London like a honeymoon? You are always so kind, but in London you leave no stone unturned in trying to make life pleasant for me, always fearing that I may not feel at home there.'[32]

By the time he caught the train from London to Plymouth, on 9 July, Ettore was feeling much happier, having now heard that Livia would soon be joining him in England. He was delighted to find the sunshine and the scenery at Plymouth both worthy of Naples and the cream and milk the richest in England—indeed, the best he had ever tasted. He admired everything—the cricket greens, the Hoe with Drake's monument, and even 'a ventriloquist such as I have never heard'. He would gladly set up his factory here!

Ettore preferred to be a 'commercial room customer' at the Royal Hotel in Plymouth, rather than pay extra in the 'coffee room' for waiter service and an *à la carte* menu. He zestfully described the curious customs of the exclusively male 'commercial room', where convention allowed even strangers to greet one another as they entered to take their places, according to seniority, at the dining-table. Residents appeared to know automatically which of their number should be President and Vice-President. Food was served according to an elaborate ritual by the President 'who generally has before him a joint of roast beef comprising a fair section of an ox, a landmark that can be seen from kilometres around'. Ordering a drink, and even raising your glass, was attended by equally formal rituals.

While waiting for his paint to arrive, Ettore spent the next few days smoking more heavily than ever and preparing an estimate of the cost of setting up and operating a factory in England. On Sunday 14 July he went to church, under- stood not a word of the sermon, but was inspired with the notion of bringing Livia's marriageable sisters, Fausta and Dora, to find English husbands to look after the factory in England in place of himself and Livia. His prolonged separation from Livia and the presence of those officers at Levico were tor- menting him more fiercely than before. This was aggravated by his lack of English. In Plymouth he was unable to resort to French, as at the Admiralty or with Frantzen (now in Ireland) and the young French gallants. He found he had completely misinterpreted the pronunciation key in his dictionary and promised Livia that she would be less surprised to discover how little English he had picked up in a month than how little she herself knew, though her English had always been better than his. There were comic scenes in Devonport dock:

I'm leading a dog's life here. Imagine yesterday I noticed 30 workmen making the same mistake. I started yelling and in my rage I completely lost the little English I know. I spoke or rather yelled Italian, German, French. The workmen had a whale of a time. The deck officers actually came out to listen to the strange sounds and I, all choked up, piped down.[33]

Ettore went to meet Livia at Dover around 22 July.[34] In London they stayed at 'a splendid hotel on Russell Square' for their fifth wedding anniversary.[35] Livia replenished Ettore, as he had requested, with heavy trousers, black boots and 'perfectly laundered shirts and collars without the tiniest crease' which were indispensable when mixing with English gentlemen. No doubt she also joined forces with him in learning English. She describes their tour of Ireland, 'whose landscapes enchanted us with their wild beauty'. They stayed at Queenstown (Cobh, the outer harbour of Cork, near Carrigoloo), where Ettore had to supervise the painting of Lord Muskerry's yacht.[36] This second 'honeymoon' turned out a better cure for Livia than her visits to Salsomaggiore and Levico.

Ettore's odyssey, as he predictably called it,[37] at last brought to an end his ties with the Revoltella Institute, as he had been unable to hold the examinations that June. He was now playing no mean part in enhancing the efficiency of the world's most powerful war navy, at the very time when Great Britain was becoming alarmed by the growing naval and colonial ambitions of Germany and by Russia's swift eastward expansion towards China and the Pacific. These fears were drawing Britain closer to an understanding with France as a safeguard against the former threat and with Japan against the latter, and out of the far from splendid isolation in which it had found itself during the bloody South African wars against the Boers. These had not yet ended while Svevo was engaged on this first English mission.

39

THE LITERARY MOLE

While Ettore was away, Olga had a furious row with Gioachino, followed by one of the worst and longest of her nervous crises.[38] Perhaps this was why the Schmitzes after their return from Britain moved down a floor in Villa Veneziani 'so as to live communally with [Livia's] parents', unless it was because the expanding Bliznakoff family needed more room on the second floor.[39] From now on, Livia generally went with Ettore to Murano, unless she was indisposed, presumed pregnant, taking the waters at Salsomaggiore or on holiday somewhere, or unless Ettore's visit was a very short one. Only on these relatively rare occasions do we catch a glimpse of Svevo's life through his letters to Livia. For the whole of 1902, we see nothing of him except in August, when Livia was on holiday at Tarvis in the Carnic Alps. Ettore could spare no more than a week there. The Schmitzes went there again in 1906, when Ettore and Livia climbed nearly 2,700 metres to the top of Mount Manhardt.[40] They generally took mountain holidays, mostly in Austria in places near the Italian border— Schrattenberg in 1907, Scheifling in 1908 and, in 1911, with Ottavio Schmitz and his family, Bad Ischl, favoured by the Emperor Franz Josef himself. It was probably in 1904 that they stayed at Villach, where Ettore absent-mindedly lost little Letizia at a country fair.[41] Sometimes they stayed nearer home: in 1903, when Letizia was in indifferent health, Livia took her to Sesana on the Carso;[42] in 1905 they went no further than the Hotel Obelisco at Opicina, overlooking Trieste.

Apart from Livia with her gynaecological problems, there were now two other invalids in the Schmitz family: a real one, Adolfo, apparently suffering from gout and 'now very well resigned to his gammy leg', who in 1901 was already in calipers and was having a special shoe made, and who had bumps on his hands which he put down to rheumatism; and an imaginary one, Ottavio, who was convinced he had nephritis.[43]

Ettore, in spite of his excess of last and other cigarettes and the vagaries of his diet, kept in pretty good health; though, in the August heat of 1902, he wrote to his wife: 'I'm not practising the violin, I'm not writing plays.'[44] A year later, on 14 June 1903, he completed *Un marito*. That is an eloquent date, as it contradicts the resolution, recorded the previous December, to eliminate from his life 'once and for all ... that ridiculous and damaging thing called literature'. This was the 'iron resolve' referred to in *Profilo autobiografico* but never long adhered to as that account would have us believe. At this point what is more interesting in the note of December 1902 than that wishful 'renunciation' is Svevo's equally oft-repeated intention to write 'the diary of my recent life', the desire to 'get to understand myself better ... through these pages'. He proclaims himself one of the 'impotent' who 'cannot think except pen in hand (as if thought was not more useful and necessary in the moment of action)'. He dwells on this point:

So, once again, this crude stiff instrument, the pen, will aid me in getting to the ground, which is so complex, of my being. Then I will cast it aside for ever and I mean to learn the habit of thinking in the very attitude of action: Racing to flee an enemy or to pursue him, my fist raised to strike or to parry. These are similes which ...[45]

Never was a statement more significantly broken off. Svevo realizes that his similes betray a slide into the rhetoric of the most hackneyed pseudo-Darwin-ism, and he casts aside his pen before ever getting to the ground, which is so complex, of his being, where all the contradictions of his time and ours coexist: the being of a writer turned industrialist; of a populist, who had insisted on being married in the working-class parish of San Giacomo, turned master of workmen and housemaids; of a bourgeois against the bourgeoisie and a Socialist against Socialism; of an indefatigable dreamer forever in danger of falling into the docks of the world's mightiest war navy who yet yearns to be a man of action; an Austrian Italian and a baptized, anticlerical, atheistical Jew; a patriarchal feminist and a jealous husband; an Irredentist who helps sustain the Triple Alliance by painting the hulls of Italian and Austrian battleships; a governor Ariosto who identifies more and more with the opportunist Equicola. Svevo's conscience is a muddle that can only be sorted out if he has the courage to live up to his own ideals and ethical impulses, but he remains still and forever split between 'dream' and 'struggle'. Herein lies Svevo's 'impotence', an impotence which is both personal and historic and which no pen can cure. The pen can do no more than displace this muddle to a fictive level, the 'literary' level, in fact, the Schopenhauerian level where everything remains a make-believe which will end when the curtain falls; a detached level, somehow objective and scientific, where perhaps that muddle may be sorted out, subjected to judgement, and overcome. But this will take years, and a world war.

Meanwhile, mole-like, unseen, Svevo went on writing. Precise dating of the pieces he wrote up to the war is usually impossible. On 4 May 1904 he declared himself the inventor of Annin,[46] referring to his scientific fantasy 'Lo specifico del dottor Menghi' (The Menghi Formula).[47] This work fully bears out Benco's remarks about Svevo's astonishing medical knowledge (pharmacological, in this case). It is no less striking for its notion of biological or physiological 'relativity' (to do with metabolic rates), and is also Svevo's earliest attempt at first-person narrative fiction. The narrative framework shows greater subtlety and sophistication than in any of his previous works, not excluding the novels, being more sensitive to the play of narrative irony and to the probing of the conscience.

On 19 January 1905 he informed Livia, from Murano, that he was neither reading nor playing his violin and was so 'busy from morning to evening with the most varied tasks' that he could hardly leave the factory long enough to write to her. Yet that very same day he dashed off a page of writing that might be the outline for a play, perhaps an early scheme for *L'avventura di Maria* (Maria's Adventure),[48] and more notes followed in February, though he was still telling Livia that he was too busy to write her long letters. Yet he himself let her know of a 'splenetic product of my chilled intellect', a 'disquisition on my own and Cimutti's vegetarianism', and at the same time asked her to toss into his *Pult* (bureau) his study on *polenta* (the maize-porridge which was the staple food of the poor in northern Italy).[49] We have a fragment of the vegetarian work,[50] which centres on the conflict of interests of Schmitz the wealthy vegetarian employer who eats meat 'out of habit' and the poor workman Cimutti who is an 'enforced vegetarian'. Cimutti 'might even think I disapprove of meat simply to put him off it, because he hears me talking this way but he sees that I go on feeding off cadavers'.

These two lost dietary essays show that Svevo was still something of the 'eccentric' that Benco had seen in him. Another lost work brought him 'genuine literary success'. It was 'something like a school essay entitled: The manufacture of men suited to play second violin in a classical quartet'. They were to be made out of wood and iron, as the presence of a soul would inevitably have led to an apoplectic fit. This essay was written as a 'vendetta' against the other three members of the family string quartet which performed in Villa Veneziani and in which Svevo was of course second violin—an 'owl' or 'mole', so frightfully fumbling and tuneless that he set the whole quartet squeaking 'like an assembly of serpents': 'I would curl up and like a real serpent I'd grope for my tail to sink my teeth into it and punish myself': a brazenly Freudian image, penned in 1926. Yet already in 1902 he had linked his impotence with that 'crude stiff instrument, the pen', which was to be cast aside. The Veneziani string quartet included Dr Giuseppe Oberti di Valnera, a first-class cellist (he married Dora Veneziani in 1903, and joined the family firm), Raffaele Levi as first violin, and Giulio Romano as viola.[51] It must have been formed after Dora and Oberti were married, as in February 1903 Svevo was still studying a Beethoven trio.[52]

40

THE FACTORY IN CHARLTON

In the summer of 1903, while Livia was relaxing at Sesana on the Carso with Letizia, Ettore was enduring the heat, the factory fumes and the mosquitoes at Murano, though also enjoying spells of leisure in the company of his young nephew, Aurelio Finzi, Paola's son—who narrowly escaped drowning on one occasion when their lagoon punt nearly capsized. In July, Marco Bliznakoff set off, highly disgruntled, for a three-month visit to London to set up the Veneziani factory there. It was to be in Anchor and Hope Lane in Charlton, a few yards from the Thames, halfway between Greenwich and Woolwich. The Greenwich Libraries Local History Collection has established that 'It consisted of a small brick built factory, a corrugated iron shed and an older dwelling house which was occupied by the Foreman or Manager.' Next door was the Sofnol Company and opposite, a Siemens factory. Kelly's 1905 *Directory* for Woolwich has the entry: 'Veneziani, Gioachino, anti-corrosion composition works' between Charlton Parish Depôt and Richards, D. D., smith and fitter.

Nella Bliznakoff joined Marco in August, along with two workmen, but things kept going wrong. Ettore, meanwhile, was most lethargically engaged in raising a mortgage on the Murano factory, possibly in order to finance the one being set up in London.[53] Delays and setbacks kept Marco in London for six months. Nella returned to Trieste. Left on his own, Marco found everything too much for him. The firm decided that Ettore should help him out, and so he set off on his second trip to England on 19 November. He ruefully remarked after arriving in London that this was the third time he had *not* seen Paris.[54] All he had time for there was to put on his 'leggings'—a complicated manœuvre—in the railway station lavatory, leaving his umbrella behind.[55]

When he reached London with his baggage and violin, the cabbies enquired

with respect: 'Albert Hall, Whigmore Hall [*sic*] or Queens Hall?' In answer to
which, from now on, he had to name 'the drabbest and most out-of-the-way
suburb'.[56] In Charlton, he found Marco touchingly overjoyed to see him, and
they got on surprisingly well together. Marco's only fault, according to Ettore,
was that he heard, talked and loved nothing but factories and machines. In
fact, a second fault, connected to the first, appeared: acute hypochondria and
neurosis which followed the ups and downs of the installation work. 'If he is
ill, his only affliction is the inability to take his mind off things,' with the result
that 'He lets himself be knocked down by every straw that crosses his path.
Then he neither sleeps nor eats.' Ettore therefore considered it his first task to
keep Marco's spirits up, but he couldn't get him to take a quarter of an hour's
rest without leaping up every five minutes to 'make sure that the workmen
hadn't made off with any stones!' A creaking window at night would make
him cry burglar, and he got Ettore up just to check a detail in the operation of
the boilers. Marco was forever in despair over the machines which he had
designed: 'Let's get rid of all these contraptions and make paint as we do in
Trieste.' Finally Ettore sent him off to spend a few days at St John's Wood on
the other side of London with his fellow Bulgarian, Cristo Tchaperoff, who
was now, with Frantzen, an agent for the firm. That way, both Marco and
Ettore might get some peace.

Ettore was delighted with the new machines: 'The factory is magnificent ...
stately and massive, iron and stone.' He daydreamed about erecting a second
Villa Veneziani on the spot, 'surrounding it with trees and plants', but the wet
ground was never drained and County Council permission to build dwellings
on it never obtained. He was not perturbed when the great boiler had to be
winched over and into its shed. On Monday 23 November production started
on the first batch and 'the machines seem to be working well'; but the next day
'on account of our inexperience with the new work and machines ... the motor
on which the whole operation depends broke down'. The workforce too was
inexperienced and the paint-barrels were leaking. The second batch proceeded
more smoothly and Svevo thought that 'the automatic mixers have even
improved the quality of the paint'. But the main advantage was that 'we no
longer personally handle the powders ...; I no longer have a metallic taste in
my mouth.' There was a great saving in managerial effort: 'Today with Marco's
machines I took ten minutes to set up tomorrow's batch (21 tubs); now the
workers are busy and so are the machines but I have no more to do except take
the boiler readings.'

Already by 5 December the improvements in efficiency could be assessed:

results for the future—that is after some small and quite inexpensive modifications to
the cleaning-out system have been made—are as follows: With little labour, that is,
without fagging ourselves, with 6 to 8 workmen (depending on the amount of accessory
work) we could turn out 60–80 tubs a week. Over a hundred even without pushing
ourselves too hard (compared with 54 in Trieste) which, as Olga and Gioachino know,
is pretty hard work.

It was not until 16 December that he revealed to Livia that he had slightly
cut his hands twice while instructing the workmen to handle the equipment,
and added: 'they followed my instructions. so accurately that their hands are
bruised all over, but I'm better now'. All in all Ettore had some cause to write
complacently on 11 December:

Altogether the clerk and man of letters Ettore Schmitz, more or less at the close of his
life, showed a good bit of practical sense and when I shave I look at myself most
admiringly in the mirror: 'Bravo, dear Ettore, bravo! Now you should change your
trade yet again so as to see how many more small talents there are in you.'

On 3 December, he whimsically associated Livia with the new machinery:

Yesterday I was unfaithful. I fondled the bottom of the gas motor. It has a regulator
and when you squeeze it the motor races madly as if it were ticklish which is very
pleasant. Having nothing better available, that's what I do.

Still, the proximity of their birthdays—with Svevo turning forty-two twelve
days after Livia turned twenty-nine—reminded him of their difference in age
('An ugly number 13') and led him to renew yet again his offer to 'allow you
the liberty to find yourself another husband, younger and more serene': which
Livia as always flatly declined. She felt far more demoralized than Ettore. She
felt useless: 'I just want to weep to solace myself and I have a lump in
my throat.' She was so upset that on 16 December she wrote him a tearful
remonstration just in time for his birthday:

I don't understand where all these clouds you keep talking about come from . . . . . . you
will beg my pardon in full repentance for all the insults which have lately been going
through your head. In truth a lover of your calibre is no true lover; you are so afraid
of being robbed of the object of your love that all your love turns to torment for you
and partly for me too. Trust, Ettore, I won't stop repeating it. What filth do you think
I am made of to consider me capable of lying to you with such effrontery?

This is one of the few letters of Livia's—usually her most passionate or warmly
affectionate ones—which Svevo did not destroy as she instructed. In this
particular case Livia's rancour seems disproportionate, as none of Svevo's
letters had accused her of deceiving him. Perhaps she had been needled by
reading in his letter of the 14th, which she had just received: 'I don't understand
the point of bothering people with rehearsals [with Kugy's choir for the
Palestrina Mass] and then missing the performance.' Perhaps Livia's condition,
and not merely in the physical sense, was less sound than her husband's. It
would not be surprising if she were in a nervous state, with Olga going through
a very bad patch, with the Bliznakoffs in quarantine (though for nothing very
serious), and her absent husband demanding that she should account for her
every movement.

So Ettore Schmitz appeared the healthiest (or least unhealthy) of the
Veneziani circle. At the practical level, Ettore's self-satisfaction with his image
in the shaving-mirror was justified. He had been precipitated into the most

uncomfortable conditions which he had ever had to live in, and managed to
turn the whole thing into a joke. The small terraced house in Charlton was not
properly furnished, lacking even a cooking-stove, and the windows did not
shut: 'Our house is still in such a state that we spent the whole of Sunday in
the little factory office which is a great deal more comfortable.' Marco, Ettore
and Nicoletto Bravin (the Charlton foreman and son of the Murano foreman)
had to fend entirely for themselves. Or rather, Nicoletto acted as factotum,
cooking up meals of a sort without any recipes after a long day's work in the
factory: 'You cannot imagine Nicoletto's kindness, his energy to the point of
heroism, his intelligence.' His cooking was rudimentary: 'Meat and fish, fish
and meat and bacon and eggs and milk. We've found some celery which we
eat raw (bad for Marco) and cabbage which we haven't yet got round to
boiling.' 'On Saturday Marco and I went to Woolwich, ten minutes from here,
to the market. It was very lively, quite ordinary, and we found some excellent
vegetables which we ate on Sunday and Monday.... Nicoletto always makes the
same supper, ringing the changes with tinned sardines, mustard and preserves.'

The lack of heating was the worst hardship. The weather was extremely
cold: either rain which pervaded everything, or else three or four degrees of
frost. By day Ettore wore three pairs of drawers. In bed he piled on not only
all the blankets but also his overcoat and fur coat and slept almost fully dressed,
'clad all in mail like Lohengrin'. On one night it was so cold that neither he
nor Marco nor Nicoletto could sleep. Nicoletto had to spend a day in bed,
while Ettore had a chronic cold and kept running out of handkerchiefs, but
laboured on undaunted.

He now made his first acquaintance with the notorious London smog: 'All
of a sudden I see a dirty yellow cloud coming across the Thames. Apparently
it's fog, for the river is full of lights and hooters.' He even attributed to it the
special quality of English portraiture: 'Those delightful faces of English girls,
ideal and proud, must have been viewed through fog.' Once through the clouds
he caught a glimpse of the moon, which turned out to be the sun.

For the first time in his life, Ettore was making his own bed, which he
described as 'a sort of catapult', and he also regaled Livia with minute accounts
of how, in this exclusively male bohemian existence, he contrived to brush his
own coat and sew his own buttons on to his fur coat. He revealed the leg-pull
only just before his return to Trieste: 'all I ever did in my bedroom was to
occasionally empty the chamber-pot and occasionally make my bed. The room
is now so full of newspapers and cigarette butts that you can hardly get in or
out.' Ettore's maladroitness was legendary in the family, and in any case he
was so busy that he never had time even to touch his violin until 17 December,
and then barely for an hour. Three days earlier he had gone into Charlton to
buy a string and 'had a pleasant diversion, finding the shopkeeper playing an
ordinary piano by machine'—no doubt, the inspiration for his piece about the
mechanical second violin player made of iron and wood.

Even now, he always found time to read. Newspapers. He bought the

Morning Leader and *The Times*; he asked Livia to send him *Il Piccolo* and all the newspapers covering the Ferri–Bettolo suit, as he was short of political news. He also asked her to pay his subscription to *Critica Sociale*. On receiving a parcel of newspapers he closely read a whole speech by Felice Venezian about the clashes between Austrian Italians and Germans at Innsbruck and about the university question: 'Very fine but it made little impact here in Charlton.' This is Svevo's only known written comment on Triestine politics. Frantzen also brought political tidings, but Ettore affected to take them very casually:

Against Marco's wishes, I made him stay to lunch, and we spent a merry half hour. He told us about Irredentist demonstrations and I know not what about which we know nothing. He even said there was a threat of war between Austria and Italy. He taught us to cook potatoes and promised to send us recipes from Chatham for ragout and suchlike dishes.

Only on one Sunday, 29 November, did he dine out, as the guest of the Tchaperoffs. Cristo Tchaperoff had married an English girl of good family (the Gambles). Ettore found the company better than the food, but best of all was 'a magnificent white Persian cat'. He entertained the ladies with his comic English:

Having for so long had no opportunity to devote myself to my favourite occupation, that of gossiping, which makes up for and replaces my former one of writing, I made the ladies laugh a great deal and when I left I was able to say to them: 'You can be happy that I can't speak English.' ... Certainly, if it goes on this way I shall never speak English as I don't let the natives speak.

In Trieste, little Letizia had taken to writing love-letters to a mysterious T. F., who could conceivably be her future husband Tony Fonda. Her father wrote to her: 'When you can read Dante's *Paradiso* and *Inferno* then you can get married because you'll know where to send your husband,' but he promised to find her a pretty ring in London.

On the afternoon of his forty-second birthday, Sunday 20 December, Svevo started on his way back to Trieste with Marco and reached home on the following evening, regretting only that he had not had the time to take up Veruda's invitation to stop and visit him in Paris.[57]

All this travelling had its effect on him. Within a month of leaving Charlton, he was off to Murano again, and wrote to Livia: 'Last night, finding myself awake, I had to collect myself in order to decide whether I was in Trieste, Murano or Charlton. In fact, I was on board ship.'[58] The crossings to Venice always remained a nightmare. Three weeks later, he was sea-sick all night. In August he found the heat in his cabin in the *Hungaria* overpowering, and the following year he wisecracked that the firm should offer the Lloyd steamship company cheaper paint 'on condition they *don't* allow us free passage any more'.[59]

The anti-fouling compound had been drawn into international *Realpolitik*. In February 1904 the Russian thrust towards China, Korea and Far Eastern waters was answered by a surprise naval attack by the Japanese, now allied to Great Britain, against the Russian base of Port Arthur in north China. The Venezianis were supplying both the Russians and the Japanese. Ettore's first reaction to the attack was: 'What do you say about those Japanese devils? Who knows how upset Marco will be. To tell the truth, of the two sides I don't know which I'm on.'⁶⁰

Ettore's letters to Livia exploited everything for humorous ends, even the Russo-Japanese war. He issued an ukase which had nothing to do with Tsarist policy, domestic or foreign, but concerned only the Schmitz family and—predictably—yet another wager that he would stop smoking. He declared himself determined to thwart his faithful wife's natural tendency to wish for her husband's death and the blonde's natural desire to wear mourning. More seriously, the proposed three years' abstinence from smoking would pay for Letizia's education. (It lasted a month.)⁶¹ The ukase did not refer to the bloody defeat of the Russians in the fifteen-day battle of Mukden in Manchuria in March 1905, nor to the destruction of the Russian Baltic fleet at Tsushima in the same month after its historic voyage round the world, nor to the Russian revolution of 1905.

Neither did his letters mention another tragic and more personal episode that occurred in 1904—the collapse and death of his friend Veruda.

41

VERUDA DEAD

The two friends never met in England. Veruda had promised to advertise his presence in London by scrawling his name in charcoal on all the walls. He painted the portraits of the Churchills at Blenheim Palace. In 1901, Svevo promised to send Veruda's mother postcards from every British town he visited. In December 1903, as we have seen, he did not find time to stop and see Veruda in Paris on his way back home. Veruda had turned acutely neurotic. He had written to Svevo that he had gambled away every penny he had at Monte Carlo. He couldn't stop his mother from drinking, and was near to suicide. In the winter of 1903–4 he felt he was slowly dying in Paris and stuffed his pockets full of documents, fearing that he might die unidentified in a strange city. Svevo invited him to Murano and tried to cheer him up, and in fact Veruda started painting again and produced two masterpieces—*Comments* and *Fondamenta at Burano*—for the 1905 Venice Biennale exhibition. But he was never to see them displayed. His mother died at Bad Villach, cursing him and slapping him for refusing her a glass of water,[62] leaving him distraught (this incident was to be incorporated into the scene of the death of Zeno's father). Veruda then had an attack of appendicitis for which, demoralized as he was, he refused treatment. It developed into peritonitis, which finished him in Trieste on 29 August 1904. He was thirty-six.[63] Livia recollects: 'That day I saw Ettore collapsed on his bed crying for the first time like a child.'[64] His grief may have been sharpened by guilt at having done too little too late for his best friend. Ettore's sister Ortensia had had her child called Umberto after the painter. Having lost Ettore's close friendship, Veruda might well have felt isolated. Livia suggests that his collapse may also have been due to his sense of failure as an artist, and mentions that he gave up painting for a considerable period.[65]

Veruda failed to come to terms with the new art which appeared with the new century. He had to live and support his parents by painting portraits of the wealthy, working fast without the leisure to develop his artistic resources or to experiment. By 1901, Picasso had already given his first personal exhibition and 1903 saw the great exhibition of the *Wiener Secession* and the Gustav Klimt exhibition. Veruda may well have felt outdated. Ottavio Schmitz in Vienna was 'laughed out of court' for admiring his art.[66] Veruda's paintings still figure nobly, however neglected, among the post-Impressionists, but he had the misfortune to apply himself to draughtsmanship, which he had always scorned, just when everybody else was giving it up.

Veruda left Ettore many of his paintings, which he hung 'religiously' in his apartment and which he ordained in his will should not be scattered after his own death. Livia narrowly saved them from the maelstrom of the Second World War. Aided by their common friend Enrico Schott, Ettore organized an all too successful posthumous exhibition and 'aroused the unanimous admiration for the dead painter which had been denied him while he lived.'[67]

42

A HALF-ENGLISH SCHMITZ

Svevo's visits to England became frequent after 1903. Livia usually accompanied him, so there are no letters and few references. By Svevo's sixth visit, in March–April 1906,[68] both the factory and the house in Charlton were in good order and the Schmitzes felt quite at home there, or rather better—on a sort of honeymoon. Svevo felt that he had recorded nothing about his journeys—as if his letters to his wife did not convey his *real* experiences. He was alarmed by the unretentiveness of his memory,[69] and when he made two short visits to

England without Livia in 1906 (the second in September) his letters showed a vista which had shrunk back to the scale of the microscopic epic of everyday life. They tell of his snoring which deafened poor Nicoletto, who was seriously ill. They relate how he tussled with the housekeeper Meggie over her duties, her cooking, her pay. On one evening 'At 6 I'm going to the Dylkeses next door, who are very fond of me, to tell them some tall stories about our country.' He sent advice to Gioachino about the poultry incubator called 'Foster-Mother' which he had in Trieste. He played snakes and ladders at his landlords', the Francises. He tried to avoid their company, but this was difficult owing to the warm attachment that had sprung up between Nicoletto Bravin and their daughter Nell (whose name Ettore phonetically transcribed as *Neu*). On Saturday he and Nicoletto went to the Colyseum, but he found it far more entertaining to lose his way in London and ask the policemen for directions back to Charlton. The same evening he went to play the violin at the Streeters, self-taught musicians somewhat less skilled than Ettore himself. He did not seek to cultivate their society. The Tchaperoffs repeatedly invited him over to St John's Wood, and he felt bound to invite them back for champagne at Church Lane, though he did not greatly care for their company either. After the day's work he sought relaxation by taking a long walk with Nicoletto as far as Greenwich, and then amused himself by reading *The Pickwick Papers*.

It was the factory that provided the most interest. On 4 April there was a visit by the Admiralty factory inspector: 'I rushed out to buy a bottle of wine, biscuits and cigars (7s/6d). The firm will foot the bill, but I will eat, drink and smoke the lot because he's a teetotaller and wouldn't take anything.' The inspector turned out to be most solicitous and an ardent Whig, as Ettore himself was. He urged Ettore to read the *Daily Mail* rather than the *Morning Leader*. Indeed, as a foreigner, Ettore should read a variety of newspapers, eat oranges and boil his drinking water to avoid catching colds, and stick to the United Church, whether of England, Austria or Italy. Schmitz, the inspector explained, was the Italian form of Smith. He nearly forgot to question Ettore about paint production and had to take his word as to the various dimensions and other details regarding the factory and plant, 'because in some places the stench was too strong and he was weeping like a calf'.

The following day brought an even more instructive visit. 'Two chevroned merchant navy petty officers' turned up, offering furs 'which they themselves had collected at the South and North Poles, at Trebizond, in Alaska, California and Zanzibar'. Partly in the hope of getting a free English lesson, and partly perhaps also because he had a weakness for good cock-and-bull stories, Ettore haggled over the price and finally handed over three pounds (over seventy crowns) for a muff that was supposed to be made of sable fur but that subsequently turned out to be worth seven or eight shillings at most.

When Ettore was in Charlton again in September, he found the factory yard full of the chickens produced by Tchaperoff's incubator. However, they were dying off at the rate of three or four a day and producing no eggs. There were also two dogs, but Ettore's favourite was another animal:

Lastly, and this is what I wanted to tell you, there's a little cat, strange and nimble ... like all cats. He's my greatest friend and we play together a real treat. I get a few scratches and he gets a bit ruffled but we're still attached to one another and some of the smudges you see on the paper are due to his stalking across the paper as I write, sticking his tail up my nose. I take him a bit of meat every day, despite Nicoletto's theory that cats should live on mice, and he prances around me like a dog ... You'll wonder why I'm telling you all these things but I'm trying as best I can to give you some idea of the life I'm leading and the cat is an absolutely important part of my life. The only thing that divides us (and he also resembles you in this) is that he can't stand smoke.

In the world's largest city, Ettore Schmitz always remained, as Giulio Ventura was to tell Silvio Benco, 'a small-town man ... his cosmopolitan life didn't change him'.[70] He made himself a home from home in Charlton. He did not seek the sort of high society which frequented Villa Veneziani, nor even any literary or artistic set. He made no close friendships in London, and, for that matter, he did not do so in Trieste either, after the loss of Veruda, preferring to keep within the extended family. In London, he fairly regularly saw the Tchaperoffs, with whom he had business connexions, and the Francises. He also made up a violin trio with a workman from the Woolwich Arsenal and a Charlton shopkeeper (possibly Streeter). They met on Sundays, and Svevo remarked that he was deservedly first violin in the trio. Ettore's London relationships, which he could choose more freely than those in Trieste, suggest a predilection, in keeping with his bachelor preferences of the years with Veruda, for unpretentious humble folk as opposed to the genteelly respectable.[71]

The language always remained something of a barrier in Svevo's relations with the English. For this he blamed his dreamy absent-mindedness, which impeded any systematic learning. The Londoners' Cockney he found 'an insuperable difficulty', especially over the telephone: he only had to name the person he wanted to speak to, and there would be a barrage of impatient questions yelled at him. He couldn't make out the bus-conductor's 'Hold tight!', which sounded to his Italian ear like 'Oltai'.[72]

He read a great number of English newspapers and followed the crime columns as eagerly as he did in Trieste, as raw material, so he said, for his writing. In 1903 a girl was killed on a train not far from Charlton. He kept track of the investigations carefully: 'And one day I discussed it so fervently with an Englishman that he all but rushed off to the nearby police station to report me. I reflected bitterly: that blessed literature. It won't let go of me. It will end up by landing me on the gallows.' He even got his friends and neighbours in Charlton to collect newspaper cuttings from the crime and divorce columns. Macabre murders are occasionally referred to in his letters.[73] The death of Guido Speier from veronal poisoning in *La coscienza di Zeno* is not unlike the too well-faked suicide of one Trevannion in Hove in September 1912, which his friends Baines and Rowe could have prevented. Svevo never mentions the name, but Trevannion, like Speier, had quarrelled with his family and squandered a fortune. His accidental suicide caused a considerable stir, and the case led to veronal being classified as a poison. Trevannion's tragedy, so complexly representative of the world of his social set, is perfectly transposed and integrated into Svevo's novel, which is no less complexly representative of that same world.[74]

Rather than forging any close personal bonds in England, Svevo thus preferred to study the nation at arm's length through the newspapers and the commercial travellers who chanced to visit his factory. He was always glad to offer these a cup of tea as 'they brought the real English pronunciation to my doorstep'. So he played the amateur sociologist. He listened to everyone's religious views, passionately held in a country that proliferated with sects.[75] But Italo Svevo always expressed himself guardedly, never completely divulged his real feelings. His frankness was always conditioned by his readership, whether in his letters to his wife or in the articles he wrote for *La Nazione* after the war, or else what he said might be instrumental to some immediate or incidental purpose (such as a dialogue with an increasingly Fascist Trieste). He revealed himself fully only to his ideal literary readership, and then only through the complex web of his ironies. The only mention of England in Svevo's fictive writings comes in one of the tall stories recounted by Zeno during his courtship of Ada.

Even as a sociologist, then, Svevo is disappointing, though an alert and lively observer. He was too bound to the old-fashioned positivist notion of the national 'character' or stereotype, though aware of its limitations:

And I walk along forever accompanied by all these stereotypes from 67 Church Lane, where I live, down to Anchor and Hope Lane less than half a kilometre away, where my factory is. In the space of that half kilometre I change my mind ten times according to the people whom I come across. One person strikes me as being worthy of the Romans, another as an indigestible morsel for the Ocean and so on. I've been floundering among these conflicting views for a dozen years. On my arrival I revel in the bracing air of freedom, great freedom; then certain formulas which one cannot escape in that blessed country form around my head a leaden hood which lightens, to my great delight, when I set foot on sacred Latin soil. This indecision makes me unhappy because in England I miss my Trieste and very often when I'm here [i.e. in Trieste], I miss that same leaden hood.[76]

He described Church Lane, 'a neat street on a slope' consisting of two rows of houses which were all shops. He analysed its social topography:

Church Lane becomes more common the further down you go. Each house has a back garden and a shop in front. As you go up Church Lane, on the other hand, the appearance of the houses improves; each one has a front garden too.[77]

The better-off people escaped out of the industrial areas and away from the higher rates levied in those same more populous districts. The result was 'the depressing phenomenon of large houses left empty' and 'rates on a sliding scale the wrong way round', that is, bearing most heavily on the poorer areas. Svevo deplored 'the present division' between rich and poor:

The Englishman to whom I confided my sentimental notions remarked: Just try to raise your workmen's pay and for every extra shilling a day you give them they'll move their homes at least a mile further away from your factory. Naturally, I didn't undertake the experiment...[78]

Meanwhile, 'my Church Lane is one of the most variegated streets in the Realm', its little station, halfway up, crowded at six in the morning by workers heading for the docks and factories and the Woolwich Arsenal, at seven by City clerks, and patronized during the day by ladies and gentlemen from as far afield as Blackheath, the adjoining district. 'The most exalted family in the district lives at the top of the hill in a huge estate which is all meadows and greenwood.' Everyone in Charlton recounted the story that this family was descended from a lady who 'supposedly had the good fortune to catch the eye of a king of England'. He, 'in order to induce her to satisfy his desires, offered her all the land which she could see from the hill up which Church Lane climbs. This lady, besides her other attributes, had excellent eyesight, and a great deal of land became hers.' Svevo also described the little Gothic church at the top of the street. It has a graveyard and an attractive fountain and watering-trough erected by the descendant of that lady for the day of King Edward's coronation. He could not describe, however, 'the stateliness and tranquillity' of the lawns and woods of the estate[79] which can be seen in period photographs of The Heights, with a small lake with ducks and boats and a tiny island inhabited by rabbits. Charlton House itself is one of the finest built by Inigo Jones. Below it, along the railway cutting, the great chalk quarries are rich in fossil remains. We may well imagine that the author of 'L'uomo e la teoria darwiniana' went to potter and muse there.

Between 1903 and 1913 Svevo saw the streets of London taken over by the internal combustion engine. By 1913, he was writing: 'The stench of petrol is so bad that everyone's eyes stream as if over some national calamity.' He remembered the rapid spread of the London double-decker trams, and also the growth of the underground railway system from the first line at twopence a ride at the beginning of the century to the tenth line constructed after the war.[80]

Svevo never mentioned English humour. He was more struck by English manners, or what he called 'kindness'. He dwelt on the refined queueing conventions of the English: every one of them 'knows his exact place' even when there is no formal queue at the less frequented bus-stops. In attempting to be 'kind'—that is, not to shove the other passengers—Ettore might let his wife board first only to have the conductor declare the bus full and bar him from joining her: so he would 'ruthlessly' push his way on. He also attributed to the 'kindness' of the English their propensity in the company of strangers to discuss that non-committal topic, the weather, as a way of inculcating 'a friendly feeling' in both parties.[81]

The London theatre was a great disappointment for Svevo: 'show business' had taken over. He found the West End musical comedies indistinguishable from one another. The war swept away the 'select little theatres' in London where good plays were to be seen, and one of which, run by Lena Ashwell, was a stone's throw from Charlton, in Greenwich. There Svevo went every week and saw plays by Shakespeare, Sheridan, Shaw, Galsworthy and others.[82] Generally speaking, however, literature, he said, left him alone in Charlton.

In *Profilo autobiografico* Svevo summed up life in the London suburb:

All in all, he thought that in the country of great adventures, adventure was rejected more than elsewhere. Everyone in that suburb worked away quietly in his place within his own class into which he fitted more or less actively but with little inclination for rebellion or adventure. And he thought he had discovered that the strength of a nation was due more to such elements and that indeed the exploits of a Clive, a Rhodes or a Nelson would be unable to produce so much wealth if adventure were not something exceptional in a nation's life, an ennobling graft upon the ancient trunk of quiet, regular, daily activity. Wasn't the literary adventure which he had attempted itself a diminution of his own strength as an ordinary useful citizen? Certainly, life in the factory in England was for Svevo a cure and a tonic, and his resignation became still more cheerful.[83]

Even so, his two brief references to his lost vocation as a writer in 1906 seem less than cheerful: 'A shame that I no longer know how to write! I don't care so much about the violin.' 'I would have the opportunity to have another go at noting things down. I doubt my ability to do it and I shan't try.'[84]

But in 'Soggiorno londinese' (London Sojourn) also he insisted that 'the Anglo-Saxons had rejuvenated me', or rather, 'calmed me', with their total lack of interest in dreams of glory. 'It is true I met the king of football of the district and that I was also shown someone who was famous throughout England in the rough game of rugby,' but Svevo thought that such sportsmen had no thought for glory. As for him, he became a fanatical supporter of Charlton Athletic, which was founded in 1905 and won the English championship in 1913. Writers in England were far less regarded than sportsmen:

Even the popular libraries are better stocked with good works on economics and law than with good literature. Nobody knew Kipling, everybody knew Cobden. Herbert Spencer died in Brighton in 1903, a few miles [*sic*] away from us. I cried out with surprise and grief but my neighbour Mr Francis, a Thames barge-owner, who died leaving a fortune of £6,000 and owned a magnificent book to which he devoted a quarter of an hour every day: The book of the English nobility with portraits of all the members of the House of Lords, took his pipe out of his mouth and asked: 'Who's he?'[85]

Francis, it will be remembered, was also Svevo's landlord, and must have belonged to that category of Englishmen who owned 'two reading books, the Bible and the Peerage', whereas the other category, more to the liberal Svevo's liking, owned 'the Bible and the life of Gladstone'. Then there was also 'my smith', D.D. Richards, whose workshop was next door to the Veneziani factory, 'who agrees now with one and now with another of these two'.

Richards perfectly typified in Svevo's eyes the image of 'perfidious Albion'. An extremely strong and hard-working man, though he was over fifty by 1903, he worked fourteen hours a day, while his men, who were in trade unions, worked eight. This is how he responded to Svevo's 'political survey':

He would vote for Lloyd George because he wanted to see the right of veto of the upper house abolished; then he would vote for Lloyd George again to secure landed property reform and obtain the right to purchase the premises where he had been working for twenty years and finally, but only then, he would give his vote to Chamberlain because he wanted tariff protection as retaliation against Germany's tariff policy.

Ettore was tempted to 'kiss my neighbour's honest face' for this frank perfidy.[86] He called the study of English politics his 'favourite pastime',[87] and certainly came to be highly sensitive to the political colour of the various British newspapers, always showing his dislike for the Conservatives and Imperialists:

London is said to be the least English city in the Empire. Before the war it was nevertheless the most Imperialist. Northcliffe's newspapers have the greatest circulation there so one must believe that its political allegiance has not changed.[88]

In 1908 Northcliffe added *The Times* to his already extensive newspaper empire.

From 1904, Svevo had been an interested observer in the debate over Tariff Reform which had been recently opened by Joseph Chamberlain, in the teeth of the overwhelmingly popular Liberal view that 'any protective tariff would mean a lowering of living standards'.[89] The Liberals were triumphant in the elections of January 1906, a few months before Svevo's exchange of views with the factory inspector, when both men declared themselves Liberal sympathizers. The Liberals were also less committed to the naval race with Germany and the Dreadnought programme, which saw the first ship launched that same year. Ettore Schmitz was in rather the same case as the workers in Woolwich Arsenal (or their opposite numbers in Trieste), who were torn between opposition to military expenditure and attachment to the livelihood which it provided.

Woolwich was in the forefront of the British Labour movement. In 1903 it elected one of the first Labour members of Parliament, Will Crooks. The district had a certain revolutionary tradition, having been the birthplace of Tom Paine, one of the few Englishmen who actively supported the French Revolution and whose motto was 'The world is my country and to do good my religion.' In 1903 began to appear one of the earliest Labour publications, the *Borough of Woolwich Labour Journal*, and Woolwich was also the first borough in England to have a Labour mayor (Revd L. Jenkins Jones) with an overall Labour majority. British Labour as a political force lagged behind working-class movements in other countries of Europe, partly because Marxism had never properly established itself in the United Kingdom, and partly because the trade unions had long supported the considerably powerful radical wing of the Liberal party, but also because many reforms were more readily granted in Britain, thanks to a well-developed public opinion and a relatively enlightened and far-sighted entrepreneurial class.

However, after some improvements in living standards in the 1890s the first decade of the new century brought stagnation or worse, especially to the working classes, for whom conditions were often miserable. Many workers at the Woolwich Arsenal had been dismissed:

Soon were seen processions of the workless rattling collecting boxes as they shuffled along singing:

> What will become of England if things go on this way,
> Thousands of honest working men are starving day by day,
> We cannot find employment, for bread our children cry,
> What will become of England if things go on this way?[90]

The population in the district declined and houses were left empty, as Svevo also observed. The year 1908, and the bitter winter that followed, brought increased misery to Thames-side. A National Right to Work Council was formed and in 1909 the children of Labour supporters were singing in the streets, to the tune of 'Nuts in May', a song against Protectionism:

> Tariff Reform means work for all [thrice]
> Chopping up wood in the workhouse.

43

SVEVO AND THE CULTURE OF THE FIRST DECADE

On 29 September 1902 died one of Svevo's culture-'gods', Emile Zola. The front-page obituary in *Critica Sociale* must have held some interest for Svevo, upholding as it did Zola's independent stance, as a writer rather than a politician, *vis-à-vis* both Socialism and the world in general. It would be all too easy, the article observed, to claim Zola for Socialism:

Has he not plunged, perhaps more deeply than anyone, the analyst's ruthless scalpel into the carcass of modern capitalism, laying bare its sordid profiteering, its brutal vampirism in politics, the double moral standard of family law (*L'Argent*, *La Curée*, *Pot-Bouille*, etc.)? Has he not made millions of readers shudder with his descriptions of the horrors of militarism in *La Débâcle*? Is *Au Bonheur des Dames* not a chapter of Marxist philosophy on the concentration of business enterprises?

Such a temptation is resisted: 'Too easy it is to clamber upon the corpses of giants and lend them all the trappings which they are at last no longer able to reject!' But the same result is obtained by inverting the relationship:

Emile Zola does *not* belong to us: we might rather say that *we have belonged to him*, for he saw into us, and he saw into our doctrines and our movement as he saw, with terrible clarity of gaze, into every fold of this great billowing Penelopean tapestry which is everyday social living. [Emphasis in the original.]

Zola had indeed prophesied that he would one day turn from being an old Republican into a Socialist—

But he did not have, nor could he have had, the capital characteristic of the party man, in the best sense of the word; the ability to isolate a cluster of phenomena of social life, of extracting their essence, of identifying with them, catching their drift, making himself their bulwark, their instrument, their weapon, their banner, their grave. The eyes of Emile Zola took in too many things at once for that; in the breathless rush of existence his attention fixed too much on details, on shape, on emotion, on psychology, on the individual; this is what made him a novelist—a great novelist.[91]

The novelist is thus absolved from action, from direct involvement in life (though the same article speaks admiringly of Zola's political campaigns, especially the 'sublime' one on behalf of Dreyfus, and Zola remains the classic type of the 'committed' writer). We may perhaps relate this distinction between novelist and man of action to the intention expressed by Svevo two months later. He vainly hoped that an account of his recent life would give him a better understanding of the so complex ground of his own being and enable him to assert himself as a man of action rather than a mere man of letters. Svevo's failure in this, his compromise with his literary inferiority and superiority complex and his impotence, seems inevitable. He was too unlike Zola. He could not commit himself either to literature or to action.

We have seen how the literary demon kept on pursuing the paint manu-facturer in these opening years of the century. Yet his major literary work of this period was his most socially 'committed'. The focal point of Svevo's play *Un marito* was still a live issue into the 1970s. In 1966 one could still read an article in *Il Corriere della Sera* about changing the law on 'crimes of honour' entitled 'Withdrawing right of wife-slaughter from the deceived husband'.[92]

As so often, clues to Svevo's cultural interests at this time are scant and sporadic, mostly bare mentions to Livia of authors and titles. It is no surprise to read in 1903 that he knew Praga's play *La moglie ideale* (The Ideal Wife) and *Tutto l'amore* (Total Love) by Lopez. In 1905 he referred flippantly to a verse-tale by Wilhelm Busch, the popular anti-Catholic humorist, whose last writings have something in common with Svevo's last writings, balancing as they do an underlying pessimism with the cheerful wisdom of old age.[93] In 1907 and later Svevo was taking a lively interest in the debate over Darwinism, with a distinct preference for the Darwinian thesis, though he embroidered upon the theories of parasitism in those quite un-'scientific' and purely 'literary' fantasies, 'L'Evoluzione' and 'La corruzione dell'anima'.[94] In these writings, and par-ticularly in the brief 'Lo sviluppo' (Development), Svevo virtually inverted Darwinian anthropology. Or rather, he displaced it from the zoological to the ethical plane, arguing that 'The excessive development of the lower faculties, all those which are of direct use in the struggle for life, leads to a dead-end'; that 'the animal most capable of evolving' is that which does not follow a single irreversible line of development; and that 'In my own absolute lack of any marked development in any direction I am that man' (that is, capable of further evolution). And he went on: 'I sense this so clearly that in my solitude I glory loftily in that knowledge and I live expectantly in the assurance that I am no more than a rough cast.' The 'inetto', the 'impotent' Ettore Schmitz thus got his own back and indeed stole a march on the winners in the 'struggle for life' and the 'supermen'. The true winner now was that mean, sullen, discontented 'soul', equipped with its 'ordigni' (tools, devices, weapons) about which he theorized here.

It was probably also around 1907 or 1908, or shortly after, that Svevo wrote the unfinished essay 'Ottimismo e pessimismo',[95] which makes much play of the celebrated scientist Metchnikoff, who was appointed director of the Pasteur Institute in 1904 and won a Nobel prize in 1908. The opposition set up in this piece between youth and old age connects the theme of metabolic relativity explored in 'Lo specifico del dottor Menghi' to Svevo's late works. In 1906 Svevo had asked himself: 'Why the devil do I talk so much about my old age?' Not, he said through fear of death, but because he regretted not having recorded all his dreams and all his recent life. Time and again, the autobiographical urge seized Svevo, even though it was not acted upon: 'a fine business if many other people felt as I do! Poor humanity! All those autobiographies!'[96]

The outwardly impersonal 'Ottimismo e pessimismo' gave ample vent to Svevo's frustrations. He too must have been a 'pessimist ... who can laugh and enjoy life without in any way losing his character as a pessimist'. He revealed himself through the first person plural: 'Midway through life's journey ... we shut our eyes in slumber to shattered delusions, forgotten desires, renunciations forced upon us by the imperious claims of our milieu, of people, of time.'

The truly great advances in Western culture at this time were in the scientific field. Perhaps Svevo had already heard of Freud, who had published his two books on dreams and in 1904 gave the world The Psychopathology of Everyday Life. That same year Pavlov won the Nobel prize for his work on conditioned reflexes and in 1905 Einstein published his theory of special relativity. Vienna had much to offer besides Freud, notably Ernst Mach's notion of the unrettbar, the 'irredeemable self' as a quite fictitious entity resulting from manifold but discrete functions—close to the way in which Zeno Cosini was to be presented.[97] Unfortunately, thanks especially to the destruction of Svevo's library, it is impossible to establish any firm link (other than the Freudian) between Svevo and the so-called Mitteleuropa.[98] There is one strong piece of negative evidence: while Berlin discovered Kafka in 1913, Svevo appears not to have done so until 1927. He had to struggle with the parochial limitations of Triestine Irredentist culture, its frontier mentality of which the Triestine historian Fabio Cusin has written.[99] Vito Levi talks of 'the passive but secretly hostile attitude maintained by the town towards its best minds, which might suggest a fratricidal complex', and said in Svevo's case that hostility could be partly explained in terms of 'the climate of the era which was permeated by aestheticism. Trieste was definitely the most D'Annunzian of our towns, not only because D'Annunzio was the acclaimed poet of modern Italy, but because, more seductively than Carducci, he had raised Irredentist hopes.'[100]

Svevo always showed his dislike of D'Annunzio (which did not mean lack of interest). His 1995 epigram, 'He is a man who writes too well to be sincere',[101] sounds as if it was aimed at D'Annunzio or one of his tribe, though the vice of fine writing was pretty widespread in Italy. Svevo was to write to a friend in 1927: 'We are a living protest against the ridiculous conception of the superman which has been foisted upon us (and especially upon us Italians).' He was clearly referring to D'Annunzio.[102] Stefani agrees that 'Gabriele D'Annunzio was by definition the poet of Irredentism.' He had earned that definition as early as 1893 when he wrote what was immediately to become an anthology piece, 'A una torpediniera nell'Adriatico' (To a Torpedo Boat on the Adriatic), which opens:

> Vessel of steel, darting swift and straight
> beautiful as a bared weapon,
> palpitatingly alive
> as if your metal hid a terrible heart...

Svevo, now manufacturing paint for torpedo boats of various nations, including those of the Austrian foeman, must have had mixed feelings about that vessel, 'death's foremost messenger', which the poet called upon to avenge the naval defeat of 1866 which Austria had inflicted upon Italy.

In May 1902 the 'poeta imaginifico' visited Trieste in person, accompanied by his mistress, the outstanding Italian actress of her time, Eleonora Duse. A packed house at the Teatro Comunale saw D'Annunzio's grandiose pseudo-historical fantasy dramas, *La Gioconda*, *La Città Morta* and *Francesca da Rimini*.

D'Annunzio's eloquence, gave birth in 1907 to the highflown rhetorical dramatic legend in verse, *La Nave* (The Ship), a celebration, in a spirit of Irredentism and naval imperialism ('Mare Nostro') of Venice's seafaring past. Stefani observes:

in the *sirventese** which precedes the tragedy, the poet, standing outside the myth, reaffirms in its ultimate synthesis the will-to-power of the Italian people:

> 'Of all the Oceans make Our Sea!'

Irredentism, then, and Imperialism, projected through legend into contemporary living reality...

In 1908 *La Nave* was triumphally staged first in Rome and then in Venice. It highlighted the rebirth of Italian Nationalism and Imperialism in a newly aggressive and politically organized form. The Triestine Irredentists Hortis and

---

* The *sirventese* or *serventese* is a metrical form originally used by the troubadours.

Pítteri attended the Venice showing of the drama and the banquet given by the Lega Navale for D'Annunzio and Duse:

The banqueting table was adorned with flowers picked from the interstices of the amphitheatre of the 'unredeemed' city of Pola. The menu, printed on parchment, bore on the front cover the Lion of St Mark rampant beside an angel with wings outspread, reproduced from the St Mark's Basilica. The back cover showed a Byzantine mosaic tile. The inner pages were decorated with the reproduction of the picture of a ship, also Byzantine, taken from another mosaic in the Basilica, along with other Byzantine devices, Gabriele D'Annunzio's line: 'All the Adriatic homeland to the Venetians' and the dedication: 'His Venetian friends and admirers pay this tribute to Gabriele D'Annunzio under the auspices of the Naval League—Venice 27 April MCMVIII'. The fascicle was sealed with an original Murano pearl.[103]

Svevo, having always been critical of D'Annunzio, was bound to be made more critical of this showy and potentially aggressive Irredentism with which D'Annunzio identified himself. We have seen how in 1903, even when there was talk of war between Italy and Austria, Svevo hopped light-heartedly from Irredentism to boiled potatoes. Calling the feckless anti-hero of his third novel Zeno may have been partly intended to deride D'Annunzio and the Imperialists: in the speech he gave at the banquet for *La Nave* in Venice, D'Annunzio had spoken in highflown terms of the historic exploits in the naval war against Genoa of the fourteenth-century Venetian admiral, Carlo Zeno.

D'Annunzio had a particular friend, admirer and follower in Trieste in the person of Silvio Benco, who was steeped in D'Annunzian aestheticism and rhetorical nationalism, and was the only Triestine writer so far to win Svevo's attention. Svevo certainly knew the novels which Benco published during this period: *La fiamma fredda* (The Chill Flame) of 1903 and *Il castello dei desideri* (The Castle of Desires) of 1906, both published by Treves. Marinetti regarded the second as inferior only to D'Annunzio's own masterpieces.[104] Benco, like his idol, also composed dramatic 'legends', librettos set to music by the Triestine Antonio Smareglia. And he had by now written a great number of the four and a half thousand newspaper articles which were the fruit of his career as a journalist, as well as a book on Veruda and various others about Trieste and about Italian and German literature. With his qualities and his limitations, Benco stands as a foil and a contrast to the more than ever invisible Italo Svevo, yet another token of the latter's isolation.

Svevo missed the last two of Benco's three lectures at the Società di Minerva in 1908 on 'The three literary crises of the nineteenth century': 'How man discovered himself to be Romantic'; 'How man fell in love with truth'; 'How truth was torn to shreds'.[105] The Minerva was still ailing. Of the few noteworthy lectures, Svevo may have got to 'The woman of the future' by the Neapolitan playwright Roberto Bracco; a tribute to Emile Zola by V. Morello (Rastignac); 'The art of taking a wife' by A. Testoni; and three days later a talk by the extremely youthful Giacomo Braun on the sixteenth-century German poet Hans

Sachs.[106] But now all this could have only a marginal impact on him. Had the 'Minerva' offered discussions on Freud or Einstein or Pavlov or Stanislavsky or Gide or Henry James or even William James or Henri Bergson, it might have been a different matter, but since about 1890 Trieste had been a cultural backwater.

Music and drama fared better. In 1905, for example, Gustav Mahler came to present one of his symphonies. In the theatre, Naturalism was still in its heyday, though increasingly challenged by the poetic drama of D'Annunzio and Sem Benelli. The Triestine stage benefited from a cultural offensive by the Socialists against the Italian National Liberal hold on the theatre in Trieste. In 1906 the 'Circolo di Studi Sociali' resolved to make serious drama available to a wider public, in the hope that this would help the Socialists to win the forthcoming parliamentary elections, in which there was to be genuine manhood suffrage for the first time in Austrian history. A first season, with the Rome Teatro Stabile, was a success, thanks partly to the modestly priced tickets at the usually costly Politeama Rossetti. The following year, the Liberals did all they could to impede a repetition of the Socialist success (although, be it noted, it was always Italian companies that the Socialists invited). Nevertheless, forty thousand spectators in all saw the twenty-five works on offer, which included classics like the *Oresteia*, Shakespeare's *Julius Caesar* and Calderón's *El alcalde de Zalamea*, and fifteen new works.

The Liberals countered this Socialist cultural onslaught with an initiative of their own, the 'Teatro Popolare', but, according to Slataper, 'they did not deign to notify *Il Lavoratore*, which alone had influence with the people: a people's theatre has no need of the people'.[107]

Slataper was similarly contemptuous of the 'Università del Popolo' which the Liberals had set up to compete with the educational activities of the 'Circolo di Studi Sociali'.[108] The Liberals had in fact lost their cultural monopoly in Trieste: the Socialists had opened up new ways of thinking to the younger generation, who might not necessarily be Socialists but were stimulated by the perspectives which Socialism offered. This was the generation of the young Triestines who were from 1908 particularly associated with the Florentine journal *La Voce* and through its pages gave Italy and their own city a fervent but mature and sophisticated forum of debate on Irredentism and other issues affecting Trieste. Slataper was a major contributor to these discussions. His generation had completed their education outside Trieste, some of them evading Austrian conscription, others, Italian nationals like the poet Umberto Saba, doing their military service in Italy. Nearly all of them, even those who were Austrian subjects, were to fight for Italy against Austria in the war to 'redeem' Trieste. Many died at the front. Saba, born in 1883, and Giotti, born in 1885, spent the pre-war years in Tuscany. Guido Voghera, born in 1884, studied in Vienna before becoming a Socialist schoolteacher in Trieste. Scipio Slataper was born in 1888 and also went to Florence. He wrote a thesis on Ibsen, which was published in 1916, after his death. Giani and Carlo Stuparich (born in 1891 and 1894) went first to Prague and then to join the *Vociani* in Florence. Alberto Spaini, born in 1892, studied in Rome, Berlin and Florence and also joined *La Voce*. Biagio Marin, born in 1891, studied philosophy in Vienna, Rome and Florence.

While this new generation was still in bud—what bloom it produced we shall duly consider—Svevo was sweating away patiently at his paint, plying between Trieste, Murano and Charlton, scribbling occasionally, browsing through the newspapers and what else it is impossible to tell, tasting the joys and pains of family life, going to the theatre and the opera. We can only surmise as to what might have interested him. The poetry which was soon to be christened 'crepuscular' was beginning to erode (and implicitly deride) the D'Annunzian grandiloquence. Outstanding examples of this new tone were such pieces as Guido Gozzano's 'La via del rifugio' (Escape Route) which apostrophized and mused upon 'this living thing called guidogozzano' and the butterfly pierced by a pin, Time concentrating in Space such intensity of pain; or his ineffectual, harmless, self-deprecating, ironic Totò Merùmeni (a name that puns on *Heautontimoroumenos*, the Self-Tormentor) with his scanty morals and appalling perspicacity which seem perfectly attuned to Svevo's timbre.

And then there was Pirandello, who hardly tried his hand at theatre until the war, but who had achieved considerable celebrity in 1904 with *Il fu Mattia Pascal* (The Late Mattia Pascal), his fourth of a series of impressive and original novels. Despite the difference between Pirandello and Svevo, the coincidences between them are remarkable. Unfortunately, there seems to be no evidence at all as to whether either noticed the other before the Great War (apart from the near-certainty that Ettore read Goethe's *Roman Elegies* with Livia in Pirandello's translation, which may have inclined Svevo to read Pirandello's stories and novels also).

Pirandello, like Svevo, had absorbed a good deal of German culture and combined a problematical Naturalism with a clearly, though not avowedly, Schopenhauerian perspective—a total fidelity to observable reality with a total disbelief in it. Svevo in 1925 heard Pasini lecture on Pirandello and wrote back excitedly to the lecturer: 'yesterday's talk was new stuff to me. Pirandello's definition of humour is identical with Schopenhauer's.'[109] (Pirandello's essay *L'Umorismo* had been published in 1908 and was based in essence on the preposterousness of all that is 'real'.) Pirandello publicly avowed an antipathy towards D'Annunzio even more marked than Svevo's.

The consonance between Svevo and Pirandello is most evident in *Senilità*, which hinges on the very issue that is central to Pirandello's writing—the conflict between a person's inapprehensible 'real' being and other people's perceptions of it. There are also several intriguing coincidences between the two writers. In 1895–7, just when Svevo was going through the choices imposed by his marriage, and particularly the choice between his literary vocation and his business career, Pirandello was writing his 'Dialoghi tra il grande me e il piccolo me' (Dialogues between my Greater and my Lesser Self) on precisely those issues.

Central to both writers is what Svevo had written in his betrothal diary in 1896 about a 'something' in his 'soul' which warns him 'Take care! All is not as you think, everything is still a make-believe, for in the end the curtain will fall.' This theme, so prominent in Svevo's life though not made explicit in his work, is close to the explicit sense in Pirandello's works of 'the game played by the mocking demon inside each of us who amuses himself by displaying to us as a reality outside ourselves what he himself a moment later unmasks as our own illusion ... as there's no other reality left outside these illusions ...'.[110] Svevo does not philosophize so directly in his own narratives, but articulates them according to this basic perception.

The theme of Pirandello's story 'Volare' (Flying) coincides with that suggested by the title of Svevo's 'La Novella del buon vecchio e della bella fanciulla' (The Story of the Nice Old Man and the Pretty Young Girl); Pirandello's Serafino Gubbio* fantasizes on cosmic destruction as Zeno Cosini does; and Pirandello's story 'Soffio' (Breath), of 1931, closely resembles in its central idea Svevo's unfinished 'Il malocchio', which Pirandello could not have read (though by then he had met Svevo).

All that can be said with any certainty is that the literary phenomena represented by such writers as Gozzano and Pirandello, show that at last, a decade after the publication of *Una vita* and *Senilità*, an important current in the Italian literary *Zeitgeist* was beginning to swing Svevo's way.

Getting hold of books, at least, should not have been a great problem for Svevo, as, since 1900, Trieste had had a flourishing 'Biblioteca Circolante Popolare', thanks to which, according to Slataper, the Triestine reading public was far better served than that in Italy. By 1906 it boasted 8,000 volumes, 1,675 members, and 122,021 loans in a year.[111] Art was not so well served. The museums had next to nothing by Trieste's best painter, Veruda.[112] Once in 1901 Svevo had met in Venice Felice Venezian, Aristide Costellos and Giuseppe Caprin who had come to buy a picture for the Revoltella art gallery: 'I don't know', he remarked drily, 'if their choice was a very happy one.'[113] Triestine artists had had to set up their own permanent exhibition. There was no entrance charge and it was well frequented. But it represented a commercial rather than a cultural arrangement, Slataper explained: 'People buy few pictures in Trieste, and artists have a struggle.'[114]

Ettore Schmitz played a minor Maecenas, helping out his artist friends quite generously, in proportion to his means, which, up to the war, appear to have remained quite modest. In July 1905, for instance, he wrote:

---

* The novel of which Serafino Gubbio is protagonist and narrator, known in English as *Shoot!*, first appeared as *Si gira!* in 1916—exactly coinciding with the fictional date of Zeno's fantasy of global destruction—and came out in a revised version as *Quaderni di Serafino Gubbio operatore* in 1925.

My dearest Livia and most unfortunate woman, I've sent Rietti 600 Lire. I had no alternative. At worst, he'll paint your portrait. This is the fourth or fifth blow we've received since we took this spell of leave. But now I'm tying up my purse-strings and I'll strangle anyone who asks me for money.

Six hundred lire was a tidy sum—almost a month's pay for Ettore, who at this time also had to spend 100 lire on a mosquito net.[115] A year later, at the unveiling of Veruda's bust—'a truly Triestine affair, with not much blood in it'—he met Rietti, very embarrassed to be so much in Ettore's debt, but bold enough to chide him: 'Rietti told me that my falling away from literature isn't the result of my business but my sloth. Just as well that I know that but it doesn't help at all.'[116]

Yet Svevo was still writing bits and pieces, though how regularly we do not know. Pasini, who saw a good deal of Svevo from 1924 onwards, took Gianni Calvi to task in 1931 for describing Svevo as 'totally absorbed in his trade', and retorted that Svevo was a writer first and last, that writing and publishing were not the same thing, and that 'The 25 years' silence is not to be taken literally.'[117] The writer Italo Svevo battles on unseen beneath the simulacrum of Ettore Schmitz.

44

TRIESTE: THE 1907 SOCIALIST ELECTION VICTORY

That Ettore Schmitz could still hold an audience. Haydée remembered him as remaining always witty, original, charming; 'from being a modest clerk he had become a great industrialist and a millionaire',* but financial success had not spoiled him: 'he was still the same dear boy of times gone by'.[118] He was not as concerned as in 1889 to feign an interest in other people's concerns—at least not when it came to politics. Livia told Lina Galli after the Second World War that 'Ettore Schmitz was a stranger to political passion, but regarded the Austrian authorities with a gently mocking smile.' He confined himself to 'mimicking perfectly the speech and mannerisms' of his instructor in the one-year volunteer course for the Austrian army, 'a real original who used to address his students in hybrid Italian as *pantigane*' (dialect slang for 'rats').[119] We may wonder what Ettore Schmitz made of the 1901 election address by Felice Venezian, that 'swayer of crowds' who 'held in his hands all the threads

---

* Ettore never became a millionaire, though he was extremely well off after the Great War.

of the Irredentist struggle, flanked by a committee of wealthy elderly men, the secret patrons of the "Circolo Garibaldi" ':

If tomorrow evening we were to deny our flag, we should be ashamed of being Triestines. Tell the citizens that on the field of battle those who desist are punished by death. Tell them that we have no rifles, but that those who desert the ranks tomorrow will be struck by civic death.[120]

The Liberals controlled local government and were frequently accused of tampering with census and ballot returns, so this may not have been a merely rhetorical threat.

When it suited him, however, Venezian himself appealed to the civic right to personal freedom and privacy:

Here's a story about Svevo: a little girl related to him (his daughter Letizia, I believe, but I'm not sure) telephoned a friend of her own age, and in an excess of patriotic fervour they started singing over the telephone a song that was absolutely banned in Austria, some anthem (a plague on anthems), either Mameli's or Garibaldi's. A telephonist ... hearing them singing, butted in, in broad Triestine: 'Watch it, lassies, mind what you're doing.'—The little girl told the story to Svevo, Svevo told it to Felice Venezian (one of the bosses of Triestine Irredentism), who, beside himself with joy at having such a weighty grievance against the oppressors: 'violation of telephone privacy', rushed straight off to the director of the Austrian Post and Telegraph to lodge a violent protest because a telephonist had butted in while the two girls were singing an anthem which was absolutely banned in Austria—the director of Post went pale, sacked the woman on the spot (violation of telephone privacy!), crisis of conscience of Zeno, of Svevo, through whose fault that poor devil had lost her pensionable post, so he went to parley with the director of Post who remained adamant (violation of telephone privacy!) and Svevo, so as to set the conscience of Zeno at rest, found another job for the telephonist who had been sacked for having violated telephone privacy with two little girls who were singing an anthem which was absolutely banned in Austria.[121]

Slataper expressed his unrestrained contempt for what he called the phoney 'Freemasons' Irredentism' led by Venezian, whose 'Liberal party in Trieste' was 'the anti-Irredentist par excellence', and, like Bazlen, he dwelled on the Austrians' honest, impartial and efficient administration, which compared very favourably with that in Italy.[122] The Triestine Liberals were also often accused of making common cause with their supposed adversaries, the Germans and Czechs, against the Socialists, even voting in the Vienna Parliament in favour of the military spending which would be turned against Italy in a war for the redemption of Austria's Italian territories. Large sections of the middle and lower middle class were affronted by the blatant disregard for democracy with which the Liberals tried every means to prevent the introduction of genuine manhood suffrage in 1906. As for 'Schmitz, Ettore (Italo Svevo), writer', the Trieste Guide for 1908 no longer shows him in any political or public position. No doubt his frequent absences from Trieste were a good enough reason for disengagement.

For all the scorn shown towards the Liberals by Slataper and Bazlen, it needs to be borne in mind that the Austrian authorities themselves, by their clumsy interference, often provoked and encouraged Italian nationalism in Trieste. The poet Umberto Saba relates that his wife Lina had a previous admirer who was exiled to Fiume for having exclaimed that he wished Oberdan's attempt on Franz Josef's life had succeeded.[123] In 1904 the president of the Società di Ginnastica was arrested and the Società closed down because bombs were found on its premises, but it was established that the bombs had been planted by outsiders and the defendants were acquitted. This may have been an early device on the part of the new Lieutenant, Prince Konrad von Hohenlohe, to break the hold of the Liberal-Nationals on Triestine politics. In fact, he caused a crisis in January 1906 by stripping Trieste of its delegated responsibilities for conscription, education and other important administrative matters, which were of course managed by the Liberals. The Socialists supported Hohenlohe's move, on the grounds of partisan and other malpractices by the Liberals, and also because they were enraged at the delaying tactics employed by the Liberals to impede progress towards manhood suffrage.[124]

The Habsburg State was still sustained by its efficient administrative and judicial system, but in political terms it was a precarious and explosive equilibrium of sharply opposing forces: dynastic autocracy, aristocracy and army were ranged against civic society; half a score of nationalities were at daggers drawn—Czechs against Germans, Poles against Ruthenians, Italians against Slavs or Germans, not to mention the even worse Babel in the Hungarian half of the Empire; the bourgeoisie was locked in battle with the Socialists and the clericals with secular forces. Manhood suffrage was introduced supposedly as a means of superseding national divisions, especially that between Czechs and Germans, but the new constituencies were to be drawn up along national lines and in fact only added further fuel to the rivalry. The monarchy exploited these new contentions to refine the traditional Habsburg art of so-called 'electoral geometry' by which it sought to make the various Parliamentary groupings neutralize one another.

The Socialists in Austria had themselves been unable to avoid the trap of division by nationality and the Austro-Marxism of Otto Bauer and Karl Renner became in the last resort a helpless tool of the Monarchy and its associated financial interests. Internationalism should have been one of the great strengths of the Socialists in a State so nationally divided. Self-discipline was another, notably in the massive demonstrations and parades in support of manhood suffrage during 1906, particularly in Vienna. The Socialists might therefore have represented—perhaps even for Ettore Schmitz—a real hope for peaceful progress towards a solution of the tensions and problems of the Habsburg State.

The fourteenth of May 1907 marked the greatest triumph of Austrian Socialism especially in Trieste; but also the limit of its achievement. For this was the day of Austria's first Parliamentary elections that could claim to be genuinely democratic. The old five-tier system, of which only one tier was based on manhood suffrage, was now done away with for the elections to Parliament (though it was cynically retained for local elections, which, for most practical purposes, were more important). Now everyone voted together. The electoral campaign was intense. The Liberals, whose heart had never really been in democracy, made some blunders, one of which was Venezian's revelation of his social outlook in the remark: 'We will give our superfluous wealth to the poor.' The Socialists responded with a poster caricaturing Venezian sitting at a banquet and eating the flesh off a chicken while tossing the bones to a poor woman carrying a child. Another Liberal, Luigi Ziliotto, ill-advisedly paid a call to an Austrian Archduke. The electors returned the Socialist leader, Valentino Pittoni, on the first ballot, but none of the Liberals. These latter refused to enter into a second ballot, alleging intimidation by their adversaries. The Socialists thus ended by taking all four town seats, while the Slavs took both the country seats. The forty-year political monopoly of the Trieste Liberals had been broken, though under the electoral system for local government they retained municipal control of Trieste until the outbreak of war.[125] Felice Venezian died the following year.

Triestine Liberalism was also losing its financial hegemony in Trieste. The modern port facilities had led to a huge increase in the transit of goods, but entrepôt trade had shrunk, the era of spectacular profits was over and Italian capital was losing ground to Slav and German banks, as well as those outside Austria-Hungary. Trieste had now ceased to be a major financial centre, second in the Empire only to Vienna, and the influx of Slav capital was such that in 1911 an Italian crowd assaulted the Živnobanka.[126] Italian nationalism in Trieste, weakened now both politically and financially, was moving steadily beyond its bland cultural terrorism and embracing the fierce antagonism of the twentieth century.

The Socialists had gained ground partly thanks to the cultural and educational activity of the previous decade, but mostly on account of their ability to organize industrially and politically, on account of the economic infrastructure of their increasingly successful co-operative movement, and on account of their skilful championing of the interests of working people within the government sickness benefit scheme.

Life was still hard for ordinary people, though, and deteriorated with the 1903 recession. Prices rose, and as they did so less meat and more wine were consumed. Alcoholism increased, and with it the alarmingly high mortality rate from tuberculosis and the incidence of venereal disease, as well as acts of violent assault, particularly among unskilled Slav labourers. A statistical study has shown that chronic alcoholism saw a fourfold increase between 1903 and 1905. Absenteeism after Sundays and feast-days was rife. Bazlen mentions all this, somewhat flippantly, apparently viewing the phenomenon nostalgically through the perspective of the relatively prosperous years after 1910. The suicide rate was still high.[127]

45

ENTER JOYCE

By 1907 Ettore Schmitz had settled down to an easy regular pattern of life. The writer in him sank deeper and deeper within the persona of the industrialist. Connexions between the two surfaced only occasionally. In 1907, for instance, there was a curious gathering in the Murano house, a spiritualist séance which threw Gilda Moravia into a panic[128] and no doubt provided Svevo with material for the spiritualist sequences in the play *Terzetto spezzato* (Broken Trio) and in *La coscienza di Zeno*.

Livia now generally accompanied Ettore on his trips to London, and they would occasionally take the opportunity to stop in Paris on their way back, or come back by another route taking a little holiday somewhere—perhaps at Würzburg for an excursion as far as Marktbreit and Segnitz, where Ettore had been to school.

Svevo soldiered on rather ineffectually with the English language. He was still taking English lessons in Trieste in 1903.[129] He resumed them in 1907, with far from negligible literary consequences. This may appear to have been arranged by a higher destiny, but it was, at least in part, an inspired little rebellion by the writer Italo Svevo against the social and economic determinism to which he appeared to have made his final surrender.

In March 1907 a twenty-five-year-old Irishman came back to Trieste. He had already been there in 1905–6 and had good recommendations in Triestine society—from Count Sordina, Baron Ralli and Roberto Prezioso, the editor of Teodoro Mayer's newspapers *Il Piccolo* and *Il Piccolo della Sera*. These former pupils and faithful friends found the young man new private pupils among well-off Triestines to round out his salary as a teacher of English, a post which he shared with his brother at the Berlitz School in Trieste. The young Irishman, James (or Giacomo) Joyce, soon attracted attention: in the thick of the election campaign he published in *Il Piccolo della Sera* a series of articles on Irish nationalism and gave some evening lectures at the 'Università del Popolo' on Irish culture and literature, ancient and modern. The Irredentists saw Ireland's case as similar to their own, though their struggle was directed more against the Socialists and Slavs than against Habsburg Imperialism. The incorrigible writer, Italo Svevo, however, was most likely to have been impressed by the assurance, authority, acumen and independence, the sheer originality, above and beyond the anti-British and anti-Catholic rhetoric, which the young man displayed. If the businessman Ettore Schmitz had really wanted to improve his English, he could long before have taken lessons from the younger Joyce, Stanislaus, who had been in Trieste for a year already and would have taught him a far more practical brand of English than his brilliant but eccentric brother. Under cover of learning the language, Italo Svevo was acquiring a literary ally such as Murano, Charlton, Trieste or even Venice could not provide.

It was not only Joyce's culture that intrigued Svevo. This self-assured young man, so unconventional in attire, in his 'free socialist union' with a working-class girl, Nora Barnacle, must have reminded him on the one hand of his lost friend Veruda and on the other of the ideal self he had so often imagined: Joyce was independent, thoroughly consistent, a fighter and a voluntary exile (like the Triestine chiropodist whom Svevo had met in Marseilles), and yet a writer, a man who lived for writing, in the endeavour to effect a wholly original renewal of the culture and consciousness of his country, that poor Ireland which had often been described by observers of undoubted impartiality as the most miserable and down-trodden country in the world, the most exploited of colonies.

In 1907 Joyce began giving thrice-weekly lessons to Ettore and Livia (and, later, to Letizia). The poet Virgilio Giotti saw him frequently in the café Stella Polare, wearing his shabby mackintosh, 'very English', and he was always struck by Joyce's 'confidence that he was a great writer'.[130] Letizia describes him as 'tall and lanky with blue eyes that looked enormous through his glasses'.[131] He wore his broad-brimmed hat askew, unmatched jacket and trousers and over-long shirt-cuffs. He was forever penniless and asking for loans or advances on lessons, was a formidable drinker and, in the taverns of the working-class areas around his frequently shifting lodgings, Città Vecchia, Barriera Vecchia and San Giacomo, made a magnificent contribution to Triestine alcoholism, which rivalled the Dublin variety. Poor Stannie often had to go out after him at night and drag him home from the gutter where he had collapsed unconscious. His teaching inevitably suffered, as one of his female pupils later recalled:

He was tall and skinny as a wraith and frightfully serious . . . He kept on his grey gloves, his mackintosh and his muffler even indoors. One day while teaching he slumped to the ground without a word. The family, from the respectable middle class, urgently sent for a doctor in panic. He diagnosed alcoholic poisoning, possibly complicated by malnutrition.[132]

Those who went to Joyce's lodgings for lessons found a little parlour curiously arranged somewhat like an art shrine furnished only with twenty wooden chairs which Joyce had had made from a Danish design.[133]

Joyce vigorously applied himself to becoming a Triestine. Triestine dialect was spoken in his household, even after they moved to Zurich and then to Paris, and 2 November, feast of St Justin, was always celebrated. He related to the Schmitzes, 'with devilish brio', how he had alighted with Nora at Ljubljana thinking it was Trieste, and had to wait until midnight for the next train; then, reaching Trieste, he had left Nora, who could speak nothing but English, on a bench outside the station while he set out to find the Berlitz School, but was arrested after trying to settle a quarrel between some British sailors and some prostitutes and could not rejoin Nora for several hours.[134]

Livia herself suggests that 'Ettore, besides learning the language, was looking for an expert to introduce him to modern literature in English', and relates that in Joyce's English lessons 'There was no mention of grammar, the conversation turned on literature and touched on a hundred different topics.'[135] Joyce had at that time only published the very slender verse-collection *Chamber Music* and a few literary and journalistic articles, and enjoyed a modest reputation in Dublin—which was a good deal less than Svevo could boast, with his two novels, a small miscellany of other writings, and several plays, though these latter lay hidden in his drawer. But Joyce was near to completing *Dubliners*. He showed the Schmitzes his writings and, towards the end of 1907, read them 'The Dead', which so moved them that Livia went into the garden and picked him a bouquet.[136] His autobiographical *Portrait of the Artist as a Young Man*, on the other hand, was making painfully slow progress. The friendship between the two writers, twenty years apart in age, was, however, to prove invaluable, artistically, to them both. As Furbank remarks, each was for the other the only close literary contact of any consequence during the eight years between 1907 and 1915.

The stimulus which Joyce gave to Svevo, especially in terms of encouragement, is immeasurable. They shared certain basic ideas and attitudes: Joyce championed Ibsen, who always remained one of his tutelary deities, and also admired Hauptmann's Naturalist dramas. Like Svevo, he too made a hero of Giordano Bruno, who was revered by all nineteenth-century progressives as a martyr in the cause of freedom of thought. And *Dubliners* was the product of an austere and refined Realist method which, Pound was to claim, advanced English narrative technique in a single leap to the level of Flaubert's impersonal narration.

These shared sympathies can only have rendered more stimulating the striking differences between the two men. Joyce too was a Socialist of a sort, a Wildean sort, as sketched out in 'The Soul of Man under Socialism', which Joyce contemplated translating into Italian. This was a Socialism that was to flower into perfect individualism, with Christ as its prophet and art as its religion.

Svevo, with consummate delicacy, is bound to have conveyed to Joyce a certain cool reserve and irony towards all these things—Socialism, individualism and the mystique of art, a reserve which he had expressed in his articles on Péladan and Wagner and an irony which gleams throughout his novels.

Does Joyce's artistic maturation owe anything to Svevo? There is one clue to such a debt in Joyce's transition from *Stephen Hero* to the *Portrait*. In 1903 Joyce had enthusiastically reviewed Marcelle Tinayre's novel *La Maison du péché*, admiringly quoting a passage from it.[137] This passage, and one sentence in particular ('Nothing lived in the vault of heaven but the man and woman intoxicated by their kiss'), is close to that describing the setting of the first kiss which Emilio Brentani gives to Angiolina in *Senilità*:

Everything around was enormous, boundless, and the only motion amid all that was the sea's colour. His sensation was that in the vastness of nature, at that instant, he alone was active, loving.[138]

The difference is that Emilio's Romantic sensibility is undercut by the narrative irony which invests Svevo's entire novel and which is lacking in Tinayre.

Svevo restrained Joyce's tendency towards aesthetic mysticism; just as, within limits, he cannot fail to have interested Joyce in his peculiar mixture of Schopenhauer and scientific positivism, against which Joyce in his turn was sufficiently inoculated by his own peculiar mixture of Aquinas, Vico and the modern realist writers including Ibsen. Svevo's scientism may have been partly assimilated into the scientific whimsies that grace *Ulysses*. Also, Svevo served Joyce as an antidote to D'Annunzio: he challenged Joyce to find any page by D'Annunzio which did not contain at least one meaningless sentence and, opening one of the Pescarese writer's books at random, read the following: 'The smile which pullulated inextinguishably, spreading among the pallid meanders of Burano lace . . .'.[139] Joyce did of course learn from D'Annunzio's verbal and musical magic, but he also learnt to keep both the style and the ideas within ironic bounds, so that his hero Stephen Dedalus in *Ulysses* defines himself wryly as 'toothless Kinch, the superman'. Still, as late as 1912, when Joyce published his article 'L'ombra di Parnell' (The Shadow of Parnell) in *Il Piccolo della Sera*, the impression it made on Svevo was, not that Joyce presented himself as Superman, but that he seemed a 'Zarathustra carrying the great man's corpse on his back'.[140]

With his usual generosity towards unjustly neglected writers, Joyce immediately set about telling the Triestines what an excellent novelist they had in Italo Svevo. He was simply laughed at and given the eternal refrain that Svevo could not write good Italian. 'There is no unanimity so perfect as the unanimity of silence,' Svevo told Joyce sadly,[141] and Joyce found he could not disturb this silence. Niccolò Vidacovich, president of the Società di Minerva, more honestly told him that Svevo's writing was too negative and unpatriotic to be acceptable in Trieste.[142] The silence about Svevo in Trieste was politically motivated and conspiratorial.

Joyce hit back by giving his pupils the following absurd but largely justified description of modern Italian literature:

beggared orphans and hungry people (will these Italians never stop being hungry?), battlefields, cattle and patriotism. Italians have a strange way of going through the gymnastics of patriotic ambition. They want to impose, by their fists, the recognition of their intellectual superiority to other peoples.[143]

This is a surrealistically jumbled critique of the social humanitarians, Triestine 'Gymnastic' Irredentism and the scuffles over the university issue, and the fist-fights of the Futurists. Joyce always singled out Svevo as the only modern Italian writer who interested him.

When Joyce, after reading Svevo's two novels, told him that 'some pages of *Senilità* could not have been better written by the greatest masters of the French novel', Svevo 'stared at him wide-eyed, amazed and overjoyed' at such unexpected praise for his forgotten works. 'That day he was unable to tear himself away from Joyce, but accompanied him back to his lodgings in Piazza Vico, telling him the story of his literary disappointments on the way.'[144] They had more of these long walks together: Ettore Settanni remembered seeing them 'clinging to the ropes fixed along the steep side-streets of Trieste under the *bora*'s blast as if they were climbers roped together' and relates how Joyce used to tell him affectionately of Svevo:

He was a great man before being a great writer, because he learnt to bear the weight of his *coscienza* in solitude. We travelled a long way together and Svevo is to my mind the first Italian novelist to introduce the technique of the interior monologue. But that is not the only thing that will make him endure in your literature: he was the Italian novelist with whom the generation born at the dawn of the new century can identify.[145]

The reference to the 'interior monologue' brings us to what Joyce had to offer Svevo, beyond his invaluable encouragement. His most precious gift was a sheer sense of artistry, both instinctive and cultivated, which he had refined into an exquisite technique. The artistic principle of 'impersonality', of the artist's divine self-effacement within his creation, adopted by Joyce in *Dubliners* and explicitly enunciated in *A Portrait of the Artist as a Young Man*, had been familiar to Svevo from as far back as his brief essay 'Del sentimento in arte'. There he had commented upon the failure by Dumas *fils* to observe this principle in his play *La Visite des noces*. Svevo had also shown appreciation of that principle in the comments on Balzac's *Louis Lambert* which he had slipped into *Una vita*. It was precisely the 'absence' of the author that most appealed to him in the theatre, but in his own novels he had reserved a rigorously restricted place for the author as the source of an impassive, 'objective' and 'scientific', critical control over his narrative and his characters (especially his partly autobiographical protagonist). However, since then he had gone further in 'Lo specifico del dottor Menghi', where he experimented with a new narrative framework which completely eliminated the author's *apparent* responsibilities by delegating them to narrators *within* the tale. He must certainly have appreciated instantly Joyce's finesse and immediacy in *Dubliners*, and I see in his Murano narratives ('Cimutti', 'In Serenella', 'Marianno') evidence of a convergence of method between *Senilità* and *Dubliners*. But both writers were in the course of time to travel a great deal further.

Joyce's English lessons were highly idiosyncratic. Stanislaus relates that Svevo once asked his brother to explain the line 'And brass eternal slave to mortal rage', in Shakespeare's sixty-fourth sonnet. Joyce's answer was 'I don't know what it means, but I suppose Shakespeare was thinking of German bands'—perhaps an Irredentist joke.[146] As one of his first tasks, Joyce asked Svevo to describe his teacher in English. The result was linguistically mediocre, but a characteristically Svevian piece of literary virtuosity. Svevo was fascinated by the way Joyce walked: 'he does not want to reach an aim or to meet anybody. No! He walks in order to be left to himself ... He walks because he is not stopped by anything,' considering things 'as points breaking the light for his amusement'. Svevo ended with a shrewd psychological observation: 'Surely he cannot fight and does not want to. He is going through life hoping not to meet bad men.'[147] Svevo was always teased by the contrast between Joyce's formidable moral courage and aggressiveness and his aversion to physical violence, and twenty years later he was to remark that 'from close to he does not give the impression of being the tough fighter that his courageous work would lead you to expect'. And he continued: 'I can't help imagining that his eye would be no less coldly curious as it rested upon an adversary against whom Joyce had to measure himself. There I go, myself slipping into the error of imagining Joyce to be physically combative.'[148]

Joyce had done what Svevo had lacked the courage to do. Or maybe the two writers had two different kinds of courage and pursued two different projects. Joyce, consciously following Dante, had chosen open exile. Svevo, like Ulysses, had entered the bourgeois citadel hidden inside the horse's belly.

46

ULYSSES SCHMITZ

Joyce had long been interested in Ulysses. He was also interested in the figure of the wandering Jew, and while still in Rome in November 1906, he had conceived a story for *Dubliners* about a Dublin Jew but had got no further than the title: 'Ulysses'. Nor did the story make any further progress for an entire year, until Joyce took it up again in the autumn of 1907. This does not look like a coincidence.

Stanislaus Joyce it was who had first suggested, in his preface to the English edition of *Senilità*, *As a Man Grows Older*, that Svevo may have been one of the models for Leopold Bloom in *Ulysses*, and Furbank, following Harry Levin and others, gathers plenty of evidence: the twenty-year age gap between Bloom and Dedalus matches that between Schmitz and Joyce; Schmitz had married a Catholic and, if only for literary reasons, had changed his name; he had a sense of humour and was well-informed about Jewish custom; he loved both cats and dogs; like Bloom, he enjoyed eating offal; also, his father, like Bloom's, originated from Hungary and had earned a living as an itinerant vendor of knick-knacks; and Schmitz too had had himself baptized for practical motives. Beyond this point, however, Furbank agrees with Ellmann in seeing in Teodoro Mayer, owner of the *Piccolo* newspapers and one of the grey eminences of the National Liberal party, a more important source for the characterization of Bloom.[149]

This seems unlikely. The forceful and influential Mayer was a man of altogether different calibre. Svevo was more like Bloom, a good-natured and self-effacing daydreamer. If Molly Bloom had lived in Gibraltar, Livia had been brought up in Marseilles, and, like Molly, she spent much of her time shut up at home looking after her health. She was also a singer and caused her husband some jealousy by reason of the interest she aroused in Julius Kugy's choir. All this is quite close to Joyce's book. But there is even more to link Bloom with Schmitz. It must have crossed both Svevo's mind and Joyce's that the name of the wandering hero Ulysses would have suited Schmitz much better than that of Hector, seeing that much of his time was spent travelling away from home through many lands, often leaving his wife behind. (The word 'odyssey' had slipped from Svevo's pen during his first trip to England.)[150] Bloom mourned over his son Rudy, who had died an infant. Livia had several times tried to give Ettore a son, tried at least twice more in 1908, and was close to childbirth in early 1909. Ettore wrote to her from Murano: 'By this time you'll know whether you are [mother of a second child] or not. A pity we didn't agree to cable: "Franz" for a boy "N" for a girl.'[151] The child must have been stillborn.

In Svevo's lecture on Joyce in 1927[152] he seems almost to see himself in Bloom, 'the assiduous reader of newspapers' and the daydreamer: 'He is a magnificent liar. He believes everything he says.'[153] He also quotes Bloom reading about a 'planter's company. To purchase vast sandy tracts from Turkish government and plant with eucalyptus trees. Excellent for shade, fuel and construction. Orange-groves and immense melonfields north of Jaffa.'[154] And so on. So Ettore had fantasized in 1900 about resinous pine plantations in France.* I think, therefore, that in Leopold Bloom we have in large part a moral portrait of Ettore Schmitz. Stan Joyce related that after the war Svevo asked him for information about the Irish so as to get even with Jim, who, before the war, had pumped him for information about Jewish practices.[155] Svevo may also have made another small contribution to *Ulysses*. In the notes for his Joyce lecture he remarked of Bloom:

A practical man. In the funeral carriage he considers advising the town council to arrange for corpses to be transported by tram: Practical. Non-stop to the cemetery

* See p. 181 above.

entrance in special coffins. As they do in Milan, he says. The elder Dedalus ridicules the idea: Pullman, restaurant car? But Bloom likes it. He is the practical fantast.[156]

Brian Moloney has linked this with one of the series of articles entitled 'Noi del tramway di Servola' (We of the Servola Tramway), published in *La Nazione* in 1919 (when Joyce was back in Trieste from Zurich), in which Svevo had satirically associated the tramway with a funeral and with restaurant cars and sleepers.[157]

After the war Joyce also borrowed from Svevo's wife her name and her hair for the character of Anna Livia Plurabelle in *Finnegan's Wake*, where he associated her with Dublin's river, the Liffey, whose waters were reddened at one point by industrial effluent and could thus be linked to the reddish lustre in Livia's otherwise blond, long thick hair. Even this idea may have come from Svevo, who in 1900 had written of a dream in which Livia lay dead with her 'long hair like a golden river'.[158] The entire thematic of dream, which grew increasingly important in each successive book by Joyce until it dominated the whole of his last work, may have been innocently suggested to him by the chatter of his older friend who, in life and literature, was so obsessed with dreams and daydreams. Livia found Joyce odd and could not see what the Liffey washerwomen had to do with her hair: 'He might have written something more poetic.'[159]

If Svevo did inspire Joyce to proceed with his 'Ulysses' story in 1907, Joyce may well have provided the stimulus for Svevo to plan a story on an old man and a girl, which Stan ascribes to this same year.[160] Svevo himself makes no mention of this. He may have conceived the story in the spirit and style of *Dubliners*, though the finished story was to emerge as something quite different and, while thoroughly Svevian, unlike anything else of his: moreover, it was to be dominated by the thunder of cannon on the Isonzo and the conditions, material and moral, of wartime Trieste. In the meantime Joyce was introducing Svevo to literature in English. We hear only of *The Second Mrs Tanqueray*, by Pinero, which Livia liked and looked forward to reading with Ettore upon his return from one of his London trips, but Joyce must have also guided the Schmitzes to his own favourite authors, particularly the Irish—Swift and the Restoration and eighteenth-century playwrights Congreve, Sheridan and Goldsmith—as well as English writers such as Defoe and Blake (on whom Joyce lectured at the Università del Popolo).[161] The form, tone and hero-narrator of Sterne's *Tristram Shandy* have much in common with those of *La coscienza di Zeno*, and Svevo paid tribute to Sterne's *Sentimental Journey* in the title of one of his last works, 'Corto viaggio sentimentale'. Nor should we forget Oscar Wilde, another of Joyce's heroes.[162]

In June 1908 Joyce required a deposit of six hundred crowns for new lodgings, having been thrown out of his last ones, and asked Svevo to lend him the money, maybe judging from the appearance of Villa Veneziani that he was better off than in fact was the case. Svevo advanced him only two hundred crowns, and this may explain why Joyce declined, after Svevo's death, to write the preface to *As a Man Grows Older*, saying that Svevo had been rather tight with him, that he had never been in the Schmitz household as a guest but only as a teacher, and that Livia wouldn't speak to Nora in the street.[163] So the Joyces can never have attended Olga's Sunday afternoon receptions, to which all polite Triestine society and many illustrious visitors were invited, and the letters between the two writers, though cordial enough, show a certain formality. They always addressed each other as 'Mr', even when Joyce was writing to Svevo in racy Triestine.[164] The Joyces' maid Mary Kirn did remember, however, Ettore and Livia around 1910–11 visiting their apartment at 32 Barriera Vecchia. Ettore always tipped her, and some of his visits lasted till late at night.[165]

Part VII

THE ENCOUNTER WITH FREUD
1908–1914

47

NEW MACHINES

Despite Joyce's encouragement, nothing substantial written by Svevo can be firmly assigned to the year 1908. In November and December of 1907 he was talking of a lecture which he was too busy to prepare;[1] this must be 'L'uomo e la teoria darwiniana', which mentions the Wasmann debate which took place in Berlin in 1907. On 10 April 1908 he addressed to Letizia, 'the only poet I love', in answer to some verses composed by herself which she had sent him, the delightful fable concerning the silent carpenter who makes fine cupboards and the poetic carpenter who invents them, and invents such fantastic, even living, ones that the poor silent carpenter cannot hope to match them.[2] Then came the brief dialect scene in which Svevo has the eleven-year-old Letizia and her five Bliznakoff cousins give grandmother Olga a joyous welcome back from her 'discovery of America' (she had gone to set up a factory in New York).[3]

In July and August 1908 Svevo was in Charlton supervising the installation of what he called, as Zeno Cosini was to do, new 'ordigni' (meaning here plant or machinery). 'I'm overwhelmed with worries, with business and preoccupations,' he wrote to Livia:

The new machines and the old ones ... My God! Who will free me from so many, so very many machines? I go to bed, as you can well imagine, very early. But I also wake up very early and my head whirls with ventilators, mixers and the very devil and worse. The ventilators blow on the feeble flame which is all I have left, the mixers stir up from the depths of my soul sad stuff that I gladly forget and the condensers turn into liquids all the gases that have always been in my head. After lunch I'm off to Shepherd's Bush [where some of the Olympic events were being held] to watch some gymnastics but I'm sure my 'ordigni' won't let me be.

It is hard to tell whether Ettore's problem was more an industrial or a literary one. The machines, at least, did turn out all right. Ettore wrote to Livia from the 'filthy office full of flies' that he quickly expected to recover the five thousand crowns which they had cost. He had a hectic time checking everything single-handed:

I'm having a mighty struggle with my clothes. In the morning I put on my blue suit and new boots. Ten minutes later, in the factory, my factory clothes and boots. Several times a day it's off with my jacket and waistcoat to put on the dressing-gown which I've brought here—a white overall handed down by a Vestal Virgin. At one o'clock it's lunch. Out with my suit and boots, change money, cigarette-holder and cigarette-paper, all the necessaries of life, from one pocket to the other. In a word, a real Fregoli [Italy's best-known quick-change artist]. Every ton of paint costs me several divestments. At least the priests only have to turn their frock round in order to say Mass.

But worse was to come:

I've had a visit from the health inspector. He made me buy tooth- and nail-brushes for every workman. This alerted the workmen to the danger they run and they're making a proper song and dance. It is true that what with the heat and the arsenic, one of them has had an enormously swollen face. I've had to buy zinc ointment and then boric acid and zinc powder. What is worse, my workmen keep washing themselves all day long so that I feel at times that I'm not a factory manager but a bath attendant.

And three days later:

This time the work is going badly. Many of my workmen have arsenic poisoning and I'm having some bits of bother. Today (it's only the second time) I had lunch in the factory so as to keep up the pace of work; but it doesn't do me much good.

Some ventilator, mixer or condenser must have given trouble, and Ettore was hard put to it trying to set things right and make up for lost time by requiring his men to work eighteen hours over the holiday. He was even driven to complain about Tchaperoff's mother-in-law dying in far-off Keswick and calling away his colleague at such a busy time.

His English was still indifferent. Joyce's Dublin accent did not help with Cockney. He was even writing 'July 21th', but he did manage to send Livia a long letter in English on 3 August. Despite some curious turns of phrase, it was a fluent and lively account of a day's holiday in London, dwelling mostly on the many different forms of transport which Ettore used, at a time when transport was changing very swiftly: a horse-drawn tram, an electric tram, a horse-drawn omnibus, the threepenny underground, and finally a double-decker bus that made him feel as if he were crossing the English Channel and made him quail in terror of lurching into the houses flanking the roadway. With enormous numbers of cars now circulating, the few remaining horses were engulfed in the streams of motor traffic, and even worse than the petrol fumes was the danger of being run over.

Svevo's progress in English was to be crowned the following year when he wrote Livia another letter in English,[4] informing her that he had dreamt he had been 'translated' wholly into English so that, by the intervention of the Holy Ghost, he had eaten beef, and been stiff and well educated. Then, 'By awakening I found myself re-translated in Italian.' His fantasy had its serious side, however: both he and Livia had been educated abroad and consequently lacked a sure command of their own language. He said that Livia had been translated into French and that he had tried to translate her back into Italian, but with dubious results. Now he was afraid that the same might happen to Letizia.

Livia was also concerned for Ettore's education: specifically, in religion. She had left for him in Charlton a copy of one of her own favourite books, *The Imitation of Christ*, hoping that he might learn intellectual humility, disdain for worldly fame and for a corrupt nature, and self-abnegation in Christ.

When he was not browsing through the crime columns or *The Imitation of Christ* or eating with Tchaperoff or strolling with the Francises, he would take an outing in London with Nicoletto and his fiancée Nell Francis, especially to watch the Olympic Games at the splendid Wembley Stadium, which held eighty thousand spectators. He was greatly impressed by the spectacle. 'An American won, looking like one of Homer's heroes in flight.' 'Splendid it is to hear so many people yelling all together.' An Italian, Dorando Petri, was disqualified in the marathon having effectively won the race in brilliant style: he became for the moment 'the real king of London'. Svevo, as a fellow-countryman, thoroughly enjoyed his reflected glory: 'I do like to see my chemist's eyes light up as I enter his shop.' He also went to the White City: 'it looks as if it's made of Parian marble whereas in fact it's reinforced concrete. But the effect is extraordinary.' It has 'an enormous crystal stairway' with a waterfall lit up at night by 'an ever so delicate filigree of electric light bulbs'—an unforgettable effect beheld by two hundred thousand people at once.[5]

The paint-manufacturer was at last 'freed' from his machines in London, but, when he was back in Trieste in October 1908, rumours of war came to remind him of the relationship between his work and the world of *Realpolitik*. That month nearly thrust Trieste and the Balkan peninsula back thirty years or forward to 1914. In the wake of the Young Turks' revolution in Istanbul, Bulgaria declared its independence. On the following day, Austria-Hungary annexed Bosnia and Herzegovina, which had been under its administration since 1878. Austria's warlike posture alienated all the Powers except Germany and made an implacable enemy of Serbia. It divided Europe firmly into the two blocs that were to fight the Great War. Italy was particularly concerned, as it had already effected a swift economic penetration of Albania and was seeking further economic expansion into the Balkans. Italian and Austrian economic imperialism were thus heading towards collision. Europe generally had been growing more nervous about the possibility of war as a result of the feared rise of German imperialism during the first Morocco crisis in 1905–6.

48

TWO WRITERS IN A TORMENTED TOWN: SVEVO AND JOYCE

There was no war in 1908–9 over Austria-Hungary's annexation of Bosnia-Herzegovina, but there had been mobilizations both in Austria-Hungary and in Serbia. In October 1908 the Triestine Socialist Angelo Vivante published in *Critica Sociale* an article entitled 'Has internationalism failed? (The Socialist debate on the Balkans)'.[6] This showed up the apparent inability of Socialists in various European countries and in the various national provinces of the Danubian Monarchy to restrain militaristic imperialism (though the Triestine Socialists had convened congresses including Socialists from both Italy and Austria which had jointly protested against the warlike postures and military expenditure of both countries and called for peaceful relations between them).

Vivante's article was prophetic, in more ways than one. In November, Emperor Franz Josef dismissed Prime Minister Beck and resorted in effect to government by decree, with the military more prominent than ever. Show-trials of Croat nationalists and the notorious Friedjung affair* demolished the vaunted moral foundations of the Habsburg monarchy and also compounded the distrust and hostility between itself and Serbia, which now broke off all economic relations with its powerful neighbour.

While the mobilization crisis was still on, on 13 February 1909, the Austrians officially burnt 4.7 metric tons of Italian books and periodicals in the Servola blast furnaces (almost next door to Svevo). The local elections were fiercely contested. Nationalists in Italy such as Oriani and Federzoni passionately denounced Trieste's Italian Socialists as traitors and despicable toadies of the Empire. The National Liberals won 59 of the 80 seats, but the Socialists captured twelve out of the sixteen seats allotted to manhood suffrage. This highlights a curious situation. On the one hand, as Giani Stuparich was to recollect, to be a Socialist in Trieste between 1900 and 1914 was almost natural; on the other hand, as Angelo Vivante observed, Triestine Irredentism was more a state of mind than a political phenomenon. Clearly, there was a fairly sharp class divide, the upper and middle classes being mainly Irredentist, the working classes preferring Socialism. Italian intellectuals often stood somewhere between the two. Some of them were even Socialists: but when events put them to the test they turned out at heart more nationalist than Socialist, and in 1915, when the Socialists were still opposed to Italy's entry in the war, men like Scipio Slataper and the brothers Stuparich were quick to enlist and offer their lives for Italy.

The national question caused a split in the Socialist ranks at the height of the 1909 election campaign also, and there were accusations by dissident Socialists that the leadership had been colluding with the Imperial authorities and even engaging in corrupt practices.[7] One can sense the tendency in Triestine Socialism to become institutionalized as part of the Austrian establishment, growing more and more ineffectively reformist. This was inevitable from the moment that 'Austro-Marxism' chose to evade the question of the power of the monarchy and its associated ruling structures and ceased to think in terms of radical change, which it publicly renounced.

Triestine Irredentism was also being ridiculed. The young Scipio Slataper, a

---

* Heinrich Friedjung was tried and convicted in Austria for publicly bringing false charges against Serbia, having been himself deceived by fabrications passed on to him by the Foreign Minister, Aehrenthal.

Triestine, had joined the staff of *La Voce*, the Florentine journal just launched by Prezzolini and Papini. This set out to rejuvenate Italian cultural and political life, to bring it up to date, to strive to get at the truth about the nation's situation, sweeping it clear of myths and rhetoric. So determined were the young men of *La Voce* to arrive at unvarnished truths that they proscribed from its pages imaginative literature, fiction and poetry. Slataper's polemical writings about Trieste, which began to appear in February 1909, certainly bore the mark of youthful impatience, yet they caused consternation among the Triestine National Liberals, especially since the elections were so close. Slataper's unceremonious critique of the Triestine Liberals, their culture and their institutions, their newspapers, the Trieste library and its librarian Hortis, has already been amply illustrated. His appreciative treatment of the Socialists and of their educational and theatrical ventures must have enraged the Liberals even more. His acknowledgement that Trieste's Liberal cultural institutions were no worse than those in Italy compounded the insult still further.

Slataper's 'Triestine letters' provoked replies to *La Voce* from Giuseppe Vidossich (Il Cerbo) and a debate between the latter and the Socialist Angiolo Lanza about the 1909 elections. There were also contributions from other Irredentists, such as Ferdinando Pasini, and Socialists like Vivante (whose book on *Irredentismo adriatico* was published under the imprint of *La Voce* in 1912). The more rational Irredentists admitted that geography and economics were against Trieste's union with Italy, but still preferred union even if it meant the town being relegated to an insignificant fishing port, and they were ready to resist Slav inroads tooth and nail. But on the whole the Liberals preferred not to engage in what they saw as an unprofitable debate, and tried instead to stifle *La Voce* with silence and subterfuge. They spread the rumour that the Austrians had banned the journal, hoping to transform the issue along their favourite nationalist lines. But this move only made the Triestines terribly eager to have the forbidden merchandise, so that a number of copies of several issues were disguised under the title of *La Cultura* specially for sale to Austria's Italian subjects;[8] Giani Stuparich afterwards recalled how the leading Triestine bookseller Eugenio Borsatti, then a bookshop assistant, 'used to get me the banned issues of *La Voce* from under the counter'.[9]

In its pages Slataper introduced to Italy a Nietzsche very different from D'Annunzio's, as well as Hebbel. It was in *La Voce*, as a result of its enquiry into Irredentism, that Prezzolini launched his appeal to the Triestine Italians to learn Slovene and to try to understand Slav culture.[10] In Trieste itself only the Socialists cared for an understanding with the Slavs, but the Triestines in Florence variously acted upon Prezzolini's call. Giani Stuparich wrote a book on the Czechs, which was published when Italy was debating whether to intervene in the Great War; while Slataper's *Il mio Carso* (My Carso), which appeared in 1912, displayed a curiously protective feeling of brotherhood towards the Slavs, a 'new race' with the primitive peasant virtues and yet the adaptability to take over the seas from the Venetians; slaves long spat upon yet ready at last to come into their own as masters, burning the forests and preaching the new gospel of Christ in their new Venice, Trieste.[11]

Like a true *enfant terrible*, Slataper also wrote several satirical sketches of *Characters* for *La Voce*, among them 'The earnest Irredentist', contrasted to 'The dried figs and sultanas Irredentist', of whom he wrote: 'as I sketch him I have before my eyes Mr Fiftypercent of Trieste. I therefore instantly beg all the other members of the Triestine family not to see any resemblance to themselves in the portrait.'[12]

The limitations of Slataper's idealism were shown up in his article 'Trieste's national and political future' of 30 May and 6 June 1912, where he affirmed that the political superiority of both individuals and nations is a matter of culture: 'there is a hierarchy of social values ... Not all have the same rights.'[13]

Yet Svevo was to remark of *La Voce* in 1927 that 'what little good we now have passed through it'.[14] Youthful bravado notwithstanding, the journal contributed more in seriousness and depth to Italian culture than did the noisier Futurist movement which swept across the land at about the same time. The thirst for sincerity and truth of the *Vociani* developed in the direction of autobiographical writing, though of a kind—somewhat naïvely lyrical and moralistic—which was a far cry from Svevo's, so detached, ironically controlled, and self-critical. Yet it was the closest that mainstream Italian culture came to Svevo's characteristic concerns until the very last years of his life. *Il mio Carso* may at least have encouraged Svevo by its bold disregard for 'correct' Italian: it incorporated often long passages in raw Triestine dialect, a variety of other unashamedly local usages, colloquialisms and ungrammatical speech in a lively linguistic expressionism all its own.

Another autobiographically based and linguistically untrammelled work, incomparably more sophisticated, but otherwise bearing an uncanny resemblance to some of the work of the *Vociani*, had dropped right into Svevo's hands late in 1908. Joyce had been stuck at the third chapter of the *Portrait* since the spring, and asked Svevo's opinion about what he had written up till then. Svevo reassured his young friend about the second and third chapters, and in particular about the extended treatment of Father Arnall's sermons in the third chapter, which was what most concerned Joyce. Svevo fully appreciated Joyce's study of the formation of his hero's young mind and of the power which religion exerted over it. Here lay much of Joyce's originality, and here it was most in tune with Svevo's: both writers were concerned with an objective study of subjectivity. Svevo missed—or resisted—another side of the book's originality, however, though, again, it was his own peculiar terrain too. He found the first chapter, dealing with the hero's earliest childish impressions, too trivial, and argued that Joyce's 'rigid method of observation and description' could not give his subject-matter a force and an importance which it did not possess. And here Svevo almost seemed to challenge Joyce to produce that epic of the everyday which was to be his masterpiece, *Ulysses*. He wrote (in English):

I must say that if you had to write a whole novel with the only aim of description of everyday life without a problem which could affect strongly your own mind (you would not choose such a novel) you would be obliged to leave your method and find artificial colours to lend to the things the life they wanted in themselves [i.e. to lend things a life which they did not themselves possess].[15]

Coming from the author of *Una vita*, this has a paradoxical ring. But it is the critically ironic autobiographer warning the lyrical and epic autobiographer, Joyce, of the perils of aestheticism and narcissism that lie in wait for him.

Perhaps reading Joyce's chapters spurred Svevo on with his own study of the formation of a young mind in that remarkable Muranese fragment, 'Marianno'.[16] Here Svevo transfers the autobiographically derived procedures of *Una vita* and *Senilità* to a child of very different experience, background and outlook from his own. Marianno is an orphan adopted by a poor cooper and his family living on the Venetian lagoon. The story of his 'everyday life' certainly offers 'problems which could affect strongly' Svevo's own mind. These problems proved too much for Svevo: he abandoned the story at the point where a technological advance makes the cooper's trade an anachronism, proletarizing him and his family. To confront directly the problems of class and economic determinism was something he never attempted except perhaps in the one-act play *Inferiorità*, in 1921. The fragment thus represents one of the great missed opportunities of twentieth-century Italian narrative literature, for the study of Marianno is very fine indeed. It contains, among other things, a passage which is strongly suggestive of something which was just coming to birth in European literature. The passage describes a dream:

He was poling away on one of those stern-driven punts which require so much strength and such steady balance from the polesmen. He slid out of a narrow side canal on to the main Canalazzo which was flooded by the sun's light and heat. And his punt shot ahead as if he had given it an over-powerful thrust or as if the water was carrying him along; he trailed the pole but his efforts were of no avail and soon it would leap out of his hands. A steam ferry was heading straight at him and alongside his punt a gondolier standing erect and calm on his oars said: 'You're poling when you should be sucking.' Marianno burst out howling with fright and shame. Berta promptly leaned over him and for many years afterwards the family laughed at Marianno's words: 'Help! The pole's jumping out of my hands!' When he was better Alessandro told him: 'Drop the pole and pick up your cooper's knife!' It was after this illness that a little shadow came between him and his adoptive family. The little boy would have liked to see the attentions which had been lavished on him during his illness kept up after it. But Alessandro had need of labour.[17]

Here the Freudian flavour is all the more extraordinary for blending perfectly into the milieu and the local idiom. The sexual overtones of the passage are reinforced by the connotations of the verb *vogare* for 'poling', and even the term for the stern punt, *sandolo popparino*, involves a pun on 'teat'. The fragment is unfortunately undated, and thus throws no light on when, how and by what degrees Svevo approached Freudian thought.

49

ITALO SVEVO AND PSYCHOANALYSIS

Svevo was the first to muddy the waters in the matter of his interest in psychoanalysis. All his own statements on this subject belong to the last two and a half years of his life, from 1926, when he was writing 'Soggiorno londinese'. In this he gave two different dates for his first contact with Freud's ideas: 'I read some books by Freud in 1908 if I'm not mistaken';[18] 'But what writer could forgo at least thinking in terms of psychoanalysis? I came to know it in 1910.'[19]

This marks a distinction between *reading* Freud and having practical knowledge of psychoanalysis. As regards reading books by Freud and his school, 1908 seems a very likely date indeed. Given his interests, Svevo was bound to get wind of psychoanalysis via both public and private channels. In the spring of that year the first international psychoanalytical congress was held in Salzburg; and on 7 October a nineteen-year-old Triestine student, Edoardo Weiss, who happened to be an old schoolmate and good friend of Svevo's brother-in-law, Bruno Veneziani, met Freud in person at the university of Vienna, having gone there with the express purpose of studying psychoanalysis.[20] The importance of the date, 1908, is that it testifies to Svevo's long-standing interest in the psychoanalytical school, extending over at least fifteen years.

What Freud had published up to 1908 must have had an irresistible appeal for Svevo. He could read *The Interpretation of Dreams*, first published in 1900, and the briefer *On Dreams* of 1901. Burlesque and absent-minded mishaps like Svevo's own were mirrored and examined in *The Psychopathology of Everyday Life*, of 1901, and in the same year Freud published his investigation into *Jokes and their Relation to the Unconscious*, putting his finger on this most striking of the strategies adopted by Svevo in his relations with existence and with those around him and baring the character of the joke as the 'impotent' man's compensation (which Svevo no doubt had already sensed).

But the appeal which Freud's works must have had for Svevo goes beyond even these aspects, which are of such capital importance to his personality. Freud went straight to literature, taking ideas from it and taking his ideas to it. He was a man of formidable education, similar to Svevo's, perhaps stronger on the classics, but for the rest centred on the great tradition of German thinkers and writers (among whom, besides Goethe, Schopenhauer had pride of place), and on the literary classics of modern Europe. He had a strong interest in Italy not only as regards literature, but even more as regards art. More than this, Freud used literary parallels and even direct probes into literary and artistic works for his enquiry into the unconscious, and posited an extremely close relationship between the unconscious and the artistic imagination.

Freud's most celebrated case-study in this direction was *Delusions and Dreams in Jensen's 'Gradiva'*, which appeared in 1907. Svevo referred to this nearly twenty years later, suggesting that a similar study be undertaken of the far worthier works of James Joyce.[21] (His remark must be taken into account by anyone wishing to minimize the importance attributed to psychoanalysis by Svevo in elucidating not merely literature as such but literature, above all, *as life*.)

'But what writer could forgo at least thinking in terms of psychoanalysis?'— even if this psychoanalysis was to be treated in the same way as the theory of relativity, on which Svevo also dwelt at some length in 'Soggiorno londinese':

The artist, I mean both the literary artist and the non-literary, after vain attempts to approach [any new idea], puts it aside in a corner, where it troubles and disturbs him, a new basis of scepticism, a mysterious part of the world, without which one can no longer think. It's there, not forgotten, but veiled, caressed at every instant by the artist's mind.[22]

Svevo never renounced psychoanalysis as an instrument of knowledge. He rejected it as therapy, as we shall soon see more fully. As regards the relationship between Freud and literature, Svevo had only one objection, the most unexpected: he didn't like Freud's style: 'I read some of Freud's works laboriously and with full antipathy. One wouldn't believe it, but I like in other writers purity of language and a clear elegant style.' Nevertheless, he continued, 'psychoanalysis never abandoned me. I was easily held, as I was not committed to anything else.'[23]

In *Profilo autobiografico* and in his letters of the same period to a young admirer, Valerio Jahier, Svevo emphasized his purely 'scientific' motive in first approaching Freud's works, wishing to know whether psychoanalysis offered any hope of curing a relative of his.[24] But in writing to Jahier, Svevo added further details:

A great man our Freud, but more for novelists than for invalids. One of my relations was quite destroyed on leaving treatment after several years. It was on his account that I came to know Freud's work about fifteen years ago. And I met some of those doctors who surround him. But as to my experiences with psychoanalysis I would rather talk to you face to face (if I have such a desirable opportunity) because it's a long story. I shall only say that after reading the works, I undertook treatment in solitude without a doctor.[25]

That 'treatment' carried out 'in solitude without a doctor' was to take place during the war, and this statement testifies that Svevo never had any real first-hand experience of psychoanalytical practice. As for the initial date, that vague 'about fifteen years ago' would point to the rather late date of 1912, as the letter to Jahier was written in December 1927. It is clearly a loose indication, but might seem less puzzling and more useful if we consider that here again Svevo is not referring to his reading of Freud's works but to his practical knowledge of psychoanalytical treatment. He seems to be saying, in other words, that he learnt of the psychoanalytical technique from his relative upon the latter's return from Vienna.

This relation was Svevo's brother-in-law and Weiss's friend, Bruno Veneziani. Weiss has related that during the years 1908–14 he frequently saw in Vienna Freud's colleague Victor Tausk: 'I once sent him as a patient a neurotic young man who was a conscious homosexual in whom I knew it to be impossible to arouse heterosexual feelings.' In the end Tausk could think of no better advice than to try to rid the patient of his sense of guilt.[26] This sage advice, however, did not recommend itself to Olga. In 1911, therefore, Bruno, on Weiss's recommendation, applied to Freud himself for a radical cure.[27]

This treatment, to judge by the 'two years' mentioned by Svevo, must have covered most of 1911 and 1912. Bruno undertook further courses of treatment by Freud and others of his school, even after the Great War. Svevo complained that 'Freud himself, after years of costly treatment, declared the patient incurable and dismissed him. I do admire Freud, but that verdict, after so long a period of life had been wasted, left me feeling disgusted.'[28]

Svevo's stricturers on Freud's behaviour were confirmed by Weiss: 'I had the impression that Freud developed strong positive and negative countertransference feelings towards his patients and pupils.'[29] This parallels Dr S.'s attitude to Zeno in La coscienza.

As we have seen, Svevo wrote to Jahier that he had met 'some of those doctors' who surrounded Freud. Not only Weiss, then. Possibly, through Weiss, he met Tausk. In the thick of writing La coscienza di Zeno he accompanied Bruno and Olga to see Groddeck in Baden-Baden.[30] And in 1911 he met one of the most flamboyant members of the psychoanalytical school, Wilhelm Stekel, while on holiday in Bad Ischl.[31] Letizia Svevo recollects that her father and Stekel shared a liking for dogs.[32] No doubt exercising their pets together gave them opportunities for long chats about even more absorbing interests. Stekel had just published his massive Die Sprache des Traumes (The Language of Dreams), and in 1908 Nervöse Angstzustände und ihre Behandlung (Anxiety Neuroses and their Treatment). Svevo would probably also have been interested in Poetry and Neurosis, of 1909. Die Sprache des Traumes, as the title hints, is a reductive, rigid and mechanistic application of Freud's ideas, offering a ready-made symbolic code for the interpretation of dreams never sanctioned by Freud.

Stekel is one of the candidates for the doubtful honour of having served as a source for Dr S. in La coscienza di Zeno. Freud was to write to Weiss in 1923 that 'admiration for Stekel shows weak judgement and perverted taste', attributing such admiration to what he saw as Stekel's over-use of self-analysis.[33] Dr S. does just that in treating Zeno Cosini, and Elizabeth Mahler-Schächter has pointed out numerous correspondences between the highly unorthodox psychoanalysis practised in the novel and that professed by Stekel,[34] who is quoted by J. A. C. Brown as saying: 'Day after day I attack the patient's system by storm, showing that he can get well betwixt night and morning if only he will discard his fictive aims.' Brown summarizes an important part of Stekel's approach as follows:

Resistance is seen not as an unconscious opposition to the emergence of forbidden wishes, but as a defence against the treatment itself, since the patient dreads being cured, or rather he dreads the adult responsibilities which being cured would imply.[35]

Stekel's view of the analyst–patient relationship as outlined here closely matches that shown in the novel, and it seems clear that Svevo was fully—and no doubt critically and ironically—cognizant of Stekel's ideas, as he was of Freud's.

Those who stress Svevo's links with the culture of *Mitteleuropa*—essentially, German culture—are wont to play down the best-documented link and, in literary terms, the most productive of all—that with the Freudian school. As if to admit such a link would be to diminish Svevo. The writer exploited Freudian ideas as freely and imaginatively as he had exploited Schopenhauer's. Svevo himself defined his relationship to Freud and his school by means of a sly simile:

This intimate relationship between philosopher and artist, a relationship resembling legal matrimony in that the two partners fail to understand one another and yet produce splendid children ... achieves a renewal in the artist or at least gives him the warm glow and sensation of renewal as would be the case if it were possible to change part of our vocabulary and give us new words which have not mouldered through antiquity and long use.[36]

Svevo is referring here to the relationship between Einstein's theory and literary approaches to it and the relationship between Schopenhauer and Wagner, but the entire drift of his argument in 'Soggiorno londinese' is clearly towards justifying his own literary exploitation of Freudianism.

Svevo was to raise the question of the possible influence of Freud on Joyce, only to dismiss it out of hand:

I can prove that Sigmund Freud's theories did not reach Joyce in time to guide him in the conception of his work [*Ulysses*]. This statement will astonish those who discover in Stephen Dedalus so many traits that seem actually to have been suggested by the science of psychoanalysis: his narcissism which will (probably) be attributed not to his being an artist but to his being a first-born son, the adored mother who changes into a haunting spectre, the father despised and shunned, the brother forgotten in a corner like an umbrella, and finally the eternal struggle in him between his conscious self and his subconscious.

There is something more. Did not Joyce borrow from psychoanalysis the idea of communicating the thoughts of his characters at the very moment in which they are formed in the disorder of a mind free from all control? On this head the contribution of psychoanalysis can be ruled out, for Joyce himself has told us from whom he learnt this technique. In fact his word was enough to confer celebrity on the venerable Edouard Dujardin, who had used this technique in his *We'll to the Woods no More*. For the rest I can bear good witness. In 1915 when Joyce left us he knew nothing about psychoanalysis.

Moreover his knowledge of current German was too weak. He could read some poets, not scientists. Yet at that time all his works, including *Ulysses*, had already been conceived.[37]

Svevo was wrong. Ellmann reports that one of Joyce's pupils between 1911 and 1913 was a young man called Paolo Cuzzi, who had come to him upon a recommendation by Svevo. Teacher and pupil discussed a myriad subjects, among them psychoanalysis, which Cuzzi knew from the *Five Lectures on Psychoanalysis*.[38]

Though not quite as guarded on the subject as Joyce, Svevo was careful not to give too much away about his own literary exploitation of Freudianism. Critics of *La coscienza di Zeno* have shown that Svevo's Freudianism runs deep; it is complex, far-reaching, subtle and elusive. And it is all very well for Svevo to protest that until after the war his interest in Freud was purely scientific. At least two of his pre-war stories bear at least some imprint of the theory of the unconscious. The better known is 'Vino generoso' (Generous Wine),[39] which Joyce may have seen before 1914.[40] The other, 'Il malocchio',[41] is hard to date. Its hero's looks can kill (literally). He dreams of a Napoleonic career, and anyone who thwarts him or rouses his envy dies. This hero, who kills involuntarily (that is, by unconscious will), is another of Zeno's precursors.

Svevo's other pre-war writings do not show a marked Freudian character, though 'La madre' gains still more interest from a psychoanalytical reading.[42] Svevo seems to have absorbed Freud into his literary awareness rather slowly, whilst the psychoanalytical movement was rapidly gaining ground in the world at large. It made its first timid appearance in Italy in 1910, when Roberto Greco Assagioli wrote a brief outline of Freud's ideas on sexuality for the issue of *La Voce* of 2 February, which was entirely devoted to the 'sex question'.[43] In that same year the second international psychoanalytical congress was held at Nuremberg, and Freud and his colleagues were also causing more stir in the various psychological and psychiatric congresses. Freud's *Five Lectures* of 1910 arose from an invitation to him to visit the United States in that year. In 1910 he also published his study on *Leonardo Da Vinci and a Memory of his Childhood* and in 1913 he extended his method to anthropology with *Totem and Taboo*. There were also many varied and interesting articles, such as those on psychoanalytical technique (1912–15), on 'Creative Writers and Day-dreaming' (1908), and 'The *Moses* of Michelangelo' (1914). This added up to a massive scientific and cultural presence whose originality and rich scope for development affected not only Svevo's outlook, but that of Europe as a whole.

Svevo's greatest tribute to Freud's importance not merely to literature but to life was made in connection with a story he had written many years before but which acquired significance when it was incorporated into *La coscienza di Zeno* precisely through the Freudian context, and there became one of the book's illuminating moments. Svevo mentions this in another of his letters to Jahier:

And if I believe Freud to be a great master it is because I believe that he attributes due importance to our experiences. Long before I knew Freud I related my adventure of the wrong funeral in a story which conveyed nothing but great good-humour. It became much more serious in the novel and Ada grasped all its significance. But Freud can have no other importance for literature than Nietzsche and Darwin had in their day.[44]

That teasingly negative last sentence says everything: Freud's influence on literature, like Nietzsche's and Darwin's, is incalculable.

Freud's paper 'Creative Writers and Daydreaming' might well have touched Svevo on the quick. Freud traces the development of childhood fantasies into the adult psyche: 'the adult ... is ashamed of his phantasies and hides them from other people. He cherishes his phantasies as his most intimate possessions ... a happy person never phantasies, only an unsatisfied one.' The scientist treats daydreams as projections of desires which do not find satisfaction in reality: 'they are either ambitious wishes, which serve to elevate the subject's personality; or they are erotic ones.' And he makes a point which is as relevant to the pre-Freudian *Una vita* as it is to *La coscienza di Zeno*, namely, that in male daydreams the conquest of the woman is associated with social and material success. Such daydreams may be the precursors of the morbid symptoms exhibited by the patients who resort to psychoanalytical treatment, or on the other hand may find a harmless outlet in the flood of romantic novels where there always sits enthroned the real protagonist of every episode, 'His Majesty the Ego'.[45] Any good writer is aware of all this, and so was Svevo. His own writing had in fact always been a conscious antidote to the fantasy literature of wish-fulfilment. But to have the issue thus explicitly set out within the framework of an organic theory might well reassure Italo Svevo that the approach which he had always followed with the rigour of a scientist could in fact claim true 'scientific' validity. It was not, however, until the Great War, from 1916 onwards, that he was more actively to turn his Freudian insights to account. Apart from the social encounter with Stekel in 1911, there is no recorded mention by Svevo of psychoanalysis, Freud, or any of his school until the writing of *La coscienza di Zeno*.

50

ITALO SVEVO VERSUS ETTORE SCHMITZ

Svevo's perseverance with psychoanalysis was in part due to his affection for his young brother-in-law, Bruno. Olga Veneziani had had, besides her four daughters, two stillborn male offspring before the birth of Bruno, her last child.

As the youngest, and the only boy, he was smothered with attention and affection by his mother, as well as by his sisters. Great expectations rested upon him, and he also had to live with the hysterical fits caused in his mother, as often as not, by Gioachino's philanderings. All in all it is not surprising that Bruno was not drawn to women.

He rebelled not only against sexual totems and taboos. Though a virtuoso pianist and a top-class Bologna chemistry graduate, he showed no interest in any 'career' or in joining the Veneziani firm. He indulged now in psychoanalysis, now in Buddhism. Anzellotti assigns the end of Bruno's first lengthy course of psychoanalytical treatment to 1911. That treatment must have been one of the major expenses which Olga never spared where her incomprehensible son was concerned. 'Olga bought pianos and paid for everything else. Bruno was to cost her two million lire in ten years, ten times as much as her industrious sons-in-law cost her in salaries and dividends.'[46] There is certainly something of the brilliant dilettante Bruno in Zeno Cosini.

Svevo's letters seldom mention Bruno. In 1908 the lad refused Ettore the favour of taking a water-melon to Livia in Schrattenberg, but Ettore still wrote with affectionate mock-concern: 'He has long hair and if they don't know at Schrattenberg that he is related to me they might take him for a Jew and massacre him.'[47] The friendship between the brothers-in-law was hallowed with a ritual wager to give up smoking in 1911. Ettore hoped to get eighty crowns out of Bruno in return for going without a smoke for one year.

Svevo noted after a month's abstinence:

I'm well, but not as well as I deserve to be. It's never enough for me. My stomach pains have ceased completely even though I'm eating like a hog. I'm suffering slightly from insomnia as I'm getting only 8 hours' sleep a night. I'm a lot more serious and don't laugh much, which should be bad.[48]

Whatever Freud had to say about it, Svevo was determined to love his own ego, to accept as he found it 'the ground, which is so complex, of *his* being'. If he was not healthy, he had learnt to love his illness, protecting it behind a screen of laughter. And if that did not work, he would write.

His defences were put to a hard test in September 1910. His laughter wore thin. Once more, Salsomaggiore was to blame. Things went smoothly enough for the first few days after Livia had left Trieste. Ettore lazed in bed till late: 'We're having a sort of festival over the arrival of the horses. Gioachino is waiting impatiently. Nico [young Bliznakoff] is doing his homework as he has to, but at the villa entrance so as to see the new beasts'. The following day turned out so busy for Ettore that he had only ten minutes with Letizia, during which he did not even see her, as they went out together after dark to release the dog Turco, 'she leading me by the hand up the hillock like Antigone with Oedipus'.

At this time Edmondo Oberti (brother of Dora Veneziani's husband Bepi) was in prison under suspicion of complicity in an Irredentist plot by La Giovane

Trieste (Young Trieste), and on 10 September was removed to Graz in German Austria for trial. He was to be acquitted, along with his companions; his fellow-conspirator the historian Tamaro's explanation was that the authorities were not crafty enough to lay their hands upon the incriminating documents.[49] The day before Edmondo was transferred to Graz, Ottavio Schmitz, his wife Frizzi, her old mother, and their daughter Tenci (Ortensia), 'a beauty of markedly Jewish type', arrived from Vienna. The palace belonging to Fortunato and Emma Vivante was put at their disposal. Frizzi, afraid of encountering cholera if they went on to Italy, persuaded Ottavio to stop in Trieste.

Ettore and his nephew Aurelio Finzi stayed up with Ottavio and Frizzi the first night until midnight at the Caffè degli Specchi in Trieste's great square. Ettore found Ottavio something of a revelation, and felt himself shown up badly in contrast. This seems to have been the reason for the beginnings of discontent which now stirred within him, sapping away at those smiling defences. He wrote to Livia:

Ottavio is in excellent humour. He told me the story of the money he had lost with Rothberger who had changed his name from Goldberger and had now changed it to Geldborger and he said that he now wants to spend all he's got left so that at least he'll have nothing more to lose. Then he told me about his battles with the school authorities. So far Tenci has never heard a single word about religion from any teacher. Every year she takes her exams and passes with flying colours except in religion of which she says that she doesn't know what it is. Everything has gone fine so far. Ottavio says that if they don't let her move up to the next class he won't care a hoot and he'll send her to finish her schooling in Italy. There's a fine difference between the brothers. What do you think?

One fundamental difference between the two brothers was that Ottavio had to defend his and his daughter's freedom from religion merely against the authorities, whilst Ettore had to reckon with his wife. That 'What do you think?' was a rather feeble challenge to Livia: at this very time, in fact, as Letizia approached her thirteenth birthday, she was being prepared to receive her first Holy Communion and also to take the entrance examination for the school run by the nuns of Notre Dame de Sion in Trieste, which Livia had also attended.

Livia confirms that she and Ettore were at loggerheads over Letizia's education, which Livia wanted to be Catholic and Ettore wanted to be secular, like that which Ottavio secured for Tenci. They compromised: Letizia attended the non-religious Liceo Femminile but also received full religious instruction and spent just one year at Notre Dame. She grew up and always remained a steadfast Catholic, though of decidedly liberal outlook.

Livia gives a carefully nuanced account of the relationship between father and daughter:

He had been too absorbed during those years in his work and in his ideas to succeed in establishing a close and continuous communion with his daughter. Sometimes tiredness made him impatient, but when he discussed serious matters with her he did so without a trace of authority, as a friend. He taught her to face life's problems with unvarnished sincerity. Even during her merry infancy she had not been able to enjoy his company very fully. The happiest times were those spent travelling, on holiday by the sea ... on long walks in the mountains or on the Carso ... Once we walked for ten hours so as to reach the summit of Mangart. Then the communion between father and daughter became closer and happier. He took her to visit the places where he had spent his carefree adolescence, the romantic landscape of the Rhine and the boarding school at Segnitz, near Wuerzburg, and he took her with us to our little house in London. The girl's physical and inner resemblance to her father grew more and more marked: the same shining eyes, the same broad forehead, the same thick knitted eyebrows, the same smile full of humanity, the same free spirit. Letizia's temperament however lacked the vein of pessimism that pulsed in his ... He watched her grow up by herself and even if he was occasionally severe he did not let his personality crush hers. Letizia attended the Liceo Classico and practised a great deal of sport. At twelve years of age she had cycled as far as San Pietro del Carso; she loved roller-skating and tennis ... Letizia had inherited from me a great love of order and a strong sense of duty. To her intelligence, school learning was easy as play. Her inclination was more to the exact sciences than to the literary disciplines.[50]

This sounds objective enough and hints at Ettore's mild irritation at his daughter's religiosity and conformity ('love of order', 'sense of duty') and also at his deliberate avoidance of infecting her with his own doubts and with his problematical view of life, even at the cost of being half a stranger to Letizia, as he had long been to Livia.

The unnatural strain of this relationship appeared in the letters he wrote in September 1910. Just as Livia's first visits to Salsomaggiore made Ettore acutely aware of the limitations of the partnership between himself and Livia, particularly in terms of mental outlook and social values, this one brought home to him the gap between himself and his only child, which was thrown into even starker relief by contrast with the relationship between Ottavio, Frizzi and Tenci.

Money, too, was still a problem. After all his years' work for the Veneziani business, Ettore still could not afford to pay for his wife to go for treatment to Salsomaggiore, let alone accompany her there (though he may have used a bit of special pleading so as not to miss a rare opportunity of spending some time with Ottavio). What he wrote on 12 September was: 'It seems to me that having saved ourselves the cost of your trip thanks to Olga it's not very reasonable to replace it with mine.' A smile still masked his irritation when he wrote that it irked him to have registered Letizia to enter Notre Dame on the 13th and for a fee of 13 crowns. And he tried a half-hearted defence of his own bad conscience regarding Letizia's education by dint of a double-edged comparison between himself and Ottavio:

To tell you the truth, among all our relatives the ones who came closest to my ideal of life are Ottavio and Frizzi. Were he only a little less dogmatic he'd be perfect. Sometimes he gets heated about his ideas and I listen to him with pleasure because he speaks to me from his soul. But contrariwise when he draws rigid logical conclusions I withdraw into my shell and cease to follow him. If I'd had him near by, perhaps I'd be stronger and he ... weaker, which wouldn't do him any harm.

Ettore, lacking the forcefulness to live up to his own ideals, thus maintained his rightness in denying his inmost soul. In this same letter of 12 September he confessed to an 'excited state of nerves', attributing it to insomnia, the present disruption of the domestic routine, and, of course, Livia's absence. In fact his letters show that he was having a pretty good time with Ottavio and Frizzi: he went with them to visit an exhibition at Capodistria, took them to the race-course and, on another occasion, to see old Aunt Marietta, who 'gobbled them alive' and killed them with laughter with her far-fetched tales about the adventures of the Schmitz grandparents at the turn of the previous century. In company with his other brother and sisters—Paola, Natalia and Adolfo— Ettore was up till the small hours chatting and ruining his health and his sleep by drinking wine and coffee. But as soon as Livia reproached him for having refused to go and join her in Salsomaggiore he took to complaining about the 'beastly life' he was leading, about his inability to get to sleep until four in the morning and about Livia's failure to inform him about the numerous acquaintances she was making at her spa.

So the habitual battle broke out between husband and wife. On 18 September Livia wrote chiding him for his inability to express his affection towards her and for his jealousy, a 'vilaine maladie' of which she thought he had been cured once and for all. There is also an undated fragment of a letter (which could really belong to any year from 1898) in which she revealed her doubts as to Ettore's fidelity, doubts which she had tried to suppress on the basis of his explanations.[51] After fourteen years of marriage punctuated by so many frequent separations, Ettore remarked: 'my state is absolutely reminiscent of every other time when you left me on my own', partly on account of the 'danger which I face of your leaving your old ancient to attach yourself to some young fellow' whilst at Salso, 'which has also been the black cat [i.e. unlucky omen] of our marriage'. As for expressions of affection, he told Livia, if she re-read his letters she would find no lack of them: 'Otherwise I'm really done for as a man of letters because it would mean I can't even express what I feel. I've always disliked the sugary word that is so easy to pen and says nothing.'[52]

This little crisis came to an end upon Livia's return, though the question of Letizia's education was to drag on for a few years more. On 30 November Ettore pointed out to Livia that there was no misunderstanding between them on the subject, but plain disagreement: 'It's the same disagreement which at certain moments came within a hairsbreadth of preventing our marriage. Let's rejoice that it is our only one.' He went on:

I believe that our family—given our situation (or rather, mine)—is Catholic enough and does not need to be any more so. Naturally if you believed that it could never be Catholic enough I would eventually give way, seeing that a girl's upbringing is more the mother's business than the father's, but I would always remain inwardly convinced that you had committed an injustice. So let's wait for this year to go by which I've freely conceded to please you and then we'll see about returning to our former arrangement.[53]

After Letizia's school year 1910–11 at Notre Dame, where instruction was in French, Ettore had his way and she attended the Liceo: 'I'm also absolutely convinced that a real education is imparted in one's own mother tongue and so I have wanted Letizia to have it.'[54] Svevo never approved either of his own German education or Livia's French education and was not having his daughter too 'translated' into other languages.

In 1912 Letizia brought her parents a fresh problems. She and a young man scarcely older than herself, Antonio Fonda, fell in love. This love was to know no doubt or hesitation or to find any alteration throughout their lives. But the lovers' tender age gave the parents some concern. Tony Fonda tells their story:

I knew Ettore Schmitz from my youth. I was seventeen when I fell in love with my wife who was fifteen and returned my love. We were virtually engaged without consulting our parents ... Letizia's mother was worried by my attentions to Letizia and by Letizia's own attitude and begged her husband to intervene by requiring me to leave the girl in peace. After all, she was quite right: we were mere children; there was every reason to fear that mine was a fleeting infatuation and that Letizia would be hurt. Her husband saw the matter in a more relaxed fashion, and promised to speak, not to me, but to his daughter. He did so good-naturedly, to bring her to take the matter seriously, examining her own feelings thoroughly. He did this by telling her a kind of parable. A peasant had gone to the fair to buy a horse, but, not finding one, had come home with a donkey, naturally feeling disgruntled. 'You,' he told her, 'now that you've committed yourself to a precocious attachment, must try to understand clearly what it is you want, so as not to jeopardize your future. Make sure you make up your mind after mature reflection and that you don't opt for the donkey if you're really after a horse.'[55]

Letizia had already made her choice, though the interference of history was to prolong the engagement to nine years. For his part, Ettore had already accepted the suitor by 1913, and was even relying on him to make sure that he was registered to vote in that year's municipal elections. His name did appear in the third category of voters in the still brazenly preferential local electoral system, but Tony Fonda failed to locate it, and the bearer of that name felt more embarrassed than ever, both as a Jew and as a writer:

He probably refused to admit my name is Aron. He's still at the age when everybody seems Christian to him. I'll do my best to delete the Aron from the electoral register and the 'Italo Svevo' from the Guida. My life really does look like a muddle.[56]

All Svevo's political connections were with the National Liberals. This applies, as we have seen, to his own and Livia's family and also to his future son-in-law, who was to fight on the Italian side in the Great War. As regards registering himself as an elector, he dealt with the leaders of the National Liberal party, the Aras. He too, then, seems to have seen the national question and the redemption of Trieste from Austrian rule as the most urgent political issue. But he still had Socialist sympathies, and in 'Vino generoso', which he first drafted at about this time, he gives his protagonist a bad Socialist conscience which he flourishes only out of petty resentment and envy towards his rival, Giorgio.[57] On May Day 1913 Svevo masked and displayed his political and religious embarrassment with the remark: 'Tomorrow is a holiday. A real holiday. This time it is demanded both by the religious and by the socialists and I who agree with the socialists and with the religious also for your sake, will celebrate the holiday.'[58] As to religion, in 1913 we see him in solidarity with Carlo Finzi, who was engaged to Olga Bliznakoff, Marco's daughter, against Marco: 'And to think that that poor Jew will have to put up for his entire life with an unceasing *grognement*. Out of solidarity, I ought to warn him off.' Marco in fact 'is unable at any instant to restrain his outbursts of impatience at the sight of the happiness of that Jew whom he'd gladly see in Kiev where they are massacred . . .'.[59] The engagement lapsed.

The writer Italo Svevo continued to lead his double life. As we have seen, he contemplated removing his pen-name from the town guide, and once in conversation with a businessman who 'broke off the serious negotiations in which we were engaged' in order to ask whether he was the author of two novels, he denied this outright and said it was his brother. 'I blushed as an author blushes in such circumstances', the culprit recollected. As for his 'novel-ist' brother, whom the businessman then approached, 'he was not gratified by the attribution, which clearly impaired his professional respectability'.[60] But Svevo still went on writing. Shortly after the upset of September 1910, he scribbled down a few ideas,[61] of which the first and most important appears to have been the germ of one of Svevo's brilliant curiosities, 'Argo e il suo padrone' (Argo and his Master), on a man who learns to interpret his dog's language.[62] This device exposes the hypocrisy and egoism of the mutual relationship between dog and master, employing a procedure not far removed from that of Zeno's 'unreliable' confession.

In a note of late 1912 the writer announced that he had now given up the name of Italo Svevo and any hope of the 'gloriola letteraria' ('a little, proud literary fame') for which he had striven in his youth.[63] But he still intended to speak his 'own word', and a year later he was at work on a play: 'I'm quite fed up about the play (you know the one). As usual these plays in the end damage the company and us personally.' This must be *Atto unico* (A One-Act Play), which can be dated to 1913 on internal evidence, and is a burlesque in racy Triestine dialect on Olga's high-handed treatment of her domestic servants. (We see her sacking two of them in 1912.)[64] A gang of four thieves who have broken out of gaol find it preferable to give themselves up and return to prison rather than be enslaved to the lady of the house.[65]

Svevo's other farcical play, or 'one-act fantasy', as he himself called it, was *Terzetto spezzato*,[66] the only play to be staged during his lifetime. Its source may have been the spiritualist experiments which Svevo began in Murano in

December 1907.[67] They seem to have led first to an undatable narrative effort 'Un medio ingenuo' (An Ingenuous Medium),[68] which points forward to the table-turning scene in *La coscienza di Zeno*. *Terzetto spezzato* sardonically dramatizes the pettiness and mercenary egoism of the dead Clelia's husband and also of her lover. Bored and dejected without her, they can do no better than quarrel as to which of them she really loved. The dead woman visits them, wishing to pacify them, but in the end, disenchanted by their low selfishness, she ends the play by departing with a sardonic burst of laughter. Svevo's irony has become here at once caustic and light, elusive as in *La coscienza di Zeno*. The author was later to mention that he had written the play around 1912 and that 'a friend pinched it off me'.[69]

The most important work undertaken by Svevo during the entire period between *Senilità* and *La coscienza di Zeno* was the play *L'Avventura di Maria*.[70] It deals with his persistent sense of guilt at having feebly betrayed his artistic vocation in exchange for a comfortable bourgeois existence, suppressing his true essence as a man and the 'adventure' which every person's life could be and should be. Along with *La rigenerazione*, this is the most autobiographical of Svevo's plays. Here Schmitz-Svevo divides himself into his component halves: the well-to-do businessman, Alberto Galli, capable only of an undemanding little affair, and the violinist, Maria, who is finally forced to choose between her rich lover and her art. There is something too pointedly demonstrative about the play, especially in the bohemian tirades of Maria's uncle, Tarelli, against the humdrum, philistine respectability and materialism of the bourgeoisie. The play is more quietly devastating in revealing the emptiness and the deformations of bourgeois life in its scenes of typical domesticity, in the paltry corruptness of Alberto's spoilt child, and even in the dignified closing speech of Alberto's wife, Giulia. Svevo shows his sharp awareness of the conflict between the claims of his art as a writer and the claims which bourgeois comforts bring with them. Written by a man who purports to have given up writing in favour of an easy life, the play seems a living paradox. But it is worth repeating that Svevo's originality, his unique 'realism' (which may equally well be called his imagination), lies precisely in his living out the conditions of bourgeois life to the full, with all the compromises—psychic, moral, social, political, cultural—that that involves; in his *not* being able to shelter behind the alibi of an artistic calling. If his conscience plagues him for having betrayed that calling, so much the better. He will go on writing on the sly, he will not cease to sense, to note, and to reveal the drama that lurks in the most microscopic creases and seams of our social existence.

Apart from the discovery of Freud, little can be said about Svevo's cultural experiences at this period. He could hardly miss the Futurists. After launching their first manifesto in the Paris *Figaro* on 20 February 1909, Marinetti and his associates kept themselves regularly in the news, causing uproar and exchanging blows; their unpredictable shows became all too predictable but were still 'happenings', and particularly pleased the Triestines by reason of the movement's swashbuckling Irredentist enthusiasm. One of the earliest Futurist 'serate' in fact took place in the Trieste Politeama Rossetti on 12 January 1910, culminating in the usual free-for-all.

But Svevo was not likely to be greatly enamoured of a movement that cried death to the intelligence and made an ingenuous cult of the machine and of war. Alone among Italian writers, he was on intimate and far from sentimental terms with machinery. In 1913 it engendered another of his bad dreams:

Last night I had a nightmare. I had invented a machine for stirring barrels and I wrote nothing to anybody so as to give people a surprise with my ingenuity. The workmen were there intent on watching the miracles of electricity and I plunged the screw into one of the batch of twenty barrels. The instant I touched a button the barrel began to dance, then to totter, and finally flew into pieces in a lake of paint. Cimutti stepped out from among the works and remembered that he had forgotten to oil the machine. You know that in an emergency one takes advice even from underlings and we tried out the machines dripping all over with oil. It was worse! The barrel started up an infernal jig and before it got destroyed it overturned all the other barrels. The workmen fled without touching another button that was supposed to stop the machine which had run amuck and I was almost drowning in the paint which was rising swiftly. Such a stupid business made me sweat with terror.[71]

Nor is it probable that Svevo was impressed by the 'Technical Manifesto of Futurist Literature', written by Marinetti in 1912 and prefixed to his *Zang-Tumb-Tum (Bombardamento di Adrianopoli)*, in which it is proposed that literature be purged of syntax, grammar, logic, psychology, in the interests of immediacy, concreteness and simultaneity. Svevo's subtleties are those of one whose roots were in positivism, and he could not readily avail himself of the revolutionary possibilities which some younger writers could see in Futurism. There may be a humorous reference to Futurist attitudes in Zeno Cosini's impulse to smash the Venus de Milo to smithereens,[72] though Livia attests to Ettore's also having had the same impulse.[73]

But it was mainly a story of mutual indifference. In 1930, when Svevo was dead, Marinetti was addressing a packed but drowsy audience in the Politeama Rossetti in Trieste. He is reported as having at one point roused it to wild applause:

'Since I'm here in Trieste, I'd like to mention Italo Svevo, the novelist from your town who is now so often spoken of. I too have tried to read his works. But what am I to tell you. I got the impression I was eating chocolates. Well,' he cried, thrusting out his chin in his characteristic manner, 'I am a lion and do not eat chocolates!'[74]

Poles apart from Futurism, the Triestine poet Umberto Saba was hardly more likely to attract Svevo's interest. Saba's unostentatious poetry of emotion, traditional in appearance despite its originality, counterpointing the 'lightly wafting' images of Trieste against his own painful but jealously guarded solitude, was a far cry from Svevo's analytical and satirical irony, and not calculated to overcome his rooted antipathy to verse. Trieste had more to offer him in the theatrical field, where it kept so up-to-date that he could see Shaw's *Candida* and *Mrs Warren's Profession* at the Teatro Popolare almost before the Lena Ashwell players brought them to Greenwich, where he had to try to follow them in English.[75] Hauptmann and Sudermann, Gorky and Chekhov were likewise quickly on the Triestine stage, alongside older established play-wrights, and produced at such a high level of artistry that James Joyce once leapt up during the performance of a Turgenev play, crying out in Italian in his enthusiasm over Ermete Zacconi's acting: 'Nobody back home has any idea there are artists like these!'[76] The spectacular set after the manner of Stanislavsky and Gordon Craig was now coming in, especially in the opera. For the showing of Richard Strauss's opera *Salome* in 1909, Joyce wrote an article in *Il Piccolo della Sera* on Oscar Wilde as author of the original play, dwelling on the shameful persecution which his fellow-Irishman had been made to endure. Strauss's work was acclaimed by an immense crowd at the Teatro Verdi. It was seen as 'a landmark in modernism previously considered utopian and incapable of realization', and Gemma Bellincioni's performance was greatly admired.[77] She 'astounded the theatre', say Coceani and Pagnini, 'robed in flame, and red-headed'.[78] Ettore Schmitz, who had adopted the pseudonym of Herod for another Gemma nearly thirty years earlier, was not so impressed. He was to ask Livia in 1911: 'Shall I be seeing *Salome* next week? Ugly as it is, I'd like to hear it once more. Perhaps with a different baritone la Bellincioni will be livelier.'[79]

A more teasing cultural opportunity was the visit by the German-language writer from Prague, Rainer-Maria Rilke, who was guest for the winter in Duino castle of its feudal owner, Princess Marie von Thurn und Taxis (Di Torre e Tasso in Italian). Here in Duino 'The members of the "Quartetto Triestino" often came out for the day and played chamber-music for us on the great terrace.'[80] The hospitality of the ardently pro-Habsburg Thurn und Taxis miraculously transcended national enmities: Duino sometimes saw gathered together Gabriele D'Annunzio and Eleonora Duse (who were also fêted by Trieste's Irredentists), Carlo Placci, Dr Rudolf Kassner, Horatio Brown and Count Hermann Keyserling. Rilke had been to Duino for a brief stay in April 1910, when he was contemplating whether to write a book on the Venetian admiral Carlo Zeno, having perhaps conceived the idea from D'Annunzio's famous panegyric on Zeno in Venice. The year 1910 had seen the appearance of the novel which Rilke had completed in 1904, *Aufzeichnungen des Malte Laurids Brigge* (Notebooks of Malte Laurids Brigge). The book has a close affinity to *La coscienza di Zeno* and (if Svevo read it) would represent an exquisitely 'mitteleuropean' influence. In terms which could almost apply to Svevo's works, Claudio Magris sees this 'novel on the collapse of individuality' as a bridge 'between aestheticism and experimentalism'.

Malte is an individual who writes to preserve his own identity which is threatened by the proliferating flux of phenomena, but in the end he finds himself to be what is written down on the page, turned into an object among other objects, something immobile.[81]

The ageing Zeno likewise will remark: 'And now what am I? Not the person who lived, but the person I described.'[82]

51

DEATH IN VENICE, AND OTHER COMPLAINTS

The issue of Irredentism was still following its now well-worn track. The Socialists argued that the Irredentists were obscuring the fact that Trieste's destiny was bound to be tied by economic geography to the lands lying along the Danube. It was pointed out that the National-Liberals themselves had insisted that Trieste's new direct railway link with the heart of Europe should take the route which most tied the town to Austria and tied it least to Italy.[83] This new railway, completed in 1909, greatly shortened the journey between Trieste and Salzburg and Munich and enabled the Italian port to compete with its formidable northern rival, Hamburg, for the trade of central Europe. Increased prosperity, unfortunately, was not Austria's only motive for building this railway. Military and economic competition with both Serbia and Italy in the Balkans and the Mediterranean was also involved. Svevo must have been aware of the same dilemma that confronted both the Triestine workers and those in the Woolwich Arsenal, near his London factory: the competition in armaments provided work, but also increased taxation, living costs and the danger of war. The Triestine Socialists were decisive: they again called a conference of Italian and Austrian Socialists to emphasize their opposition to nationalistic rivalries and to protest against the rise of militarist attitudes and expenditure in both countries. Angelo Lanza, editor of the Triestine Socialist newspaper, *Il Lavoratore*, but a citizen of Italy, had to fight a duel with the leader of Italy's Nationalist Party, Luigi Federzoni, who had called Lanza a traitor. Lanza's second was a Moravia.[84]

Those Irredentists who cared more for facts than for rhetoric were ready to admit that the standard of living in Trieste was higher than that in Italian cities and that the Irredentists in Trieste never amounted to more than about fifty activists with perhaps five thousand sympathizers, and that the real aim of 'redeeming' Trieste was to further Italian economic penetration into the Slav lands beyond.[85] This cool assessment must be balanced against the hot devotion of the two thousand volunteers from the Austrian Littoral (half of them from Trieste) who fought for Italy in the Great War.

Politics was not Svevo's only worry. An astrologist might have read trouble in store from the passage of Halley's comet in 1910. Ettore, from Murano, had this to tell Livia:

People here in Venice are comet-crazy. They say that thousands and thousands of people are spending the night on the lagoon, and not for the purpose of scientific observation. We've been advised to shut the dog inside tonight as they're going to sing a serenade to the comet opposite the bridge.[86]

Troubles had started in Murano even before this, however. Since 1908, Gilda Moravia had been engaged to one Giuseppe Cappellotto and Ettore had rashly embroiled himself with Gilda and Olga by raising Cappellotto's hopes of employment in the firm. Olga brusquely dismissed these expectations, and Gilda never forgave her for it. After threatening resignation several times, she gave up her position as secretary at Murano in 1911 and went off with Cappellotto. The dressmaker Italia De Luca left with her.[87] Gilda was replaced in April by a Signorina Hitti, who at once turned out highly efficient and besides, not being one of the family, pleased the Schmitzes by not joining them at meals.[88]

This was when cholera appeared, the same epidemic as that described in Thomas Mann's *Death in Venice*. That description fits in with what Italo Svevo reported in his letters. While the cholera was raging he spent three fairly long spells in Murano, and remained almost unduly unperturbed. By 1 June, when the alarm was at its height, Ettore was happily making fun of *siora* Pina, wife of his labourer Cimutti, who insisted that at Saõ Paolo in Brazil she had seen cholera victims turn black, and that the Venice ones must be typhus cases, as they were turning yellow. Svevo was also amused by one of his men, whose only precaution against infection was to drink wine from the South, instead of the local juice, and who warned Ettore that his tea-drinking would give him convulsions.[89]

Ettore was back again in Murano in July, to find that there was cholera in Venice again. The only loss to his workforce was that of a casual labourer required at the hospital for his skill as a grave-digger. His place was taken by a seafood vendor who was still selling his wares covertly in defiance of the health regulations. As for Ettore: '*I'm not in the least worried*. I'm afraid of old age, not cholera' (his emphasis). Signorina Hitti boiled water for him on the samovar and then left it to cool. He had given up coffee, as well as smoking, so he felt rather better than usual and his main concern was over paving the kitchen floor in the house of one of the labourers so as to keep out the damp. He risked a visit to a strangely deserted Lido for a sea-bathe, and asked Livia for news of one of his few readers: 'That invalid who was reading *Una vita*— is she dead?' The Venetian working-class was equally happy-go-lucky about the cholera: despite a public ban on celebrations, they honoured the day of Christ the Redeemer, one of their great feast-days, in the customary way, with gargantuan feats of drinking. The absenteeism from work on the following morning was due solely to wine. By the time Ettore made his third visit to Murano on 30 August, the cholera epidemic had receded.[90]

But death did not go away. At Murano again on 12 December, Ettore was faced with two fatalities: the child of one of his labourers fell ill and old Bravin, his foreman, collapsed at work. Both died. In Bravin's case, Ettore did not realize the seriousness of his condition until the two men he had sent to help Bravin at the Venice dockyard, where he had fallen unconscious, came back to say that it would take four of them to bring him back home: 'only then did I forget my perverse egoism which was driving me to try to complete today the batch which I started late yesterday.' He now went along with the men carrying Bravin to the latter's home, accompanied also by Hitti, who spent the night watching over the invalid. Bravin lingered on, paralysed, for a few weeks, and Svevo endeavoured to secure some sick-pay for him through his insurance. In the case of the child, it was Svevo who first noticed that the infant 'was no longer sucking, because he was well and truly dead'. He described the pathetic corpse: 'He was tiny, quite stiff in the same clothes I had seen yesterday ... I can't tell you how beautiful he was ... The stiffness of death gave him a certain air of strength.' He was buried the following day: 'Four pretty little girls, very nicely got up in white dresses, carried the tiny bier. And I could imagine the white infant proceeding in triumph across Murano.'

Ailments were common that December: Cimutti's little girl had pneumonia, another workman's wife caught a fever. Nevertheless, Ettore, though separated from his family, cheerfully celebrated his fiftieth birthday. 'I was born with Italy!' he exclaimed. 'I'm curious about the present which I'm so keen to have. Are you pregnant maybe?' Mere possessions did not interest him, and in 1913 he was to write in similar circumstances: 'It would be interesting if you had discovered in me a desire for some *thing*.' Now he sent Letizia a curious fable, telling Livia: 'Don't give it to her if you don't think it's suitable.'[91] It is the story of a cage-bird that feels it is free only inside its cage.[92] Svevo may have meant it as an emblem of his wife's conformity to convention, or his daughter's or his own.

In December 1913 there was another death in Murano: it was Cimutti's child Olga ('Here I find tragedy as usual'), and the following month, when Cimutti's other little daughter Teresina fell ill, Svevo called in the doctor at his own expense.[93] In June 1913 it was Hitti who caught a fever. Typhus was suspected, and the doctor had the lavatory thoroughly disinfected, and, indeed, the whole house. But the girl refused to go to bed and worked through the whole month even when she was running a temperature of 40°C (104°F). Svevo was amazed.[94]

There were tragedies in Trieste, too, and one at least concerned Svevo quite closely. It involved his father's sister, Peppina Tedeschi, whose miserable life came to a miserable end in 1911. Two years earlier, not for the first time, Svevo had appealed to Peppina's son Steno to be more humane towards his mother.[95] She had saved and scraped and sacrificed herself to enable him to go to university in Vienna and in Graz. Steno had qualified and then obtained a post as a high-school teacher of natural history, first at Pisino, in Istria, and then in Trieste itself. He had moved back to Trieste in order to be near to his mother. He was devoted to her and could not bear to leave her (as Svevo suggested it would be merciful to do), but he could not help treating her with impatient contempt. The relationship was torture to both mother and son. Then, on 2 July 1911, he paid her a visit to find that she was dying of a paralytic stroke and, before her very eyes, took strychnine, which he kept on his person. Peppina died two days after her son.

In his letter to Steno of 1909, Svevo had shown some respect for his learning. In particular, Steno Tedeschi had brought to Italy the ideas of the Graz school of philosophy—Witasek's aesthetics and Meinong's 'theory of the object', which pointed towards formal logic and Husserl's phenomenology. Steno's writings, published posthumously in 1913, form a contribution to the Triestine cultural 'melting-pot' and we must suppose that Svevo read them during the enforced leisure of the war years, if not earlier, and that they contributed to the sophistication of his thinking. He might well have read his young cousin's enthusiastic review of Weininger's celebrated *Geschlecht und Character*, published in *L'Indipendente* in 1905—though, as we have seen, he was to make characteristically ironic use of Weininger's ideas in *La coscienza di Zeno*. In 1908, Tedeschi had also reviewed Witasek's *Grundlinien der Psychologie* and in January 1909 he had given four lectures at the Università del Popolo on 'The Psychology of the Senses'. This attempt to build a bridge between abstract Idealism and Rationalism and the empirical method was, however, to be swamped, for Svevo, by the Freudian approach, which was at one and the same time infinitely more concrete and more imaginative.[96]

Ettore's life, commuting between Trieste, Murano and Charlton, did not vary much. There is no record as to whether he acted upon his own suggestion of going to meet Livia at some point along her return route from Riga, where she had visited her sister Fausta.[97] He had mooted the idea of a visit to Rome and Naples,[98] but he was not to see Rome until after the war. He had been to Tuscany in 1909, staying in Vallombrosa and paying a visit to Florence,[99] and went there again in July 1913 for a cure at Montecatini with the Obertis. Their collective 'intestinal crisis' was the subject which 'holds sway in every conversation'. Ettore's letters quipped away about toilet paper and related topics, hinting at a veritable mock-heroic epic entirely worthy of Joyce's Leopold Bloom.

He admired the cathedral in Pisa and the Valdinievole countryside. Montecatini itself offered variety shows (including one with Sacha Guitry) and a great number of magnificent *cocottes*:

There's always something to see. Old M. has one [a *cocotte*] staying in the room next to his at the Hôtel della Pace. He told me: 'I don't think about her because a woman who spends 50 francs a day at the Hôtel (it's a very pricey Hôtel) is too expensive.' And when I gazed in amazement at his openness he added: 'But there's a hole in the door and through it I've been able to see her naked. So I've had all I wanted.'[100]

The visits of a month or two at a time two or three times a year to England mostly produced no letters, as Livia accompanied Ettore. Sometimes Letizia went with them, and they took her to hear the Pankhurst sisters campaigning for women's suffrage at Speakers' Corner.[101] In 1912 Ettore was in Charlton on his own and wrote to Livia complaining about the housekeeper Maggie: 'The so-and-so gets 25s. a month when we're away and she wants 30.'[102] Thirty shillings (about thirty-five crowns) does not seem much. Life in London was getting easier, after the hardship of the first decade of the century. Yet, despite Lloyd George's 'People's Budget' and the Liberals' two general election victories in 1910, Britain lagged behind Austria and Germany in its social legislation and workers' insurance, and was more in step with Giolitti's Italy. The Irish question had now grown acute. With Home Rule imminent in 1914, Protestants and Catholics were arming and fighting the first skirmishes of a civil war from which they were saved for a few years by the First World War.

Svevo now had a personal interest in Ireland, thanks to his friendship with Joyce, and wrote to him in 1910 that he was trying to correct Livia's Anglomania.[103]

Joyce's literary and financial fortunes were still in near-desperate case. In 1909 he paid two visits to Ireland. One was to further his project of opening a cinema in Dublin. It was a flop, and Joyce felt that his business partners had cheated him. Concerned at his dejection, Svevo tried to cheer him up by writing that his surprise at being cheated proved him to be 'a pure literary man' and urged him to concentrate on getting *Dubliners* published.[104] This was the business of Joyce's second visit to Dublin, repeated in 1912 with equal lack of success. On this occasion, Nora had left Trieste first, with her daughter Lucia, to see her parents in Ireland. After seeing her off, Jim strolled jauntily over to tell Svevo how much better life was with only men at home. But within a few days he was back again to ask Svevo for an advance on twelve lessons so that he could join his womenfolk in Ireland. Nora's absence had caused him a most Zeno-like pain in the side. He also asked Svevo to look after his somewhat misshapen dog Fido, who then disappeared, to Svevo's consternation, only to be found in due course with the twelve pups which 'he' had littered.[105] Joyce made up for this by sending Hector Schmitz, Esq., a postcard from Galway showing an aged fisherman who bore a strong resemblance to the thirty-year-old James Joyce. He inscribed on the back: 'Portrait of the artist as an old man'.[106]

Svevo's relations with Joyce were still half-hearted, rather like those with Veruda, and perhaps for the same reason—namely, peace with Livia and with the highly respectable Veneziani household generally. Svevo was (or pretended to be) embarrassed when Joyce took up his invitation to come to Murano in 1911:

I'd never have believed that Joyce would accept my invitation. They are right in China, where good breeding dictates that one does not accept invitations. For the rest, I'm not at all sorry about it. I'll hire him a gondola as our own boatmen only go in pairs and I cannot spare two men.[107]

Joyce took the degree examinations at Padua University, hoping to obtain a better-paid and less time-consuming post in Italy, but Italian bureaucratic nationalism thwarted this plan and Svevo and some other friends tried to mend matters by finding him a post at the Revoltella Institute. It took a considerable time to obtain this and in the meantime, just while Joyce was in Ireland, the proofs of *Dubliners* were destroyed by the publishers, who deemed the work immoral. On his return to Trieste, Joyce vented his scorn and anger: 'I am certainly more virtuous than all of them, I who am truly monogamous and have loved but once in my life.' Svevo himself was once reproved by Joyce's 'virtue', probably after the war, when the former made a *risqué* joke. Joyce told him: 'I never say such things although I write them.' Svevo drew a characteristic conclusion: 'It seems therefore that his works cannot be read in the author's presence.'[108]

Svevo, then, still cultivated the art of the *Witz*, often with a Freudian flavour. Ottocaro Weiss, brother of the psychoanalyst Edoardo and friend of Joyce, remembers one of Svevo's witticisms: 'There are three things I always forget: names, faces, and—the third I can't remember.'[109] This absent-mindedness still occasioned the often ludicrous mishaps and blunders which are plentifully documented in Livia's biography. He mismanaged matters farcically on one occasion in 1913 when his brother Ottavio had asked him to look up his superior at the bank, Bernhard Popper, who was on holiday with his wife at the Venice Lido. When Ettore found them, they had already lunched, but he entertained them for some hours on a painfully empty stomach. He eventually got away and back to Murano, where he gorged himself into a state of gastric shock, and then had to telephone the distinguished visitors to make his excuses for declining their dinner invitation, though for Ottavio's sake he spared no effort to make their holiday agreeable.[110] This may have helped Ottavio's name get into the handbook of the Austro-Hungarian Monarchy for 1915 as 'Prokurist-Direktor-Stellvertreter' of the Wiener Lombard-und-Escompte Bank.

On 26 June 1914 Svevo was at last able to congratulate Joyce upon the publication of *Dubliners* as well as upon the serialization of *A Portrait of the Artist as a Young Man*. He found the latter much easier to understand in print than he had in his friend's handwriting, which was hardly less terrible than his own. He took the opportunity to encourage Joyce to write a book about Triestiners.[111]

But before the serialization of the *Portrait* was complete, Europe was in the grip of war.

Part VIII

WAR AND PEACE

1914–1922

52

SARAJEVO

In July 1911, an international crisis was caused when Germany, for the second time within the space of a few years, backed up its claims to share in economic investment and exploitation in Morocco by sending a gunboat to Agadir. And for the second time, unable to rely on support even from Italy, her partner in the Triple Alliance, Germany was obliged to give way in the face of the combined naval might of Britain and France. The naval rivalry between Germany and Britain had now turned into a race. The former's Naval Acts of 1908 had spurred the latter to build yet more Dreadnoughts and other vessels and to maintain a war navy equal to the next two largest put together. The British mercantile marine was also impressive, still comprising 60 per cent of the world's merchant shipping. Gioachino Veneziani's London factory was therefore thriving, and with other nations, including Italy and Austria, vying with each other for naval power, the other Veneziani factories contributed proportionally to the ever-rising fortunes of the firm.

Italy profited from her refusal to support Germany over Agadir. She was allowed a free hand by Britain and France to wrest Libya from the Turks and thus secure her interests in that territory lying between French North Africa and British Egypt. The action against Turkey started in September 1911, and marked the failure of Giolitti's policies. For a decade Giolitti had been striving to modernize his country's economy and society through industrial development, co-operation between capital and labour, liberal reforms in taxation, education, electoral suffrage, health and retirement insurance and other social provisions. His grand design was unfortunately undermined, however, by many weaknesses, in particular by his resorting to the devices of *trasformismo* or political transvestism to keep himself in office. He continued the deal with the great landowners of the South, the use of *clientelismo* or political patronage and straightforward corruption and malpractices of various sorts. He failed to win the principled support of the nation: the Socialists were not interested in liberal reform within the capitalist system and liberal democrats were shocked by his corrupt and money-minded *Italietta*. The Catholics remained hostile to his secularism, and right-wing circles were coalescing behind an increasingly aggressive nationalist movement which wanted to see a warlike Italy living up to the heroic legend of the Risorgimento and acquiring a colonial empire and the status of a great Power.

Giolitti's introduction of male suffrage (which extended the electorate from three to eight million voters) did not gain him either of the hoped-for results—a majority for his own party, or wholehearted Socialist support. He was thus induced to secure the support of the Nationalists by embarking on war in North Africa. The Futurists jubilantly acclaimed this as the 'Futurist war' and Marinetti accompanied the troops to Tripoli as a war correspondent.

The Libyan war was very largely a naval war. It began with the naval bombardment of Tripoli and then a sea-borne invasion, and extended to include the capture in 1912 of Rhodes and the Dodecanese islands, which had formed no part of Italy's original war aims.

Italy, then, was responsible for Europe's first war since 1878, and was the first nation to use force to change the European balance of power in her own favour. She was now bound to seem a threat to her nominal ally, Austria. Both nations were vying for political and economic influence in the Balkans, where they were building roads and railways and expanding trade and investment. On Austria's other flank, Serbia emerged from the two Balkan wars of 1912 and 1913 with her territory doubled.

These developments, though they receive scant mention in Svevo's letters are the necessary context for the most elementary understanding of the Great War (which was to play a crucial but problematical part both in his life and writing and in the history of his town). 'I hope you won't be agitated by further warlike reports,' he wrote from Murano on 18 December 1912. 'The newspapers here in the Kingdom [of Italy] continue to discuss the Austrian mobilization but they don't give it much weight and all these millions are clearly being spent just to frighten us.'[1] In 1913, he wrote of the Bulgarian reverses:

I'm sorry for Marco but I too am beginning to believe that the Bulgarians have put their foot in it. If they don't win they were obviously in the wrong. And I'm sorry that authoritative sources are taxing them with atrocious cruelty.[2]

Europe was thus growing accustomed to the idea and the reality of war, and of gain through war. Germany and Austria's thirst for colonies had been thwarted by the established colonial powers, and now Italy and the Balkan nations had hacked off portions of the Ottoman Empire with a further loss to German and Austrian prestige.

Austria-Hungary's warlike plans were revealed early in 1914. The Vienna parliament was dissolved in March on account of obstructionism by the Czech deputies opposing the bill to increase Austria-Hungary's army by 30,000 men, presumably for a war against Serbia or Russia. In Trieste, on 13 March, shots were exchanged between rival Italian and Slovene nationalists among the students of the Revoltella Institute.

In that spring of 1914 Trieste saw the entire Austrian fleet in review off Miramare to welcome the German Kaiser Wilhelm on board the *Hohenzollern,* with the German battleships *Goeben* and *Breslau* as escorts. At Miramare, the Kaiser was the guest of the Archduke Franz Ferdinand, who had been on the Austrian Littoral since February on a military tour of inspection. The implications of all this for Italy and Serbia were all too obvious. After the Kaiser's visit, Franz Ferdinand sailed away for naval exercises in the Adriatic and then went on to supervise military exercises in Bosnia-Herzegovina, where he was also to make an official visit to the capital, Sarajevo.

The Slavs of Trieste held further violent demonstrations on May Day against the Italian monopoly of political power in the local administration thanks to the local electoral system. The Slavs of the Littoral had held a congress at Opatija (Abbazia) in Istria in 1913, declaring in favour of Trialism (turning the Dual Monarchy of Austria-Hungary into Austria-Hungary-Slavia). In Trieste they appeared a real threat: 3,700 out of the 4,600 government officials were Slav, since the Italians disdained to learn Slovene. Moreover, in thirty years the Slavs had doubled their proportion of the population of Trieste, increasing from 15,755 out of a total of 133,019 recorded in the 1880 census to 51,108 out of 220,540 in 1910.[3]

On 28 June the Archduke Franz Ferdinand and his wife were shot dead in Sarajevo by Ivo Princip, a member of the 'Young Bosnia' secret society. The flagship *Viribus Unitis* brought the bodies back to Trieste on 12 July and there the state funeral was held. The Serbian government disclaimed responsibility for the Sarajevo assassination, but the Austrian general staff had resolved on war. Austria-Hungary's ultimatum to Serbia came on 23 July. Trieste and the world waited anxiously. Serbia substantially accepted the terms of the ultimatum, but Austria declared herself dissatisfied and effected a partial mobilization. In Trieste there was a riot, encouraged by the authorities, outside the Serbian Consulate, whose coat-of-arms was defaced by the mob.[4] The Italian Irredentists in Trieste greeted the war against Serbia with enthusiasm and presented themselves for call-up crying 'Long live Austria!' and 'Death to the Slavs!'[5] On 29 July the Italian consul was able to report to Rome that Trieste was wholeheartedly in favour of war and the Triple Alliance.

This was an exaggeration. The Socialists, even in Trieste, were internationalists and opposed the war. But, like most Socialists in every country, they failed to make their opposition to the war effective. Mere appeals and proclamations could not stop the machine of war. For the Socialist movement, this was incontrovertibly the greatest missed appointment with history.

So one nation after another was able to mobilize and declare war, silencing internal opposition to war by pointing to similar actions carried out by rival nations. Austria and Germany rejected the offer of mediation made by Great Britain on 27 July and on the following day came Austria's declaration of war on Serbia and full mobilization. The ultimatums and declarations of war from the allies on each side rained down during the following days. On 3 August, the day on which the German invasion of Belgium started, Italy declared her neutrality.

Italy indeed had grave problems of her own. Weakened by the war against Turkey and by the Messina earthquake, she had undergone the insurrection of the 'Red June' of 1914, when for a week the people had swept away the whole structure of public administration and authority over a broad belt of central Italy. The modest prosperity of the Giolitti era had not by any means eliminated the country's social or political ills. Mass emigration had become the safety valve for social and economic tension, reaching a peak in 1912, when 800,000 people had left the kingdom. Even so, strikes and agitation, often violent, continued. Rural landlords had already resorted to the use of motorized squads to combat the peasant unions of the Leghe, while the police persisted in repressing workers' demonstrations with gratuitous violence. The June insurrection was in fact precipitated precisely by the quite pointless death of a demonstrator at the hands of the police, when the demonstration had already passed off peacefully.

This was a confusing situation for many Triestines, made more so by the institution of press censorship and the consequent lack of reliable information. Mail was also censored: 'from that point on', writes Gaeta, 'letters had to be sent unsealed, had to bear the sender's name on the envelope and were franked by the security police.'[6] A general blackout was ordered and the administration even prepared to move inland.[7] Italian newspapers were banned, but a contraband supply was quickly organized through the Caffè Milano, which also became 'one of the headquarters for the issue of false passports to those wishing to cross the frontier'.[8] The passports were to help Austrian citizens evade conscription. The draft-dodgers included Letizia Schmitz's fiancé, Tony Fonda, who, when Italy entered the war in 1915, signed up as an infantryman.[9]

Both for Austria and for Trieste, naval incidents were prominent in the opening stages of the war. The very first action was a naval bombardment of Belgrade by Austria-Hungary's Danubian fleet, while news reached Trieste that an Anglo-French naval force was heading towards the town.[10] The waters were at once sown with mines, but their first victim was the *Baron Gautsch,* an Austrian vessel bringing refugees from Albania and Dalmatia, which was sunk by a drifting mine with the loss of a hundred lives. The Austrian Adriatic fleet itself saw action only during the conquest of Albania and Montenegro in 1915. Otherwise the only Austrian naval activity was carried out by submarines.

53

ETTORE SCHMITZ'S AUGUST 1914

Paint was still required, however, even when the fleet did not put out to sea, and soon after war was declared the Austrian naval authorities carried out an inspection of the Veneziani works to make sure that supplies would be available.[11] Nor was the need for ship's paint limited to Austria-Hungary. At six o'clock in the morning of 22 August, Ettore took the train for Germany.

The Germans had by now invaded Belgium and fighting was raging on every front. The Russians were suffering their first great defeat at Tannenberg in Prussia but were at the same time sweeping the armies of Austria-Hungary out of Galicia.

Having travelled all the first night and chattered a good deal, Ettore was tired and dirty as he waited several hours at Salzburg the next day. The next night he spent at Munich, and then proceeded to Frankfurt 'on the first express to run since the war broke out', which was of course extremely crowded. Before drinking his jug of beer and going to bed, he wrote to Livia (all his letters were in German, so as to reduce censorship delays) and described the mood in the country: 'Enthusiasm reigns in this nation, but it is calm and there is perfect order. They display calm coupled with a will to work which must lead them to their goal.'

On the 26th he reached his destination, Mülheim, near Essen, in the Ruhr— the industrial heart of Germany. Three weeks later the tone of his comments on the country had not changed:

What I have seen here of real, strong enthusiasm is beyond description. I have never admired and understood the power of Germany as I do now. There can be no doubt! Here lies victory. Science is the guide and all that is necessary is carried out, sacrifice being considered natural.

Svevo does not sound as if he is buttering up the censors. He clearly thought he was witnessing a heroic spectacle and felt quite ridiculous when, upon his arrival at Mülheim, not finding any missive from Livia, tears came to his eyes:

all this time I've been thinking mostly about the war. I can't take my mind off it although I'm in a country where order prevails to such an extent that the only ones who suffer from the war are those who are ordered to do so. And even they go off to war all bold and singing as if it were a holiday. They are certainly less concerned than I am.

That last remark hints at the seriousness with which Svevo regarded the war, a seriousness which is carried over, mostly in oblique ways, in many of his major post-war writings, and which undercuts the irresponsibility of Zeno Cosini's wartime behaviour.

His conscience was troubling him more than usual: 'You know how dear I hold the interests of the firm, but this time I cannot bring myself to desire its interests.' There was some secrecy surrounding the customer's identity that suggests the transaction had something to do with the war and perhaps even involved the German navy, which had up to now not figured among Gioachino's customers. This would help to explain Svevo's misgivings about his German mission, the first by the Veneziani firm, which had been planned before the war. The quantity ordered, totalling eight and a half tons, was quite considerable.

During the idle spells of waiting for the arrival of the arsenic and solvent naphtha, Svevo smoked and daydreamed as ever: 'I'm smoking like a mobilized Turk and so I cough busily away especially in the morning.' Otherwise he had no complaints: he devoured all the newspapers he could lay his hands on, and in the factory he found himself very much at home with the four Müllers and the three Schmitzes.[12] His associates, the Lindgenses, proved hospitable, though he was slightly embarrassed to find himself wearing his travelling clothes among ladies in evening dress. He took a great liking to the Foppes, employees of Lindgens's firm, with whom he was staying and who took him to Cologne to the cinema, to an open-air charity concert and to the zoo, where Svevo took 'real pleasure in seeing the good beasts (tiger included)'.[13]

Svevo was back in Trieste by about 25 September. On the 20th, rumours had been rife that Italy was about to enter the war, and the Socialist parties in Italy and Austria responded by calling for Italy's absolute neutrality. The end of the month brought news of Austrian defeats in Galicia and Serbia, and casualties from the 97th regiment on the Russian front started pouring into Trieste.[14] Trieste had already suffered a sharp reduction in trade from the mine-strewn seas and now the wounded soldiers returning from Galicia brought cholera, which took twenty-eight lives in 1915, twice as many as the 1911 epidemic.[15] Touring companies and orchestras cancelled their theatrical and musical visits to Trieste and cultural life gradually starved away as men were drafted for military service. No wonder Zeno remarks in his diary entry for 3 May 1915: 'Since war broke out, this town has become more tedious than usual. . .'.[16]

In November 1914 Ettore spent several days in Vienna to negotiate with the naval authorities there.[17] He was met by Ottavio who, although over forty, had been called up in August, no doubt to serve in the army's financial administration.[18]

The exact nature of Ettore's business in Vienna is unclear. Olga and Gioachino may have sent him to avert the possibility that the navy might requisition their factory or materials or even demand the surrender of the secret paint formula, or he may have been haggling over prices or the quantities to be supplied. Since 1909 Gioachino had pressed the Austrian navy to appoint him its sole supplier of paint and on 22 November of that year had gently hinted that the price would go up unless he was invited to supply two thirds instead of only one third of its total requirement. His argument was that the Austrian government ought to encourage home manufacturers in the face of foreign competition. The precise situation was that for several years the Veneziani firm had been receiving two fifths of the orders for paint from the Royal Imperial Navy, which recognized the superior quality of Gioachino's product but did not care to grant him a monopoly.

Ettore's present mission was probably precautionary in character, rather than expansionist. The records in the Vienna Kriegsarchiv mention, for the time being, only the inspection of the Veneziani factories and stock, on which a report was conveyed on 29 November by the Trieste Seebezirkskommando (local naval headquarters) to the Pola Seearsenalskommando (Naval dockyard headquarters).[19]

54

TRIESTE'S MAY 1915

Christmas briefly brought hopes that Austria-Hungary would agree to an armistice. Already on Sunday 25 October 'the young lads whose conscription was brought forward [those aged 19 and 20] were called up to go to their training camps at Ljubljana.'[20] Edoardo Weiss was serving in the medical corps on the Russian front. The Venezianis, Italian nationals, were not yet directly affected. Bruno Veneziani was receiving treatment in Germany.[21] Just before the war began, Livia's sister Fausta lost her husband and returned to Trieste from Riga with her two infants. Marco Bliznakoff had left for Bulgaria while Svevo was on his way to Mülheim, but his family had stayed behind in Trieste. And still opinion in Italy was divided over the war. At the outset the nationalists had been for supporting Italy's partners in the Triple Alliance, but middle-class opinion was clamouring ever more loudly to take the opposite side. The pro-Entente interventionists mounted increasingly massive and excited dem-onstrations, often clashing violently with the counter-demonstrations in favour of neutrality. The government repressed the agitation by both sides with an equally heavy hand. The Catholics and Socialists remained opposed to Italy's entry into the war, with insignificant exceptions—until the sensational volte-face by the Syndicalist Socialist Benito Mussolini.

By early 1915 preparations were being made in every quarter against a possible Italian intervention. Italy got her forces into a state of readiness, while Austria strengthened her frontier defences. Camillo Ara, the leader of the Triestine Liberal Nationalists, undertook a risky journey from Rome to Trieste to entrust Italian nationalist interests in Trieste to Edmondo Puecher, a nationalist Socialist who had joined Pagnini in breaking with the Triestine Socialists. 'The two men,' argues Rino Alessi, 'though adversaries, esteemed one another. They quickly reached an understanding.'[22] Ara must certainly have known the intentions of the Italian government and conveyed them to Puecher, who passed on the information to the leading Italian citizens in Trieste. There was a mass exodus of these in the days immediately preceding the Italian declaration of war.

Italy had been negotiating with both sides in the conflict. She sought from Austria, as the price of her continued neutrality, the cession of the province of Trent, and the establishment of Trieste as a Free City. This proposal—which exactly suited the interests of the Triestine Liberals—was indignantly rejected by Austria. Instead, Italy secured from the Entente Powers, by the secret Treaty of London, signed on 26 April, the promise of Trent, Trieste and its territory, Istria, and much of the coast and islands of Dalmatia, whose population was mainly Croat.

On 5 May, D'Annunzio made a triumphal return to Italy from France, where he had taken refuge from creditors, to add his eloquent voice to the interventionist campaign. Excitement now ran high in Italy, but Zeno Cosini's belief, on the very day of Italy's declaration of war, that such a thing would not happen, is no mere fiction.[23] James Joyce was also caught out. He wagered a case of wine on it with the bookseller Borsatti. Borsatti crossed the frontier just in time and volunteered for Italy, while Joyce sought refuge in Zurich in June. The wager was not forgotten, however, and the case of wine arrived for Borsatti in 1919, when both he and Joyce were back in liberated Trieste.[24]

Austria-Hungary, including Trieste, had not been prepared for total war and long-term shortages of essential supplies. Prices shot up, bread all but disappeared. On 20 April the women of Trieste—most of the men having been called up—took to the streets waving white flags from the ends of their umbrellas, crying 'Down with war! Surrender! White flag!', demanding bread and pillaging the shops well into the night. Troops eventually restored order, but on the following day angry rioters swarmed aboard the ship Trieste, which was loaded with provisions for the Austrian forces based further south at Kotorska Boka (Cattaro), and scuttled it where it lay at anchor in the harbour. The Italian Irredentist and interventionist press presented this riot as a demonstration of Italian patriotic feeling against the Austrian oppressor and an invitation to Italy to declare war on Austria. The Irredentist Minutillo, an eyewitness, deplored this as mere propaganda, very far from the truth.[25] In the Triestine press there was a complete censorship blackout on the riots.

The new lieutenant, Alfred von Fries-Skene, took steps on the very day of the riot to improve the supply of flour. As the war dragged on and wheat grew scarcer, all sorts of ingredients were added to make up what had to pass for bread: maize and rye, chestnuts, potatoes, and beetroot. Even with this mixture, the daily ration of bread per person had diminished by the end of the war to 140 grams. There was a thriving black market.[26]

The excitements and alarms of war continued to mount. On 4 May Italy denounced the Triple Alliance. On the 6th, German submarines claimed their most celebrated victim, the transatlantic liner Lusitania, which was sunk with the loss of hundreds of passengers, including many from neutral countries. An Austrian victory over the Russians once again raised hopes of an early peace, as long as Italy did not enter the war. The Austrians strengthened the fortifications of Trieste and the land frontier with Italy, and on 13 May men up to the age of fifty were called up. Amid anxious uncertainty, there was a mass exodus of Italian citizens on 18 May, including the Venezianis and the Obertis. There was a series of false alarms, especially on 20 May, so that when the

Italian ultimatum and declaration of war finally did arrive on 23 May most people could hardly believe it had really happened.

In *La coscienza,* Svevo has Zeno Cosini return from the frontier on the very last train to find Trieste once more in a state of riot. This might seem like a continuation of the riots of a month before, but this time popular wrath was turned against the Italian party, who were blamed for this extension of the war. Even the neutralist Socialists, however, dissociated themselves from these fresh disturbances and concurred with Irredentist charges that the Austrian authorities themselves had encouraged the rabble to burn or loot Italian property, while the police and firemen looked on and some individuals were even seen holding lists of names from which they directed the mob as to which premises they should destroy. They burned down the offices of *Il Piccolo,* of the Ginnastica, the Lega Nazionale and other Italian nationalist institutions. The cafés frequented by the Irredentists were also devastated, including the Portici di Chiozza, the Milano, and one of Joyce's favourites, the Stella Polare. Many Italian-owned shops were also looted and burned down. The rioting went on throughout the night of the 23rd and into the following day, and it was not until the 29th that a state of siege was declared. The mob's slogans this time had been: 'Long live Austria! Down with the pine-cones [i.e. the Italians]!'[27]

One of the fullest accounts of the rioting of the night of 23 May was written by Italo Svevo.[28] Never published except in collections of his works, it tallies precisely with other accounts and adds many interesting details of its own. First of all, no one believed the news of Italy's declaration of war. The Italian lady who had brought the news suddenly felt a sister to an Austrian lady sitting beside her on the tram, each of them having a husband or a son at the front, and the two women came very near to tearfully embracing one another:

Moreover, the Italian woman felt a burden of conscience about this war. Hadn't she been longing for this war from her earliest youth! She had been longing for it up to ten months ago. Those last ten months of her not so brief life had given her a more accurate notion of the war. Now—when she no longer dared invoke it—the war was on its way.

Svevo's conscience, as well as the woman's, is speaking here. He must also have been the one to suggest a Schopenhauerian formula for the Italian ultimatum: 'I exist, you exist, therefore I make war on you.'

Svevo describes the confusion in the telephone system and on the streets. He went to the centre of town to witness the disturbances and encountered a female looter:

It strikes me that something is stirring in her conscience because she comes up to me and feels the need for my approval: 'We be all Italians. But they done the dirty on us. Makin' war on us after we bin sufferin' so ten month long.'

Svevo encouraged a fireman, whom he took to be 'just an ordinary labourer', to turn his hose on the fire. He turned out to be 'a law student who had been serving his town as an unpaid volunteer fireman for ten months'. Mistaking

Svevo in his turn for a representative of authority, he immediately burst into a rage of self-justification.

Svevo's account reads like something written from impressions still fresh in his mind. He may have considered publishing it in the new Triestine newspaper *La Nazione* after the war. If so, he must have realized that his account was incompatible with the one-sided nationalism of the newspaper. His failure to have it published amounts to another case of the self-censorship of Svevo's conscience, its displacement from direct historical responsibility to the literary plane.

Meanwhile, the police were rounding up Italian nationalists in Trieste. Public meetings were banned. *Il Lavoratore,* the Socialist daily newspaper, now remained the only independent Italian-language newspaper, and even this appeared with many blank spaces where it had been censored. Even official Austrian military reports were censored if they concerned the Italian front. Many Italian sympathizers were arrested on the basis of anonymous denunciations, which were often quite false. These arrests culminated in a large round-up on 20 December, the anniversary of Oberdan's execution. A sinister Major Loneck was behind these secret operations until he committed suicide in February 1916 by hurling himself out of a train on the way to Ljubljana.[29]

The climate of the time is conveyed in an anonymous denunciation of Ettore Schmitz. It is dated 27 December 1915, and written in barely literate Italian. It says that Bruno Veneziani was an Italian officer; that Gioachino, having ruined all his Triestine competitors by underhand methods, had now fled to Italy; that the 'filthy Jew' and 'dyed-in-the-wool Irredentist' Schmitz, as an Austrian subject, had secured permission to carry on the business under his own name by dint of making a corrupt payment to a fellow Jew in Government service dealing in metals.[30] All these factual assertions are confirmed or at least supported by evidence from other sources, excepting only the allegation that Schmitz had bribed a government official. The denunciation, however, had arrived too late, as matters had already been settled between Ettore Schmitz and the naval authorities of Austria-Hungary.

55

ETTORE SCHMITZ'S PAINT
AND THE AUSTRIAN NAVY

Immediately after Italy's entry into the war, the Austrian security police took an active interest in Gioachino Veneziani, and the Pola naval dockyard in his paint. On 8 June the Marinesektion of the War Ministry in Vienna received a telegram defining Gioachino as a politically unreliable *Extremnational*,[31] and a second telegram on 24 June reported that he was now in Turin and that his verdigris factory at Bolliunz (Dolina) had been placed under the supervision of naval engineer Rudolf Hermann.[32] Hermann promptly sent naval headquarters in Pola a detailed description, dated 8 July, of the Bolliunz factory and of the method by which the verdigris was produced, which was quite simple. This led Admiral Kirchmayr in Pola to ask Vienna, on 18 July, for permission to move all the plant and materials from the Bolliunz factory to Pola so that verdigris could be manufactured on the spot. The requisition was carried out on 7 August.

The Venezianis reacted swiftly. Olga and Gioachino sent a telegram from Lugano in Switzerland on 9 August confirming power of Attorney for Livia over the firm. Wartime regulations required that all business concerns must be headed by an Austrian citizen, and Livia qualified as such by virtue of being married to Ettore Schmitz. On 13 August a telegram from Pola to Vienna confirmed that the Veneziani firm had been registered under the names of 'Ettore Schmitz and wife' before the requisition had been carried out, and asked whether compensation should be paid at pre-war or wartime prices.

An intricate bureaucratic wrangle now ensued, with Ettore Schmitz and his lawyer Giulio Sandrini facing Admiral Kirchmayr, first over the compensation to be paid (including loss of profit due to the closure of the factory), and then over the question of producing both verdigris and paint at Pola, the restitution of the requisitioned materials, and payment overdue from the Navy for previous consignments of paint. In September 1915 Ettore went to Vienna, where he applied for support in the highest quarters before presenting himself at the Navy Office, and where he also met Marco Bliznakoff who had travelled there from Sofia.[33]

One step which Ettore and Marco took was to suggest, no less, that the firm's operations should be transferred to Linz on the Danube, right in the heart of Austria, on the grounds that Pola was no less vulnerable to enemy attack than Kirchmayr claimed Trieste to be. This proposal, in French, was conveyed to the Austrian Navy Office by the Royal Legation of Bulgaria in Vienna and was one of the documents discussed by the Navy Office in a meeting on 30 October. The meeting ratified the agreement reached in Pola on 22 October at a meeting comprising Vice-Admiral Kirchmayr, the naval officers Franz Roland and Teodor Novotny and, on the other side, Ettore Schmitz and Giulio Sandrini. The agreement shows that the Navy could not do without the Veneziani paint, all production of which had ceased on 7 August. The Navy agreed to pay for all the requisitioned material at current prices—a total of over 200,000 crowns in place of the original offer of 85,000, not counting the copper-plate. It also envisaged a huge sum (several hundred thousand crowns) in compensation for the loss of profit arising from the factory closures. Since Ettore Schmitz, as director of the firm, refused to produce paint or verdigris at

Pola, he was allowed to resume production at Trieste and Bolliunz, but the Navy would assure its own supplies by holding the raw materials in Pola and releasing them to the firm in small amounts at its own expense.

Under the direction of Ettore Schmitz the Veneziani firm thus continued to supply paint for the warships and submarines of Italy's enemy. He cut off supplies only briefly towards the end of 1915 because the Navy had left its bills unpaid for several months. Ettore Schmitz signed a letter on 15 November 1915, demanding payment of over 100,000 crowns due on seven invoices made out between 24 June and 4 October—all of them, that is, post-dating Italy's entry into the war, and three of them post-dating the requisitions. It was not until 22 December that Ettore threatened to withhold further supplies.

This does not square—particularly as regards chronology—with the version furnished by Livia in *Vita di mio marito:*

Work in the factory had ceased. A sudden tempest had disturbed the atmosphere of our lives for some days. In August 1915 Austrian military experts and technicians came to the factory to requisition the machinery and merchandise, also demanding the surrender of the jealously guarded secret formula for the paint and threatening Ettore with internment. He swiftly devised a ruse. During the night, aided by some old workmen who were bound to the family by ties of long-lasting loyalty, and deeply devoted to him—he knew how to make the humble worship him—he feverishly walled up the secret material in a tiny chamber and on the following day solemnly consigned to the military commission fake formulas which were tried out with imaginable results in the factory which the Royal Imperial Austrian Navy had set up in Pola.... In reprisal, the Austrians stripped our factory. No less than nine wagonloads of plant and raw material were seized and transported to the stronghold of Pola.[34]

A letter of Ettore's of 9 January 1919 makes it clear that there was no long-term closure of the paint factory during the war years, though production was of course diminished: 'this past year will again show a fair profit.'[35] After the war the firm declared to the Italian revenue office an ordinary profit of 35,000 lire for 1916, 48,000 for 1917, 42,000 for 1918 and 87,300 for 1919, with a war profit (taxable at a higher rate) of 4,000 lire for 1917 and 11,300 for 1919. These are modest figures, but certainly do not denote any complete shutdown. Furthermore, the tax assessment, while reducing the figures for the ordinary profits, arrived at much higher figures for the war profits, mostly on production at Murano: 72,000 lire for 1916 and again for 1917, 74,000 for 1918 and 152,000 for 1919. For 1919 the firm declared a profit of 70,647 lire from the Trieste factory on its own, though its internal accounts showed nearly 200,000.[36]

These figures are still modest in comparison to the firm's pre-war income. In his *Referat,* presented to the meeting of the Marinesektion of the Kriegs-ministerium in Vienna on 30 October 1915, Franz Roland calculated that Bliznakoff's share alone came to 60,000 crowns a year.

All this suggests that the decline in production was due to the wartime scarcity of raw materials and of customers, rather than to patriotism. The London factory, and the one in Murano for much of the war, were of course still adding to the family wealth. Certainly, Ettore Schmitz could not escape being involved in the war, economically, politically and morally, no matter how much he may have hated it, just as for fifteen years he had been involved up to his neck in the capitalist system which he himself, as will be shown, saw as the cause of the Great War. Not only was he profiting from the war, but he was also serving the enemy power. How not to compromise oneself—this was the knot that Svevo's guilty conscience failed to unravel but was to project with critical irony into Zeno's *coscienza*. Svevo leaves his hero suspended at the height of the war, when the outcome is most uncertain, announcing the apocalypse even as he rejoices in the new-found 'health' or well-being brought to him by the wonderful profits of the war.

A word must be said about the patriotism of the Venezianis. It is incongruous that a couple like Olga and Gioachino, who liked to present themselves as passionate Irredentists, should have tried to sell as much paint as they could to the very Power that stood in the way of Trieste's 'redemption', even at a time when Austria and Italy were partners in the Triple Alliance. But as soon as Italy was at war with Austria, one would expect the firm to ensure that the Austrian Navy would not get a single kilogram of its paint, let alone seven consignments worth a total of 100,000 crowns. Even the complete loss of the Trieste factories would have left the firm extremely well off on the proceeds from its operations in the countries of the Entente. As to the concealment of war-profits, it seems highly unpatriotic to try to avoid paying to the Italian nation a share of the cost of the longed-for redemption for which nearly half a million Italians had lost their lives. The inevitable inference is that the highflown and complacent rhetoric of nationalism was a hypocritical sham, a mask for money-grubbing egoism. Ettore Schmitz also played along with this sham—that same Ettore Schmitz who gently chided his brother Ottavio for being too consistently logical, too 'dogmatic': that is, principled and true to himself. Having started along the path of compromise, Ettore Schmitz found himself compromised through and through—except on paper. Only on paper, in writing, is he utterly uncompromising, utterly ruthless with himself and his world. Still and always, it is only on paper that he can realize himself; once again Ettore Schmitz will succeed in becoming Italo Svevo by pillorying himself, parodying himself, in the figure of Zeno Cosini, a figure torn between the thirst for truth and innocence and the eternal, irresistible temptation to cheat his own conscience and other people. As we shall see, Svevo himself asserted that the war determined his return to literature. We shall see also how large the war loomed in his thoughts and writings during the crucial period which includes the composition of *La coscienza di Zeno*. Svevo made a characteristically ironic joke out of his sense of war guilt: he liked to relate, according to Saba, that 'he never enjoyed a beefsteak so much as towards the end of the first war, when he was (or thought he was) the only person in town who could afford it.'[37]

56

SVEVO AND THE WAR

Svevo's last extant letter for two years is dated 10 December 1915. It was addressed to Letizia, now staying with the Obertis in Florence, where she could see her fiancé Tony whenever he was on leave from the front. Letizia had sent her father good wishes for his impending fifty-fourth birthday. He replied:

The best wish would be to see this period over. It is far too long. Do you remember how you left after a few moments' discussion? You seemed to be going off on holiday and instead you were off for a long spell at school. I no longer write fairy-tales. Reality is far too distracting for my daydreams—if one can put it that way. I'm becoming a very serious businessman. Papa used to say that I'd settle down at 40. He was 14 years out. I hope for your sake that this precociousness is not hereditary. Up to a couple of weeks ago I played the violin a little while every day. Then fresh preoccupations came up, nothing serious, just business difficulties which had to be tackled, and that too was abandoned.[38]

That very day Svevo had picked up his violin again to find all the strings broken. To replace them he would have had to cross 'a sea of mud', meaning, presumably, the battle-front of the Isonzo. So he dwelt for half a page on the misfortunes of his violin and attributed his preoccupations to nothing more serious than business. And indeed he was still awaiting the payment of 100,000 crowns from the Austrian Navy and the compensation for the forced factory closure in August. The letter gives barely a hint of how the war was affecting him, nor was this apparently due to official censorship. As usual, Ettore Schmitz did not share his inmost thoughts even with his own wife and daughter, just as he did not disclose his views fully in his newspaper articles.

In May 1915 the Venezianis, like most other Italians who had left Trieste at that time, thought that Italian forces would reach the town within a few weeks. But during the following two years eleven massive attacks were launched across the Isonzo and only a few kilometres were gained. So Gioachino and Olga had settled in London, the Obertis with Letizia in Florence, and Nella Bliznakoff with her children, like James Joyce, in Zurich. Silvio Benco had been arrested, but the Socialist leader, Valentino Pittoni, saved him from the concentration camps and he spent the war years in Vienna translating novels for *Il Lavoratore*.[39] The less fortunate Irredentist journalists, Giulio Césari and Riccardo Zampieri, 'were languishing among the political internees in an Austrian castle'.[40] The Socialist Angelo Vivante, broken-hearted at Italy's entry into the war, committed suicide on 1 July. Valentino Pittoni was called up—though over forty, and despite his parliamentary status—after an altercation with the police over the cruel and arbitrary measures they were taking. Over 30,000 Triestines were conscripted in all. One of them was Svevo's nephew, Aurelio Finzi.[41]

On the night of 28 May 1915 Trieste first heard the sound of cannon from the front a bare twenty kilometres away. The artillery barrages resumed with every fresh attack or counter-attack, until the frightening cannonade of 24–5 October 1917, when the Austrians and Germans made their great thrust towards Caporetto. Then followed an even more terrible silence as the routed Italians fell back first on the Tagliamento and then on the Piave in the space of a few days. For Svevo's Nice Old Man, war and conscience are closely bound together:

Every sign of war which the old man witnessed reminded him with a pang that he was making plenty of money out of it. The war brought him wealth and degradation.... He had long grown accustomed to the remorse occasioned by his successful business deals and he went on making money in spite of his remorse.[42]

It is the sight, from Trieste's great pier, of the flaming battle on Mount Hermada that leads him to make a good resolution. (The autobiographical basis for this is confirmed in 'Soggiorno londinese').[43] But his good resolutions go by the board, and the old man is left alone with his bad conscience: 'The guns could be heard rumbling and the nice old man asked: "Why haven't they yet invented a way of killing each other without making so much noise?" '[44] He falls into the most consummate and selfish hypocrisy:

That was the time of Caporetto ... the old man saw nothing but good in what had happened: the war was moving away from Trieste and therefore from him. The doctor wept: 'We shan't even see their aeroplanes any more.' The old man muttered: 'True, we mightn't see them any more.' His heart swelled with the cheering hope of quiet nights, but he tried to match on his own countenance the grief which marked the doctor's.[45]

Air raids on Trieste by sea-planes, aeroplanes and dirigibles were common enough, and Villa Veneziani, being situated near the wharves, in an industrial district, was quite exposed. One of the first raids was led by Gabriele D'Annunzio on 7 August 1915. He showered the town with leaflets carrying a wordy message from the fatherland, which ended: 'Courage, brothers! Courage and constancy!' Then bombs were released over the Lieutenancy and on two destroyers moored in the harbour. Despite severe police prohibitions, the leaflets circulated clandestinely through the town.[46] On 24 October two sea-planes released their bombs over S. Andrea, close to the Veneziani villa.[47] Civilian casualties sometimes occurred. On 20 April 1916 eight Italian aeroplanes bombed the Austrian sea-plane hangars at Servola. Two sea-planes were destroyed, nine people killed and five injured. A few days later the steamer *Iskra* was torpedoed in harbour.[48] Svevo was to hear from commander Rizzo after the war that, if he had succeeded in blowing up a huge ammunition dump at Servola, Svevo with his house and factory would have been blown sky-high.

'I clasped his hand firmly,' recollected the latter, 'as if I wanted to restrain him—how shall I put it?—retrospectively.'[49]

Political repression in Trieste sometimes took grotesque forms. Gaeta writes: that 'Maria Gianni went to prison for writing a patriotic poem which she enclosed in a bottle and threw into the sea, and which was carried to the other side and published in the newspapers of the Kingdom...'.[50] In 1916 the high school teacher Ferdinando Pasini, one of the more serious Irredentist publicists on the university question and a member of the *Voce* group, was convicted of high treason on the basis of a premature obituary published in the *Corriere della Sera* which disclosed the part he had played in the clandestine opposition against the Austrians. Pasini was to play a far from negligible part in promoting Svevo's fame, and in 1924 the latter was to write to him: 'You certainly knew nothing of the anxiety with which I followed your vicissitudes during the war nor of my sympathy for your literary and cultural work.'[51] Most tragic of all was the fate of Austrian citizens who had enlisted on the Italian side and then been captured: they were hanged as traitors. The most celebrated of these was Cesare Battisti, who had been the Irredentist deputy for Trent in the Vienna Parliament.

Throughout the war there were still those who continued to plead for peace. The Pope made frequent appeals, and dissident Socialists gathered to call for an end to hostilities, in the teeth of the official Socialist parties of the belligerent nations. Throughout 1916, governments remained bent on war. The German Chancellor, Bethmann-Hollweg, declared, only a month later than the date of Zeno Cosini's last diary entry with its apocalyptic prophecy, that Germany would be defeated only at the cost of the destruction of mankind. At almost the same time British forces were pounding Dublin and exacting a fierce revenge for the Nationalist uprising which had begun on Easter Monday. On the plateau south of Trent the Austrians advanced into Northern Italy and were threatening Venetia.

Another connection, in lighter vein, can be made between Zeno's diary and the chronology of wartime misery, for it was precisely in March 1916, the date of his last diary entry, that tobacco ran out in Trieste: 'Supplies arrived periodically, but they were rare and scanty to the point of absurdity. Famished smokers were awesome in their first assault upon the newly replenished tobacconists. Their windows were often smashed...'.[52]

Triestine memoirs about the Great War single out a type closely resembling Zeno Cosini (whom we may therefore consider representative of a significant section of the town's inhabitants) and also—less closely— bearing some resemblance to Ettore Schmitz. The most concrete historical portrait of this type was drawn by Alessandro Minutillo, a high-minded Irredentist who was disgusted by the ignominious behaviour of many supposedly pro-Italian Triestines. He emphasized the courage of those who were truly fighting and suffering for Italian Trieste by contrasting it to the hypocritical egoism, the mean and petty opportunism, of so many others. He portrayed the Triestine businessman as being Italian in tongue and Austrian in politics—a portrait somewhat reminiscent of Slataper's caricature in *La Voce* of the 'dried figs and sultanas' Triestine. Minutillo wrote that after the riots and arson of 23 May 'The most sickening thing is the volte-face of some Italians'; and he, like Svevo, made it clear that it was an Italian mob that burnt down the offices of *Il Piccolo* and looted Italian-owned shops.[53] His portrait of the obtusely self-interested Triestine was corroborated by a note published by Silvio Benco in 1918 in his literary periodical *Umana*:

Remaining within the field of the obligatory themes of popular satire ... we have the series of sketches drawn against the drab atmosphere of the city during the war years. These images and ideas form a refrain, day by day, even in the minds of those who are not creative writers, and they are picked up by the writer as documents of the times through which he has lived, times which some day will seem incredible and strange. Those who profit from the war and have their own philosophy:
> 'What I say is, war makes the world
> go round, it brings life and movement.'[54]

Italo Svevo must certainly have read these words, and I for one see the figure of Zeno Cosini as in part one of those 'documents of the times ... which some day will seem incredible and strange', a figure in whom many Triestines would fail to recognize themselves and many others would *refuse* to recognize themselves, and whom they would consequently smother in silence, or worse.

As for Ettore, he was often subjected to police interrogation, sometimes even being taken away in the middle of the night.[55] But the most memorable experience of the war for Ettore and Livia was of a naval character:

On the night of 4 December 1917, with a terrible *bora* blowing, we heard a tremendous explosion in front of Villa Veneziani: it was a torpedo fired by Luigi Rizzo which hit the quay instead of the ironclad *Budapest*. The frightful crash was followed for about ten minutes by the howling of crazed voices and then a tragic silence: it was the seamen of the *Wien* drowning in the tempestuous seas.

Ettore, touched to the depths of his human feeling, and in spite of the strict blackout regulations, immediately ordered all the powerful lights in the garden to be turned on so as to allow the floundering men the encouragement and the guidance of the illumination in that stormy night.

The Schmitzes thus facilitated the rescue of eighteen seamen, all from Istria.[56] Livia mentions their bitterness towards their officers, and in fact on 1 February following there was a mutiny in the Austrian fleet which had been bottled up in Kotorska Boka for nearly the entire duration of the war. No longer able to endure their immobility, the arrogance of the officers and their increasingly short commons, and spurred by the progress of the Bolshevik Revolution in Russia, the sailors raised the Red Flag and demanded an improvement in their conditions. They were disarmed without violence by dint of false promises and punished by the execution of some of their leaders and the imprisonment of others.[57] The Schmitzes may have heard details of the mutiny as families of Austrian officers were billeted in Villa Veneziani. Among them was the Royal-

Imperial Commissioner, of Czechoslovak nationality and anti-Austrian sentiments, who became a good friend of the Schmitzes.[58]

The war—indirectly at first—set Svevo back on the literary path. He relates in *Profilo autobiografico* that in 1918, 'to please a doctor nephew of his who was ill and staying in his house, he embarked with him on the translation of Freud's work on dreams.' Svevo's co-translator was Paola's son, Aurelio Finzi, not himself a psychoanalyst. The *Profilo* adds:

Then it was that Svevo attempted to psychoanalyse himself—entirely on his own, which is in total contradiction with Freud's theory and practice. The entire technique of the procedure remained unknown to him, as everybody reading his novel will realize.[59]

In fact, several remarks made by Dr S. and by Zeno in the course of the novel reveal a much better understanding of psychoanalytical treatment on Svevo's part than is suggested here. And though Svevo's letters to Jahier corroborated the account given in the *Profilo*[60], in 'Soggiorno londinese' (which was written over a year earlier than the letters to Jahier and the *Profilo* and was not published until after Svevo's death) he let slip that he read Freud's 'celebrated Introductory Lectures' from 1916 onwards, immediately upon their first appearance.[61] Svevo's collaboration with Aurelio Finzi was thus not the beginning of his wartime interest in Freud but, on the contrary, one of its culminating points, and it is legitimate to suppose that Svevo also read other new works by Freud as they came out—for instance, his reflections on war and death in 1915 and, after the war, *Beyond the Pleasure Principle* (1920).

The *Profilo* offers more 'literary' information on the war years:

Svevo undertook a quasi-literary work, a project for universal peace suggested by the works of Schücking and Fried. Naturally one cannot in this world follow any idea without getting back to the father of all literature, Dante Alighieri. With a slight shudder, Svevo resigned himself. The resulting work no longer exists.[62]

Now there are at least two puzzling things about this passage. The first is the 'shudder' experienced by Svevo on returning to Dante's *De Monarchia* or *Divina Commedia*, perhaps caused by the anachronistic and authoritarian Utopianism of Dante's solution. The second is that no less than three pieces by Svevo of varying length under the heading of 'Sulla teoria della pace' have survived—so why disavow them?[63]

Writing the *Profilo* in the Fascist Italy of 1928, Svevo draws attention to a work in which, following the two pacifist writers mentioned (Fried won the Nobel Peace Prize in 1913), he proposed to dilute national rights based on force by strengthening international powers of jurisdiction, and which, therefore, was then unpublishable. A similar reason may explain why Svevo failed to publish the longest of the three pieces, which is a carefully finished work.[64] Internal evidence shows that he must have completed it in 1919 after a visit to England. His proposal to open 'the frontiers between neighbouring countries so as to try out free competition'[65] must have been quite unacceptable to his Italian nationalist friends who were then engaged in resisting Yugoslav claims to

Trieste. Also, much of what Svevo was urging was achieved in 1919 when Italy became a founder member of the League of Nations. Finally, Svevo himself avows: 'I have no great confidence that I have got anywhere.'[66]

Still, it remains puzzling that the *Profilo* should draw attention to this work only to disavow it. Why not simply ignore it? Svevo seems to have felt that it was important for the readers of *La coscienza di Zeno* to be aware of his feelings against the war, the great victorious war which was central to the mythology of Fascism. He is stating a link between his pacifism and the novel, invoking Dante himself. It was Svevo's conscience insisting on making itself heard, and it rang out even more clearly in what appears to be the earliest draft of his pacifist work, which opens: 'War is and remains a foul thing for every balanced and moral person. Its foulness is not diminished either by patriotism or by heroism.' And the piece tails off, ending incoherently: 'it is the possession of markets which makes war inevitable. When human wickedness then falls my   '.[67] These alternative diagnoses ('markets' and 'wickedness') have nothing to do with either Schücking and Fried or the League of Nations. One derives from revolutionary socialist critiques of capitalism, the other from the metaphysics of the churches or of Schopenhauer. Svevo cannot accept either. He quietly drops both diagnoses and returns to compromise, in keeping with his habitual bourgeois liberalism. But this, he recognized, means accepting the winners' law, the rights of the strongest. Svevo's conscience remained unappeased.

Svevo spent 'entire nights reading Green's history of English literature' and, after having abstained from writing for some time, 'he began to collect his ideas on numerous scraps of paper for a book of memoirs which was never completed.'[68] Livia cites the autobiographical annotation of 13 June 1917.[69] We are clearly entering the pre-history of *La coscienza di Zeno,* which combines autobiographical elements with psychoanalytical theory and the theme of war—components which all take shape between 1917 and 1918. The war theme also receives imaginative treatment in the narrative fragment 'Trommelfeuer',[70] strangely suggestive of the plot of Heinrich Mann's pre-war novel *Der Untertan* (Man of Straw), which was published in 1918, and two tiny dramatic fragments.[71] All these pieces develop the theme of war in a humanitarian direction, stressing the anguish of the parents of combatants living or dead. But Svevo dropped such humanitarian pacifist motifs, which could be all too easily countered by the rhetoric of heroism. What makes war foul is not simply the suffering of its victims, but its very nature, and its object—control over markets. The mercenary theme was to dominate all the writings of Svevo's last phase.

57

REDEMPTION

Austria-Hungary underwent an internal shock when the prime minister, Stürgkh, hated for having dissolved parliament and abrogated political liberties, was assassinated on 21 October 1916. A month later, the Emperor Franz Josef died after reigning for sixty-eight years. His successor Karl attempted to loosen up the political situation. Austria and Germany proposed peace negotiations at Christmas 1916, but the Entente Powers turned them down. In 1917 political activity was reopened in Austria-Hungary and political detainees started to be released, including, after the Austrian breakthrough at Caporetto, some Italian ones. In Russia there was the Liberal Revolution in February 1917 followed by the Bolshevik one in November (by the Gregorian calendar), which took Russia out of the war. This was counterbalanced by the entry of the United States, who announced their peace objectives in January 1918. They consisted principally in the self-determination of small nations and the creation of a League of Nations: eminently equitable objectives, but not calculated to bring Austria-Hungary, with its Babel of nationalities, to the negotiating table.

Life in Trieste, as throughout war-torn Europe, grew harder month by month. The excess of deaths over births rose from 741 in 1915 to 3,518 in 1917. Those Italians in the town who were less egoistic than Svevo's Nice Old Man were quite downcast by the Italian rout at Caporetto: 'What dismayed the Italians in Austria, whether in Trieste or in the interior, perhaps more than anything else,' wrote Gaeta, 'was hearing Italian prisoners cursing Italy.'[72] In Trieste the Socialists were now openly calling on the authorities to bring the war to an end. On 14 January 1918 supplies of gas ran out and there was a spontaneous general strike in Trieste and Muggia. The people cried: 'We want bread! Down with the war! Down with Germany!' When the gas failed again on 27 January, the strike lasted five days and the cry this time was: 'Down with Austria!' The daily ration of the curious substance that passed for bread was down to 100 grams per person.[73] In April a conference of the subject nationalities of Austria-Hungary was held in Rome, but the Austrian Italians stayed away from it as also from a similar congress held in Prague in May.[74] Already the old quarrel between the Italians and Slavs of Austria's Adriatic seaboard was taking a new form as the two sides vied for territorial sovereignty within the new Europe of the nationalities which could be sensed struggling to be born from the ruins of the old Europe of the dynasties. The Slavs of Julian Venetia held a political conference in their Narodni Dom in Trieste on 30 May, at which the Slovene Wilfan claimed for the future Yugoslavia all the territory east of the Isonzo, including Trieste.[75] The Triestine Socialists, still entranced by the largely fictitious and Habsburgical internationalism of Austro-Marxism, failed to oppose a new and more dynamic internationalism against the resurgent Italian and Slav nationalisms. It was not until after the collapse of Habsburg power that Bolshevism took off in Trieste.

In June 1918 came the last Austrian offensive on the Piave, nicknamed the 'starvation offensive', because the soldiers were no better fed and clothed than the civilian population. Within three weeks it had disintegrated, to be succeeded by the Italian counter-offensive which was to culminate in the decisive victory of Vittorio Veneto in the last few days of the war. In Vienna and Budapest there were strikes and cries of 'Bread and peace!' Parliament reopened at last in Vienna in July, but the confused political situation was now slipping beyond the control of the dynastic state. In Trieste, as early as 2 August, an action committee was formed comprising various groups which acted in part individually and partly in concert, but the Socialists seem to have scented an Italian victory and were now making common cause with the Italian nationalists against the Slav claims. It was this Committee that agreed on the statement by the Italian deputies to the Vienna Parliament on 25 October to the effect that their territories no longer formed part of the Habsburg Empire.[76] Meanwhile, hearing that the American conditions for peace included the creation of an independent Poland, Czechoslovakia and Yugoslavia, the constitution of a federal Austria-Hungary was belatedly announced. This included a statute for an autonomous Trieste.

On 28 September there had appeared the first of three numbers of Edmundo Puecher's periodical *La Lega delle Nazioni*. Puecher declared himself an independent Socialist and his magazine a forum for free and open discussion. The Socialists, however, justifiably saw it as a vehicle for propaganda against the Slavs and pro-Soviets, who tended to band together in the face of the solid front presented by the Italian nationalists.[77] It must have been in this increasingly confused situation that Svevo started on his pacifist essay. On 30 October, the Triestines had their revolution; that is, they liberated themselves by taking over their town, simultaneously hoisting the Italian Tricolour and the Red Flag over the Town Hall. On the following day a Committee of Public Safety was formed, composed of twelve Italian nationalists and twelve Italian Socialists, two Slav nationalists and two Slav Socialists. The Lieutenant, Fries-Skene, handed over the municipality to the Committee and set out for Vienna taking with him the local exchequer of 60,000,000 crowns, of which, however, he was relieved on his way through Ljubljana by the local revolutionary Committee.[78]

With disbanded soldiers of various nationalities running riot, the confusion in Trieste was such that the Slovene citizens themselves prevailed upon the predominantly Slav crew of an Austrian submarine to bear a message to Italy inviting Italian forces to come and take the situation in hand. So troops under

General Petitti di Roreto disembarked from the destroyer *Audace* on to the great pier now named after it, at four o'clock in the afternoon of 3 November.[79] Trieste had been redeemed. Among the excited crowd welcoming the Italian troops was Ettore Schmitz, who was photographed blissfully smoking a cigarette (see Plate 15).

He had joined in the meetings of the previous weeks held by the Italian nationalists in the house of deputy Edoardo Gasser. The Italian tricolour was raised over Villa Veneziani, to the consternation of the sister of the Austrian Field-Marshal von Cicerich, who was staying there. Adolfo Schmitz had died there of cardiac disease on 13 August, less than three months before the redemption for which he had longed all his life.[80]

Il Lavoratore welcomed the arrival of the Italian forces with high-flown Irredentist rhetoric and was immediately taken over by indignant young Socialists. The imagery (though not, of course, the tone) of that welcome may well call to mind Svevo's story of disillusion, 'La madre' (*The Mother*), which has always been associated with the writer's desire to belong to an Italy that so persistently rejected him:

Our great mother Italy now fulfils her vow and that of all her children who have been redeemed from the foreign yoke and comes to us to receive us beneath her protecting wings and unite us to the nation from which until now heinous frontiers divided us.[81]

The Fascio Nazionale (National Union) put out a wall-poster, almost delirious in its enthusiasm, which called for national unity among the entire population. It carried fifty signatures, including those of Benco, Furlani, Gasser, Carlo Hermet and of several men close to the Venezianis and the Schmitzes, such as Marco Samaia and Marino Szombathely. It did not include Ettore Schmitz or Giulio Césari nor the Socialists of differing tendencies, Edmondo Puecher and Valentino Pittoni.[82]

The twenty-first of November saw the first appearance of the newspaper *La Nazione*, whose editors were Silvio Benco and Giulio Césari and to which Svevo was to contribute several articles. It aimed to mobilize Triestine public opinion against the rising tide of Bolshevism. In December was held the constituent assembly for a political grouping called Rinnovamento (Renewal), professing a political programme inspired by democratic principles and aiming to safeguard the interests of the world of work, 'so that', writes Silvestri, 'many people thought it to be akin to that of the Italian Radicals.' The new movement, however, proposed that in place of the Italian manhood suffrage system, Trieste should retain its old municipal electoral system based on privileged colleges.[83] It was simply an attempt to renew the old National-Liberal establishment. Trieste's political battles were starting anew, only now under an Italian government.

Svevo was then travelling across Italy. He and Livia had gone to see Letizia in Florence, then on to see the Finzis in Milan. After long delays caused by the general confusion of transport and communications, all the occupants of Villa

Veneziani were reunited there for Christmas. But the family was soon on the move again: Livia and Olga went to see Bruno in Italy, while Ottavio Schmitz was expected in Trieste.[84] Little by little, a new normality was established.

58

THE CREATOR OF ZENO
AND THE RISE OF FASCISM

The years 1919 to 1922, during which Svevo conceived and wrote his masterpiece, *La coscienza di Zeno,* were historic years for Trieste, for Italy, and for Europe. During these years the effects of the Great War established patterns for the next generation as the issues raised by the peace were variously settled. This was the period of Svevo's great re-awakening from the dormancy of the war years and those preceding. He still did not deal directly with public history and issues, though he was more closely and visibly concerned with them than ever. An indication of this is the more than casual wartime setting of several of his works of this period. Zeno is left at the height of the war declaring himself 'cured'. Likewise, 'La Novella del buon vecchio e della bella fanciulla', (which Stanislaus Joyce says had been sketched out as far back as 1908) is set against the background of the war, and Svevo lets the Old Man die between the Italian rout at Caporetto and the final Italian victory at Vittorio Veneto. And 'Una burla riuscita' (A Hoax) reaches its dénouement in the closing days of the war. All these are Svevo's contributions to his own distinctive kind of war literature, a literature of non-combatants, and to a no less original kind of historical narrative whose protagonists hide in the shadows in the delusion that they can give history the slip.

In 1923 Svevo was to write of his experience of the war years:

During that long period of repose, my old phantoms [*fantasmi*—artistic figments] haunted me once more, but, distrustfully, I did not set them down. I had to hold myself in readiness to resume my normal life whenever that became possible. After the armistice and our redemption my industry made a slow recovery and until its lungs strengthened sufficiently to deafen me I wrote ... I regarded myself as having been convicted and sentenced and certainly if Italy had not come to me, I would not even have thought I could write. It is a curious thing which I myself, to whom it is happening, cannot explain. Our milieu has not changed all that much! And yet, I set to work writing my novel four months after the arrival of our troops. As if it were quite natural! At 58! I think that with the impertinence of anyone who has been liberated I believed that I and my sub-language [*linguetta*] had been granted right of citizenship.[85]

Who can explain the highly suggestive fact that Svevo wrote his third novel, almost from historical necessity, *as a result* of Trieste's redemption? Such an explanation would clearly have to form part of the far from straightforward task of interpreting the work in its multifarious relations with its context, and I will attempt this in due course.

In 1927 a complete stranger introduced himself to Svevo, saying, 'I belong to that generation whom the war tore away from their studies only to drop them later, dazed and irresolute, almost without any path to salvation, in the midst of a humanity all of whose values had been shaken.' *La coscienza di Zeno*, said this young man, was the only Italian book that rendered his own experience.[86]

Svevo's letter of 1923 quoted above tells us that he began the first draft of the novel by March 1919. He may have received a stimulus to write it from *La Nazione*, which on 15 December 1918 had offered a prize of 2,000 lire for the best novel 'displaying scenes and characters from the epic of the past four years of the life of the Italian nation'. The closing date was 1 April 1919. But, beyond any such consideration, *Profilo autobiografico* stresses the sense of necessity, both historical and, as it were, biological, which produced the new novel: 'It was an instant of powerful, overwhelming inspiration. There was no escape. That novel had to be written. Of course, one need not publish it, he used to say.'[87] Unfortunately Svevo never explained what he meant by that 'inspiration'. He must have shared in the general feeling of exhilaration remarked upon by many in the newly 'redeemed' Trieste in the months following the 'outbreak of peace', perhaps a feeling that everything was possible—though Svevo was clearly sceptical about many fundamental aspects of both the 'war of redemption' and the peace which followed.

Two years after publishing *La coscienza di Zeno* Svevo confided in Dora Salvi, a journalist with *La Nazione*, about his urge to write:

It was one of his weaknesses, one amongst others, and, as with the others, he was unable to reform and abjure them, he could only accuse himself. Besides, his real life had begun with writing, he wanted to end it writing. He was not even ambitious and knew it was his own fault if the general reading public failed to take an interest in the meticulously expounded experiences of his characters who bore such a resemblance to a single person, the real protagonist of his novels.

'I started with *Una vita*,' he said then, fixing his slightly protruding Silenus eyes on the lights moving across the bay, 'and I end with *La coscienza di Zeno*. In Zeno I discover myself. His defects irritate me, but I do not attempt to excuse them. I know full well that if I were to recommence the complicated web of life I would allow myself to be carried away by the same irresistible errors.

'How can one not be oneself on the first day as on the last and how can one wish not to be?

'I have never intended to produce literature...'.

And Svevo continued in the same vein, explaining that his pseudonym was meant to indicate his deep-wrought fusion of Southern 'passion' and German 'urge to analyse'.[88]

The autobiographical foundation of *La coscienza di Zeno* was avowed, in these recollections of Dora Salvi's, by the author himself. As we have seen, Svevo had embarked during the war on a 'book of memoirs'. [89] No doubt these memoirs were the starting-point for the novel.

Like everything which Svevo wrote, *La coscienza di Zeno* underwent a lengthy process of elaboration and revision, about which we are little better informed than in the case of the first two novels. Césari states that a complete draft was ready by the end of 1920 and that the final draft was written during the summer holidays of 1922 at Villa Israeli at Opicina.[90] Livia confirms this. In June 1922 Svevo had taken with him the materials for his novel when he spent a fortnight at the spa of San Pellegrino, but never wrote a line.[91] Yet the novel was certainly ready by November, when Svevo started negotiations with the publisher and bookseller Licinio Cappelli.[92] So, by an extraordinary coincidence, the maturation of *La coscienza di Zeno* exactly corresponds in time to that of Fascism, which was born in March 1919 and took Benito Mussolini to the head of the government at the end of October 1922. The relationship between the literary and the political phenomenon is a delicate one, not one of cut-and-dried connections or reactions, but nevertheless a firm one. It is essentially the same relationship which there had always been for Svevo between living and writing: writing is self-indictment and self-castigation on the fictive plane for guilt on the behavioural plane.

Benco's daughter, Aurelia, remembers a visit she paid to Villa Veneziani to see the Veruda paintings which Svevo kept in his apartment. The war was just over. Aurelia was only fifteen. That house made her feel that there had never been a war:

It struck me that the adults had shrugged off the experience of war with frightening casualness, and, with alarm and horror, I watched them tying together the strands of the present to the outworn values of the pre-war era. As if everything had not changed radically.

It was a Sunday afternoon in spring. Svevo chatted away, leaning against the desk in his study. The garden was full of frolicking children, whilst Olga presided over tea for the adults. Letizia burst into the house glowing from a game of tennis. Aurelia felt like an onlooker at a family scene among the Forsytes or the Buddenbrooks in one of the novels which she had just been reading.[93]

For the Schmitzes, family life had entered a new phase. On 23 April 1919, after waiting through the war, Letizia and Tony Fonda were at last married. It was a proper Catholic wedding. Tony had served with distinction in the war and earned several decorations and the privilege of adding Savio to his surname. He now entered the Veneziani firm, greatly lightening the burden of Svevo's work and thus facilitating the composition of his new novel. The young couple presented Livia and Ettore with Piero, the first of three grandsons, in June 1920.

As Aurelia Benco remarked, the world had changed radically. Three empires had disappeared. In Germany and Austria the revolutions had gone no further than the establishment of Parliamentary republics and of new nation-states— Austria, Poland, Czechoslovakia, Hungary and Yugoslavia; but in Russia Bolshevism was on the way to victory, despite military intervention by Germans, Czechs, British, French and Japanese. On 2 March 1919 the Third International set up the Comintern in Moscow and governments everywhere were now concerned that Bolshevism might spread to their own countries. On 22 March Béla Kun set up a Hungarian Soviet Republic in Budapest, but this lasted no more than four months and was replaced by the right-wing dictatorship of Admiral Horthy. In the following March Kapp's attempted right-wing military coup was crushed in Germany, and shortly afterwards the German government bloodily suppressed unrest among the workers in the Ruhr. In May Poland invaded the USSR, but the Soviet counter-offensive almost reached Warsaw. The whole of Europe might indeed have appeared to be crumbling in the two years following the end of the war. The post-war tensions were no less strong in Italy, and they emerged first and most fiercely in Trieste.

'Trieste is crazy with joy,' reported Ugo Ojetti, who arrived with the liberating troops in November 1918.[94] On 13 March 1919, when the Socialist Aldo Oberdorfer returned, he put down the city's exhilaration to causes which had little to do with Irredentist feeling. And while his first impression was that Trieste needed only a fresh coat of paint, he soon sensed an underlying emptiness and an irreversible decline.[95] Now that the Nationalist goal had been achieved, there was a loss of political momentum. The Liberals sought to regain this with their shortlived Rinnovamento (Renewal) movement (which Svevo supported by contributing to its newspaper La Nazione), and campaigned against the railway strike, followed by a general strike, in February, as being 'anti-national'.

More vigorous movements took shape in April. Piero Jacchia formed a 'Fascio di Combattimento' in Trieste a few days after the first Fascio was founded in Milan (though Jacchia soon rejected Fascism and died fighting it in Spain). Fascism was backed by the industrialists but in its early stages adopted a revolutionary rhetoric calculated to appeal to the demobilized non-commissioned officers and to the lower middle classes. And April also saw the opening of a branch of Federzoni's more openly right-wing Nationalist Party, which appealed to the upper and middle classes. While, in the same month, the maximalists (Bolshevists) in the Trieste Socialist party displaced the entire reformist leadership, including both Pittoni and Puecher, who were derided as the 'firemen' of the bourgeois State.[96]

That Svevo lacked the courage to publish his project for a Liberal pacifist Utopia seems significantly related to the conception, very soon after, of his novel, and to his anti-hero's final apocalyptic prophecy of universal destruction. As so often, writing is Svevo's substitute for direct involvement—even political involvement—with the world around him. His ironic fictions are an implied critique of his own inability to live up to his own convictions, as well as of the world he did not dare to challenge. Italy's joining the League of Nations could have been scant satisfaction to him, as he had already observed it to be a League of Victors. As for his more radical proposal to abolish frontiers as far as movement of goods, persons and ideas was concerned, that would have been far from welcome to his nominally 'Liberal' friends in a Trieste for whom aggressive nationalism was the ace of trumps. Even so, Svevo did not completely withdraw from political commitment. As ever, he adhered officially to the party of Triestine capital, the old Liberals, when they tried to launch another group in 1920, as Benco, who was likewise involved, records.[97]

The tangle of Triestine politics began to look ominous about midway through 1919. Poverty and Bolshevism led to frequent strikes which doubled wage-rates by the end of the year, and prices with them. Wages went on improving, even in real terms, until 1921, and Coceani cites this as a factor in the crisis in Triestine shipbuilding in that year. From late 1921, wages started a slow decline and were never again to catch up with prices for the whole of the Fascist period. The Veneziani workers were included in a Labour Contract in 1920 which set wages at 1.30 to 1.65 lire per hour for a labourer and 2.25 to 2.75 lire for a machine operator (the lira was worth about fivepence or ten US cents).[98]

Economic conditions were not the only cause of strikes and of discontent. Italy did not formally annex Trieste until 20 March 1921. Thus, in May 1919, the elections to the *Comune* were held under the system of voting in four privileged categories, as in Austrian times. The inevitable Liberal victory was answered by a general strike which forced the dissolution of the new Council and a re-election by proportional representation.[99] The Italian Government also sent Senator Antonio Mosconi as a Civil Commissioner to take over responsibility for governing Trieste and its territory from the military command and the *Comune* itself. Mosconi kept this post until August 1922. He professed impartiality but stressed the 'gravity' of a situation in which the Socialist party 'was much more widespread than any other', and saw the rapid growth of Bolshevism as Italy's greatest danger. By his own account, he set out to defeat Socialism in the province, and succeeded. He admits that he found it impossible at first to unite the various nationalist forces in Trieste but that, as early as the beginning of 1920, only Fascism could provide the necessary binding force 'to combat the lures and poison which cunning Bolshevist propaganda succeeded in spreading steadily and widely among the mass of people'. Thanks to Fascism, he argued, the situation in Trieste was transformed more quickly than in the rest of Italy. Mosconi is ambiguous, if not downright hypocritical, about the unbridled violence of the Fascists. He himself readily resorted to force and repeatedly boasted that he had restored order with cannon.[100] The Schmitzes, and the Veneziani circle as a whole, were on good terms (at least in 1922) with Mosconi and the military commander in Trieste, General Castagnola.[101]

It was Commissioner Mosconi himself who first resorted to violence, when, on the evening of Sunday 3 August, 1,500 Socialist schoolchildren paraded in Trieste on their return from their group holiday. Mosconi claims that Bolshevist slogans were chanted and that there were some scuffles between Socialist supporters and police, and he generally seems to have seen the occasion as a celebration of the recent and resounding Socialist election victory and a challenge to his own authority.

Perhaps he welcomed the challenge. The police fired on the crowd and wounded several people. Some workers were arrested, but later released without being charged. The Nationalists assaulted the Socialist party headquarters but were repelled and turned their anger against the Slavs instead. There was an almost complete general strike in protest the following day. When it was over, the police made several arrests and wrecked the Camera del Lavoro. Oberdorfer found the police far worse under Italy than they had been under Austria.[102]

Trieste was bound to be excited by D'Annunzio's seizure of Fiume in the following month. The real model for Italy proved to be, however, not the farce of Fiume, but the tragedy of Trieste. The town did not participate in the Italian general election of 16 November 1919, in which, thanks to manhood suffrage, there were large Socialist gains and somewhat smaller gains by the (Catholic) People's Party, while the Fascist poll was 2 per cent. This led the Fascists to take a more unashamedly right-wing position and to resort to armed squads to combat other parties, and especially working-class organizations, with open violence. The truncheon and the litre of castor oil were soon just the mildest of their instruments of persuasion or intimidation. Raids were organized on a larger and larger scale, using motorized convoys like veritable military operations.

Trieste quickly became familiar with the new form of political struggle. Francesco Giunta was sent there by the Fascists early in 1920 to crush the trade unions after another railway strike had led, in Mosconi's words, to a great victory for the 'Reds'. There was a whole wave of strikes at this time. Mosconi lists: primary school teachers, clerks, industrial workers, seamen, shop-assistants, chemical workers, metal workers, bank-clerks. He complains that the majority of citizens not only did not react against this, but seemed to sympathize with the strikers. On 11 April the Fascist leadership instructed Giunta to prepare the Fascio of Trieste for either an operation in support of D'Annunzio at Fiume or the pre-empting of a possible takeover in Trieste by the Slavs and Communists. They appealed throughout Italy for funds to help D'Annunzio, but on 7 August Gaetano Salvemini revealed in the Italian Parliament that the Fascists had used nearly half a million lire of the funds for their own election expenses.[103]

Organized violence on a large scale broke out in Trieste, as in Italy, in July 1920. The pretext used in Trieste was the territorial dispute between Yugoslavia and Italy. In October 1919, the Slavs of all political colours in Trieste had jointly declared that Trieste must not be detached from its Slav hinterland. Now a violent incident which took place in the Dalmatian seaport of Split

(Spalato) between Slav nationalists and Italian naval officers led to a Fascist demonstration in Trieste on 13 July, at which Giunta addressed the crowd, promising to take 'an eye for an eye and a tooth for a tooth'. Fighting broke out on the spot and a man was killed, variously claimed by both Slavs and Fascists to be one of their own supporters. The Fascists led the excited crowd into the city centre to attack the Balkan Hotel, which was the chief meeting-place for the Slav nationalists. Unimpeded by the military, the Fascists stormed and burnt down the extensive six-storey building. They prevented the firemen from approaching and the Balkan went on burning for a whole week. Among the dead were a foreign honeymoon couple and other people quite unconnected with Triestine politics. Giani Stuparich, who lived nearby, first heard some shots, then 'a crackle of rifle-fire amid the screams of the crowd and the burst of hand-grenades'. A few minutes later he was aware of the roar of the blaze, the acrid stench, and smoke and flames rising above the tall Post Office building. The Fascists then rampaged through the town wrecking Slav property—banks, shops, schools, restaurants, lawyers' offices, the *Edinost* presses. Stuparich said that that day in Trieste gave him an uncanny premonition of the future horrors that were to afflict Europe and Trieste itself, a vision of 'an array of millions of innocent victims':

In the tragic spectacle of that afternoon I sensed something monstrous [*immane*]: the confines of that square opened up to me an ominous vision of collapsing and ruined cities, as if something far fiercer still than the past war were threatening the very foundations of our civilization...[104]

Stuparich had been awarded the Medaglia d'Oro, Italy's highest decoration for bravery in war. Senator Mosconi was evidently more patriotic than Stuparich: he excused the Balkan fire, almost defended it.[105] And many upper-class Triestines, Irredentists before or after the 'redemption', saw Fascism as a perfectly natural sequel to Irrendentism.[106] The Veneziani family were to support Mussolini's regime more or less spontaneously. As for Svevo, he accepted it in perfect bad faith, though we occasionally see his antipathy show through. As far as one can divine his views, he seems to have shared the fear of Bolshevism which was so widespread among his class and to have regarded Fascism as a lesser evil if not a positive good. Certain old Liberals held out at first against Fascism, some of them very bravely, and some of them to the bitter end. In Trieste's first general election, in 1921, Camillo Ara, the leader of the Trieste Liberals, refused to stand for election in the 'National Bloc' with the Fascists which had been agreed nationally.[107] His house was raided by the Fascists—though, according to Alessi, 'he admired [Fascist] organization and counsel to the extent of recognizing the need to make use of them in matters of State.'[108]

Typically, however, the Triestine Liberals, like those in the country at large, had little scruple about cynically exploiting Fascist violence to suit their own interests. When their newspapers *La Nazione* and *La Nazione della Sera* proved incapable of drawing the mass readership away from the Socialist *Il Lavoratore*, they revived *Il Piccolo*. The first number appeared on 20 November 1919 under the editorship of Rino Alessi (who was to remain a Fascist all of his long life). Alessi boasts that Benco was welcome on the staff, although an avowed anti-Fascist, but that Benco's anti-Fascism did not amount to much clearly appears from his history of *Il Piccolo*.[109]

Giulio Césari also seems to have been from the start an enthusiastic supporter of Fascism, as all his writings which touch on the subject demonstrate. Before *La Nazione*, its task done, closed in 1922, he had moved over to the official Fascist newspaper *Il Popolo di Trieste*.

Fascism in Trieste eliminated the Socialist movement, which was split between maximalists (soon to call themselves Communists) and reformists, and every other party, such as the Republicans and Radicals, which refused to band together with it. No opportunity was missed to assault Socialists or workers in shipyards and factories, in Party offices and clubs, at the Camera del Lavoro or at the presses of *Il Lavoratore*, or simply in public places. Whether the victims defended themselves or not, their premises were devastated and their persons mauled or worse, either by the Fascists themselves or by the *guardie regie* ('Royal Guard' or security forces) or by the police who would restore order at the expense of the Socialists. This violence reached a peak on 6 September 1920, at the funeral of a Socialist who had been killed by a Fascist. As usual, provocation led to disorder and the police opened fire and killed a Republican. The angry crowd then lynched an unfortunate *guardia regia* who just happened to have alighted from a tram, and Commissioner Mosconi decided that the time had come to clear Piazza San Giacomo by calling in the artillery.

Firearms and hand-grenades became the normal currency of political debate, particularly on the Fascist side, but it was only after the damage to Trieste had been done that the Fascist headquarters were searched, a hundred or so hand-grenades and several cases of gelatine found, and Giunta and some of his comrades imprisoned.

Meanwhile, the Italian Communist Party had been formed in January 1921 in Livorno, when the maximalists finally left the Socialist congress which was being held there. The Communists immediately won the upper hand in the Triestine Socialist movement and seized *Il Lavoratore* on 26 January. This was followed by a full-scale siege of the newspaper offices by Fascists, *guardie regie* and *carabinieri* combined. The Communists finally surrendered and the premises were gutted. Other Socialist establishments in Trieste, which had already been repeatedly wrecked, were burnt down, with the wholehearted approval of *Il Piccolo* but not without some vigorous opposition by the workers that included the burning down of the San Marco shipyard.

This was the context in which Trieste held its first elections for the Italian Parliament in 15 May 1921. Seventy per cent of the Triestine electorate voted. Under the manhood suffrage proportional system, the National Bloc, composed of Liberals, Fascists, Nationalists and Catholics (Partito Popolare), won three of the four seats with 16,295 votes, or 47 per cent of votes cast. The Communists polled 6,637 votes, the Republicans 4,473, the Socialists 4,154 and the Slav nationalists (Edinost) 2,930. The fourth seat therefore went to the Communist Bombacci, who, however, was later to go over to the Fascists.

It was now only a matter of time before what was left of the infra-structure of the Socialist and other dissident movements in Trieste was systematically obliterated and a general lowering of real wages effected. The Fascists turned on the Slavs with fire and sword more fiercely than before. So, more than a year before Mussolini's March on Rome and assumption of office, Fascism had triumphed in Trieste. What they had done in and around that town, the Fascists were also doing throughout Italy, but Trieste and its province took precedence not only in time but also in the intensity of Fascist violence. Two thousand armed Fascist legionaries from the province paraded before the King when he visited Trieste in May 1922. In the same month a convoy of 20,000 Fascists occupied Bologna, which had just had the temerity still to elect a Socialist council. It is estimated that between 1919 and 1922 about 300 Fascists and 3,000 anti-Fascists were killed in Italy.[110]

The *Profilo autobiografico* mentions that Svevo wrote for *La Nazione* during the first few months of its existence from the end of 1918 and also refers to eight humorous articles about the Servola Tramway.[111] No signed articles have been found earlier than 23 August 1919, the date of the first of four of the 'Tramway' articles, of which the fourth came on 21 October 1919, and the fifth and last that is known of, as late as 11 February 1921.[112] If Svevo really was contributing anonymously to *La Nazione* (probably editing its foreign news), then, as the *Profilo* would have it, he stopped doing so in order to start writing *La coscienza di Zeno* at about, or perhaps exactly, the time when he completed the pacifist essay to which he so quizzically alludes and which he did not publish. It is possible that that essay made him realize that he must dissociate himself from the editorial policy of *La Nazione* and contribute to it only signed articles on an independent basis. Certainly, his first signed articles on the Tramway ('Noi del Tramway di Servola') appeared shortly after the grave disturbances of 3–4 August 1919, when the Socialists had won a remarkable victory in the local elections and when strikes and wage-claims were rife. But no explicit point is made in these brief good-humoured satires on the deficiencies of the tram services between Trieste and the Servola suburb other than the very fact that they appear in a newspaper which was attempting to challenge the Socialist *Il Lavoratore*. They are literary squibs signed, as between 1880 and 1886, simply 'E. S.' The same tone of civic conviviality continues in the fifth article, but in the meantime the situation had altered, with the unforeseen escalation of violence, the Balkan Hotel fire, virtual Fascist control and all the rest. The Tramway itself had been turned from a private company to a municipal concern, and E. S. jokes about the workers wanting to turn this *comunale* tramway into a Communist one and about the Triestines (his sort, of course, the readers of *La Nazione*) 'having a good laugh over the burning of *Il Lavoratore* and even over the strike'. This E. S. panders all too cynically and callously to the prejudices of his own social set, though he may perhaps have intended to soothe political passions by humorously ignoring the clash of opposing social and economic interests. Such an intention appears more clearly in another humorous article, also signed 'E. S.', which filled two front-page columns of *La Nazione* on 2 August 1921, under the heading 'Summer fantasies' and ironically entitled 'Storia dello sviluppo della civiltà a Trieste nel secolo presente' (A History of the Development of Civilization in Trieste during the Present Century).[113]

This foretells the history of Trieste from 1921 to 2021 and Svevo takes the opportunity to propose, as an alternative to the politics of the bomb, his own mild Utopianism and the efforts of Italy's reformist Socialist prime minister, Bonomi, to prevent his country from being torn apart by Right and Left. It is hard to say how honest, serious or thoughtful is Svevo's presentation of a future 'great Triestine who made a sensational discovery' (meaning perhaps himself?), a discovery which represents that very Liberal perspective which was now in crisis in post-war Italy:

he proved with serried logic that no blame in the world attached either to those who were wealthy or to those who were not. They could contend and yet respect one another. All had been born to their station or achieved it without political designs. There they were, ready to yield their places if they were forced to do so, but until that moment they could perfectly well shake hands with one another, as long, of course, as those hands were not encumbered by dangerous devices.

And Svevo bravely points, not too explicitly, to the terrorist tradition within Triestine Irredentism as the source of the post-war violence. A brief sequel on 11 August joked about Trieste's traffic and alcohol problems.[114]

Money and class relations—which E. S.'s summer fantasies approached in such a facile spirit—were very much on Svevo's mind, and in a more serious spirit, at this time while he was working on the novel. The tiny fable 'Un artista', dated London, 25 July 1920,[115] about an artist whose soul has been thoroughly poisoned by money, matches the sceptical irony of the close of *La coscienza di Zeno*, where the rejoicing narrator-hero declares himself 'cured' by financial success. Svevo was to pursue the theme of the conflict between financial and artistic success in 'Una burla riuscita', and that of the relationship between the businessman and his money in 'La Novella del buon vecchio e della bella fanciulla' and in the later 'Corto viaggio sentimentale'. These latter two were to involve the conflict between haves and have-nots, which Svevo treated unconvincingly in the one-act play *Inferiorità*, dated 27 August 1921.[116] Here two bourgeois friends of the wealthy Alfredo wager with him that he will lose his wallet, and then persuade Alfredo's servant Giovanni to carry out a mock robbery. There is a furious scene between Alfredo and Giovanni, which leads to real shots being fired and Alfredo being killed. Giovanni is left crushed by horror and guilt. The play's plot and drawing-room naturalism make this too flimsy a parable of proletarian revolution, but reveal Svevo's troubled social and political awareness as he was writing *La coscienza di Zeno* in strife-torn Trieste.

Through all this—the troubles in Trieste and the gestation of the novel—Ettore and Livia were still visiting England frequently, though there are few traces of these visits. One of their nieces speaks of having had a thoroughly entertaining time in their company—no doubt a welcome relief from the tense situation in Trieste. Not that Britain was without its own grave troubles—unemployment and strikes and a situation in Ireland on the very verge of civil war, leading, a couple of years later, to the creation of the Irish Free State. These and other problems are by no means ignored in the series of five articles on 'Londra dopo la guerra', signed 'E. S.', which appeared in *La Nazione*, three of them on the front page, between 18 December 1920 and 6 January 1921. They show Svevo to be well-versed in a whole range of topics to do with London and its post-war life—transport (the subject of the first article), music, theatre and cinema, politics, economics, manners and crime.

An unemphatic strategy seems to be at work in the five articles. A comparison is discreetly suggested between England and Italy so as to convey, with the greatest delicacy, the need for tolerance and peaceful intercourse both between and within nations. That is, the very opposite to the overweening nationalism and factionalism then rampant in Italy and at its highest pitch in Trieste. So, after the politically neutral opening article on transport, the second, entitled 'Odio' (Hatred), is balanced by the third, under the English title 'Kindness', which appeared very appropriately on Christmas Day.

In 'Odio' Ettore Schmitz (whose surname probably involved him in some personal experience of the phenomenon) sadly describes the marks of hostility by the English to things German—but only to show how mild that hostility was in comparison with the hatreds between nationalities in Trieste, and how far removed from the genuine character of the English, which is the subject of 'Kindness'.

This opens with the words: 'English kindness and good manners are quite unique.' Svevo implies that civilized living in a nation is based on 'kindness' at all levels, even the most humdrum, as in the ritual exchanges about the weather for which the English are so famous. He draws on a personal experience to illustrate this thesis and prove that 'To describe such kindness is as easy as to imitate it, if the will is there.' He recounts the following incident:

I had the misfortune, while climbing on to an Imperial, of kicking an old gentleman and making him tumble out of the vehicle. Profoundly upset, I too leapt out, intending to help him and dust him off. The old man stared at me wide-eyed, unsure of my designs. I should have said: sorry, and let him be. As it was, we both missed the omnibus and the old man really could not have been grateful to me. You simply have to utter the sacramental word to show that you meant no mischief.

After several other examples, Svevo compares political funerals in England to those in other countries—which must have clearly brought to the minds of his Triestine readers the Socialist funeral in September which had ended with the use of cannon by Commissioner Mosconi.

Svevo is careful not to present England uncritically as the paragon of civilized living, but rather conveys his own conception of civilization through his judgements on that country. He does not hide his scorn for the 'bad manners' that were gaining ground there too in the self-regarding memoirs of such people as Lady Asquith and Colonel Repington and the chauvinist attitude of G. K. Chesterton; nor does he hide his views on London's responsibilities for the misfortunes of Ireland; nor on the Conservatives, whom he calls 'the worst party'. He is sarcastic about the British government's attitude towards the war between Poland and the Soviet Union and voices his antipathy towards the Imperialistic editorial policy of the Harmsworth newspapers and his sympathy towards the Labour party. Yet the fourth article, despite its title 'La perfida Albione', is inspired by a well-restrained but none the less apparent admiration for English political life, which Svevo sees as being vigorously and stubbornly democratic and yet always tolerant, moderate and lawabiding.

Svevo presents England, then, if not as a Liberal Utopia, certainly as a working model of liberalism, no doubt imperfect, but vital, and these five articles thus constitute Svevo's main political contribution (given that he did not publish his pacifist essay) to his unhappy town.[117]

In January 1924 he wrote to Césari from London showing every sympathy for the first Labour government precisely because it was so unrevolutionary that the new Ministers went to be sworn in at Buckingham Palace wearing wigs and top-hats. He knew that the Socialists and Communists saw them as traitors and he shared the establishment fear that 'MacDonald might do too well and that the next elections might produce an overall Socialist majority and God knows of what Socialists'. Still, the following month he did not seem unduly perturbed about the dock strike that was holding up production in the Charlton factory.[118]

If Svevo saw England as a model of civilized political life, he found that its theatre and cinema had been turned into a cultural desert of show-business. Five years later he wrote, but never published, 'Soggiorno londinese', which gives a more personal view of London life and dwells particularly on the most important feature, for him, of the suburb of Charlton, which was 'the absence of any and every kind of literature'.[119] He regularly went to cheer Charlton Athletic, preferring the trams favoured by the workers to more genteel forms of transport; and 'was never more content than when, having boarded a workman's tramcar, he engaged in earnest deliberation with some honest shagbelching dock labourer'. So reported a young friend, Cyril Ducker, who also relates that Svevo once dragged him and his brother 'to a completely undesirable cinema in the depths of Greenwich, to enjoy himself even more than we did.

His deep and persistent laughter provoked among the audience almost as much amusement as the film itself.'[120]

59

SVEVO AT HOME

Charlton offered Svevo a holiday from Villa Veneziani, but his home in Trieste of course had countervailing advantages, mostly music and high society. Casals, Caruso, the conductor Rodolfo Ferrari and many other musicians visited there and the Quartetto Triestino played there when they had a free Sunday. Svevo still scraped away as second violin in the family quartet. He remained interested in all sorts of music and was particularly struck by the later Richard Strauss, from *Ariadne auf Naxos* onwards. 'Soggiorno londinese' also singles out 'Beethoven's great last quartets'. He listened to everything, which included other people, whom he would allow to lead the conversation. Reading Freud had made him a better listener than ever. He still practised the art of the *Witz*: 'Some of his remarks, some of his witticisms,' writes Vito Levi, 'were taken as paradoxes by the serious-minded, and he took care not to make them change their mind.' As a writer, he remained forgotten. Once after hearing a Tchaikovsky quartet he gave a copy of *Senilità*, 'with a humorous dedication in which the gift was presented as a punishment', to the very young and very promising violinist. The violinist was told that Svevo couldn't write and did not bother to read the book. Svevo pressed him for a reaction to it, but could get no more out of him than vague and vacuous praise.[121] Voghera says that even his wife and daughter affectionately tolerated as a 'strange mania' his 'insistence on being a writer though he couldn't write Italian'.[122]

In this unreceptive atmosphere Svevo could not have felt completely at home, and the politics of Villa Veneziani must have made things worse for him. The Venezianis were Fascist sympathizers both before and after Mussolini came to power in 1922, like most of their class. 'In Trieste Fascism was almost a family affair,' wrote Alessi,[123]* but he saw Svevo as an exception: 'Italo Svevo always refused to get mixed up in politics. He lived as a good Italian and a free spirit within a family which ... oozed patriotism.'[124]

Alessi too attributed the resistance to Svevo's writings among the Triestines to his novels' total lack of political commitment or content, and we have already seen that the Triestine nationalists sensed that the novels implied a

---

* Alessi is clearly referring here to a certain class of people.

critique of their own particular type of political commitment. Perhaps it is this Svevo who made the remark, one of those which 'serious' people refused to take seriously, recorded by Tony Fonda: 'He often said that the better he came to know men, the more inclined he was to love animals.' And yet, Tony went on, 'he inspired in us that faith in life which he did not feel in his own heart'— which could also define the paradoxical effect produced on many readers by *La coscienza di Zeno*.[125]

Svevo's writings amply testify to his love of animals: not only cats and dogs, but also sparrows and swallows, which figure in the fables in 'Una burla riuscita'. He always sees in animals a naïve egoism, undisguised by rationalizations. Tony mentions his analogous love of children, too, and Quarantotti Gambini remembers that once as a boy, around 1923, on the ferry between Trieste and Capodistria, he saw a very correctly dressed gentleman entertain a swarm of small boys with his jokes. This nice old man, it later emerged, was Ettore Schmitz.[126]

Photographs present a rapidly aged Svevo compared to the smiling and quite youthful-looking man of the day of Trieste's liberation. Benco reported him as going on foot at least once a day the long way from Villa Veneziani to the stock exchange 'with the regularity of physical exercise that was part of his system for keeping fit'. But maybe after the enforced rest of the war the quicker pace of factory life, the constant shuttling between Trieste and London, grief over the turn which politics had taken at home as well as the death of his sister Paola in 1922, had worn out Svevo as he entered into his sixties. On 10 August 1921 Gioachino Veneziani had died, and on the 14th, the day of the funeral, Svevo resolved to spare Livia the affliction caused her by the death of anyone she loved: so he wrote her 'a word of greeting and comfort' for her to read in case of his death, sending her 'a last affectionate kiss', and the same to his daughter and son-in-law, gently urging them not to mark his death with 'mourning, tributes and suchlike' and stipulating: 'Let my funeral be simple, modest and *civic*.' Svevo emphasized this last word, no doubt, in a reaction against the, solemn Catholic ceremony which had accompanied Gioachino's burial. For himself, Ettore wanted 'no ostentation of any kind, not even of modesty'. Warm affection towards his family pervaded the entire message and extended to his orphaned nephew Umberto Ancona and his handicapped nephew and niece, Angelo and Carmen Vivante, whom Svevo entrusted to the care of his family.[127] Already, death was no remote eventuality for Svevo: around 1922 or 1923 Benco often met him on his long walks on the Carso and was alarmed at his laboured breathing as he mounted a rise, trying to cover his wince with a smile.[128]

When he was at the spa of San Pellegrino in 1922 Svevo mentioned his 'chronic catarrh' or pharyngitis, which sea-bathing and sun-bathing no longer managed to clear. One doctor was worried by his difficulty in breathing and instructed him to give up smoking! Svevo's big toes were also giving pain and, if he wanted to sleep at night, he had to abstain from meat at his evening meal or, better still, altogether. He tried hydroelectric treatment and massage, but they served only as subjects for jokes. Writing the novel had proved an additional strain.

Ettore was not alone in the family in having health problems: most of them continued to go to health resorts and Olga and Livia were again contemplating a visit to Salsomaggiore for their nerves.[129] Around 1920 Svevo made his first visit to Rome.[130] His business trips to London continued until 1926 and, until he died, he went on working from 9 a.m. until midday and from three to six in the afternoon.[131] He indulged in picturesque philanthropy: Césari relates: 'One day a gondolier in Venice was bewailing the fact that he could no longer make a living with a gondola that was falling apart: Svevo simply bought him a new boat.'[132] Then there is a lighthearted incident from a nocturnal fishing expedition with Tony in the boat of the 'delicate Triestine poet Ettore de Plankenstein':

Svevo, though maladroit by nature, had most of the luck. After a thousand adventures with hooks, bait and line, which got all tangled up, he landed on board, with Plankenstein's help, a magnificent *corbello* weighing a few kilos. Naturally, when we returned home that morning, my mother-in-law swore that the fish had been caught ... in the fish-market.[133]

The incident appears, brilliantly transposed, in *La coscienza di Zeno*.

On his walks on the Carso with Svevo, after the publication of *Zeno*, Benco divined that 'while he makes a show of rebelling against Freudianism, he is steeped in it through and through. It is the ritual that he rebels against,' thought Benco, 'the contrived and cumbersome box of tricks; not the shaft of light which he drew from it to look into man's being.'[134] Svevo's Freudian adventure came to a head in the years of *La coscienza di Zeno*. As soon as Joyce returned to Trieste from Zurich in October 1919, Svevo eagerly pressed him for his experience in the second capital of psychoanalysis and was dumbfounded when Joyce dismissed the subject with the words: 'Psychoanalysis? Well, if we need it, let us stick to confession.'[135]

We have seen that autobiography and self-analysis, during the last two years of the war, constituted the prehistory of *La coscienza di Zeno*. Then came the pacifist essay and other evidence of political concern over the next three years. The maturation of the novel also owed a good deal to Bruno Veneziani's continuing experiences with psychoanalysis. It was in October 1920 that Freud wrote to Edoardo Weiss expressing his amazement at his choice, for co-translator of the *Introductory Lectures on Psychoanalysis*, of Dr Veneziani, whom Freud saw as being all too self-assured, unashamedly homosexual, a narcissist capable of outwitting the psychoanalyst and beyond hope of cure. Freud wrote this letter after his second failure to cure Bruno and, as a forlorn hope, suggested treatment with another psychoanalyst, Groddeck, in Baden-Baden. Ettore accompanied Bruno and Olga there in late June 1921. This treatment also failed.[136]

It was from the end of the war that Freudianism became part of Triestine culture, especially among Jews, as Giorgio Voghera, Socialist schoolteacher and writer, and himself Jewish, relates with gusto:

The fanatical adherents of psychoanalysis in Trieste were constantly swapping stories and interpretations of dreams and telltale slips, carrying out amateur diagnoses of their own and other people's neuroses, attempting to fit them into one or other of Freud's three 'phases' (oral, anal, genital, as we then used to say), continually finding other people's 'id'—but really their ego as well—guilty of the nastiest intentions and the foulest sentiments.[137]

Likewise, both Dr S. and Zeno in *La coscienza di Zeno* show an easy familiarity with psychoanalytical thinking, however unorthodox the psychoanalyst's behaviour may be. And Svevo's cunning is greater even than that of his characters. So the novel always implies the possibility of interpreting along Freudian lines, in terms of the unconscious, any detail of the patient's auto-biographical account or of his relationship with the analyst. The possibility of such an interpretation becomes all the more ironic when either party (patient or analyst) is unaware of it. The whole novel therefore provides potential grist to the psychoanalytical mill, but without either allowing or denying any validity, absolute or relative, to the Freudian enquiry or excluding alternative viewpoints such as those of traditional morality or of social Darwinism, to which Zeno himself occasionally and variously appeals.

This means that *La coscienza di Zeno* defies Freud's vigorous attempt to decipher reality. The 'science' of psychoanalysis, on which Svevo dwells so much in 'Soggiorno londinese', does not exhaust all possible science or knowledge but, on the contrary, lays a 'new basis of scepticism'.[138] The locus of knowledge shifts instead to the elusive, perhaps ambiguous, level of the literary act itself. After he was 'discovered', Svevo was to protest his lack of reading and say that the most recent writer he had read was Anatole France, but Eugenio Montale insisted that Svevo was capable of 'critical insights that most of our men of letters have no inkling of' and that he 'sometimes engaged in discussing Meredith, James, and numerous foreign writers, right up to Kafka, with rare penetration'.[139] This confirms and amplifies what has already been said about the literary relations between Svevo and Joyce. The mention of James particularly suggests an interest on Svevo's part in the refinements of the narrative technique of the 'unreliable narrator', which James had developed in both theory and practice. Svevo's novel deliberately draws the reader's attention to the unreliability principle, as both Dr S. and Zeno accuse one another of falsehood or error and of an oedipal complex. So Svevo sets us a puzzle, challenging us to solve it. By doing so, he implies that a solution *is* possible, which he leaves to the reader's judgement. For Svevo does seek a positive morality and desires 'truth'. He remains the scientist of the human heart of venerated nineteenth-century memory, though his notion of 'science' has grown infinitely more subtle and complex.

Svevo was writing his final draft of the novel through much of 1922. There was a break in June while he was at San Pellegrino, then he forged ahead during the summer at Opicina. Livia recalls:

He shut himself up in the drawing-room and typed all day. No one interrupted or disturbed him. He smoked extremely heavily. When he came out, he would be totally engrossed, almost in a trance. He never spoke about the work he had done. Sometimes, though seldom, he would carry on at night too. He would take a break from his labours by going on short walks in the pine-woods with his grandson Piero ... He destroyed the first draft as he went along with the revision. I don't think he let anyone read it before publication.[140]

The typescript of the novel has never been found, though Svevo's family and the present author have made enquiries with the publishers. Svevo always destroyed previous drafts once he felt he had achieved the final product. Only those works which did not reach a definitive form can be studied at various stages of composition.

Svevo vouchsafed the closest glimpse of the creation of *La coscienza di Zeno* in his first letter to Montale. It shows a sort of comic but delicate ballet in which Svevo hovers between autobiography (which he admitted when talking about the novel to Dora Salvi) and invention:

it is an autobiography, yet not my own. Far less than *Senilità*. I took three years to write it in my spare time. And this is how I proceeded: When I was alone I tried to persuade myself that I was Zeno. I walked like him, I smoked like him, I planted into my own past all his adventures which might resemble my own only because the re-evocation of an adventure of your own is a reconstruction that easily turns into a completely new construct when you succeed in setting it within a new atmosphere. And it does not thereby lose the flavour and the value of memory, nor its sadness ...
... I know of one or two points where Zeno's mouth was replaced by my own and is jarringly loud [*e grida e stona*].[141]

The novel was written by the autumn of 1922 and for the third time in his life Svevo could not find a publisher who would buy, so that again he had to publish it at his own expense. The Bolognese Licinio Cappelli, who had opened a bookshop in Trieste after the war and published many works by Triestine authors, agreed, in a conversation with Svevo, to an edition of 2,500 or 3,000 copies, but after he had read the book he sent Svevo a contract for only 1,500. Svevo was deeply hurt by such eloquent criticism, though Cappelli expressed his admiration for the work apart from a few linguistic blemishes and some *longueurs* which he himself offered to amend by discreet corrections and small cuts under Svevo's supervision. In fact, as the correspondence between author and publisher proceeded in December, Cappelli's reservations and his talk of amendments and cuts dwindled progressively until on 5 January he was expressing his unconditional admiration. He had already sent eighty folders of typescript to the press, and his heightened admiration was the result of the enthusiasm of his literary reader and corrector, Attilio Frescura, 'one of the most formidable of critics' who was all praise for Svevo's work and wanted to meet the author: 'never have I heard him express such a judgement', Cappelli concluded in awe.

Svevo instantly fell in love with his admirer—as he was to do with every future admirer—and hastened to buy, read and admire Frescura's three novels and to write to him telling him the whole story of his own literary misfortunes.

But fame played Svevo a cruel trick. When Frescura's reply arrived a month later, his admiration had cooled. Impressed by the opening of the novel and the chapters on smoking and the death of Zeno's father, he was disappointed to find that thereafter Zeno progressively lost his fascinating originality and became 'normalissimo', and that the book's 'prolixity' did not lead to a logical conclusion. Frescura still recognized Svevo's talent and suggested a re-drafting of the final chapter that corresponds exactly to the published text, which may therefore owe a great deal to him. He also complained about the difficulty of the linguistic revision of the text, which he had not yet completed.

Is *La coscienza di Zeno*, then, partly the work of Attilio Frescura? Does this partly explain the gap between 5 January, when Cappelli announced that the first eighty folders had already gone to the printers, and 19 May, when he wrote to say that the book was ready for publication?

In the absence of Svevo's autograph typescript, this question cannot be answered with certainty. But in 1926 there appeared one telling piece of evidence in an article by Bino Binazzi, the literary critic of the influential Bolognese daily, *Il Resto del Carlino*. It exemplifies the reception of Svevo's novel in that Binazzi admits that he had to overcome a resistance in himself to four features of the work: its prolixity, its hybrid language, its scientism, and the pseudonym 'Svevo', which sounded so unpatriotic in a country which had waged a terrible war against the Germanic Powers. Yet, the further he got into the book, the more it held him. Its 'defects' vanished and the book revealed riches enough to fill at least ten saleable Italian or French novels! But the point here is that, according to Binazzi, who was a close friend of Frescura's, the latter had eventually recognized the quality of the book and had made no corrections of any kind.[142] 'Frescura was perfectly right,' remarked Binazzi. ' "Rewrites" are always failures, if undertaken by others: they are often failures even when done by the author himself.'

So it would seem that Frescura respected Svevo's text and that the first four months of 1923 were taken up simply with the setting of the type and the printing and proof-reading of Svevo's long book. However, the correspondence between Frescura and Svevo came to an end with the letter in which Frescura let Svevo know that his admiration for the novel had cooled.

'In this world one must write, but one needn't publish,' Italo Svevo used to say. The publication of this third novel did indeed bring vexations. One of these was the method of promotion. Cappelli wrote on 19 May:

The Florence newspapers will certainly discuss it because I have instructed a friend of mine, promising him payment in proportion to the reviews which he writes. Nowadays you get nothing without paying for it. I am footing these expenses as I wish to give the book the widest publicity.[143]

With or without these expenses, *La coscienza di Zeno* was to occasion its author even greater vexations.

Meanwhile, in November 1922, Mussolini had been constitutionally accorded dictatorial powers, with the approval of both Chambers of the Italian Parliament (though not without opposition from the minority parties) and of the Sovereign. Italy had entered upon the Fascist Era.

Part IX

RESURRECTION OF ITALO SVEVO AND DEATH OF ETTORE SCHMITZ

1923–1928

60

ZENO'S WORLD

La coscienza di Zeno appeared at about the end of May 1923, priced at 10 lire.

Its protagonist, Zeno Cosini, has many identifiable characteristics in common with his creator: the compulsion to smoke and to give up smoking; the grating violin; an indulgent mother and an authoritarian father; a loving but conventional wife (though Augusta lacks Livia's magnificent hair and eyes); awe-inspiring parents-in-law; an enviable brother-in-law (Giuseppe, or Bepi, Oberti di Valnera, otherwise known as Höberth von Schwarzthal, who resembles the novel's Guido Speier in his Germanic origins and his virtuosity with the violin).[1]

As already seen, in conversation with Dora Salvi Svevo stressed the auto-biographical core of his three novels; with Montale, the element of invention in *La coscienza di Zeno*. The characterization of Zeno Cosini, he remarks in *Profilo autobiografico*, in an exposé of the novel which is over-full and over-explicit, even one-sided, 'borders on caricature'. 'But', he goes on, 'it has been acknowledged that when one leaves Zeno after having seen him in motion one is forcibly struck by the ephemeral and insubstantial character of our will and our desires.' And Svevo equates Zeno's character with 'the nature of all men': his anguished impotence, his mis-spent life, his misdemeanours, delusions and self-deceptions are those we all share.[2]

No naïve imaginary autobiography, then. Svevo treats his own life and personality with complete artistic freedom, as raw material, and as being representative. He does so courageously, in showing up considerable depths of meanness, fecklessness, hypocrisy. Perhaps he is even too hard on his unfortunate prototype Ettore Schmitz. But, if he condemns what he shows, he does so with compassion, as one who sees no alternative, who does not believe in human freedom; one who can write the truth in all its tortuousness, but not live it, not carry through his judgement from the page back on to the stage of life. All Svevo's writings are about an unrealized ethical impulse. The only place where they suggest that impulse can be realized is in the transcendent act of writing (and of reading). Schopenhauer's presence can more strongly than ever be felt in Svevo's self-exegesis.

From the raw material of his own experience Svevo extracts broader meanings which amount to an arraignment (as the *Profilo* would have it) of the ego as such, undifferentiated and beyond the reach of history; and, concomitantly, an arraignment of society (responsible for the Great War) also seen in a timeless, universal perspective. Yet the representation is sharply specific in space and time and specifically concerns a *rentier* bourgeois individual in a mercantile bourgeois society which almost unthinkingly precipitates itself and its own world-order into a war of unprecedentedly frightful scale and intensity. *Profilo autobiografico*, published in Fascist Italy, was not at liberty to make the point. It is open to every reader's judgement whether that point is part of the intention and effect of *La coscienza di Zeno*.

If the novel is no naïve autobiographical fiction, still less is it a naïve psychoanalytical fiction. The ingenious narrative machinery of *La coscienza di Zeno* is so open-ended that it would be presumptuous here to attempt to open it in any particular direction, let alone to close it up. Freudian theory itself is exploited and integrated within this open ironic structure, with patient and analyst accusing one another, with the Oedipal diagnosis as a foregone conclusion, a tautology, yet nevertheless disturbing, revealing, unanswerable. Freudianism, 'a new basis of scepticism', remains 'a mysterious part of the world without which one can no longer think' and which may illuminate that mystery of the self discussed in 'Soggiorno londinese'. How else explain our character, our weakness, our sense of guilt, the world war?

This freedom in the treatment of Freudianism earned the novel its second rebuff (after Frescura's). Svevo tells the story in 'Soggiorno londinese', weaving into it one of his characteristic flights of fancy:

Just then, Trieste's only psychoanalyst, my very good friend Dr Weiss, turns up at my house and, uneasily, looking me in the eye, asks if the Trieste psychoanalyst I had made fun of in my novel was himself. It emerged at once that it could not have been him as he had not practised psychoanalysis in Trieste during the war. Relieved, he accepted my book, dedication and all, promised to study it and report on it in a Vienna psychoanalytical journal. For a few days I ate and slept better. I was close to success because my work would be discussed in a world journal. But when I next saw him, Dr Weiss told me that he could not talk about my book because it has nothing to do with psychoanalysis. At the time I was sorry because it would have been a fine success if Freud had telegraphed to me: 'Thanks for having introduced psychoanalysis into Italian aesthetics.' I would have sent the despatch to Dr Ry of the *Corriere della Sera* and I would have been made. I am no longer sorry. We novelists are wont to play with great philosophies and are certainly not fitted to clarify them: we falsify them but we humanize them.[3]

Until Weiss's rebuttal, Svevo was quite convinced that he had been faithful to Freudian thinking: even now, he remained convinced that the underlying ideas on which the novel turned were more Freudian than might appear. Weiss's rejection related mostly to the final chapter, on account of the misrepresentation in it of the analytical relationship.[4]

Weiss, who always remained a faithful follower of Freud and later founded the Associazione Psicanalitica Italiana, and also himself wrote or translated several major psychoanalytical works, always refused to discuss Svevo.[5] Freud himself, a close observer of things Italian and of literature in general, likewise never published anything about Svevo. Freud's biographer, Ernest Jones, reviewed *Senilità* in 1949 without mentioning *La coscienza di Zeno* or psychoanalysis.[6]

La coscienza di Zeno is clearly a work which has been enriched by a great variety of cultural and scientific currents. 'Sources' and 'influences' could be (and have been) pursued in the most diverse geographical and historical quarters of Western culture. The novel itself is studded profusely with cultural references which span the whole range between the Oedipus of Sophocles and that of Freud. The name Zeno, for instance, implies a reference to the two Zenos of ancient Greece—the Stoic and the paralogician from Elea—and to the early Christian saint who is venerated throughout the area of Venetian influence. It recalls, too, an illustrious Venetian family of travellers and admirals which included the eighteenth-century tragedian Apostolo Zeno, who was poet laureate in Vienna. Zeno Cosini also echoes the name of Svevo's contemporary the Turin professor Zino Zini, who wrote many books calculated to interest Svevo and was sympathetic to Freudianism. From the 1890s, Zini had written books on Lombroso and Spencer, on individual and collective property, on repentance and morality; he translated Ibsen and, in 1921, published, through the Communist press, *Il congresso dei morti* (The Congress of Corpses), attacking the reformist Socialists. This is not to suggest Bolshevist influences on Svevo, but, at most, to emphasize how open his horizons were. Perhaps the most interesting coincidence is with Zini's most ambitious work, *La doppia maschera dell' universo. Filosofia del tempo e dello spazio* (The Two-fold Mask of the Universe. A Philosophy of Time and Space), which came out in 1914. This too could have been at most a stimulus, particularly the chapter entitled 'L'illusione del progresso' in its contrast of the conquest of space, which is feasible, with the purely illusory conquest of time, where the 'mondo della coscienza' is defined as 'pure time and actuality':

The conquest of time, if we wish to call it that, achieved by a perfected system of recollections and anticipations, resolves itself into a contradiction, the tragic antinomy of the possession of the unreal; or better, it becomes an obsession with a part of ourselves. Rather than victors, we should here confess ourselves vanquished. Consciousness [*coscienza*] is the *nunc semper stans*; whereas we delude ourselves that we possess the totality of time, in reality, chained to the present moment, we navigate the great river, ascending or descending its course towards its sources in memory or its outlet in desire.

Memory gives us the past and with the shadow of the past we compose the phantom of the future . . .[7]

Bethmann Hollweg had threatened world destruction in 1916. The celebrated apocalyptic (perhaps prophetic) close of *La coscienza di Zeno*, taken in isolation, could be called a commonplace which, stemming originally from biblical and chiliastic texts, has spread through modern literature and consciousness. There are, as previously remarked, close parallels with Ugo Ojetti's *Il vecchio* and Pirandello's *Shoot!*. André Thérive was to suggest another in Moritz Hartmann, and Attilio Frescura claimed a resemblance to 'an image of my own, of the last, solitary man (*Diciotto milioni di stelle*) . . .'.[8] The last page of *La coscienza di Zeno* also echoes Nietzsche's Zarathustra, who says that man is merely one of the diseases of the earth's crust. That same final page contains a more cryptic motif: 'That busy, unhappy animal—man—may discover and harness new forces. There is a threat of this kind in the air. The result will be a great abundance—of people!'[9] A Fascist candidate in the 1921 general election in Trieste had declaimed: 'There are signs—and many scientists predict this—that the discovery of new sources of energy will increase production.... Then ... the workers can demand a greater share of the common product.'[10]

As for the rather more evident theme of the Great War as the symptom of universal disease and culmination of the *mal du siècle*, Diomede Carito's 'Riflessioni di un medico napoletano', published in 1916 under the title *Come lo spirito della nostra epoca (Darwin—Nietzsche—Beard) ha concorso all'attuale guerra* (How the Spirit of Our Age—Darwin, Nietzsche, Beard—has led to the Present War) is a fair non-literary example. Besides the three writers in his title, Carito dwells on others—Strindberg, Eduard von Hartmann—who are very much part of Svevo's cultural hinterland. Moreover, Carito takes the businessman as the very embodiment of modern 'business fever', lingers on Trieste as a hotbed of this fever, and quotes none other than Prince Konrad von Hohenlohe-Schillingsfürst, then Chancellor of Austria-Hungary and for several years previously Habsburg Lieutenant in Trieste:

'What most alarms me is that Darwinism and Nietzscheanism are making life lose its normal rhythm and become a Fever, which turns it into a continuous convulsion, an incessant gasping ... If we do not change course, the day might not be far off when supreme authority will be vested in neuropathologists and psychiatrists.'[11]

No less than Joyce's *Ulysses*, Svevo's *La coscienza di Zeno* is woven out of the life of its time. In Zeno's confession Svevo has crystallized the anguish of his world, of which Zeno is in part conscious victim and in part hysterical mouthpiece. Between the two poles of autobiographical individualism and anthropological universalism fixed in *Profilo autobiografico*,[12] Svevo actually maps out, in Zeno and the society to which he belongs, a circumstantial and well-differentiated portrait of mankind, distinctive in its geographical, historical and sociological attributes. The ingredients that make up Svevo's world coalesce in the novel into a perfect synthesis which betrays no discontinuities and yet, from the lexical level upwards, expresses nothing but contradictions.

61

WAITING FOR ZENO

It is hardly surprising that the failure of such a masterpiece affected the author's health: 'He grew morose and his heart trouble grew worse.'[13] His literary activity followed the ups and downs of his health: in June, full of hope for his novel, Svevo started writing again—though only the sombre story 'Proditoriamente' (Traitorously) in which a failed businessman is confronted with the death of his successful friend (or rival). As the utter fiasco of *La coscienza di Zeno* became clear, he wrote absolutely nothing for a whole year.

The book came out in the wrong season, too late for most critics to read such a long work before their summer holidays. This diluted the impact on the reading public. Nine reviews have been traced, all but one of them on balance favourable. But there was a three-month gap between the first five in June–July and the last four in October–December. The real leaders of critical opinion did not read the book.[14]

Of the five earlier reviews, three appeared in Triestine newspapers. They were quite full, but seemed reluctant to praise local wares. Most at fault in this was the extremely long review by Svevo's old friend Benco: it bristled with reservations—on grounds of style, of prolixity and of whimsicality—and was not particularly perceptive.[15] On the same day the book was anonymously reviewed in another Trieste newspaper, *L'Era Nuova*, and in the Rome *L'Epoca*. The former found only the first half of the book to be an 'accomplished grotesque', with the second half losing its character and falling short. The latter more briefly spoke of the book's 'wealth of talent and story-telling skills, its rigorous structure and the artistry of its development and its acute psychology', without even a rebuke about its style: kind, but vague. By contrast, D. D'Orazio in *Il Popolo di Trieste* of 15 July shot the book to pieces, apparently subscribing to the conservative aesthetic of the influential Roman literary magazine *La Ronda*, or of Benedetto Croce. Unaccountably, he said it lacked 'a genuine capacity for introspection', as well as being too complex and impure and far inferior to Pirandello's *Henry IV* or Borgese's *Eliseo Gaddi*.

The review signed 'fr. st.' in the Potenza newspaper *Basilicata* of 1 July was laudatory: 'The book grips you from the very first pages, if only by the way it is cast.' But the reviewer voiced a widespread misgiving about the pseudonym 'Italo Svevo' (which Benco had felt it necessary to account for). No Italian father, the reviewer said (forgetting the thirty-year-old Triple Alliance), could have so unpatriotically combined such a name with such a surname. It is this sort of reaction that explains why Svevo opened his *Profilo autobiografico* with a defence of his pseudonym, and it emphasizes his quixotic and quirky courage in retaining it for his third novel, published so soon after the Great War.

The more influential reviews did not come until well into the autumn. Willy Dias, in the Genoa *Il Caffaro* of 16 October, though complaining about the book's form and style, recognized in its author a formidable analyst and fully grasped the importance in the novel of 'apparently unimportant actions' which really make up 'the life of every one of us', and magnificently illustrated the book's 'perfect logic of the illogical', quoting liberally.

The Bergamo *Il Popolo* of 7 November also reviewed favourably. Then, on 9 and 11 December respectively, followed the more prestigious Milan *Corriere della Sera* and Bologna *Resto del Carlino*. The former merely listed it under books received, gave a short summary and characterized it as 'a somewhat ramshackle and fragmentary novel, perhaps over-prolix, but not without psychological interest'. The latter carried a longer review, also anonymous, headed 'A paradoxical novel', which found that the novel's original approach held the reader's attention right from the opening chapters.

These nine reviews did not suffice to make the book a success. Near despair, Svevo played his joker, James Joyce. Joyce had moved to Paris in 1920 and had left behind in Trieste some of his manuscripts and notes for *Ulysses*. This gave Svevo the opportunity to do him another favour. A zestful letter came from Joyce in January 1921, written partly in Italian and partly in colloquial Triestine and reeking of Trieste as *Ulysses* reeks of Dublin. In it, Joyce begged Svevo to fetch to Paris, from the apartment of Joyce's sister in Trieste, 'an oilcloth folder fastened with a rubber band the colour of the abdomen of a Sister of Charity, having the approximate dimensions of 95 cm by 70 cm', in which 'reposed the sign-symbols of the languid lightning which sometimes flashed upon my soul'.[16] This contained the notes for the 'Ithaca' and 'Penelope' episodes, which Svevo personally delivered to Joyce in Paris on his way to London in March.[17]

At last Joyce was in a position to help Schmitz. He had become a member of the world's foremost literary circle, a friend of Pound and Gide, Valéry and Eliot, and an acclaimed hero of the new literature. *Dubliners* and the *Portrait* had won him fame and in 1922 *Ulysses* had enshrined him as one of the most original of modern writers. Svevo sent him a copy of *La coscienza di Zeno* and arranged to meet him at the Gare de Lyon early in 1924. Joyce found that 'no trains were due or even announced as overdue for the hour which had been indicated'. But he wrote to Svevo at his Charlton address on 30 January pressing him to stop in Paris on his way back to Trieste.

Despite that bungled appointment, Joyce's letter marks the slow birth of Svevo's fortunes. *La coscienza di Zeno* was already making a conquest of him: 'I am reading it with great pleasure. Why do you despair? You must know that it is by far your best book.' He gave Svevo the addresses of Valéry Larbaud and Benjamin Crémieux, experts on Italian letters, as well as those of T. S.

Eliot and Ford Madox Ford, and of Gilbert Seldes in New York, telling him to send them copies. He promised that he himself would press upon them the novel's claims. As for himself:

For the time being, two things interest me. The theme: I would never have thought that smoking could dominate someone in that way. Second: the treatment of time in the novel. There is no lack of wit, and I see that the last paragraph of *Senilità* 'Yes, Angiolina thinks and sometimes cries etc . . .' has blossomed out greatly on the quiet.[18]

While Italo Svevo sought recognition, Ettore Schmitz was an absorbed spectator of the British political scene. On 22 January, just before he arrived in London, the first Labour government had taken up office under Ramsay MacDonald. He wrote a long letter to Giulio Césari on the subject. He must have stayed in London till mid-March or later, as a strike delayed supplies to his factory. Food was short too, but the Schmitzes had acquired 8 kilograms of ham. Whenever the factory was idle, Ettore's health immediately deteriorated: 'If I heeded this strange old body of mine', he wrote to his brother-in-law Marco, 'I'd be condemned to forced labour for life.' But he had other things to keep him busy, such as modifying his plant in line with the regulations to reduce atmospheric pollution.[19]

Svevo was still over-timid in his own cause, and Joyce had to write to him again on 20 February: 'Send the books, simply. I've already told Larbaud and Crémieux about you.' He assured Svevo that his novel would be appreciated. He also said that he had given Livia's name to the heroine of what was to be *Finnegan's Wake*, Anna Livia Plurabelle, the Irish Pyrrha whose hair forms the river Anna Liffey.[20] Now Svevo plucked up the courage to call on T. S. Eliot in London. He was not at home, but wrote inviting Svevo to lunch in a Fleet Street pub.[21]

The Schmitzes must have seen Joyce in Paris in March. On 1 April he wrote to Trieste: 'Good news. M. Valéry Larbaud has read your novel. He likes it very much. He will review it in the *Nouvelle Revue Française*. He has also written to a friend of his, Signora Sibilla Aleramo of the *Tribuna*, about it.'[22]

But two months later there was still no sign of Larbaud's review. Svevo, again close to despair, wrote to Joyce once more. Joyce received his letter on 6 June and wrote to Larbaud that same day, urging him to write the review or translate a section of *La coscienza di Zeno* for another journal, *Commerce*. Svevo himself did not dare write to Larbaud, having lately received not the slightest acknowledgement in response to the three copies of his book which he had despatched to Italian men of letters. He was now virtually resigned to seeing his third novel sink into total oblivion and proposed instead to bury himself in reading his newly acquired copy of *Ulysses* with the help of Stan Joyce.[23] No wonder he began to doubt whether Larbaud really existed and conceived the long story 'Una burla riuscita' by way of melancholy humour and examination of his literary conscience about his predicament.

Throughout this affair Svevo appears strangely divided in himself between his thirst for recognition and a bashful reluctance to press himself on others. Just as in publishing *Una vita* and *Senilità*, so now his behaviour seems to indicate either a lack of practical sense or of the will to prevail. He seems to have done almost as little as he could to advance his book. He himself denied that he was ever much of a businessman, being much more at home running the factory.[24]

It is not certain whether he and Joyce saw each other on Svevo's London trip of June–July 1924. Joyce was having problems with his health, especially with his eyes, which had to be operated on over and over again. Larbaud had quarrelled with the Princess Bassiano (who was financing *Commerce*), and was engaged in numerous other literary projects, including the translation of *Ulysses*. Svevo's novel seemed to have been totally forgotten.[25]

Then, at the height of summer, it was unexpectedly, though briefly, resurrected. It was reviewed in the Trent newspaper *La Libertà* on 10 August, in very laudatory but slightly naïve terms. Zeno Cosini was seen as a cheerful and almost unproblematical figure, with Benjamin Constant's *Adolphe* and Kierkegaard's *Seducer's Diary* as literary precedents. Augusta was read as a splendid portrait of moral health. The reviewer could not see why the novel ended halfway through the Great War.

This reviewer was Ferdinando Pasini, a notable educationalist and man of letters, associated with *La Voce*, who taught at the Trieste University (created after the war with the old Revoltella Institute as its core) and had suffered for his patriotism during the war. Svevo's son-in-law, a former pupil of Pasini's, had pressed the book on him. Though the firm's business and extensions to the apartment which the Schmitzes shared with the Fondas interfered with Svevo's social life, he managed to cultivate a cordial friendship with Pasini and they exchanged visits. He lent Pasini his last remaining copy of *Senilità*, surmising that most of the thousand copies of the edition must be mouldering away unsold in bookshops all over Italy.[26]

Pasini's review made no difference. Over three months later an article appeared in *Il Popolo di Trieste* under the title 'Di uno scrittore triestino— Ettore Schmitz'. This took up a puzzled remark of Pasini's about the pseudonym in order to attest to Svevo's—or rather, Schmitz's—patriotic and Irredentist credentials, suggesting that the pseudonym referred to the writer's style, resembling Stendhal's *code civil* style in its plain matter-of-factness. The article probably came from Svevo's friend Césari, and quite probably at Svevo's own instigation. In any case, this attempt to create a politico-literary issue hardly amounted even to a storm in a tea-cup and could not mitigate Svevo's literary misfortunes.

It was, however, directed against the prejudice, so strong in Trieste, that held Svevo unworthy of being considered an Italian writer because he was un-Italian in style and in the subject-matter and characters chosen for his novels. This wall of disapproval confronting Svevo was the subject of a two-column article by Pasini, entitled 'Note retrospettive', which appeared in *La Libertà* on

14 May 1925. Pasini now revealed that everyone in Trieste had done the utmost to dissuade him from reviewing Svevo's novel, which was seen as being, in every conceivable way, an insult to the town. Pasini admitted that he himself, as a passionate Irredentist, had had to struggle hard not to reject outright Svevo's portrait of Trieste.[27]

Given these circumstances, there is something all the more symbolic—and defiant—about the publication (though in mutilated form) of Svevo's tale 'La madre', first drafted in 1910, in the Trieste newspaper *La Sera della Domenica* of 7 December 1924. The tale is a perfect example of the outgrowth of diverse meanings from and around a modest, indeed downright banal nucleus. The narrative nucleus is the story of the incubator chick, Curra, who seeks his 'real' mother in a broody hen only to find in her a terrifying enemy. This typically Svevian animal fable is so developed as to lend itself from the first to being interpreted as an expression of Svevo's distressing experience of rejection by 'mother' Italy even after Trieste's 'redemption', or of literary failure as such. It can also be read along classical Freudian lines in terms of an Oedipal fixation. On the most general plane, it suggests Svevo's whole experience of reality, which turns out hostile instead of maternal.

Reality now played yet another trick, mocking his failure as a writer by according him success as an industrialist. On the night of 6–7 April 1925 there was great anxiety in the family over scarlet fever among the grandchildren, and a telephone call was expected from the clinic to report how the crisis of one of them had developed. At dead of night, the telephone rang. Svevo woke up and answered it, his heart in his mouth. It was his friend Césari, unable to restrain himself from giving Svevo the exciting news, which had just reached his newspaper office, that Ettore Schmitz had been awarded the honour of Cavaliere del Regno (Knight of the Realm—the lowest Court honour) for his services to Italian industry. Svevo was not thrilled to have been woken up on that account.[28] The newspaper announcement on the following day said that Svevo's literary and artistic merits had also played a part in earning him the decoration (though it was probably intended as a tribute to Olga, who, as a woman, was not eligible for State honours).[29] Political recognition of the Veneziani family's services to Fascism may have played a larger part than strictly industrial merit.

Svevo was bound to be involved, if only tacitly, in the Venezianis' connexions with Fascism. Bruno Maier has written: 'though the writer was officially a Fascist, or passively acquiesced in the regime, for political or patriotic reasons … he appears, contrariwise, inwardly and ideologically, as a man and as a writer, distinctly anti-Fascist, European, "mittel-European".'[30] Svevo never became a Fascist party member, but as an industrialist he belonged to the Fascist Confederation of Industrialists and held card Bn. 41009.[31] He occasionally made jocular references to Fascism in his letters. What his real views were it would be hard to divine in the quizzical disquisition 'Sulla critica italiana', written in 1926 or 1927:

We lacked political parties because we lacked followers and had only leaders. This is the national character. Everyone is a born leader. And I—frankly—do not see this as a shortcoming. In politics it caused, and still does, a bit of confusion which is sorted out when somebody at last compels our great men to co-operate as subordinates or to remain very usefully idle. At the same time, this milieu encourages strict selection which brings to the fore the best adapted to rule in such a land.[32]

This is at least a markedly different Svevo from the reader of *Critica Sociale* and *Avanti!* who had cried out against 'that rascal', Admiral Bettolo, accused by the Socialists of corruption. Here, his elusive tone could indicate either sober maturity or veiled irony, authoritarianism or self-preservation, naïve 'social Darwinism' or brazen bad faith.

Opposition to Fascism, whether overt or covert, whether in word or in deed, was not unheard of. Svevo, with his social and economic standing and his Irredentist past, was in a far stronger position than an Edoardo Weiss, a Stanislaus Joyce, or an Eugenio Montale, who were not afraid to refuse the Fascist card and to voice their dissent and were removed from State employment in consequence. The worst that Svevo might have had to fear was a litre of castor oil. But, as ever, he accepted the *fait accompli* and melted into the Veneziani milieu. The curious thing is that he should have brought politics into a paper on literary criticism.

Fascism certainly went clean against his liberalism and his pacifism. Having been granted dictatorial powers in 1922, Mussolini swiftly dismantled the Liberal State and crushed any remaining resistance with a new wave of violence. The Socialist deputy Giacomo Matteotti protested in Parliament against Fascist violence during the 1924 election campaign. A few days later he was kidnapped and murdered in obscure circumstances in which Mussolini appeared to be implicated.

The ensuing outcry nearly brought down the Fascist government, as respectable opinion was belatedly outraged. Mussolini used censorship to stifle criticism, but the situation continued precarious until 3 January 1925, when the Duce addressed Parliament, taking upon himself full responsibility for everything that had happened and cynically braving the opposition. This was the signal for yet another Fascist terror campaign, which succeeded in turning Fascism from a dictatorial regime into a totalitarian one. The decoration awarded to Ettore Schmitz in April 1925 can be seen as a tiny move in the consolidation of the Fascist regime with the support of the ruling class. The enquiry into excess war profits had already been shelved in 1923 and the law requiring the publication of shareholders' names had been repealed. Direct taxation on income and property had been sharply reduced. The alliance between Fascism and property was sealed.

April 1925 also saw the Fascist intellectual and cultural offensive. On the 21st, every newspaper in the country carried the 'Manifesto of Fascist intellectuals', drafted by the ideologist of the regime, Giovanni Gentile, and signed by about 250 men of culture, including Pirandello and the poet Ungaretti. On May

Day *Il Mondo* published the riposte, 'The Manifesto of Italian anti-Fascist intellectuals', drafted by Benedetto Croce and carrying several hundred signatures, including that of the young poet Eugenio Montale. Their voice was soon to be stifled and Fascism's most dogged opponents hounded to death, even if, like Piero Gobetti and Giovanni Amendola, they sought refuge abroad.

Italy's swift transformation into a police state in which liberty and justice were twisted so as to serve the interests of power and its beneficiaries presented an acute new challenge to Svevo's highly sensitive and yet equivocal *coscienza*. It revealed itself only hedged about with literary fictions, and kept well out of sight in his workaday writings, letters or articles for publication as they might be, carefully ducking awkward responsibilities or principled commitment.

This non-commitment on Svevo's part must be seen however not only in the light of his hesitation and timorous character and his day-to-day conformity, but also of the atmosphere in which he lived, both at the domestic and at the cosmopolitan level. The spectre of revolution still haunted Europe, and the Fascist brand of authoritarian conservatism might well have seemed the lesser evil. Also, national rivalries were as ferocious as ever. A still impotent Germany had to endure French military occupation of the Ruhr in 1923. In September 1923, Communist risings were bloodily put down in Saxony, Thuringia and Hamburg, and in November, less bloodily, the *putsch* by Hitler and Ludendorff in Munich. Many people felt that the Italian solution offered order and security. In England—the country which Svevo knew best outside Italy—Baldwin's Conservative government defeated the General Strike over wage cuts, in 1926. Churchill was to write to Mussolini in 1927 saying that, were he Italian, he would have followed the Duce 'wholeheartedly' in his 'triumphant struggle against the bestial appetites and passions of Leninism' and that Italy had provided the 'antidote' to 'the cancerous growth of Bolshevism'. In 1928 the press baron Lord Rothermere acclaimed Mussolini as 'the greatest figure of our age', 'the antidote to a deadly poison'.[33] Likewise, Sir Frank Fox's *Italy Today* (1927) was a panegyric to the Fascist State. Fox regarded violence as justified for the sake of order and found everyone he questioned in Italy, whether Italian or foreign, united in approving the regime and not in the least inclined to criticize it in the name of liberty or legality.[34]

These were of course only the views of a certain class of people, but Svevo belonged to it.* This was the class that Orwell during the Second World War was to call 'the real war criminals'. History can repeat itself, and Svevo, after finding himself involved through his business interests in the First World War, was still involved with the very same interests which were blindly creating the conditions for the Second. Perhaps his return to literature after the Armistice was an attempt to shake off his ties with the world of business so tainted by

---

* Livia, in common with the other Veneziani women, was an active member of the women's Fascio, and the firm also supported the regime financially.[35] The workers' bargaining power was severely curtailed under Fascism.[36]

the guilt of war. Writing was his only defence against the determinism of his surroundings.

62

OPERATION SVEVO

Svevo's Knight's Cross arrived three months after another tribute which he valued far more highly. One morning in January 1925, Livia relates, the Schmitzes and the Fondas were having their breakfast and Svevo 'absent-mindedly opened a letter from Paris. He began reading it out loud and the heading itself made his voice fail.'[37] The letter, in Italian, was from Larbaud, and opened 'Esteemed Sir and Master'. It spoke of Larbaud's solely verbal, but effective, propaganda on behalf of *La coscienza di Zeno* amongst the circle of the Princess Margherita Caetani Bassiano, which included Paul Valéry and Léon-Paul Fargue.[38]

Svevo thought the letter was a hoax. For the past year Larbaud's name had been mentioned to him repeatedly by Joyce but he had had no direct proof that the man existed. He went to see Giulio Césari in his newspaper office and showed him the letter: Césari just happened to have Lalou's history of contemporary French literature, which informed them that Larbaud, born in 1881, was the author of several novels, of which the best known was *Barnabooth*, and of excellent translations from English, including Samuel Butler's *The Way of All Flesh*.[39] Svevo replied immediately, promising to send Larbaud a copy of *Una vita* and, if he could borrow one, of *Senilità*.[40]

A month went by without further word from Larbaud. So, on 16 February, Svevo wrote again. This time Larbaud replied immediately, with sober enthusiasm, suggesting that an excerpt from *Senilità* should also be published, as he had 'read it to several friends and it was received with applause and some people pronounced the name of Marcel Proust'. Only the title was wrong. The Svevo material was to appear in the fifth number of *Commerce* in October.[41]

But Svevo, old and impatient, would not remain silent until October. When Larbaud was nominated Chevalier de la Légion d'Honneur a month later, he seized the opportunity to write his congratulations and chatter away to Larbaud about the latter's controversy with Boyd over Joyce; about Proust, whom he had never heard of until Larbaud's last letter but on whom he had now read the information contained in Lalou's *Histoire*; and about his own books which he was re-reading through Parisian eyes. He remarked that James Joyce had always said that a writer's pen contained only one novel, and that his own one and only novel, though so badly written as to be in need of wholesale revision, was *Una vita*. A first draft of Svevo's letter also reveals that he was reading Proust's *Recherche*, which he had just purchased.[42]

Only three days after he had sent this letter, on 19 March, Svevo had a pleasant surprise which may have allayed his anxieties over the delay in launching his works in Paris. The Trieste *La Sera* published an article by Dora Salvi entitled 'A tireless Italophile—Benjamin Crémieux'. Crémieux had told Salvi that the Triestines were not even aware that they had in their midst a great writer, the author of three novels marvellous in their psychology though stylistically flawed, densely packed with rich content. Crémieux was shrewdly preparing the ground for the impending 'Svevo affair'. This must be when Svevo, guessing that the article referred to him, sought out Dora Salvi for an evening stroll along Trieste's great pier, during which he confessed to his lifelong literary vocation and the autobiographical basis of his three novels.

But still another two months of 1925 went by without further news from Paris, and in the meantime the publisher Cappelli had sent from Bologna the all too abundant remnant of his edition of *La coscienza di Zeno*. Svevo feared the books might bring the attic down on his head.[43]

This time he personally took destiny by the horns. In May, he and Livia departed for London. 'We stopped in Paris,' Livia relates,

to make the personal acquaintance of the two illustrious French men of letters who had taken such a lively interest in the Svevo affair. Joyce arranged dinner in a restaurant close to the Gare Montparnasse. Nino Frank, a young French writer, was also there. My husband, who was generally extremely sociable and kind and affable with everybody, at once hit it off perfectly with his new friends, who displayed towards him an admiration which amazed us. As if slightly inebriated, he spoke a very great deal that evening. He liked to have an audience, all the more so if composed of his peers.

On the following evening we were invited to one of the most aristocratic of literary salons, that of the patroness of *Commerce*, Princess Bassiano Caetani, in her 'Villa Romana' at Versailles. Larbaud and Crémieux were there too. During the long and sparkling conversation, my husband mentioned a story on which he was working.[44]

On 3 November Svevo was to write to Larbaud: 'Heartened after my first visit to Paris, I started in London on an extremely long novella: "Corto viaggio sentimentale".' The nucleus of this story may have been a crime report in *Il Popolo di Trieste* in February about a businessman who was drugged on a train and relieved of 35,000 lire.[45]

In this year Svevo enjoyed a striking revival of creativity. The unfinished 'L'avvenire dei ricordi', in which past and present are fused together as the first visit to Segnitz is recalled, bears the date 1 May 1925;[46] and by November Larbaud was in possession of the only story completed since the publication of the novel, 'Una burla riuscita',[47] in which Svevo complicates the theme of the imaginary literary success, drawn from his own current vicissitudes, with two of the themes of the novel—war, and the financial killing. Larbaud gave January as the date of publication and asked Svevo's permission to offer the story to the Princess.

Svevo was rather sheepish about his petulance and 'infantile impatience' and told Larbaud that he needed to be propped up with continual encouragement if he were not to 'collapse'. This state of affairs was often to be hinted at in Svevo's letters.[48] These became frequent in November, when pressure of work in the factory was holding up progress on 'Corto viaggio sentimentale'. Comnène persuaded him to sign a contract with Giuseppe Prezzolini's literary agency for the translation and publication of his works abroad. (Prezzolini, now a political exile in Paris, had been eminent in pre-war cultural movements in Italy, especially *La Voce*.) *Le Navire d'Argent* was now chosen to carry Crémieux's Svevo article and translation. Svevo confided in Comnène:

If *Le Navire d'Argent* proves worthy of its name, I might (perhaps) rid myself of all my commitments to do with underwater paint. In my family (I exclude my wife),* they'd have to see some cash to make them believe in literature. Then I'd also find the time to mend my language a little.

So this sixty-four-year-old baby repeats his youthful daydreams of a literary success which would enable him to devote himself entirely to literature and— worse and worse—to 'improving' his language. But once again he was to be disappointed. The contract with Prezzolini was to yield nothing but wrangles. Meanwhile, Crémieux was intending to get his article on Svevo published in Italian in *Il Corriere della Sera* and Svevo indulged his fantasies: 'It would be splendid to visit you as a literary man. To arrive in Paris and find the band at the station!'[49]

In December the correspondence lapsed anew. Svevo went to Pasini's lectures on Pirandello and mentioned that he had at last got hold of twenty copies of *Senilità,* which he was passing round to interested parties.[50] On 31 December he was off again to London, scribbling notes on the way for 'Corto viaggio sentimentale'.[51]

He did not realize that at that very moment fame was already smiling on him, and from an unexpected quarter—in Italy itself. The December issue of the Milan little literary magazine *L'Esame* published a ten-page 'Homage to Italo Svevo' by Eugenio Montale. It was followed on 30 January by a shorter 'Introducing Italo Svevo', also by Montale, in another Milanese little literary magazine, *Il Quindicinale*.[52]

Montale had only a few months previously published his first book of poems, *Ossi di seppia* (Cuttlefish Bones) and signed the anti-Fascist manifesto. He had got wind of the Paris discovery of Svevo from Prezzolini, who had heard about Svevo from Joyce at the PEN Club dinner in honour of Pirandello. Prezzolini had brought this news to the *Convegno* literary circle in Milan, to which Montale belonged. But no one could find anything by or about Svevo either in the well-stocked *Convegno* library or in the Milan bookshops. 'There was a

* This aside does not appear in the first draft of the letter.

full-scale hunt for the Unknown One', according to Carlo Linati, and Montale felt obliged to assure the readers of his first article on Svevo that he was not writing an 'Imaginary Portrait'.

One fine day Montale had turned up to see his Milanese friends with a dog-eared copy of *Senilità* tucked underneath his arm but made a great mystery of how and where he had laid his hands on it.[53] His supplier was Roberto Bazlen, known as Bobi, a friend of his from Trieste.

Like Joyce in Paris, Bobi acted as midwife to Svevo's fame in Italy. He was born in 1902, the son of a German Lutheran. Bobi had the gift of cultural divination, scenting out for his friends all that was most new and strange and intriguing, yet keeping himself out of the limelight. 'What Roberto Bazlen thought, it would be arbitrary to say,' remarks his editor Roberto Calasso; 'what remains certain is that his presence forced other people to think.'[54] In the Svevo affair Bobi, as another critic, Zampa, put it, had 'all the air of a director invisibly pulling the strings of the operation.'[55] This to some extent bears out the claim by Giulio Caprin, the *Corriere della Sera* critic who was such a staunch opponent of Svevo's fame, that it was due in good measure to 'familiarity with some brotherhood for the mutual manufacture of celebrity'. Svevo had indeed found in Bazlen, Montale and company a circle that was at the same time discovering and creating a new literary world. Ahead of their time in the Italy of the 1890s, *Una vita* and *Senilità*, as well as the startlingly modern *La coscienza di Zeno*, found their readership and their platform among the advanced young writers emerging as the first quarter of the twentieth century elapsed.

Svevo's literary life now became quite hectic. He and Livia were in Paris for the New Year and met Adrienne Monnier, editor of *Le Navire d'Argent*, who was going to devote an issue to Svevo. They planned to dash over from London for a brief visit to Paris at the end of January to coincide with its publication. Svevo's euphoria made him more garrulous than ever and he felt obliged to apologize for having spoken so much 'twaddle'. Comnène sent on to him in Charlton a letter from Caprin turning down the article on Svevo which Crémieux had written for *Il Corriere della Sera*. *Profilo autobiografico* asserts that 'In 1925 a mutual friend recommended Svevo to Giulio Caprin, who received him courteously in Milan. Caprin however then told the old gentleman that *Il Corriere della Sera* did not have enough space to discuss his book.' After Svevo's death, Caprin was to deny that the meeting had ever taken place or that he had been responsible for burying the announcement on *La coscienza di Zeno* 'in a couple of lines among "Books Received"'.[56] Whatever really happened, Caprin, though he lived in Milan, was a Triestine and clearly shared the hostility towards Svevo characteristic of establishment Trieste.

In that January of 1926 Ettore and Livia went on a hilarious shopping expedition to the West End of London. Wearing a bowler, overcoat and a celluloid collar that came up to his chin, Svevo walked into a Regent Street photographer's proclaiming, in his foreign accent, that he was a ballet dancer and performing an unsteady pirouette before the eyes of the disconcerted shop-assistant. Then he set out again with Livia into the cold wind to look for a hat shop, where he tried one top-hat after another without finding one that would fit his head, which, he told Livia, fame had made bigger than ever.[57]

He was enjoying a late bath towards midday on 27 January in the house in Charlton, when there was an excited cry from Livia. He rushed downstairs in his bathrobe to be handed a copy of *L'Avenir* which had just arrived from Paris and contained Léon Treich's notice of Crémieux's article on Svevo which was due to appear in the forthcoming issue of *Le Navire d'Argent*, and which billed Svevo as the Italian Proust.

The Schmitzes' triumphal entry into Paris was slightly marred by Larbaud's absence in Lisbon and the Crémieuxs' on the Riviera.[58] However, they made the acquaintance of Prezzolini, who on 8 February brought out in the Milan *L'Ambrosiano* an article opening with the words 'I had lunch today with Italo Svevo' and summarizing Crémieux's article and its remarks about Svevo's courageous use of Freudianism and his lack of fine style: 'He can't write. But he has something to say.'

So burst the Svevo 'affair'. From 30 January, Italian newspaper reports about the French discovery came thick and fast. *L'Ambrosiano* of 9 February published a letter from *L'Esame* staking its own claim to the discovery through Montale's 'Homage to Svevo'. This Italo-French rivalry could only advance Svevo's cause; but two days later an article by Caprin in *Il Corriere della Sera* delivered a hostile blast. Entitled 'A proposed celebrity', it did at least have the merit of devoting a full quarter spread to a detailed analysis of *La coscienza di Zeno*, picking out what Caprin saw as the book's defects of form, style and language and deploring its 'all-embracing analysm' (i.e. minutely analytical method), its total dissolution of the narrative material ... into the indefinite series of its moments', its 'deliberately banal events', its flouting rather than missing of unity, its 'method of art which professes to reproduce the methods of science'. In short, Caprin saw what were in fact the novel's most original achievements as faults. That same evening *La Sera* in Milan, while agreeing with Caprin, concluded a brief report on the Svevo 'affair' with the remark that Svevo's new-found celebrity had been manufactured by that 'phalanx of Jewish writers who devote themselves particularly to pricing up their literary co-religionaries in various European countries' and that 'in real life Italo Svevo bears a Semitic name—Ettore Schmitz', which 'might in part explain the far-fetched praise'.

Benjamin Crémieux was indeed a free-thinking Jew, like Svevo himself, though more outspoken than Svevo, not least in his solidarity with fellow-Jews. When only twenty he helped to found the Institut Français in Florence in 1908 and worked there for several years, becoming one of the most formidable French experts on things Italian, particularly literature. He had recognized, and strove to have recognized by others, the genius of Pirandello as far back as the appearance of *Il fu Mattia Pascal* in 1904. It was he who had translated Pirandello's *Sei personaggi in cerca d'autore* (Six Characters in Search of an

Author) and ensured its sensational success on the Paris stage in 1923, which was the beginning of Pirandello's fame. He had been familiar with the *Voce* circle and translated Slataper's *Il mio Carso*. But precisely on account of his qualities of frankness and critical acumen, Crémieux was not the man to win over the Italian literary set unanimously to his side: in 1920, when the provincial preciosity of *La Ronda* ruled literary fashion in Italy, *La Nouvelle Revue Française* had brought out a panoramic article by him 'Sùr la condition présente des lettres italiennes', in which he castigated Italian literature in the period immediately following the war as a deadly bore and a mere subsidiary of foreign literatures, particularly French and English. Crémieux's name was therefore bound to rouse some rancour in Italy, rancour which now attached itself to his new protégé, Svevo. A European at heart, and a great lover of Italy, Crémieux was slow to recognize the threat which Fascism presented both to French security and to the liberty of Italian letters. The situation was, however, beginning to arouse his concern by 1925, and in the thirties he was to attack Italian cultural policy vigorously. He joined the French Resistance during the Second World War, was captured by the Nazis and died in the Buchenwald extermination camp in 1944. Most of his papers, including the letters he had received from Svevo, were seized and destroyed by the Gestapo.[59]

Crémieux's four-page article of 1 February 1926 in *Le Navire d'Argent* emphasized Svevo's isolation as an Italian writer, his foreignness to the Italian literary tradition. The commercial and bourgeois atmosphere of his novels, his 'analysm', his admitting everything in life, great or tiny, outside any pre-conceived scheme (an aspect of *La coscienza di Zeno* particularly admired by Joyce), his eternal interior monologue which so impressed Larbaud, and his humour, which produced in the character of Zeno a sort of middle-class Triestine Chaplin—all these characteristics, argued Crémieux, marked him out from other Italian writers. The article briefly touched on the first two novels, mainly to point out the continuity and indeed identity of the central figures, and it also remarked on the vitality and wealth of significance of the secondary characters. The almost forty pages of translations from Svevo included the finale of *Senilità* and the opening of *La coscienza di Zeno*, with the entire chapter on 'Il fumo'. An Italian version of Crémieux's article was published in the Milanese *La Fiera Letteraria* of 28 February, with a disclaimer by the editor.[60]

Crémieux's role in the Svevo operation was rather like that of a lightning conductor in the Italian critical storm. Meanwhile, out of the limelight shed on the paraliterary 'Svevo affair' Svevo's properly literary reputation advanced quietly, mostly through the circle of Montale's young literary friends centred in Milan. These included Somarè, Lodovici and Ferrieri, respectively editors of the little magazines *L'Esame*, *Il Quindicinale* and *Il Convegno*. Svevo was not to win a wide readership success until long after his death, either in Italy or abroad, but the *succès d'estime* which he won in 1926 took his books (as soon as they became available) straight into the European literary consciousness.

Svevo did not see Montale's articles until 17 February, when he was back in

London after his brief visit to Paris. On 24 January Bazlen had written to tell him about the interest aroused in Milan by Montale's first article. He had given away several copies of Svevo's books and wanted more, and he pressed Svevo to stop in Milan on his way back home and look up Somarè or Lodovici. Bazlen wrote again from Trieste to say that 'the Milanese' wanted to republish *Una vita* and *Senilità*.[61]

On 15 February Svevo did Joyce a small favour by sending him a report on the London premiere of *Exiles*. He had struggled to read Joyce's manuscript several years before and still had not yet been able to follow the play as he and Livia were sitting too far from the stage to catch all the dialogue, though they were delighted to get such 'magnificent' free seats. As Svevo explained to Joyce:

In London we usually sit so close to the actors that, when we say: 'I beg your pardon', the actors, if they're decent, repeat the phrase. I am eager to have the book because on Thursday I'll be trying to get into the 'Debate on *Exiles*' gratis and I would like to have understood the work thoroughly.[62]

Montale's two articles expressed astonishment at the modernity of Svevo's tone, even in his novels of the 1890s, and at the novelist's sense of the independence of his art from any demonstrative purpose. Montale thought that Svevo 'reflects, as very few other writers, the impulses and the drifting of the contemporary spirit', that he transcribes 'the epic of the drab causality of our day-to-day life' (and here Montale more clearly reveals his own affinity with Svevo's world, tacitly associating it with the metaphysic which suffuses all his own poetry) 'interrupted by the sudden flashing of a no less blind and mysterious contingency...'. He argued that Svevo's superficial stylistic blemishes could not affect the essential value of this work, which consisted in his 'ardour for human truth', his 'continuous desire to sound out, far beyond the phenomenal semblances of being, that dark subterranean zone of *coscienza* where the appearances that are most readily taken for granted wobble and blur'. He recognized the originality of *La coscienza di Zeno* but considered it less 'perfect' than *Senilità*. (He was to change his mind as he got to know the third novel better).[63]

These articles of Montale's (rather than Crémieux's decisive, but more polemical, propagandist and journalistic piece) clear the path to an understanding of Svevo, and Svevo realized this. He immediately showed great fondness for Montale, as he did with all his admirers, and initiated a close, though slightly formal, friendship with him with the very first letter which he sent Montale on the day he received the journals containing his articles. What seemed to concern him most in this first letter, apart from his smarting resentment towards Caprin, was that *La coscienza di Zeno* should not be read as straightforward autobiography, as Crémieux's article might have suggested.[64] The writer without a face did not want his various masks to be confused.

On Wednesday 24 February 1926, the Schmitzes left London for Paris, and on the following day they again lunched with Prezzolini and Crémieux to discuss new editions of the novels. They must almost certainly also have seen Joyce and Adrienne Monnier.[65] On the 27th they reached Milan. Eugenio Montale tells the story of how he met Svevo:

Towards the close of the winter of '26, on a spring-like morning, a rather elderly gentleman, not tall, quite portly but elegant, had stopped outside the entrance to La Scala in Milan to read the poster for *Lohengrin*. With him was a lady several years his junior, who in her day must have been very beautiful. The elderly gentleman bore a striking resemblance to the portrait of the Triestine industrialist Ettore Schmitz, which I had seen a short while before in *Les Nouvelles Littéraires*. Accompanied by a friend, I followed the couple some way along Via Manzoni, then plucked up my courage and hazarded the question: 'Signor Schmitz?' I was not mistaken ... Signor Schmitz (for such he remained for me until his death) invited us to take a seat with him in a café and barraged me with questions which were not exactly of a literary kind. He was curious about my name. A resin and turpentine importer with my name had for years and years been supplying him to his great satisfaction; was he related to me? I admitted that it was my father, little guessing that this would win merit for me in his eyes, as in fact was the case. From then onwards there was always a whiff of turpentine in our relationship, which I could never keep on a literary level for very long. Our first conversation was brief, because the friend who was with us—a pompous, dyed-in-the-wool hair-splitter—fired at Schmitz one question after another about his 'peculiarly Triestine character', with the predictable result of putting him to flight; but I remember that I was immediately struck by the resemblance between Schmitz and his characters. . . . Everything about Italo Svevo was ... Svevian from top to toe.[66]

Montale did not let Italo Svevo escape so easily. Svevo went round to the Treves publishing house to see Dall'Oro, to whom he had already sent his novels in the hope of correcting the unfortunate episode of 1889, when Treves, against Dall'Oro's recommendation, had rejected *Un inetto* before it was re-named *Una vita*. This time Dall'Oro raised his hopes that there would be a re-edition of *Senilità*.[67] From Treves, Svevo called in at the offices of a press-cutting agency, L'Eco della Stampa, and paid a subscription to enable him to follow his own literary fortunes. Upon leaving, he found himself surrounded by Montale and his friends—Lodovici, Somarè, Ferrata, Tallone, Ferrero—all of them aged around thirty.[68] They took him first to the office of *L'Esame* and then *Il Quindicinale*, where Svevo's vivacity galvanized the editorial staff. 'I felt that Svevo, who was still capable of grasping certain prismatic truths, was the youngest of us all,' recollected Lodovici. This was everybody's impression, though one or two glimpsed or divined in him an underlying sadness. Svevo's joviality cost him an effort: as he left *Il Quindicinale* he whispered gaily to Lodovici that he felt as if he had been to *L'Esame*, or an examination.[69]

63

A NEW LIFE

After a lifetime of obscurity, Svevo now had to face the hardly less distressing frustrations brought by his stunted fame.

He hit it off best with the younger devotees of literature—those around thirty, like Montale, or even younger, like Leo Ferrero. With older admirers, even those born in the 1880s like Crémieux, Larbaud and Joyce himself, relations were more distant and, with the touchy Saba, even difficult. Yet, though all Svevo's new literary friends were at least twenty years his junior, he was to appear the most youthful. He played father to them and child at the same time.

This *vieillard terrible* was an old man in a hurry. He knew that his days were numbered and that his 'miracle of Lazarus' (as he was to call it in prefacing the second edition of *Senilità*) was far from complete. He had still to win himself a readership and bring out new editions of his novels—of which the first two were totally unavailable, while *La coscienza di Zeno* was fast becoming so (*Il Secolo* of Milan reported on 15 March that Cappelli's stock of 700 copies had gone in a flash). He set about revising *Senilità* for Treves and trimming the chapters on 'The Story of My Marriage' and 'A Business Partnership' in *La coscienza di Zeno*, as requested by Crémieux, for the French translation. By 16 March he had already sent Crémieux his copy of *La coscienza di Zeno* 'short-ened by ten pages, two lines and one and a half words',[70] but he later had to yield to pressure from Crémieux and the publisher Gallimard and agree to have a hundred pages cut out.[71]

Svevo devoured the press cuttings (by no means exhaustive) sent to him by L'Eco della Stampa, and was delighted whenever he came across a long and favourable review. One such was that by Bino Binazzi in *Il Resto del Carlino* of 2 March. Binazzi did have some reservations, especially regarding what he considered the old-fashioned scientism of *La coscienza di Zeno*, and he rather too naïvely accepted the 'cure' claimed by Zeno at the end of his diary. But Svevo was particularly pleased that Binazzi had boldly acclaimed the validity and efficacy of his style. 'A real caress,' wrote Svevo to Montale, and remarked that it was better than having Rigutini and Fornaciari (authorities on Italian usage: Svevo mis-spelt both their names) thrown at him.[72]

Svevo's long-standing linguistic inferiority complex had now begun to turn into a sense of his own stylistic originality, individuality, truth and rightness—

thanks to the vindications of it by Montale, Crémieux and Binazzi. Of course, Svevo had always had a clear sense of the necessity and character of his own style. This is shown by his consistency as a writer from the very first. But only now that he had prestigious support did he feel strong enough to justify his literary—or rather, anti-literary—style, and he was to do so publicly and forcefully in *Profilo autobiografico*.

Binazzi's encouragement was timely: Svevo was revising *Senilità* with the help of Tony Fonda and a schoolteacher friend, Marino de Szombathely. Montale warned him 'not to spoil the text's straightforwardness with literary frills', but simply to 'get rid of a few exclamation marks and one or two anacolutha in all'. When Svevo paid a brief visit to Milan at the end of April his literary friends there were still concerned that he might turn the book into a model of fine writing. In his preface to the new edition he was to speak of 'a few merely formal improvements', but the case was not quite so simple. Svevo effected numerous small corrections involving punctuation, morphology, lexis, idiom and phrasing, many of them of doubtful merit, and he also cut out some details and at least one long passage which had too explicitly or heavy-handedly emphasized the process of self-deception in Emilio Brentani's daydreams. Szombathely's corrections were few and far between, and he was embarrassed at the over-generous fee which Svevo pressed upon him.[73]

On Svevo's second visit to Treves, Dall'Oro again received him cordially and promised him a decision by 15 May about the republication of *Senilità* if Svevo sent him the revised copy at once.[74] Svevo meanwhile was trying to re-establish contact with the Crémieuxs, whom he had missed when he last stopped in Paris, and who were keeping him short of news owing to the pressure of Benjamin's commitments and to Marie-Anne's migraine. Finally the latter wrote back very apologetically and informed Svevo that they were coming to Milan for the first night of Benjamin's play *Qui si balla*. Crémieux had written it in Italian, but persuaded Pirandello to pretend that he had translated it from a French original, *Ici on danse*, and it was so presented on the programme. Pirandello's own company performed the play on 24 April, and Svevo travelled across to Milan to see the Crémieuxs as well as to nudge his prospective publishers and look up his young Milanese friends. The play itself was a flop.

On 1 May 1926 Svevo, signing himself 'I. S.', paid his first tribute to Joyce by publishing in *Il Popolo di Trieste* a review of the French translation of *Dubliners*. The headline stressed Joyce's link with Trieste, and the review was mainly a summary of Larbaud's introduction on Joyce's literary career. Svevo followed Larbaud in putting Joyce on a par, in his own field, with Freud and Einstein.[75]

Svevo made further brief visits to Milan in June and in August of 1926 to negotiate with publishers and see his friends. Enzo Ferrieri of the literary club Il Convegno wanted him to give a reading of one of his works, but 'The very thought of such a thing ruined my sleep. . . . In the modern world old men may write but they must keep silent.'[76] Several memoirs recorded the image of his stout figure and large head with its bulging eyes gleaming with a mischievous wit. Carlo Linati remembers his low slow voice with its slightly German accent explaining that his underwater paint was a discovery of his own which enabled the keels of merchant ships to be painted without raising them out of the water. Svevo had not lost his passion for telling tall stories.[77]

Though Svevo had begun to act as a go-between, establishing contacts between Triestine writers and Italian and European literary circles,[78] he himself meanwhile was having a struggle with his pen: 'in confidence,' he wrote to Montale on 10 March, 'I'm no longer myself at my writing-desk. I've tried. I fear that all the praise has ruined me. I keep reminding myself: "Mind now, you've got to be good." And to be good I'd have to re-educate myself.' But on the 26th he inscribed the date on what was to have been the final draft of *Con la penna d'oro* (The Gold Pen).[79] When he began this play, it is impossible to tell. As in almost all his post-war writings, money is a central theme. It defines the conflict between the cold-hearted Alberta, a wealthy married woman, and her passionate and impoverished cousin Alice. The play also depicts the wife's tyranny over her household. This theme gradually acquires prominence in Svevo's later writings, from its first subdued appearance in the conventional domestic *ménage* which Augusta imposes on an all too willing Zeno in *La coscienza*. Yet on 27 March, all he told Montale was: 'I do have phantasms [i.e. literary ideas] pestering me every day to write. I've even drafted a few pages. But the difficulty when you're 65 is not to start something but to finish it.'[80]

In Milan he showered invitations on all and sundry to come and see him in Trieste. Montale was, fitly, the first to do so. He came to Villa Veneziani early in May with Bobi Bazlen. Livia had a bad bout of influenza. Uncle 'Eusebio' (as Montale's friends called him) was a great success with Svevo's grandsons, and with everyone else. Svevo read him 'Una burla riuscita' and later claimed that it had sent him to sleep (which Montale denied). Svevo insisted: 'It made an impression of poverty on me.' He kept tinkering with it, but was never happy with it and was not very vigorous in opposing the cuts which Crémieux made in the French version. He told Leo Ferrero, who admired the story: 'I myself feel it to be a bit old-fashioned. . . . Between friends, I can confess that I'm very fond of it. . . . It's my youngest child. A little pale, and weedy even. Poor thing! The child of an old father.'[81]

After his visit Montale wrote another article on Svevo, which appeared in the June issue of *L'Italia che scrive*. Publicity was its main object, but Svevo found Montale's observation on the similarity between Emilio's relationship with Stefano in *Senilità* and Zeno Cosini's relationship with Guido Speier something of a revelation. Montale dwelt on Svevo's 'gift' as a writer of narrative and showed a growing admiration for the stature of *La coscienza di Zeno* with 'that fluid, ambiguous *totaliste* literature which is arising fairly generally in Europe and to which Svevo relates in a highly personal manner.'[82] On 16 May, *Il Marzocco* carried a measured article on *La coscienza di Zeno* by Luigi Tonelli, which was perceptive in its treatment of Zeno's disarming humour. The *Times Literary Supplement* of 20 May 1926, on the other hand, gave a forthright condemnation of Svevo's feckless anti-hero, contrasting Zeno to the virile regime governing his country. No doubt the reviewer's admiring reference to Fascism was a reaction to the General Strike and protracted coal-miners' strike in Britain.

In June, Svevo made his last journey to London. He stopped in Milan to see his friends of *Il Convegno* and get from the publishers, Treves, a decision on *Senilità*. In London he told his friends the Duckers that he would not be able to visit London again, and advised young Cyril Ducker, an aspiring poet, not to waste time writing to him, but to achieve fame as soon as possible. He was unable to work on 'Una burla riuscita' as both he and Tony, who followed him to London, forgot to bring the manuscript. Finally, a letter from Treves arrived, dated 6 June, turning down *Senilità*. 'Those troglodytes' at Treves thus had the honour of refusing to publish Svevo twice over, at an interval of nearly forty years.

This time Svevo knew the ropes, and became increasingly tireless in furthering his own cause. He made a present to Adrienne Monnier of a sculpture by the Triestine Ruggero Rovan, 'Hill in profile', damaged but skilfully repaired. She recommended him to Gallimard for the French edition of *La coscienza di Zeno*. Bobi Bazlen wrote to say that the first three chapters of the German translation, *Zeno Cosini*, were ready, so Svevo wrote to Prezzolini, whose agency was dealing with the foreign editions of his works, inviting him to lunch in Paris on Monday 12 July.

Svevo and Livia reached Paris on 11 July, and saw Joyce and the Crémieuxs. With the latter, they watched the Bastille Day celebration fireworks. Benjamin Crémieux had found a first-rate translator for *La coscienza di Zeno*, the Swiss Paul-Henri Michel. He also sent Svevo to Gallimard to discuss publication under the Nouvelle Revue Française imprint. Gallimard refused to settle anything, however, and Svevo, rueful and bewildered, complained to Crémieux. Crémieux had heard the other side of the story, and had a good laugh over the affair: 'Gallimard told me: "Monsieur Svevo must have found me a complete idiot. That day I was fagged out and I spoke to him without properly knowing what it was all about".' As regards English and German editions, James Joyce was to give his usual businesslike help.

From Paris Svevo went to Vulpera Tarasp, in the Engadine in Switzerland, to bathe, for the benefit of his arteriosclerosis, in the natural carbonic acid waters. He stayed at the Grand Hôtel Kurhaus until early August. Even there, he still kept up a busy correspondence with Montale, Treves, Crémieux, Prezzolini and Michel. He suggested a German publisher to Prezzolini and (upon Crémieux's advice) offered Michel 2,000 francs or £180, to be paid through London, for the translation of *La coscienza di Zeno*. On his way back to Trieste, he stopped at Como, and then once more in Milan to find another home for *Senilità*, but his celebrity was not sufficient to convince the publishers.

He strolled down Via Manzoni with Linati, 'Amid the roar of traffic and the hubbub of the brightly lit shops', and told him that Mondadori had also turned down *Senilità*, while Cappelli was asking 5,000 lire for a re-edition. Svevo was tempted to take up the violin once again, or settle in Como and translate the 'Walpurgisnacht' sequence from *Ulysses*.[83]

Matters proceeded more smoothly with Michel. Svevo just once had to insist on scientific precision in a detail of the death-scene of old Cosini. He did not hide his eagerness for the translation and publication to go forward as fast as possible, nor his distress over the cuts in the text. Back in Trieste that August (though in fact spending much of his time in Villa Letizia up on the Carso), he devoted himself mainly to studying Joyce's works, having no doubt decided to make a gesture of gratitude to the godfather of his literary fame.

During September and October of 1926 he was discussing the republication of *Senilità* with Somarè, editor of *L'Esame*, whom Montale had strongly recommended as long ago as March. On 18 September Somarè had already undertaken to bring out an edition of 2,000 copies immediately, but he offered Svevo a lower price than Cappelli for the disposal of the remaining 600 copies of *La coscienza di Zeno*. The contract was slow to arrive, but was then followed by the promise that the book would be out in time for the New Year, a peak book-buying season in Italy. Then the date was deferred to late February.

The news from France was also galling. For *La coscienza di Zeno* Svevo had to accept massive cuts and a modest edition of perhaps no more than 6,000 copies. *Commerce* eventually turned down 'Una burla riuscita', finding it too long and slow, and then the brief 'Vino generoso'. Prezzolini's agency exasperated Svevo by its apparent total lack of effort on his behalf. In January, its Rome representative, Rendi, wrote to complain to Svevo that the latter was negotiating independently for a German edition, and Svevo blew his top. The angry exchanges which followed did not come to an end until two months later with Rendi's withdrawal.

The opening months of 1927 brought more 'agonies' (*dolori*) over *Senilità*, as Svevo wrote to Montale on 14 February:

A friend (Manager of Treves Zanichelli in Trieste) actually circularized the offer of *Senilità* to the various Italian publishers. They demand between seven and ten thousand lire to publish it. There seem to me to be two base circumstances in this business: My own, the vanity of an old man capable of spending so much, and that of the publishers . . .

Somarè seems to have dropped out because of personal difficulties.[84]

64

NEW TRIESTINE FRIENDS

Svevo was having a trying time.[85] The poet Umberto Saba (himself a notoriously difficult man) described to Pier Antonio Quarantotti Gambini a brush he had with him at around this time:

'One day when we were discussing business together, suddenly Svevo lost his temper, which I wasn't at all expecting, though I thought I knew him pretty well. "What do you know about it," he yelled [in broad Triestine], "when it comes to business you're just a newborn chick: and I, if I care to, could just go like this," he went on at me, "and squash you!" I can't forget,' concluded Saba, 'the satisfaction, the relish, with which Svevo, imagining I was under his heel (his heel, mind you!), went through and repeated the motions of squashing me!'

Quarantotti Gambini mentions another explosion which took place when Svevo was introduced to an artist and thought that he was going to be touched for a loan.[86] No doubt this happened when Svevo was having to fork out thousands of francs for the French translation of *La coscienza di Zeno* and thousands of lire besides for the new edition of *Senilità*, not to mention other publishing projects which involved some initial outlay. But the outbursts were in character, as on other occasions when Svevo felt that things were slipping out of his control.

Giani Stuparich's lively picture of the literary and artistic company that gathered at the café Garibaldi at that time noted acutely that 'Svevo knew how to win over even Saba' and how these two senior members of the group (Saba having been born in 1883) 'joined hands across the edges of their ego-centricities'. Svevo used to entertain everybody with reminiscences of his various 'adventures', but, even when he was telling stories about London or Paris, his tone always remained utterly Triestine. With his 'garrulous and deep-flowing spontaneity, halfway between that of an *enfant terrible* ready to cock a snook at anyone and the old sage full of Socratic finesse', he loved to 'dissect psychological conditions, starting always with his own, laying bare his own human nature'. He wore his 'halo' like a high-spirited child, revelled in drinking the sharp *terrano* wine of the Carso in that congenial company, and would put on his act as a conscript in the army of Franz Josef for their amusement.[87]

In *Giochi di fisonomie* (Physiognomical Games) Stuparich gives a more detailed and multi-faceted portrait of Svevo.[88] He dwells on his tireless chit-chat, his curiosity about any and every topic, his child's heart and sage's head, his formidable perception of human motivation in its complex articulations, his unforced kindness and modesty, his 'nineteenth-century simplicity and sanity, reared and matured in the school of positivism' and remote from all posturing, whether as refined aesthete, or systematic sceptic or mercurial wit. 'Perhaps there really never was a writer who so revelled in fame and remained so uncorrupted and untroubled by it.' Like so many others, Stuparich emphasized that the man Ettore Schmitz was all of a piece with the writings of Italo Svevo, and that in the man, as in the writings, the world with all its problematic was mirrored, 'so crooked, contradictory, painful, disjointed, that one would feel impelled to cover one's eyes so as not to see it'. And yet, Svevo the chatterbox, the egocentric, 'is also a good listener, and how he listens!—when his great head tilts to one side and his eyes smile . . .'.

Svevo was now at the centre of the Triestine literary circle, and in close touch with Italian and European circles. Many young Italian writers wrote to him or came to see him, and when Luigi Pirandello visited Trieste for a season of his plays at the Teatro Verdi (as the Comunale was now called) in November 1926, Svevo 'invited him home and also took him on an outing by car to see the Postumia caverns'. This information comes from Anita Pittoni, who continues:

> Svevo's daughter Letizia, who was always present at the meetings between him and Pirandello, attests that Svevo's literary work was never mentioned ... During these meetings Pirandello always kept the tone of the conversation banal and somewhat non-committal.[89]

Pirandello was always non-committal except with close friends. There was also a shadow between him and Svevo, as the latter had written to him in 1925 sending a copy of *La coscienza di Zeno*, without getting a reply. Svevo remarked that he could not bear the man.[90] No doubt he had extended his hospitality to him in token of their common friendship with the Crémieuxs, but it is strange that there should be so little communication between two writers whose interests were so closely akin and who shared a certain debt to Schopenhauer.

Svevo was now turning out fables, some miniature ones, others merely short, like 'Rapporti difficili' (Difficult Relationships) and 'Piccoli segreti' (Little Secrets), about the old man and the birds.[91] The 2nd of January 1927 is the date which appears at the beginning of the fragment 'Le confessioni del vegliardo',[92] a false start to his planned sequel to *La coscienza di Zeno*, of which only some polished segments were completed. A jumble of other jottings and sketches from these last two years of Svevo's life occupies the last thirty pages of the third volume of the *Opera Omnia* edition. The themes are varied: the problem of the novel; time and 'Einsteinian' relativity; old age, disease and death; animals; and even a waterspout. There is also the fantasy about the smooth-cheeked American who offers a hundred thousand dollars for the manuscript of *La coscienza di Zeno*. The 'final tense' of one whose life is done dominates Svevo's last great lease of literary life. His protagonists try to cheat this final tense by donning the false dress of the relationship between old and young ('La Novella del buon vecchio e della bella fanciulla') or of the 'rejuvenation' experiment (in Svevo's last play, *La rigenerazione**). 'Corto viaggio sentimentale' is not mentioned again after 1925.

After a long gap, Svevo eventually heard again from Montale. He had been made quite ill by his misadventures as regards employment, and sought Svevo's commiseration over the long hours of clerical work he now had to put in. Svevo pulled his leg over this (though making a serious point): 'It will be an outsize literary cure if it works.' Svevo himself had been almost in despair, sweating over *Ulysses* and the Joyce lecture he had eventually promised Enzo Ferrieri for the members of Il Convegno. He facetiously referred to it as a dose of (Fascist) castor oil, both for himself and for his audience. He felt he was no critic: 'In my lecture Joyce fiddles away in the air all on his own as if no one else had ever written anything either before him or alongside him.' The date fixed was Tuesday 8 March 1927, five o'clock in the afternoon. Svevo promised to go in 'pompa magna'. He took with him to Milan his corrected copy of *Senilità*, with the preface dated 1 March 1927, for the star-crossed second edition, but he spent a whole week looking for a publisher in Milan without success.

The lecture was a non-event. It was held during working hours and the audience was almost wholly female. Livia assured Svevo that it was a good lecture, but Svevo resolved that it would be his last. He sent the text to Joyce, and a copy also to *La Fiera Letteraria*, where it was published in mutilated form.[93] Though it consisted mainly of exposition of Joyce's works, it was the exposition by one artist of the works of a brother artist. Rather than merely describing Joyce's works, Svevo re-lived them, and in the case of Bloom identification takes place almost before our eyes. For an Italian reader this could still rate as the best short introduction to Joyce. For the student of Svevo it is interesting that Svevo discreetly but insistently surveys Joyce's work from a point of view that is at least tendentially Freudian, and concludes quite explicitly:

Joyce's works, therefore, cannot be credited to psychoanalysis, but I am convinced that they can be the subject of its study. They are nothing but a piece of life, of great importance just because it has been brought to life not deformed by any meticulous science but vigorously hewn with quickening inspiration. And I do hope that some thoroughly competent psychoanalyst may venture to study his books, which are life itself—a rich, felt life, recalled with the spontaneity of one who has lived and suffered what he writes. They are far worthier of study than that poor *Gradiva* of Jensen's which Freud himself honoured with his celebrated comments.[94]

Svevo had followed the serial publication of *Ulysses* and in 1921 had made Joyce explain the 'Eolus' chapter. After having made a thorough study of the

---

* Svevo left this play untitled. The conventional title, 'Regeneration', is one he had intended for a projected play many years before. See above, p. 48.

'great poem', Svevo (presumably in July 1926) visited Joyce's home in Paris with some assurance, yet timidly, as if he were the younger man: but Joyce astonished him by showing not the slightest interest in *Ulysses*. He was now engrossed in his new book and was only interested in discussing with Svevo the meaning of a Triestine dialect expression.

The unpublished lecture-notes bring out more clearly than the lecture itself that Svevo attached particular value in Joyce's works to 'an objectivity applied with what I would call almost fanatical rigidity', to a '*scienza*' which carried on the great tradition of Flaubert and Zola.[95]

By April 1927 there was still no publisher for *Senilità*, despite the efforts made in Milan by Alberto Tallone.[96] Nor was there much progress with foreign editions of Svevo's works. There was the comfort for him of visits to Trieste by his young admirers, especially those from the Convegno circle. One of these was the very young Leo Ferrero. Svevo introduced him to Livia with the obligatory joke: 'You see, she doesn't squint'—tacitly conceding that Augusta in *La coscienza di Zeno* was based on her.[97] Ferrero described the house as 'spilling over with furniture, over-luxurious perhaps', and the dinner was exquisite. But, he observed,

one could not say that Svevo was a happy man: deep in his eyes one could perceive an obsessive gleam, an anxiety, a continuous anguish, which he sought to allay with chit-chat, with 'madrigals', with *Witzen*. One would have said that Svevo's loftiest ideal consisted in making his friends laugh at his *Witzen*. Svevo certainly cracked too many *Witzen*.

Ferrero saw a curious contradiction between Svevo's 'Latin mischief' and 'human kindness' on the one hand and that 'strange obsession' in his eyes, the Germanic mould of his head, 'a makeshift compromise between Hindenburg and Thomas Mann', with the bizarre Y of his 'Mephistophelian eyebrows' over his Semitic nose.

The afternoon was lowering and chilly. They went on a drive around town. Svevo was affable with all and sundry, he slapped Saba on the back, smiled to the chauffeur, chatted with the museum door-keeper. He confided in Ferrero, of the women in his novels, 'I've so loved them!' Ferrero himself guessed that Svevo's 'strange obsession' was the fear that he would not live to see his books published.[98]

Bobi Bazlen brought to Villa Veneziani another very young visitor, Piero Rismondo, a native of Istria who had been educated in Austria and was now a reporter for the *Wiener Allgemeine Zeitung*. He was already well advanced with the German translation of *La coscienza di Zeno* and Svevo was always to speak highly of him in his letters to Crémieux. Rismondo was invited back to dinner on the following day, but his first impression was one of gloom in the hall, in Svevo's study, throughout the apartment, which was full of dark furniture. The study itself was small and simple enough, however, with its desk and bookshelves overflowing with papers and books, prominent among them the works of Proust.

Svevo's suit was dark, too. With his rather stout build, he looked the typical businessman, save only for his eyes, which searched, enquired, and smiled mischievously. He told Rismondo of his astonishment at having been appreciated earlier in France than in the German-speaking world, with which he felt his literary ties were so much closer, and confessed his eagerness for his works to be published in German.

The table-talk, with Letizia and Tony, was all about children, vitamins and a diet of raw food. Only after the meal, fortified by black coffee and a cigarette, did Svevo return to the subject of literature and warn Rismondo of the dangers attendant on translating his works into German, particularly the danger of fine writing, of a display of artistry. He urged Rismondo to respect the fidelity to truth of his Italian style, however ungainly, to translate it into grammatically correct German, but not to beautify or improve it in any other way.[99]

Svevo was now self-confident and firm about the validity of his style. When Enrico Rocca wrote an article which was critical of his Italian, Svevo wrote him a brief but trenchant letter in which he went so far as to declare: 'I can faithfully say that I believe the discipline of G. Verga was no greater than mine: the difference was that the Italian public were more familiar with certain forms of his dialect.'[100]

There were more visits. On a fine Sunday in April 1928, Saba brought Giacomo Debenedetti, the young Jewish literary critic and academic, to see Svevo. There was the usual crowd of family and visitors at Villa Veneziani, taking tea or playing tennis. From the open window of Svevo's study could be seen the steeply climbing lanes and orchards of the hillside of Servola, while on the other side the sea was sparkling in the sunshine. Svevo joked about his gaffes at the reception which had just been held in Paris in his honour. He had sat next to the writer Jules Romains, whose books he had not read, he had bought some modern paintings which he pretended not to understand. He was contemplating an essay on Kafka, apparently forgetting his long-drawn-out ordeal in preparing the Joyce lecture. He glanced at his visitors, who were both Jews, and said: 'Yes, he was a Jew. Certainly, the Jew's position is not a comfortable one.'[101]

65

'LOVE THYSELF'

Svevo's remark suggests that he was a somewhat reluctant Jew, and echoes one he made, probably a short while before, on a wild wet day of *bora*. Sergio Solmi was then visiting him, and they also had discussed not only Proust and Larbaud but Kafka. 'It is not race, but life, which makes a Jew.' This remark was explicitly addressed to those critics who had seen *La coscienza di Zeno* as the expression of an underlying Jewish scepticism and despair. Contrariwise, Solmi, like others, remarked: 'What surprised one at first impression about Italo Svevo was his immutable youthfulness of heart'; and 'From whatever angle I viewed Svevo, he struck me as an example of a profound human harmony.' Solmi found this harmony all the more astonishing in that it did not negate or ignore that 'sharp and disillusioned science of man' which was so evident in his books but could barely be perceived in the author.[102]

Here lay that difficult self-love which Svevo discussed more openly with two other young friends. One was Cyril Ducker, then not yet twenty, who lived in Blackheath, close to Charlton. Ducker heard of Svevo's literary fame from a German friend of his who had seen Ernst Schwenk's article in *Die Literarische Welt* of 2 September 1927. He now wrote to ask Svevo's advice, as he too wanted to be a writer. Svevo's answer (in English) was: 'Stick to prose, please. It is so very extravagant to use only partly the piece of paper which you were obliged to pay in full.' The *Witz* does not hide Svevo's profound distrust of lyricism, to which he counterposes a superior narcissism:

You have not yet acquired an essential quality: to love yourself. Only after having done so can others follow your example. . . . In order to acquire this women look in a looking-glass. The writer must do the same, and write every evening the history of his day. It is the only way to get a great sincerity—the most important quality, I guess. For the first time since the creation of the world it is You that writes . . .[103]

In 1927 Svevo was asked to contribute to the National Book Festival brochure, and wrote the brief piece on 'La vera battaglia del libro' (The Real Book Campaign), bringing into the open the mutual contempt between the writer and the non-reading public.[104] Here Svevo showed himself to be well aware of the deep social and political reaction that was affecting the Western world. The publishing industry, like every other, was in a state of persistent crisis that reached breaking-point with the 1929 Wall Street crash. Not only the Italian economy, but that of the whole capitalist world, was sick. In nearly every country, to varying degrees, social reaction and economic recession went hand in hand. Capitalism really seemed bent on digging its own grave. Public education, and even literacy, were bound to suffer, especially in Italy, where the Fascists had systematically destroyed the whole educational infrastructure of the Socialist and other parties. The industrialist Ettore Schmitz, in the guise of the writer Italo Svevo, might find it all too easy to say:

The real campaign would consist in the effort to introduce to the reading of books those strong and innocent souls who are still unable to read. They have not yet scorned books, which have been denied them by destiny.

The writer must have known perfectly well that the Italian people had been denied access to books not by any impersonal 'destiny' but by well-defined social and political forces towards which he himself had been all too accommodating, and by economic interests and forces which he actually embodied in his own person, concentrating in his own hands a disproportionate measure of mankind's resources. Svevo's honesty as a writer—that is, in his narrative and dramatic fictions—lies in unmasking his own corrupt conscience and that of other people of his own ilk, men of culture and of business. He contrives to live with this bad conscience and enjoy both the pleasures of privilege and the pleasures of honesty, which is itself a privilege. This is what places him at the centre of modern experience, and this is probably why he was unable to finish 'Corto viaggio sentimentale' at which he had worked so hard in 1925. In 'La Novella del buon vecchio e della bella fanciulla', as in the play *Inferiorità*, he had resolved the relationship between haves and have-nots with the death of the haves. As long as Svevo lived, the governor Ariosto and Mario Equicola continued to walk with their arms around one another's shoulders. As if to emphasize this conjunction, the writer and industrialist Schmitz-Svevo invited all his literary friends to pay him a visit in Trieste but never invited any to repeat the visit.

Svevo's complex personality is illustrated by a young girl's memory of him. I quote from Annetta Pane's reminiscences of thirty years later:

Perhaps he too gazed at me in admiration ... not for my own sake, but simply because I was young and possessed what was for him the supreme good: a whole life still to live. While the adults were chatting, I was doing my homework at an old desk. Italo Svevo, seated on a wooden armchair, his gold chain across his waistcoat, his grey suit slightly worn, his broad, open and irregular forehead surmounted by a few white hairs, his mouth covered by a pair of whiskers which did not quite conceal it and did not conceal either, despite his drooping age, a life-long sensuality, had all the air of the eternal old man, the nice old man of the fairy stories.

Instead of goodies, however, his pockets were bulging with newspapers attesting to his fame, 'which he would not have cared to leave at home, and which he kept intact, not simply taking out the cuttings'. If he heard that a newspaper had just mentioned him by name, he would hunt all round town for it.

Svevo helped the girl with her English, lifted her off her chair and sat her on the desk:

He explained for me the simple rules that were my despair, meanwhile running his hand up and down my leg. 'You are a real *Backfisch*,' he told me, 'what a pity, still a real *Backfisch*. Do you know that that means? It's not English, it's German, and means someone like you, who is no longer a girl but is not yet a woman, neither flesh nor fish.' He sighed, and one could tell that it pained his heart to think that soon, in a few years' time, there would be one more woman in the world for him to miss.[105]

Between March and April of 1927 things at last started to make progress for Svevo. *Il Convegno* published 'La madre' and *La Fiera Letteraria* the Joyce lecture.[106] On 26 March, the actor-producer Nino Meloni wrote to ask for the script of *Terzetto spezzato*, and it was staged in Rome for a week from 1 April by Anton Giulio Bragaglia's Teatro degli Indipendenti. However, Bragaglia had used Svevo's one-acter as a filler, and on the first night the actors misinterpreted the play. To make matters worse, none of the fashionable critics were there, and their inexperienced but opinionated underlings produced a curious critical ragbag.[107] *Il Messaggero* liked the play but not the acting, while *La Tribuna* thought it a poor play well acted. *Il Corriere d'Italia* also slated the play, but *Il Lavoro d'Italia* carried an interesting review by a young man called Enrico Rocca, which led to a brief correspondence between him and Svevo. Rocca thought that irony and drama were not properly fused in Svevo's play, but was struck by its truth to life in showing that 'men's characters remain just the same even when faced by the most extraordinary happening.' The play tempted Rocca to read *La coscienza di Zeno*, on which he wrote a well-sustained article—the first serious piece since those by Montale and Binazzi, with which it bears comparison—published in *Il Lavoro d'Italia* on 26 April.

This article of Rocca's finds the novel a linguistic chamber of horrors and its conclusion 'botched and rushed', but nevertheless proclaims its irresistible appeal and, above all, the appeal of its protagonist:

He hides nothing of himself and even when he hunts for excuses and noble justification for his actions, the truth emerges, clear, repugnant and appalling. And his flashes of self-awareness are too vivid for the reader to give him up simply as a lunatic rather than seeing him as weak, hypocritical, sly, selfish and disingenuous in his own defence.

This is what, for Rocca, explains Zeno's appeal: 'One's impression, distasteful and eloquent, is precisely this: that—be the protagonist of the novel healthy or sick—a Zeno certainly slumbers deep within every one of us.'

No sooner had Svevo read this unlooked-for tribute than he wrote to Rocca offering his friendship. Not having yet gained access to the wider public, he would rejoice over every young person who from time to time issued forth 'from the mass of people to whom I do not belong.' 'I am therefore in Italy the man of many successes.'[108] Rocca's reply was to undertake an organic study of Svevo's three novels, which appeared in October in *La Stirpe*. Three exchanges of letters took place, in which Rocca went so far as to express his filial affection for Svevo and urge him to abandon business and devote himself exclusively to writing. Yet Svevo, at sixty-six, sufficiently well off and with an international reputation behind him, still refused to take the plunge:

It may even be the case that I can no longer write and that even complete freedom would not enable me to do so. And I don't know much about myself: I don't know how much of myself I communicated and how much of me died unheard. I'll ponder on that, that is, I'll try to recall ... I guess that when my work wasn't *half* auto-biographical, it did not reach completion.

Once again Svevo showed his awareness that to write is to keep in contact with *his own* life. We might say that he feels the best he can do is express his sick conscience, being unable to cure himself of it by committing himself to some other goal. A few months later he was to talk to Valerio Jahier of the need to love one's own sickness. And he now had a real physical complaint: very high blood-pressure. As for the correspondence with Rocca, it came to an end after Svevo defended his literary language against the strictures which Rocca had voiced in *La Stirpe*.[109]

Svevo's business interests had evolved slightly. Six years after Gioachino's death, his succession duties were at least agreed at 38,308 lire, and Olga decided to reorganize the firm as a joint-stock company. The new board of directors had its first meeting on 2 April. Dora's husband, Bepi Oberti, was chairman and all the working husbands in the family firm were assigned 5 per cent of the profits. The firm at once registered with the Fascist Union of Industry.[110] The signature of Ettore Schmitz appears in third place in the company's constitution, after that of the seventy-five-year-old Olga and of Bepi, and is followed by those of Marco and Fausta and of the lawyer Camillo Ara.[111]

66

SENILITÀ TWENTY-NINE YEARS ON

In April 1927, Svevo's friend Alberto Tallone at last found a publisher for *Senilità*, the Milanese Giuseppe Morreale. Morreale wrote Svevo a cordial, admiring and breezy letter offering to bring out an edition of 3,000 copies promptly if Svevo were willing to put down, 3,000 lire. Svevo gratefully agreed to the proposal without any haggling and even left it to Morreale to fix the author's royalties should the proceeds of the book actually exceed the cost of publication. He stipulated only that the book should be out in May. Morreale gaily agreed to this, but things took a bit longer. This was partly due to Svevo's last-minute decision to overhaul the punctuation at the proof stage to bring it in line with current usage. It looked as though there were more 'agonies' to come over *Senilità*, but at last, early in July 1927, while Svevo was having a mountain holiday, the book appeared on sale at 9 lire. Morreale spent much effort and money on advertising; but by February of the following year only 800 copies altogether had been moved—rather few. Morreale, however, loyally insisted on having publication rights to Svevo's other works, and agreed to reissue *Una vita* and publish the sequel to *La coscienza di Zeno*, which Svevo was writing in 1928.[112]

While awaiting the appearance of the *Senilità* edition, Svevo was joking as usual about his style to Montale: 'I hope it will be accepted as a linguistic model! I've revised it so many times.' He was convinced the novel would cost Morreale a fortune: 'It's the first time I've ever managed to drive a good bargain.' Montale had discovered a new admirer of Svevo's in Florence, Drusilla Marangoni, the daughter of a Triestine, Dr Tanzi. She possessed signed copies of *Una vita* and *La coscienza di Zeno* dedicated to her father, and now also wanted one of *Senilità*. Svevo remembered with pleasure 'Dr Tanzi, the brilliant student of Paranoia' and the connections between paranoia and genius that he had explored.

'Una burla riuscita' was also about to appear. It had been requested by the new Florentine journal *Solaria*, which was to keep alive what was best in Italian writing under Fascism into the 1930s. It devoted a double issue to Svevo's long story.[113]

Svevo and his correspondence rested in July, awaiting reactions to the new edition of *Senilità*. Michel wrote on the 22nd, however, to say that the French edition of *La coscienza di Zeno* was to appear in September or October, entitled simply *Zeno*, and that the translation of 'Una burla riuscita' was now ready. Svevo still did not really believe in Gallimard-Westermann, as he called him, jocularly alluding to the imaginary publisher in 'Una burla riuscita'.[114]

From the end of July and throughout August 1927, letters of thanks and congratulations poured in to Svevo in response to copies of *Senilità* which he had sent out. Montale intended to read the book another three or four times, making at least fifteen times in all. Fracchia asked Svevo for something to publish in *La Fiera Letteraria*, and got 'Vino generoso'.[115]

In the middle of all this, on 22 August, Svevo made his will. He left Livia the entire contents of their house, including the paintings, and divided his liquid money, shares and bonds, as well as earnings from his writing ('Should my literary works, contrary to all expectation, bring in any income'), assigning 10 per cent to Antonio Fonda ('as some slight token of my gratitude for the affection which he has always shown me'), and the remainder in equal shares to his wife and his daughter.

He charged his son-in-law with the task of seeing to the publication of his works, or actively supervising others who might do so. He expressed his gratitude to the Veneziani firm and its directors 'for the happy and pleasant life

I have spent working for it in brotherly fellowship with the other directors'.
The document ends;

> Please: no rabbis and no priests.
> Please: pierce my heart.*
> And I say no goodbyes because I hope to see everybody this evening.

Reviews of *Senilità* kept on appearing over the next few months. Some
of them were far-reaching and carried weight, like Ferrero's in the October
issue of *Solaria* and Solmi's in *Il Convegno* of 25 November. The latter put
the Italian novel itself on trial for having failed to put down firm roots and
pointed to Svevo as a genuine master from whom a narrative tradition could
spring.

Critical acclaim for Svevo thus continued to grow, but he still had no success
with the Italian public. On 2 September his fame in Germany had a small
beginning with the publication in *Die Literarische Welt* of the translated excerpt
from *La coscienza di Zeno*, 'Die Zigarette', with an accompanying *feuilleton*.
That month Svevo was spending three weeks at Bormio, in the Alps to the
north of Lake Garda. From there he wrote to Crémieux, hoping to speed up
the French edition of *Zeno*, and also pressing Crémieux to come to Trieste: 'I
don't know whether I shall see Paris again. I am struggling with all my might
to stay on this earth which contains Paris.'[116] This was the constant refrain of
Svevo's letters to many of his friends for the next twelve months. Eighteen
months had gone by since the Paris 'discovery' of Italo Svevo, and since then
nothing more had been heard of him in France, and hardly anything anywhere
else outside Italy.

But Gallimard was prompt, and on 7 October Svevo was reading his *Zeno*
in French. On the 11th, Montale wrote him a joyful letter thanking him for the
sumptuous copy he had received, and praising the skilful translation and
abridgement, and announced that he had now been definitively converted to
the third novel.[117] Svevo's faithful friend Césari reported in *Il Popolo di Trieste*
that a *de luxe* edition of 1,004 copies had been made, as well as an ordinary
one.

There was now a stream of reviews in France, while in Italy a Turin professor,
Federico Sternberg, was writing a book on Svevo, with whom he had been in
touch since the year before.[118] On 24 November the contract was signed for the
German *Zeno Cosini* by the Swiss publishers Rhein-Verlag, through Joyce's
good offices. This brought Svevo 'the first tangible recompense for his literary
labours', writes Livia. And she adds: 'A great giver of gifts, he hastened to
present me with the cheque in Marks, accompanied by an affectionate card.'[119]
His affection must have been sweetened by a sense of triumph now that
literature had at last begun to prove its worth in money to the Veneziani circle.

Svevo, who had so wished to see his book read in Germany before he died,
did not live long enough to do so, nor to see Sternberg's volume published. He

---

* Piercing the heart was a common practice in Italy to prevent premature burial.

confided to Montale on 5 January 1928: 'I grow more grey with every day that goes by.' He felt 'I am no longer capable of winning friends with the charm of my wit and joviality.'[120]

67

TRIUMPHAL MARCH

In reality, he had just made his last great conquest. Valerio Jahier was a young Italian living in France, who had left Italy in 1920 in disgust at the social, political and cultural state of the country. Jahier introduced himself as one who had been uprooted in his youth by war to find himself pitched back into a world in which all human values had gone awry. His wife Alice had read *Zeno* first, devouring it feverishly. Her husband followed suit. Enormously impressed, he had obtained a copy of *Senilità*, which he found equally superb, comparing it feelingly to the best of Stendhal. Svevo was moved and overjoyed, and sent him a copy of *Una vita*. Jahier wrote back, declaring his sense of identity with Zeno Cosini, and Svevo sent him the complete *La coscienza of Zeno* in the original Italian. 'Whatever the malicious might say, it is the best thing I've written,' he remarked. And here Svevo took up the Freudian issue, which Jahier had touched on.

Jahier was suffering a living hell because of his own inferiority complex. He had tried psychoanalysis, 'giving it up, of course, at the sixtieth sitting, at the very moment when the doctor said that things were starting to come right'. He intended to resume psychoanalytical treatment, in the faint hope of a cure, but was finding it hard to make ends meet on a risible salary. Svevo recognized that he and Jahier had much in common. He refused to take on any responsibility for his own views on the therapeutic value of psychoanalysis, but recommended that Jahier should try auto-suggestion with the school of Nancy: 'They won't change your innermost self. And do not despair on that account. I would despair if they did so.'

This led Svevo on to what he called a 'superman-type tirade':

And why wish to cure our sickness? Must we really rid humanity of the best it has? I firmly believe that my real success, which has given me peace, consisted in this very conviction. We are a living protest against the ridiculous conception of the superman as it has been foisted upon us (especially upon us Italians).

Svevo here clearly had in mind D'Annunzian and Fascist posturing. He agreed however that there is also bound to be the 'anxious hope of being cured'. That too 'is part of our life', but 'the goal is obscure'. And he continued:

But in the meantime—with some distress—it often happens that we laugh at those who are healthy. The first person who knew about us came before Nietzsche: Schopenhauer, and he considered the observer to be as much a finished product of nature as the fighter. No cure is of any avail. If it means suffering, then that's another matter: But if the suffering can disappear as a result of some success (e.g. the discovery that one is the most human man to have been created) then it's just like the swan in Andersen's story which thought it was an ugly duckling because it had been reared by a duck. What a cure that was when it arrived among the swans!

Quite apart from its paternal and protective concerns, there is much, perhaps all, of Schmitz-Svevo in this letter. The ground of his being is still complex and obscure. But there is, besides, the self-love of which he had written to that other young man, Cyril Ducker. Svevo accepts himself complete with all his contradictions and advises others to do the same, contenting themselves with clear self-knowledge. The penalty which this solution brings with it is that of forgoing independent action consequent upon and responsible to that very self-knowledge or *coscienza* in all its senses. Self-knowledge thus remains impotent, sterile, 'senile' or 'sick', capable at best only of literary self-indictment. The sacrament of literary confession, however, brings with it no heavenly absolution. Svevo is rightly warning Jahier (implicitly) against Zeno's 'cure', since the 'action' by which Zeno thinks he has achieved that cure involves loss of self-knowledge. But self-knowledge without action does not serve either. The only thing that will serve, the only 'cure', is to act according to *coscienza*, in full self-knowledge. This is what is so difficult, and Svevo himself was never really able to live up to his own *coscienza*. How the individual's *coscienza*, his self-knowledge, can come to terms with the actual conditions in which people live together and yet not betray itself—this is a difficulty for us all. It is because Svevo's writings enact this difficulty that he seems still central and relevant.

Jahier did not answer this letter until a month later, and when he did so, on 25 January 1928, he returned to the literary applications of psychoanalysis. His long letter—as perceptive as his previous ones—voiced his misgivings about a dogmatic and reductive or simplistic appropriation of literature by psychoanalysis. This drew a long letter back from Svevo, who defended his own literary use of Freudian theory, comparing it to the use that had been made of Darwin and Nietzsche, as something which certainly need not compromise the openness, freedom and integrity of art. He also mentioned to Jahier that he felt *La coscienza di Zeno* was impaired by his lack of direct experience of the Freudian therapy. Jahier, who did have this experience, was able to reassure Svevo that the novel's presentation was convincing, and felt that his psychoanalyst would approve of its Freudian content.[121]

By this time an opportunity had come Svevo's way to see Jahier, and his other friends, in Paris. He made the opportunity by getting himself invited by Crémieux as guest of honour to a PEN Club dinner. He had not heard from his literary friends in Paris for nine months, as they never answered his letters. Nor could he go to see them himself, now that he no longer visited London.

So, on 19 December 1927, his sixty-sixth birthday, he sent as a Christmas present to Marie-Anne Comnène some autographs by French musicians and writers (one of them written by Victor Hugo while he was eating sardines in Nantes). He pointedly wrote to Comnène in French. She was touched, and showed it by assuring Svevo that *Zeno* had been a great success with both critics and public in France, and by inviting him as guest of honour to a magnificent reception in Paris.[122]

Svevo was all agog. He had written to Montale not long before: 'I was thinking of hopping over to Paris too, but I wanted to be met by a band at the station.' He hinted that he would enjoy being lionized in Florence also, which Montale arranged for him.[123] So, before his conquest of Paris, he set out in February 1928 upon his conquest of Florence. His friends there, led by Montale and Marangoni, welcomed him jubilantly. Livia says they were Drusilla's guests and that 'on the door of the apartment we found a notice saying "Svevo's Club" '. There Svevo met the writers and critics Loria, Vittorini, Franchi and Bonsanti. He was invited to the famous Giubbe Rosse literary café which, wrote Montale, 'in twenty years witnessed the passage of at least half of the best and the worst in Italian literature' and of which Svevo remained 'right up to today the most exceptional visitor'. He amazed his Florentine friends with the penetration of his remarks and the breadth of his knowledge not only about the great European novelists up to Kafka, but also about the recent Italian writers whose names cropped up from time to time in his letters also: Tozzi, Pea, Boine, Comisso, Stuparich, to name a few at random. He even discussed with Bonaventura Tecchi, director of the Gabinetto Vieusseux library in Florence, the German Romantic aesthetic theorist Wackenroder—whom he had presumably read in his long-past youth. (Ferrero too had remarked that Svevo 'knew every literature in the world', which he had studied in solitude 'out of a crazy love of letters amid the amazement and sarcasm of an entire city'.)[124]

So it was by Svevo's own wish that his friendly, informal triumph in Italy's traditional literary capital should precede the rather more stilted Paris affair. The former also conveniently coincided with the publication of 'Una burla riuscita' in *Solaria*. The Florence journey in February was taxing enough, and on 2 March Svevo was on the move again. Valerio Jahier had already joyfully begged to have his company for an evening. Svevo told him that for the last three years he had fasted for nineteen hours of each day and did not dine. He was not wholly serious, but they agreed to meet for lunch at a restaurant on Easter Day, 11 March. Svevo recognized the Jahiers without ever having seen either of them before. Alice remembered Svevo as being all 'ensoleillé', radiant. The conversation was mostly in Italian (no doubt Svevo badly needed to rest his French). When Valerio confirmed that he had undergone sixty psychoanalytical sittings, Svevo looked at him with an earnest smile and exclaimed: 'And you're still alive?' Only when Valerio took his life more than ten years later did Alice understand why Svevo had tried to warn him against psychoanalysis. Valerio asked Svevo how he had managed to abstain from writing for so many years, and Svevo smiled again, wryly and uncomfortably, and replied: 'I talked a great deal.' After their meeting in Paris, relations between Svevo and Jahier remained warm, but the correspondence petered out: both men had health problems, and they had little prospect of meeting again.[125]

The Crémieuxs gave a private party for Svevo and it was also Marie-Anne who had organized the PEN Club dinner for the following Wednesday, 14 March, and had personally addressed one hundred invitations. Svevo brought her Parma violets and a Chinese flower-pattern dish.[126]

The Schmitzes were staying in great style at the Savoy Hôtel at the Tuileries. They visited the apartment of Svevo's translator, Paul-Henri Michel, with whom they established a cordial relationship. Svevo urged Michel, as he had urged the Jahiers, the Crémieuxs, and many others, to visit him in Trieste, as he himself felt he would not be able to come to Paris again. He particularly admired Michel's well cared-for library. They agreed upon a translation of *Senilità*.[127]

The great day arrived. The Russian writers Ehrenburg and Babel and the Romanian Pillat were also guests of honour. The guests included Shaw, Julien Benda, Michel, Prezzolini, James and Nora Joyce, Ivan Goll, MacOrlan, Martin Maurice, Giraudoux. Gide and Valéry were absent. Larbaud was also away from Paris. Giovanni Comisso was the only Italian author present apart from Svevo. The latter, as principal guest, was seated between the two presidents, Benjamin Crémieux and Jules Romains. He was unable to return the latter's compliments, not having read any of his books.

Goll later described Svevo as an 'old great-uncle' surrounded by grand-nephews who had never known him very well but hoped to inherit something. Ehrenburg was still more sarcastic about the occasion: he recollected Jules Romains introducing the guests of honour, not having read their works but hinting that they must be of value if they had been translated into French; he described the writers paying court to the publishers and the girls gazing 'devo-tedly' at Joyce. Everyone invited everyone else to his home, the food resembled the sort you got at railway stations, while the scene as a whole embodied to perfection 'the elect gatherings of aesthetes in M. Maurois's Utopian Kingdom'. Against this backdrop he projects a close-up of Italo Svevo:

That is where I met Italo Svevo. I saw a little flame of mischief in his eyes. Despite the poor food and his international reputation, Svevo was making fun of that choice idyll. When I saw that flame I realized that I was not looking at an aesthete but a man who was in love with life, and that, despite the praises of Larbaud, he was not a lover of rare books but an authentic man, a living man. He smoked one cigarette after another. Then I remembered *Zeno*, and smiled involuntarily. Yes, this man could make fun of things with kindness.

Ehrenburg concluded with the remark that 'Such meetings help one to live a little and hold up one's bored pen in one's hand.'

Svevo was having double fun. He was unfeignedly enjoying his fame and more quizzically enjoying the 'comedy' which everyone present, himself included, was acting with varying degrees of competence. He contributed to the entertainment with an obligatory last cigarette, or several. Prezzolini found him looking younger than on his last visit to Paris: 'Fortune and success have done him good.' His 'cheerful and charming joviality' and his 'childlike and enchanting sincerity' were a delight to all, 'as when you read in the newspapers that the first prize in a lottery has gone to a family of poor and honest workers'.

Comisso revealed that, like the other ordinary guests, he had paid twenty-five francs for the dinner. He found this too cheap, having discovered that, far from being 'magical figures exceptional in appearance', the literary banqueters were 'all free-and-easy people who, when they meet, become intensely engrossed in exchanging addresses and making appointments'. Marie-Anne Comnène was the life and soul of the party, speaking Italian with a Roman accent (though she was actually a Corsican, descended from the Byzantine Imperial family). Livia had to help out Ettore when the French talk got too fast, and he eventually turned to listen to Comisso's familiar lilting Venetian instead. Of the dinner itself, Comisso remembered that it included a salad with bananas and walnuts (not an Italian line), and that he, Livia and the Joyces talked about the fish dishes of the Adriatic. Joyce also mentioned that he was immortalizing Livia's long hair in *Finnegans Wake*. She had now had it cut ('my husband was against it'). They went into the library for coffee and there was a great clamour of voices and laughter at a Franco-Chinese woman who 'was waiting to get rich through her novels so as to ride on elephant-back, as she detested the *metro* and the taxis'.[128]

Life had now given Svevo all, or nearly all, he desired. He had proved himself, especially to the Veneziani circle and to his fellow Triestines in general. On his way home from Paris he stopped at Zurich from 15 to 17 March—whether on medical or publishing or other business, is not known. Comnène wrote affectionately to him of his simplicity and sincerity, and he also found a letter from Joyce giving him the names of two English-language publishers to whom he had praised *La coscienza di Zeno*. In gratitude for all Joyce's help, Svevo appropriately sent him Veruda's splendid portrait of Livia with her hair hanging full length.[129]

After Zurich, the Schmitzes stopped in Milan. Among their friends there they saw Ferrarin. It was the first day of spring (presumably 21 March), yet snowing. Underneath his ever-present irony, Svevo was clearly cock-a-hoop about the honour bestowed on him in Paris, and Ferrarin thought he looked ten years younger than when he had last seen him about a year before. Svevo told him that he was bursting with ambition and craving to be praised. This is how Ferrarin remembered one of his outpourings:

I've been to Paris, where there are so many interesting things, and all I could see was Italo Svevo: Italo Svevo amid the marvels of the Louvre; Italo Svevo on the stage of the fifty Paris theatres, Italo Svevo at the Elysées, Italo Svevo at Versailles, Italo Svevo everywhere. The Ville Lumière with everyone and everything in it seemed to exist solely as a function of my glory.

He had gone all round the French capital, from one editorial office to another, from one literary circle to another, so as to meet and thank the critics and writers who had discussed his work. He entertained his friends in Milan not only with the stories of his experiences but also with his own great bursts of laughter as he recalled them. One story involved a journalist whose office hours were 3.00 to 4.00 p.m. on Mondays only. There was another about 'a fat literary Frenchwoman who, in praying for the recuperation of the American composer Antheil, made a slip in appealing to the *Vierge Marie*' which Svevo thought very Freudian.[130]

68

THE OLD, OLD MAN

Reinvigorated by his ego-trip in Paris, Svevo took up his pen again. The date 4 April 1928 appears at the head of 'Le confessioni del vegliardo', the first of a sequence of chapters which resume the autobiography of Zeno Cosini, the others being 'Umbertino', 'Il mio ozio' (My Life of Leisure), and 'Un contratto' (A Contract), which form the bulk of the sequel to *La coscienza di Zeno*.[131] The date is corroborated by 'Il vecchione' (The Old, Old Man),[132] which appears to be a reworking of the opening of the projected novel and starts with the words: 'It was in April this year that it happened . . .'. Svevo had written a score of pages by 16 May and on 19 August was already speaking of 'several chapters'. But he thought they needed revising, because 'There's a certain false note creeping in.' In May he had written to Crémieux:

after some not so good weeks I'm feeling so well that, on a sudden decision, I've started on another novel, *Il Vecchione*, a continuation of *Zeno*. I've written a score of pages and I'm having a whale of a time. It won't matter if I don't get to finish it. I'll at least have had one more good laugh in my life.[133]

Svevo was still laughing his Schopenhauerian laugh of one who looks on without any illusions at the pointless make-believe or charade of life. Zeno, and Svevo with him, now in his old age, feels more alone, more powerless than ever in the face of others, and of death, the unmentioned but ever-present shadow. His only prop and defence is to communicate with and honour his own devious *coscienza* once again by writing his confessions and telling himself 'the things I don't usually say'.[134] The one last hope, the one remaining 'measure of hygiene' amid the negativity of the real world, is writing, that unreliable beacon, its subtly untruthful redress, compromised by the self-indulgence and self-deception of old age as of earlier ages.

Though the approach does not seem to be deliberately sociological, many hard and specific features of his society as it was then developing are precisely captured: one example is the 'managerial revolution' brought off by the younger Olivi in 'Un contratto' at the expense of the old *rentier* Zeno. Zeno is now more continuously subject to the unpredictable and unexpected jolts of external, objective time: of history, of the clash of generations, of developments in economics and in *mores*, of material change itself (the automobile replaces the carriage and plays a significant role). Old age, attended by impotence in its most physical senses and by the imminence of death, almost fortuitously presents itself as an apt metaphor for the reality of Italy and Europe in the twenties—a period which the Fascists were not alone in seeking to characterize under the label of *giovinezza*—'youthfulness'. Zeno's *vecchiaia* is different, then, from the *senilità* made up of self-delusion and the fear of living which Svevo had adopted in his thirties as a metaphor for the *fin de siècle* lower middle class.

On 26 April *Il Popolo di Trieste* (therefore, one presumes, Svevo's old friend Césari), reviewed the *Solaria* issue devoted to 'Una burla riuscita', and also reported that Svevo was working on a play, evidently the one we know as *La rigenerazione*.[135] This has in common with the sequel to *La coscienza di Zeno* its central motif of the rejuvenation operation, as well as other material and characters. In theatrical technique, it is Svevo's boldest play—that is, not particularly bold, as Svevo always kept much closer to the naturalist mode as a playwright than he did as a writer of narrative. It is one of Svevo's most successful plays, resolving its painful subject-matter into high farce. It is a matter of guesswork that the composition of *La rigenerazione* overlapped in time that of Svevo's most pitiless work, 'La Novella del buon vecchio e della bella fanciulla'.[136] He never mentioned this story in his letters, yet it was completed, ending with the elderly protagonist's death. Perhaps Svevo intended it to be his farewell from beyond the grave.

He was still busy tending his fame and the dissemination of his writings. On 23 May Morreale wrote to say that at the Milan book fair he had sold forty copies of *Senilità* in one day. In June and July Svevo received offers for Hungarian and English translations and editions. He was also busy re-drafting the *Profilo autobiografico*, of which Césari had drawn up the first outline and which expresses two of Svevo's complexes—that of his 'missed' literary vocation and that of his mixed national and international allegiances. Césari was also working like a slave collecting reviews of Svevo's works for republication. The material for this amounted to no less than 95 folders.[137]

In May Svevo also wrote a review of Crémieux's masterly *Panorama de la littérature italienne contemporaine*. This appeared under the title 'Mezzo secolo di letteratura italiana' (Half a Century of Italian Literature) in *Il Popolo di*

Trieste on the 20th.[138] It was the best way of repaying Crémieux for the part he had played in Svevo's literary fortunes. He criticized Crémieux only for having omitted all mention of Benco. At the same time he was fending off requests from *Il Convegno*, *La Fiera Letteraria* and *Solaria* for an article on Kafka.

The review did elicit a couple of letters from Crémieux, half-promising to take up Svevo's invitation to visit Trieste, but after several further letters from Svevo had been left unanswered, one at last came back from Comnène to say that they had decided to visit her family in Corsica instead. Svevo was deeply hurt and felt rejected:

Dear kind friend. I duly received your dear letter of 26 July and was so highly honoured at the news it contained that I have really had to accustom myself to your decision before writing to you. Do not think you neglected us in Paris. We received from you and your husband all we could reasonably have expected and certainly more than we deserved. We are no longer foreigners and we know your way of life. In fact I completed my studies of the dogs in Paris with the discovery that the reason why they so resented being looked at is that they are not used to it. In Paris no one has time to bother them . . .

After this, the tone becomes more good-natured, but the letter as a whole recalls Svevo's jealous scenes when Livia was at Salsomaggiore. That he should have brooded over this letter for two or three weeks shows his petulant old age still craving for special attention, approval, love.[139]

It was a similar story with the young writer Comisso, whom Svevo had taken a liking to at the PEN Club dinner, inviting him to lunch at the expensive Poccardi on the following day. Comisso did answer all Svevo's letters, but only to duck his invitations to visit him in Trieste or to meet elsewhere as opportunity arose. Finally Svevo ran Comisso to ground at Vittorio Veneto in August, on his way to the mountain resort of Bormio.

Comisso described how 'on the hot afternoon of the 24th I heard someone at the entrance of the house where I was living ask leave to enter and then converse with the lady of the house: "I haven't been to Vittorio Veneto for forty years . . . !"' Comisso recognized Svevo's husky voice and rushed to meet him. The two men walked over to the hotel where the Schmitzes had lunched, to find Livia and their grandson Paolo, 'amid the scent of roses and the green shimmer of the hills round about'. Though worn out by the long drive from Trieste, Svevo smoked and chatted about Joyce and urged Comisso to read Kafka. He said he was considering retiring from business by the end of the year, devoting all his time to writing, and completing a large work, *Il vecchione*. Comisso said Italy needed 'a lot of "Svevo" as a dam against the D'Annunzian onslaught'. They wanted to send some postcards to their friends—Montale, Angioletti, the Crémieuxs—but the shop was closed. Svevo said he collected every article written about him because 'it was part of his doctor's prescription'. Livia called to him, and he dragged himself off reluctantly to the car to resume the journey to Bormio.[140]

69

THE LAST CIGARETTE

Svevo was facing the ten-hour drive to Bormio in the hope that he would again find some relief there from the very high blood pressure that was troubling him. The thought of approaching death obsessed him. Livia recalled:

He often expressed his grief to me too: 'I'll soon have to leave you', so insistently that, in alarm, I had begged him to stop. He was no longer the man he once was, cheerful and full of witticisms: something in him seemed to have run down after his initial elation, as if the great flame of success had burnt up part of his life's strength. Instead of sleeping soundly, he had become restless. He did not see any doctors, which he had always avoided doing, and took no medicines (he had never managed to keep to his bed for longer than forty-eight hours), yet he brooded constantly about illness and death. He monitored his body very closely. Sometimes he would raise his right arm, fist uppermost, as if to ward off an invisible foe, and pant: 'I can feel it coming, I can feel it coming!' And if I asked him: 'What?', he would reply: 'The stroke.'[141]

Though he had given up evening meals, he was still smoking thirty or forty cigarettes a day and would clear his lungs by going on long walks among the pines and horse-chestnuts of the Carso. He usually spent the summer in Villa Letizia, on the Banne side of Opicina. He and Livia had a room on the first floor, but had their meals with their daughter's family. Letizia had furnished the dining-room in a mixture of seventeenth-century Italian and rustic styles, with brasses and wood-reliefs and an old spinet.[142]

At Bormio, fame still brought him consolation: someone, hearing that the Schmitzes were from Trieste, asked whether they knew Italo Svevo.[143] Svevo was actually writing while in Bormio. He was going over *Il vecchione* and probably drafting the nearly completed story 'La morte' (Death),[144] which reaches its climax on a stark note: 'His death was the very thing he had not wanted—a thing of terror.' It is the story of the stroke which Svevo so feared for himself. In 'La Novella del buon vecchio e della bella fanciulla' also, it is a stroke which comes in the last sentence to leave the protagonist symbolically 'dead and stiff with the pen, over which had passed his last breath, in his mouth', and it is possible that Svevo completed the story during his stay in Bormio. 'La morte' goes beyond the death of the protagonist to show him posthumously converted, in his widow's mind, to her religion. His atheistic scientism had collapsed in panic at the moment of death, when he suddenly confessed to a lifetime of guilt. This is the ultimate defeat of self-betrayal, which his widow interprets as a reaching towards faith. Perhaps Svevo wrote this story so as to fortify himself in advance against such weakness.

His grandson Paolo diverted him somewhat from these gloomy preoccupations. 'Ciocci', as he was familiarly called, was an 'adorable little frog' in the swimming-pool, and a cheeky lad. Hearing Svevo complain about his health once or twice, he dubbed him the 'prince of pains' and, when Svevo called for Livia's sympathy by exclaiming 'Poor Schmitz!' (as Zeno exclaims 'Poor Cosini!'), answered 'Lucky Schmitz!' But Ettore's blood-pressure had risen by another 15 mm.[145] While he was getting dressed in the room next to hers, Livia heard him exclaim suddenly: 'After all, I can die because I've been pretty happy.'[146]

When Livia called her husband for their departure on their last morning in Bormio, he was at work on 'La morte'.[147] It was 8 o'clock on 11 September, and the rain was pouring down. That day they drove as far as Trent, where they spent the night. The next day they continued as far as Treviso, where they stopped for lunch. The rain had grown heavier, but the driver assured Livia that it was quite safe to go on. Svevo was not afraid of car travel, only of taxis. He was always terrified of dying and always told the driver, whenever he entered a taxi, to drive slowly, because he did not know who his passenger was—meaning, of course, himself, even if he was accompanied by Saba or anyone else.[148]

Young Paolo glanced at the road map and suddenly cried out: 'Look, granny, this map ends at Motta di Livenza.' That was just where the car, having crossed the second bridge over the Livenza, skidded and swerved into a tree. All Livia heard was Ettore shouting at the driver: 'Giovanni, what are you doing?' When she came to she had fractured her forehead, and saw Paolo's face masked in blood, while 'Ettore, in the bottom of the car, was moaning: "My leg! My leg!"' The driver, who was unhurt, pulled Ettore out and sat him up on the road in the rain, and then helped out Livia, who quickly swabbed off Paolo's face with antiseptic. Two passing cars took them to the hospital in Motta, where, to Livia's surprise, the doctor dealt with Ettore first as the most seriously injured, not on account of his leg but because of the shock to his heart.

After 'a night of hell', with all three casualties in the same ward, Letizia and Tony, with Aurelio Finzi, Ettore's doctor nephew, turned up before daybreak. Ettore was already sinking:

Seeing Letizia weep, he looked at her thoughtfully and said gently: 'Don't weep, Letizia; there's nothing to dying.' His tongue was already swollen and, seeing his nephew light a cigarette, he made a gesture to have one. Aurelio refused to give him one. Then he said, with a voice already failing: 'It really would have been the last cigarette.'

Livia relates that someone offered to call a priest:

Although I was very religious, I replied that I did not think it was appropriate. He heard me and saw my hands joined in prayer. I asked him with trepidation: 'Ettore, do you want to pray?' 'When you haven't prayed all your life it's no good at the last moment,' he murmured in a voice that was already veiled. After that he said nothing else. Two hours later he had passed away. It was half past two on Thursday 13 September 1928.[149]

So Svevo did not weaken and betray himself in his last hours, as 'La morte' suggests he feared he might. For once, his literary conscience had preceded the event and guided his behaviour.

There are slightly differing accounts of his last words and deeds. Hearsay had it that he tried to cheer up Livia by joking about the bandages round her head.[150] Saba says Svevo remarked that dying was easier than writing a novel.[151] Césari a year later assured his readers that Svevo did have a puff or two of that last cigarette.[152]

Svevo's injuries might not have proved fatal if he had been physically fitter. The hospital records show confusion and puzzlement in the diagnoses made of his condition, and do not say what treatment he received. He was initially admitted with a straightforward 'fracture of the left femur', then was found to have a cranial contusion, with associated symptoms. Finally he died of uraemia and heart failure.[153]

'A life that does not look splendid but was adorned with so many fortunate affections that I would live it over again,' was how Svevo had summed it up a year earlier;[154] Saba, in the epigraph he wrote for Svevo, was to agree, almost with envy:

Fortune
was to him as far as it can be to any man
favourable
...   .
From his own consciousness and that of his race
from all that unsuspectingly surrounded him
he drew
the matter for three novels and one
gentle fable-blossomed
tale.
He lived
his last years' thousand and one days
as in a dream a sunset
of gold.[155]

Svevo was buried at four o'clock in the afternoon of 18 September in the Catholic cemetery of Sant'Anna in Trieste. Only his family and the firm's employees attended; but there was a wreath from the Mayor, Senator Pitacco.[156] He was laid to rest in the Veneziani family chapel built after the fashion of a little temple with a Florentine mosaic reproduction of the Sassoferrato Madonna. Underneath the latter is inscribed Saba's commemoration, with a small bas-relief by the sculptor Mayer, showing Svevo frowning slightly in thought.[157] Svevo, a nominal Catholic, could not have been buried in consecrated ground without benefit of clergy—a final, but fitting, irony for this atheist Jew.

Many years later Fulvio Anzellotti was allotted the task of rearranging the family coffins and bones:

My grandmother Olga* was in a zinc box with a glass window, through which one could see her face, green as on the last day of her life.

Ettore was also well-preserved. Amid the bustle his hand came into view, his coffin had somehow come open. Livia was there: 'Ettore, bless you, how you whiff,' she said lovingly in Triestine, with a last serene and affectionate rebuke for his gaucheness.[158]

70

AFTERLIFE

After the accident, Livia made a slow recovery. She received letters of condolence from the Crémieuxs, who had refused to take seriously Svevo's continual harping on his age, failing health and approaching death, who had ignored his repeated invitations to come to see him in Trieste, and had neglected him. 'Everthing has been unfair in Svevo's life,' exclaimed Benjamin, and he admitted: 'I feel nothing but remorse. I knew well enough, I could feel well enough, that what he needed more than celebrity was friendship . . .'. Marie-Anne, besides a briefer personal letter to Livia, had a 'last letter' to her dead friend published in the September issue of *Les Nouvelles Littéraires*. This was even longer and more emotional than her husband's and no less full of regret for the days and hours which they had denied to Svevo, who so needed them. Comnène's emotionalism does not detract from her tribute to the 'smiling tragedy' of Svevo's writings and to his 'constant terror of not being truthful enough and of making literature'.

Dear Italo Svevo, you who had extinguished all vanity, pretended to be vain about the success which a belated justice had brought you, when you mischievously enjoyed confounding those who had not understood who you were.[159]

Joyce wrote in more sober and businesslike fashion about practical matters to do with the publication of Svevo's works and the extension of his fame.[160] He had at first thought that Svevo's death was suicide, as was the case with so many Jews.[161] Valerio Jahier wrote to tell Livia that he felt as if he had lost his father, and Stuparich, still a young man, could hardly take in the loss of the old man who had made him feel so young. Michel was deeply distressed. Many, many others wrote to Livia and shared her grief.[162]

* Olga died in 1936.

On 26 January 1929 Pasini delivered a commemorative speech on Svevo to the Lega Nazionale and on 19 March Sternberg lectured on his works to the Società di Minerva. Sternberg had published a critical work on Svevo just after his death. Svevo had seen the manuscript before publication and thought it too laudatory.[163]

Eugenio Montale's farewell appeared in *La Fiera Letteraria* of 23 September 1928, where he stressed the 'examination of conscience' with which Svevo's works faced the reader.[164] Bobi Bazlen told Montale that he would not buy that issue of *La Fiera*:

I'm afraid your article might lend itself too much to misinterpretation and give rise to the legend of a bourgeois Svevo, intelligent, cultured, profound, a good critic, psychologist, a clairvoyant of life, etc ... All he had was genius: no more. Apart from that he was stupid, selfish, opportunistic, gauche, calculating, tactless. All he had was genius, and this is what makes his memory most fascinating to me.[165]

For me, at least, this letter sounds strangely like the posthumous conscience of Italo Svevo, that part of him which mocks itself, probes and arraigns itself: that part of him which subsists in his writings and not in any other of his life's actions. Montale faced Bazlen's charges in his brief 'Leggenda e verità di Svevo' (The Real and Legendary Svevo),[166] which appeared among thirty-odd other testimonials by friends, writers and critics in the March–April 1929 issue of *Solaria. Il Convegno* also made a Svevo tribute out of its double issue of January–February 1929.

Svevo was now a national and international figure. In 1931 his family presented Trieste with a bronze bust of the writer by his fellow-Triestine Giovanni Mayer. Svevo's home town, which had been the first and last and most persistent opponent of his fame, honoured him with a public ceremony for the unveiling in the Giardino Pubblico. This is in the area where he grew up, and had been the setting for a memorable scene between Zeno Cosini and Carla Gerco in the novel. On that splendid sunny Sunday, 26 April, all of cultured and official Trieste was present. Césari unveiled the bust and delivered the inaugural speech.[167]

But Svevo's international fame still faced stumbling-blocks and resistance. Editions of Svevo's unknown or no longer available works were very slow in coming; some of them did not appear until the 1950s or 1960s. Svevo criticism necessarily marched in step with the publication of his works: fairly active until 1931, it gradually dwindled almost to vanishing point during the Second World War, to pick up again slowly from 1950.[168] Now, more than half a century after the publication of *La coscienza di Zeno*, Svevo commands attention—by reason of his moral authority, his artistic rigour, his irresistible humour—as an inescapable part of Western culture. He is also gaining a growing readership in Italy and abroad, especially in the United States.

From the beginning, two main tendencies have emerged in talking about Svevo, amid the welter of critical observations and interpretation. Each of these tendencies enthrones one of the two indivisible aspects of his work, the comic and the tragic, which are fused in irony. One line starts with Crémieux (behind whom one senses the silent presence of Joyce) and Rossi, who see Zeno as a bourgeois Triestine Chaplin. Evolving through the agency of Renato Poggioli, especially in the English-speaking world, this interpretation presents Svevo as the redeeming champion of the bourgeois individual. Amid private and public catastrophes, guilt and failure, the Svevian hero still remains a beacon of enduring goodwill and vital good humour, in good faith or in blithe bad faith, and achieves a mature and humane sociability. In Latin countries the tendency is rather to see in Svevo an unrelenting judge of himself and the world, a suffering witness to a problematic reality. This Svevo shows human relationships to be painful or non-existent and men to be petty-minded and obtusely cynical. He exposes a dialectical failure of individual and society, over which his own smile can cast no more than a flimsy veil.

Such a coarse distinction cannot, and does not seek to, do even rough justice to Svevo criticism and interpretation. Many students of Svevo have avoided slipping into either of these sharply differentiated alternatives. To pose these alternatives is however to indicate something central and complex which necessarily belongs to the man before it belongs to the work—that is, his living in clear consciousness against conscience. The divided will is the author's before it can inform a fictional character. The tragic burlesque of his books is his own love-hate for the bourgeoisie whose life he lived.

The society to which he remained always so restlessly yet invincibly attached sent two of his grandsons to their unknown end in Russia in 1943 and made the third, Sergio, pay with his life two years later for the liberation of his city.[169] Trieste had been incorporated into the Third Reich and was equipped with an extermination camp at the Risiera di San Sabba, in which Svevo's Jewish nephew and niece perished. Livia and Letizia, both faithful Catholics, were classed under the race laws as Jews. Faced by the demand for a huge bribe to reclassify them, they sought refuge in the village of Arcade, near Treviso, taking with them all Svevo's writings and the precious Veruda paintings. History, which blotted out his blood, preserved Svevo's works. If that chestful of books and papers had stayed in Trieste, much of what he wrote would have been lost in the air-raid of 20 February 1945, with the destruction of Gioachino and Olga's factory and their villa, which contained the Schmitzes' apartment and Svevo's study and library.

ABBREVIATED SOURCES

The critical edition of Svevo's works, now beginning to appear, has not been used. References indicating only volume and page number, without title, are to the edition of Svevo's *Opera omnia* by Bruno Maier, published by Dall'Oglio, Milan, as follows:

    I *Epistolario*, 1966

    II *Romanzi*, 1969

    III *Racconti, saggi e pagine sparse*, 1968

    IV *Commedie*, 1969

    V *Lettere a Svevo. Diario di Elio Schmitz*, 1973

    VI *Carteggio con James Joyce, Valéry Larbaud, Benjamin Crémieux, Marie-Anne Comnène, Eugenio Montale, Valerio Jahier*, 1978

References to VMM are to Livia Veneziani Svevo's *Vita di mio marito* (text by Lina Galli). This was first published in Trieste in 1950, but the edition referred to is the splendid second edition of 1958, enlarged and furnished with notes, indices, etc. by Anita Pittoni. Pittoni's invaluable contributions were omitted from the third edition (Milan, 1966).

The following works have also been frequently referred to for information on Svevo's life and the Triestine milieu:

ANZELLOTTI, FULVIO *Il segreto di Svevo*, Pordenone, 1985.

BENCO, SILVIO 'Italo Svevo', *Pegaso*, I (Jan. 1929), 48–57; repr. *Umana* (Trieste), 20 (May–Sept. 1971), 64–8.

—— 'Prefazione' to 2nd ed. of *La coscienza di Zeno*, Milan, 1930; also in the Dall'Oglio eds. of the novel from 1938. The 1962 ed. has been used here.

COCEANI, BRUNO AND PAGNINI, CESARE *Trieste della 'Belle Epoque'*, Trieste, 1971.

Critica Sociale Milan, fortnightly from 1891.

ELLMANN, RICHARD *James Joyce* 3rd ed., Oxford, 1982.

FONDA SAVIO, LETIZIA SVEVO, AND ANTONIO *Ricordi di James Joyce e Italo Svevo*, private pub., Trieste, no date.

MOLONEY, BRIAN 'Italo Svevo e *L'Indipendente*: sei articoli sconosciuti', *Lettere Italiane*, XXV, 4 (1973), 536–56.

—— 'Londra dopo la guerra: five unknown articles by Italo Svevo', *Italian Studies*, XXXI (1976), 59–81.

PIEMONTESE, GIUSEPPE *Il movimento operaio a Trieste. Dalle origini alla fine della guerra mondiale*, Udine, 1961; repr. Rome, 1974. The 1st ed. is used here.

SABA, UMBERTO *Opere di Umberto Saba*, (ed. Linuccia Saba, Milan), Vol. I: *Prose*, 1964.

SLATAPER, SCIPIO *Scritti politici* (ed. G. Stuparich, Rome, 1925). The 2nd ed. (Milan, 1954) is used here.

Solaria Svevo obituary issue: IV, 3–4 (Mar.–Apr. 1929).

TAMARO, ATTILIO *Storia di Trieste*, 2 vols., Rome, 1924; 2nd ed., 1930; revised ed. entitled *Trieste, storia di una città e di una fede*, Milan, 1946. Unless otherwise indicated, the edition used here is the most recent, *Storia di Trieste*, further revised (Trieste, 1976).

NOTES

PART I
The elusive self

1 'Soggiorno londinese', III.685–98.
2 III.772–3.
3 R. Graff, 'L'uomo dalla doppia personalità. Un'introduzione per chiudere', *La Fiera Letteraria*, 11 Oct. 1953.
4 D. Salvi, 'Ricordi di giornalismo triestino nelle *Opere* di Italo Svevo', *La Patria*, 25 Nov. 1954.
5 III.818.
6 II.431.
7 III.136.
8 III.137.
9 III.799–810.
10 I.860.
11 I.816, 818.

PART II
Splits: to 1878

1 I. Zoller, *La comunità israelitica di Trieste. Studio di demografia storica* (Ferrara, 1924; repr. from *Metron—Rivista internazionale di statistica*, III), 537; G. Césari, *Sessant'anni di vita italiana 1869–1929. Memorie della Società Operaia Triestina* (Trieste, 1929), 80.
2 II.947–50.
3 III.85.
4 R. Bazlen, *Note senza testo* (Milan, 1970), 139.
5 I. Burton, *The Life of Captain Sir Richard Burton* (London, 1893), II.16.
6 Ibid. 5.
7 Ibid.
8 Quoted in A. Spaini, *Autoritratto triestino* (Milan, 1963), 260–1.
9 Ibid. 33–4; and cf. 62–6.
10 L. Veronese, *Vicende e figure dell'irredentismo giuliano* (Trieste, 1938), 15–24.
11 See files on K.u.k. Polizei, Stadthälterei, Archivio di Stato, Trieste.
12 Césari, *Società Operaia Triestina*, 19–29.
13 A. Tamaro, *Storia di Trieste* (Trieste, 4th ed., 1976), II.383, 404.
14 Cf. Spaini, op. cit. 103; for a critique of Irredentism in Trieste, see G. Negrelli, *Al di qua del mito. Diritto storico e difesa nazionale nell'autonomismo della Trieste Absburgica* (Udine, 1978).
15 III.799.
16 A. Fonda Savio, 'Ettore Schmitz (in arte Italo Svevo) nella vita di ogni giorno', in

Ricordi di James Joyce e Italo Svevo (Trieste, n.d., private publication by Letizia and Antonio Fonda Savio), 25.

17 V.195, 212.
18 I.867.
19 V.212.
20 I.552; V.195.
21 V.230.
22 V.212.
23 Ibid.
24 V.213.
25 V.196.
26 Ibid.
27 VMM.15; V.214.
28 VMM.15.
29 V.196–7.
30 V.195.
31 V.197–8.
32 III.492.
33 V.202.
34 V.203.
35 V.199–200.
36 V.198.
37 V.201.
38 V.202–3.
39 V.203.
40 VMM.16.
41 III.799.
42 Cf. III.799; V.203–5, 241; and E. Ghidetti, *Italo Svevo — La coscienza di un borghese triestino* (Rome, 1980), 48.
43 III.799.
44 V.206.
45 V.205, 240–1; I.243.
46 III.297–304.
47 Cf. G. Walter, *Von den Juden in Segnitz in 18. und 19. Jahrhundert und dem Brüssel'sche Handels-und Erziehungsinstitut* (1964), unpublished typescript, consulted by courtesy of Herr Otto Selzer of Marktbreit. This is the source of all the information on Segnitz given in these chapters, other than that derived from the brothers Schmitz.
48 V.211.
49 Cf. I.588.
50 V.241.
51 V.205–11.
52 V.246–7.
53 III.799–800.
54 Cf. W. K. Wimsatt and C. Brooks, *Literary Criticism: A Short History* (London, 1965), 378–80.
55 Ibid.
56 VMM.17.

57 Ibid. 18–19.
58 V.215.

PART III
Public and private destinies: 1878–1886

1 Cf. S. Slataper, *Scritti politici* (2nd ed., Milan, 1954), 76–80.
2 Veronese, *Vicende*, 47.
3 L. Veronese, *L'Indipendente — storia di un giornale* (Trieste, 1932), 9–29.
4 L. Galli, 'Il clima politico nella prima giovinezza di Svevo', *Voce giuliana*, 1 Mar. 1959.
5 III.800.
6 III.676.
7 Veronese, *Vicende*, 34–59.
8 Cf. L. Veronese, *Ricordi d'irredentismo* (Trieste, 1929), 59, 63–4.
9 Bazlen, *Note senza testo*, 131.
10 Burton, op. cit. II.18.
11 Spaini, op. cit. 100.
12 Ibid. 290.
13 M. Nordio, *Il Politeama Rossetti di Trieste. Storia di cinquant'anni: 1878–1928* (Milan, 1928), 6–7.
14 V.232.
15 V.224–8.
16 V.228–30.
17 V.214, 245.
18 III.800.
19 V.231.
20 Slataper, op. cit. 125. Cf. also B. Coceani and C. Pagnini, *Trieste della 'Belle Epoque'* (Trieste, 1971), 82–5; A. Pittoni, *L'anima di Trieste* (Florence, 1968), 116–21; L. Lorenzutti, *Granellini di sabbia, ovvero ricordi delle vicende triestine nel periodo dal 1850 al 1900* (Trieste, 1907), 77.
21 III.800.
22 Cf. V.219–24.
23 U. Saba, *Prose* (Milan, 1964), 249–50.
24 Slataper, op. cit. 25; (cf. also 22).
25 V.254.
26 B. Moloney, 'Italo Svevo e *L'Indipendente:* sei articoli sconosciuti', *Lettere italiane*, XXV, 4 (1973), 536–56. See 548–51.
27 C. Boito, *Gite d'un artista* (Milan, 1884), 90.
28 V.215, 221.
29 III.559, 568–71.
30 Slataper, op. cit. 43.
31 C. C. Russell, *Italo Svevo. The Writer from Trieste. Reflections on his Background and his Work* (Ravenna, 1978), 62.
32 Coceani and Pagnini, op. cit. 151–6.
33 V.217–20.
34 V.231, 247.

35 Nordio, op. cit. 10, 34.
36 Saba, op. cit. 147–8.
37 VMM.20, 233.
38 S. Benco, 'Italo Svevo', *Pegaso*, I (Jan. 1929), 48–57 (cf. p. 49). The article was reprinted in *Umana*, 20 (May–Sept. 1971), 64–8.
39 V.219–24.
40 VMM.25.
41 Private communication by Dr Stephen Kolsky. Cf.
42 V.244–5.
43 III.800.
44 V.263, 268, 284.
45 VMM.19.
46 V.243.
47 V.246, 254.
48 V.231–3.
49 V.236.
50 V.237.
51 V.239, 243, 248.
52 G. Piemontese, *Il movimento operaio a Trieste. Dalle origini alla fine della guerra mondiale* (Udine, 1961; Rome, 1974). I refer to the 1st ed. (see p. 36).
53 V.254.
54 V.256–7.
55 V.267.
56 V.284.
57 V.285.
58 V.239.
59 V.238–9.
60 III.557–8.
61 V.254.
62 V.256; cf. 242.
63 V.86.
64 V.243–80.
65 Nordio, op. cit. 8.
66 V.238.
67 Coceani and Pagnini, op. cit. 173–4.
68 F. Hermet, *La Società Filarmonico-Drammatica — Memorie compilate per cura di un socio filo-drammatico* (Trieste, 1884), 98–106; cf. 125–30.
69 VMM.12.
70 Burton, op. cit. II.250.
71 A. Gentille, *Il primo secolo della Società di Minerva: 1810–1909* (Trieste, 1910), 147–9.
72 R. Alessi, *Trieste viva. Fatti — Uomini — Pensieri* (Rome, 1954), 53.
73 Veronese, *Vicende*, 63.
74 V.264.
75 V.244.
76 V.88.
77 V.87.
78 Russell, op. cit. 125.

79 *Esposizione Aust.-Ung. Agricola-Industriale. Trieste 1882. Catalogo ufficiale*, 278, entry no. 1414.
80 Burton, op. cit. II.237.
81 Veronese, *Vicende*, 82–5.
82 Burton, op. cit. II.238.
83 Ibid. 239–40.
84 III.559–61.
85 Veronese, *Ricordi*, 77.
86 Tamaro, op. cit. II.423.
87 A. Alexander, *The Hanging of Wilhelm Oberdank* (London, 1977), 197.
88 III.562–5.
89 III.566–7.
90 III.572–4.
91 Cf. I.26.
92 Finanzarchiv, Vienna.
93 III.800.
94 V.270.
95 V.270, 273–4.
96 V.283.
97 V.286.
98 Benco, 'Italo Svevo', 54.
99 I.25.
100 V.295.
101 V.296–7.
102 Cf. Veronese, *L'Indipendente*, 45.
103 III.592–5.
104 III.583, 586, 600.
105 Moloney, 'I.S. e *L'Indipendente*', 544–8.
106 Bazlen, op. cit. 141.
107 Benco, 'Italo Svevo', 49–50.
108 Coceani and Pagnini, op. cit. 161–3.
109 III.580.
110 III.569.
111 Moloney, 'I.S. e *L'Indipendente*', 537–42.
112 III.586–7, 600–1, 607–10.
113 Moloney, 'I.S. e *L'Indipendente*', 544–8.
114 III.614–16.
115 III.800.
116 Benco, 'Italo Svevo', 51.
117 I.760.
118 III.590.
119 F. De Sanctis, *Saggi critici* (Bari, 1962), III.262, and cf. p. 289.
120 Ibid. 265, 263.
121 Ibid. 235–6.
122 Ibid. 241–3.
123 Ibid. 193–207.
124 Ibid. 203–4.
125 Ibid. 205.

126 Ibid. 195.

127 III.800.

128 III.588–91.

129 III.575–7.

130 II.726.

131 Cf. 'Cronaca della famiglia', I.65–8.

132 III.800.

133 III.600–1.

134 C. Franellich, 'Italo Svevo', *Sechszehntes Jahrbuch der Schopenhauer-Gesellschaft* (1929), 194–7.

135 I.860, 875.

136 F. De Sanctis, *Leopardi* (Bari, 1960), 465–6.

137 Ibid. 464.

138 *Senilità:* 1898 ed., II.1036; 1927 ed., II.524.

139 G. Savarese, 'Scoperta di Schopenhauer e crisi del naturalismo nel primo Svevo', *La Rassegna della letteratura italiana*, LXXV, 7th series, No. 3 (Sept.-Dec. 1971), 411–30; S. Maxia, *Lettura di Svevo* (Padua, 1965), 19–26.

140 Cf. G. Rustia, 'Il teatro di Italo Svevo—proposte per una cronologia e per una edizione critica' (unpublished degree thesis, Università degli Studi, Trieste, 1969–70); B. Maier, *La personalità e l'opera di Italo Svevo* (Milan, 1961; reference is to the revised 3rd ed., 1971), xi–xii, 137, 151; R. Rimini, *La morte nel salotto. Guida al teatro d'Italo Svevo* (Florence, 1974).

141 IV.34.

142 IV.37–69.

143 IV.44.

144 IV.127–38.

145 IV.137.

146 IV.71–126.

147 IV.126.

148 A. Famà, 'Prossimo il centenario di Italo Svevo — viveva nella letteratura mentre cercava di sfuggirla', *Il Piccolo*, 10 Aug. 1960.

149 Coceani and Pagnini, op. cit. 155.

150 Ibid. 152–4.

151 III.633.

152 *Senilità:* 1898 ed., II.1037–8; 1927 ed., II.525.

153 Russell, op. cit. 133 n.68; *Il Comunale di Trieste* (Udine, n.d.), 44–5, and cf. 50.

154 III.619–23; A. Gentille, op. cit. 75–6, 149–51.

155 III.579.

156 F. Cusin, *Un aspetto caratteristico della coltura triestina nell'opera di Domenico Rossetti e di Attilio Hortis* (Trieste, 1931), 117–18.

157 Cf. Russell, op. cit. 43–5.

158 Coceani and Pagnini, op. cit. 48.

159 G. Stefani, *La lirica italiana e l'irredentismo. Da Goffredo Mameli a Gabriele D'Annunzio* (Rocca San Casciano, 1959), 154.

160 II.715; T. Kezich gives the source in *Svevo e Zeno — vite parallele* (Milan, 1970; references are to the 2nd ed., 1978), 21.

161 Coceani and Pagnini, op. cit. 169.

162 Quotations and information are from Coceani and Pagnini, op. cit. 169–75.

163 III.567.
164 I.26–7.
165 I.25–6.
166 I.347.
167 G. Stuparich, *Trieste nei miei ricordi* (Milan, 1948), 100–1.
168 V.233, 295.
169 E. Schmitz, *Una congiura a palazzo e altri scritti* (Rome, 1978), 23–4.
170 V.233.
171 V.295–6.
172 V.291.
173 V.270, 278.
174 V.272.
175 V.274.
176 V.282.
177 Cf. E. Schmitz, op. cit.
178 III.602–6.
179 VMM.239 n.49; see also 180.

PART IV
Disillusion—The years of *Una vita*: 1887–1895

1 III.813.
2 Cf. F. Carlini, 'Uno scritto sconosciuto di Italo Svevo: *Critica negativa*', *Umana*, XXI. 1–4 (Jan.–Apr. 1972), 14–15.
3 Moloney, 'I. S. e *L'Indipendente*', 542–4.
4 Ibid. 547.
5 Rimini, op. cit. 119.
6 III.607–10.
7 Moloney, op. cit. 544–8.
8 Ibid.542–4.
9 Ibid. 547.
10 III.663–80.
11 III.673.
12 II.182.
13 III.802; cf. I.757.
14 Moloney, op. cit. 555.
15 I.649, 652.
16 II.182–3.
17 III.841 ff..
18 Cf. B. Moloney, 'Italo Svevo and Thomas Mann's *Buddenbrooks*', in *Essays in Honour of J. H. Whitfield* (London, 1975), 251–67.
19 P. Bourget, *Essais de psychologie contemporaine* (2 vols., Paris, 1883, 1885), 296–7.
20 I.101.
21 See *Una vita*, ch. 8.
22 II.204–5.
23 III.671–2.
24 Savarese, op. cit. 427–8.

25 II.329.

26 Quoted by Piemontese, op. cit. 32–4.

27 G. Timeus, *Contributo allo studio sulla diffusione dell'alcoolismo nella città di Trieste* (Trieste, 1907), 150.

28 Burton, op. cit. II.246.

29 Césari, *Sessant'anni*, 101.

30 II.1095.

31 Russell, op. cit. 211 n.40.

32 Bazlen, op. cit. 144.

33 II.876.

34 Piemontese, op. cit. 51.

35 Ibid.; Césari, op. cit. 96–7, 110–11.

36 Piemontese, op. cit. 46–7.

37 Veronese, *Ricordi*, 88.

38 Césari, op. cit. 101.

39 Ibid. 103.

40 Cf. G. Negrelli, 'Dal municipalismo all'irredentismo: appunti per una storia dell'idea autonomistica a Trieste', *Rassegna storica del Risorgimento*, LVIII.3 (1970), 408–13. This essay is included in Negrelli's *Al di qua del mito*.

41 I. De Franceschi, 'Irredentismo d'azione a Trieste negli anni 1888–89', *Rassegna storica del Risorgimento*, XLIII.4 (Oct.–Dec. 1956), 748.

42 Ibid. 739–44.

43 Benco, 'Italo Svevo', 48.

44 III.813–14.

45 Veronese, *'L'Indipendente'*, 56–9.

46 De Franceschi, op. cit. 748.

47 Veronese, op. cit. 98, 53–9.

48 Archivio di Stato, Trieste, Imperial-Regia Polizia, file 338, Clarizza, No. 3285/Res.

49 Césari, op. cit. 114.

50 C. Pagnini, *I giornali di Trieste dalle origini al 1959* (Società per la Pubblicità in Italia, 1959), 247.

51 E. Piceni, *Tra libri e quadri* (Milan, 1971), 32.

52 Benco, op. cit. 50.

53 IV.141–4.

54 III.751.

55 F. Carlini, 'Italo Svevo: *Una lotta*', *Paragone*, XXX.264 (Feb. 1972), 61–72.

56 III.617–18.

57 Cf. Coceani and Pagnini, op. cit. 23–32.

58 Slataper, op. cit. 51.

59 G. Tamaro, 'Una lettera inedita di Italo Svevo', *Adige Panorama*, 39.XI (Mar. 1980), 24.

60 Benco, op. cit. 50–1.

61 S. Benco, 'Prefazione' to 2nd ed. of *La coscienza di Zeno* (Milan, 1930), repr. in later eds. I refer to the 1962 ed., p. 6.

62 Ibid. 10.

63 Benco, 'Italo Svevo', 54.

64 Benco, 'Prefazione', 12–13.

65 Ibid. 14–16.

66 L. Galli, 'Svevo nel 1890', *Voce Giuliana*, 1 Sept. 1961.

67 Russell, op. cit. 46.

68 G. Césari, *Vigliaccherie femminili* (Udine, 1892; I refer to the 3rd ed., Trieste, 1895), 4–5.

69 Russell, op. cit. 47.

70 Césari, op. cit. 65–7.

71 Quoted in Russell, op. cit. 14.

72 I.879.

73 VMM.32–3.

74 I.771.

75 This information on Veruda comes from L. Veneziani Svevo, 'La vita e le opere di Umberto Veruda', unpublished typescript catalogued Sv Misc 107, Biblioteca Civica, Trieste.

76 VMM.63.

77 Benco, 'Prefazione', 12–13.

77 Benco, 'Italo Svevo', 52–3.

82 Césari, *Sessant'anni*, 117; Kezich, op. cit. 24–5; II.790.

83 I.616.

84 III.801.

85 III.220–40.

86 III.224.

87 III.619–23.

88 Benco, 'Italo Svevo', 54.

89 H. de Balzac, *Louis Lambert* (Paris, 1832; the ed. referred to here is undated), 58, 63.

90 *Critica Sociale*, II (1892), 21–3.

91 G. M. Beard, *A Practical Treatise on Nervous Exhaustion (Neurasthenia)* (London, 1889), 144.

92 II.939.

93 IV.141–4.

94 *L'Indipendente*, 1892: nos. of 9, 12, 14 Mar., 6 Apr., 15 Dec.

95 P. Luxardo-Franchi, 'Un inedito di Italo Svevo', *Lettere Italiane*, XXXIII (July–Sept. 1980), 351–5.

96 III.751.

97 *Pro Patria Nostra*, I.7, p. 28.

98 'Il Superuomo', *Critica Sociale*, V (1895), 350–2.

99 S. Benco, *Trieste* (Trieste, 1910), 155–6 (quoted in Kezich, op. cit. 28).

100 Alessi, op. cit. 3.

101 G. Gratton, *Trieste segreta* (Bologna, 1948), 128–9.

102 I.503.

103 M. Presel, *Cinquant'anni di vita ginnastica a Trieste: 1863–1913* (Trieste, 1913), 300.

104 Ibid. 171–2.

105 Ibid. 160–1, 156.

106 Gentille, op. cit. 80, 152–5.

107 Benco, 'Italo Svevo', 50–2.

108 III.804.

109 VMM.47.

110 Quoted by Kezich, op. cit. 29.

111 VMM.11–12.

112 III.802–3; VMM.30.

113 III.799.

114 A. Meoni, 'Svevo si sfoga', *Il Corriere della Sera*, 17 Aug. 1969.

115 e.g. *Profilo autobiografico*, III.802.

116 VMM.32.

117 III.803.

118 Slataper, op. cit. 41–2.

119 Piemontese, op. cit. 52–62.

120 Césari, *Sessant'anni*, cf. 118–33.

121 *L'Indipendente*, 15 Apr. 1892.

122 Ibid., 17 Feb. 1892.

123 Ibid., 30 Jan. 1892.

124 III.525–30.

125 Quoted in Piemontese, op. cit. 68; cf. *Senilità* (1898 ed.) II.1051; (1927 ed.) II.540–1.

126 G. Pinguentini, 'Vecchie cronache triestine (Tre mesi del 1895)', *La Porta Orientale* (1946), 31–7.

128 *Critica Sociale*, II (1892), 14.

129 Ibid. 3.

130 I.68.

131 *Critica Sociale*, II (1892), 119–35.

132 Ibid. III (1893), 71–4.

133 Ibid. IV (1894), 138–40.

134 Cf. ibid. V (1895), 106–7, 116–18.

135 Ibid. III (1893), 111–12.

136 Ibid. 160 (signed 'y').

137 Summary from VII (1897), 179–80, signed 'P. I.'.

138 Ibid. V (1895), 143–4.

138 Ibid. V (1895), 143–4.

139 Ibid. IV (1894), 120–1.

140 Ibid. VI (1896), 137–9.

141 Ibid. 317–18.

142 Cf. E. Saccone, *Il poeta travestito* (Pisa, 1977), 198–9.

143 *Critica Sociale*, III.205–7, 222–3, 236–9.

144 III.814–15.

145 *Guida Generale* (Trieste, 1894), 133–4, 170, 160.

146 Ibid. (1895), 296.

147 VMM.12–13.

148 F. Cialente, *Le quattro ragazze Wieselberger* (Milan, 1974), 11–12.

PART V
The family man: 1895–1902

1 I.29–33.

2 III.768.

3 E. Schmitz, op. cit. 24 (footnote).

4 VMM.13–14.
5 *Guida Generale* (Trieste, 1895).
6 Cf. I.35–9.
7 F. Anzellotti, *Il segreto di Svevo* (Pordenone, 1985), 40–55.
8 V.200.
9 Anzellotti, op. cit. 90.
10 Ibid. 60–1, 73, 86, 91.
11 Ibid. 73–6.
12 Ibid. 91–7.
13 Alessi, op. cit. 261–3.
14 Anzellotti, op. cit. 99–101.
15 I.34–5; V. 91–2.
16 I.56–7.
17 Anzellotti, op. cit. 126.
18 I.39–41.
19 I.45.
20 I.609, 683.
21 I.107.
22 VMM.37–8.
23 VMM.43–4.
24 III.768.
25 III.769.
26 III.773.
27 I.45.
28 III.777.
29 III.769, 794.
30 III.774.
31 Ibid.
32 III.773–4.
33 III.489–90.
34 III.771.
35 I.43 (Ettore dated the letter January in error for February).
36 III.775–6.
37 III.777.
38 III.815.
39 III.791.
40 III.778–81.
41 III.771.
42 III.781.
43 Cf. I.116.
44 III.782.
45 III.783.
46 I.43.
47 III.783–4.
48 III.785.
49 III.786–9; I.47–50.
50 III.789–90.
51 Anzellotti, op. cit. 102–3, 109.

52 III.792.
53 III.792.
54 III.795.
55 Ibid.
56 VMM.43–4.
57 Cf. I.50–2.
58 Zoller, op. cit. 548–50.
59 Rimini, op. cit. 56.
60 I.55, 74.
61 I.413, 502.
62 I.220.
63 I.150.
64 I.60; VMM.44.
65 VMM.44.
66 III.795.
67 I.52.
68 I.53.
69 The painting forms part of Svevo's Veruda collection, now in the keeping of his daughter, Letizia Fonda Savio.
70 VMM.44–5, 238; Anzellotti, op. cit. 110–12.
71 I.73.
72 I.65–9.
73 J. W. von Goethe, *Dichtung und Wahrheit* (trans. *Poetry and Truth*, London, 1948), I.155.
74 I.64.
75 I.69.
76 I.59.
77 I.60–2.
78 Kezich, op. cit. 39–40.
79 I.64.
80 I.65.
81 VMM.231.
82 M.-A. Comnène, 'Italo Svevo', *Europe* (Sept. 1960), 114.
83 P. N. Furbank, *Italo Svevo. The Man and the Writer* (London, 1966), 50–1.
84 The church wedding of Livia and Ettore is recorded in the marriage register of the church of San Giacomo in Monte (Atto III — 14/159/39).
85 I.115, 243, 348, 374, 383, 446.
86 C. Fonda, *Svevo e Freud. Proposta di interpretazione della 'Coscienza di Zeno'* (Ravenna, 1978), 59.
87 *Critica Sociale*, VII (1897), 122–3.
88 Piemontese, op. cit. 90–104.
89 II.715.
90 VMM.56.
91 III.525–30.
92 III.752–3.
93 III.858–60.
94 I.72–3.
95 I.73–4.

96 I.74–7.
97 I.104.
98 I.76.
99 III.817–18; IV.666–70.
100 I.74.
101 II.947–52.
102 I.79.
103 I.80, 83, 92.
104 U. Levra, *Il colpo di stato dell borghesia. La crisi politica di fine secolo in Italia, 1896–1900* (Milan, 1975).
105 I.80.
106 I.109–10.
107 I.99–101.
108 I.112.
109 Cf. I.107, 117–20, 125–7; V. 32–4.
110 I.119.
111 I.104.
112 I.128.
113 I.109, 116.
114 I.129–36.
115 I.139, 203.
116 I.113, 120; V.129.
117 I.139.
118 I.99–117; cf. esp. 115.
119 I.90.
120 I.112.
121 V.27.
122 I.101, 135.
123 V.20, 42.
124 I.85, 88, 130.
125 I.101–3.
126 I.106–7.
127 I.117.
128 A. Tamaro, op. cit. II.438; Piemontese, op. cit. 89.
129 Personal communication to the author by Svevo's son-in-law, Antonio Fonda Savio.
130 III.805.
131 VMM.47–8.
132 III.805.
133 II.429.
134 I.804.
135 II.431.
136 *Il Popolo di Trieste*, 15 Sept. 1928.
137 G. Cassieri, 'Una copia preziosa', *Il Giornale di Roma*, 25 Aug. 1961, and *La Fiera Letteraria*, 23 July 1961.
138 Cf. III.804 and Russell, op. cit. 135–7 and n. 74.
139 S. Joyce, *The Meeting of Svevo and Joyce* (Udine, 1965), 7–8.
140 Guido Voghera, *Gli anni della psicanalisi* (Pordenone, 1980), 18.

141 VMM.48–9.
142 VMM.48.
143 Cf. I.138–40, 145.
144 I.144.
145 I.143.
146 I.145.
147 I.194.
148 I.149–50.
149 I.141–2, 172, 139.
150 I.165, 151–2.
151 I.175–6; cf. 140, 168, 171.
152 I.145–78 *passim*.
153 I.160–4.
154 I.165.
155 I.149–55.
156 Cf. B. Michel, *Banques et banquiers en Autriche au début du 20ᵉ siècle* (Paris, 1976), 70, 72, 216, 321, 326.
157 I.149–55.
158 Cf. I.156.
159 I.154.
160 I.156; V.45.
161 I.156–7.
162 I.162–3.
163 Cf. 169–70.
164 I.173, 240.
165 I.181.
166 I.274.
167 I.177.
168 VMM.63.
169 VMM.64.
170 I.203.
171 I.341.
172 I.553, 547.
173 VMM.64.
174 III.816.
175 VMM.65.
176 Cf. Anzellotti, op. cit. 157.
177 I.191.
178 I.364–5, 377.
179 III.345–65.
180 I.590.
181 I.239, 243, 265–6, 317, 324, 446, 595.
182 I.329, 458.
183 Anzellotti, op. cit. 138–40.
184 I.245, 223, 273, 205.
185 III.815–18; cf. IV.666–70.
186 III.480–2.
187 I.222.

188 IV.145–72, 565–78; cf. I.263.
189 IV.209–70.
190 P. A. Quarantotti Gambini, 'Il cilindro di Svevo', *Il Tempo*, 26 May 1959.
191 I.186, 222–3.
192 V.61.
193 I.142–3, 147, 225; V.70, 46, 59.
195 I.229–35, 333, 337, 375, 467–8, 522, 537, 555.
196 V.57–8.
197 I.209–11.
198 V.61.
199 I.188, 192, 193, 200; V.54, 57.
200 I.217.
201 I.234, 236.
202 Cf. I.183, 345, 348, 405, 470, 527, 435, 641–2, 644.
203 I.415.
204 I.351.
205 I.412.
206 I.242.
207 I.406.
208 I.336.
209 I.339, 371, 372 fn. 2; V.71.
210 I.413.
211 I.230, 351.
212 I.413.
213 Anzellotti, op. cit. 133.
214 Ibid. 137; cf. I.605.
215 I.481.
216 I.227.
217 I.217.
218 Cf. III.350.
219 I.349.
220 I.229.
221 I.343; cf. 229, 251.
222 I.380; cf. 238, 387, and V.63.
223 Cf. Coceani and Pagnini, op. cit. 196.
224 I.204.
225 I.205.
226 I.225–6.
227 I.243.
228 I.196.
229 I.366.
230 Cf. Negrelli, op. cit. 415; and A. Tamaro, op. cit. II.441, and 1924 ed., II.542.
231 A. Tamaro, op. cit. (1930 ed.), II.226–7: quoted in E. Apih, 'Borghesia e proletariato di fronte al problema nazionale', *Trieste*, II.6 (Mar.-Apr. 1955), 22.
232 A. Tamaro, op. cit. (1976 ed.), II.460.
233 Op. cit. II.442; Piemontese, op. cit. 192.
234 L. Galli, 'Svevo non dedicò mai una riga nei suoi scritti al mito risorgimentale', *Voce Giuliana*, 1 Nov. 1961.

235 VMM.242.
236 A. Tamaro, op. cit. II.443; Césari, *Sessant'anni*, 148–9; Piemontese, 192–3.
237 L. Della Venezia Sala, 'La scuola triestina dall'Austria all'Italia', in G. Cervani (ed.), *Il movimento nazionale a Trieste nella prima guerra mondiale* (Udine, 1968), 81.
238 Slataper, *Scritti politici*, 32.
239 A. Tamaro, op. cit. II.452.
240 Slataper, op. cit. 119.
241 Bazlen, op. cit. 141.
242 *Critica Sociale*, X (1900), 4–7; cf. 20–2.
243 Slataper. op. cit. 39.
244 Piemontese, op. cit. 145–6.
245 Ibid. 147.
246 A. Tamaro, op. cit. II.452–3.

PART VI
Ulysses Schmitz: 1901–1907

1 Anzellotti, op. cit. 106–7; Furbank, op. cit. 64.
2 I.213.
3 I.226, 238, 245.
4 I.246–8; V.62.
5 V.61.
6 I.249.
7 I.253.
8 I.250–4.
9 I.254–5.
10 I.257–8.
11 I.260.
12 I.263–5.
13 I.266–7; cf. 263, 305.
14 I.278.
15 I.270–3.
16 I.273.
17 I.271–2.
18 I.274–8.
19 I.280.
20 I.281–2.
21 IV.564–78, 145–72.
22 I.283–4.
23 I.282–3.
24 I.285–6.
25 Saba, op. cit. 152–4.
26 For Ettore's stay in London, cf. I.285–303.
27 III.699–705.
28 Cf. B. Moloney, '*Londra dopo la guerra*: five unknown articles by Italo Svevo', *Italian Studies*, XXXI (1976), 59–81.
29 I.305.

30 P. A. Quarantotti Gambini, 'Italo Svevo fidanzato a Londra', *Il Corriere della Sera*, 31 Jan. 1962.
31 VMM.47.
32 V.80.
33 For Svevo's visit to Plymouth, cf. I.303–18.
34 I.316.
35 III.699.
36 VMM.67–8.
37 I.316.
38 I.317.
39 Cf. VMM.74 (where, however, the dates are muddled).
40 I.441.
41 VMM.79.
42 I.347.
43 I.322–30; V.62.
44 I.323.
45 III.818.
46 I.400.
47 III.531–54.
48 III.818–19.
49 I.409.
50 III.852–3.
51 VMM.67, 239.
52 I.336
53 I.343–50.
54 I.391.
55 I.356.
56 III.695.
57 For Svevo's second English visit, cf. I.356–93 and V.70–7.
58 I.334–5 (where Ettore even mistook the year).
59 I.395, 461, 506.
60 I.396.
61 I.398–400.
62 S. Maldini, 'La moglie di Svevo', *Il Resto del Carlino*, 14 June 1957.
63 L. Veneziani Svevo, 'Veruda'.
64 VMM.34.
65 Veneziani, 'Veruda', 8.
66 V.93.
67 VMM.35.
68 Cf. III.821 and I.410–11, and 416–22.
69 III.821.
70 Benco, 'Italo Svevo', 56; for the two visits to England in 1906, see I.425–41 and 445–60.
71 III.697.
72 III.689, 701; Moloney, 'Londra dopo la guerra', 64.
73 III.690; I.259, 503.
74 M. Raper, 'A Death in Hove' (script for BBC Radio 4 broadcast of 29 Mar. 1973).
75 III.694.

76 III.701.

77 III.702.

78 III.703.

79 III.704–5.

80 Moloney, 'Londra dopo la guerra', 62–4; cf. III.699–700.

81 Moloney, op. cit. 70–1.

82 Ibid. 77–9; III.695.

83 III.807–8.

84 I.449, 451.

85 III.693; cf. Moloney, op. cit. 73.

86 Ibid. 73–4; III.692.

87 Moloney, op. cit. 75.

88 III.691.

89 III.704; cf. Moloney, op. cit. 73.

90 The information on the Charlton and Woolwich area is drawn from E. F. E. Jefferson, *The Woolwich Story 1890–1965* (London, 1970), 55–6, 63, 104–8.

91 *Critica Sociale*, XII (1902), 289–90.

92 *Il Corriere della Sera*, 3 Nov. 1966.

93 I.367, 369, 423.

94 III.637–43.

95 III.644–8.

96 III.822.

97 C. Magris, 'Svevo e la cultura tedesca a Trieste', in G. Petronio (ed.), *Il caso Svevo* (Palermo, 1976).

98 Cf. G. A. Camerino, *Italo Svevo e la crisi della Mitteleuropa* (Florence, 1974).

99 F. Pasini, 'Italo Svevo', *La Porta Orientale*, I, 15 May 1931, p. 482.

100 V. Levi, *La vita musicale a Trieste. Cronache di un cinquantennio: 1918–1968* (Trieste, 1968), 31–2.

101 III.820.

102 I.859–60.

103 Stefani, op. cit., cf. 181–256.

104 Coceani and Pagnini, op. cit. 25–6.

105 Gentille, op. cit. 165; I.470.

106 Gentille, op. cit. 159–60.

107 Slataper, op. cit. 31–5; cf. Nordio, op. cit. 27, 35–6.

108 Slataper, op. cit. 30–1.

109 I.772.

110 L. Pirandello, cf. *The Old and the Young* (trans. C. K. Scott-Moncrieff, London. 1928), II.360.

111 Slataper, op. cit. 29.

112 Ibid. 19.

113 I.244.

114 Slataper, op. cit. 30.

115 I.414–15.

116 I.443–4.

117 F. Pasini, 'La personalità di Italo Svevo', *Giovinezza ed Arte*, II (Jan. 1931), 4–6.

118 I. Finzi, 'Necrologio — Italo Svevo', *L'Illustrazione Italiana*, Sept. 1928.

119 L. Galli, 'Il clima politico della giovinezza di Svevo', *Voce Giuliana*, 1 May 1959.

120 Ead., 'Svevo non dedicò ...', *Voce Giuliana*, 1 Nov. 1961.

121 Bazlen, op. cit. 136–7.

122 Slataper, op. cit. 99, 106–8.

123 Saba, op. cit. 226.

124 A. Tamaro, op. cit. II.464–5.

125 Ibid. 467; Piemontese, op. cit. 230–4.

126 B. Michel, op. cit. 70–6.

127 Timeus, *Contributo*, 149–53; id., 'L'alimentazione dei lavoratori a Trieste. Studio statistico-economico sociale', *Rapporto sanitario del Comune di Trieste degli anni 1906–08* (Trieste, 1908), 65–74; M. Alberti, *Il costo della vita, i salari e le paghe a Trieste nell'ultimo quarto di secolo* (Trieste, 1912), quoted in Piemontese, op. cit. 268–76; Bazlen, op. cit. 134, 144.

128 I.466.

129 I.335.

130 P. A. Quarantotti Gambini, 'A Trieste nel primo '900 — Giotti, Ferravilla e Svevo', *Il Tempo*, 28 Mar. 1960 and *Il Piccolo*, 1 May 1960.

131 E. Mo, 'Quando Svevo e Joyce litigavano', *Il Corriere della Sera*, 21 Nov. 1977.

132 B. Wall, 'Joyce e Svevo', *La Gazzetta dell'Emilia*, 16 Mar. 1954.

133 A. Todisco, 'I capelli della signora Svevo hanno ispirato James Joyce', *La Stampa*, 1 Aug. 1954; R. Ellmann, *James Joyce* (Oxford, 1982), 340.

134 VMM.83–4.

135 Ibid.

136 VMM.85.

137 J. Joyce, *The Critical Writings of James Joyce* (ed. E. Mason and R. Ellmann, London, 1959), 20.

138 *Senilità*, II.966.

139 S. Joyce, 'Introduction' to Italo Svevo, *As a Man Grows Older* (London, 1932). Also published as 'Joyce and Svevo' in *The Stork*, III (Sept. 1932), 15–20.

140 III.710: my translation is more literal and appropriate to this context than that by S. Joyce (Norfolk, Conn., 1950, unpaginated).

141 S. Joyce, 'Introduction'.

142 S. Crise, *Epiphanies and Phadographs: Joyce and Trieste* (Milan, 1967), 112–14; quoted in E. Ghidetti (ed.), *Il caso Svevo — Guida storica e critica* (Rome–Bari, 1984), x–xii.

143 Ellmann, op. cit. 218.

144 VMM.85.

145 E. Settanni, 'Ritratto di Italo Svevo', *Il Giornale della Sera*, 8 Aug. 1949.

146 S. Joyce, 'Introduction'.

147 III.748.

148 III.708; cf. S. Joyce's less complete version, cited above (n. 140).

149 Furbank, op. cit. 89–90.

150 Cf. I.316.

151 I.527.

152 The text and the notes appear in III.706–48.

153 III.719, 722, 744.

154 J. Joyce, *Ulysses* (London, 1960), 72.

155 S. Joyce, 'Introduction'.

156 III.742–3.

157 B. Moloney, 'Count Noris changes trams: an unknown article by Italo Svevo', *Modern Language Review*, LXXI.1 (Jan. 1976), 51–3; III.624, 627.

158 I.210.

159 Todisco, op. cit.

160 S. Joyce, 'Introduction'.

161 Cf. J. Joyce, *Critical Writings*, 214.

162 Cf. VMM.92.

163 Ellmann, op. cit. 636.

164 VI.26–7; Levi, *Vita musicale*, 117–18.

165 T. F. Staley, 'The Search for Leopold Bloom: James Joyce and Italo Svevo', *James Joyce Quarterly*, I (Summer 1964), 60.

PART VII

The encounter with Freud: 1908–1914

1 I.464–5.

2 I.473–4.

3 IV.663–4.

4 I.532–3.

5 For this visit to London see I.484–513; V.81–5.

6 *Critica Sociale*, XVIII (1908), 325–8.

7 Piemontese, op. cit. 257–9, 262–4; A. Tamaro, op. cit. II.468, 472–3; F. Testena (Comunardo Braccialarghe), *I.-R. Socialismo triestino* (Milan, 1910).

8 Cf. A. Romanò (ed.), *'La Voce' (1908–1914)* (Turin, 1960), 'Introduzione a *La Voce*', 80; G. Baroni, *Trieste e 'La Voce'* (Milan, 1975), 26.

9 Stuparich, *Trieste*, 211.

10 Baroni, op. cit. 41–2.

11 S. Slataper, *Il mio Carso* (Florence, 1912), 46.

12 *La Voce*, 6 May 1909.

13 Baroni, op. cit. 74–5.

14 I.840.

15 I.527–8.

16 III.329–44 and 510–12.

17 III.330.

18 III.685.

19 III.688.

20 E. Weiss, *Sigmund Freud as a Consultant. Recollections of a Pioneer in Psychoanalysis* (New York, 1970), 7.

21 III.724–5.

22 III.687.

23 III.688.

24 III.807.

25 I.857–8; cf. 863.

26 Weiss, op. cit. 9.

27 Ibid. 23–8; cf. C. L. Musatti, *Riflessioni sul pensiero psicanalitico e incursione nel mondo delle immagini* (Turin, 1976), 49–51 and n. 28.

28 I.859.

29 Weiss, op. cit. 12.

30 Anzellotti, op. cit. 151.

31 I.594.
32 E. Mahler-Schächter, 'Svevo, Trieste and the Vienna Circle: Zeno's Analyst Analysed', *European Studies Review*, XII (1982), 52–3.
33 Weiss, op. cit. 5.
34 Ibid. *passim.*
35 J. A. C. Brown, *Freud and the Post-Freudians* (Harmondsworth, 1966) 42.
36 III.687.
37 Italo Svevo, *James Joyce*, trans. S. Joyce; III.724–5.
38 Ellmann, op. cit. 340.
39 III.63–77.
40 I.839.
41 III.271–83.
42 III.129–32.
43 Cf. G. Prezzolini, *'La Voce' 1908–13: cronaca, antologia e fortuna di una rivista* (with E. Gentile and V. Scheiwiller, Milan, 1974), 439–41.
44 I.863.
45 S. Freud, *Jensen's 'Gradiva' and Other Works* (London), 143–53.
46 Anzellotti, op. cit. 140–55.
47 I.514.
48 I.573–4; cf. 569.
49 Cf. A. Tamaro, op. cit. II.475–7.
50 VMM.80–2.
51 V.85–6.
52 I.540–59.
53 I.562–3.
54 I.687.
55 A. Fonda Savio, *Ricordi*, 21.
56 I.639.
57 III.63–77; cf. esp. 65–6.
58 I.634.
59 I.664–6.
60 III.694.
61 III.822–4.
62 III.310–28.
63 III.824.
64 I.621.
65 IV.192–208.
66 IV.173–90.
67 I.466.
68 III.833–4.
69 Italo Svevo—Eugenio Montale, *Carteggio, con gli scritti di Montale su Svevo* (ed. G. Zampa, Milan, 1976), 54.
70 IV.271–329.
71 I.631.
72 II.727.
73 VMM.141.
74 P. A. Quarantotti Gambini, 'I cioccolatini di Svevo', *Corriere d'Informazione*, 21 Apr. 1962.

75 G. Hermet, 'Memorie della Società del Teatro popolare 1908–1914', *La Porta Orientale* (1943), 83.

76 Ellmann, op. cit. 266.

77 G. Hermet, 'La vita musicale a Trieste (1801–1944), con speciale riferimento alla musica vocale', *Archeografo Triestino* (1947), 228.

78 Coceani and Pagnini, op. cit. 200.

79 I.570–1.

80 N. Wyderbruck, *Memoirs of a Princess. The Reminiscences of Princess Marie von Thurn und Taxis* (London, 1959), 153.

81 C. Magris, 'Dall'estetismo allo sperimentalismo: Rainer-Maria Rilke nel I° centenario della nascita', *L'Approdo Letterario*, No. 70 (new series), XXI (June 1975) 112.

82 III.372.

83 A. Tamaro, op. cit. II.397–8; A Vivante, *Irredentismo adriatico: contributo alla discussione dei rapporti austro-italiani* (Florence, 1912; the 3rd ed., Trieste, 1945, is used here), 222–3.

84 Piemontese, op. cit. 224.

85 M. Alberti, *L'irredentismo senza romanticismo* quoted in Piemontese, op. cit. 240–1; cf. the entire section 235–48 in Piemontese.

86 I.537.

87 I.475, 493, 525, 530, 565–6.

88 I.571.

89 I.575.

90 I.576–97.

91 I.599–611, 683.

92 III.860.

93 I.681, 686.

94 I.638–47.

95 I.531–2.

96 G. Bedarida, *Ebrei in Italia* (Leghorn, 1950), 160; S. Tedeschi, *Studii filosofici ed altri scritti* (Genoa, 1913), xvii, 121–2; A. Cavaglion, *Otto Weininger in Italia* (Rome, 1982), 200–9.

97 I.613–24.

98 I.572.

99 I.531.

100 For the letters from Montecatini see I.647–58.

101 Mo, op. cit.

102 I.621.

103 I.539.

104 I.538–9.

105 Ellmann, op. cit. 322–3.

106 Crise, op. cit. 29–30.

107 I.568.

108 III.707, 713.

109 Ellmann, op. cit. 272.

110 I.665.

111 I.692.

PART VIII
War and peace: 1914–1922

1 I.626.

2 I.654; cf. 650, 657.

3 G. Gaeta, *Trieste durante la prima guerra mondiale. Opinione pubblica e giornalismo a Trieste dal 1914 al 1918* (Trieste, 1938), 31.

4 S. Benco, *Gli ultimi anni della dominazione austriaca a Trieste* (Milan, 1919), I.29.

5 A. Minutillo, *Trieste durante l'ultimo periodo di dominazione austriaca. Dal 24 luglio 1914 al 24 maggio 1915. Note, impressioni, rettifiche* (Rome–Bracciano, 1915), 7–9.

6 Gaeta, op. cit. 50.

7 Benco, op. cit. I.62.

8 V. Furlani, 'Brigate e cenacoli triestini', *Nuova Antologia* XCI.469, fasc. 1866 (June 1956), 205.

9 A. Fonda Savio, 'Noterelle di un volontario' in G. Cervani (ed.), *Il movimento nazionale a Trieste nella prima guerra mondiale* (Udine, 1968), 54–5.

10 Benco, op. cit. I.60.

11 Kriegsarchiv, Vienna, Marinesektion, 29G2/30.

12 Cf. A. Fonda Savio, in *Ricordi*, 25.

13 I.693–718.

14 Benco, op. cit. I.89–104.

15 C. Ban, *Il 1914 a Trieste e nel mondo* (Padua: the years up to 1919 are covered in this periodical, published 1973–6). For this reference, cf. *1915*, V.3.

16 II.927.

17 I.719.

18 I.709–10.

19 Kriegsarchiv Vienna, 29G.

20 Benco, op. cit. I.115, 135–6.

21 I.707.

22 Alessi, op. cit. 8–9.

23 II.947.

24 Coceani and Pagnini, op. cit. 222.

25 Benco, op. cit. I.165–81; Gaeta, op. cit. 74–6; Minutillo, op. cit. 101–5.

26 Piemontese, op. cit. 314.

27 Ibid. 305; Gaeta, op. cit. 80–1; Minutillo, op. cit. 116–71.

28 III.824–7.

29 Gaeta, op. cit. 97; Piemontese, op. cit. 306; Benco, op. cit. II.31.

30 Crise, op. cit., photograph No. 40.

31 Kriegsarchiv, Vienna, Marinesektion, 37A1/3.

32 Ibid. 29G.

33 I.721–4. Note 1 to the letter of 27 Sept., which implies that no requisition had yet taken place, is mistaken.

34 VMM.88–9.

35 I.729.

36 Anzellotti, op. cit. 257–8.

37 Saba, op. cit. 269–70.

38 I.725.

39 Piemontese, op. cit. 306.

40 VMM.89.

41 I.727.

42 III.27.

43 Cf. III.698.

44 III.34.

45 III.36.

46 Stefani, op. cit. 271–2; Benco, op. cit. II.99.

47 Ibid. II.119.

48 Ibid. II.169–70.

49 III.698.

50 Gaeta, op. cit. 98; cf. Stefani, op. cit. 279.

51 I.754; cf. 755 n.; Benco, op. cit. II.166.

52 Ibid. II.162–3.

53 Minutillo, op. cit. 5–9, 17–19, 121.

54 *Umana*, I (25 May 1918), 13–14.

55 VMM.90–1.

56 VMM.93–4.

57 Piemontese, op. cit. 318–29.

58 VMM.95, 243.

59 III.807.

60 I.859, 863.

61 III.688.

62 III.808.

63 III.649–62.

64 III.649–58.

65 III.657.

66 III.658.

67 III.661–2.

68 VMM.92.

69 III.828.

70 III.854–5.

71 IV.664–6.

72 Gaeta, op. cit. 125.

73 Piemontese, op. cit. 314–16.

74 C. Schiffrer, 'La crisi del socialismo triestino nella prima guerra mondiale' in
    Cervani (ed.), op. cit. 173–4.

75 Ibid. 177; C. Silvestri, *Dalla redenzione al fascismo. Trieste 1918–1922* (Udine,
    1959), 20.

76 Piemontese, op. cit. 340–2; Furlani, op. cit. 206.

77 Piemontese, op. cit. 345; Gaeta, op. cit. 148–9.

78 Piemontese, op. cit. 346–7.

79 Ibid. 348.

80 VMM.96.

81 Piemontese, op. cit. 350.

82 Comitato Trieste '68, *Trieste ottobre–novembre 1918. Raccolta di documenti del
    tempo* (Milan 1968), 147–8.

83 Silvestri, op. cit. 28–9.

84 I.727–9.
85 Letter to A. Frescura, pub. in A. Meoni, 'Svevo si sfoga', *Il Corriere della Sera*, 17 Aug. 1969.
86 VI.233–6.
87 III.808.
88 *La Patria*, 25 Nov. 1954.
89 VMM.92.
90 *Il Popolo di Trieste*, 15 Sept. 1928.
91 I.739.
92 I.744.
93 A. Gruber-Benco, 'Incontri e figure: Italo Svevo', *Umana*, III, 9–10 (Sept.–Oct. 1954), 18–19.
94 Césari, *Sessant'anni*, 212.
95 A. Oberdorfer, *Il Socialismo del dopoguerra a Trieste* (Florence, 1922), 7–9.
96 Silvestri, op. cit. x and 29–36.
97 S. Benco, '*La coscienza di Zeno*, romanzo di Italo Svevo', *Il Piccolo della Sera*, 15 June 1923: now in Italo Svevo—Eugenio Montale, *Carteggio*.
98 B. Coceani, 'Salari d'anteguerra e dopoguerra nelle industrie di Trieste', *La Porta Orientale* (1931), 339–76; cf. C. Silvestri, op. cit., 25–6.
99 Ibid. 37.
100 A. Mosconi, *I primi anni del governo italiano nella Venezia Giulia: Trieste 1919–1922* (Bologna–Rocca San Casciano–Trieste, 1924), 'Prefazione' and 5–24.
101 I.743.
102 Oberdorfer, op. cit. 44–6; Silvestri, op. cit. 40–1; Mosconi, op. cit. 1.
103 Ibid. 31–2; Silvestri, 48–50.
104 Stuparich, *Trieste*, 66–8; cf. Silvestri, op. cit. 54–7.
105 Mosconi, op. cit. 22–3.
106 Cf. Alessi, op. cit. 30–1 and 295.
107 Silvestri, op. cit. 106–7.
108 Alessi, op. cit. 11.
109 Cf. S. Benco, '*Il Piccolo*' di Trieste—Mezzo secolo di giornalismo (Milan–Rome, 1931), 266–7; cf. Apih, op. cit. 293; and Alessi, op. cit. 36.
110 Silvestri, op. cit. 59–148; Mosconi, op. cit. 35–155; E. Apih, *Avvento del Fascismo a Trieste* (Udine, 1957), esp. p. 21; A. Tasca, *Nascita e avvento del fascismo in Italia* (Florence, 1950), 161.
111 III.808.
112 III.624–30, and Moloney, 'Count Noris'.
113 G. A. Camerino, 'Trieste nel secolo presente. Un articolo sconosciuto di Italo Svevo': Part I, *Critica letteraria*, V.4.17 (1977), 763–70; Part II, ibid. VII.4.25 (1979), 775–8.
114 Ibid. Part II.
115 III.754.
116 IV.335–50 and 635–40.
117 Moloney, 'Londra'.
118 I.749–52.
119 III.693.
120 C. Ducker, 'Italo Svevo', *The Stork* (Sept. 1930), 28–31.
121 Levi, *La vita musicale*, 31–4; cf. III.697 and Alessi, op. cit. 266.

122 Voghera, op. cit. 18–19.

123 Alessi, op. cit. 295.

124 Ibid. 287.

125 A. Fonda Savio, *Ricordi*, 22.

126 P. A. Quarantotti Gambini, 'Guardando l'Istria', *Il Tempo*, 23 June 1949, and 'Un illustre sconosciuto', *Il Tempo*, 29 June 1959.

127 I.731–2.

128 S. Benco, review of 'La novella del buon vecchio e della bella fanciulla', *Pegaso*, I (Aug. 1929), 244.

129 I.734–43.

130 Meoni, op. cit.

131 M. Sutor (ed.), *Saba. Svevo. Comisso. — Lettere inedite* (Padua, 1968), 69.

132 *Il Popolo di Trieste*, 15 Sept. 1928.

133 A. Fonda Savio, *Ricordi*, 23.

134 Benco, op. cit. 246.

135 III.725; Italo Svevo, *James Joyce*.

136 Weiss, op. cit. 27–8; Musatti, op. cit. 49–51; Anzellotti, op. cit. 151.

137 Voghera, op. cit. 9.

138 III.687.

139 Italo Svevo–Eugenio Montale, *Carteggio*, 578.

140 VMM. 98–9.

141 I.779.

142 B. Binazzi, 'Italo Svevo', *Il Resto del Carlino*, 2 Mar. 1926.

143 For the correspondence with Cappelli and Frescura, cf. I.744–5; V.96–101; Meoni, op. cit

PART IX
Resurrection of Italo Svevo and death of Ettore Schmitz: 1923–1928

1 Other details common to Zeno and Ettore are listed in Russell, op. cit. 211–12.

2 III.809.

3 III.686.

4 I.863.

5 Voghera, op. cit. 16, 42; E. Roditi, 'Il romanzo comincia dove Freud finisce. Fascino del quiproquo', *La Fiera Letteraria*, 11 Oct. 1953.

6 E. Jones, 'A Powerful Writer', *The Nation*, 31 Dec. 1949.

7 Z. Zini, *La doppia maschera dell'universo* (Turin, 1914), 537.

8 A. Thérive, *Solaria*, IV.3–4 (Mar.-Apr. 1929), 81; V.100.

9 II.954.

10 Quoted in Apih, *Avvento del Fascismo a Trieste*, 24.

11 D. Carito, *Come lo spirito della nostra epoca (Darwin—Nietzsche—Beard) ha concorso all'attuale guerra— Riflessioni di un medico napoletano* (Naples, 1916), 8, 478, 78–9.

12 III.809.

13 VMM.99; cf. III.809.

14 Cf. Italo Svevo—Eugenio Montale, *Carteggio*, 109.

15 Benco, '*La coscienza di Zeno*, romanzo di Italo Svevo'.

16 VI.26–7; cf. Levi, op. cit. 117.

17 Ellmann, op. cit. 500–1.
18 VI,29–30; Levi, op. cit. 120–1.
19 I.749–52.
20 VI.31; Levi, op. cit. 121–2; Ellmann, op. cit. 561.
21 V.101–2.
22 VI.33; V. Levi, op. cit. 122.
23 I.753.
24 Cf. III.689.
25 Cf. Ellmann, op. cit. 564.
26 I.754–6.
27 Quoted in Russell, op. cit. 242–3.
28 A. Fonda Savio: personal communication.
29 Alessi, op. cit. 268.
30 B. Maier, *Gli scrittori triestini e il fascismo* (Trieste, 1975), 33.
31 Anzellotti, op. cit. 261.
32 III.683–4.
33 Cf. G. Orwell, 'Who are the War Criminals?', *Tribune*, 22 Oct. 1943.
34 Sir Frank Fox, *Italy Today* (London, 1927); see in particular 64–7 and 82–3.
35 Anzellotti, op. cit. 261, 270, with quotations from *Il Popolo di Trieste* of 1931 and 1936.
36 Apih, 'Borghesia e proletariato', 22.
37 VMM.101.
38 VI.47–8.
39 V.188.
40 I.757–8.
41 V.52.
42 I.759–60; cf. VI.53–5.
43 I.761.
44 VMM.109.
45 III.143–219; cf. 495–501, 829–31 and *Il Popolo di Trieste*, 27 Feb. 1925.
46 III.297–304.
47 I.766; 'Una burla riuscita' is in III.78–128.
48 I.761–3; VI.56–9.
49 VI.60–5, 105–11; I.764–72 and cf. 830–1.
50 I.772–3.
51 III.829.
52 Svevo—Montale, *Carteggio,* 71–87.
53 C. Linati, 'Italo Svevo, romanziere', *Nuova Antologia*, LXIII (1 Feb. 1928), 327–36, and 'Un giorno con Svevo', *Corriere d'Informazione*, 16 Jan. 1948.
54 R. Calasso, preface to Bazlen, op. cit. 7.
55 Svevo—Montale, *Carteggio*, xi.
56 III.809; G. Caprin, 'Italo Svevo e Giulio Caprin', *L'Ora*, 2 Oct. 1928.
57 R. Graff, 'L'uomo dalla doppia personalità. Un'introduzione per chiudere', *La Fiera Letteraria*, 11 Oct. 1953.
58 For the correspondence with France of Jan. 1926, see I.775–6, VI.112–15, III.809, VMM.114–15; the letter at VI.115 should be dated 26 Jan.
59 E. Giordanetti, 'Benjamin Crémieux, a French Critic of Italian Literature', Ph.D. Thesis, Princeton University (New Jersey, 1959): cf. introduction, 20–32, and 83;

A. A. Eustis, *Marcel Arland; Benjamin Crémieux, Ramon Fernandez: trois critiques de la 'Nouvelle Revue Française* (Paris, 1961), 79.

60 Both versions of Crémieux's article are now in Svevo—Montale, *Carteggio*, 173–85.

61 V.107–9.

62 I.776–7.

63 Cf. Svevo—Montale, *Carteggio*, 71–87.

64 I.778–80.

65 I.777, 781; VI.75.

66 Svevo—Montale, *Carteggio*, 104–5.

67 I.781, 792.

68 VMM.115–116.

69 C. V. Lodovici, *Solaria*, IV.3–4 (Mar.-Apr. 1929), 50–2.

70 I.791; cf. VI.118–19.

71 I.815, 821–2; V.128.

72 I.788, 791; cf. Svevo—Montale, *Carteggio*, 13 and VI.118.

73 I.791–3; II.431; V.114–15; VI.68–9; Svevo—Montale, *Carteggio*, 15–17.

74 I.794–5.

75 VI.121; Giordanetti, op. cit. 32–3. Giancarlo Mazzacurati (ed.), *Italo Svevo: Scritti su Joyce* (Parma, 1986), 26, 37–41.

76 I.790, 817, 835; V.110, 114, 120, 123; Svevo—Montale, *Carteggio*, 15, 36, 38.

77 Linati, 'Italo Svevo, romanziere', 129.

78 I.785–6, 793; VI.68; Svevo—Montale, *Carteggio*, 9–10.

79 IV.13, 351–440, 641–55.

80 I.787, 790; Svevo—Montale, *Carteggio*, 11, 15.

81 I.848; cf. 796, 839; VI.85; Svevo—Montale, *Carteggio*, 19.

82 I.795; Svevo—Montale, *Carteggio*, 18–19, 88–93.

83 For Svevo's journey of June-Aug. 1926 see: I.794–807; V.115–17; VI.40, 76–8; Svevo—Montale, *Carteggio*, 18–27; Linati, 'Un giorno con Svevo'.

84 I.807–43; V.117–31; VI.79–89, 124–7; Svevo—Montale, *Carteggio*, 27–53.

85 I.817–20; Svevo—Montale, *Carteggio*, 20, 36–42.

86 P. A. Quarantotti Gambini, 'Due scatti di Italo Svevo', *Il Tempo*, 15 Feb 1960, and *Il Piccolo*, 6 Mar. 1960.

87 Stuparich, *Trieste*, 9–12, 16, 100–1.

88 Idem, *Giochi di fisonomie* (Milan, 1946), 219–20.

89 VMM.252.

90 I.770; VI.109.

91 III.755–63.

92 III.492.

93 I.828–40; V.128–9; VI.85–6; Svevo—Montale, *Carteggio*, 47–50.

94 Italo Svevo, *James Joyce,* trans. S. Joyce; III.725.

95 III.726–7.

96 Svevo—Montale, *Carteggio*, 54.

97 Cf. VMM.145.

98 L. Ferrero, *Solaria*, IV.3–4 (1929).

99 P. Rismondo, 'Erinnerung an Italo Svevo', *Für Rudolf Hirsch—Zum siebzigsten Geburtstag am 22 Dezember 1975* (Frankfurt-am-Main, 1975), 155–63.

100 B. Maier, 'Tre lettere inedite di Italo Svevo a Enrico Rocca', *La Rassegna della*

letteratura italiana, LXXX, 7th series, Nos. 1–2 (1976), 151–6.

101 G. Debenedetti, 'Lettera a Carocci su "Svevo e Schmitz"', *Solaria*, IV.3–4 (Mar.-Apr. 1929) 28–34. Repr. in *Saggi critici*, 2nd series (Milan, 1950). The 1969 Milan ed. is used here: see p. 93.

102 S. Solmi, *Solaria*, IV.3–4 (1929), 67–71.

103 I.835–7; V.149–51, 155–8; Ducker, op. cit. 28–31.

104 III.832.

105 A. Pane, 'Svevo e una *Backfisch*', *Il Punto*, 6 Apr. 1957.

106 Svevo—Montale, *Carteggio*, 53–4.

107 V.131–3.

108 I.882.

109 I.846; V.144–5; Maier, 'Tre lettere'.

110 Anzellotti, op. cit. 258–61.

111 Kezich, op. cit. (1970 ed.), ill. no. 15.

112 I.844–5; V.133, 135–6, 155, 170, 178–9, 190.

113 Svevo—Montale, *Carteggio*, 55–6.

114 I.847, 849; V.138.

115 V.139–47; Svevo—Montale, *Carteggio*, 60–1.

116 I.851–2; VI.90–1.

117 I.853–4; Svevo—Montale, *Carteggio*, 64.

118 V.125, 127, 160, 163–4, 189, 191.

119 VMM.122, 243.

120 Svevo—Montale, *Carteggio*, 67.

121 I.856–8, 859–60, 862–1; VI.233–50.

122 I.858–9; VI.129–30.

123 Svevo—Montale, *Carteggio*, 66–7.

124 Ferrero, op. cit.; VMM.117 (where, however, Livia mistakes the year); Svevo—Montale, *Carteggio*, 94–7; V.159.

125 I.862–70, 875; VI.248–57; A. Jahier, 'Quelques lettres d'Italo Svevo', *Preuves*, II (1955), 26–8.

126 I.862, 865–6.

127 I.868.

128 VMM.143–4; *Solaria*, IV.3–4 (1929), 34–6 and 43–4 and I. Ehrenburg, *Il Lavoratore*, 7 Jan. 1958; G. Prezzolini, 'Di Svevo, Crémieux e Comisso' (exact source unidentified), a Genoa periodical of Mar. 1928; G. Comisso, 'A Parigi con Svevo e Joyce', *La Fiera Letteraria* (25 Mar. 1928), 3.

129 I.867, 869; VI.43–4, 134–5.

130 A. R. Ferrarin, 'Ricordi di Italo Svevo', *Augustea*, 15 Oct. 1928.

131 III.373–474.

132 III.133–42.

133 I.876–9, 888; VI.97–101, 138–9.

134 III.137.

135 IV.441–562 and 657–9.

136 III.21–62.

137 V.178–89.

138 III.631–4.

139 I.874–9, 881, 887–8; VI.95–101, 136–40.

140 G. Comisso, 'Colloquio', *La Fiera Letteraria*, 23 Sept. 1928, and 'Svevo mi consigliò

di leggere Kafka', *Settimo giorno*, 15 Apr. 1958; M. Sutor, op. cit. 53–79.

141 VMM.146–7, and cf. 155.

142 VMM.148–50.

143 S. Maldini, 'La moglie di Svevo', *Il Resto del Carlino*, 14 June 1957.

144 III.251–63.

145 I.889.

146 VMM.156.

147 VMM.156–7.

148 Saba, op. cit. 154.

149 VMM.157–9.

150 *Il Piccolo della Sera*, 14 Sept. 1928.

151 Saba, op. cit. 154

152 *Il Popolo di Trieste*, 13 Sept. 1929.

153 G. Berto, 'La morte del signor Schmitz', *Rotosei*, 19 Sept. 1958, 71–4; G. Campolleti, 'A colloquio con alcuni medici dell'ospedale in cui Italo Svevo morì—Dopo l'incidente d'auto forse potevano guarirlo', *Tuttolibri*, IV.30 (5 Aug. 1978), 12–13.

154 Maier, 'Tre lettere' (cf. Svevo's letter to Rocca of 11 Oct. 1927).

155 VMM.255.

156 Cf. *Il Popolo di Trieste*, 19 Sept. 1928.

157 VMM.180.

158 Anzellotti, op. cit. 281.

159 VMM.161–7.

160 VMM.167–8.

161 Ellmann, op. cit. 605.

162 VMM.168–72.

163 F. Sternberg, *L'opera di Italo Svevo* (Trieste, 1928), *L'arte e la personalità di Italo Svevo* (Trieste, 1929); cf. VMM.176; V.125, 127, 160–1, 163–4, 189, 191.

164 Svevo—Montale, *Carteggio*, 94–8.

165 R. Bazlen, *Adelphiana 1971* (Milan, 1971), 195–6 and L. Nanni (ed.), *Leggere Svevo—Antologia della critica sveviana* (Bologna, 1974), 162.

166 Svevo—Montale, *Carteggio*, 99–100.

167 *Il Popolo di Trieste*, 24 and 27 Apr. 1931.

168 Cf. B. Maier's bibliographies, II.1107–228, and his 'Introduzione' to the same vol., 7–128.

169 Anzellotti, op. cit. 280–1.

INDEX

The works of Italo Svevo/Ettore Schmitz are listed individually; it is indicated which of the writer's various pseudonyms or guises each work appeared under, or whether it was merely projected, fragmentary or unfinished, or appeared after his death.

It has not been possible to ascertain the forename of every individual listed here. Their surnames are included in the hope that such identification may become possible.